BloodCovered 2

Makoto Kedouin
Toshimi Shinomiya

Translation: Alethea and Athena Nibley
Lettering: D. Kim

CORPSEPARTY BLOODCOVERED Vol. 2
©2008 TeamGrisGris/ALL RIGHTS RESERVED.
©2010 Toshimi Shinomiya/Square Enix Co., LTD. First published in Japan in 2010 by Square Enix Co., Ltd. English translation rights arranged with Square Enix Co., Ltd. and Yen Press, LLC through Tuttle-Mori Agency, Inc.

English translation ©2016 Square Enix Co., Ltd.

Yen Press
1290 Avenue of the Americas
New York, NY 10104

Visit us at yenpress.com
facebook.com/yenpress
twitter.com/yenpress
yenpress.tumblr.com

First Yen Press Edition: August 2016

Yen Press is an imprint of Yen Press, LLC.
The Yen Press name and logo are trademarks of Yen Press, LLC.

The publisher is not responsible for websites (or their content) that are not owned by the publisher.

Library of Congress Control Number: 2016930997

ISBN: 978-0-316-27611-5

10 9 8 7 6 5 4 3 2

BVG

Printed in the United States of America

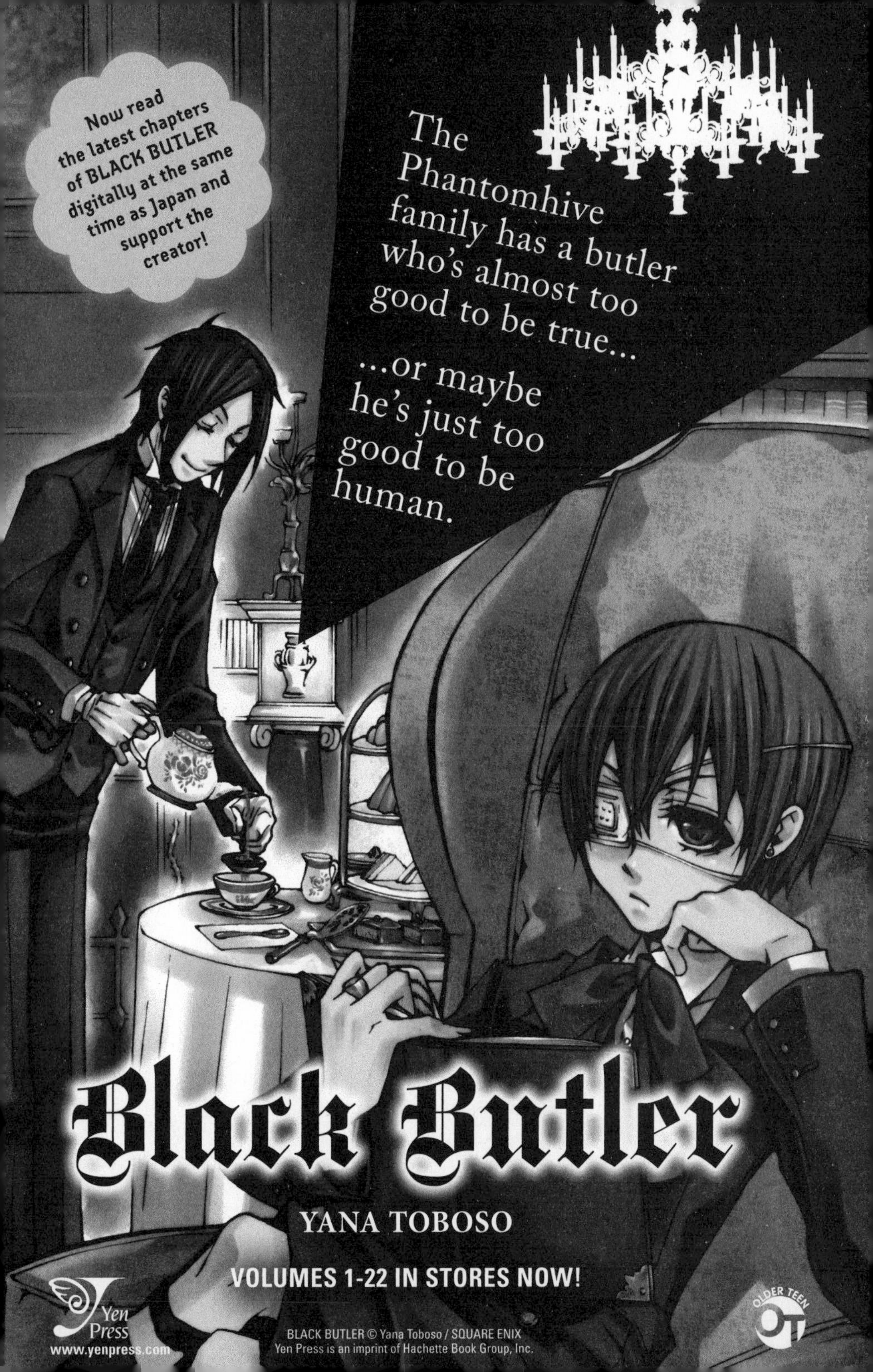

Now read the latest chapters of BLACK BUTLER digitally at the same time as Japan and support the creator!
The Phantomhive family has a butler who's almost too good to be true...
...or maybe he's just too good to be human.
Black Butler
YANA TOBOSO
VOLUMES 1-22 IN STORES NOW!
Yen Press
www.yenpress.com
OLDER TEEN
OT
BLACK BUTLER © Yana Toboso / SQUARE ENIX
Yen Press is an imprint of Hachette Book Group, Inc.

CORPSE PARTY

BloodCovered

TRANSLATION NOTES

COMMON HONORIFICS

no honorific: Indicates familiarity or closeness; if used without permission or reason, addressing someone in this manner would constitute an insult.

-san: The Japanese equivalent of Mr./Mrs./Miss. If a situation calls for politeness, this is the fail-safe honorific.

-sama: Conveys great respect; may also indicate that the social status of the speaker is lower than that of the addressee.

-kun: Used most often when referring to boys, this indicates affection or familiarity. Occasionally used by older men among their peers, but it may also be used by anyone referring to a person of lower standing.

-chan: An affectionate honorific indicating familiarity used mostly in reference to girls; also used in reference to cute persons or animals of either gender.

-sensei: A respectful term for teachers, artists, or high-level professionals.

-onii-chan, nii-san, aniki: A term of endearment meaning "big brother" that may be more widely used to address any young man who is like a brother, regardless of whether he is related or not.

-onee-chan, nee-san, aneki: The female counterpart of the above, *nee-san* is a term meaning "big sister."

PAGE 7
Tenjin Elementary School: When this school was first built, before the tragedy that occurred, it may have been named after Tenjin, the deified spirit of Sugawara no Michizane, who has become a god of education—surely this would be an auspicious name for a place of learning. However, before he was appeased with deification, Tenjin was also one of the most feared vengeful spirits in all of Japan. Additionally, the word *tenjin* can also be a general term referring to gods or spirits in heaven.

PAGE 88
Squat toilet: Because this is an old Japanese school, it has old bathrooms, including squat toilets, which were the norm in Japan for many years. As the name suggests, the toilet is used by squatting over it instead of sitting down, as with a Western toilet.

PAGE 179
pixiv: A social media site for sharing art and fiction, much like DeviantArt.

PAGE 312
Paper talismans: The pieces of paper stuck all over the door of the bathroom Yuka eventually finds should be taken as a warning. Charms like these are often used to keep evil spirits out of a home, but in this case, they are used to keep the evil confined. In other words, whatever was in that bathroom was evil enough and powerful enough that multiple magical talismans were needed to hold it back.

PAGE 334
Seiko and Yu in the bath: Bathing is not always a private event in Japan—in fact, public bathing houses are still in wide use. Here we see a private family bathroom, and because it's much smaller than a public bath, family members usually take turns, but Yu is still young enough for Seiko to pester him as his big sister. Hopefully, as he gets older, she'll learn to respect his privacy, as even public baths are usually separated by gender. The reader will notice that most of the cleaning process takes place outside the bath, before getting in the water. This is because baths are for soaking and relaxing, after one is already clean.

PAGE 340
Merry-san: Merry-san is the name of a doll from a Japanese ghost story. A girl moves and leaves her doll, Merry-san, behind. Later, she gets a mysterious phone call from someone claiming to be Merry. Believing it to be a prank call, she hangs up. Merry keeps calling back, each time reporting where she is and getting progressively closer to the girl. Eventually, Merry informs the girl that she is right outside, so the girl rushes to open the door, finding nothing there. Then she gets one more call saying, "I'm behind you." At this point, the details of the story tend to vary, but the girl usually ends up dead.

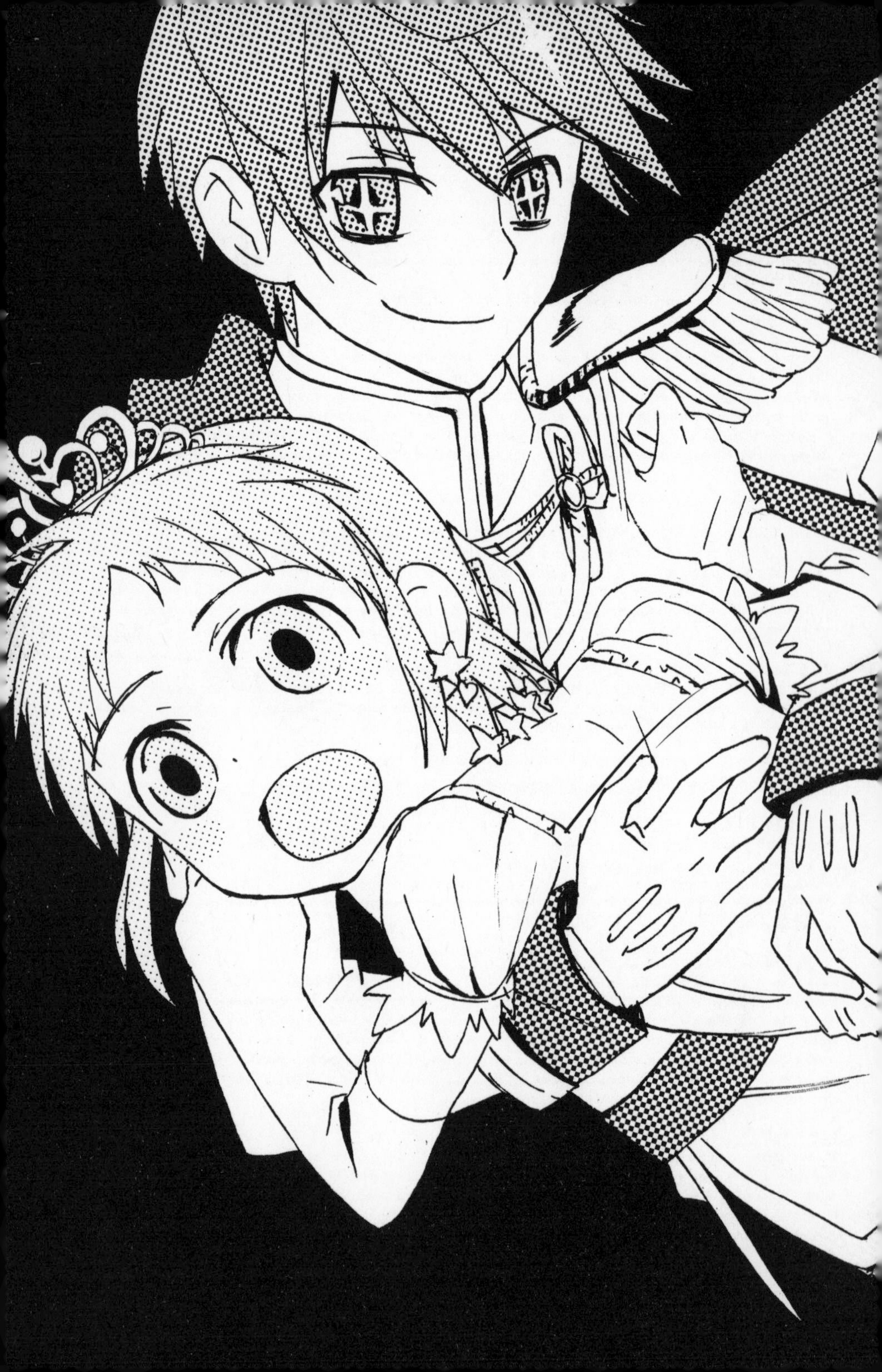

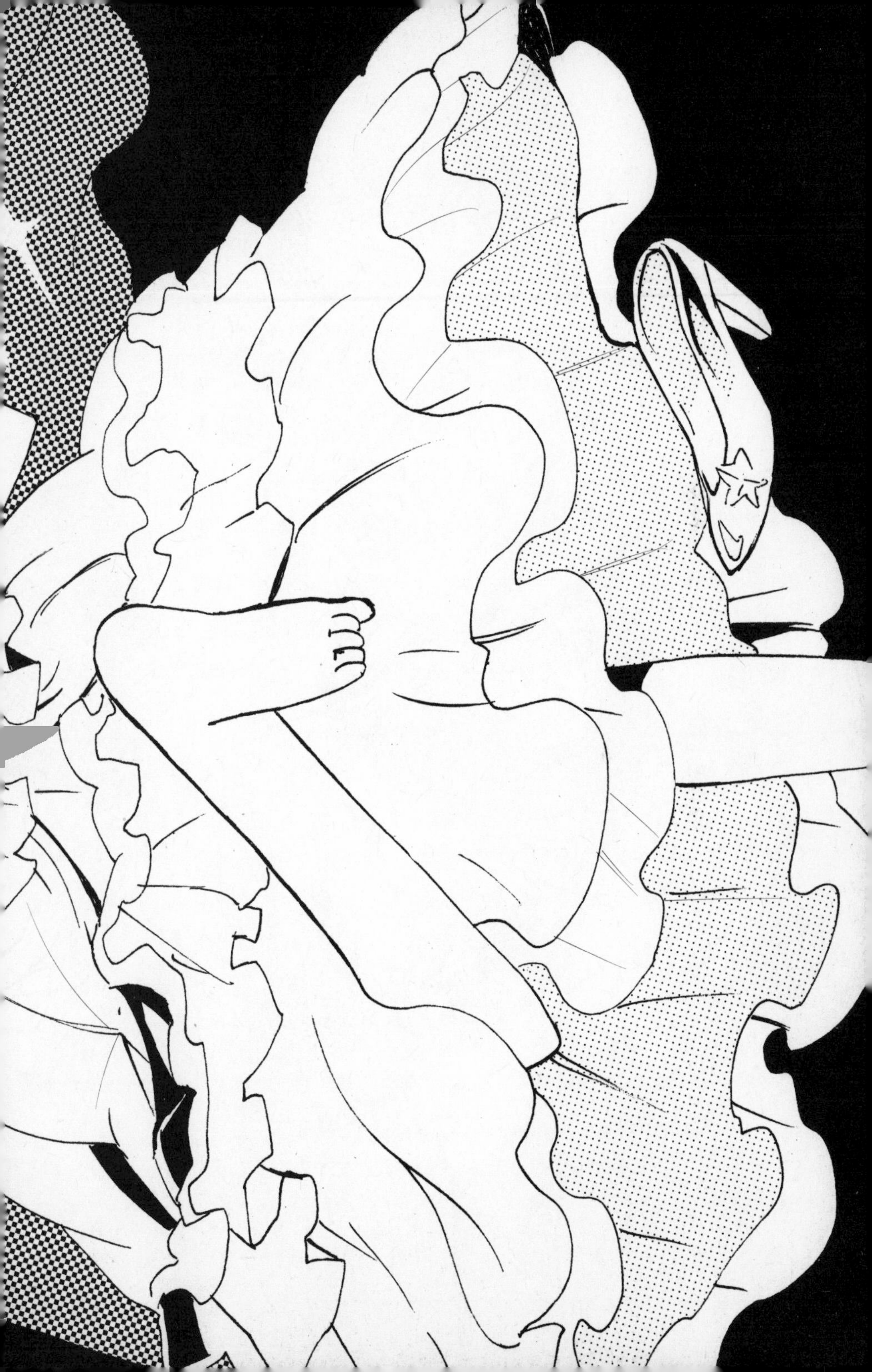

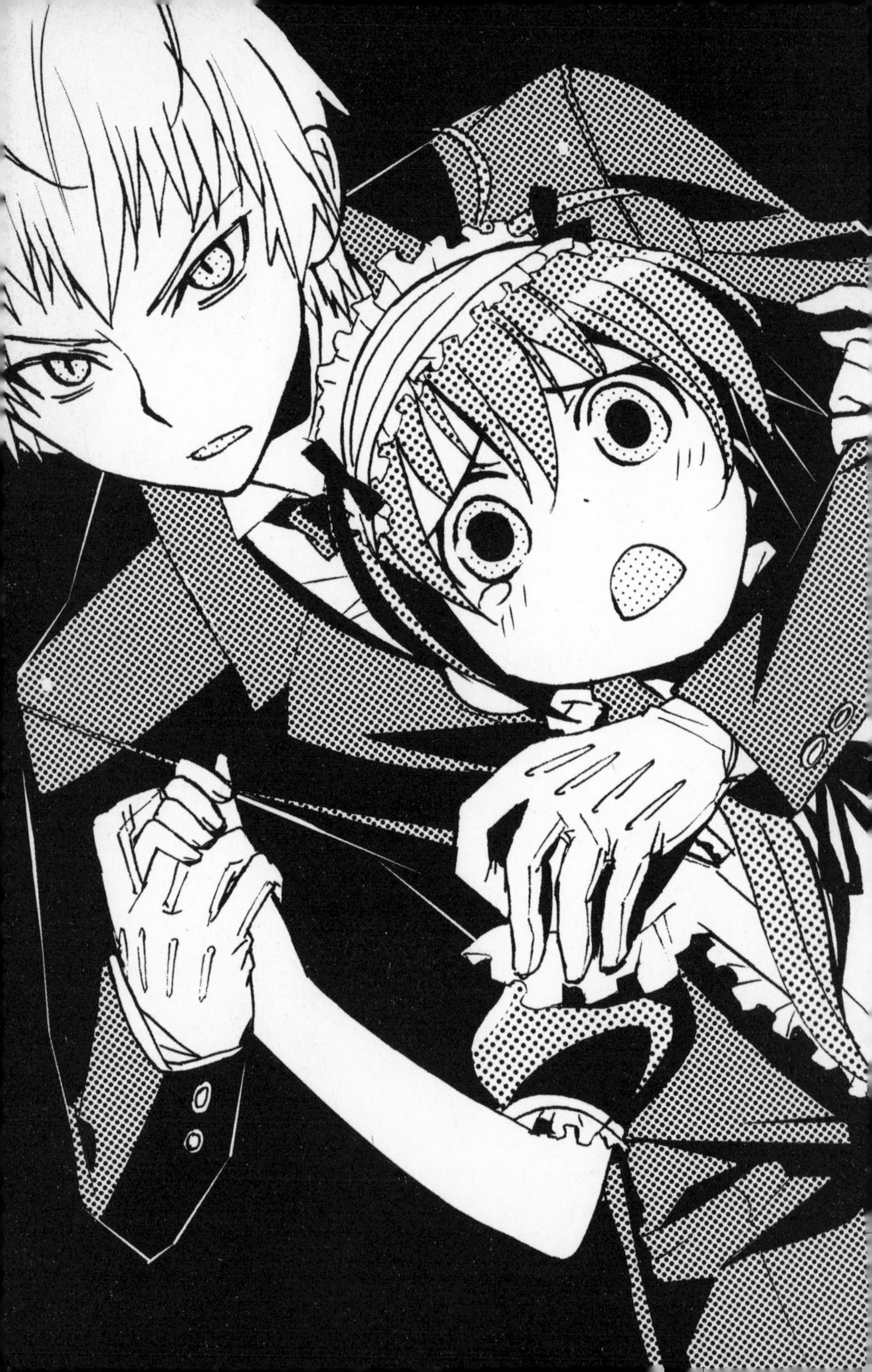

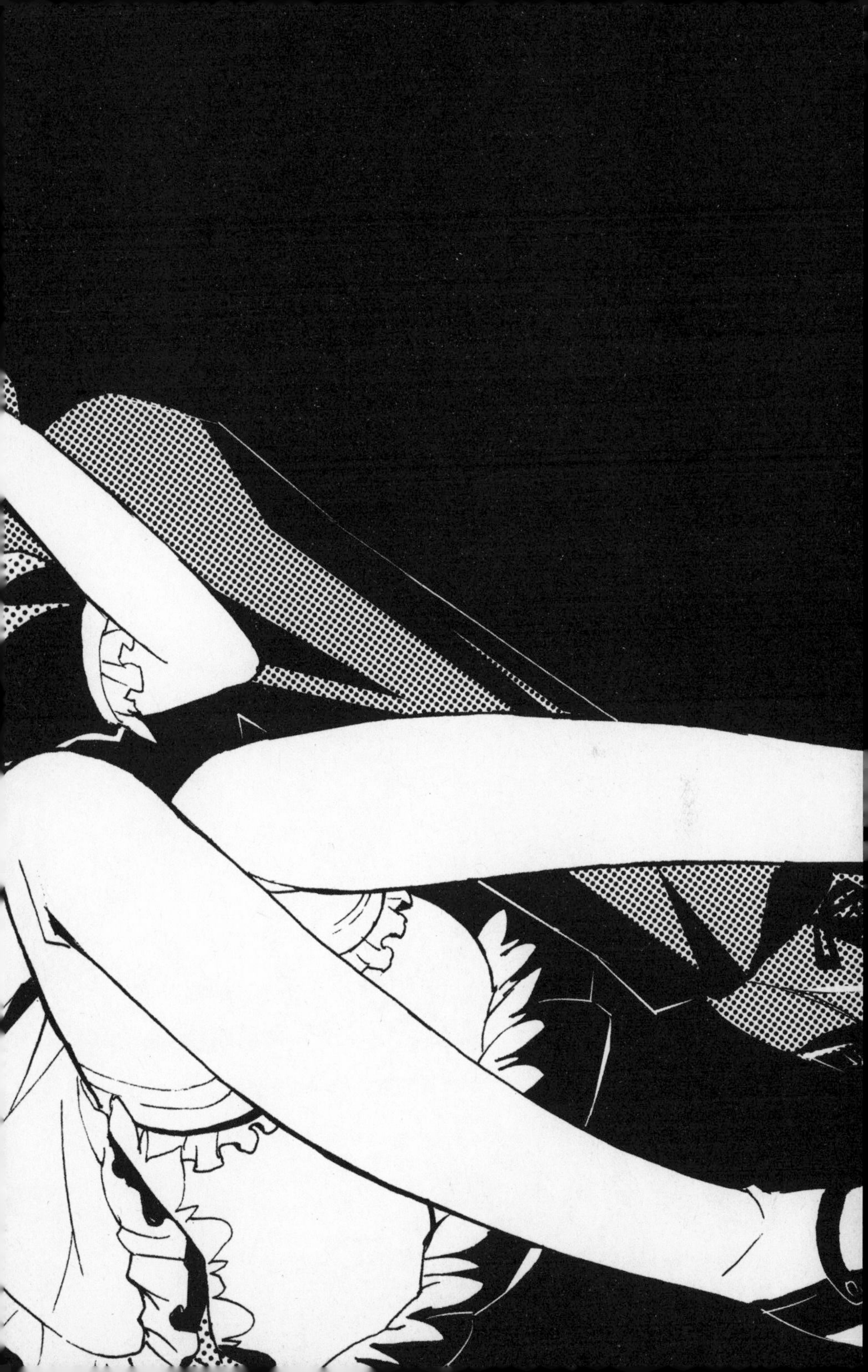

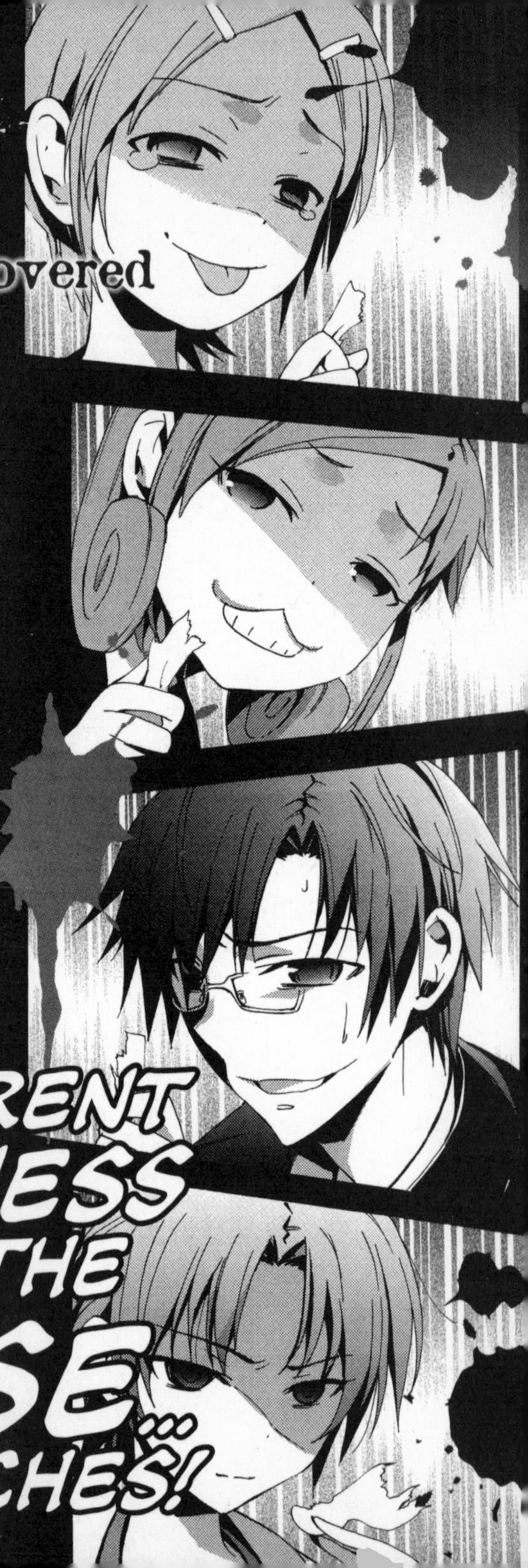

CORPSE PARTY
BloodCovered

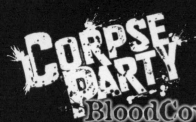

VOLUME 3
COMING
NOVEMBER
2016!

A DIFFERENT
DARKNESS
THAN THE
CURSE...
APPROACHES!

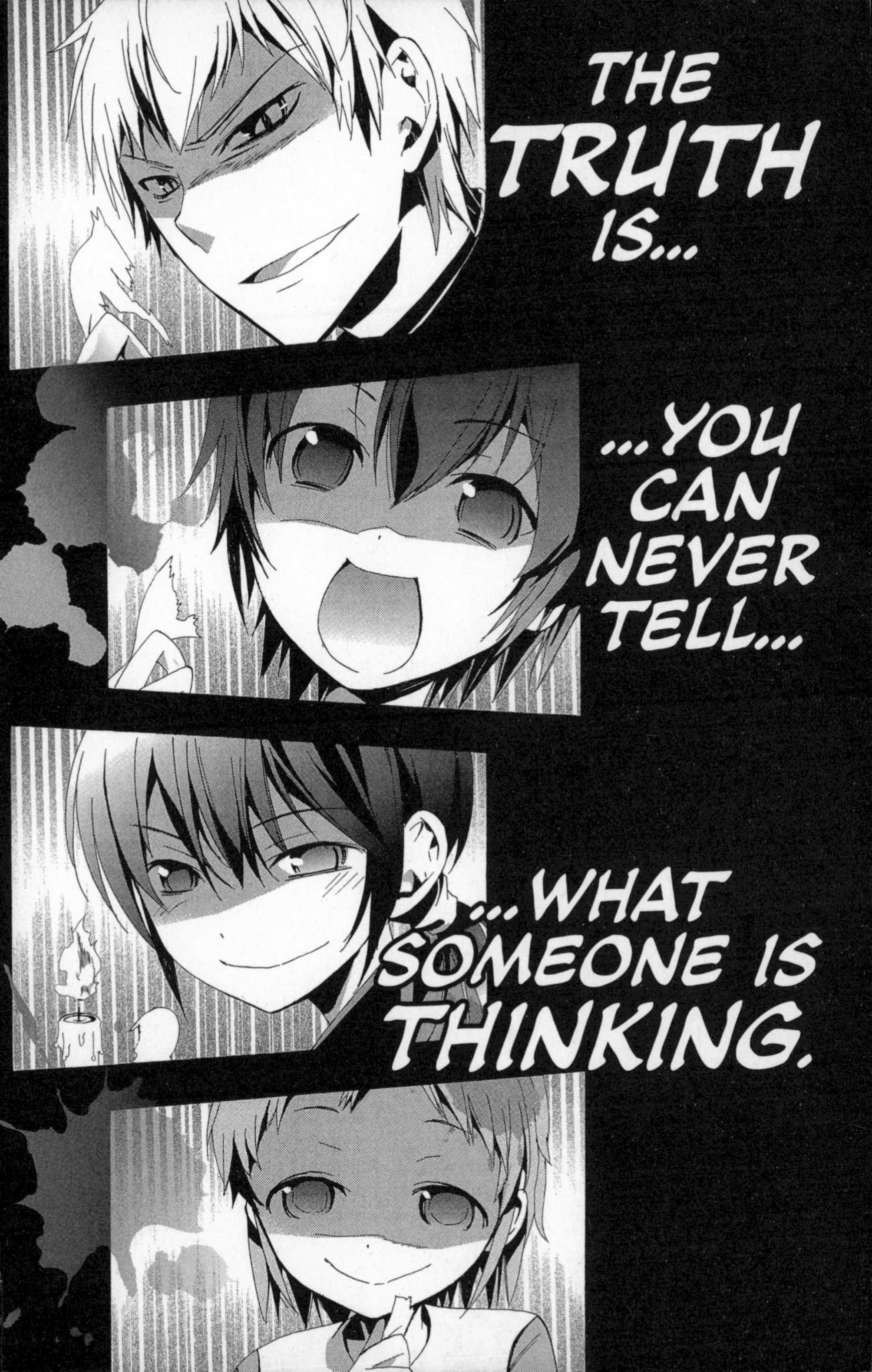
THE TRUTH IS...
...YOU CAN NEVER TELL...
...WHAT SOMEONE IS THINKING.

AFTERWORD

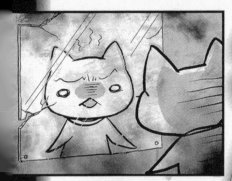

DU-DUN! CORPSE MORNING, EVERYONE! SHINOMIYA-SENSEI, CONGRATULATIONS ON RELEASING VOLUME 4 OF THE MANGA! AND THANK YOU, ALL OF YOU WHO PICKED IT UP!

IN VOLUME 4, WE GET THE MOMENT WE'VE ALL BEEN WAITING FOR (I MEAN, SERIOUSLY, HA-HA), THE APPEARANCE OF THE MAIN CHARACTER, SATOSHI-KUN. PLEASE SHOW HIM YOUR LOVE.

I'VE NOTICED THAT A LOT OF DIFFERENT WORLDS HAVE BEEN BORN FROM *CORPSE*, AND THEY'RE STARTING TO EVOLVE INTO ALTERNATE UNIVERSES. THIS MANGA VERSION IS DEFINITELY TAKING OFF AT AN ORIGINAL PACE. THIS IS THE ONLY PLACE YOU CAN SEE SHINOMIYA-SENSEI'S VERSION OF *CORPSE PARTY*, AND EVEN I CAN'T WAIT TO SEE HOW IT'S GOING TO END!

ANYWAY, THE WAY SENSEI DRAWS SEIKO IS ADORABLE... RAWR! HAVEN'T THEY MADE A FIGURE OF HER YET (HA-HA)!? I WANT TO GAZE AT IT! FROM ABOVE! AND BELOW!

MAKOTO KEDOUIN

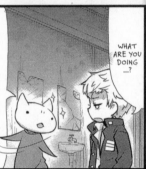

WHAT ARE YOU DOING ...?
WELL, IT'S GREAT THAT THERE ARE FOUR VOLUMES NOW, BUT FOUR IS THE NUMBER OF DEATH, SO I'M AFRAID WE'LL BE CURSED, YOU KNOW?
SO I THOUGHT I'D TRY TO BEAT THE CURSE WITH MY STARE!
FOR CRYING OUT LOUD.
LIVE A LONG LIFE.
NNNNGH!
GACHAN (KACHLUNK)
MANGA: ALBA & KEDWIN

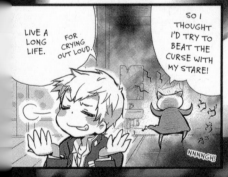

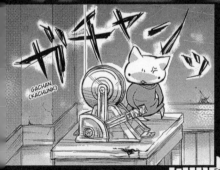

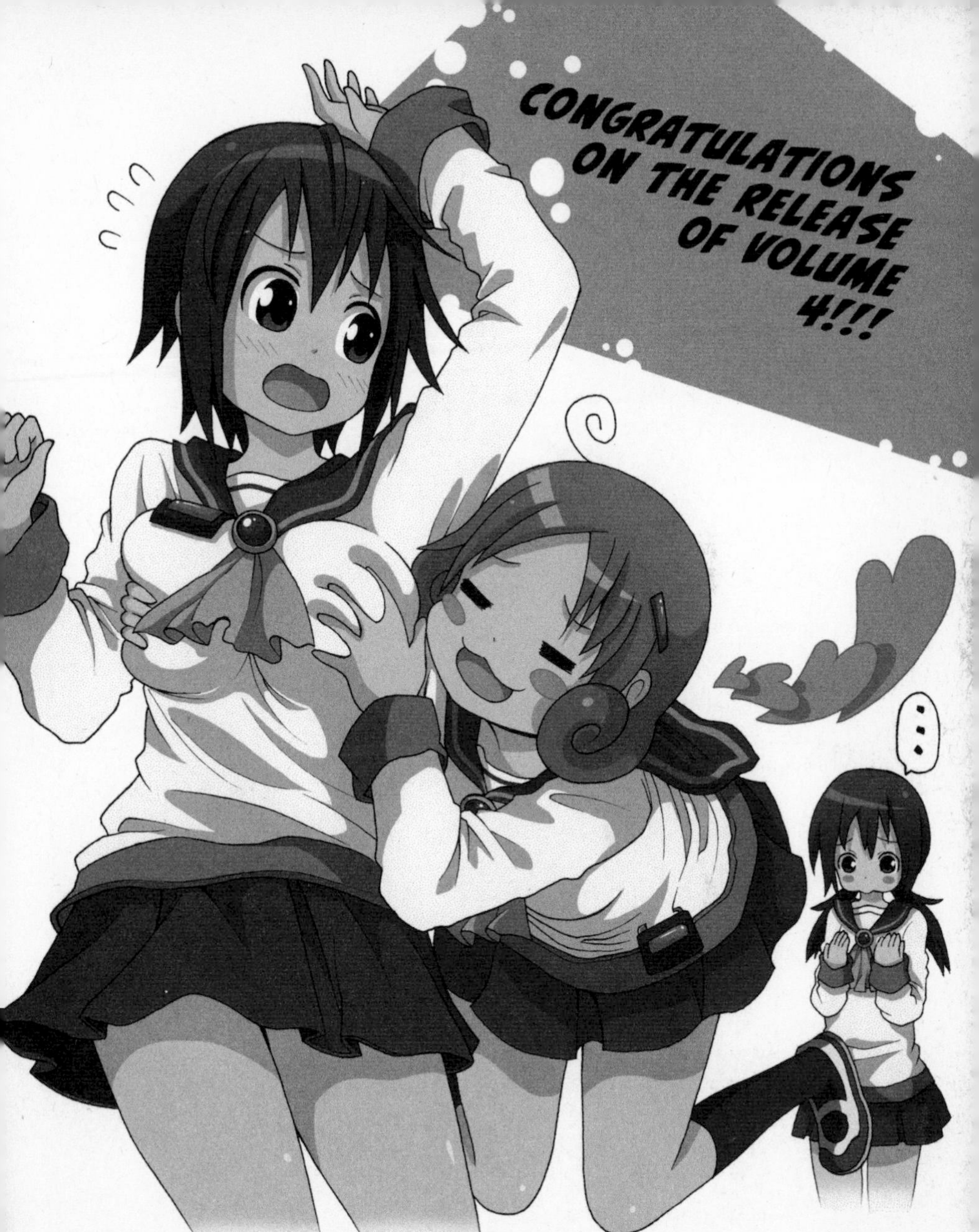
CONGRATULATIONS ON THE RELEASE OF VOLUME 4!!!!

I read every volume of Corpse Party with my heart pounding!
I'm afraid and eager to read more of Shinomiya-anesan's Corpse Party manga,
so please keep at it!! Don't lose, Yoshiki!! And I mean that in every possible way!!

Taichi
Kawazoe

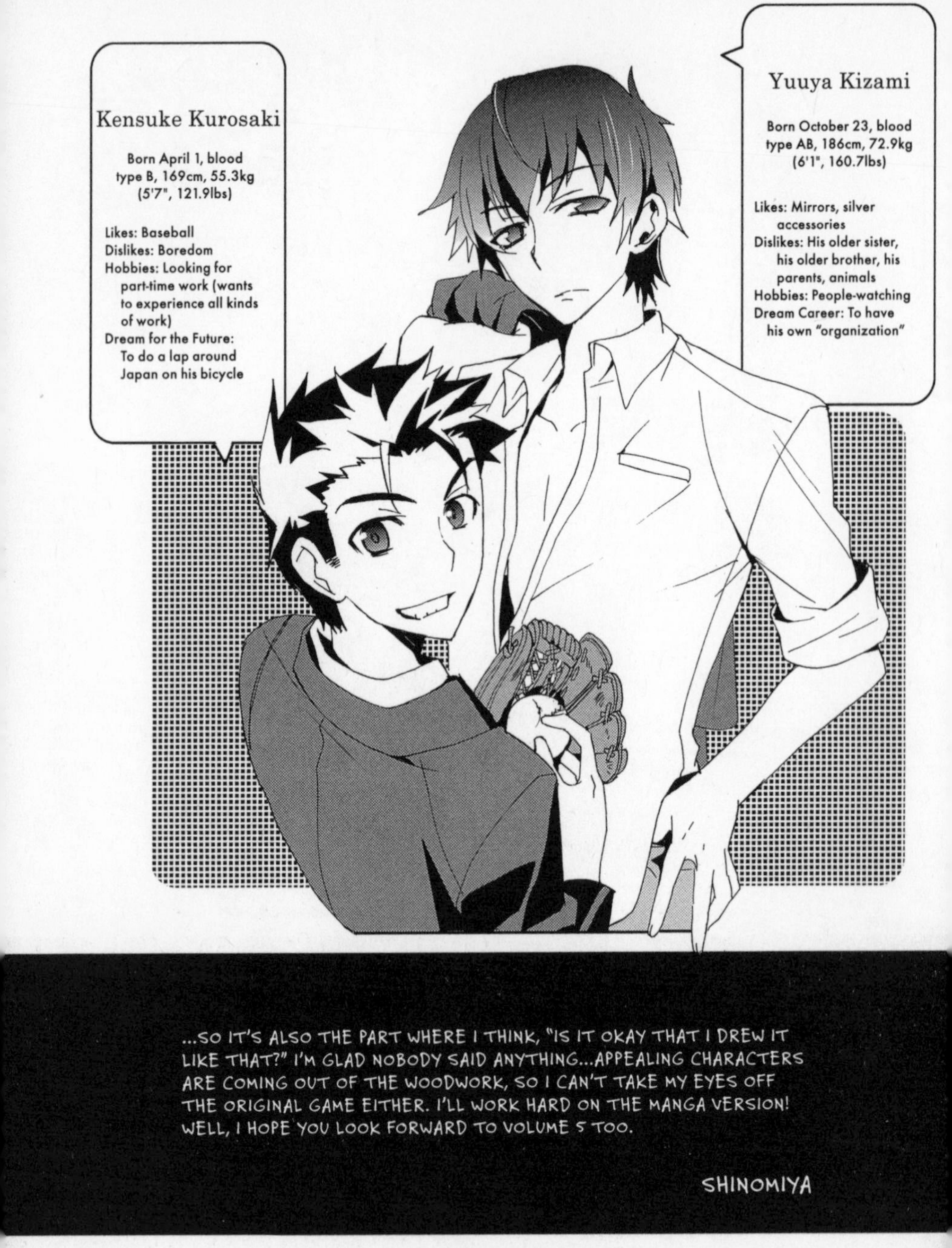
Kensuke Kurosaki
Born April 1, blood type B, 169cm, 55.3kg (5'7", 121.9lbs)
Likes: Baseball
Dislikes: Boredom
Hobbies: Looking for part-time work (wants to experience all kinds of work)
Dream for the Future: To do a lap around Japan on his bicycle
Yuuya Kizami
Born October 23, blood type AB, 186cm, 72.9kg (6'1", 160.7lbs)
Likes: Mirrors, silver accessories
Dislikes: His older sister, his older brother, his parents, animals
Hobbies: People-watching
Dream Career: To have his own "organization"

...SO IT'S ALSO THE PART WHERE I THINK, "IS IT OKAY THAT I DREW IT LIKE THAT?" I'M GLAD NOBODY SAID ANYTHING...APPEALING CHARACTERS ARE COMING OUT OF THE WOODWORK, SO I CAN'T TAKE MY EYES OFF THE ORIGINAL GAME EITHER. I'LL WORK HARD ON THE MANGA VERSION! WELL, I HOPE YOU LOOK FORWARD TO VOLUME 5 TOO.

SHINOMIYA

SPECIAL THANKS
M KOKKO-SAN, SHIN ARAKAWA-SAN, TAKATOSHI OGURA-SAN,
MASAKI KAWANO-SAN, TOMOHIRO IKAWA-SAN,
AND EVERYONE FROM TEAM GRISGRIS, MAKOTO KEDOUIN-SAN,
TAICHI KAWAZOE-SENSEI,
MY EDITORS, AKIYAMA-SAN AND KAWANO-SAN.

Character pickup

Mayu Suzumoto

Born December 29, blood type A,
154cm, 43.9kg (5'1", 96.8lbs)

Likes: Reptiles, crepes, fortune-telling
Dislikes: Her parents' fighting
Hobbies: Writing plays, making costumes, (making others) cosplay
Dream Career: Production designer

Sakutaro Morishige

Born February 14,
blood type AB,
178cm, 62.8kg
(5'10", 138.5lbs)

Likes: Rehearsing acting, collecting photo albums of Western musicians
Dislikes: Reptiles
Hobbies: Watching plays, surfing the Internet
Dream Career: An actor with his own convictions

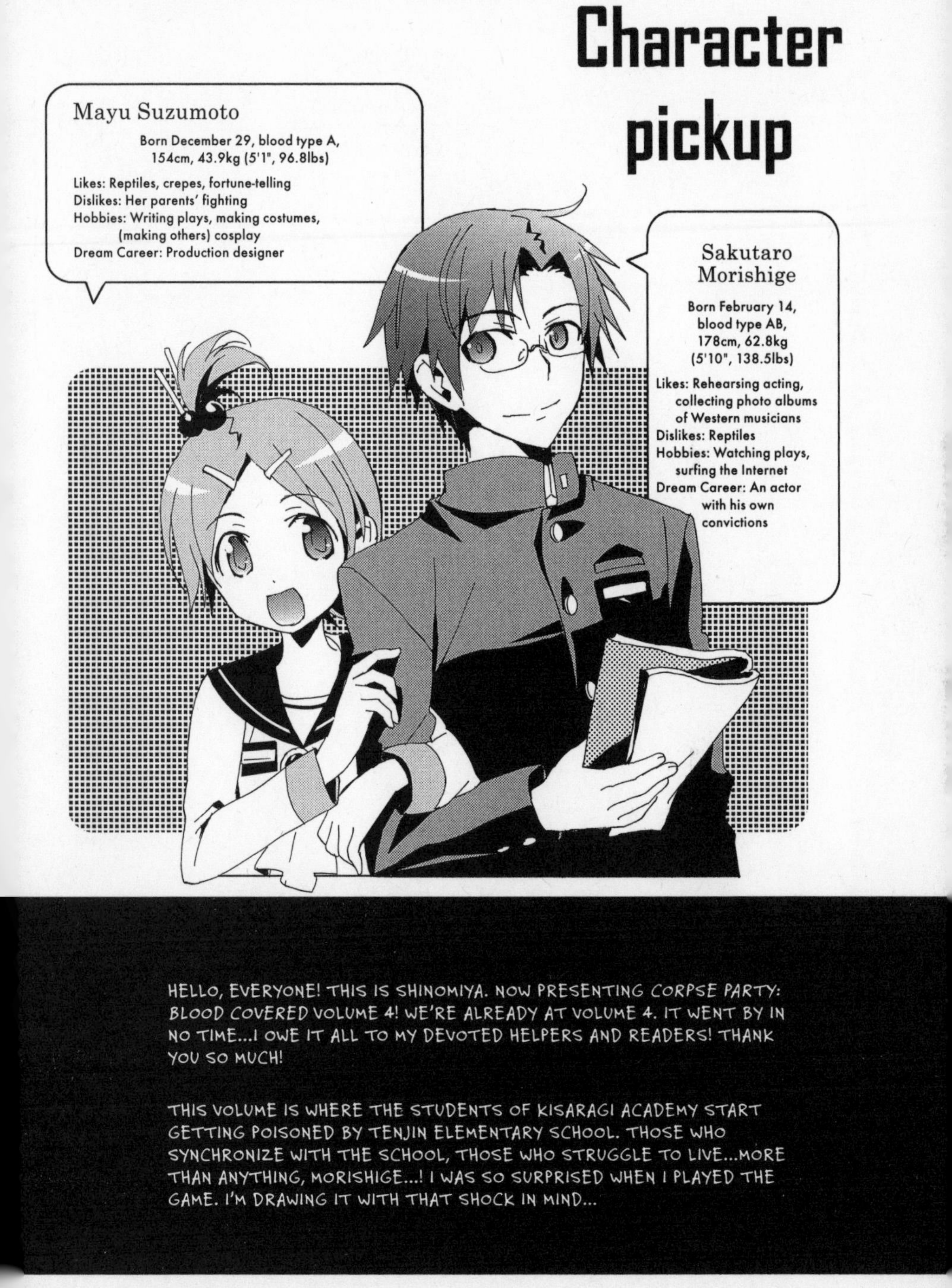

HELLO, EVERYONE! THIS IS SHINOMIYA. NOW PRESENTING *CORPSE PARTY: BLOOD COVERED* VOLUME 4! WE'RE ALREADY AT VOLUME 4. IT WENT BY IN NO TIME...I OWE IT ALL TO MY DEVOTED HELPERS AND READERS! THANK YOU SO MUCH!

THIS VOLUME IS WHERE THE STUDENTS OF KISARAGI ACADEMY START GETTING POISONED BY TENJIN ELEMENTARY SCHOOL. THOSE WHO SYNCHRONIZE WITH THE SCHOOL, THOSE WHO STRUGGLE TO LIVE...MORE THAN ANYTHING, MORISHIGE...! I WAS SO SURPRISED WHEN I PLAYED THE GAME. I'M DRAWING IT WITH THAT SHOCK IN MIND...

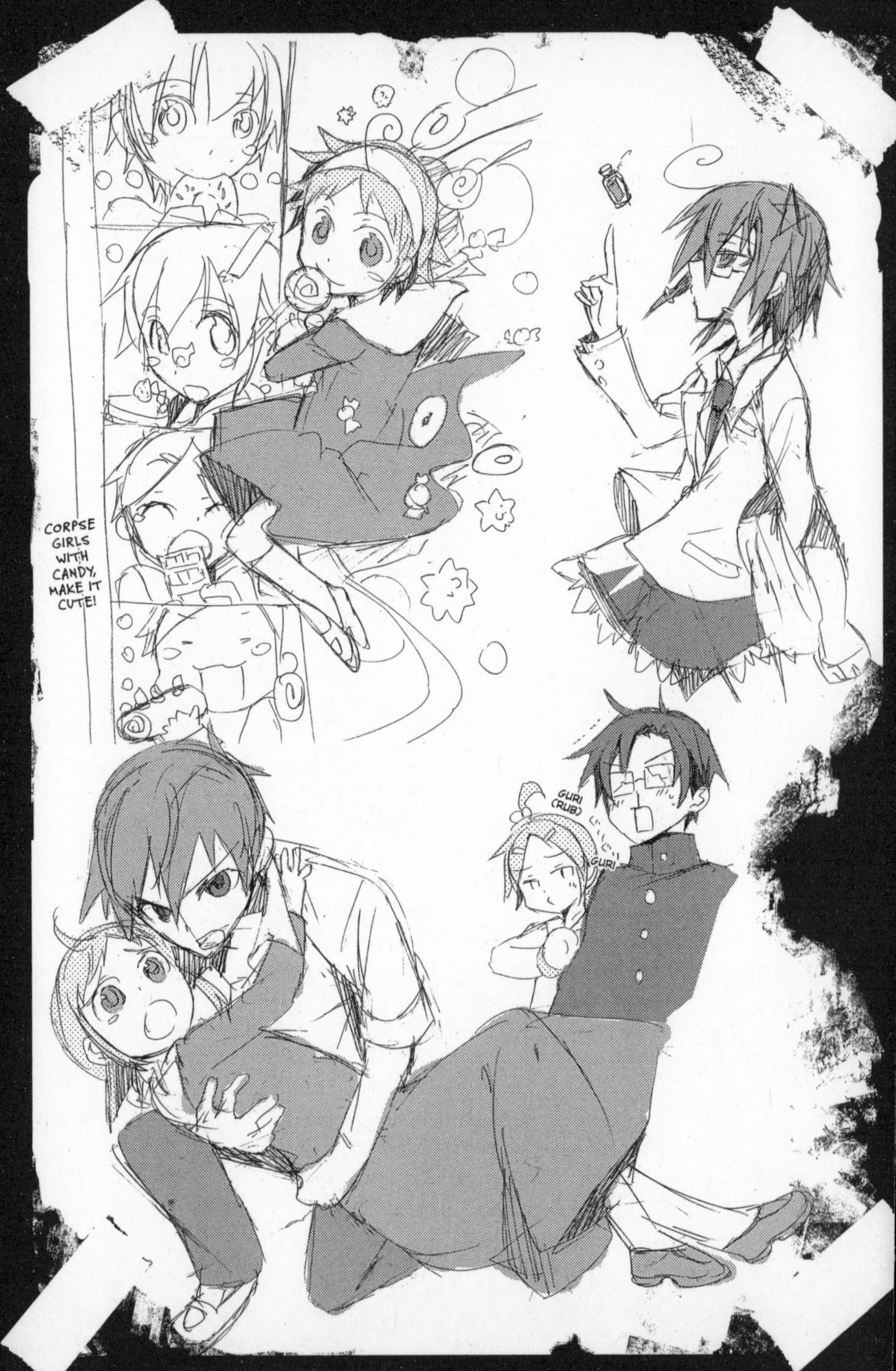
CORPSE GIRLS WITH CANDY, MAKE IT CUTE!
GURI (RUB)
GURI

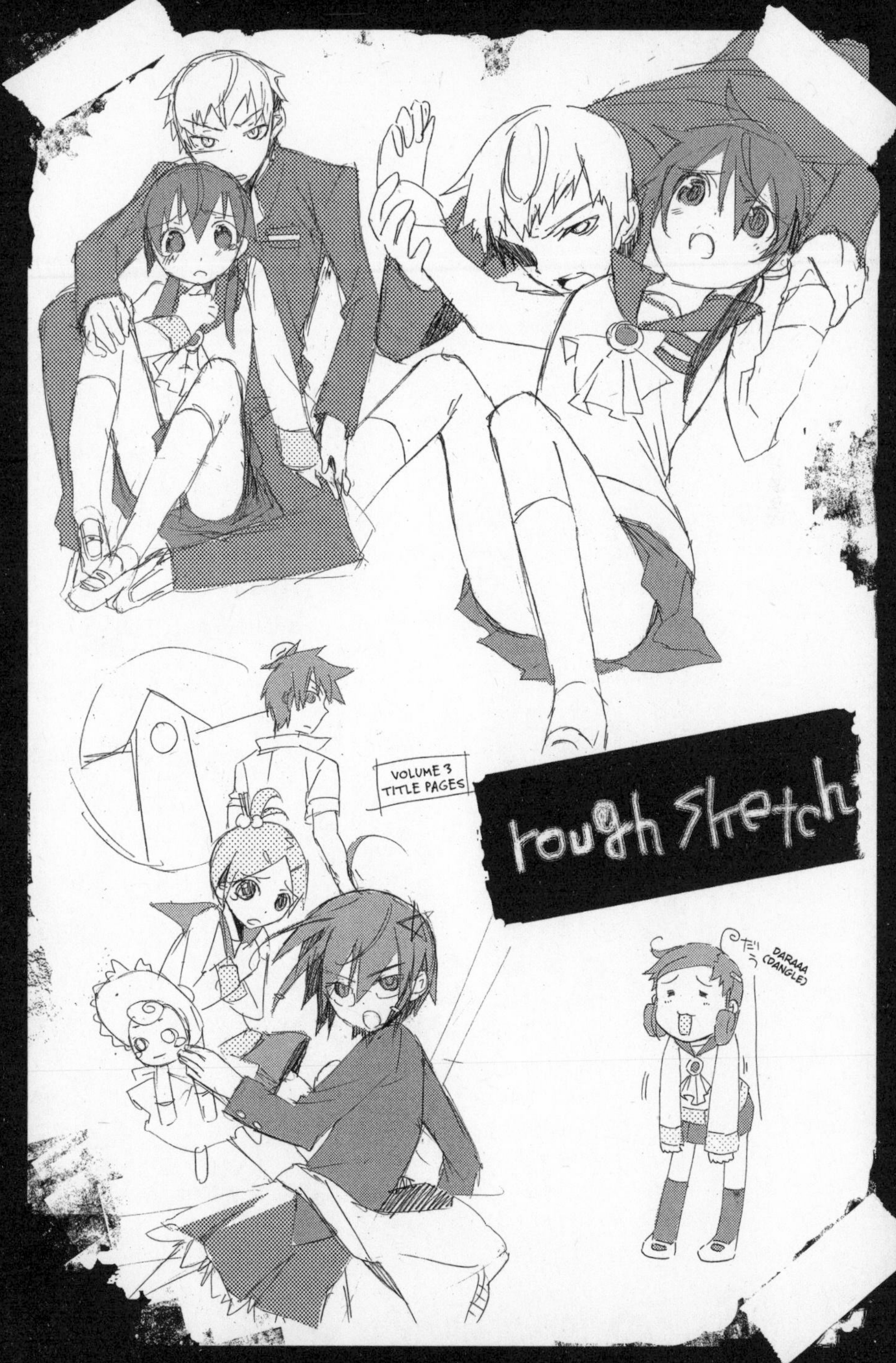
VOLUME 3
TITLE PAGES
rough sketch
DARAAA
(DANGLE)

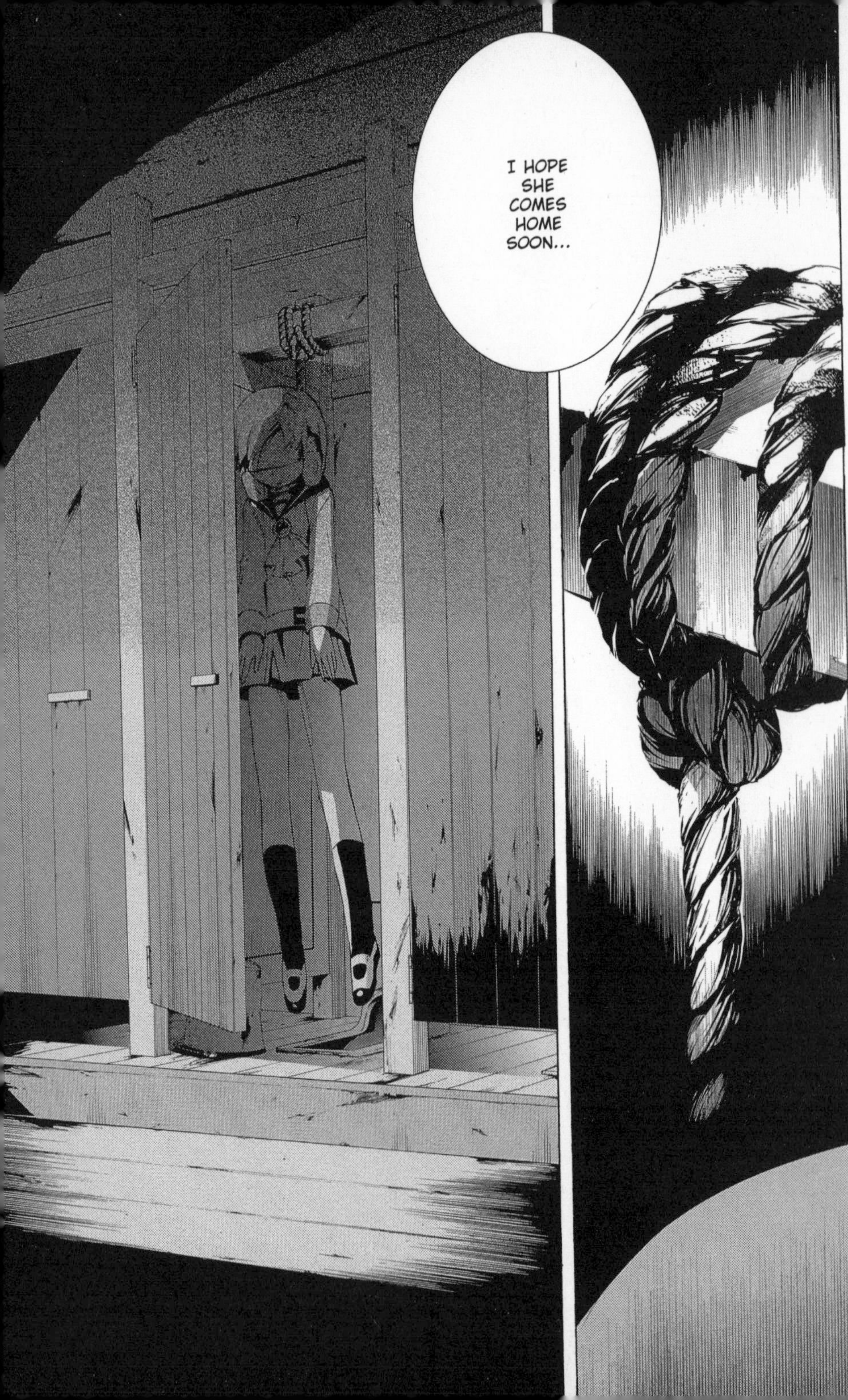
I HOPE SHE COMES HOME SOON...

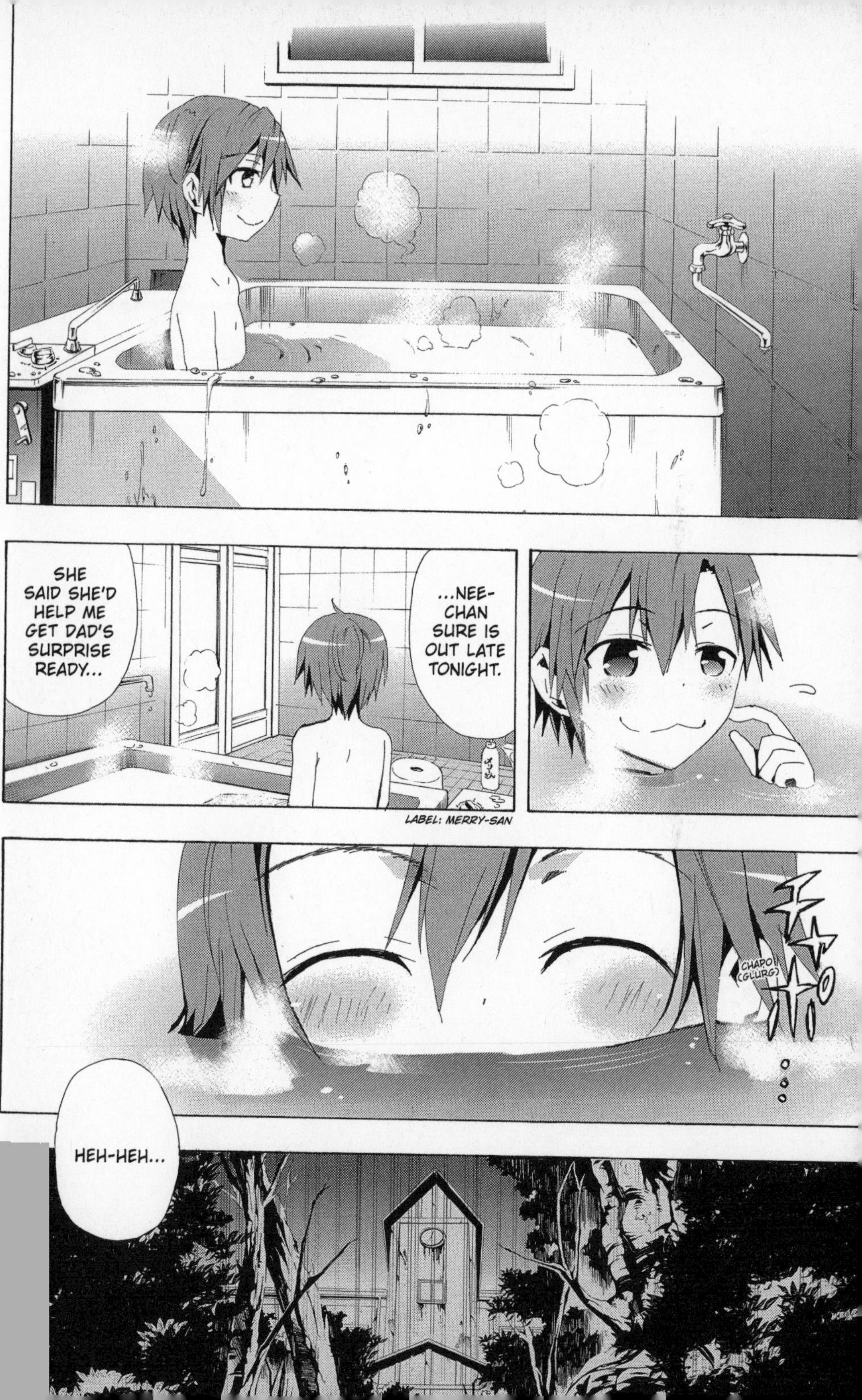
...NEE-CHAN SURE IS OUT LATE TONIGHT.
SHE SAID SHE'D HELP ME GET DAD'S SURPRISE READY...
LABEL: MERRY-SAN
CHAPO (GLURG)
HEH-HEH...

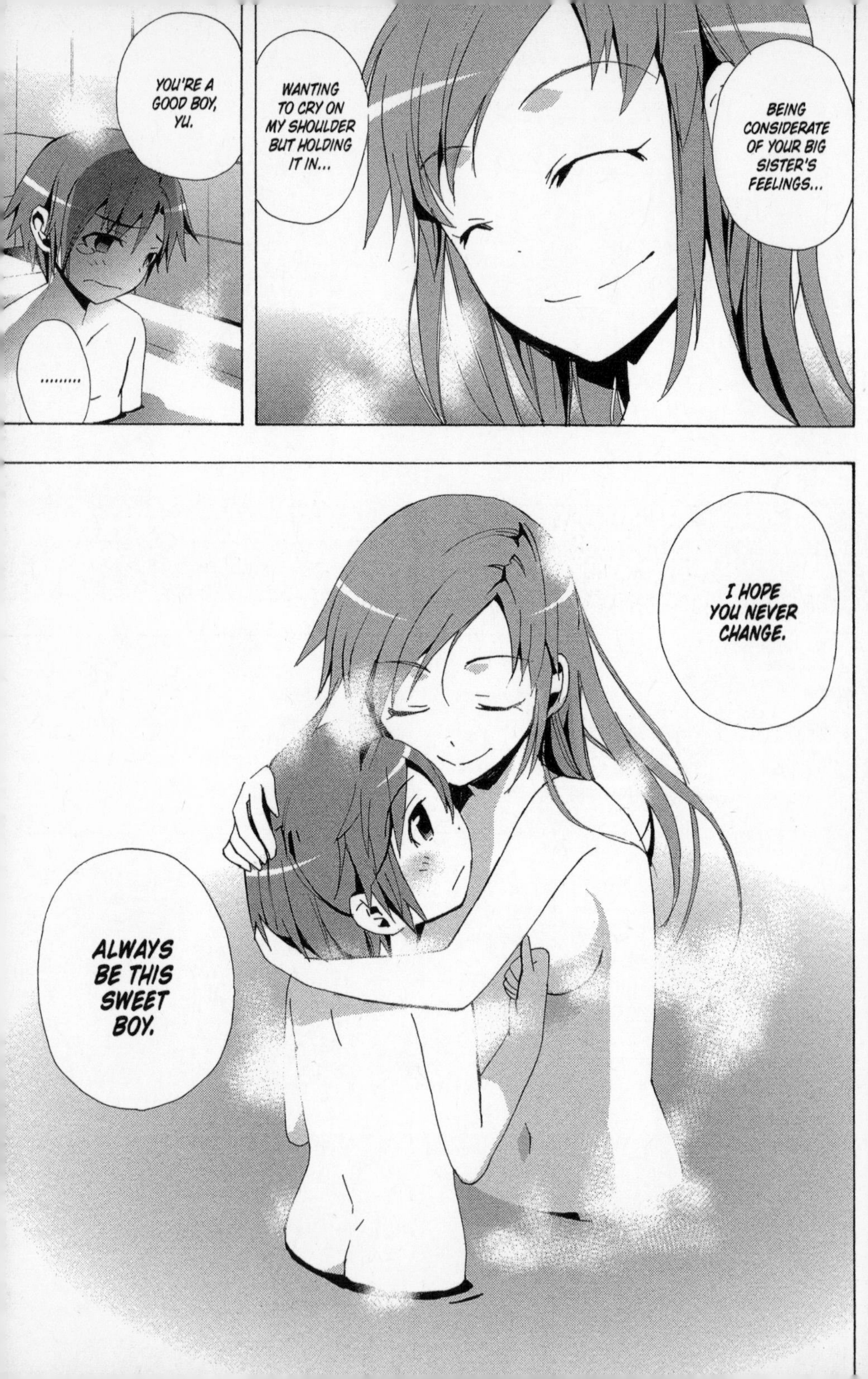
BEING CONSIDERATE OF YOUR BIG SISTER'S FEELINGS...
WANTING TO CRY ON MY SHOULDER BUT HOLDING IT IN...
YOU'RE A GOOD BOY, YU.
....
I HOPE YOU NEVER CHANGE.
ALWAYS BE THIS SWEET BOY.

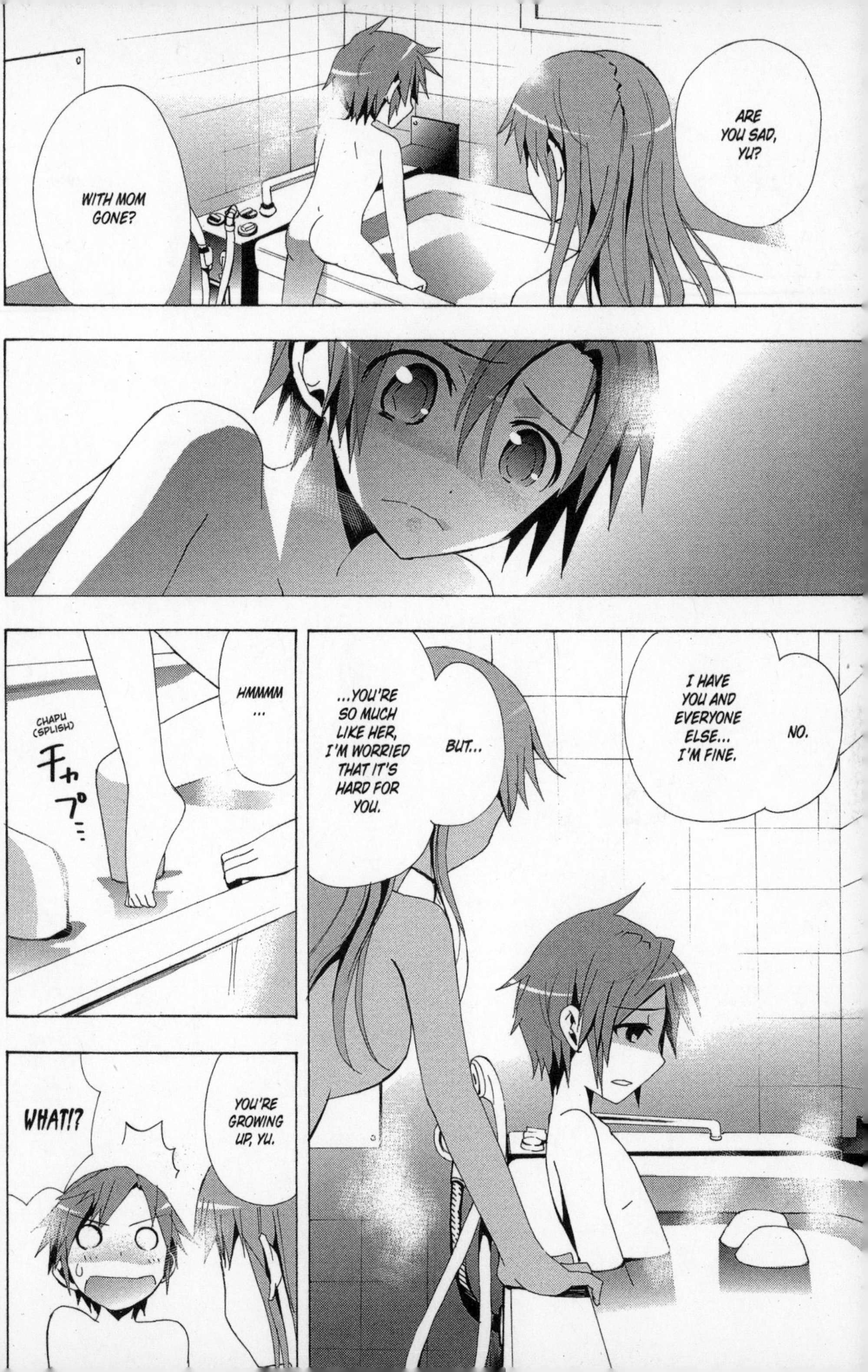
ARE YOU SAD, YU?
WITH MOM GONE?
NO.
I HAVE YOU AND EVERYONE ELSE... I'M FINE.
BUT...
...YOU'RE SO MUCH LIKE HER, I'M WORRIED THAT IT'S HARD FOR YOU.
HMMMM...
CHAPU (SPLISH)
チャプ
YOU'RE GROWING UP, YU.
WHAT!?

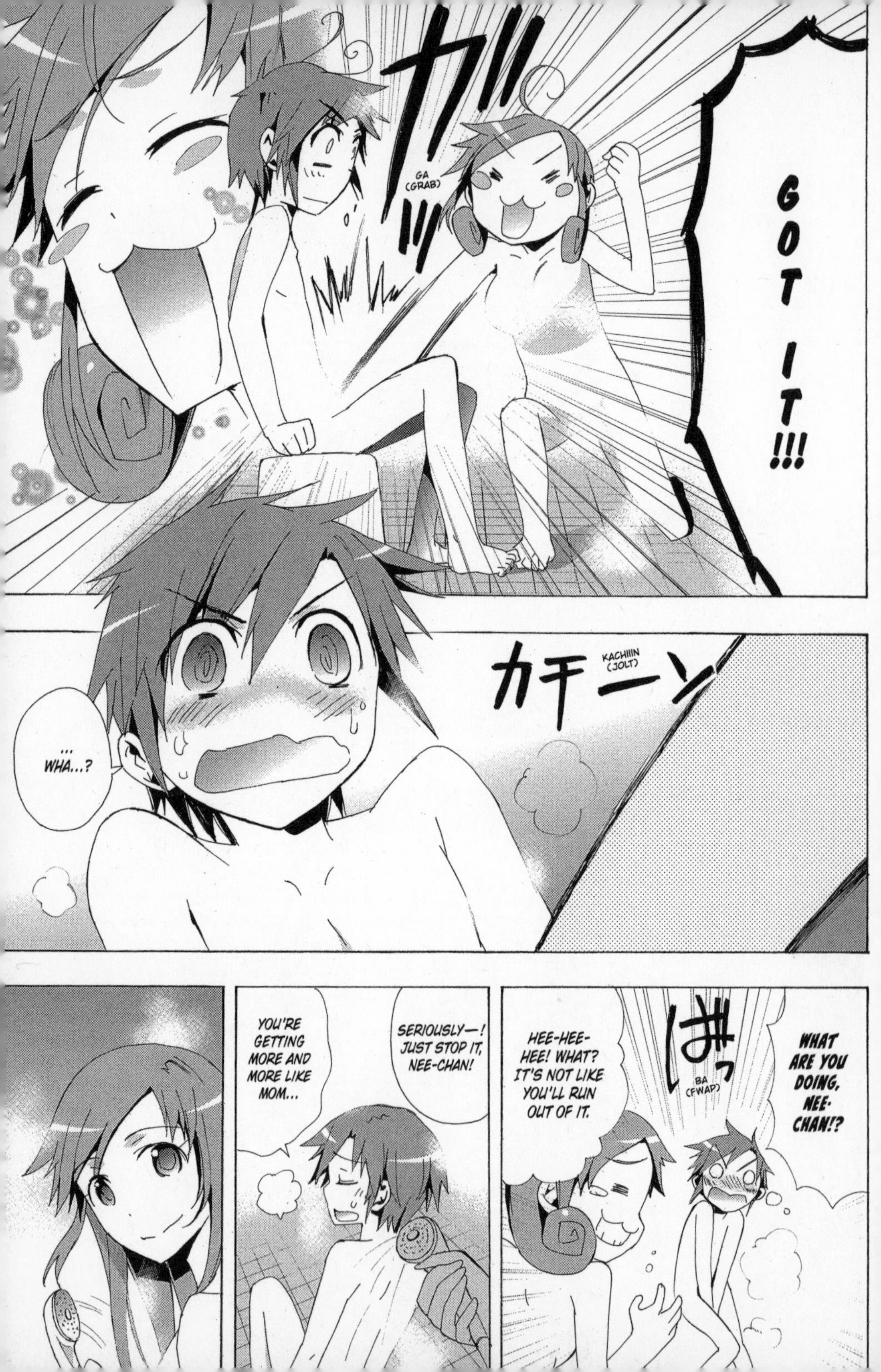
GOT IT!!!
GA (GRAB)
カチーン
KACHIIIN (JOLT)
... WHA...?
WHAT ARE YOU DOING, NEE-CHAN!?
ぱっ
BA (FWAP)
HEE-HEE-HEE! WHAT? IT'S NOT LIKE YOU'LL RUN OUT OF IT.
SERIOUSLY—! JUST STOP IT, NEE-CHAN!
YOU'RE GETTING MORE AND MORE LIKE MOM...

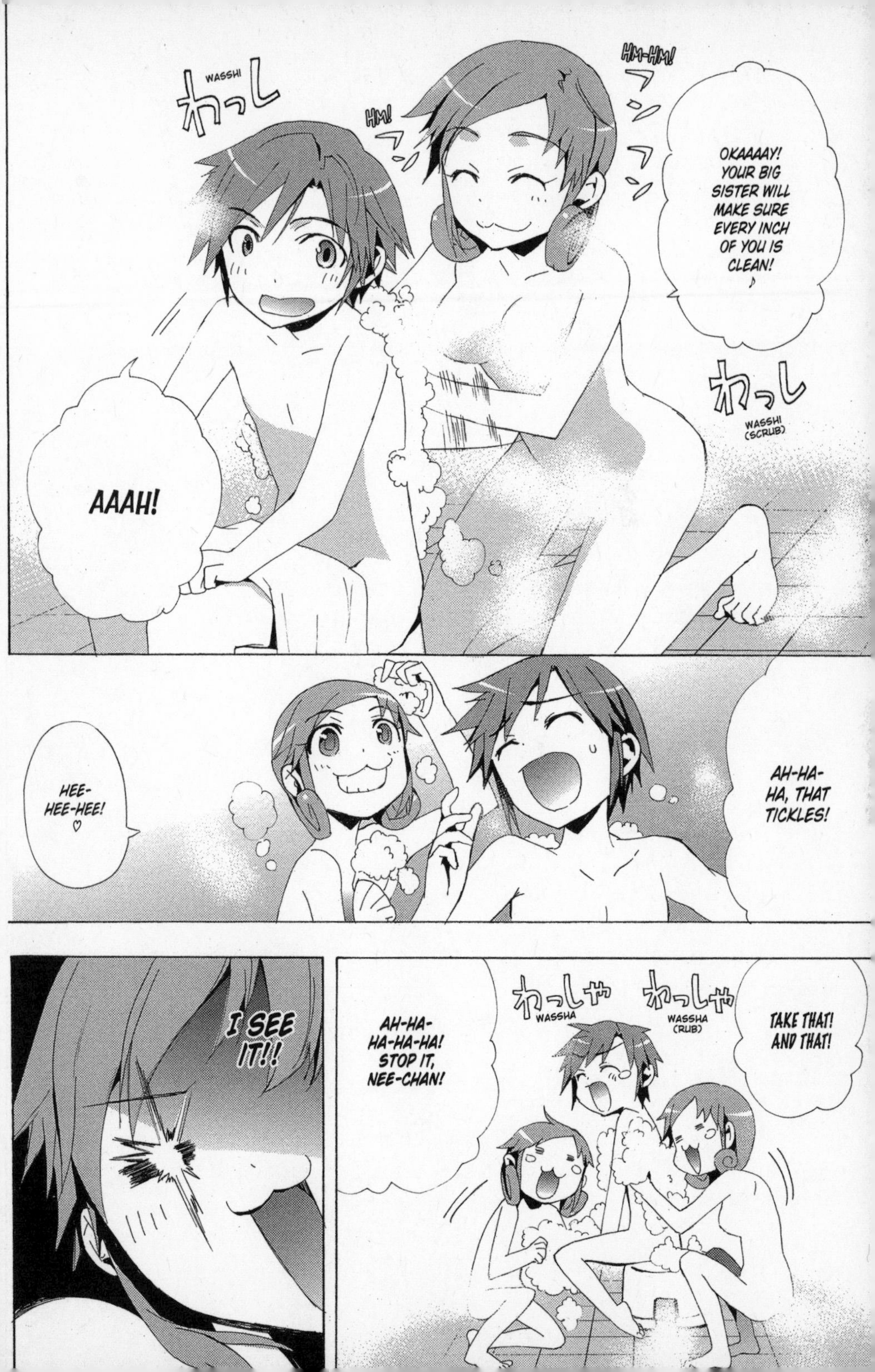
HM-HM!
OKAAAAY! YOUR BIG SISTER WILL MAKE SURE EVERY INCH OF YOU IS CLEAN! ♪
HM!
わっし
WASSHI
わっし
WASSHI (SCRUB)
AAAH!
AH-HA-HA, THAT TICKLES!
HEE-HEE-HEE! ♡
TAKE THAT! AND THAT!
わっしゃ
WASSHA (RUB)
わっしゃ
WASSHA
AH-HA-HA-HA-HA! STOP IT, NEE-CHAN!
I SEE IT!!

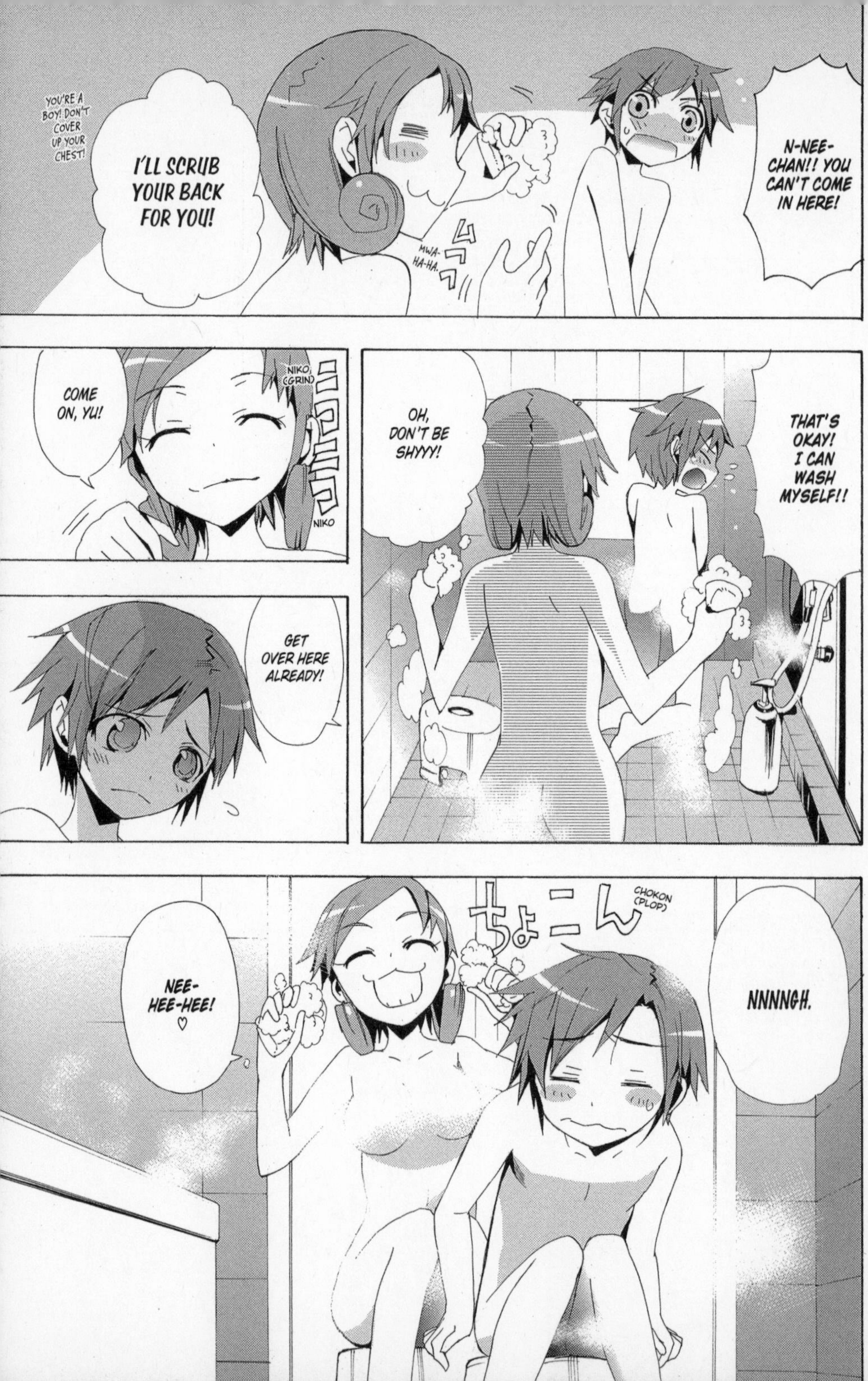
N-NEE-CHAN!! YOU CAN'T COME IN HERE!
MWA-HA-HA.
I'LL SCRUB YOUR BACK FOR YOU!
YOU'RE A BOY! DON'T COVER UP YOUR CHEST!
THAT'S OKAY! I CAN WASH MYSELF!!
OH, DON'T BE SHYYY!
NIKO (GRIN)
NIKO
COME ON, YU!
GET OVER HERE ALREADY!
NNNNGH.
ちょこん
CHOKON (PLOP)
NEE-HEE-HEE! ♡

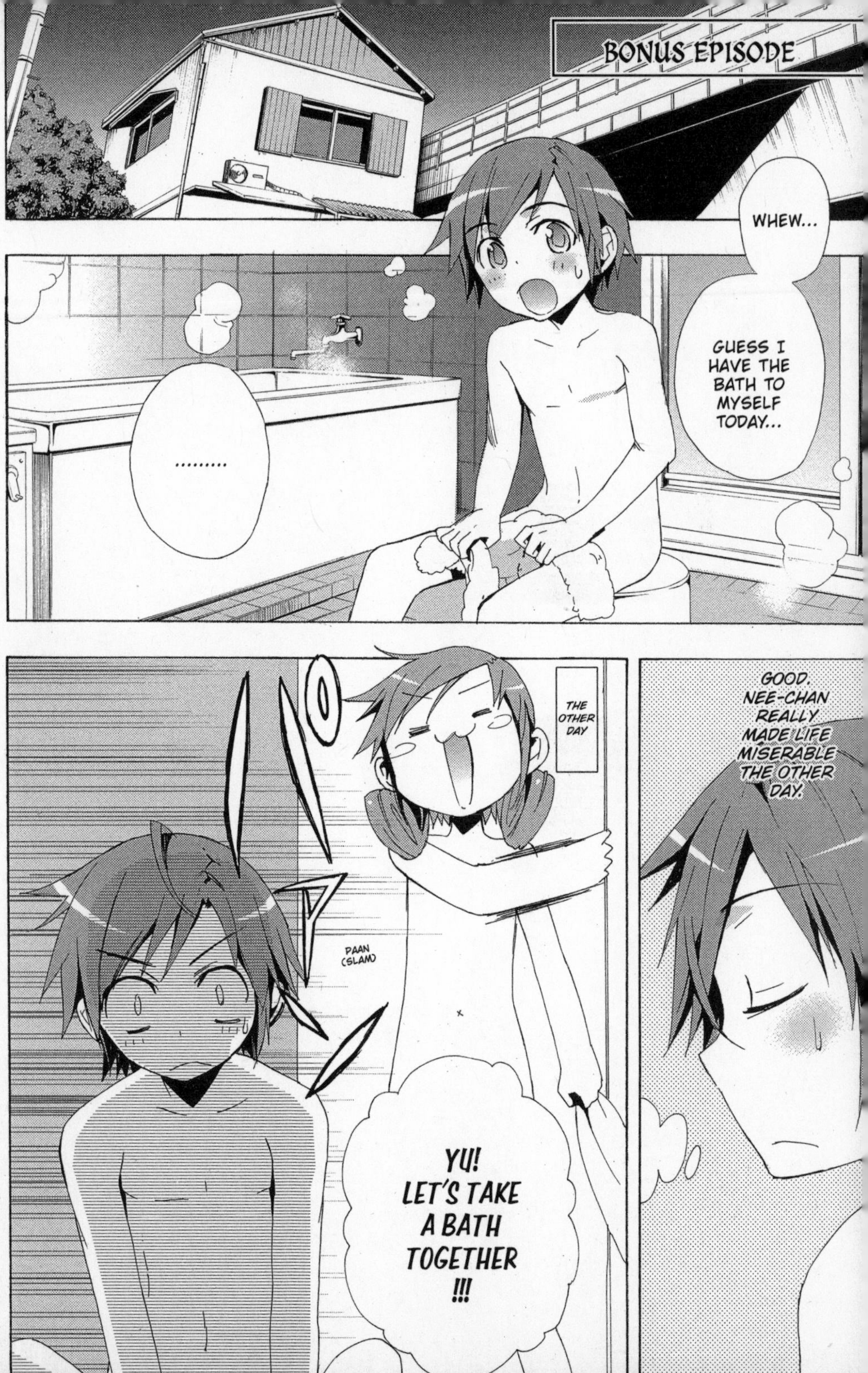
BONUS EPISODE
WHEW...
GUESS I HAVE THE BATH TO MYSELF TODAY...
....
GOOD. NEE-CHAN REALLY MADE LIFE MISERABLE THE OTHER DAY.
THE OTHER DAY
YU! LET'S TAKE A BATH TOGETHER!!!
PAAN (SLAM)

The man behind the series of kidnappings and murders that happened at Tenjin Elementary School thirty years ago

A large man carrying a sledge-hammer. Though he regrets what he did, he has gone mad and cannot stop his killing spree. He still wanders the halls of Tenjin Elementary School.

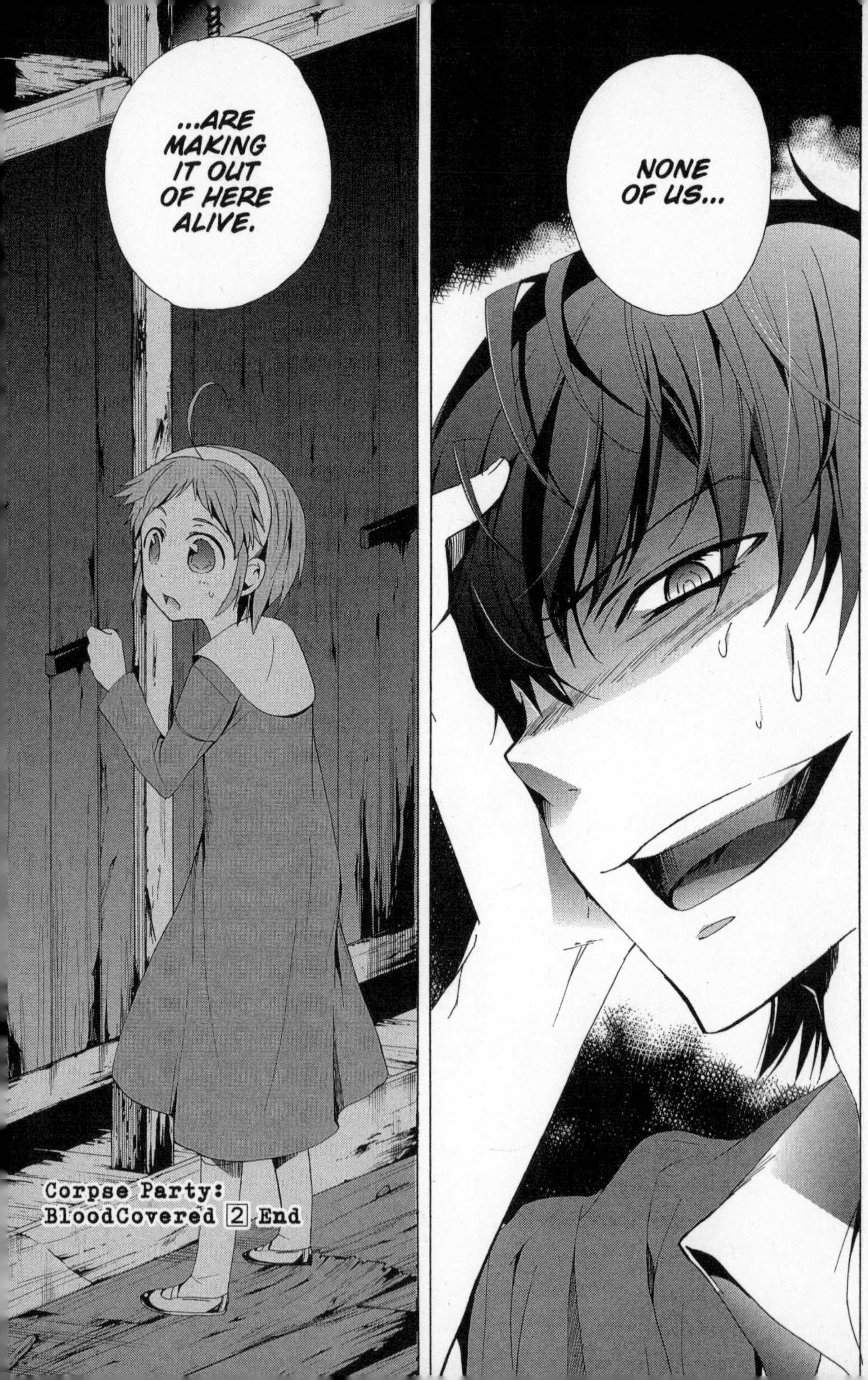
NONE OF US...
...ARE MAKING IT OUT OF HERE ALIVE.
Corpse Party: BloodCovered 2 End

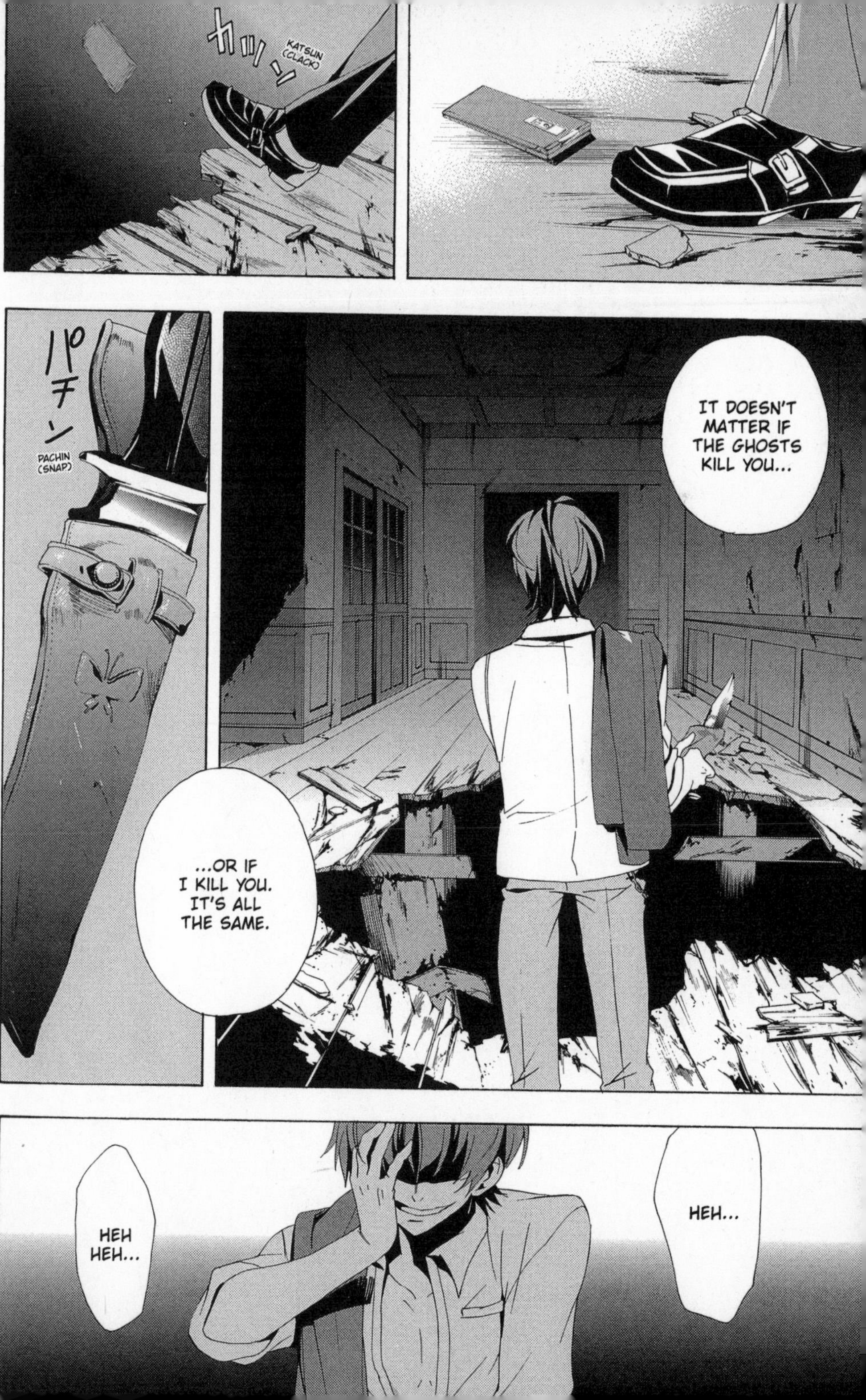
カツン
KATSUN (CLACK)
IT DOESN'T MATTER IF THE GHOSTS KILL YOU...
...OR IF I KILL YOU. IT'S ALL THE SAME.
パチン
PACHIN (SNAP)
HEH...
HEH HEH...

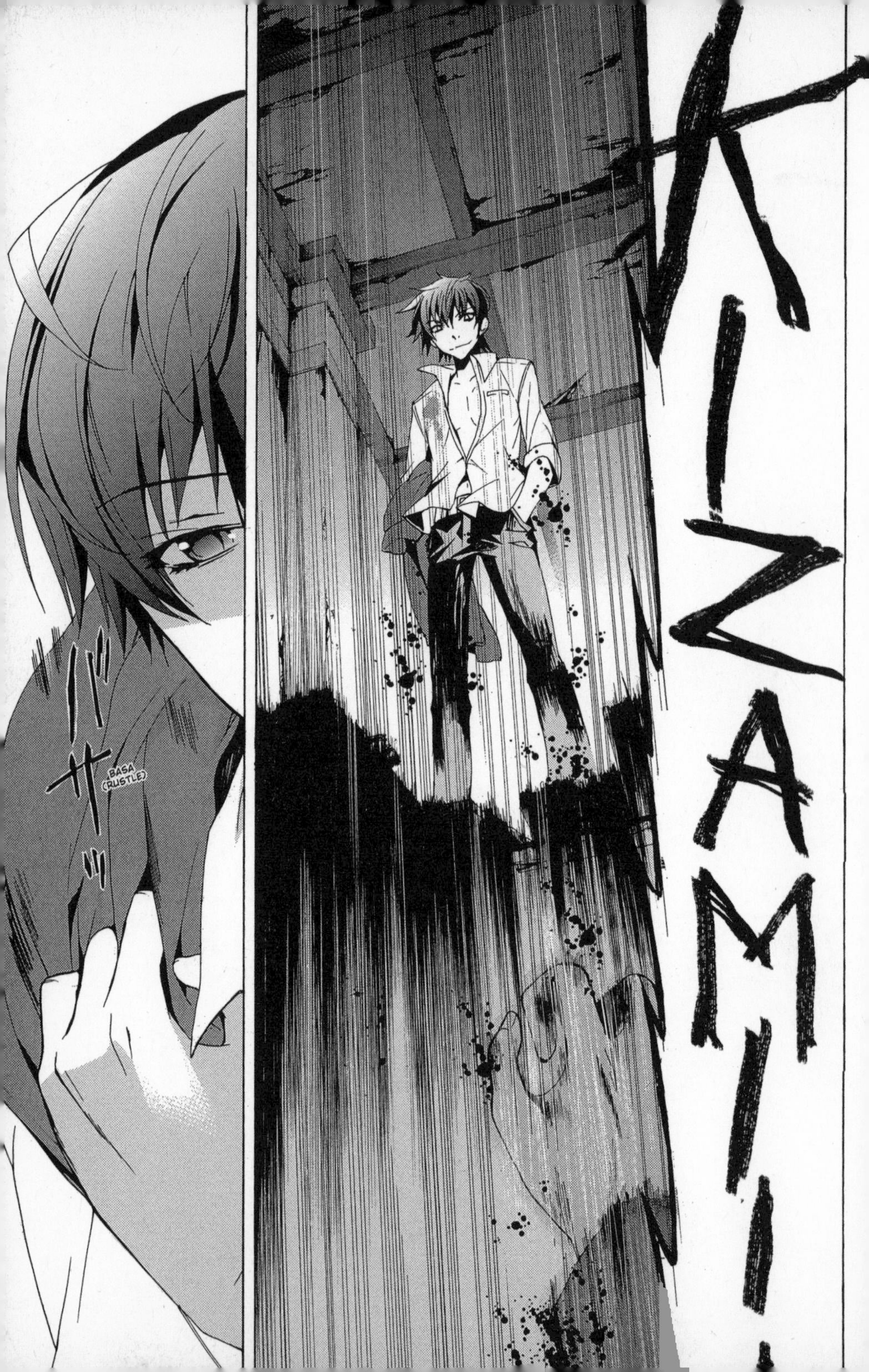
KIZAMI!
バサッ
BASA (RUSTLE)

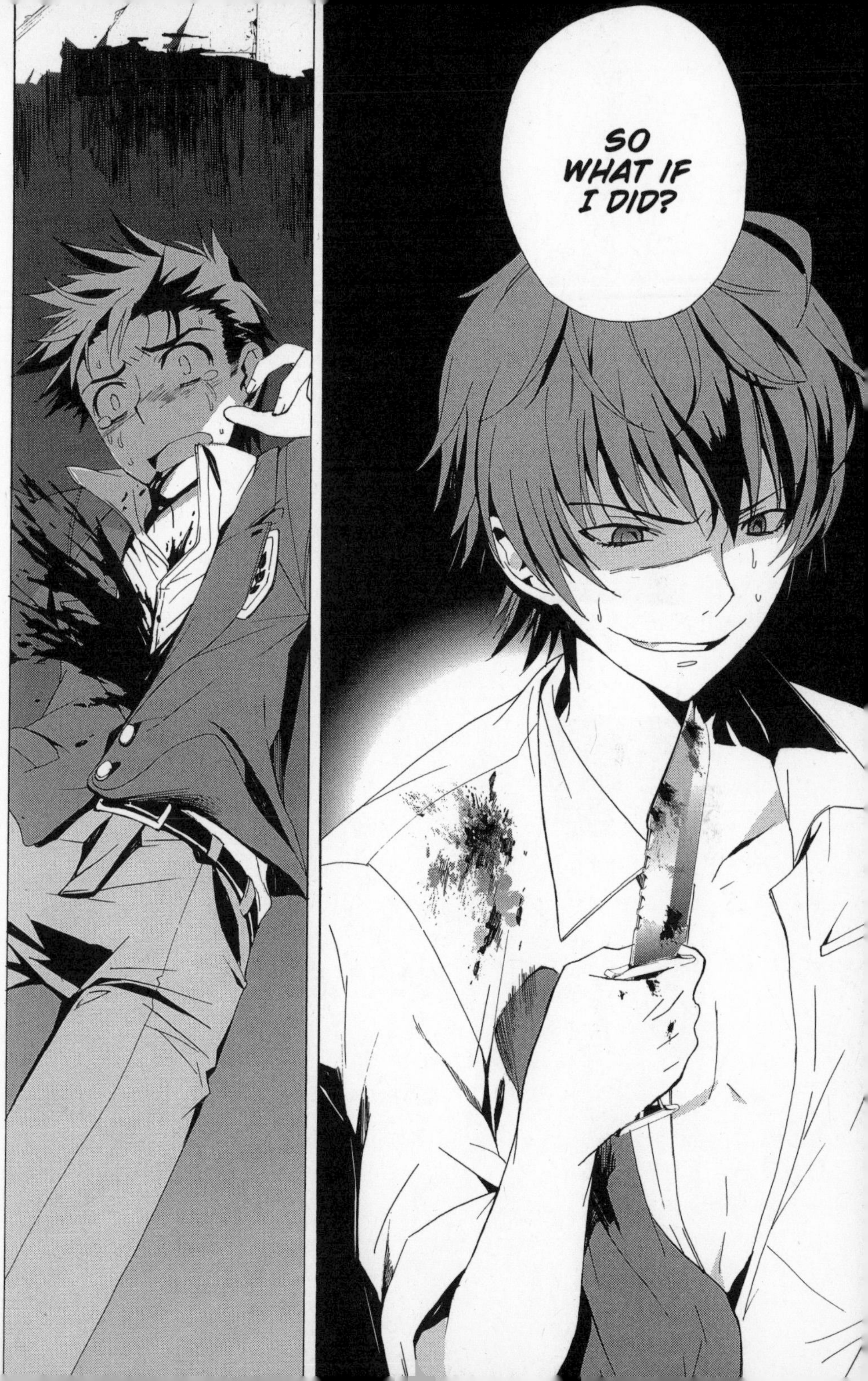
SO WHAT IF I DID?

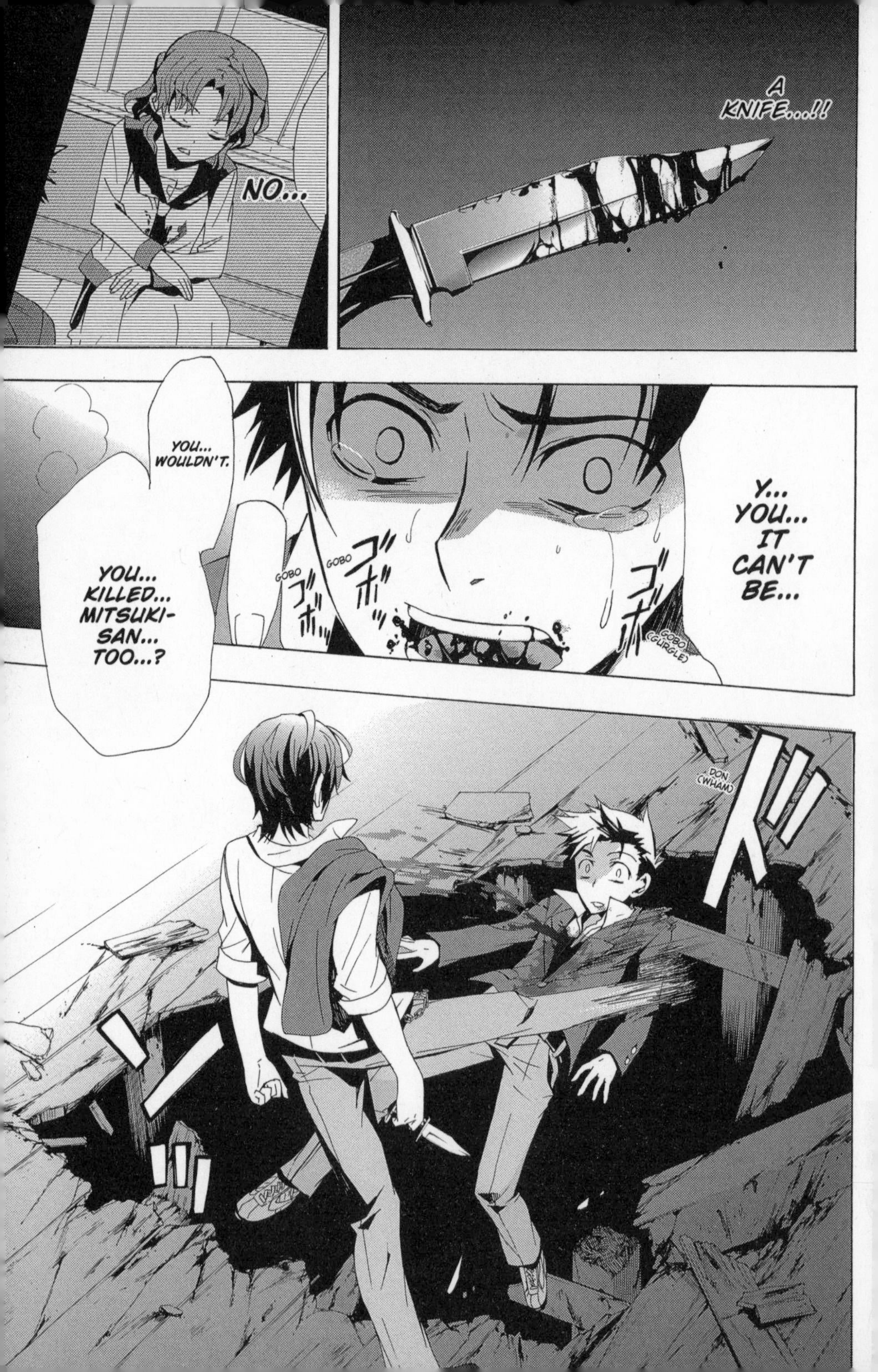
A KNIFE...!!
NO...
Y... YOU... IT CAN'T BE...
ゴボ
GOBO (GURGLE)
ゴボッ
GOBO
ゴボッ
GOBO
YOU... WOULDN'T.
YOU... KILLED... MITSUKI-SAN... TOO...?
ド
DON (WHAM)

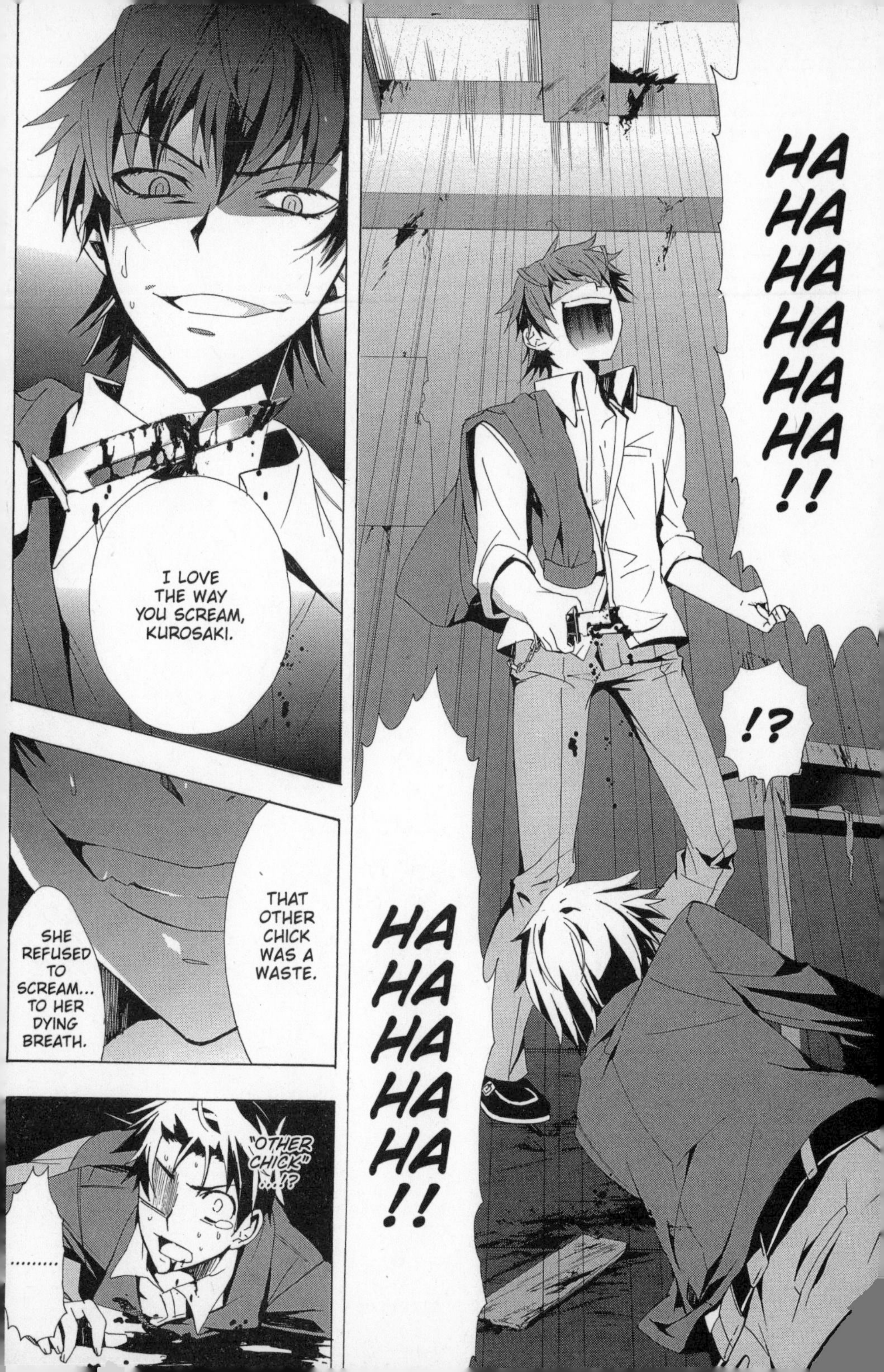
HAHAHAHAHAHA!!
!?
HAHAHAHAHAHA!!
I LOVE THE WAY YOU SCREAM, KUROSAKI.
THAT OTHER CHICK WAS A WASTE.
SHE REFUSED TO SCREAM... TO HER DYING BREATH.
"OTHER CHICK"...!?
....

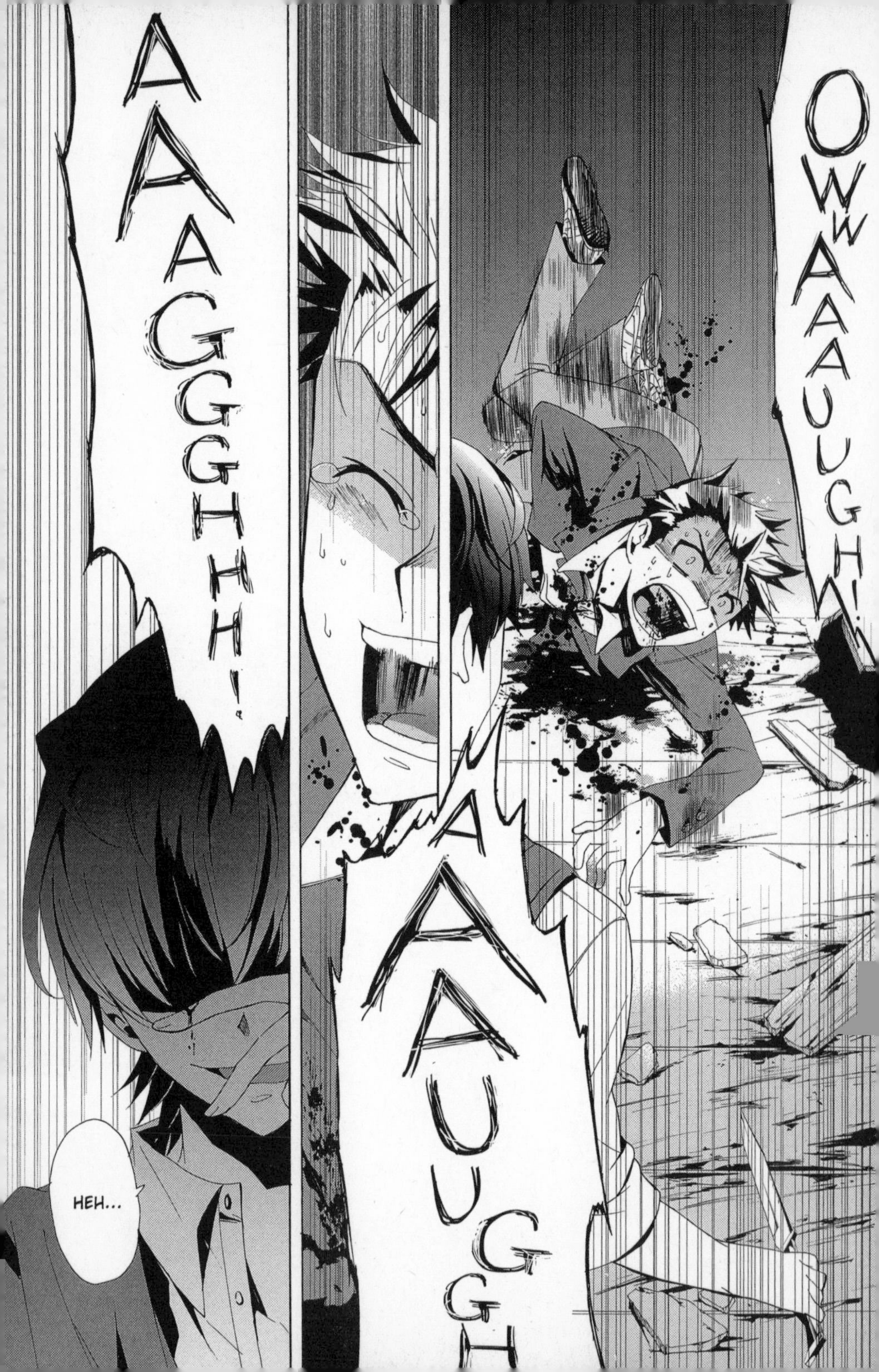
OWWAAAAUGH!!
AAAUUGGH
AAAGGGHHH!!
HEH...

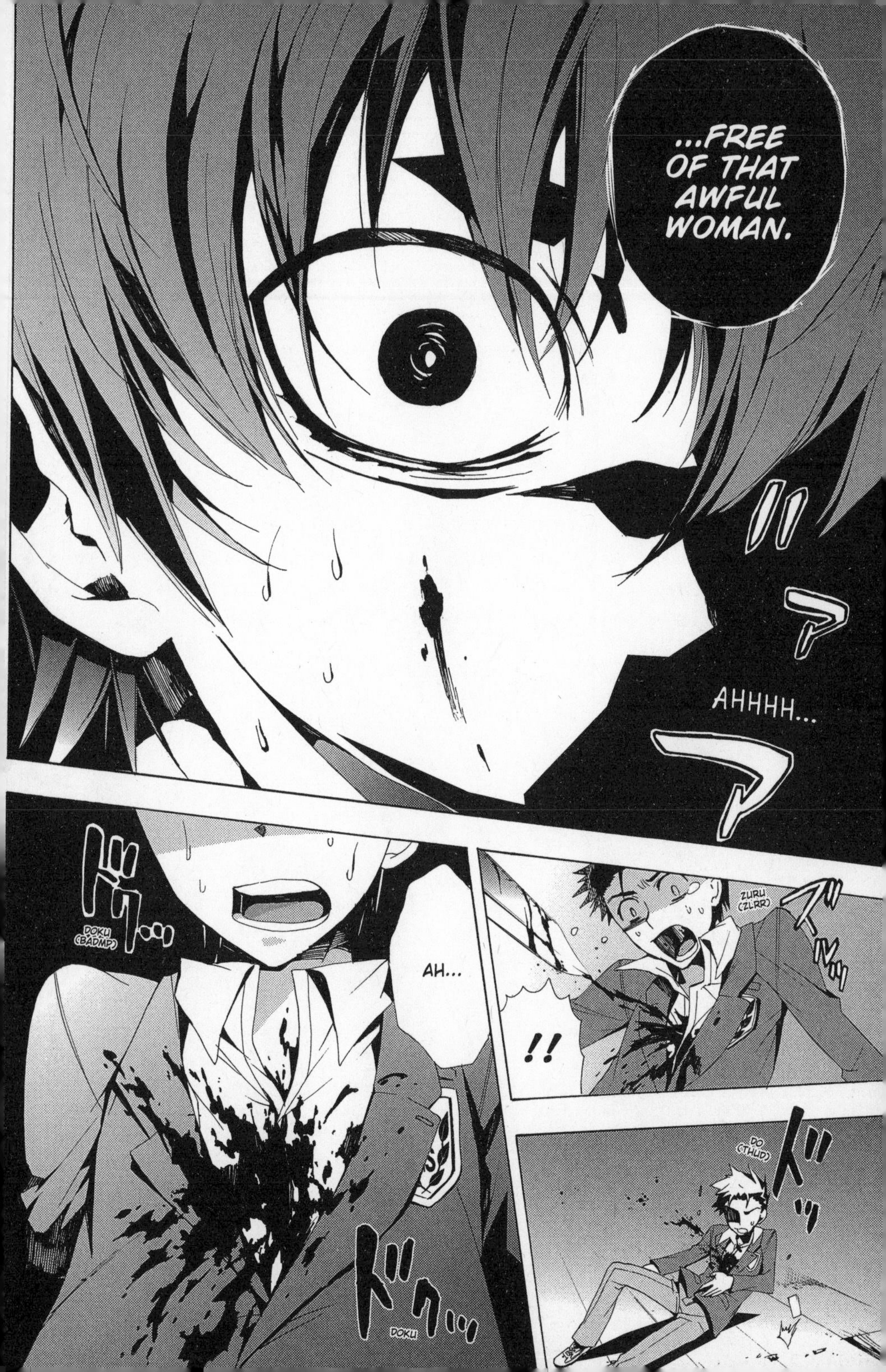
...FREE OF THAT AWFUL WOMAN.
AHHHH...
ZURU (ZLRR)
!!
DO (THUD)
DOKU (BADMP)
AH...
DOKU

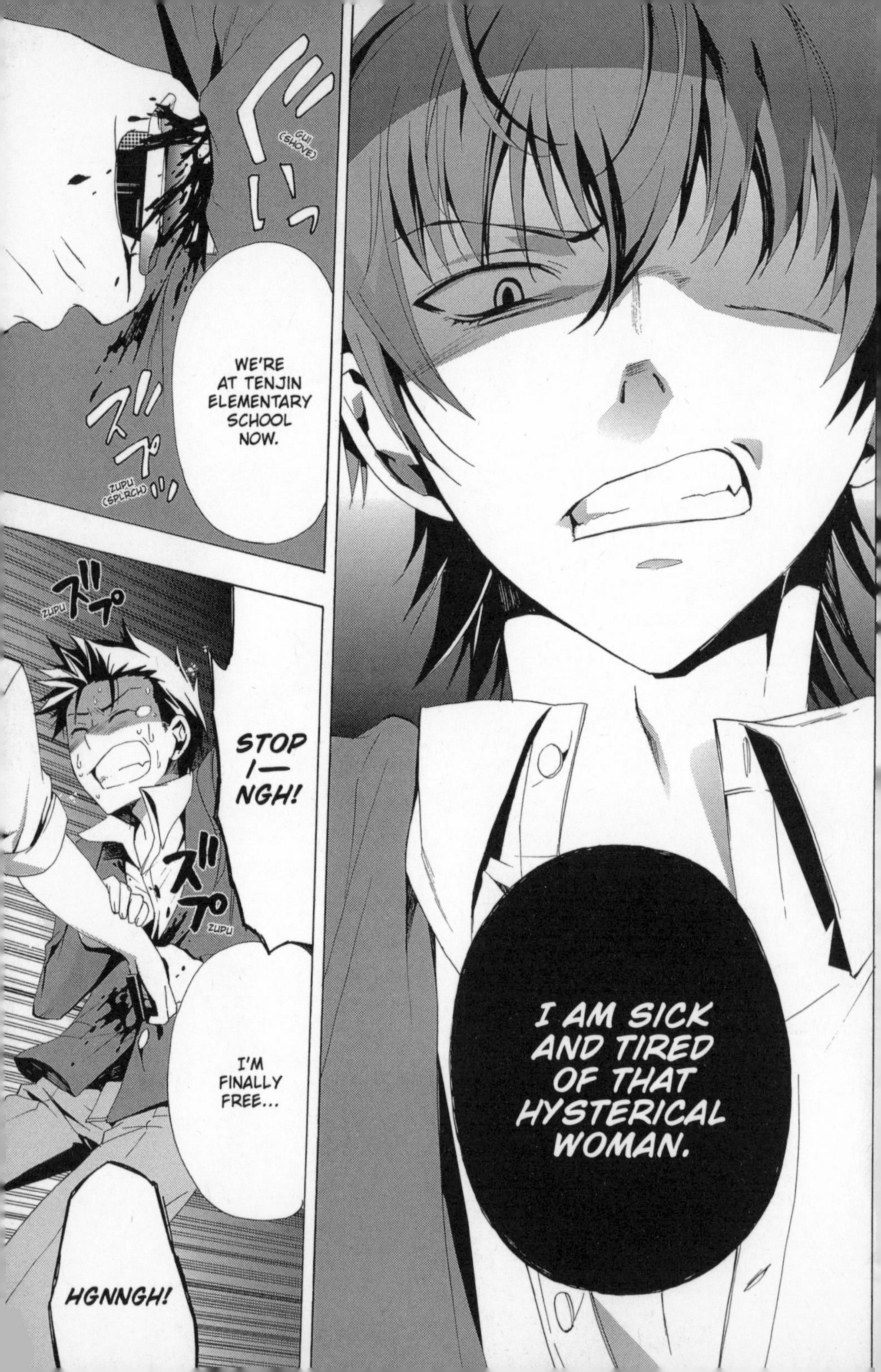
I AM SICK AND TIRED OF THAT HYSTERICAL WOMAN.
GUI (SHOVE)
WE'RE AT TENJIN ELEMENTARY SCHOOL NOW.
ZUPU (SPLRCH)
ZUPU
STOP I— NGH!
ZUPU
I'M FINALLY FREE...
HGNNGH!

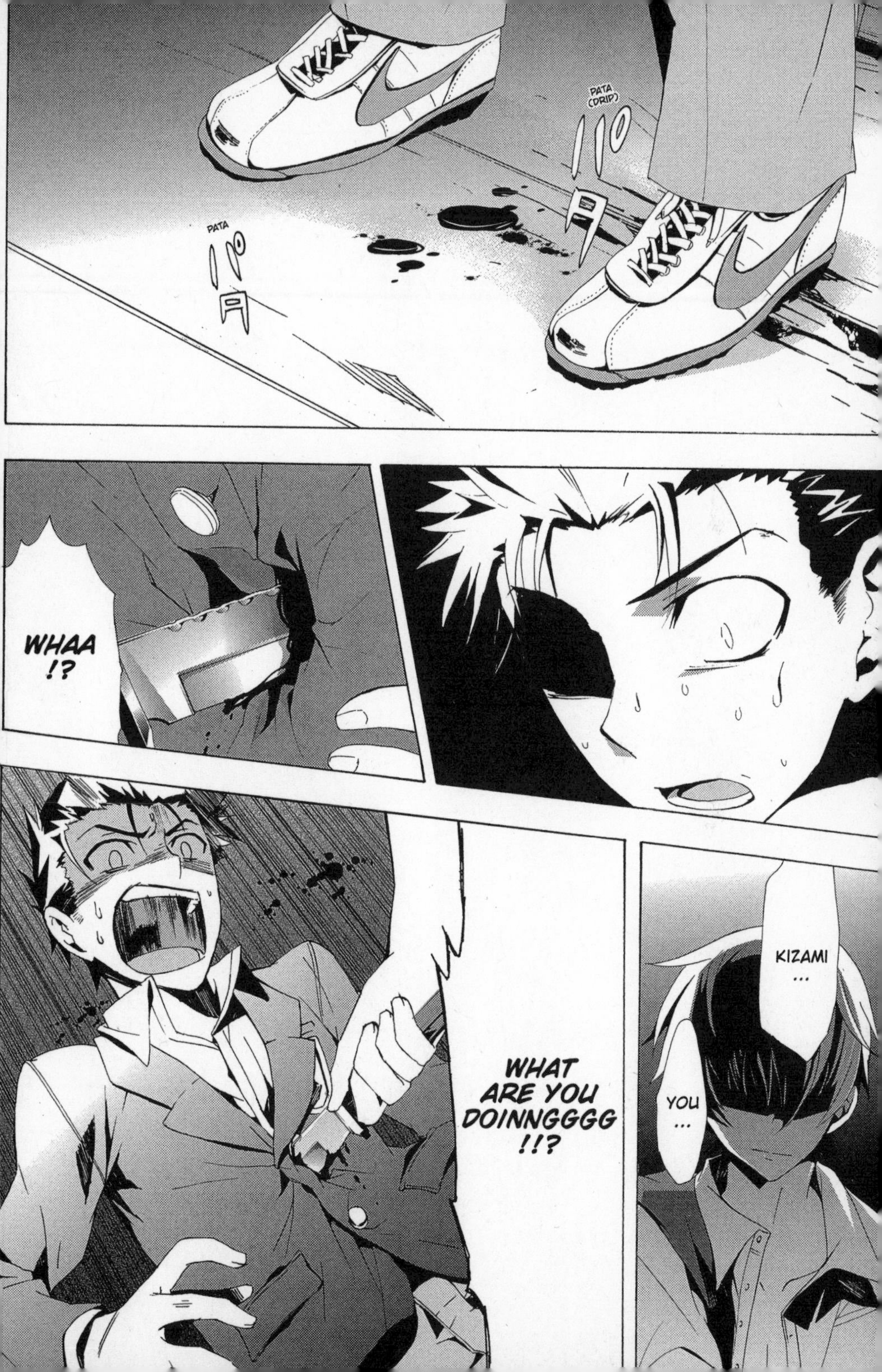
PATA (DRIP)
PATA
WHAA !?
KIZAMI ...
YOU ...
WHAT ARE YOU DOINNGGGG !!?

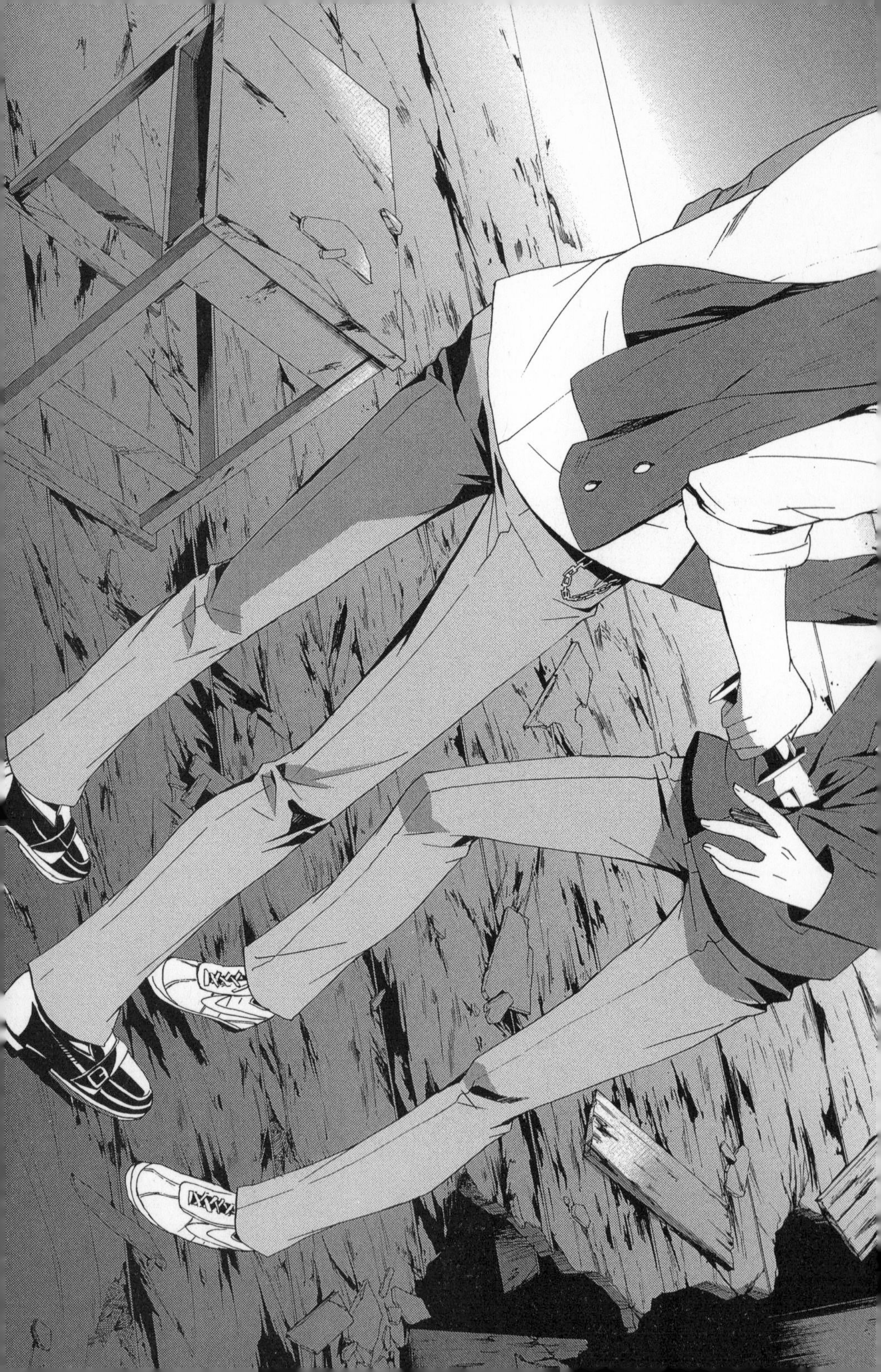

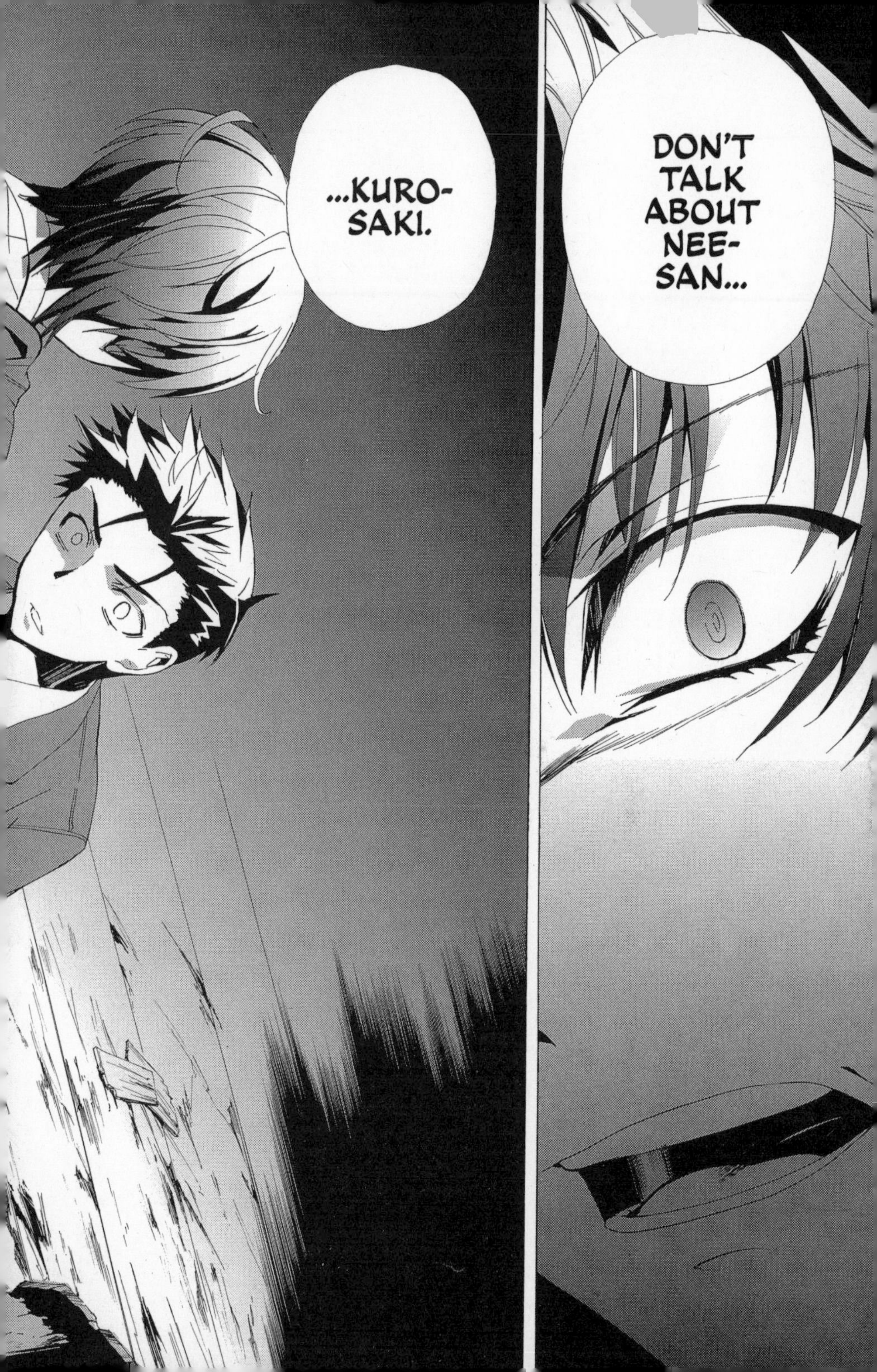
DON'T TALK ABOUT NEE-SAN...
...KURO-SAKI.

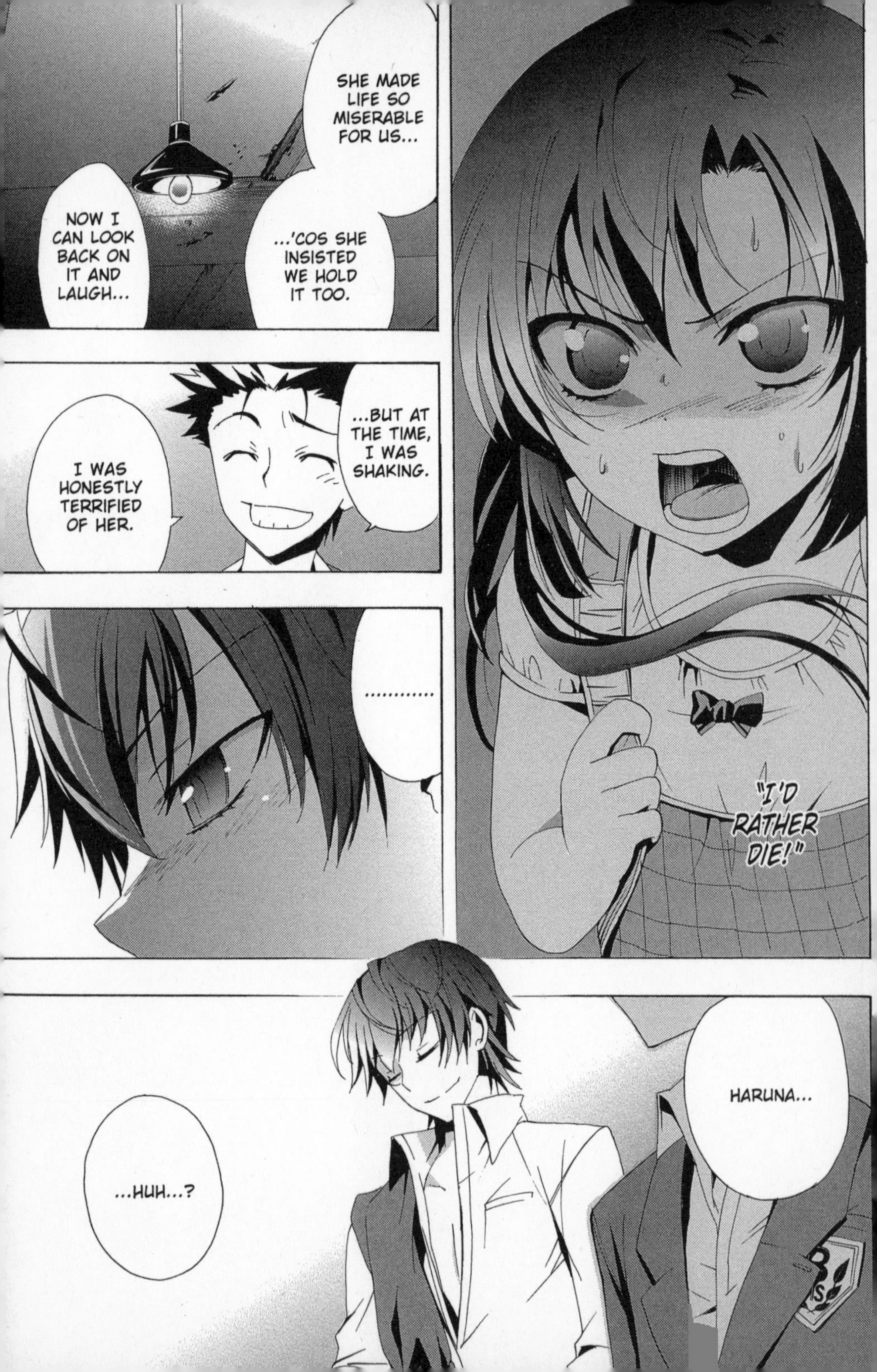
"I'D RATHER DIE!"
SHE MADE LIFE SO MISERABLE FOR US...
...'COS SHE INSISTED WE HOLD IT TOO.
NOW I CAN LOOK BACK ON IT AND LAUGH...
...BUT AT THE TIME, I WAS SHAKING.
I WAS HONESTLY TERRIFIED OF HER.
....
HARUNA...
...HUH...?

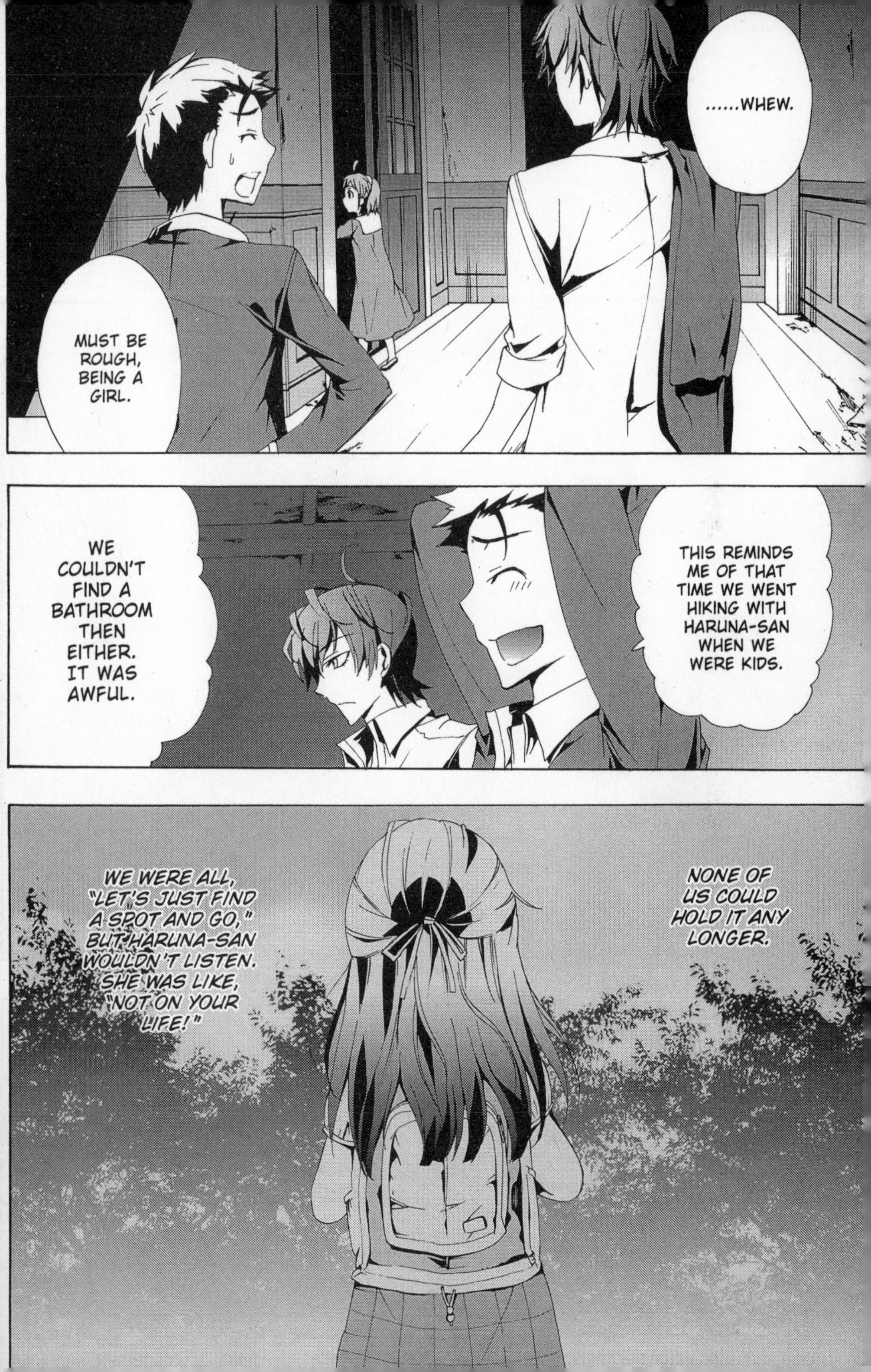
......WHEW.
MUST BE ROUGH, BEING A GIRL.
THIS REMINDS ME OF THAT TIME WE WENT HIKING WITH HARUNA-SAN WHEN WE WERE KIDS.
WE COULDN'T FIND A BATHROOM THEN EITHER. IT WAS AWFUL.
NONE OF US COULD HOLD IT ANY LONGER.
WE WERE ALL, "LET'S JUST FIND A SPOT AND GO," BUT HARUNA-SAN WOULDN'T LISTEN. SHE WAS LIKE, "NOT ON YOUR LIFE!"

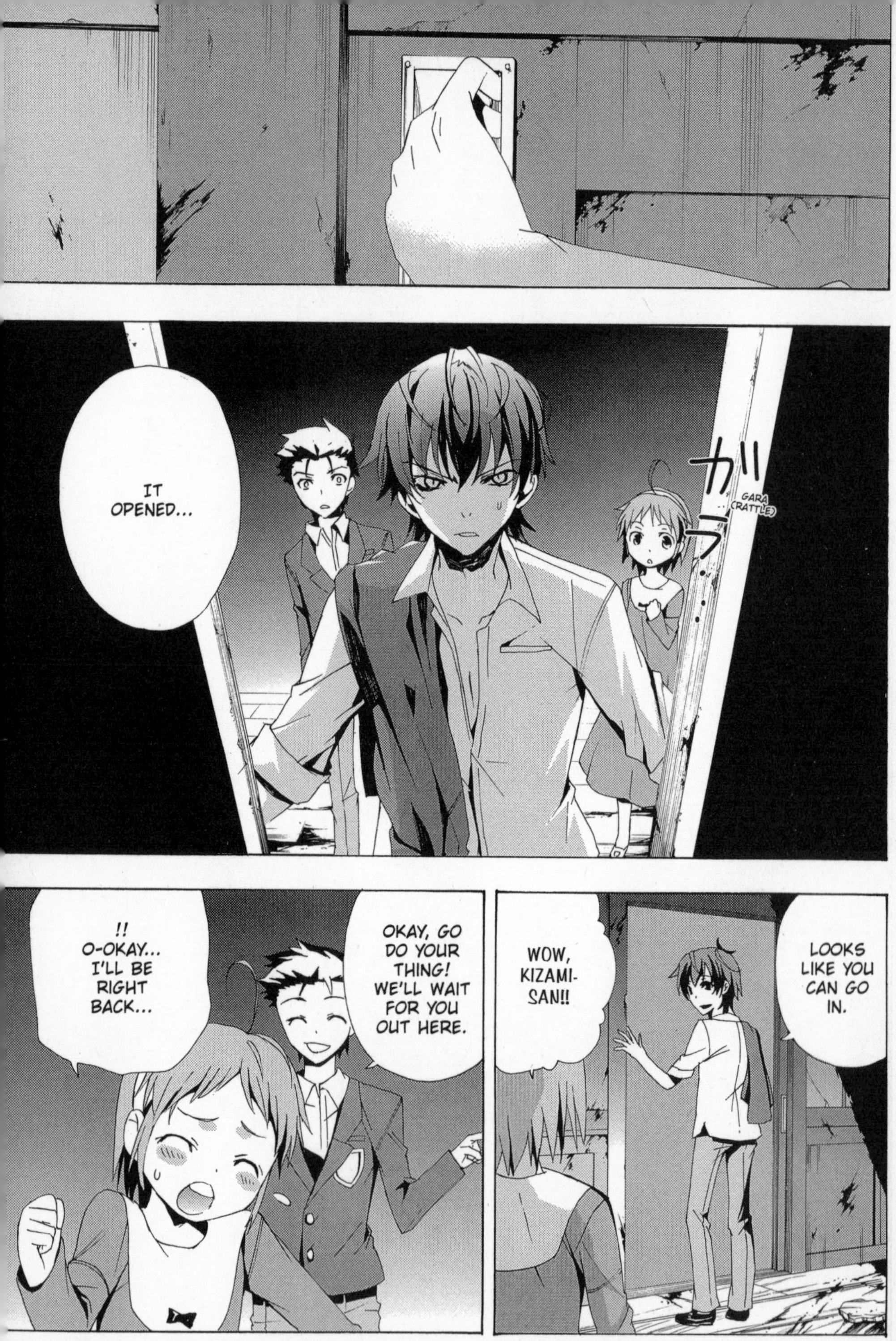

ガラ
GARA (RATTLE)
IT OPENED...
LOOKS LIKE YOU CAN GO IN.
WOW, KIZAMI-SAN!!
OKAY, GO DO YOUR THING! WE'LL WAIT FOR YOU OUT HERE.
!! O-OKAY... I'LL BE RIGHT BACK...

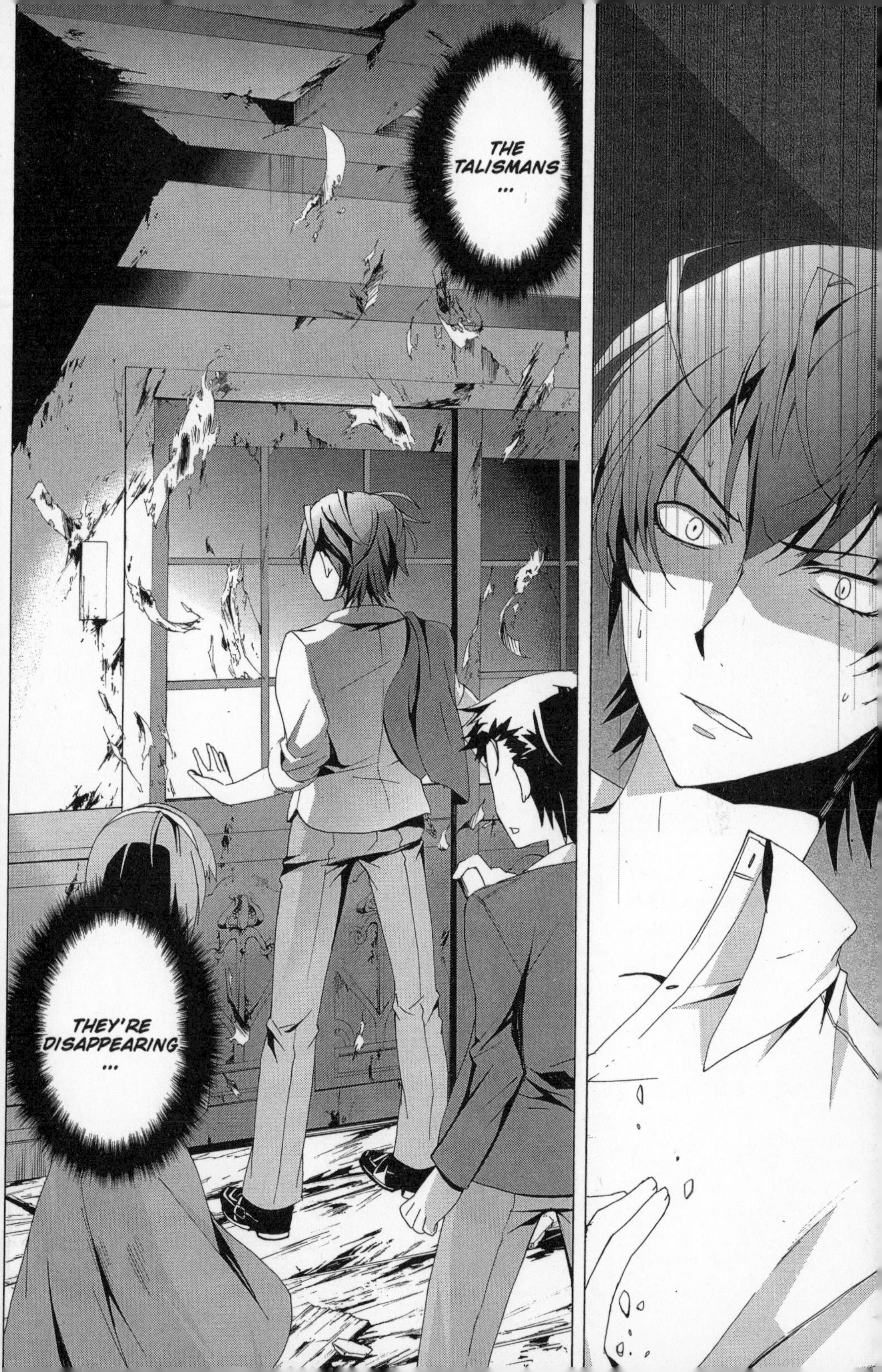
THE TALISMANS ...
THEY'RE DISAPPEARING ...

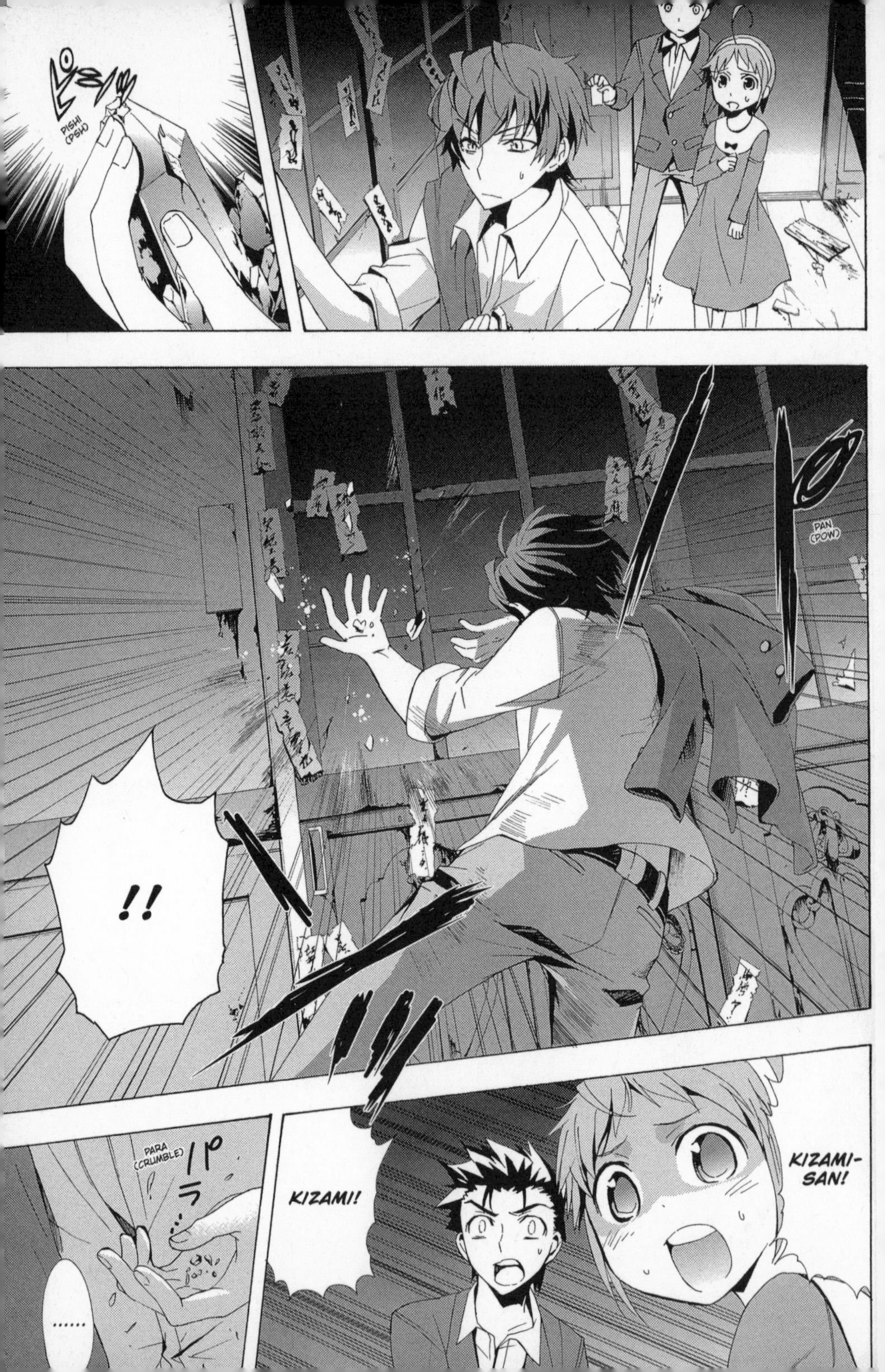
PISHI (PSH)
PAN (POW)
!!
KIZAMI-SAN!
KIZAMI!
PARA (CRUMBLE)
......

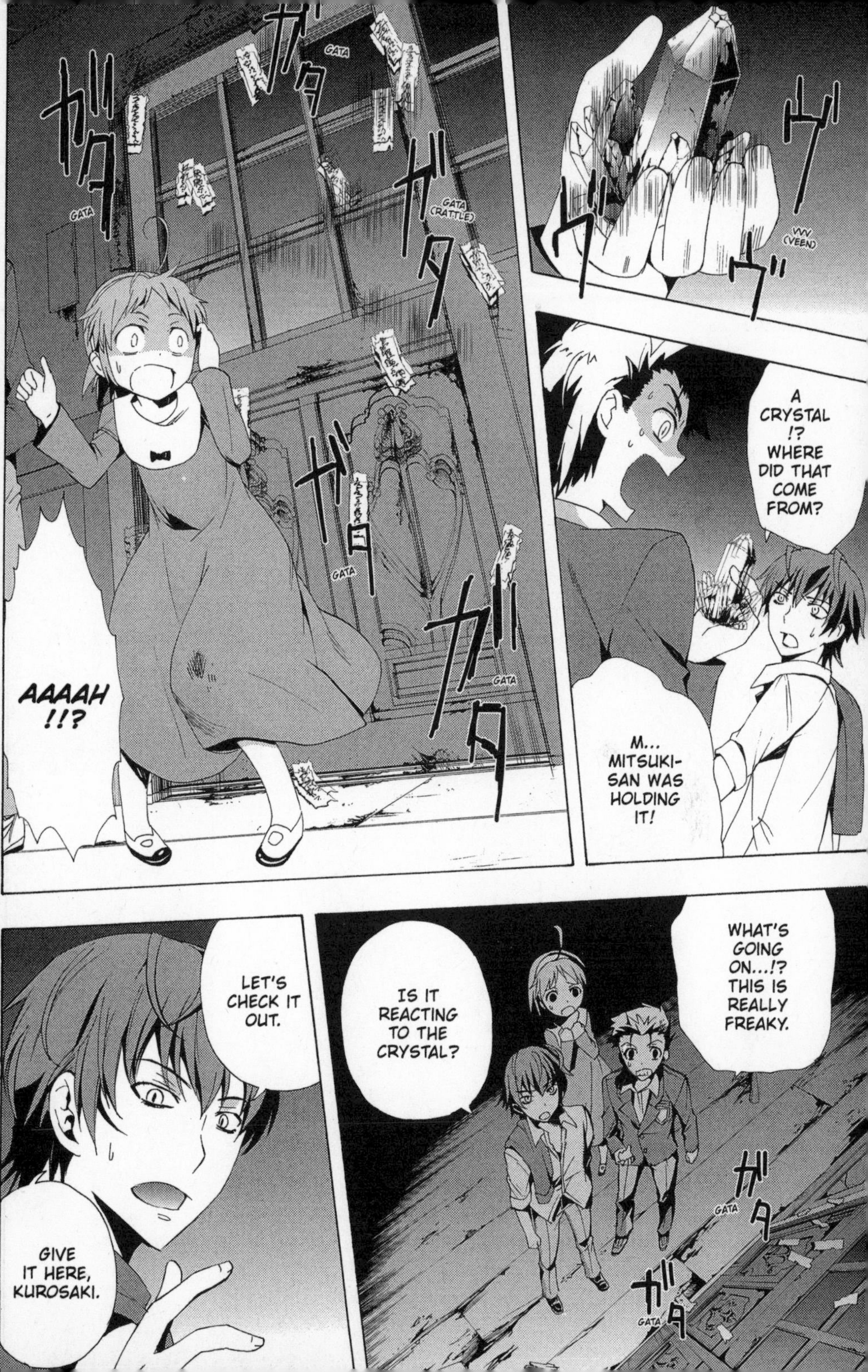
VVV (VEEN)
A CRYSTAL!? WHERE DID THAT COME FROM?
M... MITSUKI-SAN WAS HOLDING IT!
GATA
GATA (RATTLE)
GATA
GATA
GATA
AAAAH!!?
WHAT'S GOING ON...!? THIS IS REALLY FREAKY.
IS IT REACTING TO THE CRYSTAL?
GATA
GATA
LET'S CHECK IT OUT.
GIVE IT HERE, KUROSAKI.

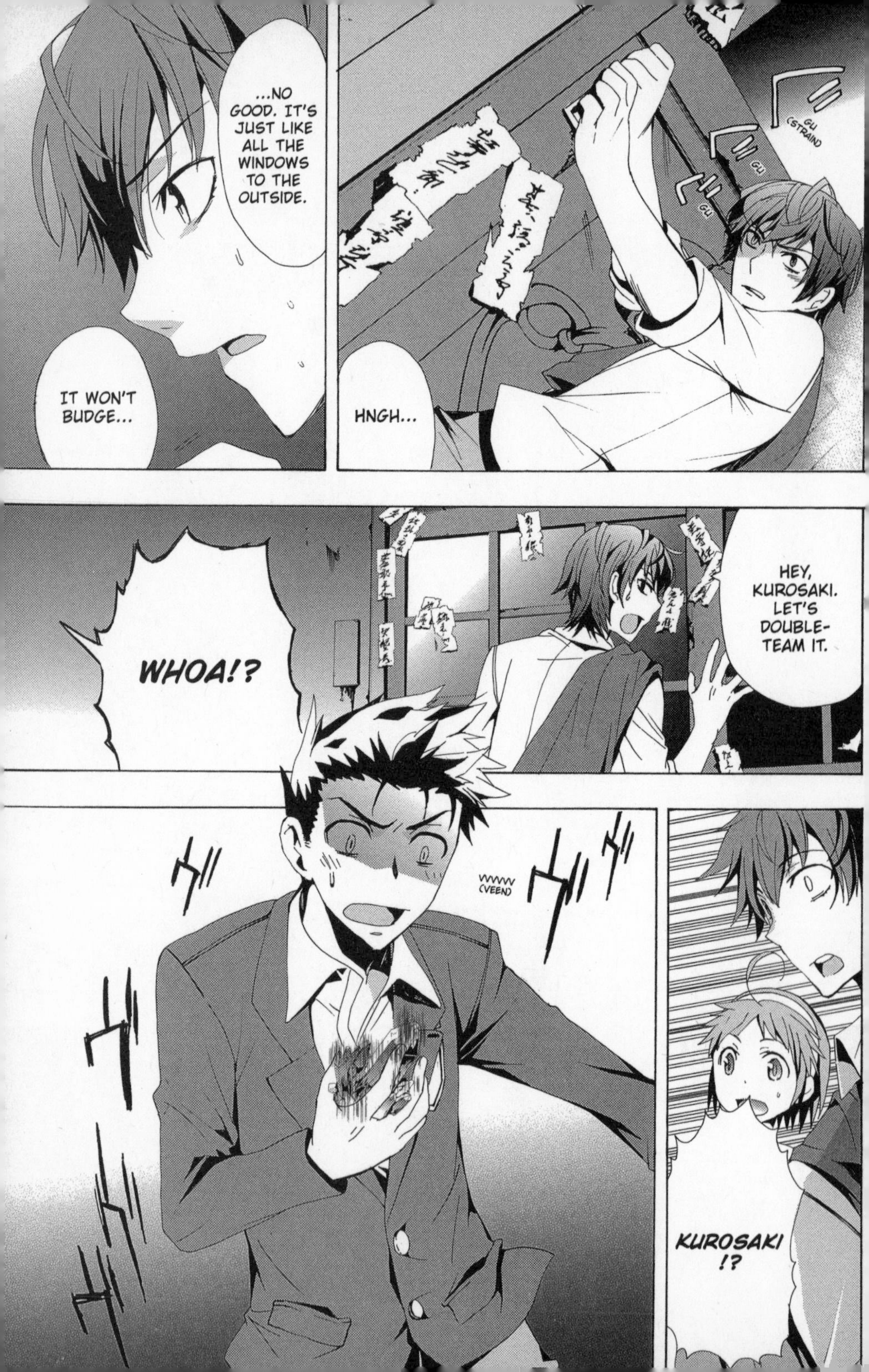
GU (STRAIN)
GU
GU
HNGH...
...NO GOOD. IT'S JUST LIKE ALL THE WINDOWS TO THE OUTSIDE.
IT WON'T BUDGE...
HEY, KUROSAKI. LET'S DOUBLE-TEAM IT.
WHOA!?
KUROSAKI !?
VVVVVV (VEEND)

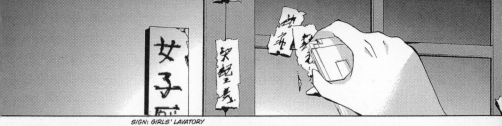

SIGN: GIRLS' LAVATORY

IS THIS IT?

WHAT ARE THESE TALISMANS FOR?

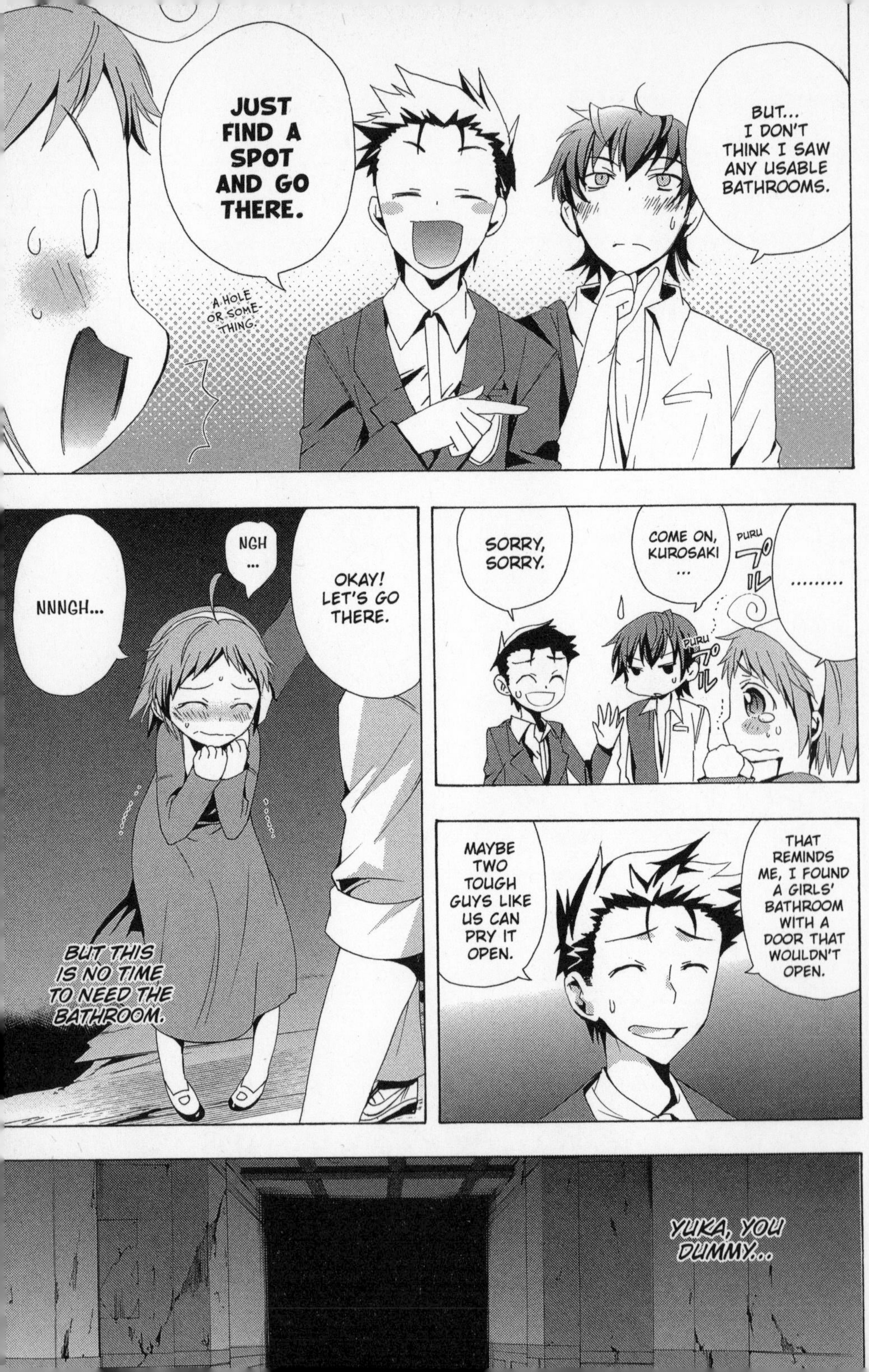
BUT... I DON'T THINK I SAW ANY USABLE BATHROOMS.
JUST FIND A SPOT AND GO THERE.
A HOLE OR SOMETHING.
....
PURU
プル
PURU
プル
COME ON, KUROSAKI ...
SORRY, SORRY.
THAT REMINDS ME, I FOUND A GIRLS' BATHROOM WITH A DOOR THAT WOULDN'T OPEN.
MAYBE TWO TOUGH GUYS LIKE US CAN PRY IT OPEN.
OKAY! LET'S GO THERE.
NGH ...
NNNGH...
BUT THIS IS NO TIME TO NEED THE BATHROOM.
YUKA, YOU DUMMY...

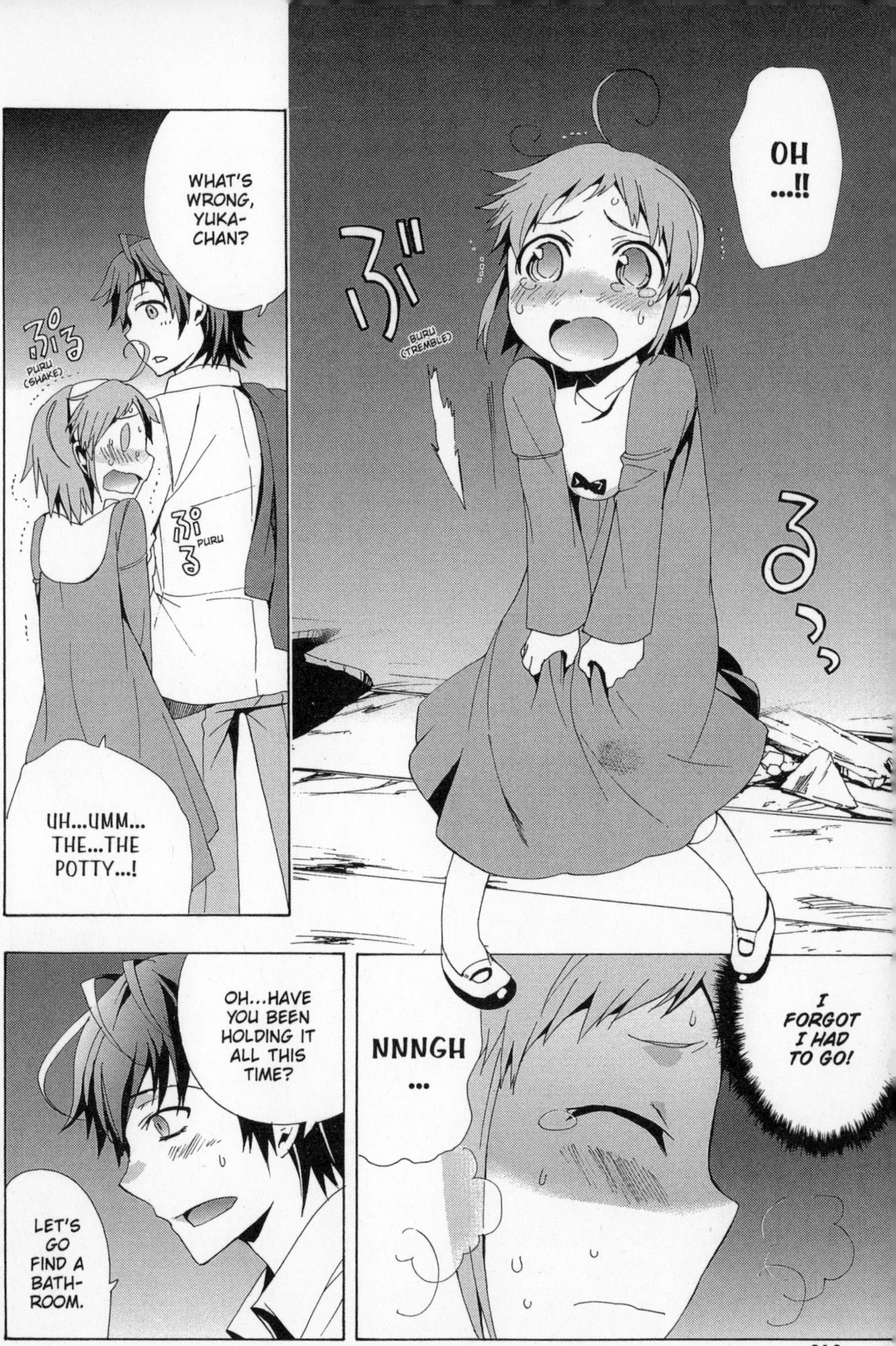
OH ...!!
ぶ
BURU (TREMBLE)
るっっ
WHAT'S WRONG, YUKA-CHAN?
ぷる
PURU (SHAKE)
ぷる
PURU
UH...UMM... THE...THE POTTY...!
I FORGOT I HAD TO GO!
NNNGH ...
OH...HAVE YOU BEEN HOLDING IT ALL THIS TIME?
LET'S GO FIND A BATH-ROOM.

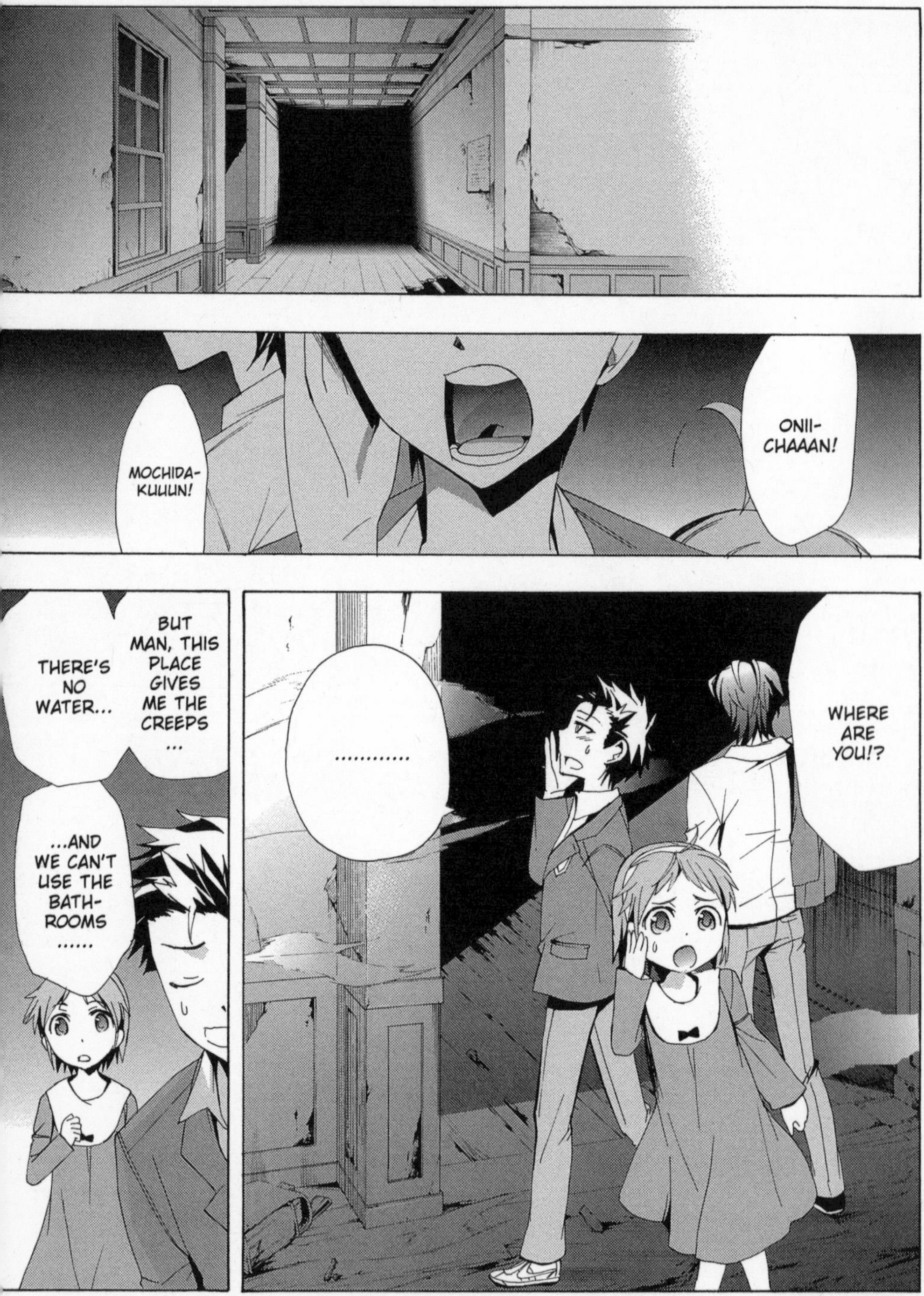
ONII-CHAAAN!
MOCHIDA-KUUUN!
WHERE ARE YOU!?
....
BUT MAN, THIS PLACE GIVES ME THE CREEPS...
THERE'S NO WATER...
...AND WE CAN'T USE THE BATH-ROOMS......

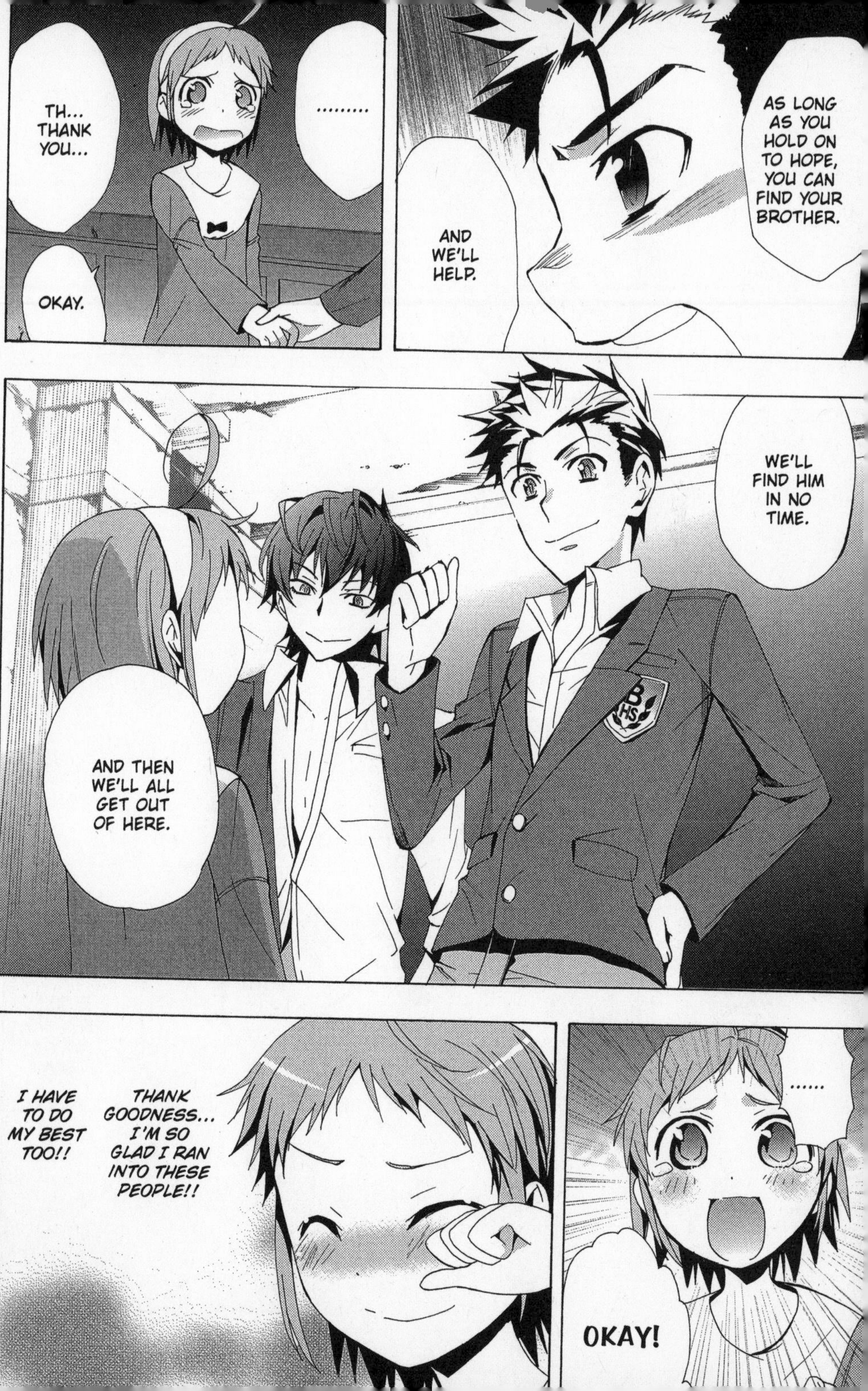
AS LONG AS YOU HOLD ON TO HOPE, YOU CAN FIND YOUR BROTHER.
AND WE'LL HELP.
....
TH... THANK YOU...
OKAY.
WE'LL FIND HIM IN NO TIME.
AND THEN WE'LL ALL GET OUT OF HERE.
......
OKAY!
THANK GOODNESS... I'M SO GLAD I RAN INTO THESE PEOPLE!!
I HAVE TO DO MY BEST TOO!!

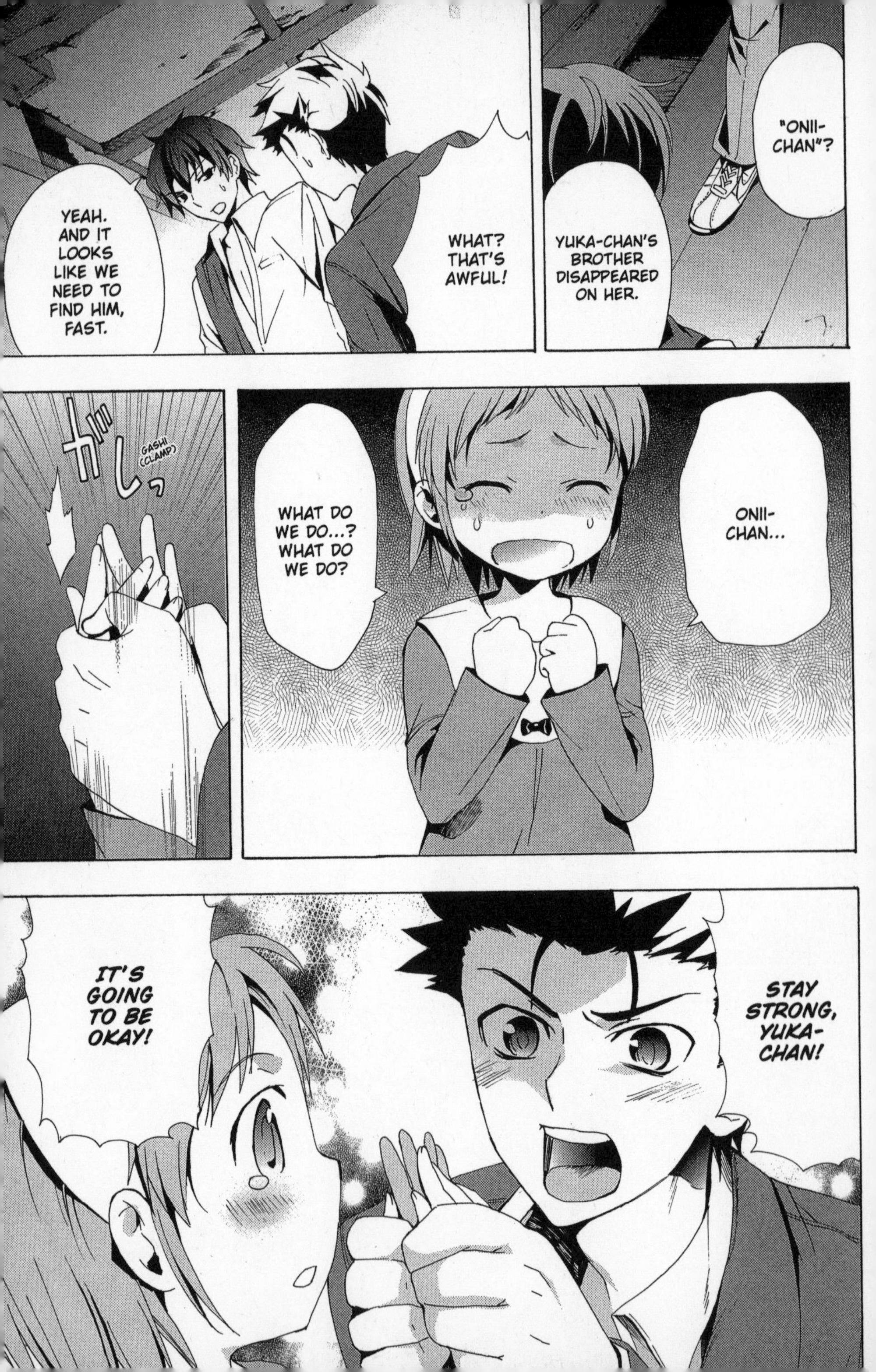
"ONII-CHAN"?
YUKA-CHAN'S BROTHER DISAPPEARED ON HER.
WHAT? THAT'S AWFUL!
YEAH. AND IT LOOKS LIKE WE NEED TO FIND HIM, FAST.
ONII-CHAN...
WHAT DO WE DO...? WHAT DO WE DO?
がしっ
GASHI (CLAMP)
STAY STRONG, YUKA-CHAN!
IT'S GOING TO BE OKAY!

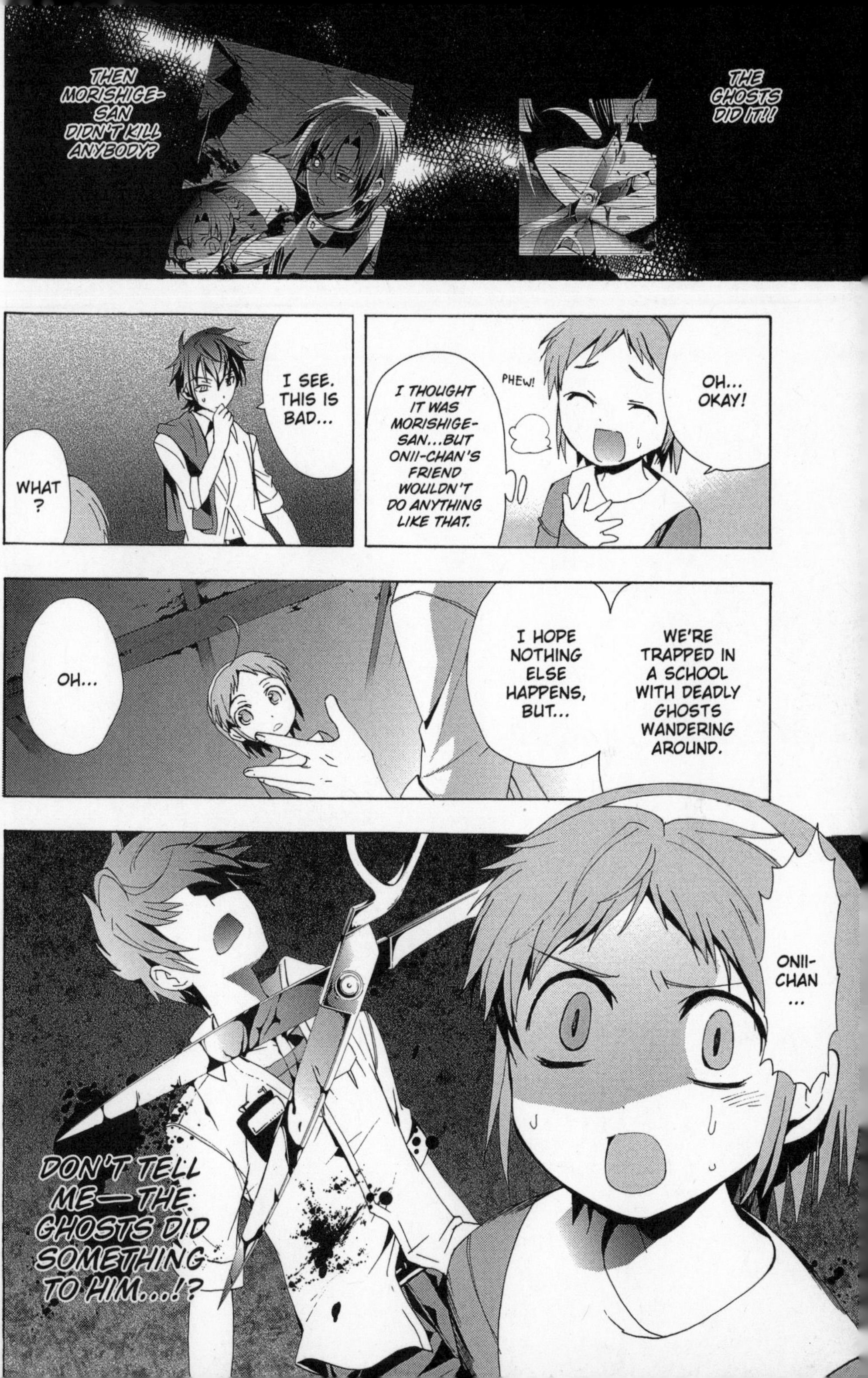
THE GHOSTS DID IT!!
THEN MORISHIGE-SAN DIDN'T KILL ANYBODY?
OH... OKAY!
PHEW!
I THOUGHT IT WAS MORISHIGE-SAN...BUT ONII-CHAN'S FRIEND WOULDN'T DO ANYTHING LIKE THAT.
I SEE. THIS IS BAD...
WHAT?
WE'RE TRAPPED IN A SCHOOL WITH DEADLY GHOSTS WANDERING AROUND.
I HOPE NOTHING ELSE HAPPENS, BUT...
OH...
ONII-CHAN...
DON'T TELL ME—THE GHOSTS DID SOMETHING TO HIM...!?

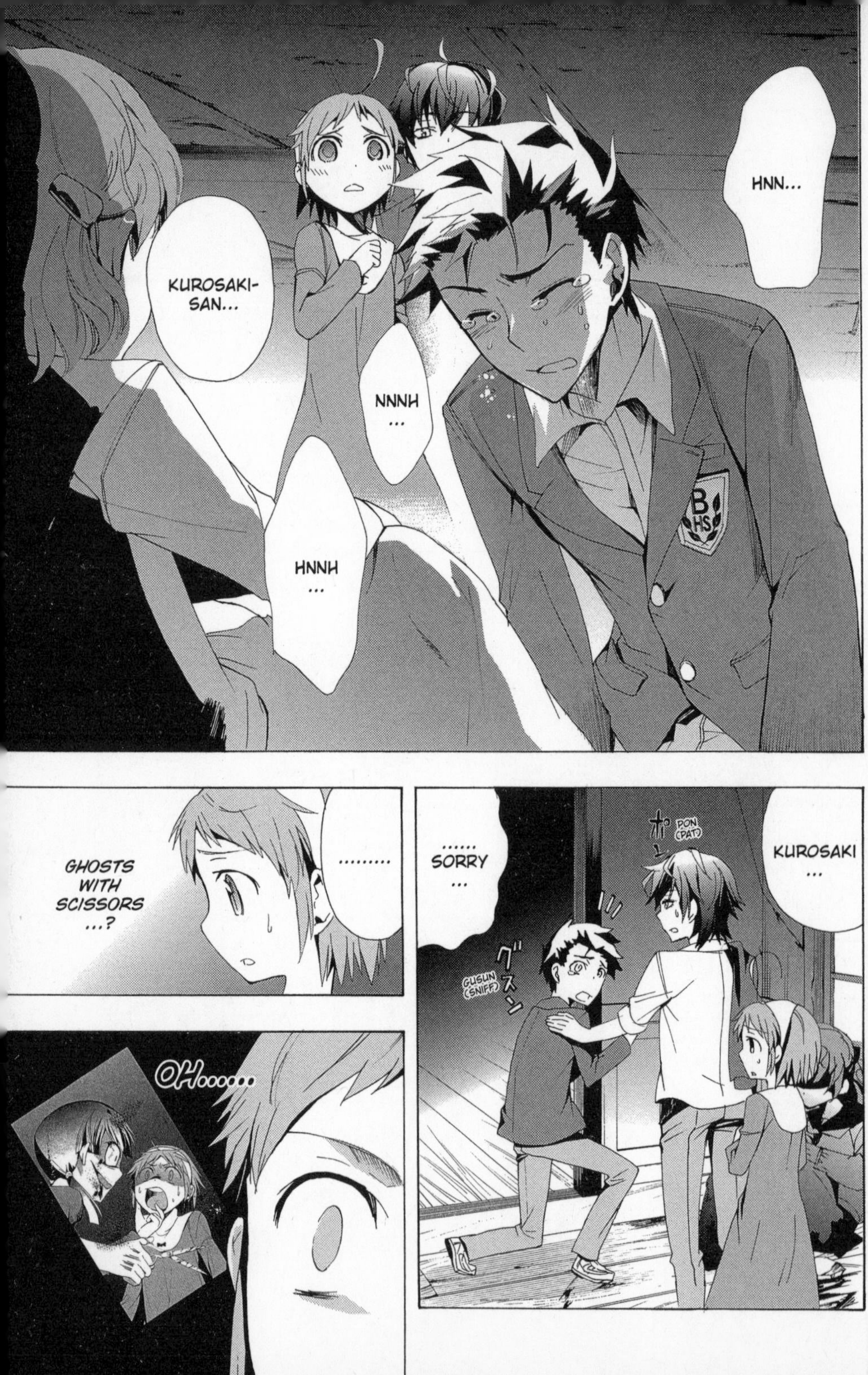
HNN...
KUROSAKI-SAN...
NNNH ...
HNNH ...
KUROSAKI ...
PON (PAT)
...... SORRY ...
GUSUN (SNIFF)
....
GHOSTS WITH SCISSORS ...?
OH.......

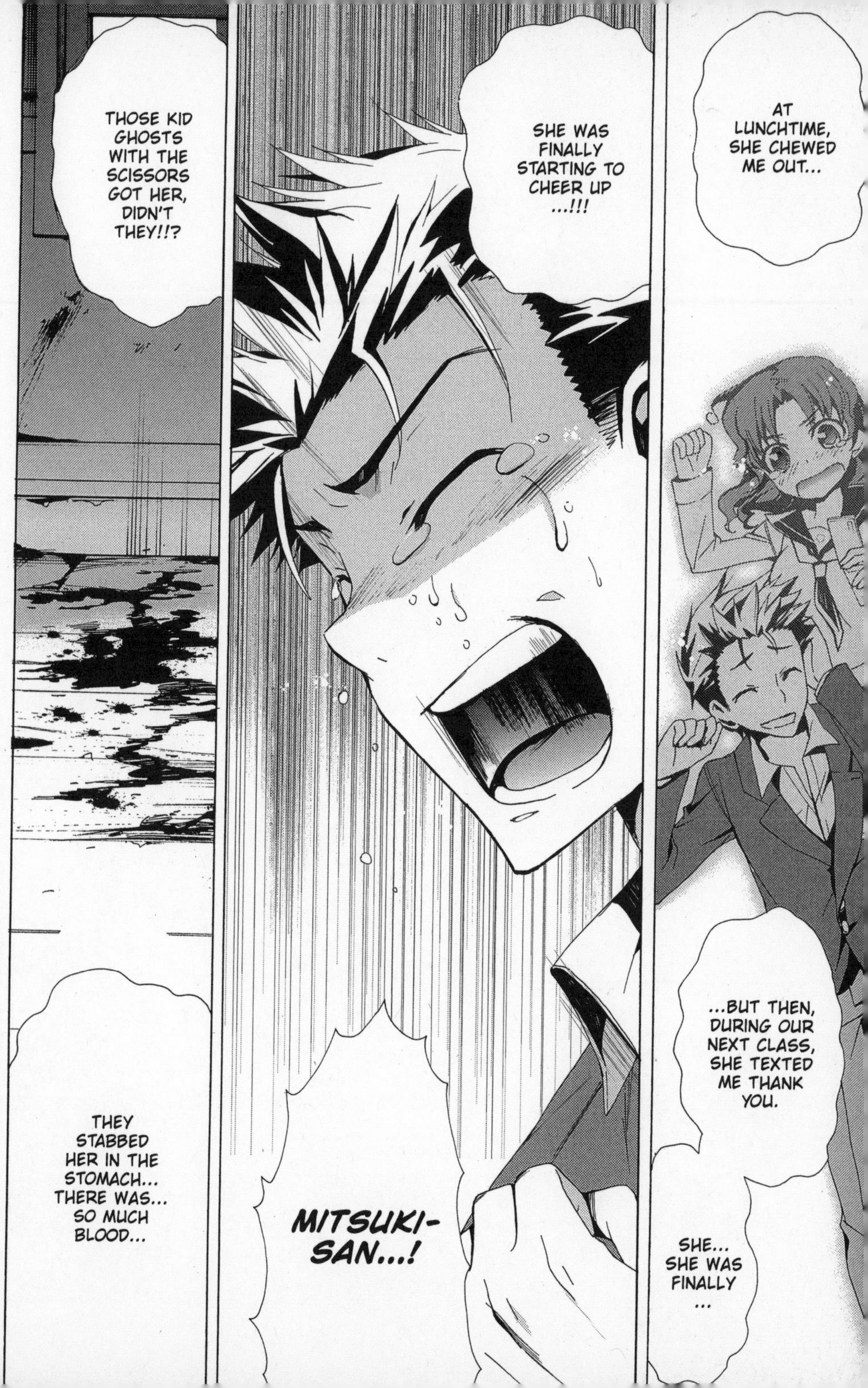
AT LUNCHTIME, SHE CHEWED ME OUT...
...BUT THEN, DURING OUR NEXT CLASS, SHE TEXTED ME THANK YOU.
SHE... SHE WAS FINALLY ...
SHE WAS FINALLY STARTING TO CHEER UP ...!!!
MITSUKI-SAN...!
THOSE KID GHOSTS WITH THE SCISSORS GOT HER, DIDN'T THEY!!?
THEY STABBED HER IN THE STOMACH... THERE WAS... SO MUCH BLOOD...

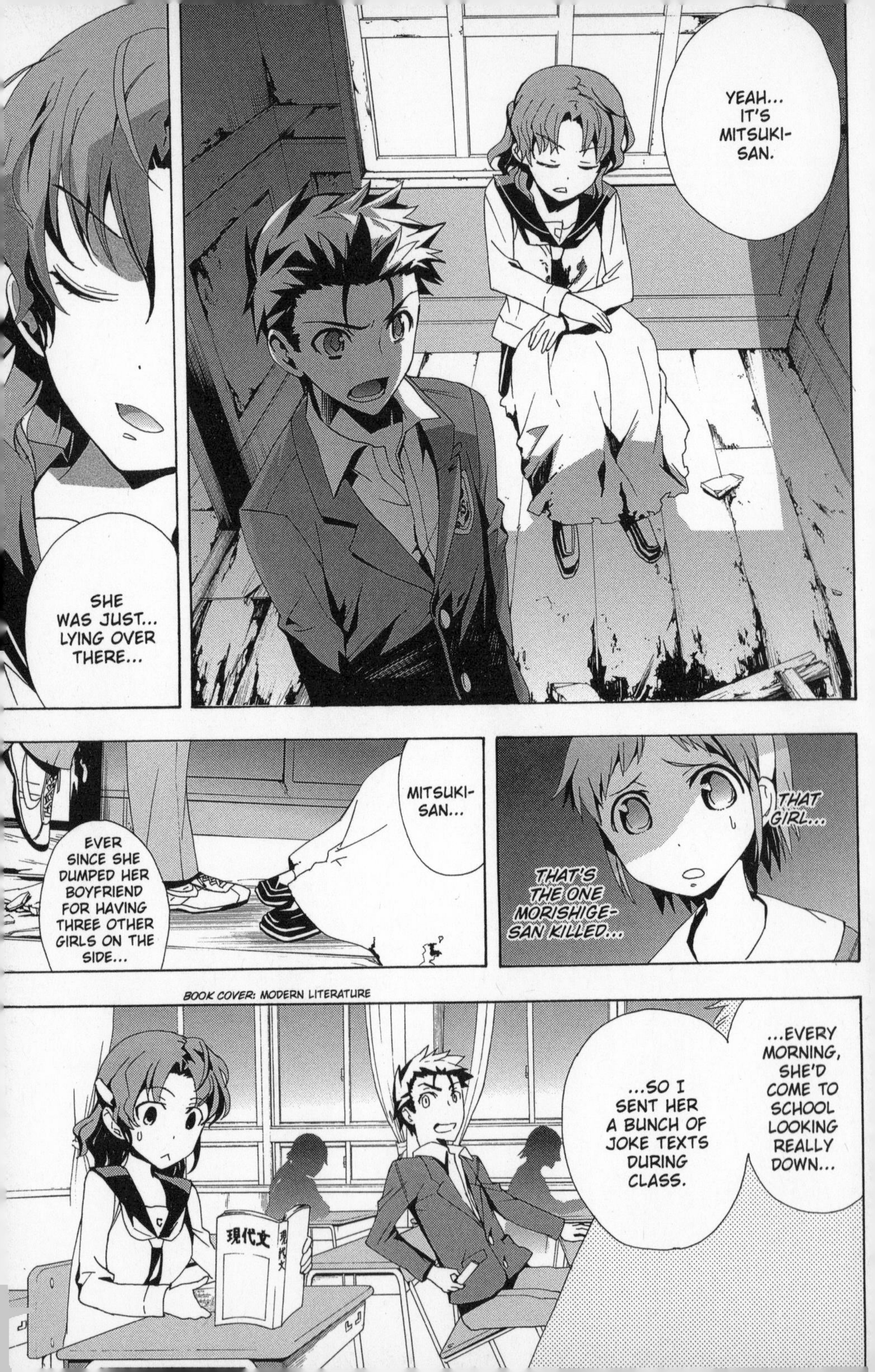
YEAH... IT'S MITSUKI-SAN.
SHE WAS JUST... LYING OVER THERE...
THAT GIRL...
THAT'S THE ONE MORISHIGE-SAN KILLED...
MITSUKI-SAN...
EVER SINCE SHE DUMPED HER BOYFRIEND FOR HAVING THREE OTHER GIRLS ON THE SIDE...
BOOK COVER: MODERN LITERATURE
...EVERY MORNING, SHE'D COME TO SCHOOL LOOKING REALLY DOWN...
...SO I SENT HER A BUNCH OF JOKE TEXTS DURING CLASS.
現代文
現代文

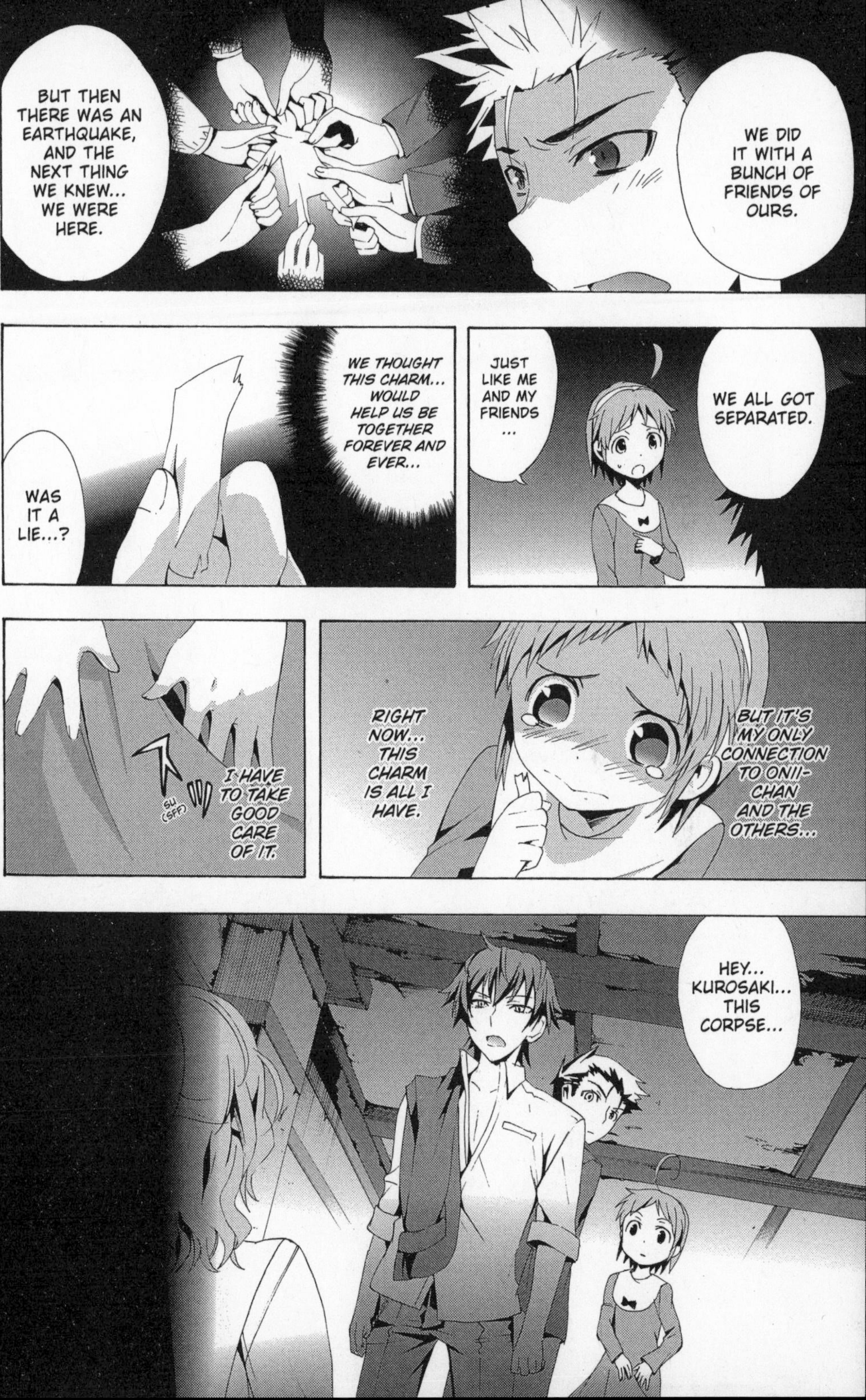
WE DID IT WITH A BUNCH OF FRIENDS OF OURS.
BUT THEN THERE WAS AN EARTHQUAKE, AND THE NEXT THING WE KNEW... WE WERE HERE.
WE ALL GOT SEPARATED.
JUST LIKE ME AND MY FRIENDS ...
WE THOUGHT THIS CHARM... WOULD HELP US BE TOGETHER FOREVER AND EVER...
WAS IT A LIE...?
BUT IT'S MY ONLY CONNECTION TO ONII-CHAN AND THE OTHERS...
RIGHT NOW... THIS CHARM IS ALL I HAVE.
I HAVE TO TAKE GOOD CARE OF IT.
SU (SFF)
HEY... KUROSAKI... THIS CORPSE...

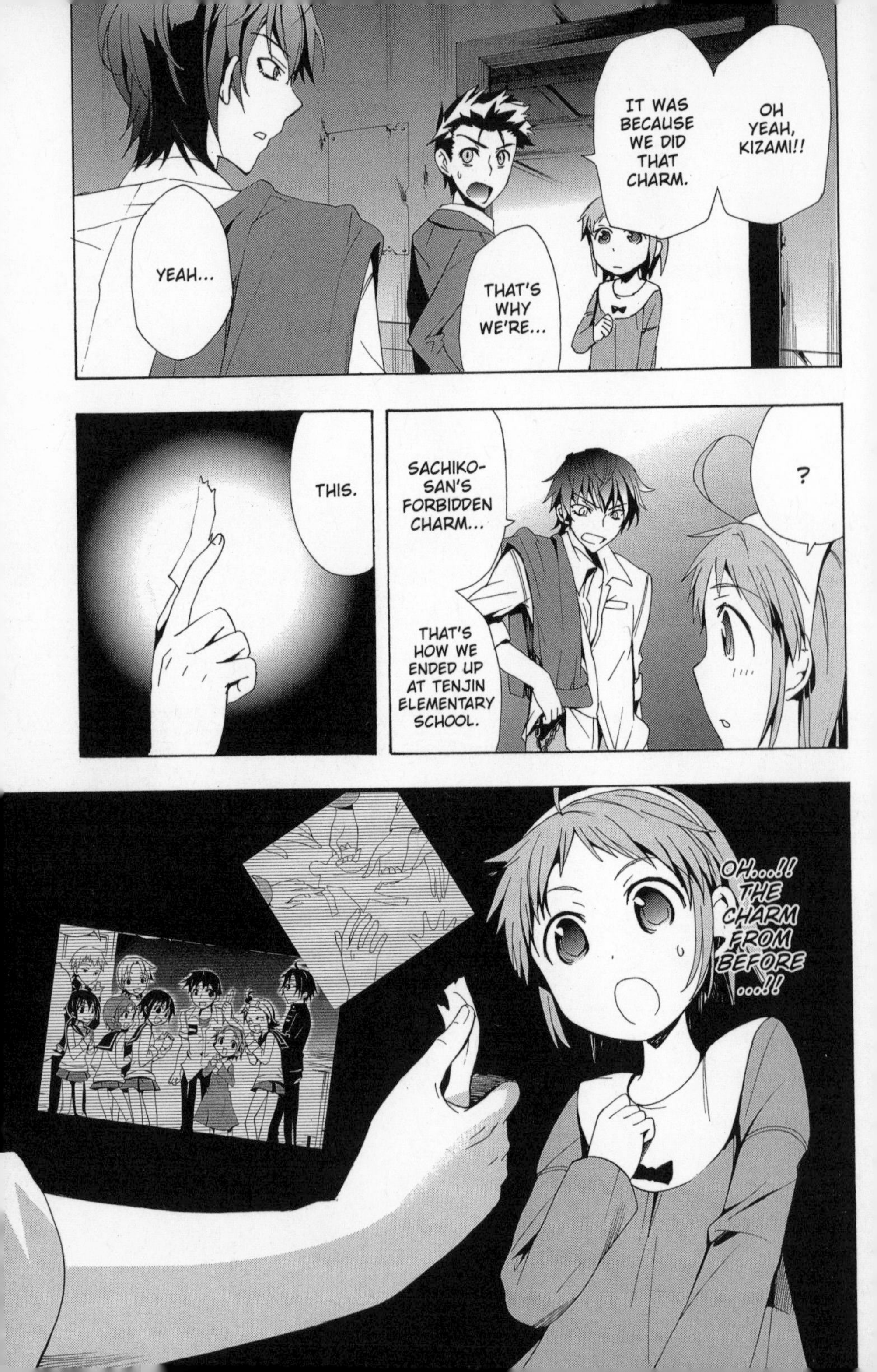
OH YEAH, KIZAMI!!
IT WAS BECAUSE WE DID THAT CHARM.
THAT'S WHY WE'RE...
YEAH...
?
SACHIKO-SAN'S FORBIDDEN CHARM...
THAT'S HOW WE ENDED UP AT TENJIN ELEMENTARY SCHOOL.
THIS.
OH...!! THE CHARM FROM BEFORE...!!

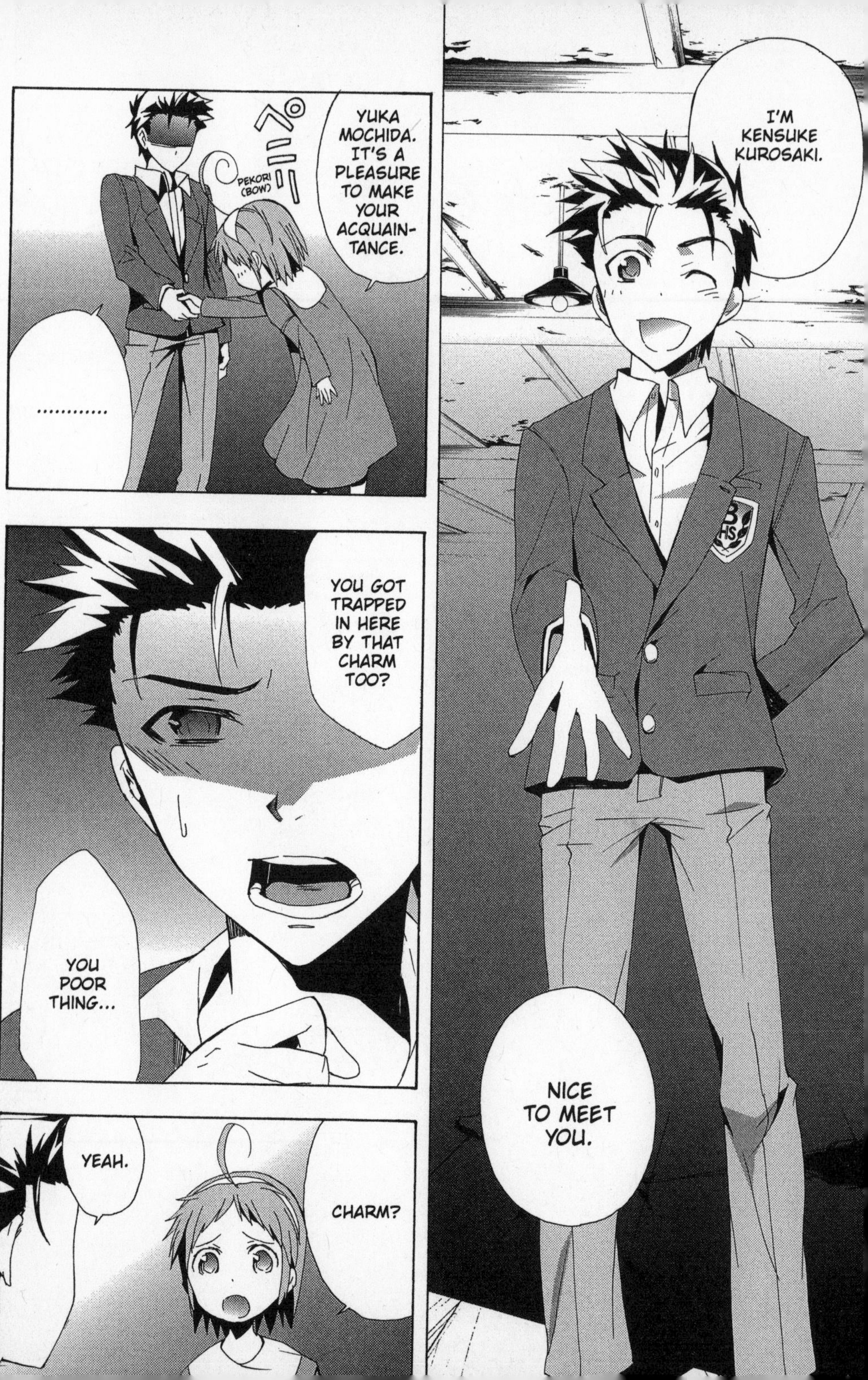
I'M KENSUKE KUROSAKI.
NICE TO MEET YOU.
PEKORI (BOW)
YUKA MOCHIDA. IT'S A PLEASURE TO MAKE YOUR ACQUAINTANCE.
....
YOU GOT TRAPPED IN HERE BY THAT CHARM TOO?
YOU POOR THING...
CHARM?
YEAH.

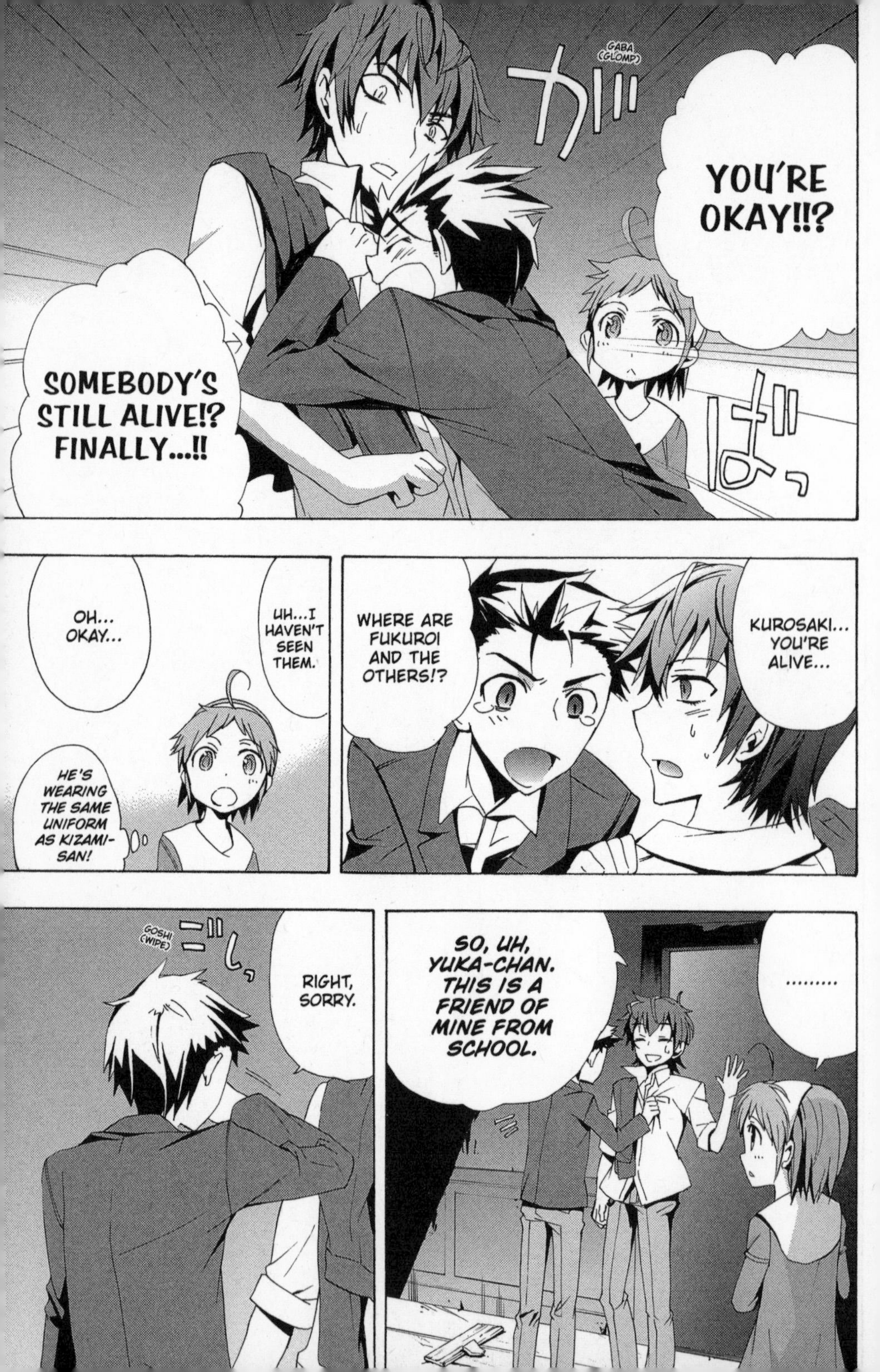
GABA (GLOMP)
YOU'RE OKAY!!?
SOMEBODY'S STILL ALIVE!? FINALLY...!!
KUROSAKI... YOU'RE ALIVE...
WHERE ARE FUKUROI AND THE OTHERS!?
UH...I HAVEN'T SEEN THEM.
OH... OKAY...
HE'S WEARING THE SAME UNIFORM AS KIZAMI-SAN!
....
SO, UH, YUKA-CHAN. THIS IS A FRIEND OF MINE FROM SCHOOL.
GOSHI (WIPE)
RIGHT, SORRY.

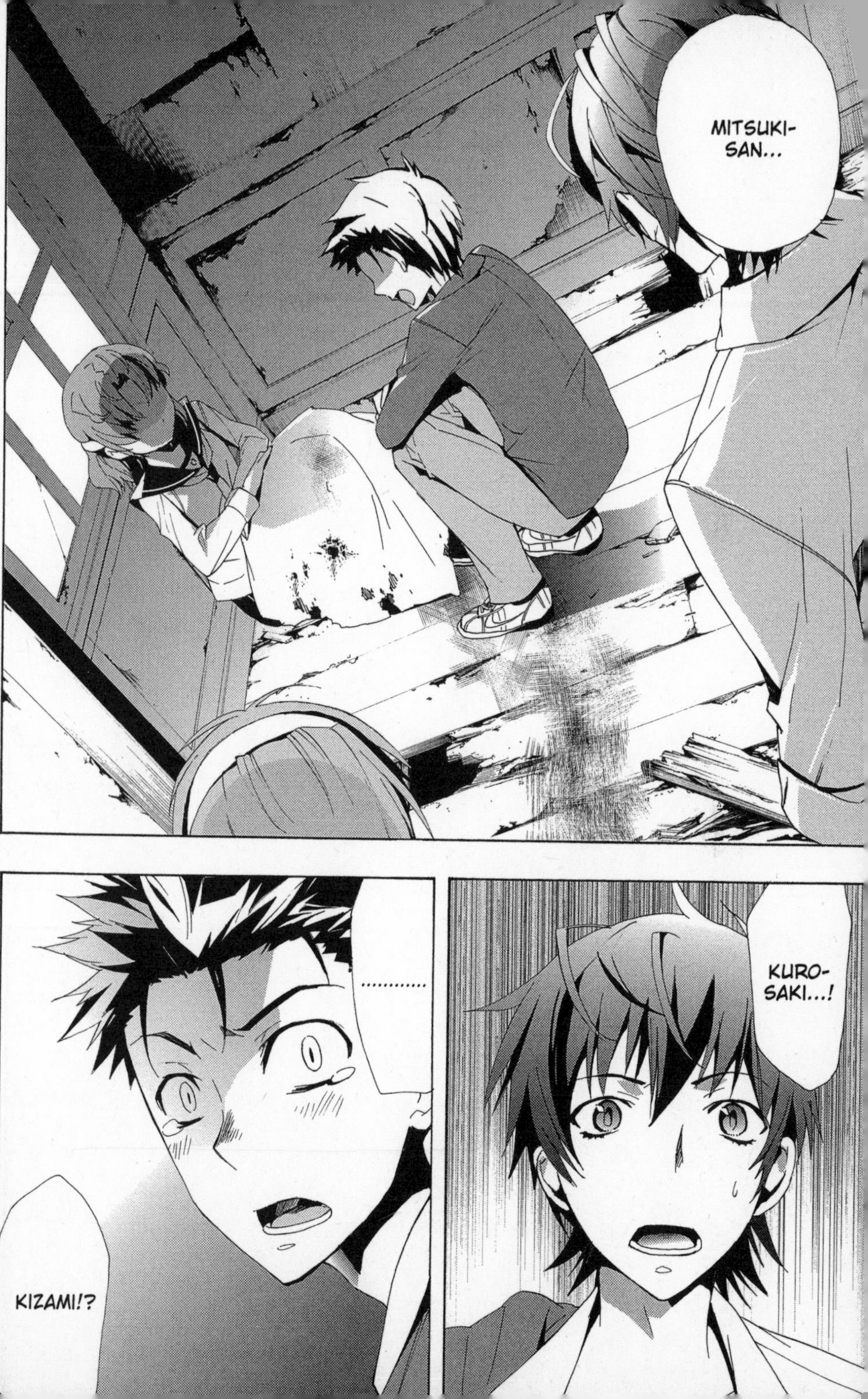
MITSUKI-SAN...
KURO-SAKI...!
....
KIZAMI!?

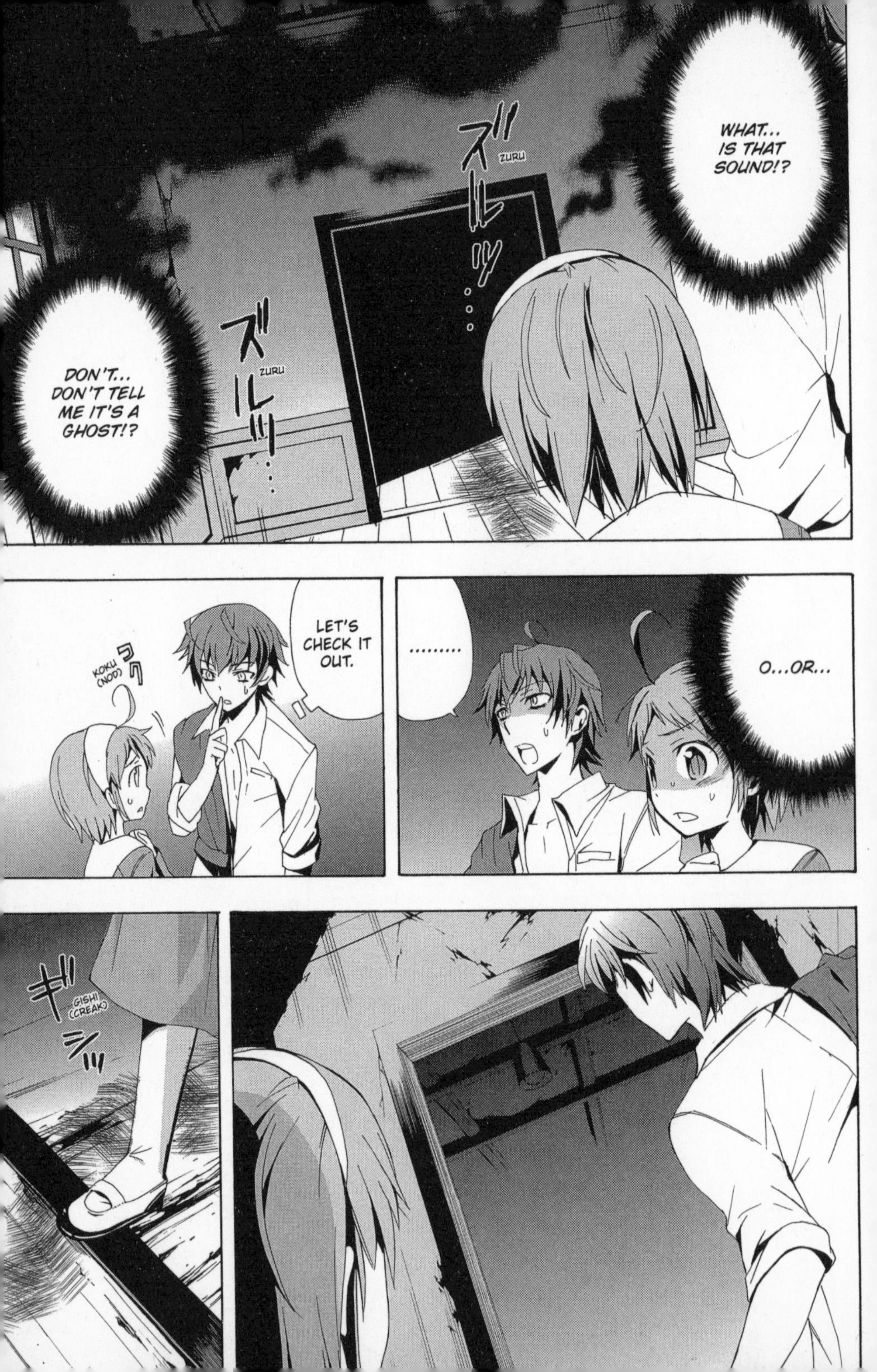
WHAT... IS THAT SOUND!?
ZURU
ZURU
DON'T... DON'T TELL ME IT'S A GHOST!?
O...OR...
....
LET'S CHECK IT OUT.
KOKU (NOD)
GISHI (CREAK)

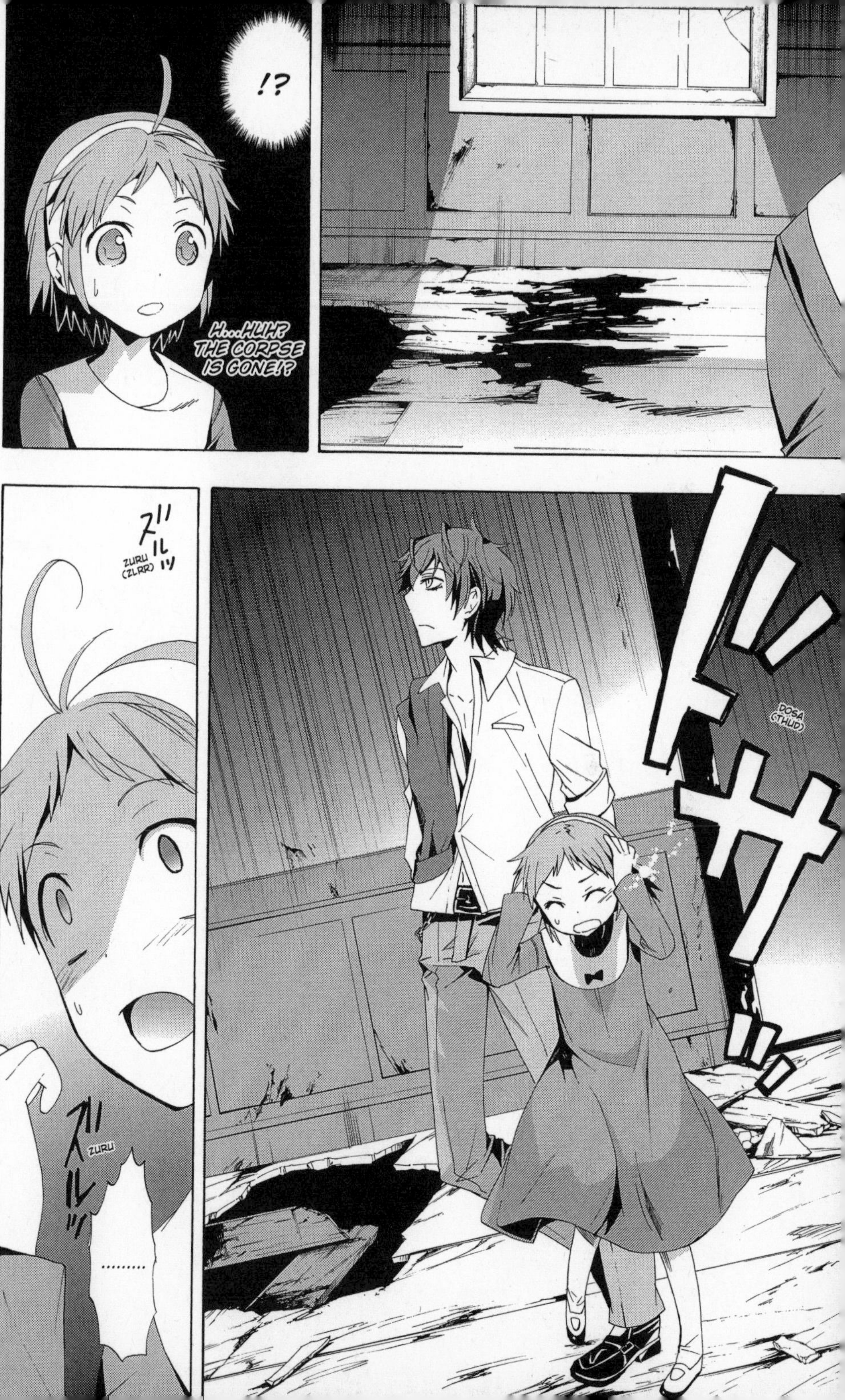
!?
H...HUH? THE CORPSE IS GONE!?
ドサッ
DOSA (THUD)
ズルッ
ZURU (ZLRR)
ズルッ
ZURU
....

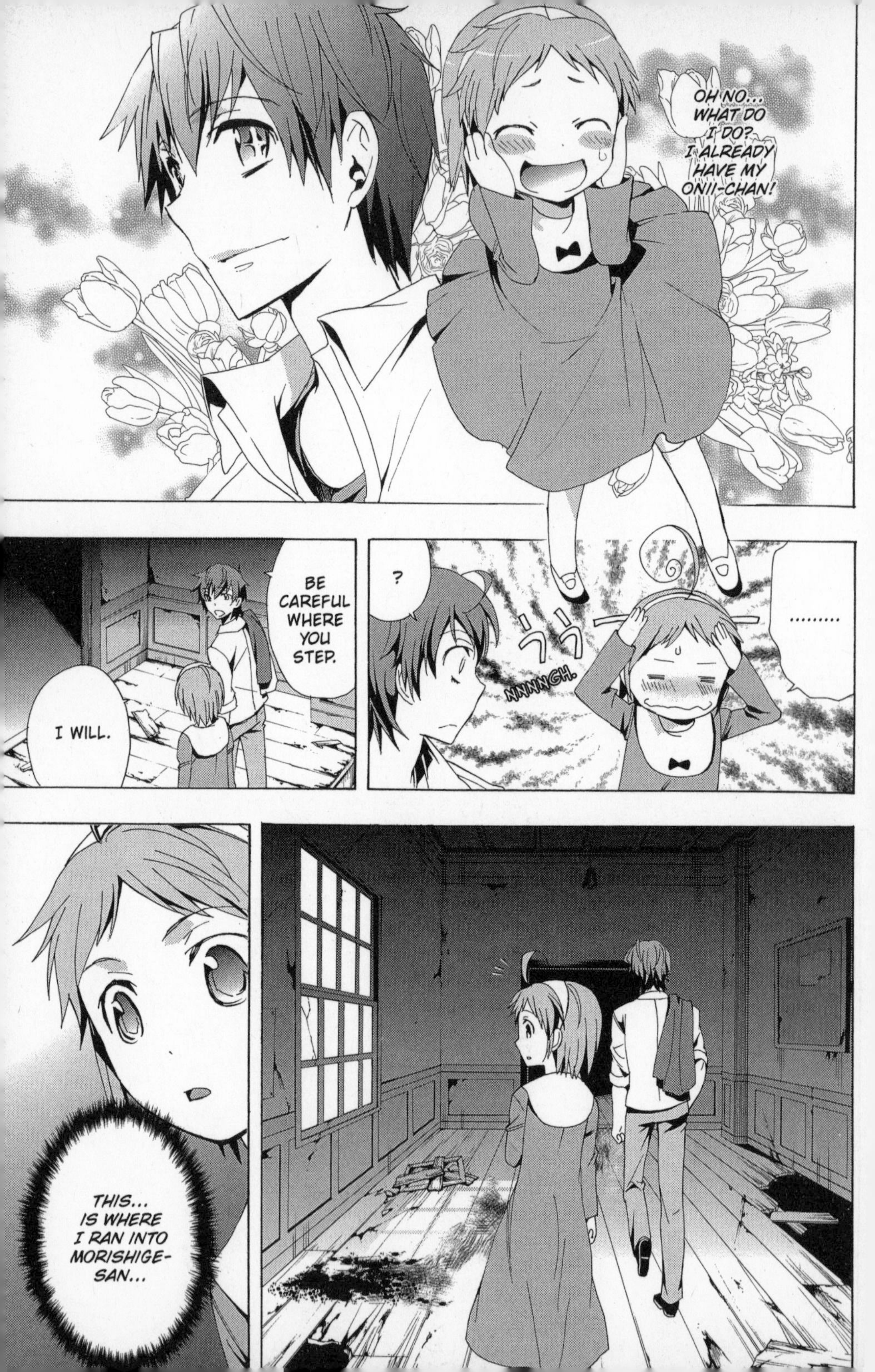
OH NO... WHAT DO I DO? I ALREADY HAVE MY ONII-CHAN!
....
?
ううー
NNNNGH.
BE CAREFUL WHERE YOU STEP.
I WILL.
THIS... IS WHERE I RAN INTO MORISHIGE-SAN...

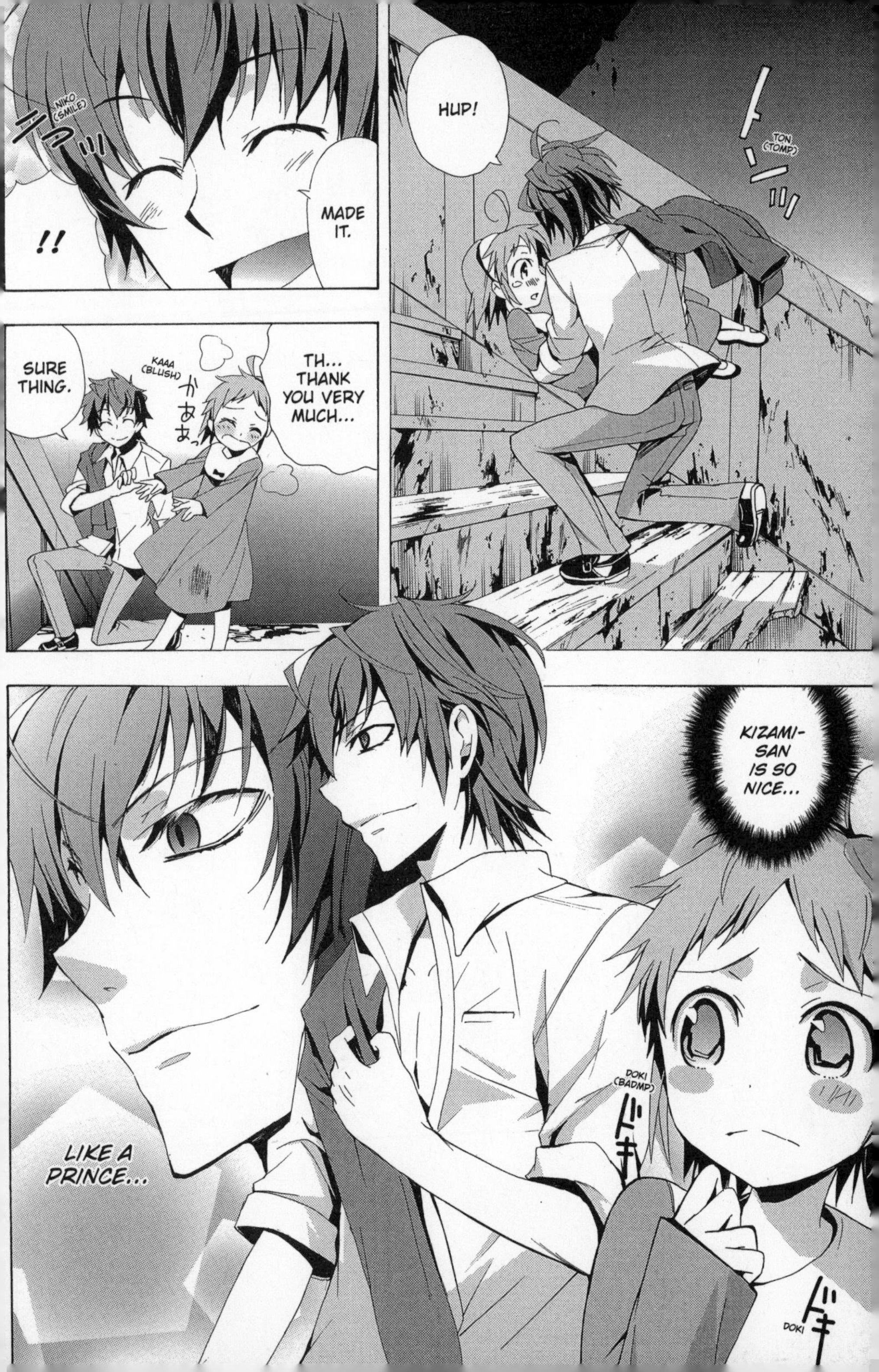
HUP!
TON (TOMP)
NIKO (SMILE)
MADE IT.
!!
TH... THANK YOU VERY MUCH...
KAAA (BLUSH)
かあぁっ
SURE THING.
KIZAMI-SAN IS SO NICE...
DOKI (BADMP)
ドキ
LIKE A PRINCE...
ドキ
DOKI

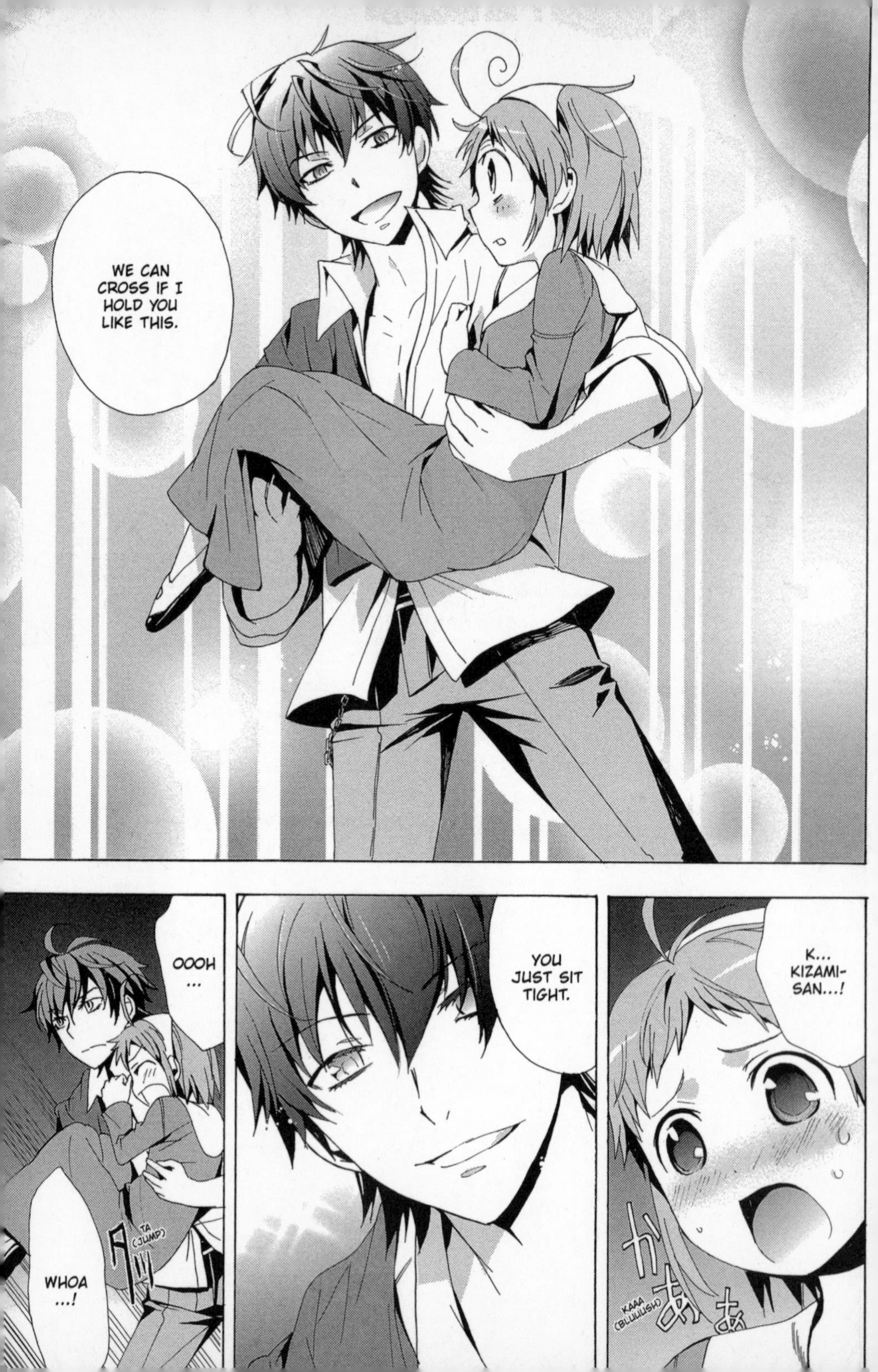
WE CAN CROSS IF I HOLD YOU LIKE THIS.
K... KIZAMI-SAN...!
KAAA (BLUUUSH)
YOU JUST SIT TIGHT.
OOOH ...
TA (JUMP)
WHOA ...!

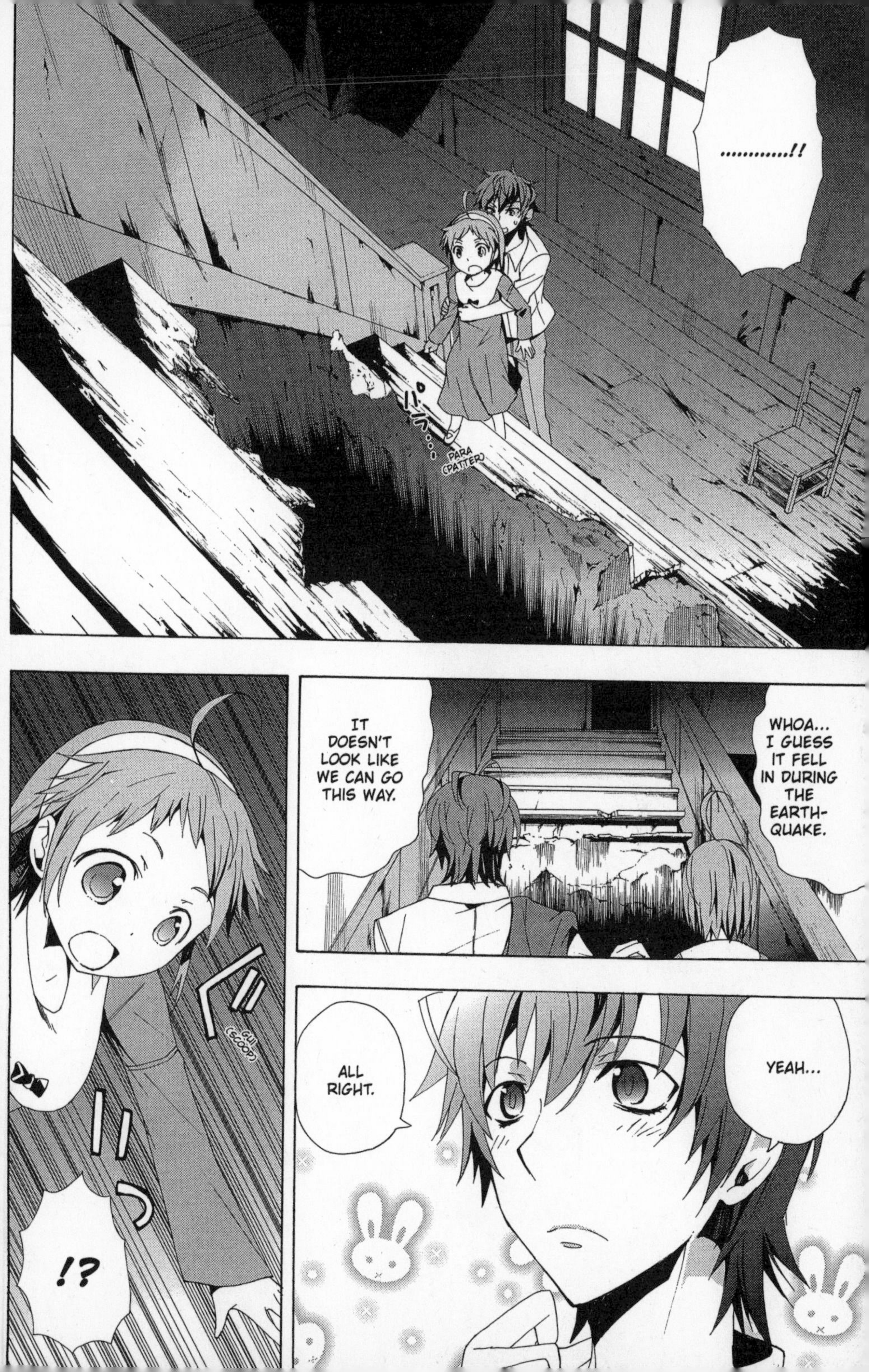
...........!!
PARA (PATTER)
WHOA... I GUESS IT FELL IN DURING THE EARTH-QUAKE.
IT DOESN'T LOOK LIKE WE CAN GO THIS WAY.
YEAH...
ALL RIGHT.
GUI (SCOOP)
!?

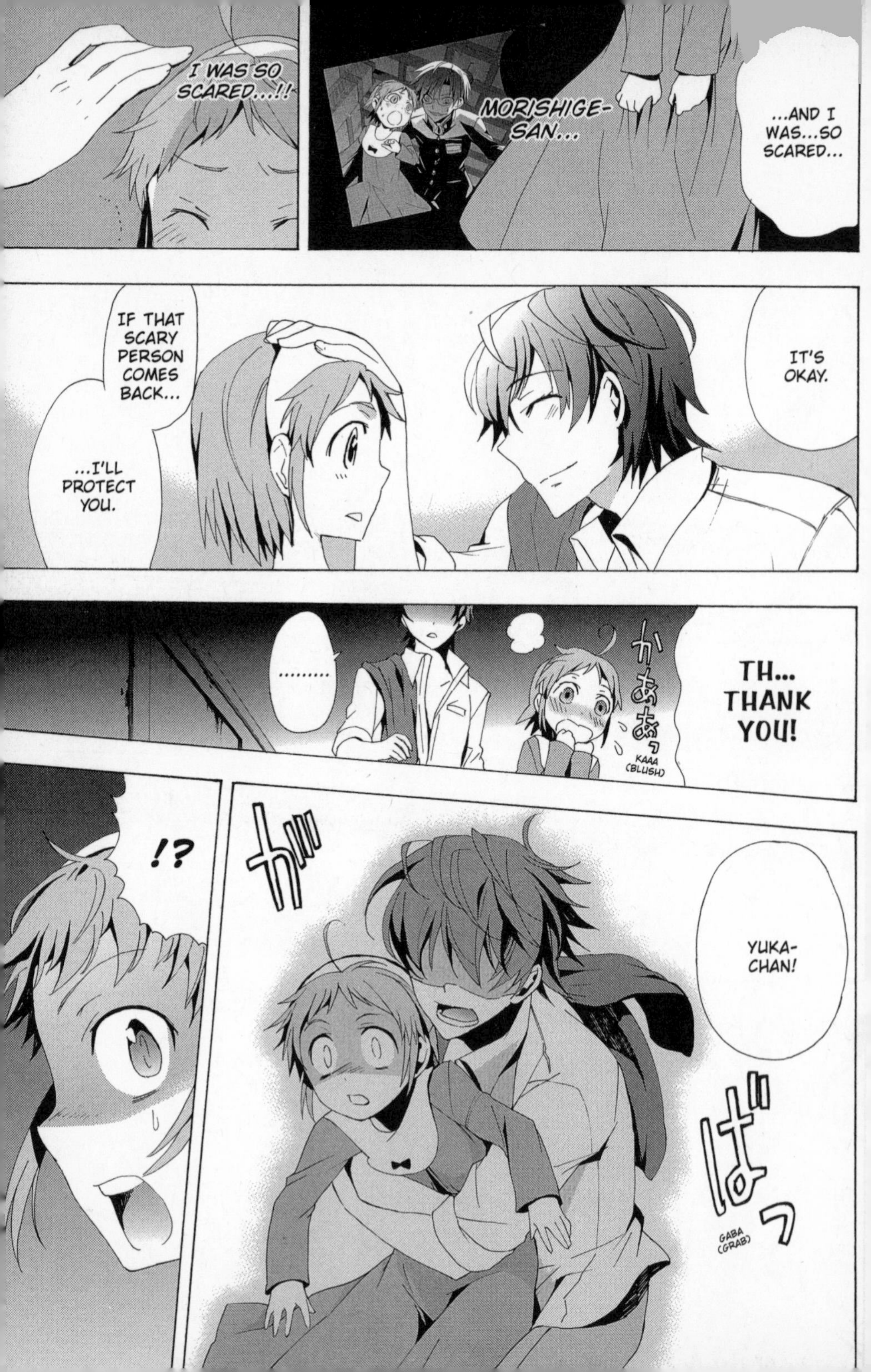
...AND I WAS...SO SCARED...
MORISHIGE-SAN...
I WAS SO SCARED...!!
IT'S OKAY.
IF THAT SCARY PERSON COMES BACK...
...I'LL PROTECT YOU.
TH... THANK YOU!
かああっ
KAAA (BLUSH)
....
YUKA-CHAN!
ばっ
GABA (GRAB)
が
!?

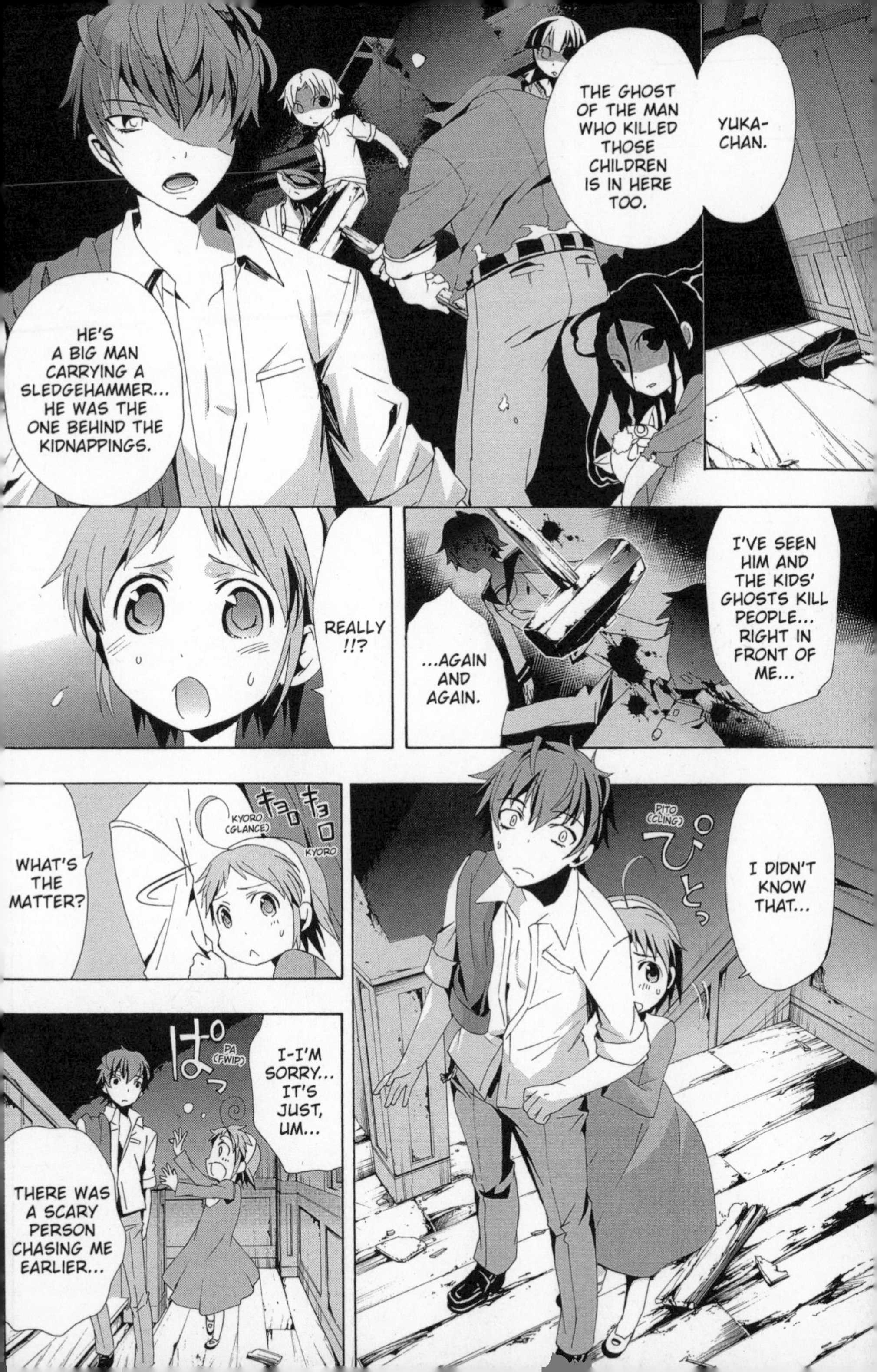

YUKA-CHAN.
THE GHOST OF THE MAN WHO KILLED THOSE CHILDREN IS IN HERE TOO.
HE'S A BIG MAN CARRYING A SLEDGEHAMMER... HE WAS THE ONE BEHIND THE KIDNAPPINGS.
I'VE SEEN HIM AND THE KIDS' GHOSTS KILL PEOPLE... RIGHT IN FRONT OF ME...
...AGAIN AND AGAIN.
REALLY!!?
ぴとっ
PITO (CLING)
I DIDN'T KNOW THAT...
キョロキョロ
KYORO (GLANCE) KYORO
WHAT'S THE MATTER?
ぱっ
PA (FWIP)
I-I'M SORRY... IT'S JUST, UM...
THERE WAS A SCARY PERSON CHASING ME EARLIER...

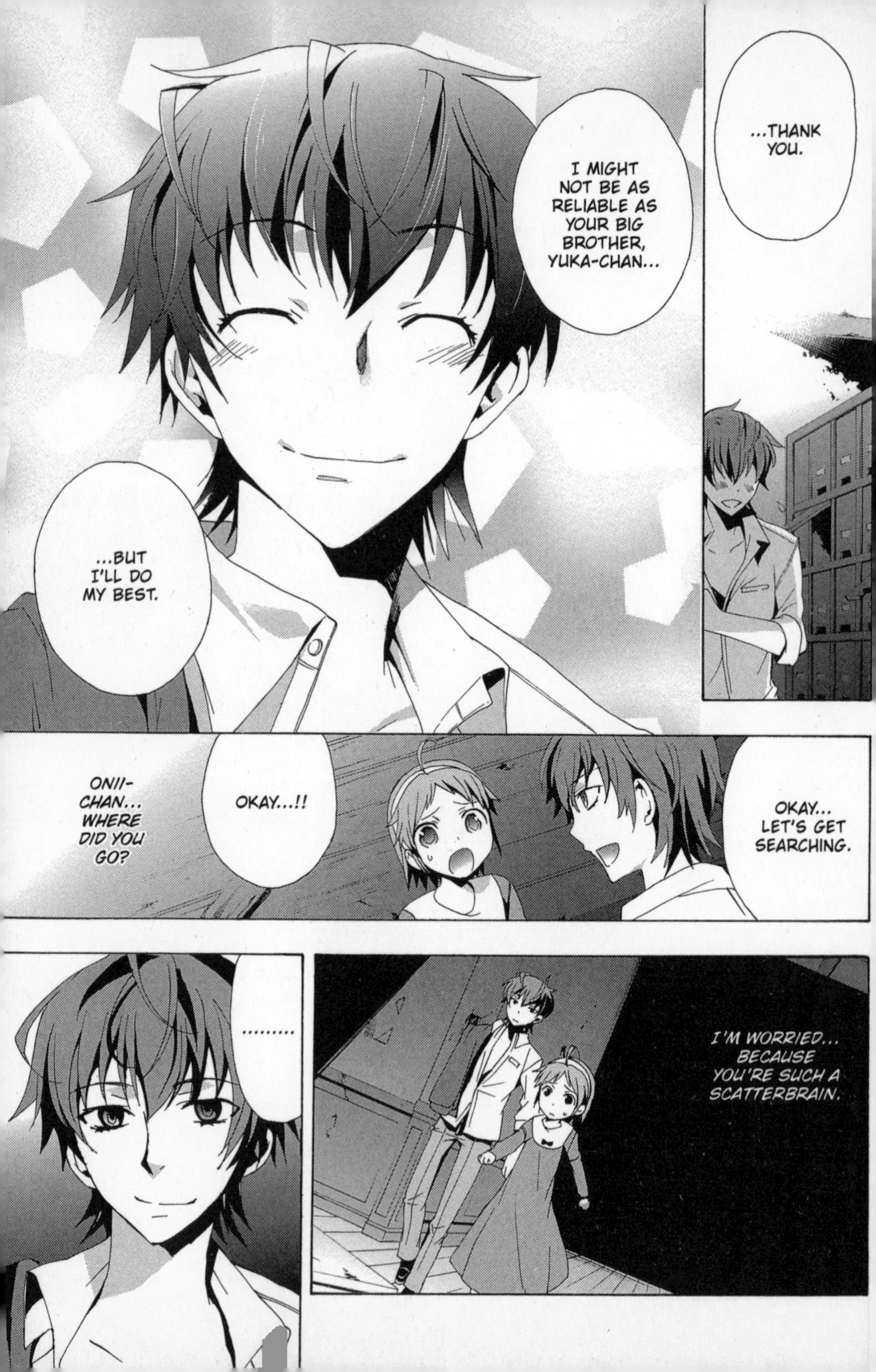
...THANK YOU.
I MIGHT NOT BE AS RELIABLE AS YOUR BIG BROTHER, YUKA-CHAN...
...BUT I'LL DO MY BEST.
OKAY... LET'S GET SEARCHING.
OKAY...!!
ONII-CHAN... WHERE DID YOU GO?
I'M WORRIED... BECAUSE YOU'RE SUCH A SCATTERBRAIN.
....

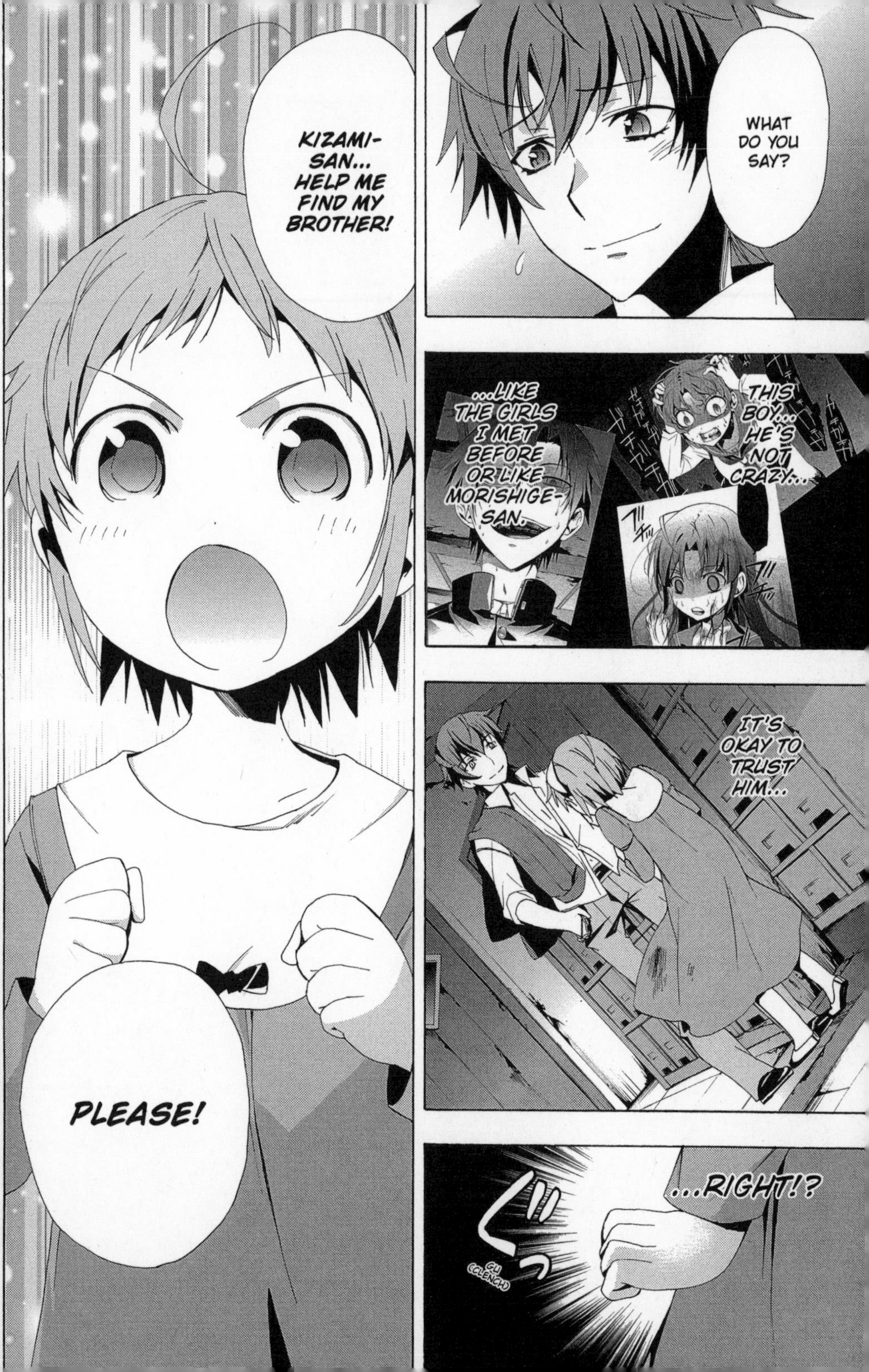
WHAT DO YOU SAY?
THIS BOY... HE'S NOT CRAZY...
...LIKE THE GIRLS I MET BEFORE OR LIKE MORISHIGE-SAN.
IT'S OKAY TO TRUST HIM...
...RIGHT!?
GU (CLENCH)
KIZAMI-SAN... HELP ME FIND MY BROTHER!
PLEASE!

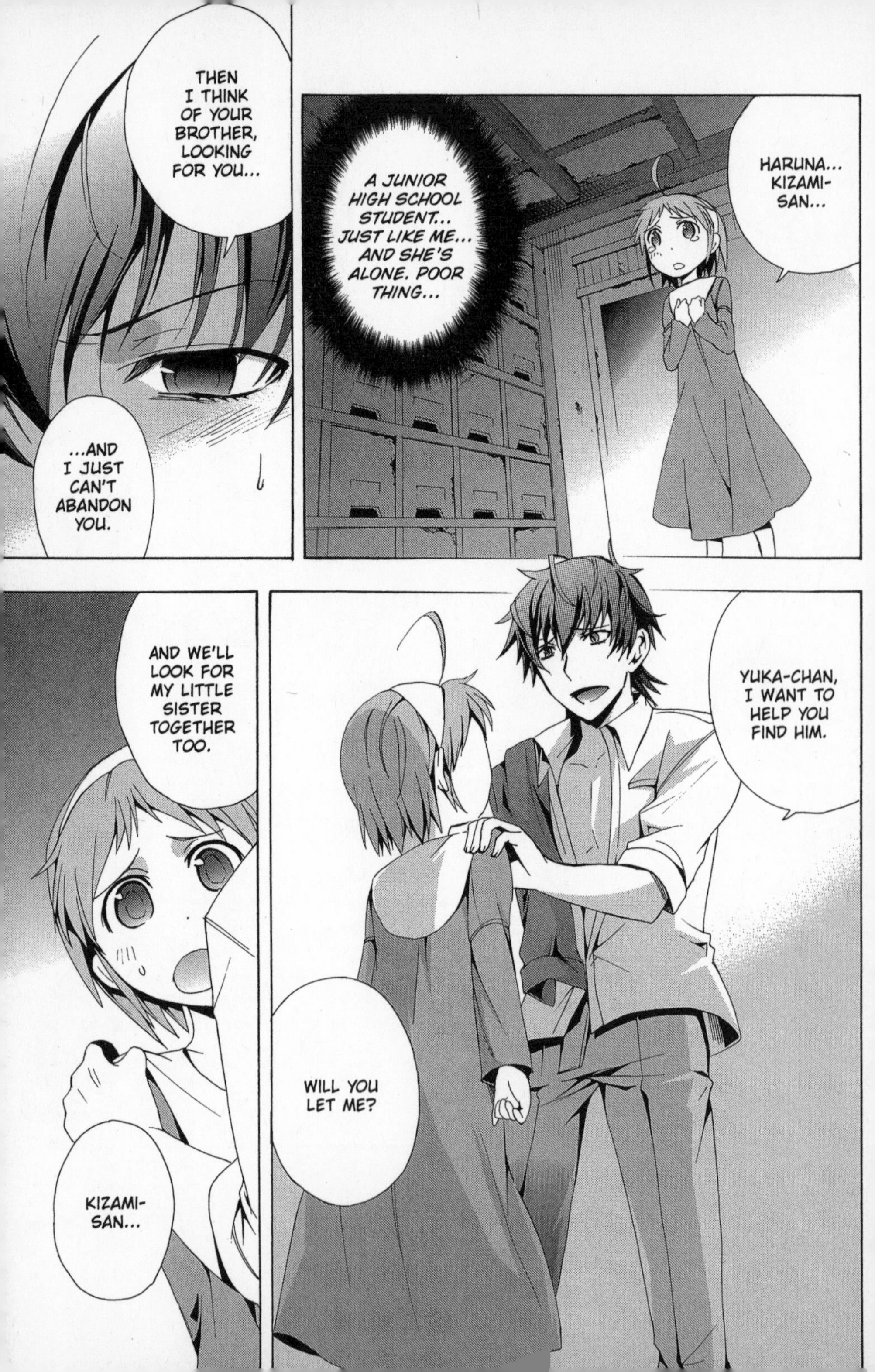
HARUNA... KIZAMI-SAN...
A JUNIOR HIGH SCHOOL STUDENT... JUST LIKE ME... AND SHE'S ALONE. POOR THING...
THEN I THINK OF YOUR BROTHER, LOOKING FOR YOU...
...AND I JUST CAN'T ABANDON YOU.
YUKA-CHAN, I WANT TO HELP YOU FIND HIM.
WILL YOU LET ME?
AND WE'LL LOOK FOR MY LITTLE SISTER TOGETHER TOO.
KIZAMI-SAN...

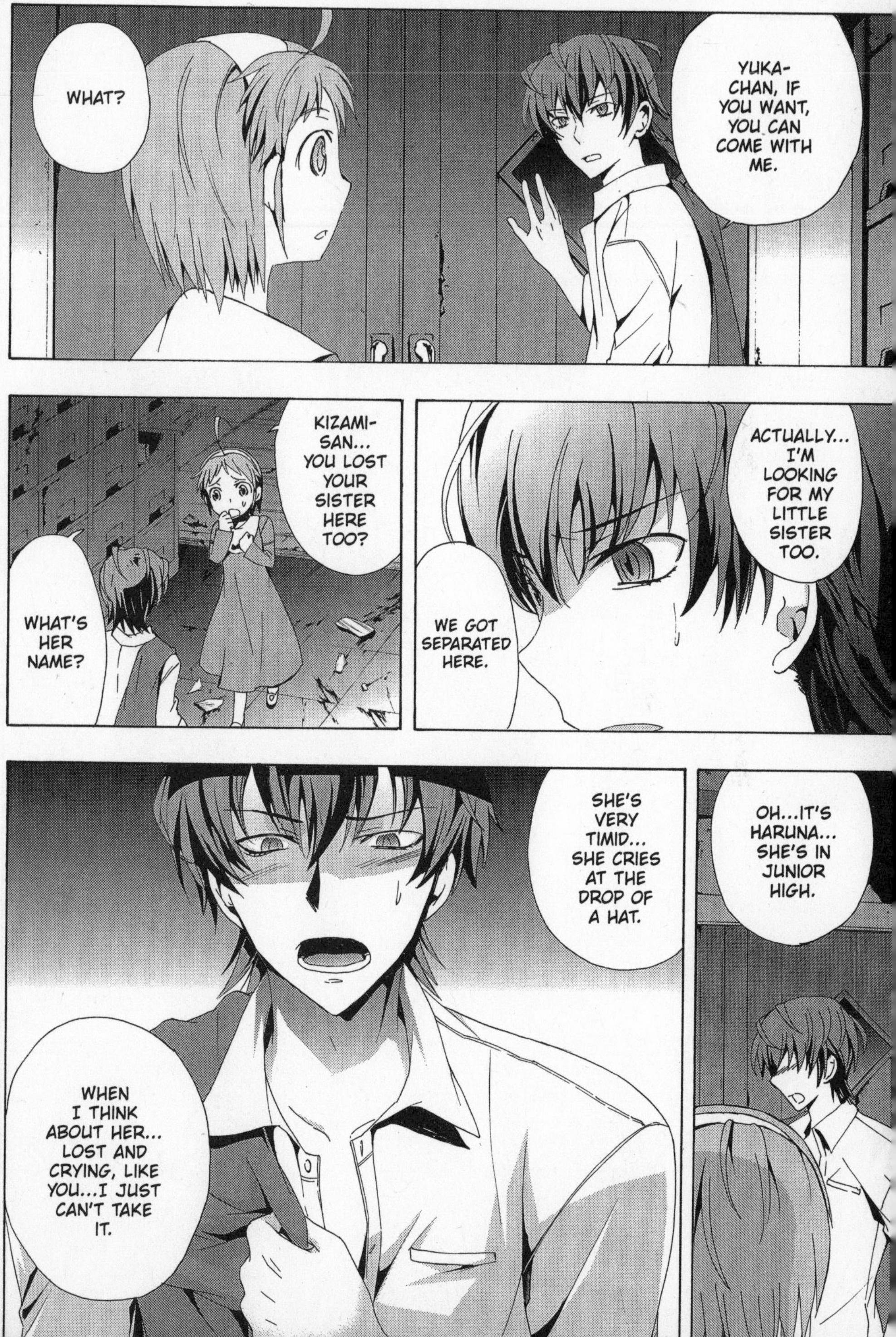
YUKA-CHAN, IF YOU WANT, YOU CAN COME WITH ME.
WHAT?
ACTUALLY... I'M LOOKING FOR MY LITTLE SISTER TOO.
WE GOT SEPARATED HERE.
KIZAMI-SAN... YOU LOST YOUR SISTER HERE TOO?
WHAT'S HER NAME?
OH...IT'S HARUNA... SHE'S IN JUNIOR HIGH.
SHE'S VERY TIMID... SHE CRIES AT THE DROP OF A HAT.
WHEN I THINK ABOUT HER... LOST AND CRYING, LIKE YOU...I JUST CAN'T TAKE IT.

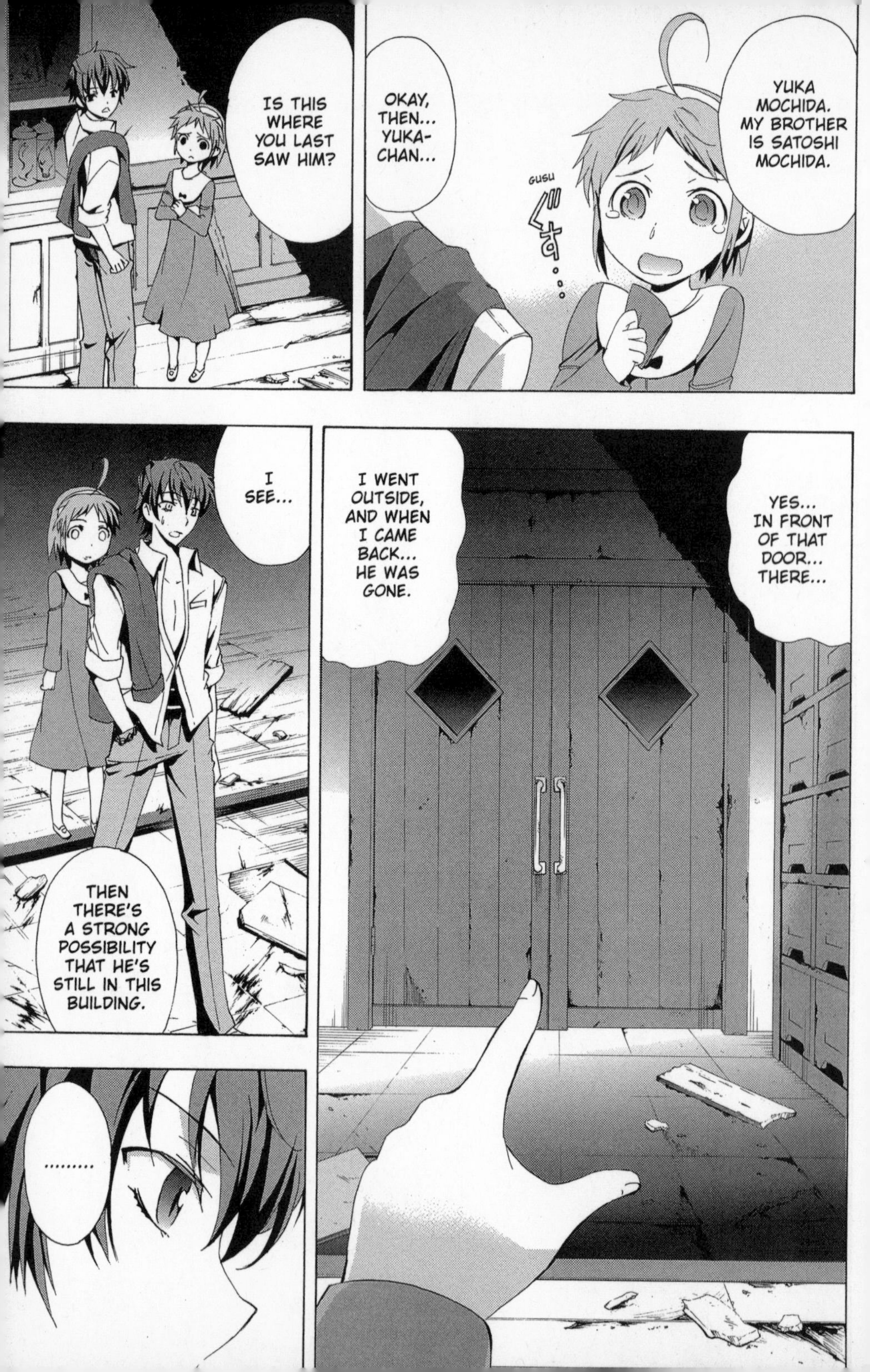
YUKA MOCHIDA. MY BROTHER IS SATOSHI MOCHIDA.
GUSU
ぐす
OKAY, THEN... YUKA-CHAN...
IS THIS WHERE YOU LAST SAW HIM?
YES... IN FRONT OF THAT DOOR... THERE...
I WENT OUTSIDE, AND WHEN I CAME BACK... HE WAS GONE.
I SEE...
THEN THERE'S A STRONG POSSIBILITY THAT HE'S STILL IN THIS BUILDING.
....

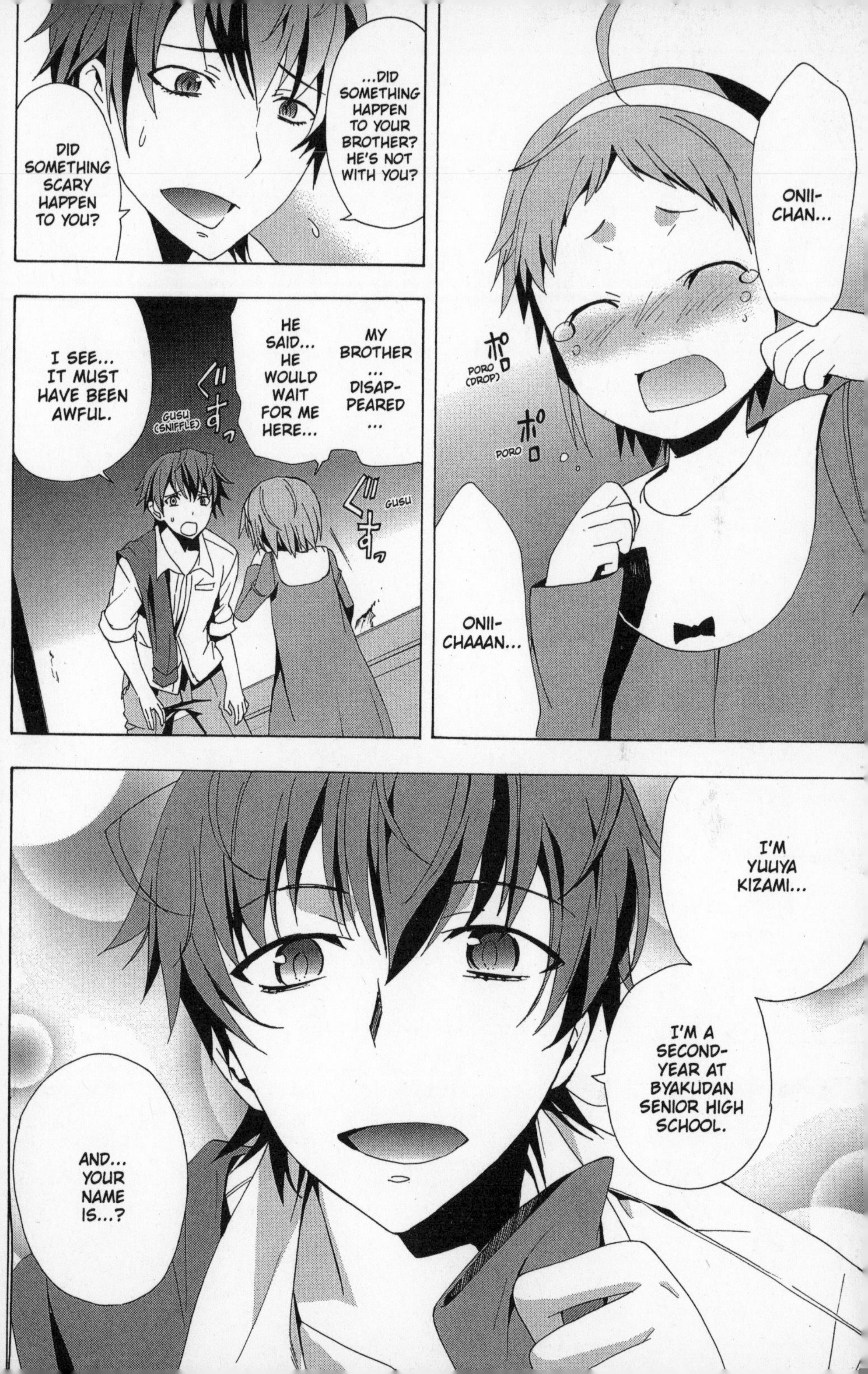
ONII-CHAN...
ポロ
PORO (DROP)
ポロ
PORO
ONII-CHAAAN...
...DID SOMETHING HAPPEN TO YOUR BROTHER? HE'S NOT WITH YOU?
DID SOMETHING SCARY HAPPEN TO YOU?
MY BROTHER... DISAPPEARED...
HE SAID... HE WOULD WAIT FOR ME HERE...
ぐすっ
GUSU
ぐすっ
GUSU (SNIFFLE)
I SEE... IT MUST HAVE BEEN AWFUL.
I'M YUUYA KIZAMI...
I'M A SECOND-YEAR AT BYAKUDAN SENIOR HIGH SCHOOL.
AND... YOUR NAME IS...?

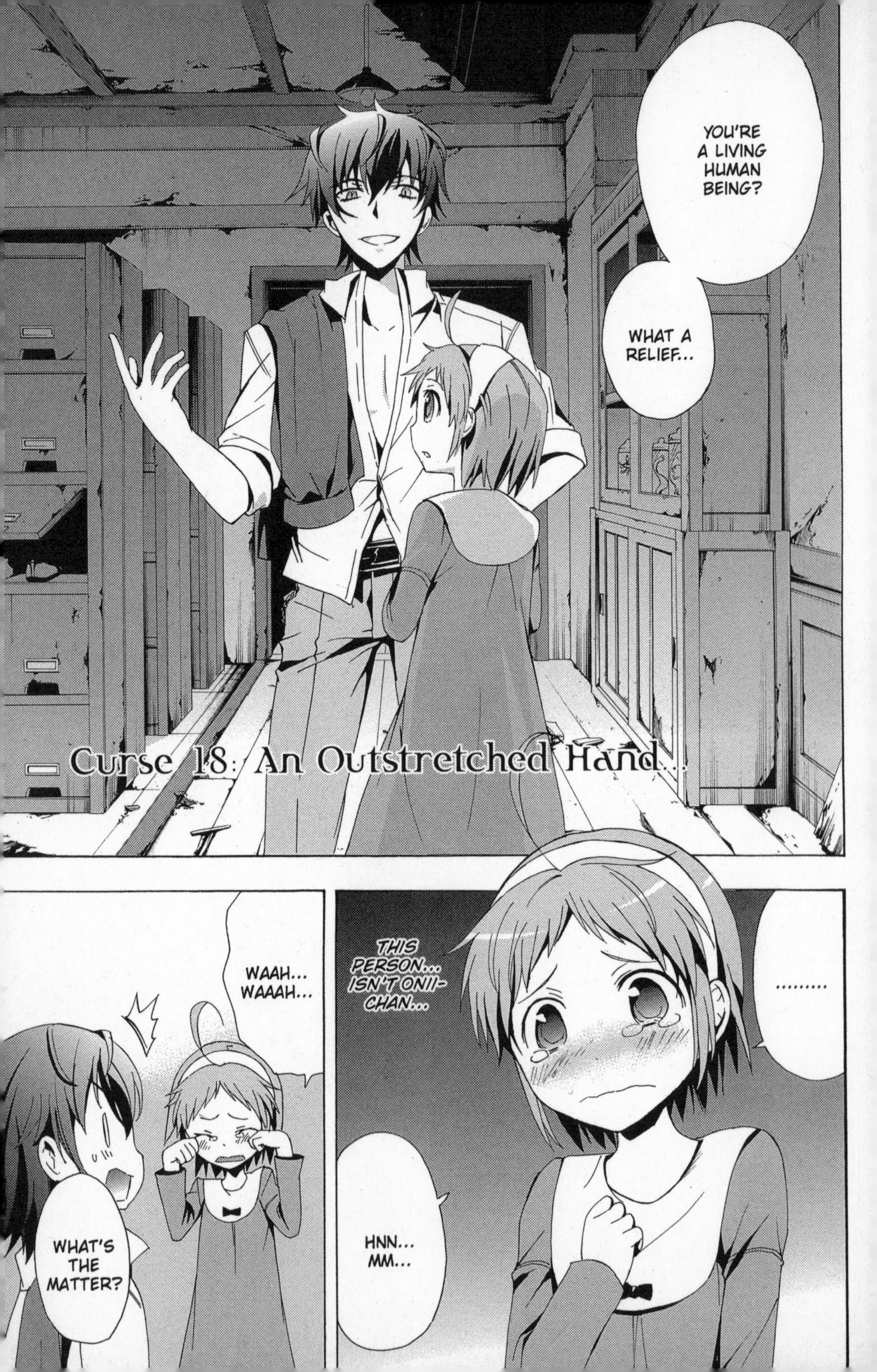
YOU'RE A LIVING HUMAN BEING?
WHAT A RELIEF...
Curse 18: An Outstretched Hand...
....
THIS PERSON... ISN'T ONII-CHAN...
HNN... MM...
WAAH... WAAAH...
WHAT'S THE MATTER?

a list of hints/02

Misato City, Hikoito Public High School,
Class 2-4, Kokuhaku Akaboshi

The girl who was hiding in the Tenjin
Elementary School annex art room.

The words she strings together no longer
make any sense. Sometime after parting
ways with Yuka, she disappears.

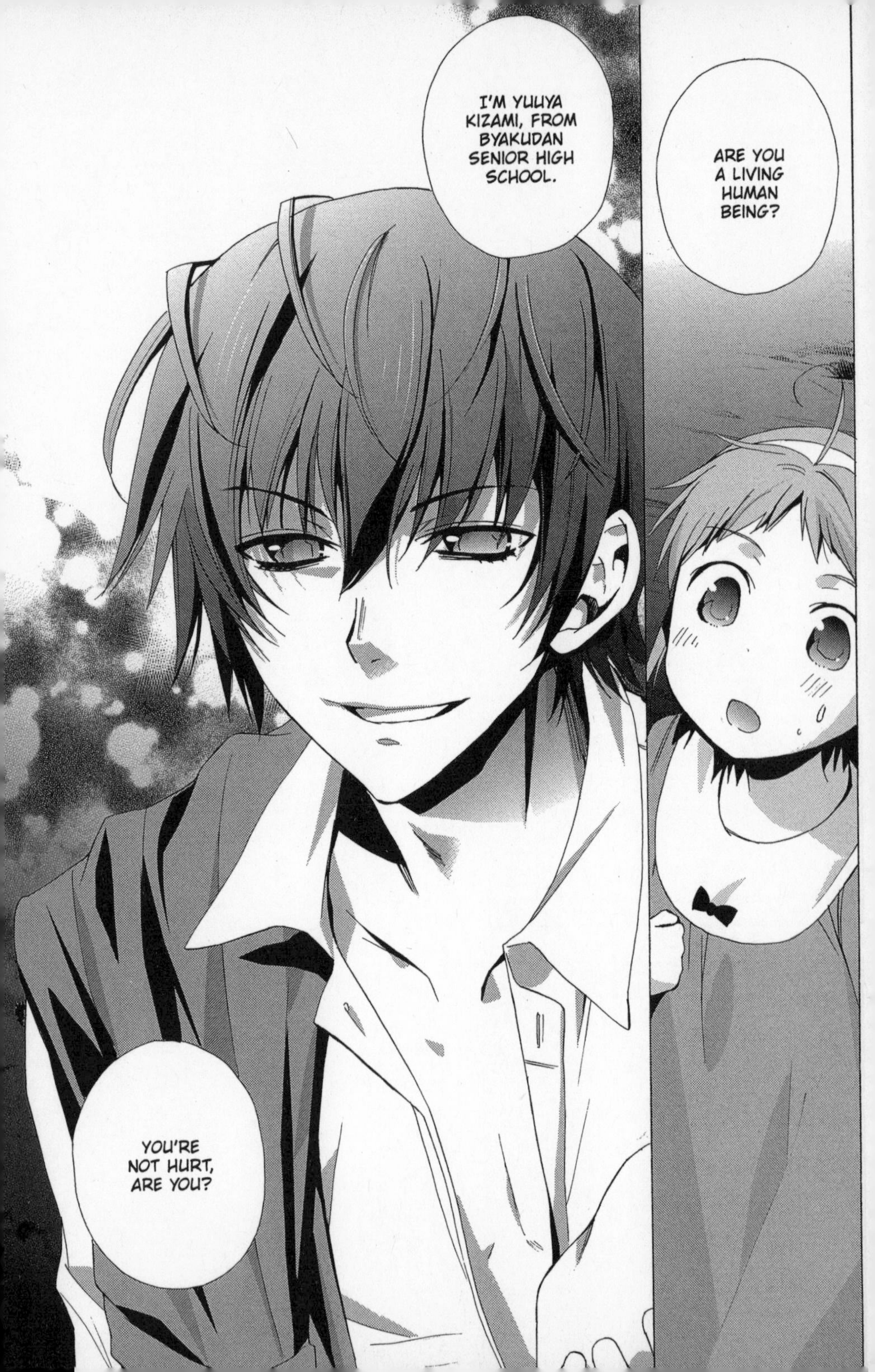
ARE YOU A LIVING HUMAN BEING?
I'M YUUYA KIZAMI, FROM BYAKUDAN SENIOR HIGH SCHOOL.
YOU'RE NOT HURT, ARE YOU?

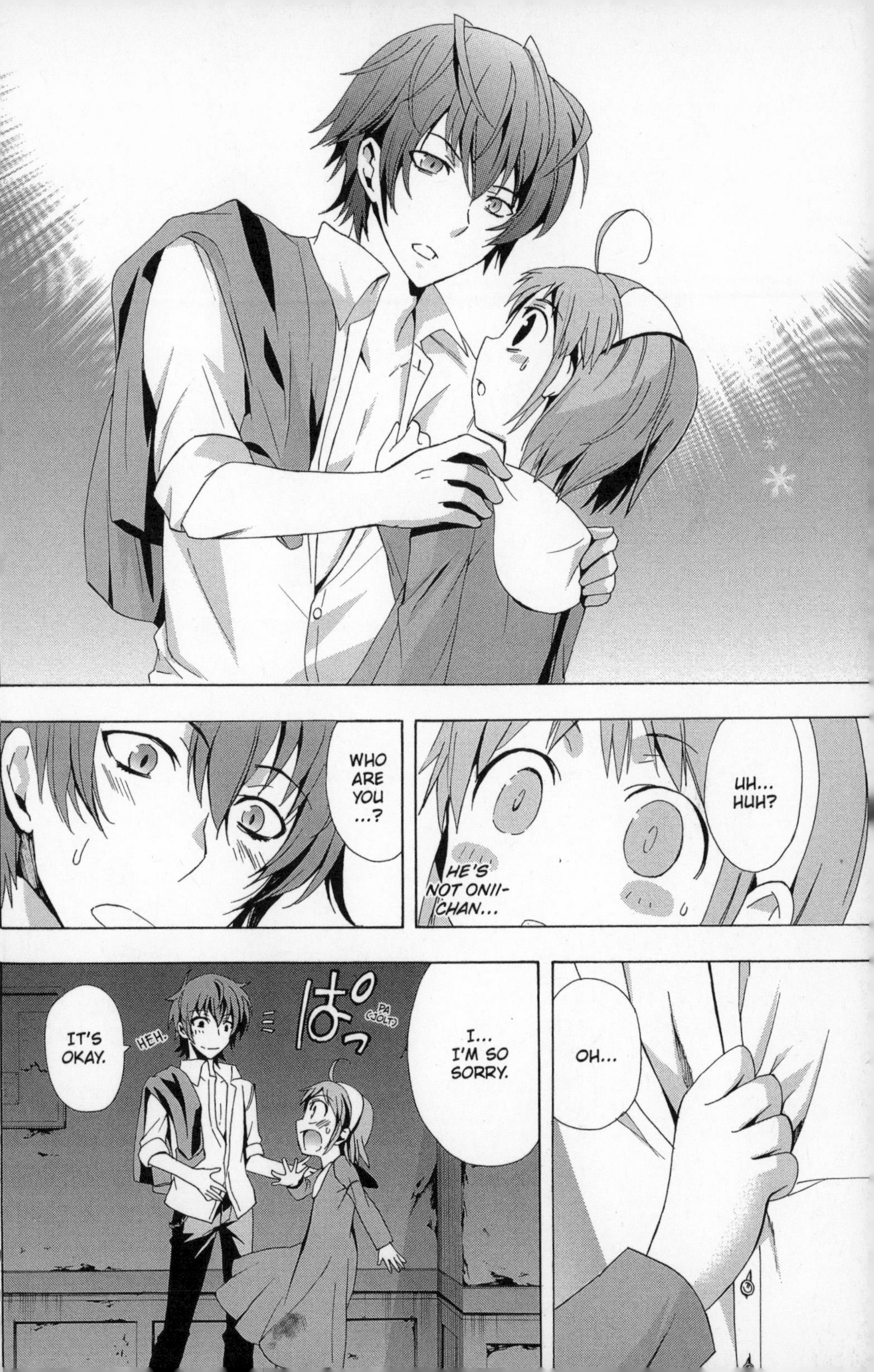
UH... HUH?
HE'S NOT ONII-CHAN...
WHO ARE YOU ...?
OH...
I... I'M SO SORRY.
ぱっ
PA (JOLT)
HEH.
IT'S OKAY.

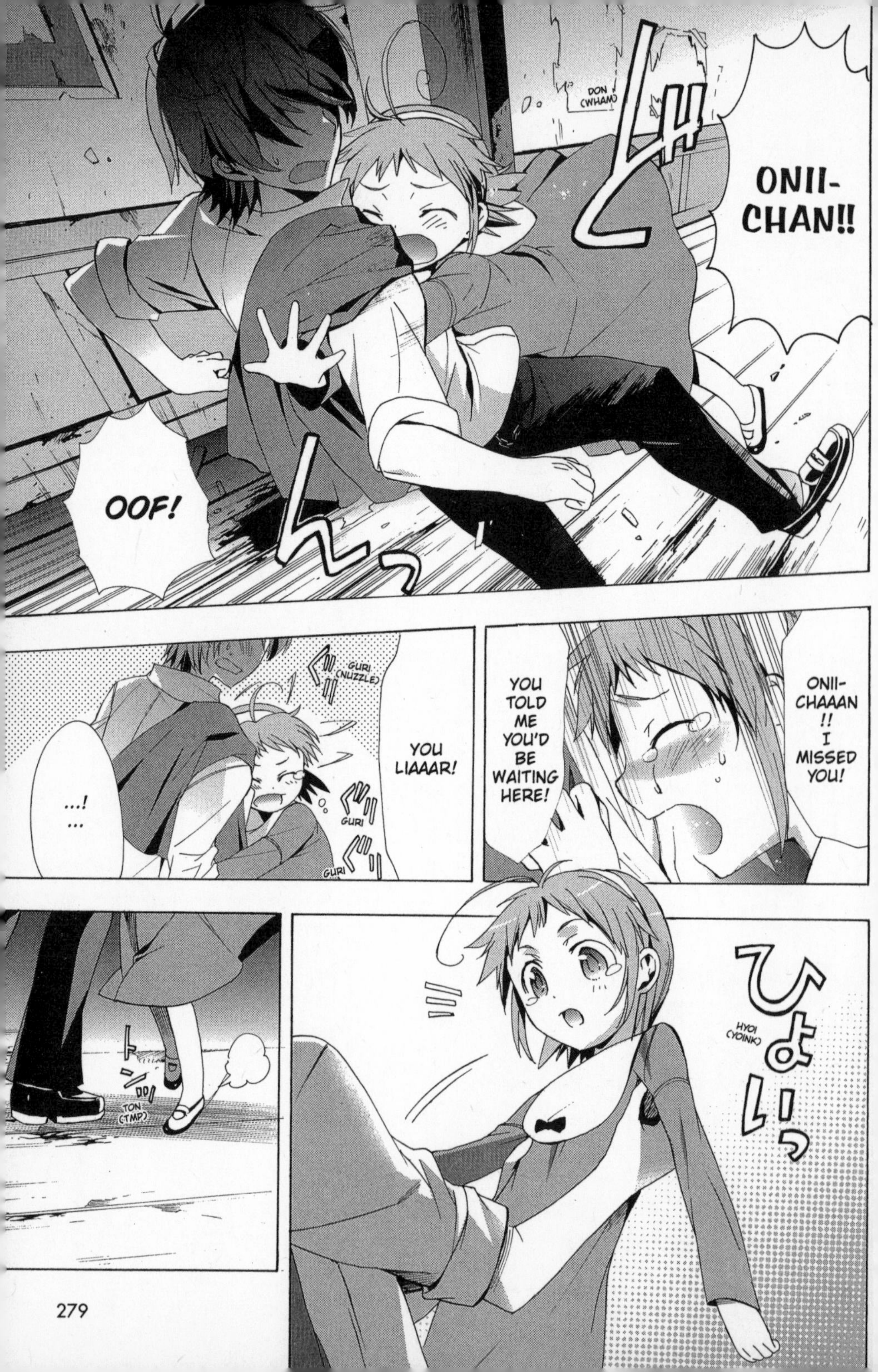
DON (WHAM)
ONII-CHAN!!
OOF!
ONII-CHAAAN!! I MISSED YOU!
YOU TOLD ME YOU'D BE WAITING HERE!
GURI (NUZZLE)
YOU LIAAAR!
GURI
GURI
...! ...
HYOI (YOINK)
TON (TMP)

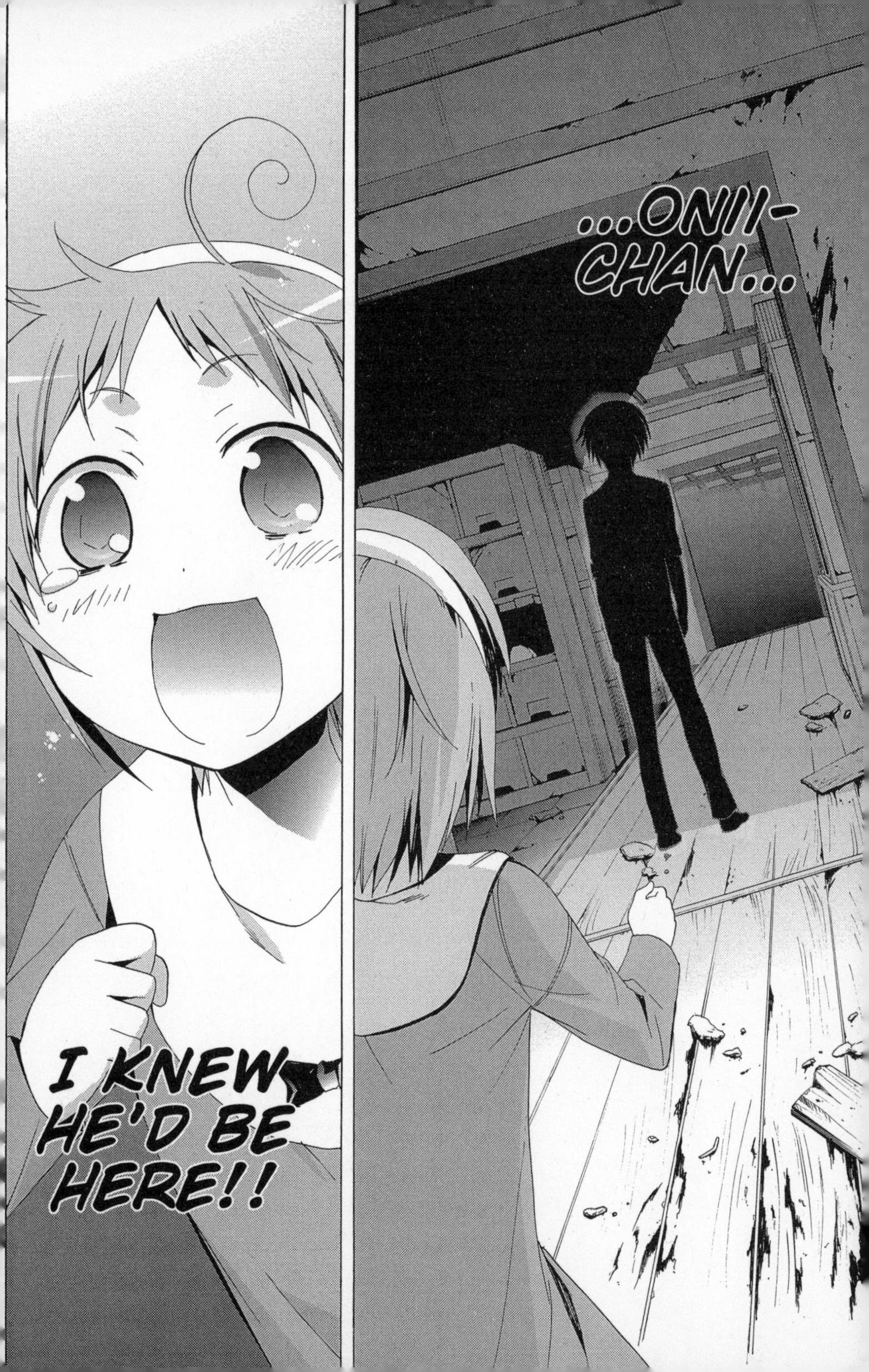
...ONII-
CHAN...
I KNEW
HE'D BE
HERE!!

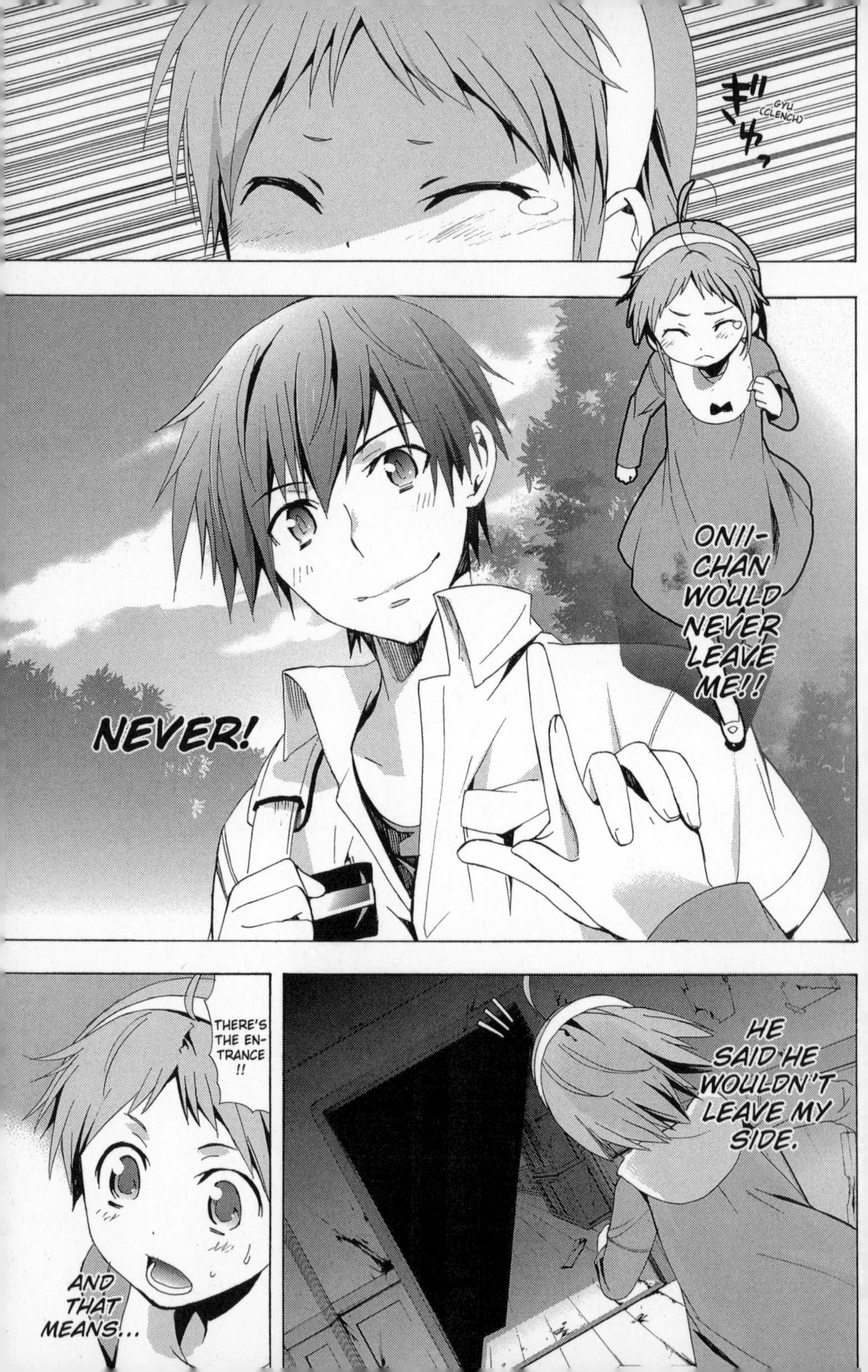
ぎゅっ
GYU (CLENCH)
ONII-CHAN WOULD NEVER LEAVE ME!!
NEVER!
HE SAID HE WOULDN'T LEAVE MY SIDE.
THERE'S THE EN-TRANCE!!
AND THAT MEANS...

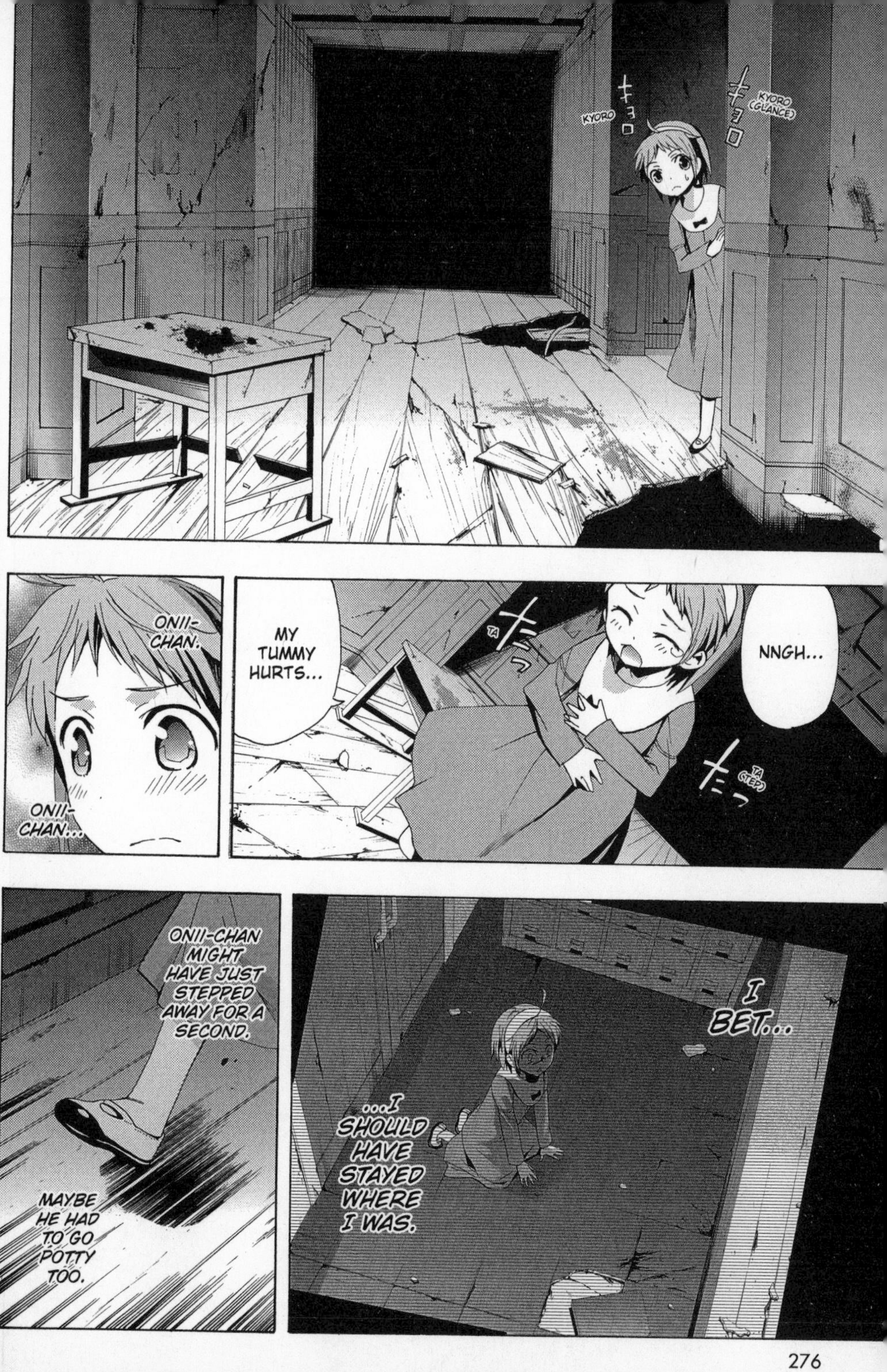
キョロ
KYORO (GLANCE)
キョロ
KYORO
NNGH...
たっ
TA
MY TUMMY HURTS...
たっ
TA (TEP)
ONII-CHAN.
ONII-CHAN...
I BET...
...I SHOULD HAVE STAYED WHERE I WAS.
ONII-CHAN MIGHT HAVE JUST STEPPED AWAY FOR A SECOND.
MAYBE HE HAD TO GO POTTY TOO.

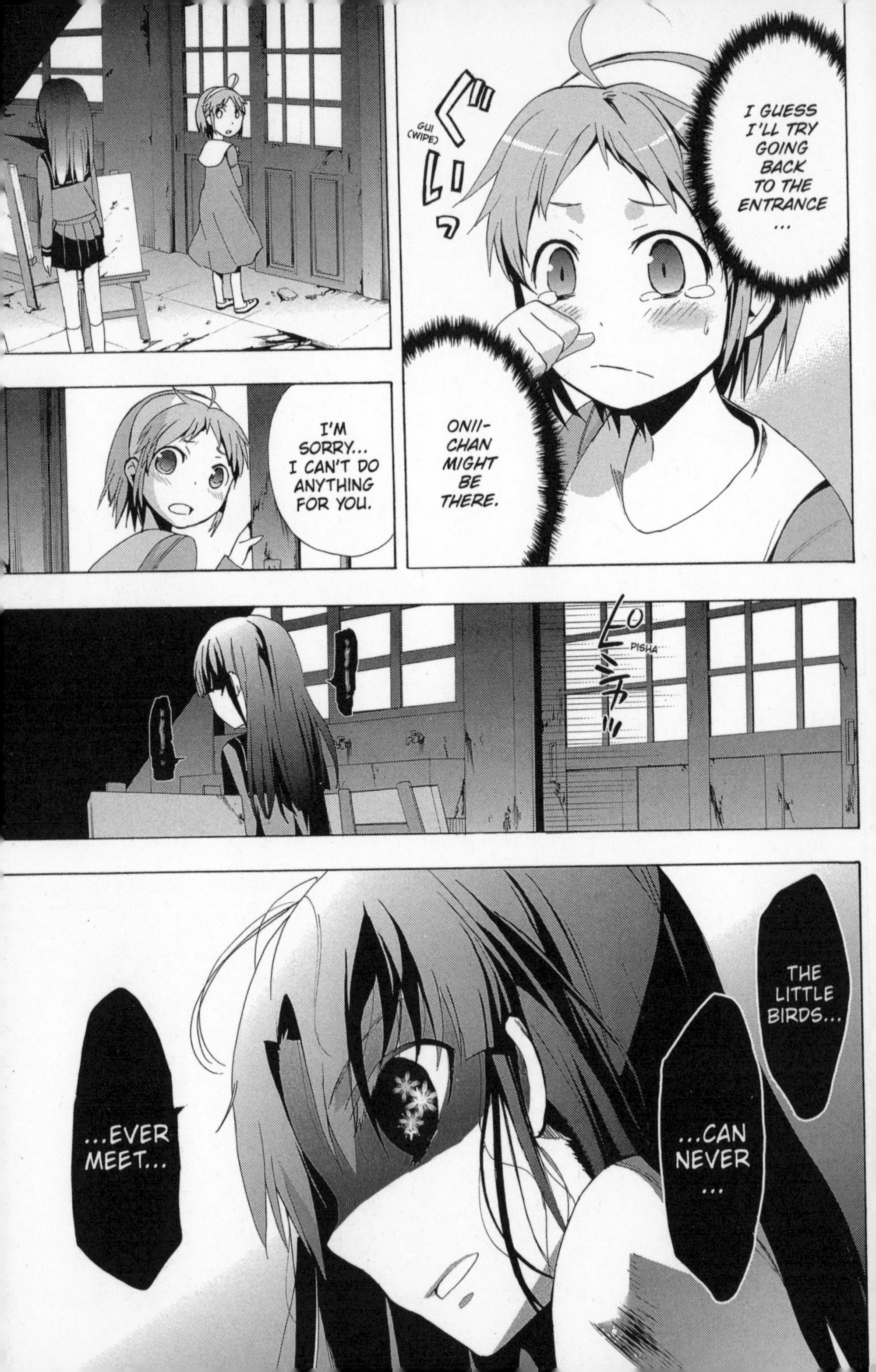
GUI (WIPE)
I GUESS I'LL TRY GOING BACK TO THE ENTRANCE...
ONII-CHAN MIGHT BE THERE.
I'M SORRY... I CAN'T DO ANYTHING FOR YOU.
PISHA
THE LITTLE BIRDS...
...CAN NEVER...
...EVER MEET...

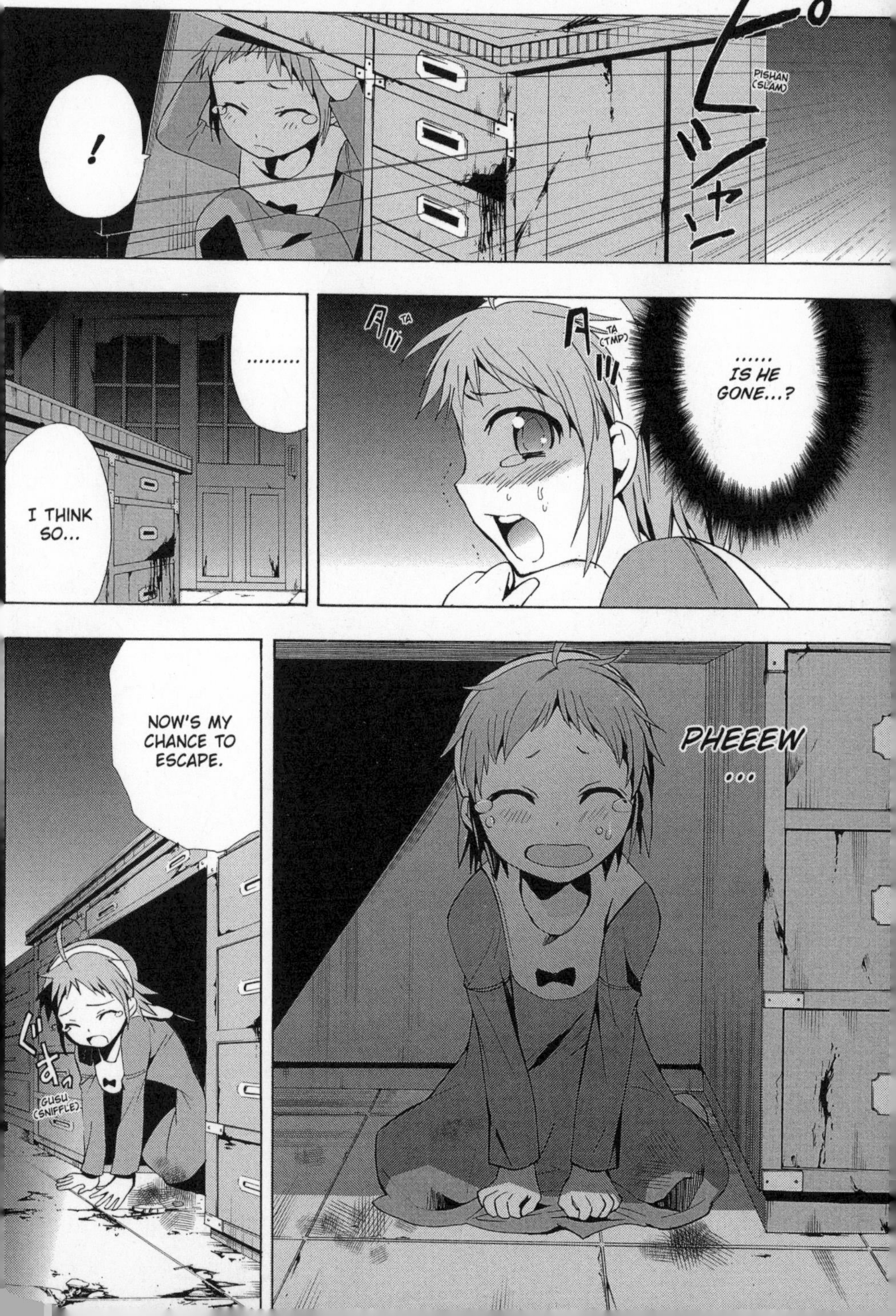
ピシャン
PISHAN (SLAM)
!
TA
TA (TMP)
...... IS HE GONE...?
....
I THINK SO...
PHEEEW ...
NOW'S MY CHANCE TO ESCAPE.
ぐすっ
GUSU (SNIFFLE)

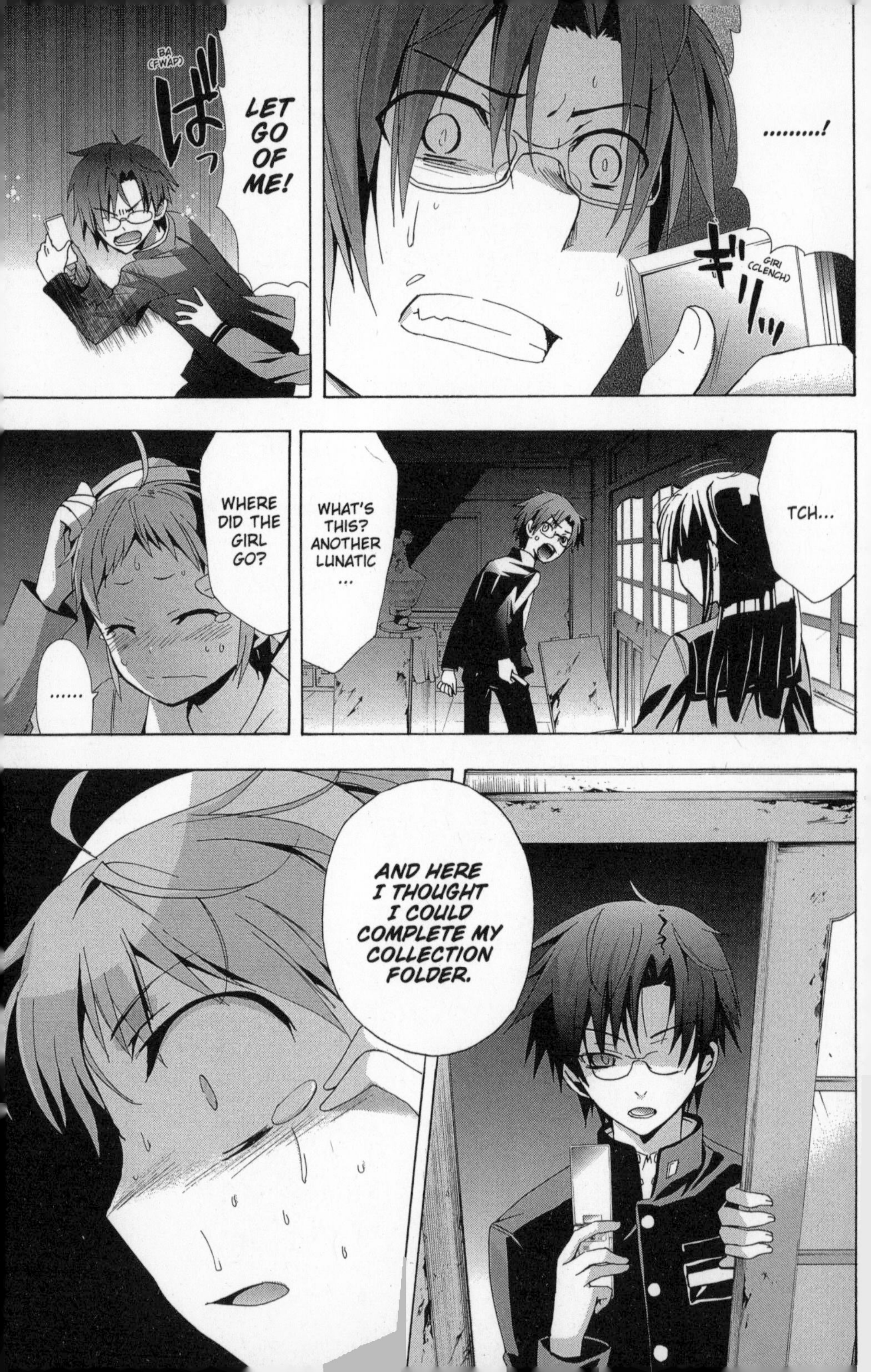
.........!
ギリッ
GIRI (CLENCH)
ばっ
BA (FWAP)
LET GO OF ME!
TCH...
WHAT'S THIS? ANOTHER LUNATIC ...
WHERE DID THE GIRL GO?
......
AND HERE I THOUGHT I COULD COMPLETE MY COLLECTION FOLDER.

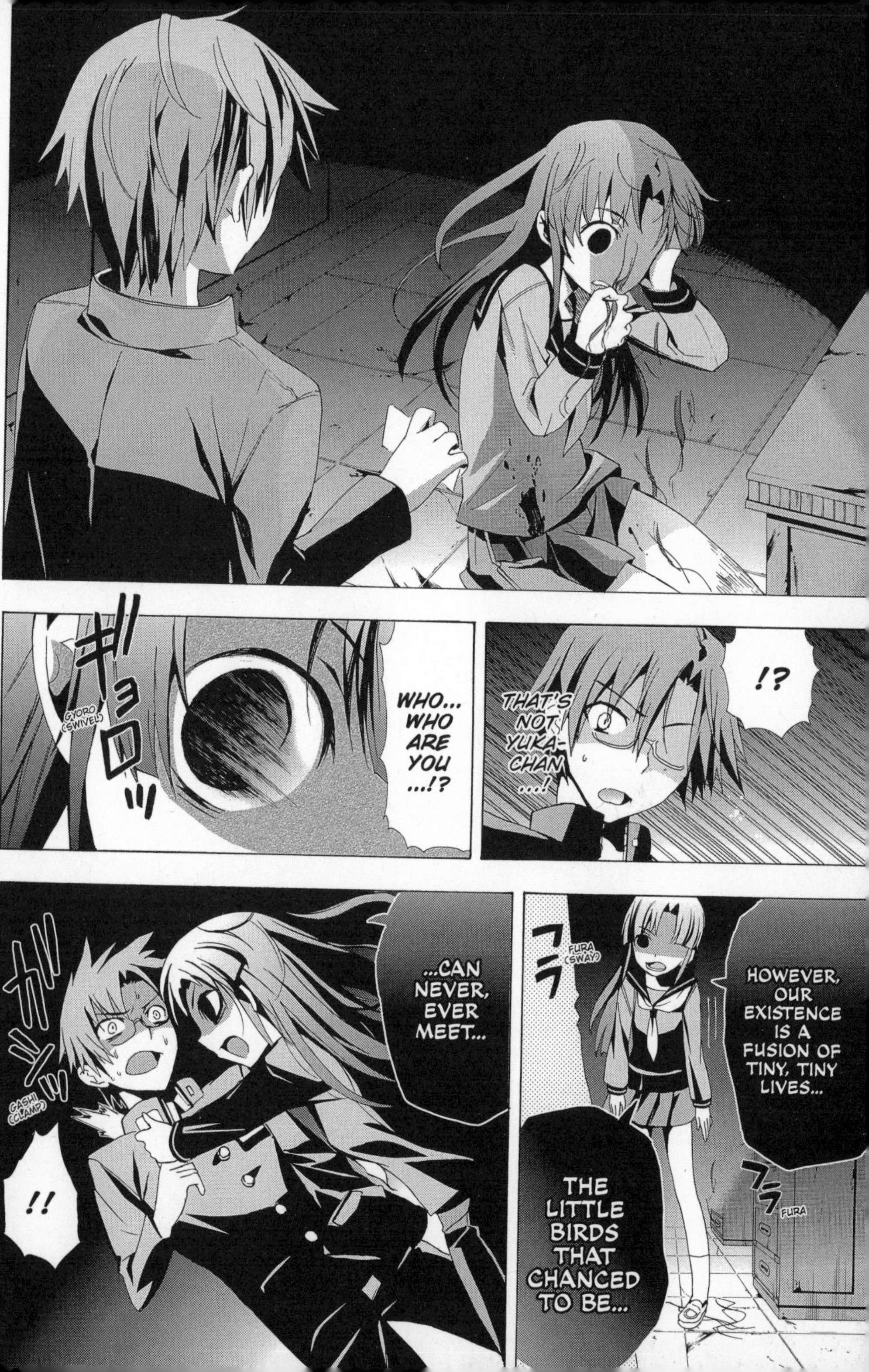
!?
THAT'S NOT YUKA-CHAN ...!
GYORO (SWIVEL)
WHO... WHO ARE YOU ...!?
FURA (SWAY)
HOWEVER, OUR EXISTENCE IS A FUSION OF TINY, TINY LIVES...
THE LITTLE BIRDS THAT CHANCED TO BE...
FURA
...CAN NEVER, EVER MEET...
GASHI (CLAMP)
!!

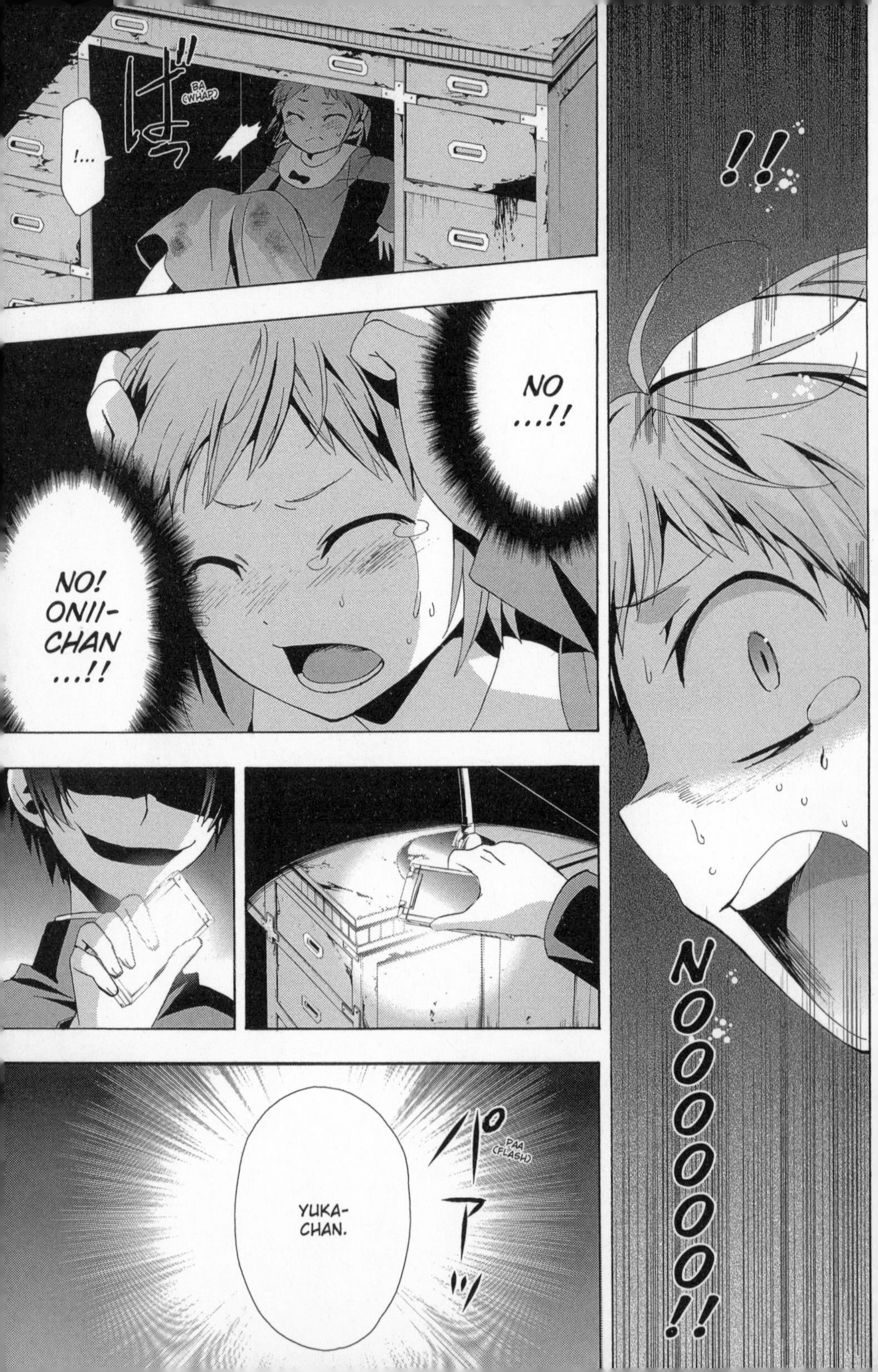
!!
NOOOOOO!!
ばっ
BA (WHAP)
!...
NO ...!!
NO! ONII-CHAN ...!!
パァーッ
PAA (FLASH)
YUKA-CHAN.

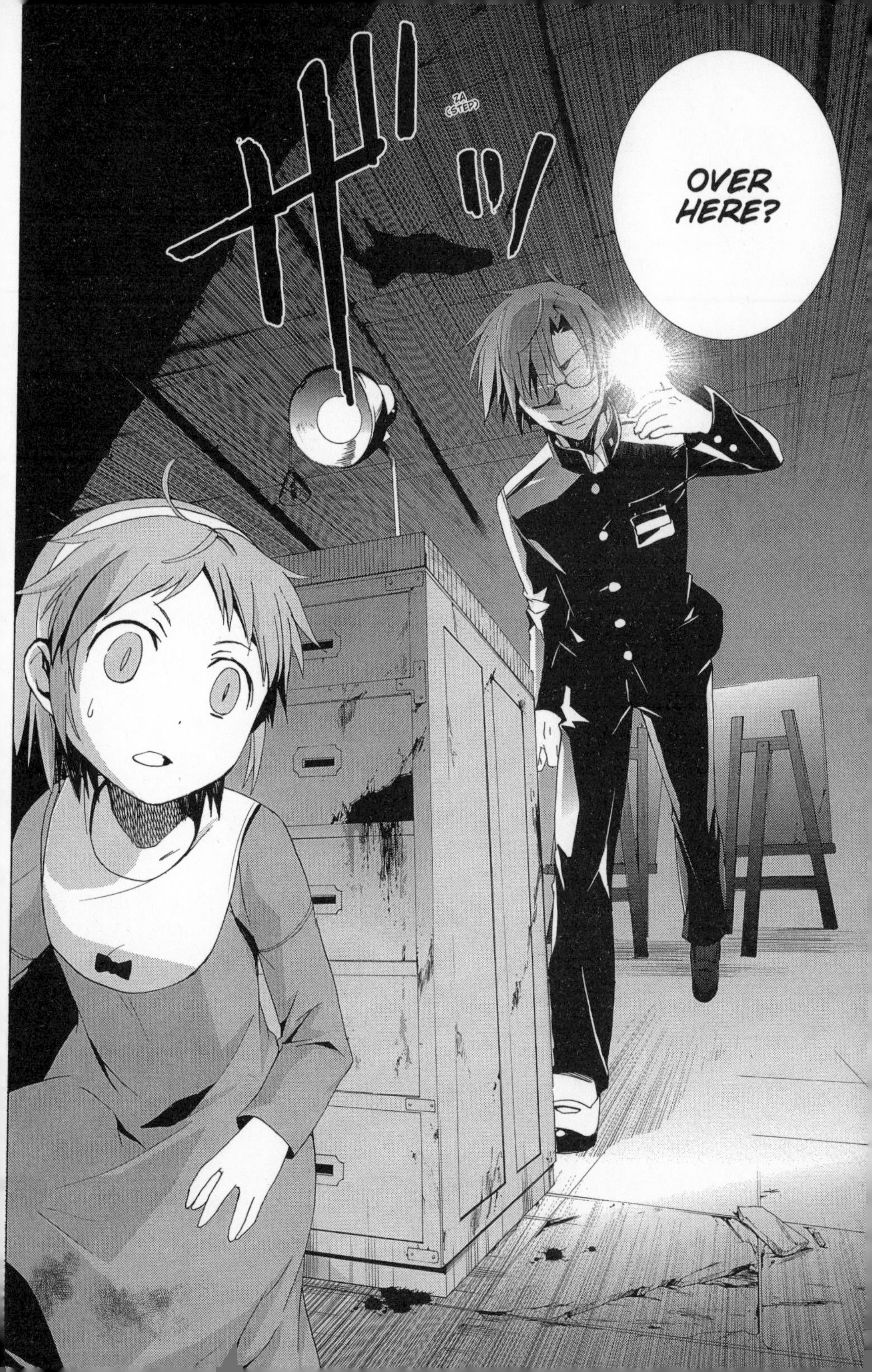
OVER HERE?
ザッ
ZA (STEP)

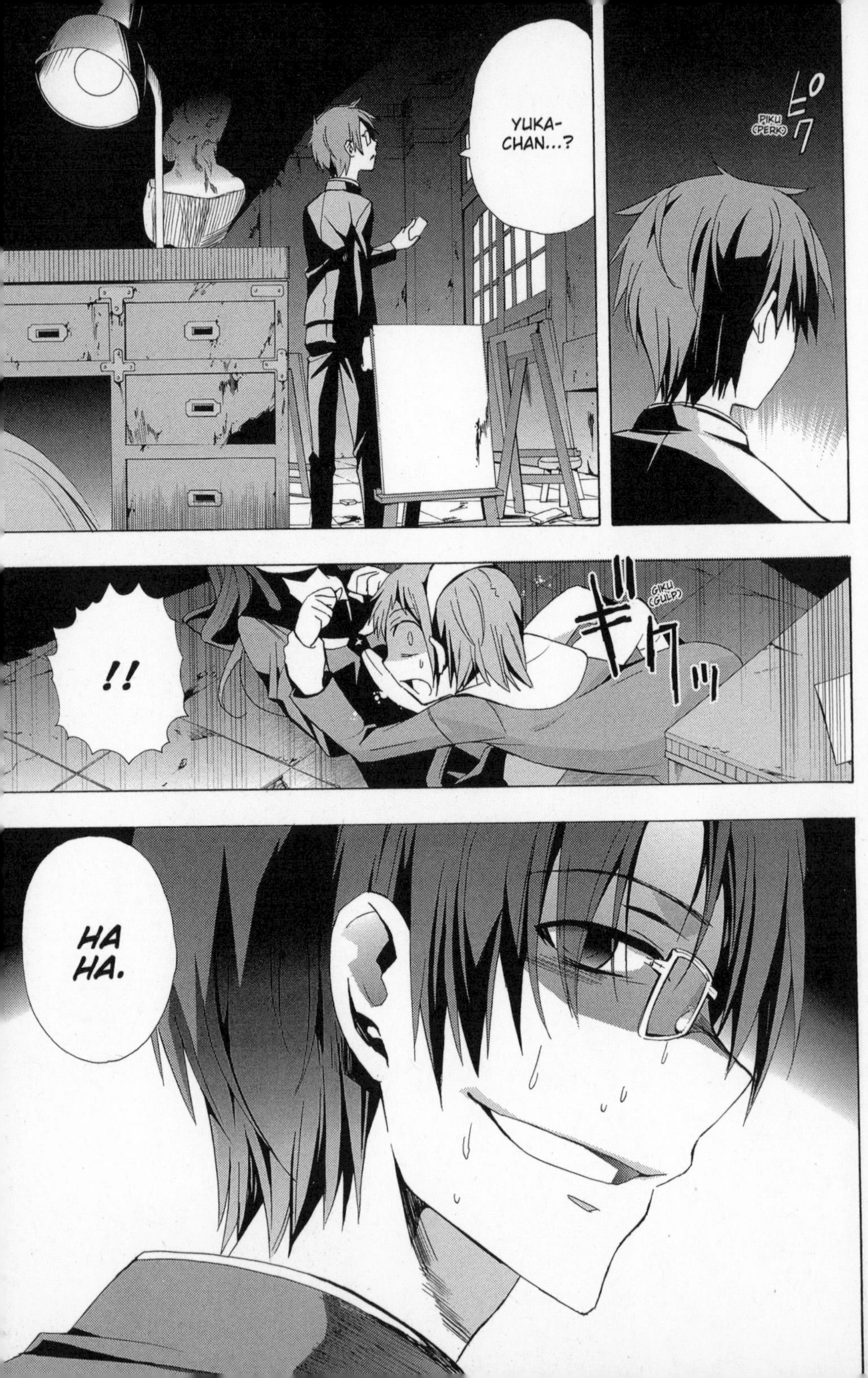
ピク
PIKU
(PERK)
YUKA-
CHAN...?
ギクッ
GIKU
(GULP)
!!
HA
HA.

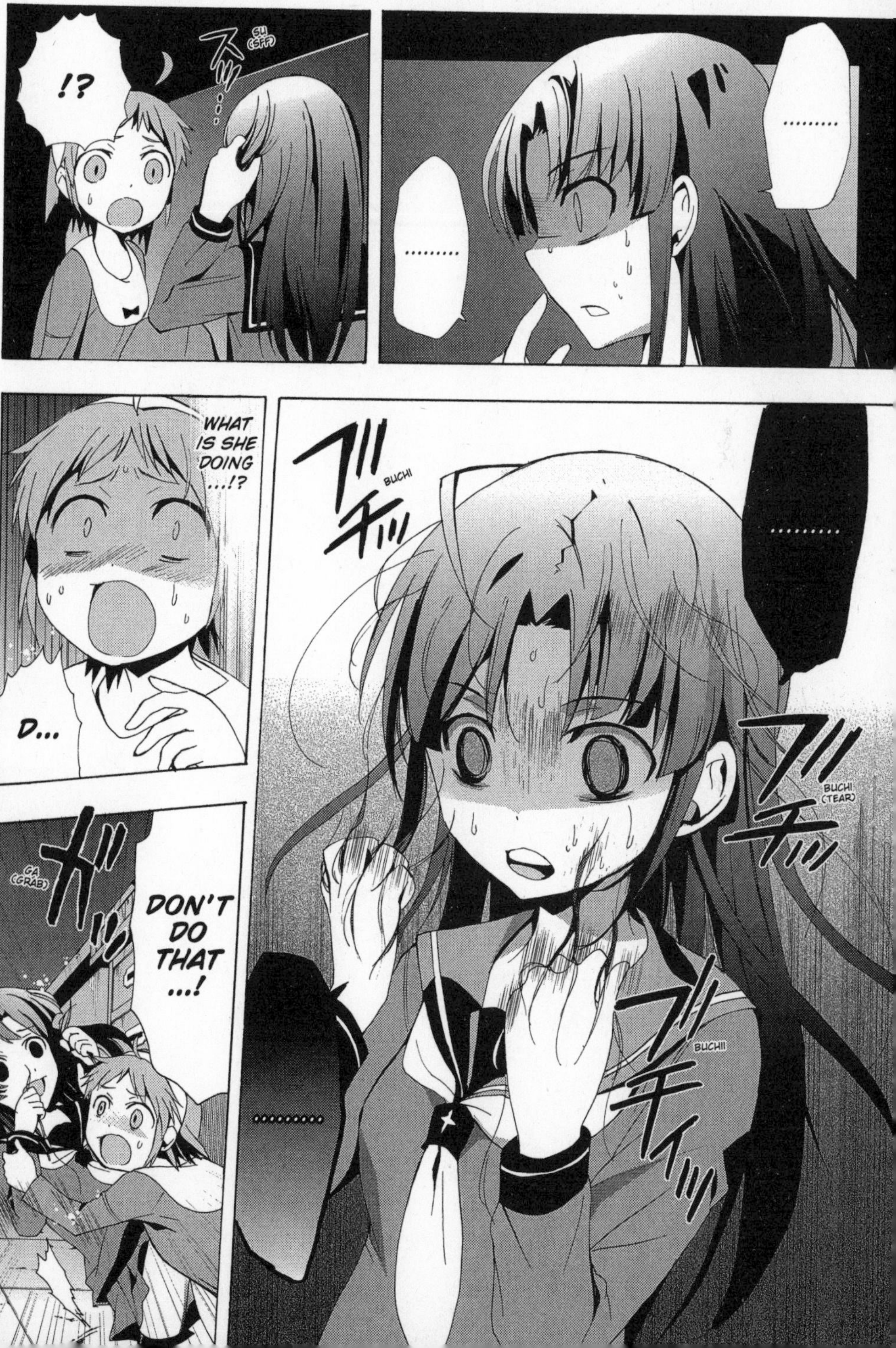
....
....
!?
SU (SFF)
BUCHI
....
BUCHI (TEAR)
BUCHII
....
WHAT IS SHE DOING ...!?
D...
GA (GRAB)
DON'T DO THAT ...!

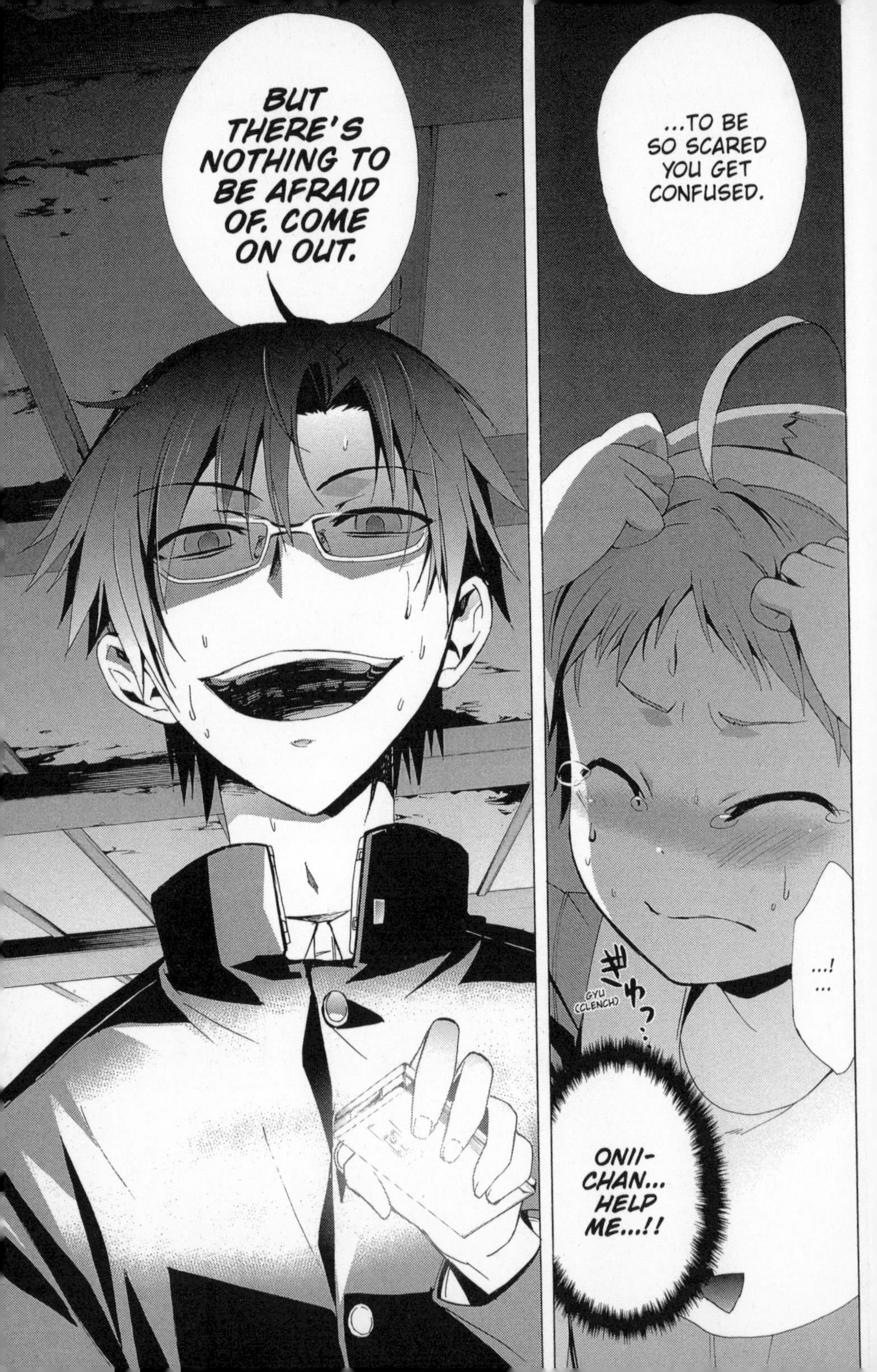
...TO BE SO SCARED YOU GET CONFUSED.
...!
...
GYU (CLENCH)
ONII-CHAN... HELP ME...!!
BUT THERE'S NOTHING TO BE AFRAID OF. COME ON OUT.

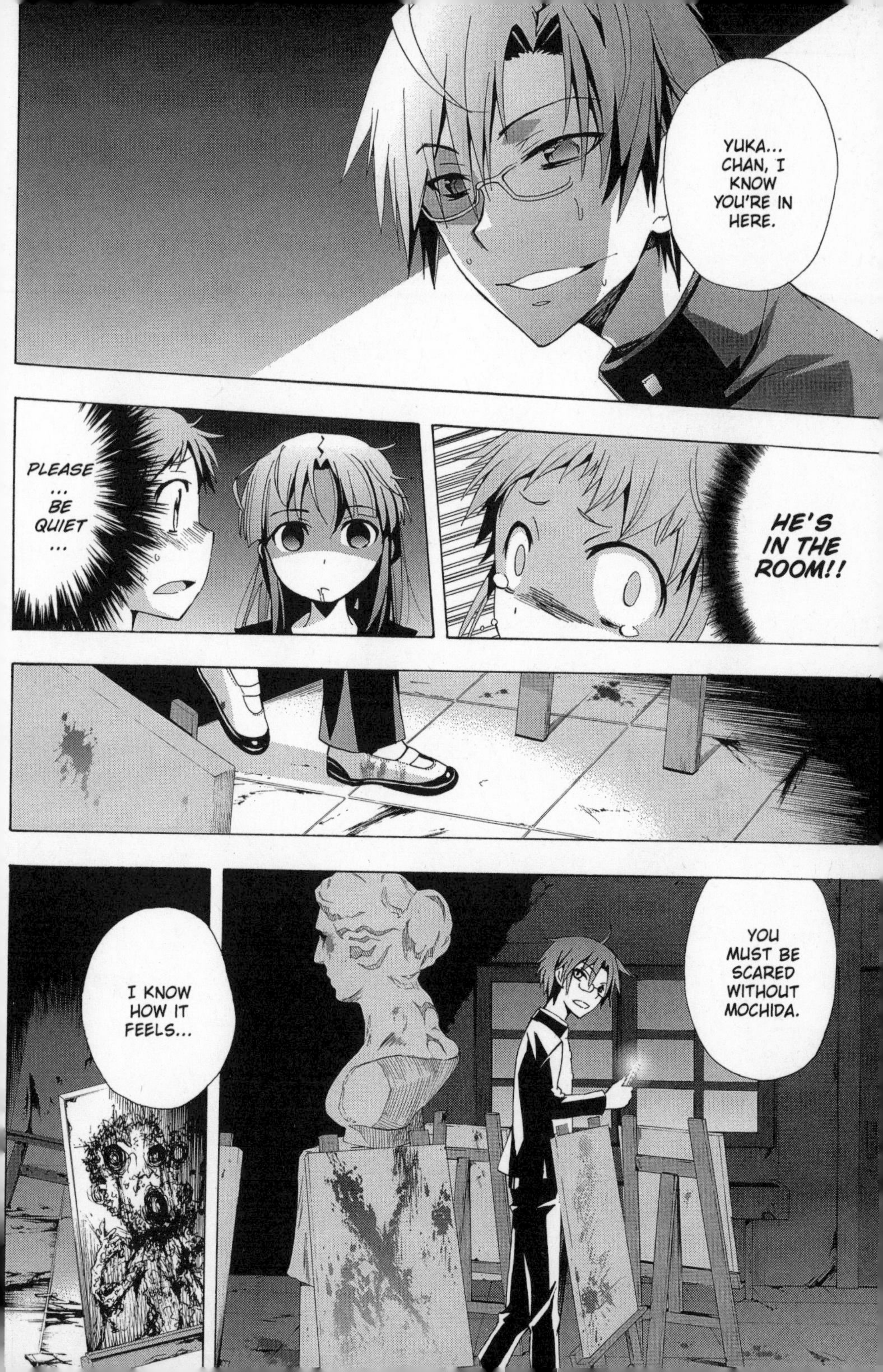
YUKA... CHAN, I KNOW YOU'RE IN HERE.
HE'S IN THE ROOM!!
PLEASE ... BE QUIET ...
YOU MUST BE SCARED WITHOUT MOCHIDA.
I KNOW HOW IT FEELS...

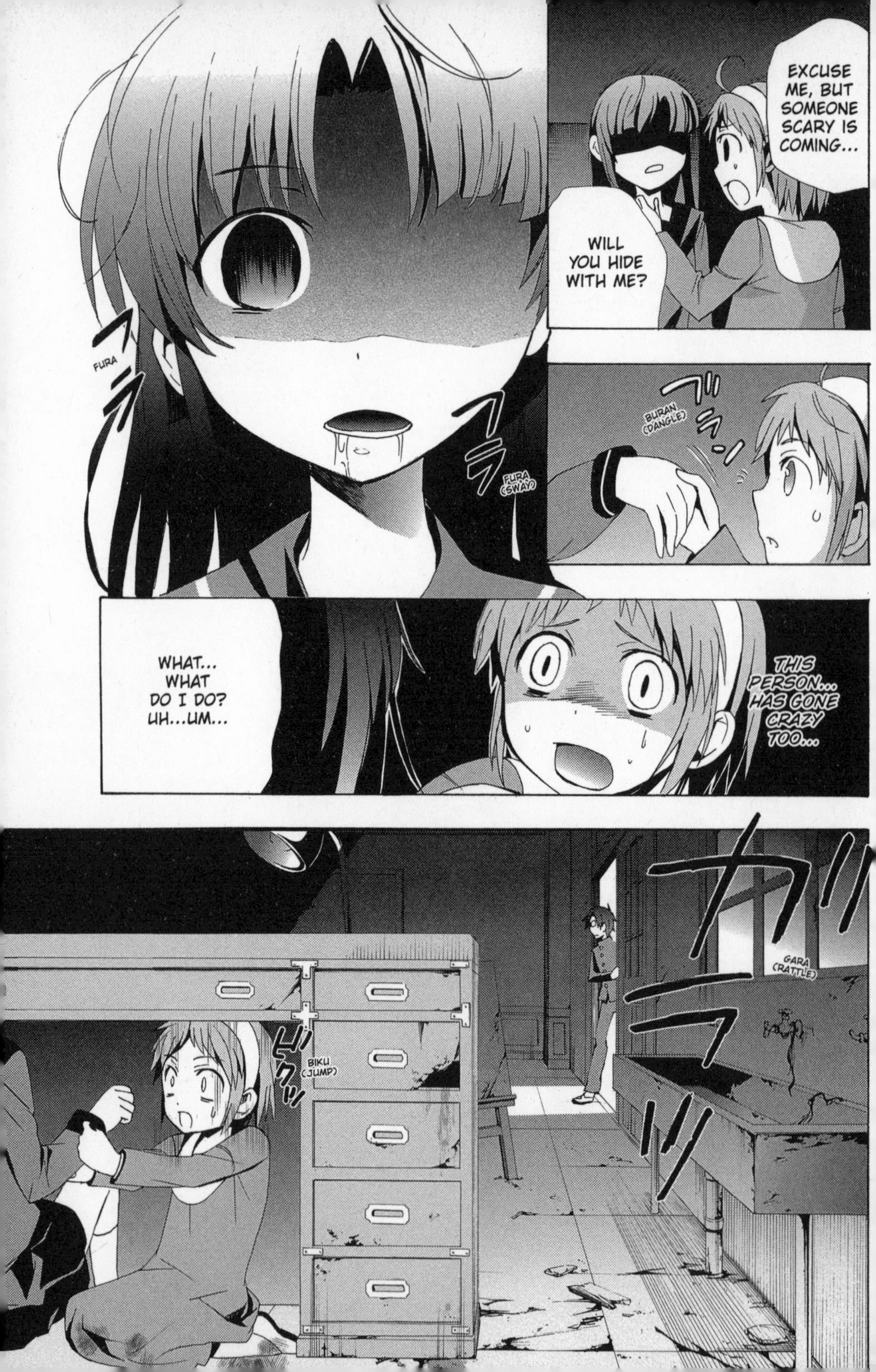
EXCUSE ME, BUT SOMEONE SCARY IS COMING...
WILL YOU HIDE WITH ME?
BURAN (DANGLE)
FURA (SWAY)
FURA
THIS PERSON... HAS GONE CRAZY TOO...
WHAT... WHAT DO I DO? UH...UM...
GARA (RATTLE)
BIKU (JUMP)

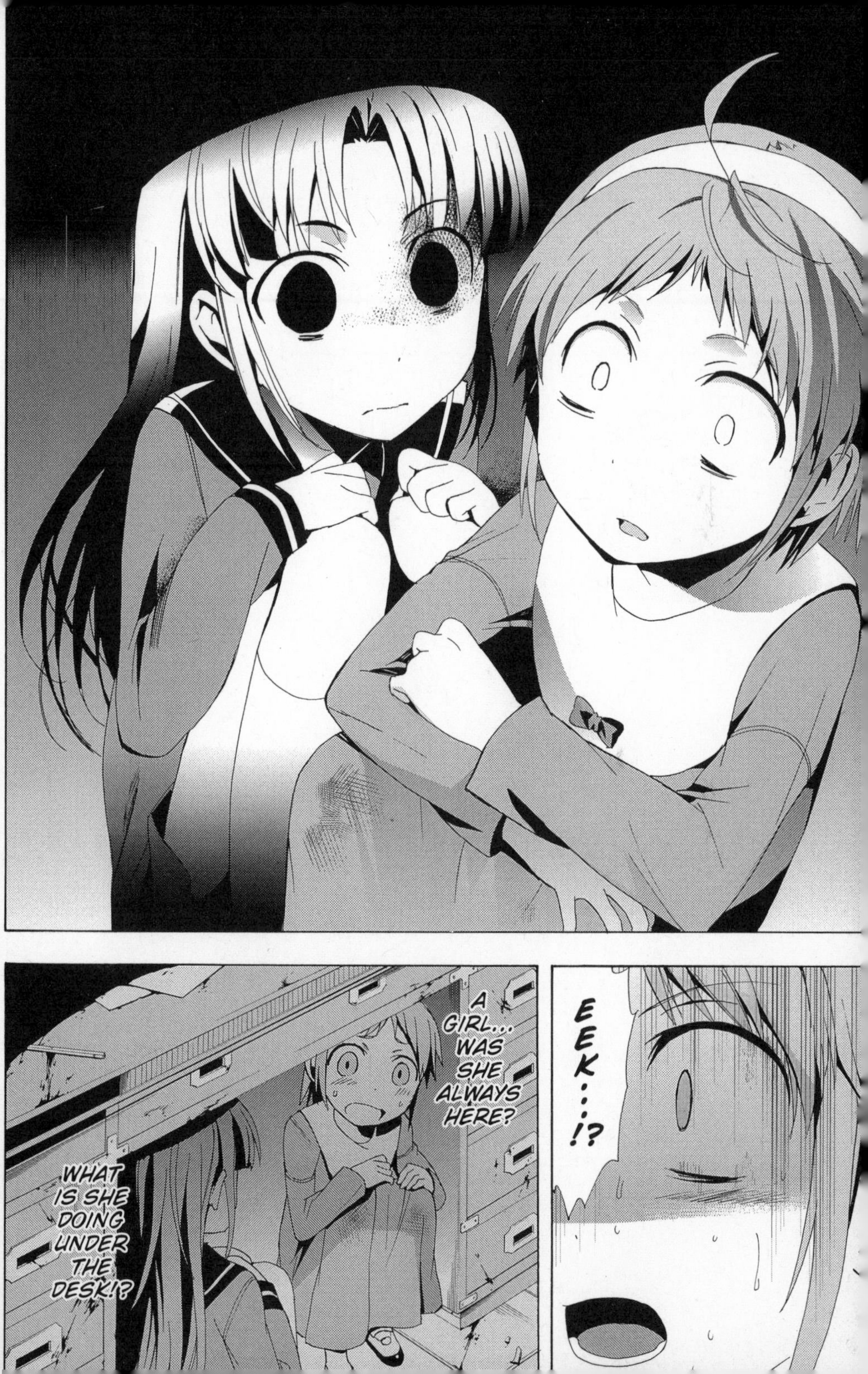
EEK...!?
A GIRL... WAS SHE ALWAYS HERE?
WHAT IS SHE DOING UNDER THE DESK!?

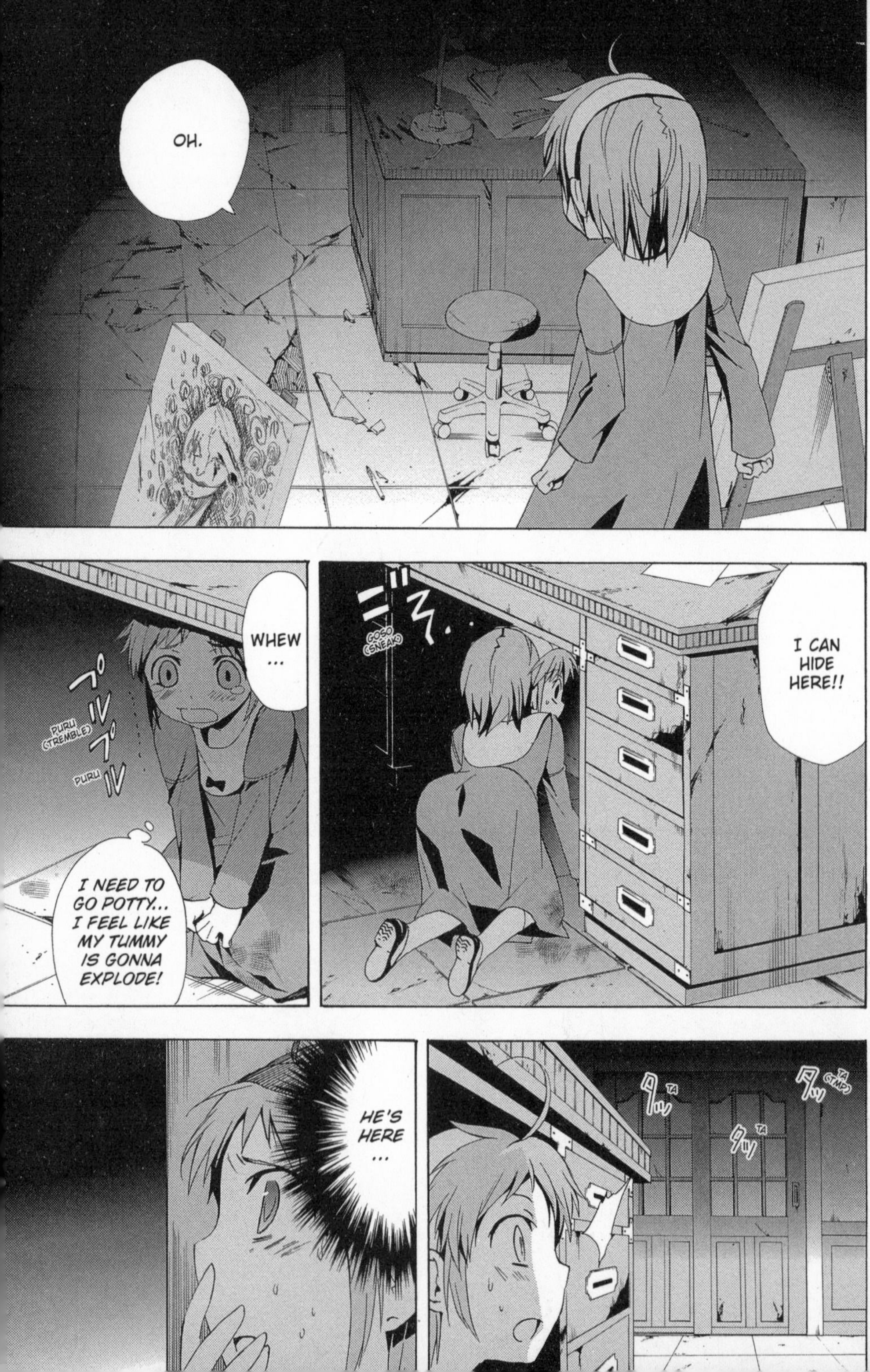
OH.
I CAN HIDE HERE!!
GOSO (SNEAK)
WHEW ...
PURU (TREMBLE)
PURU
I NEED TO GO POTTY... I FEEL LIKE MY TUMMY IS GONNA EXPLODE!
TA (STMP)
TA
TA
HE'S HERE ...

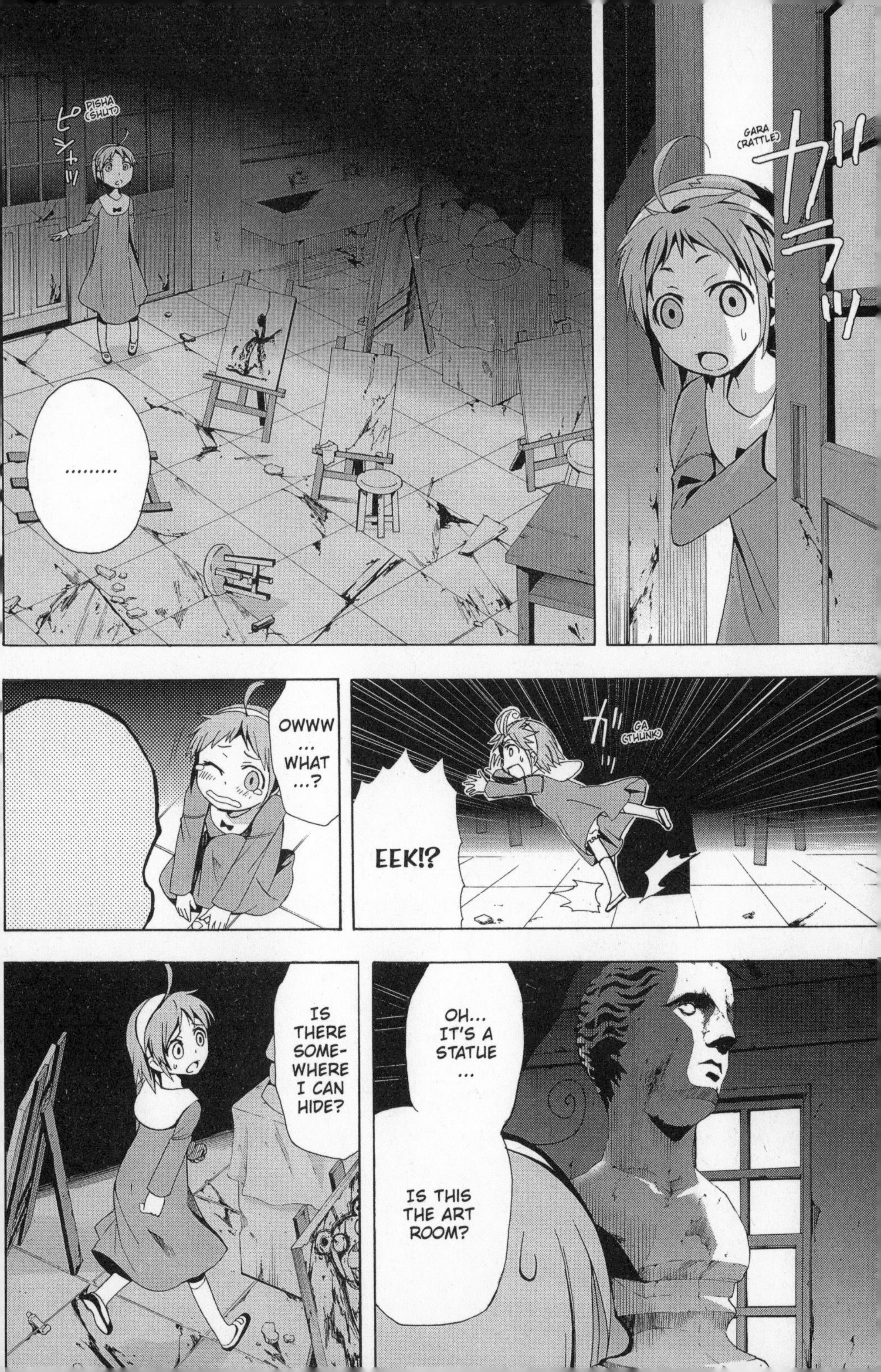
GARA (RATTLE)
ガラッ
PISHA (SHUT)
ピシャッ
....
GA (THUNK)
ガッ
EEK!?
OWWW... WHAT...?
OH... IT'S A STATUE...
IS THIS THE ART ROOM?
IS THERE SOMEWHERE I CAN HIDE?

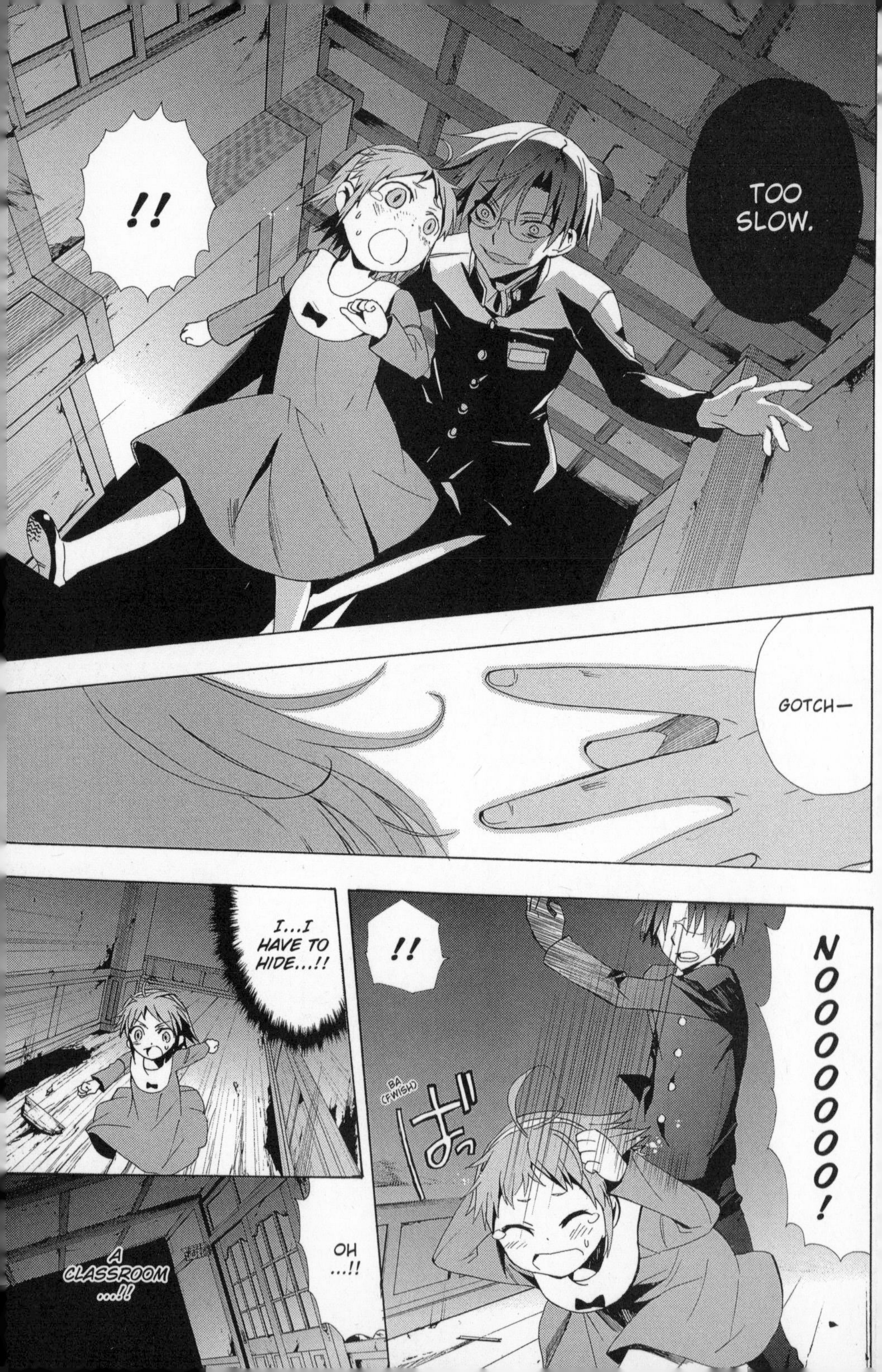
TOO SLOW.
!!
GOTCH—
NOOOOOOOOO!
!!
BA (FWISH)
I...I HAVE TO HIDE...!!
OH ...!!
A CLASSROOM ...!!

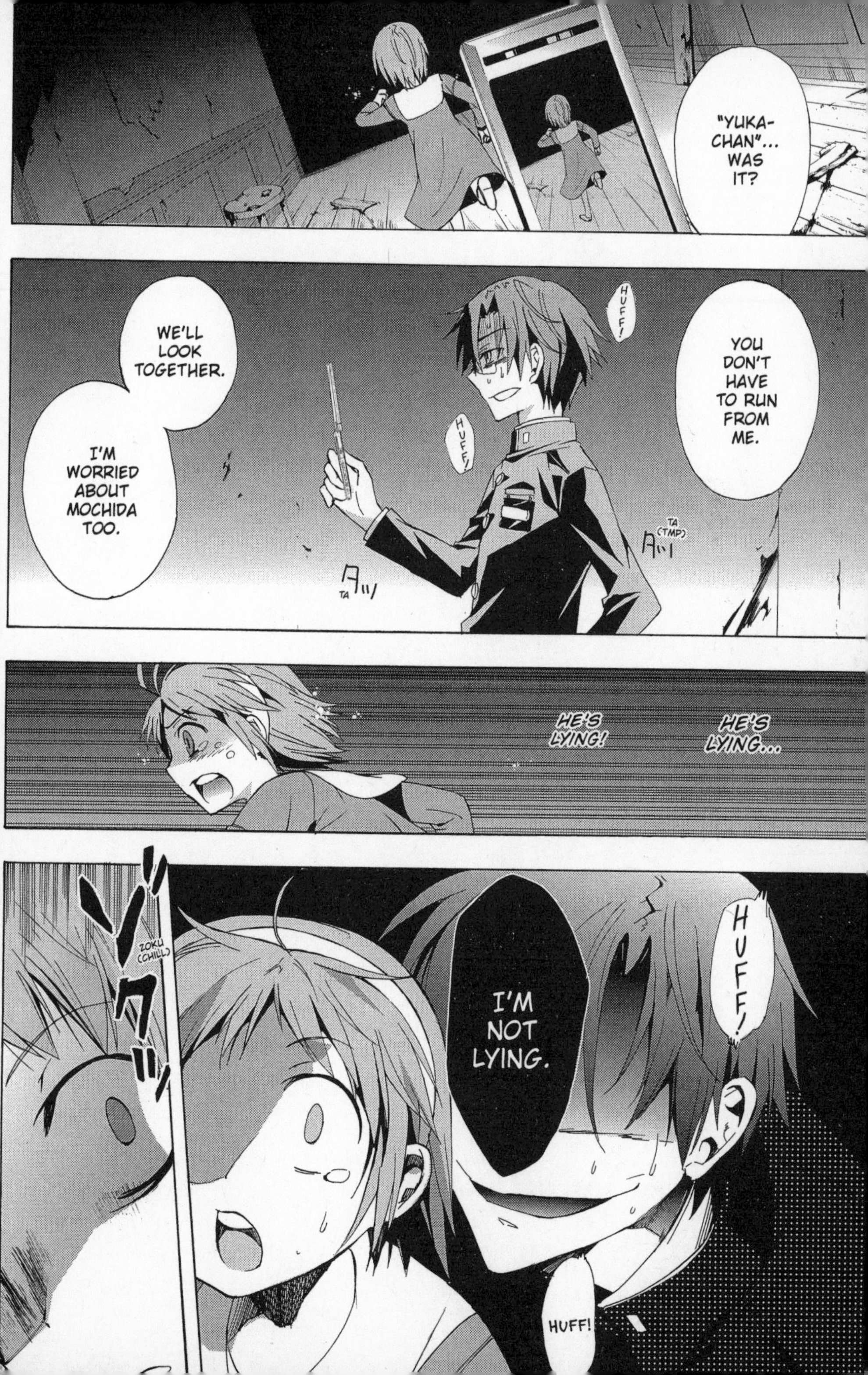
"YUKA-CHAN"... WAS IT?
YOU DON'T HAVE TO RUN FROM ME.
TA (TMP)
HUFF!
HUFF!
WE'LL LOOK TOGETHER.
I'M WORRIED ABOUT MOCHIDA TOO.
TA
HE'S LYING...
HE'S LYING!
HUFF!
I'M NOT LYING.
HUFF!
ZOKU (CHILL)

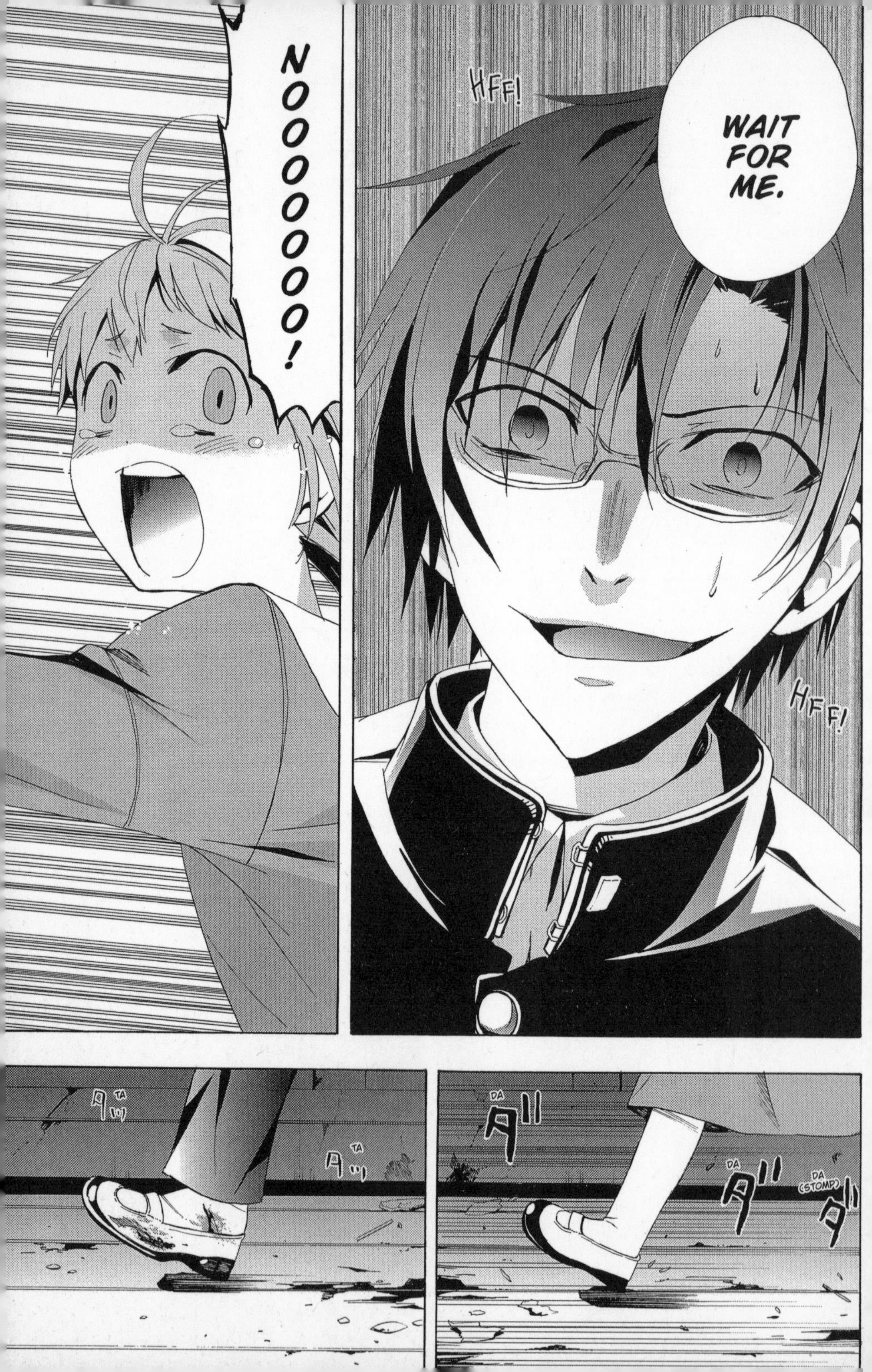
HFF!
WAIT FOR ME.
HFF!
NOOOOOOOOO!
DA
DA
DA (STOMP)
TA
TA

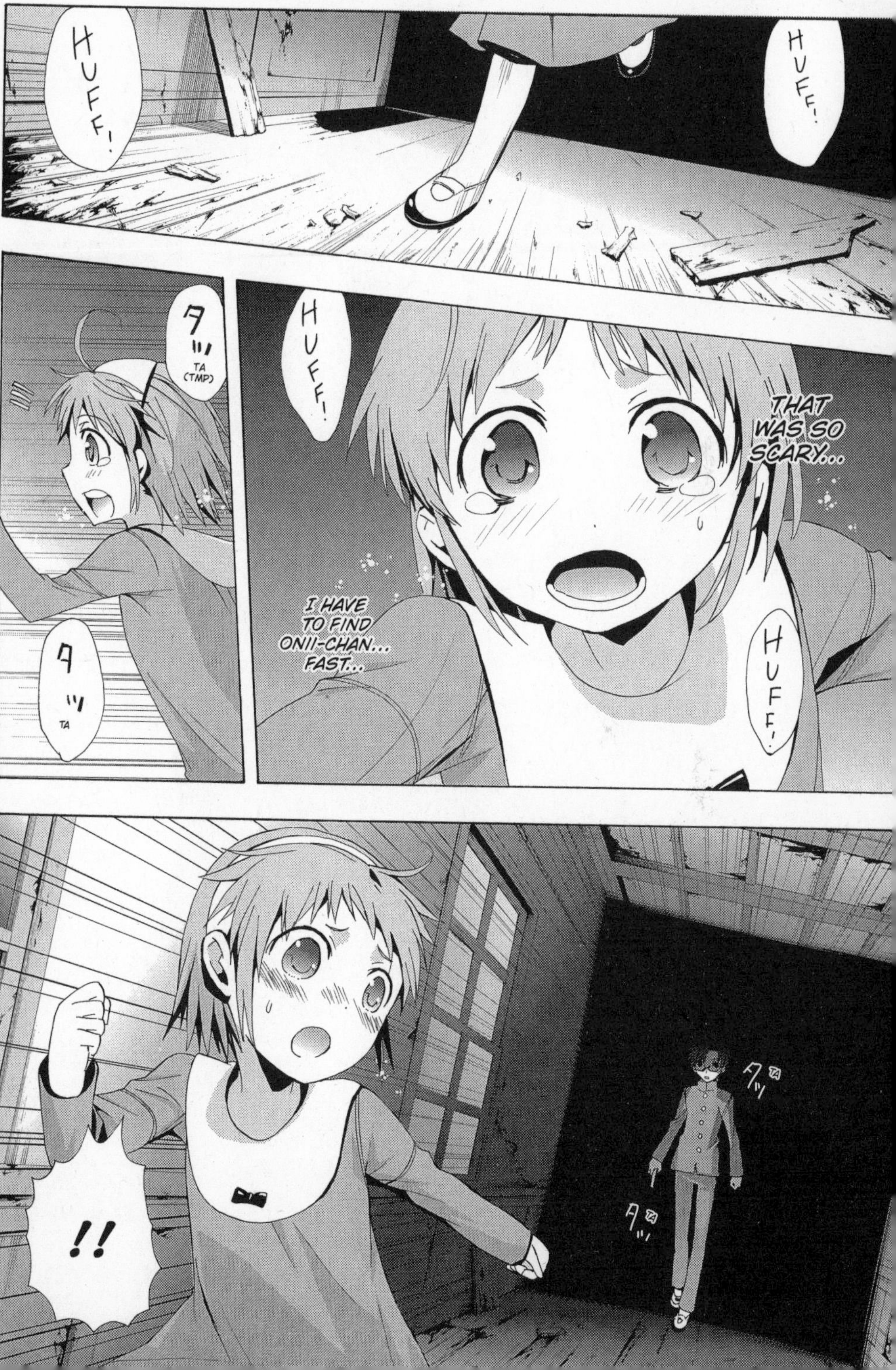
HUFF!
HUFF!
HUFF!
THAT WAS SO SCARY...
I HAVE TO FIND ONII-CHAN... FAST...
HUFF!
タッ
TA (TMP)
タッ
TA
タッ TA
タッ TA
!!

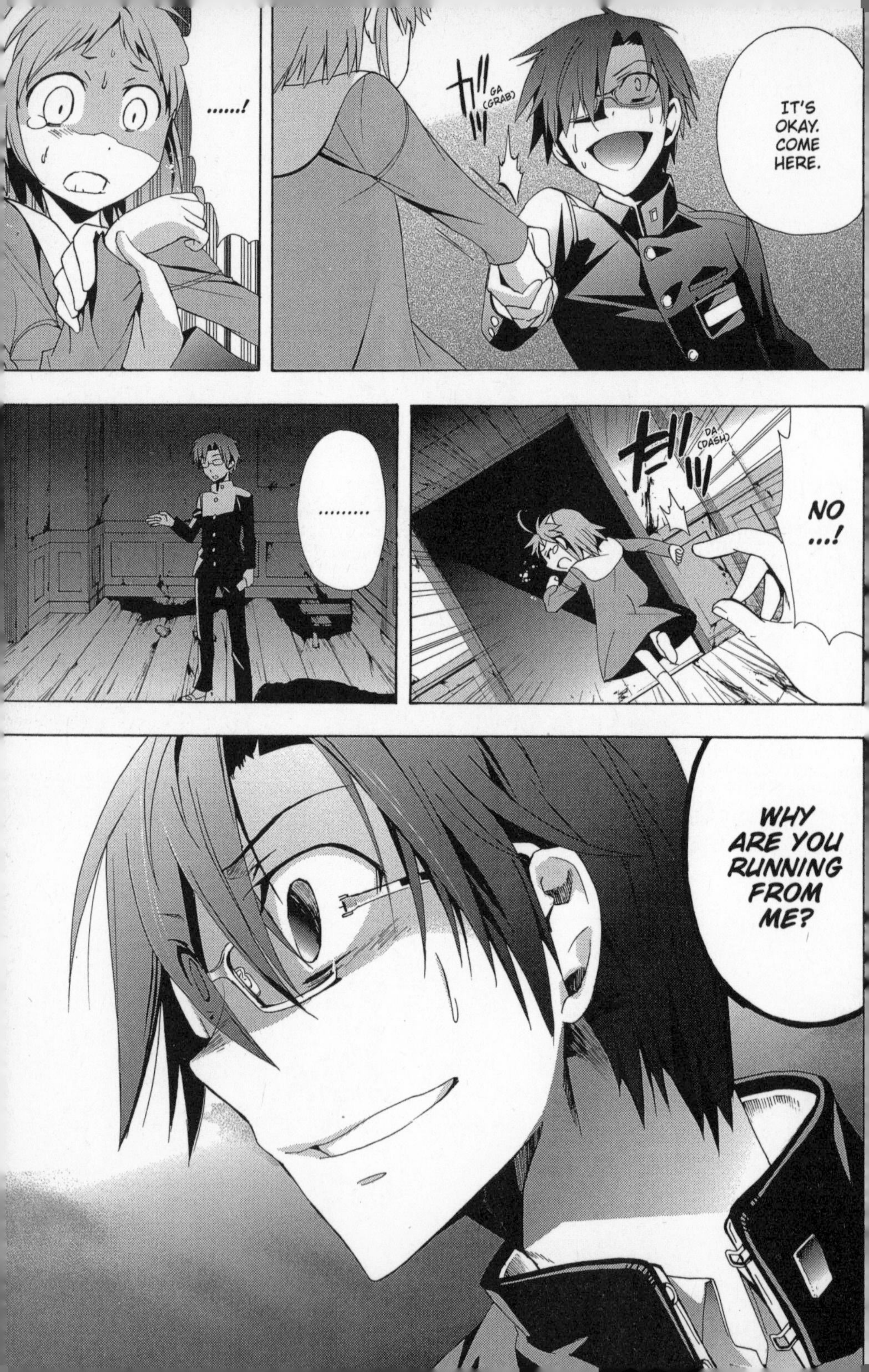
IT'S OKAY. COME HERE.
ガッ
GA (GRAB)
......!
NO ...!
ダッ
DA (DASH)
....
WHY ARE YOU RUNNING FROM ME?

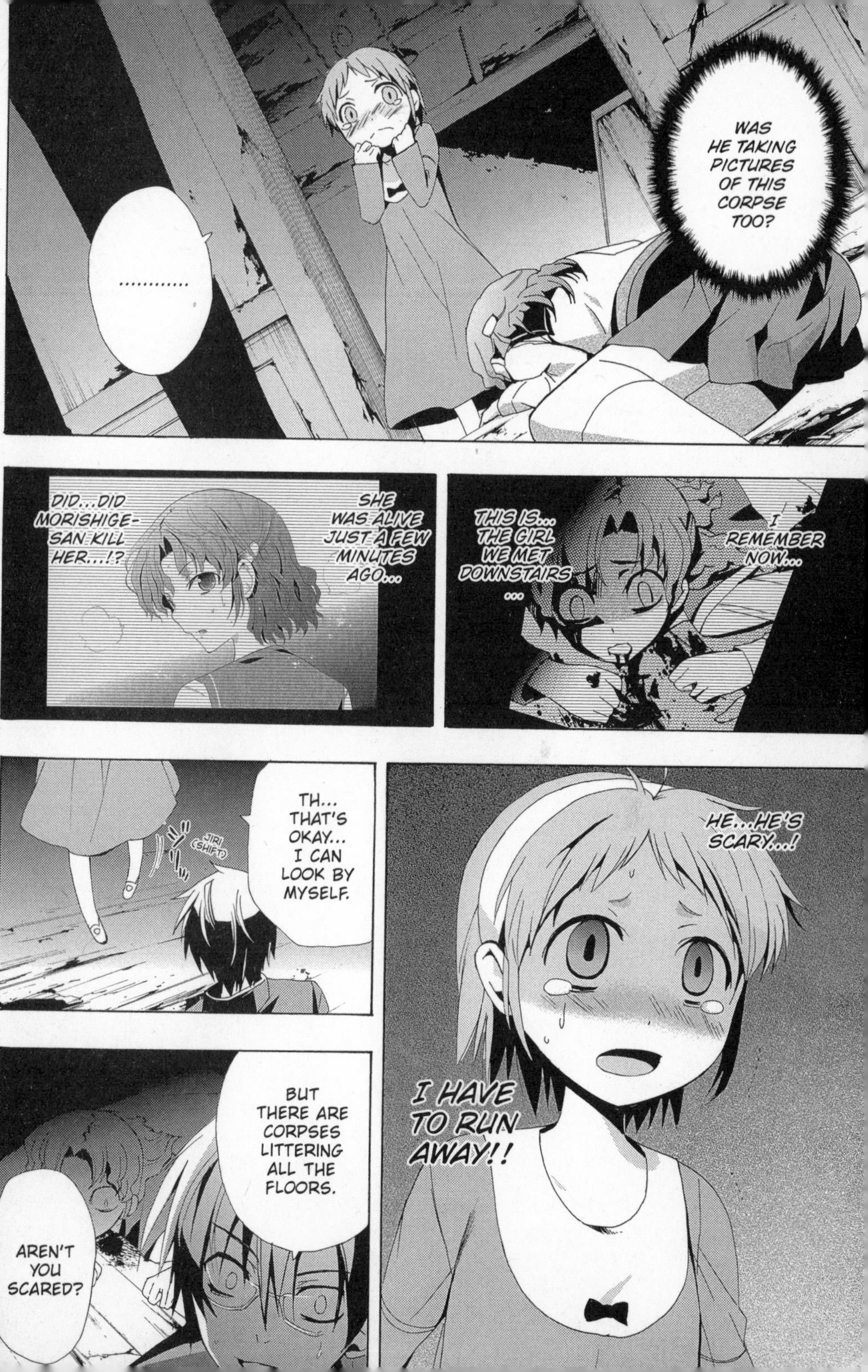
WAS HE TAKING PICTURES OF THIS CORPSE TOO?
....
I REMEMBER NOW...
THIS IS... THE GIRL WE MET DOWNSTAIRS ...
SHE WAS ALIVE JUST A FEW MINUTES AGO...
DID...DID MORISHIGE-SAN KILL HER...!?
HE...HE'S SCARY...!
I HAVE TO RUN AWAY!!
TH... THAT'S OKAY... I CAN LOOK BY MYSELF.
JIRI (SHIFT)
BUT THERE ARE CORPSES LITTERING ALL THE FLOORS.
AREN'T YOU SCARED?

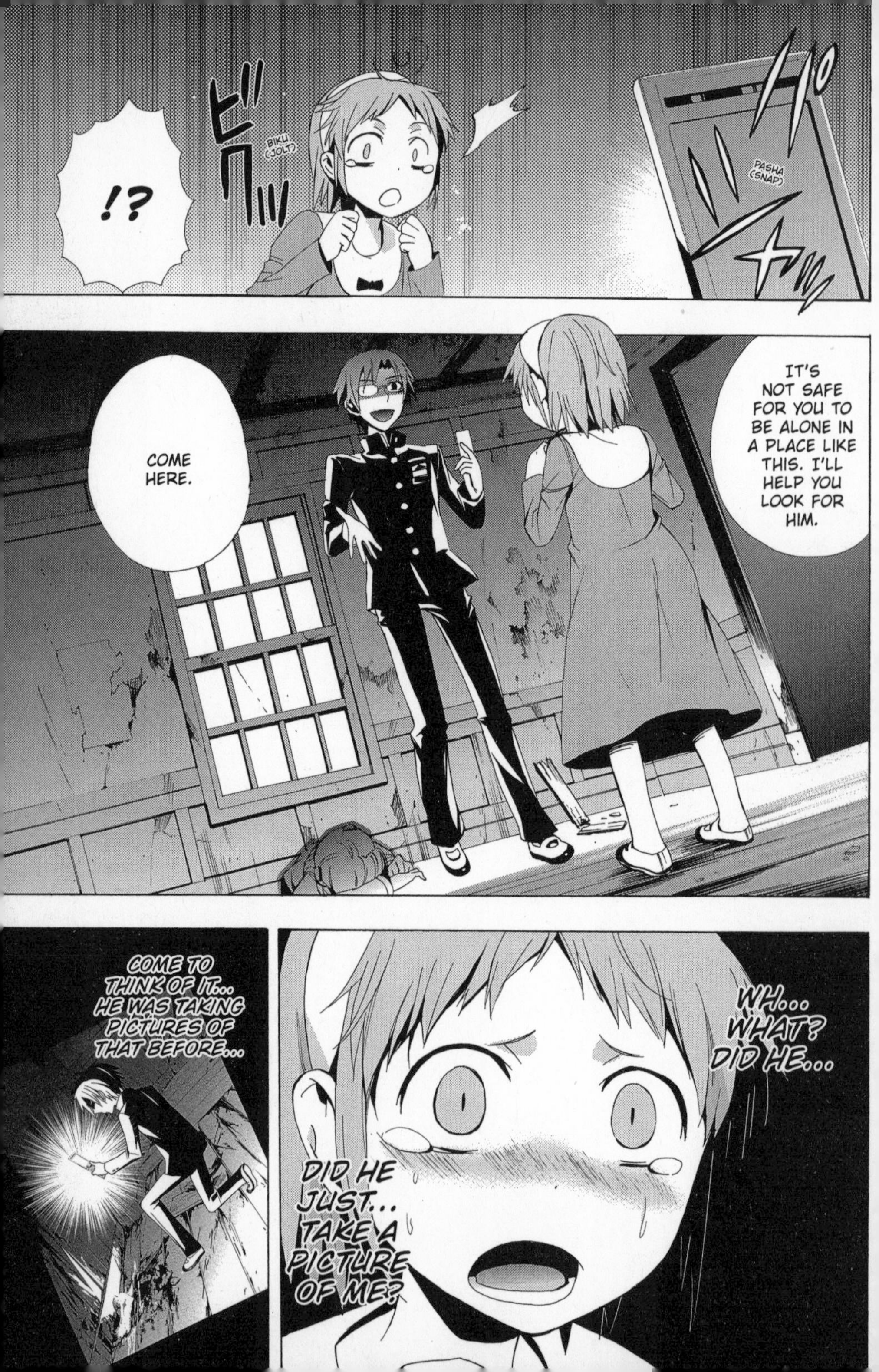
PASHA (SNAP)
BIKU (JOLT)
!?
IT'S NOT SAFE FOR YOU TO BE ALONE IN A PLACE LIKE THIS. I'LL HELP YOU LOOK FOR HIM.
COME HERE.
WH... WHAT? DID HE...
DID HE JUST... TAKE A PICTURE OF ME?
COME TO THINK OF IT... HE WAS TAKING PICTURES OF THAT BEFORE...

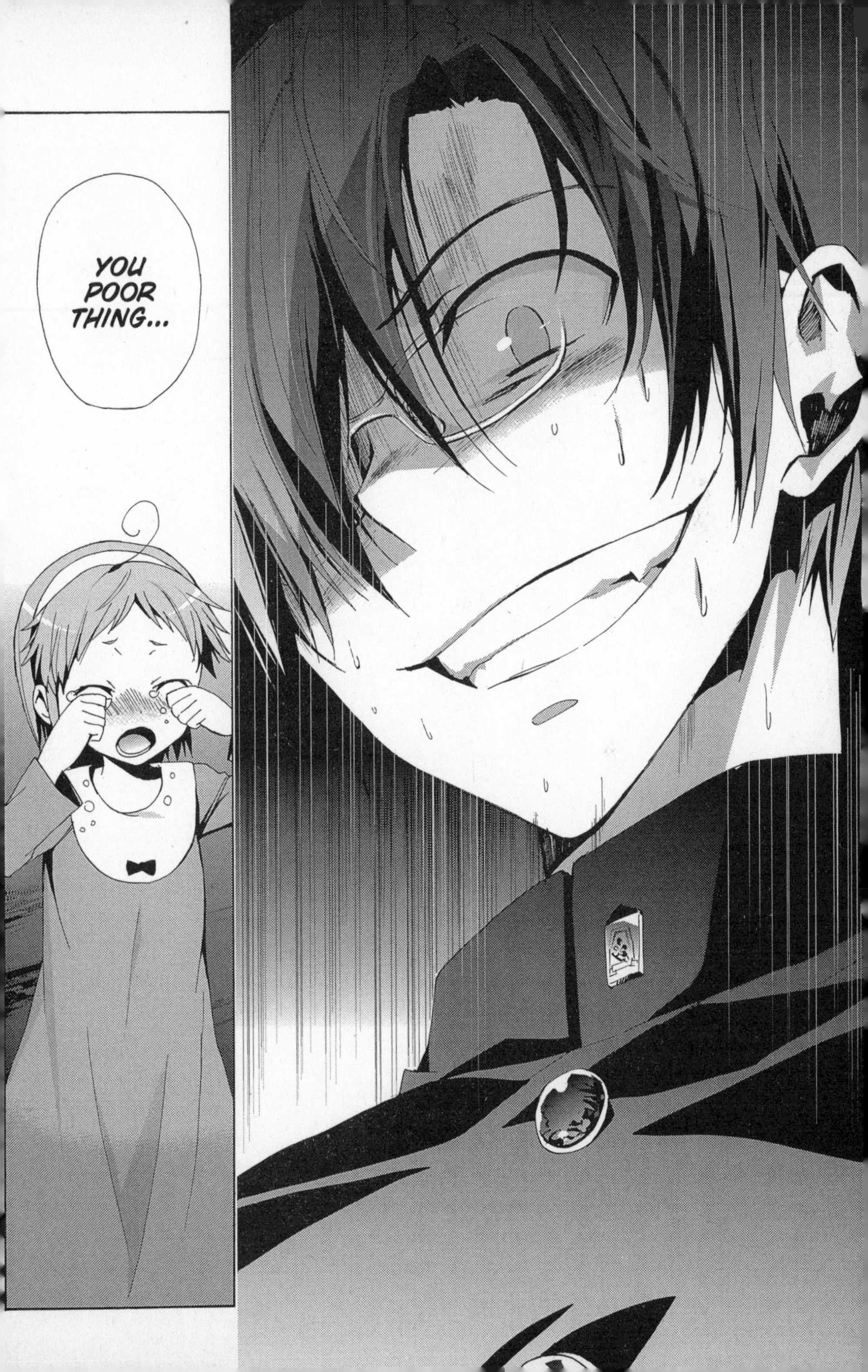
YOU POOR THING...

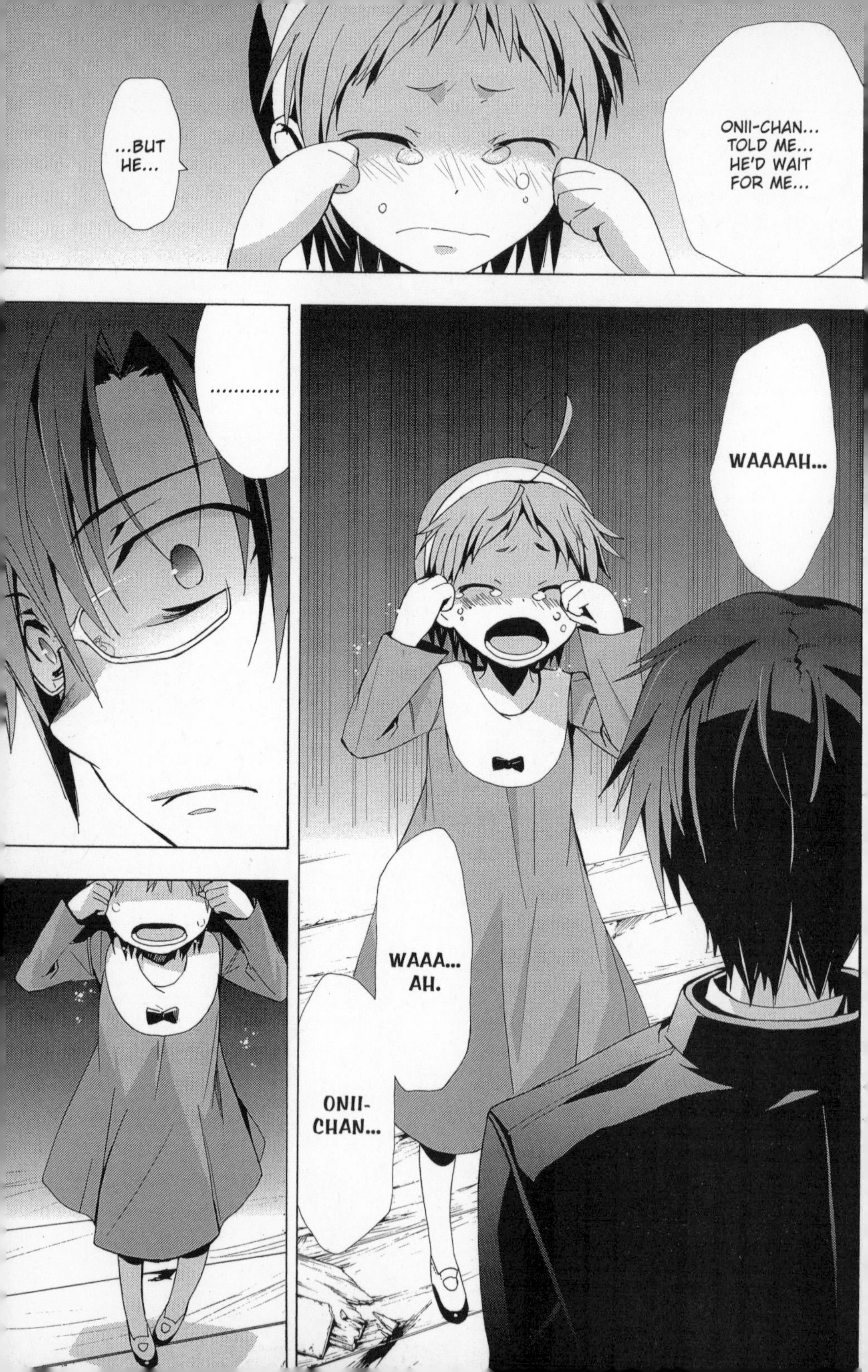
ONII-CHAN... TOLD ME... HE'D WAIT FOR ME...
...BUT HE...
WAAAAH...
WAAA... AH.
ONII-CHAN...
....

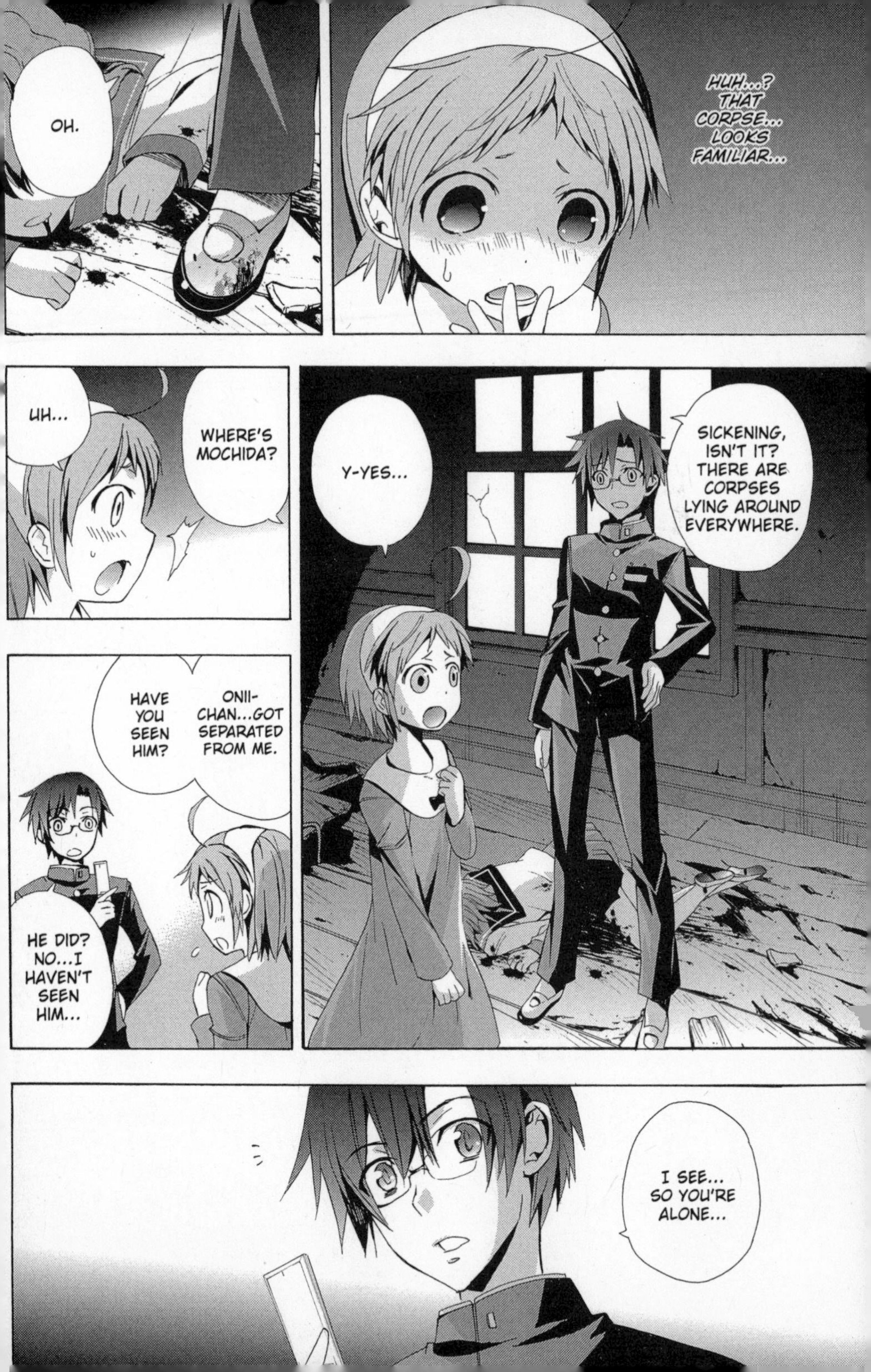
HUH...? THAT CORPSE... LOOKS FAMILIAR...
OH.
SICKENING, ISN'T IT? THERE ARE CORPSES LYING AROUND EVERYWHERE.
Y-YES...
WHERE'S MOCHIDA?
UH...
ONII-CHAN...GOT SEPARATED FROM ME.
HAVE YOU SEEN HIM?
HE DID? NO...I HAVEN'T SEEN HIM...
I SEE... SO YOU'RE ALONE...

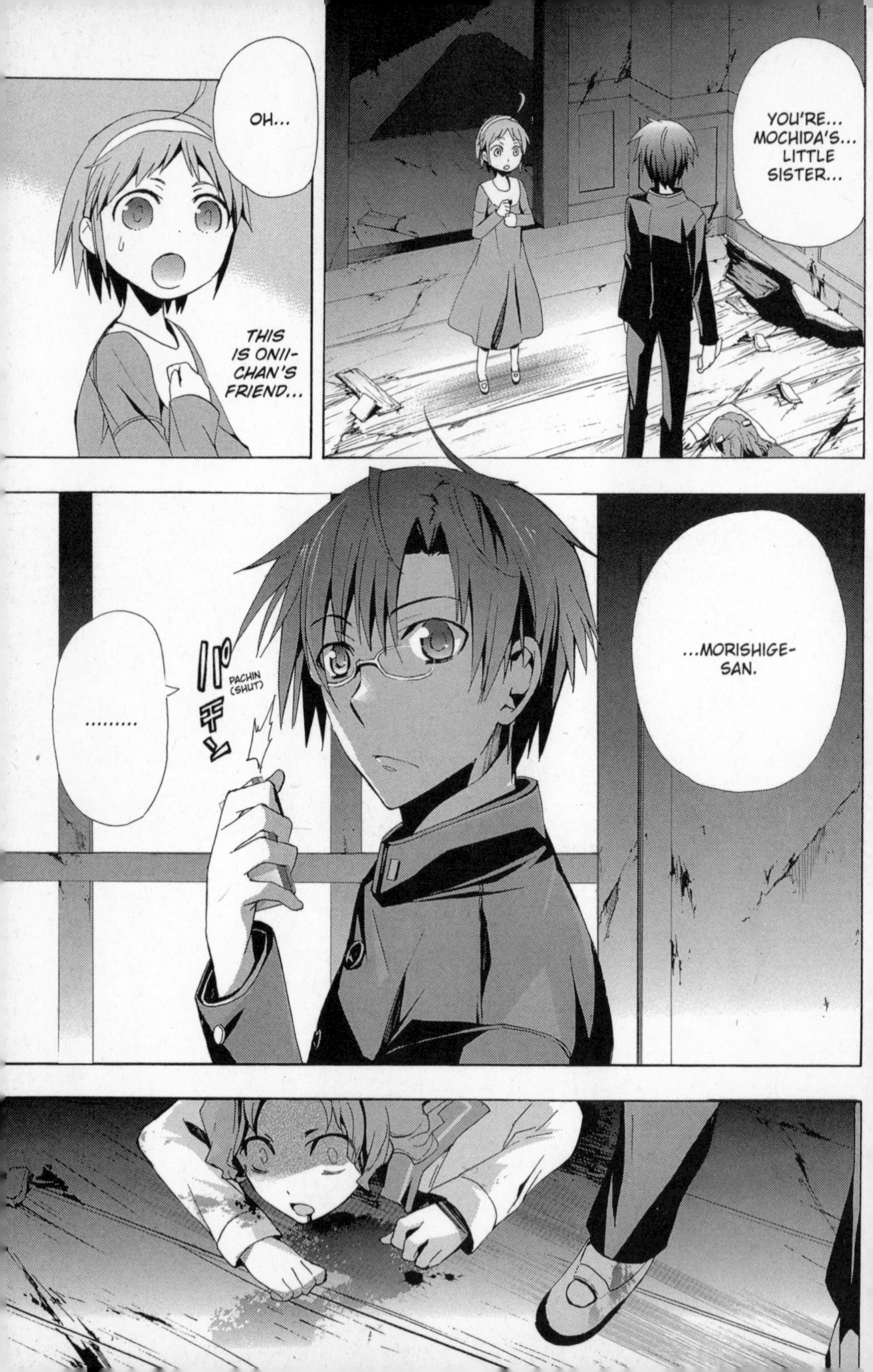
YOU'RE... MOCHIDA'S... LITTLE SISTER...
OH...
THIS IS ONII-CHAN'S FRIEND...
...MORISHIGE-SAN.
パチン
PACHIN (SHUT)
....

CORPSE PARTY
BloodCovered

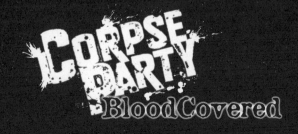

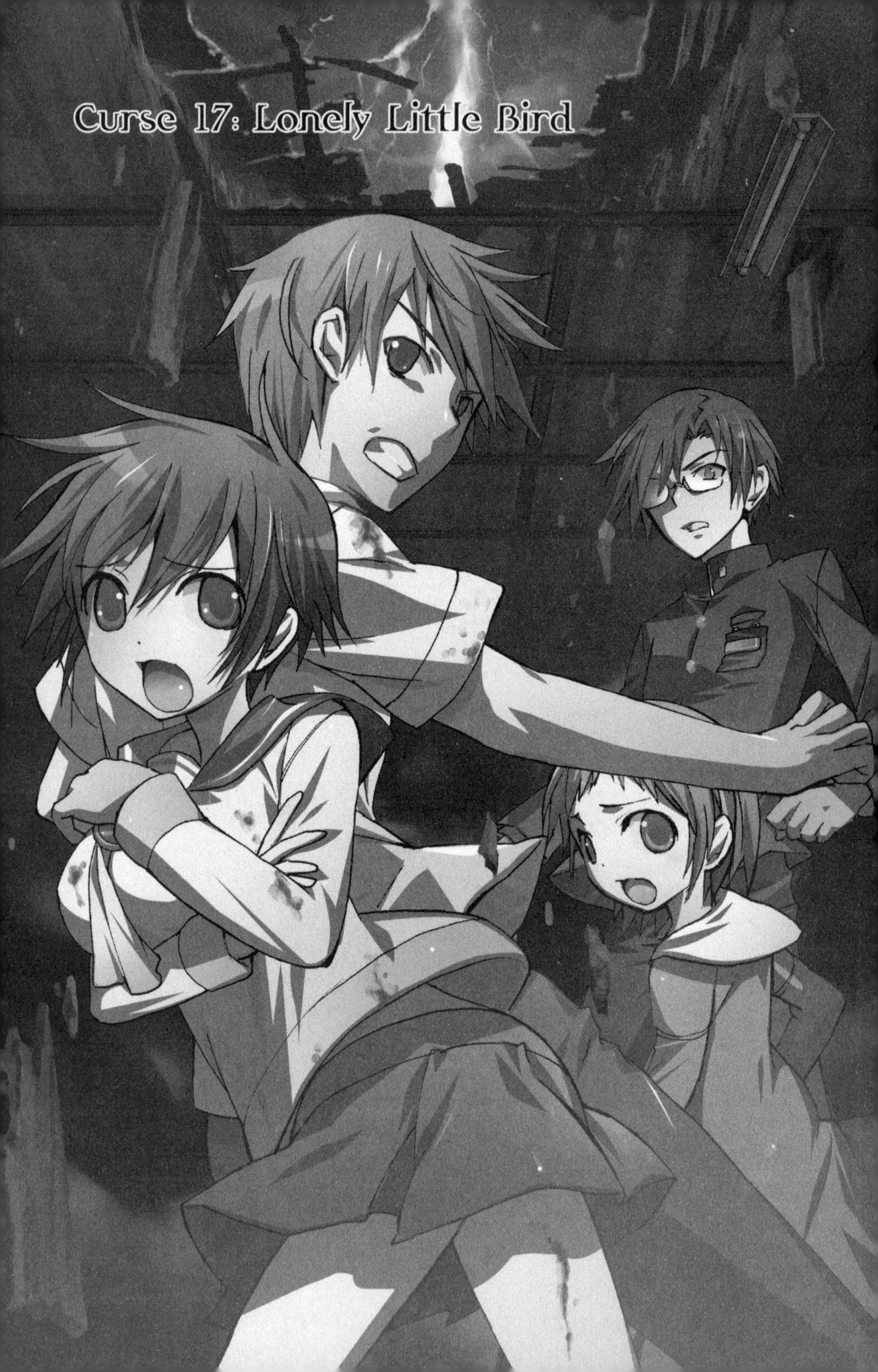
Curse 17: Lonely Little Bird

CORPSE PARTY
Blood Covered

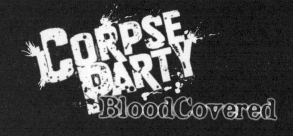

a list of corpses/07

Byakudan Senior High School,
Class 2-4, Mitsuki Yamamoto

Died of blood loss from a
wound to the abdomen.

Seems to have died very soon after her
encounter with Satoshi and Yuka.

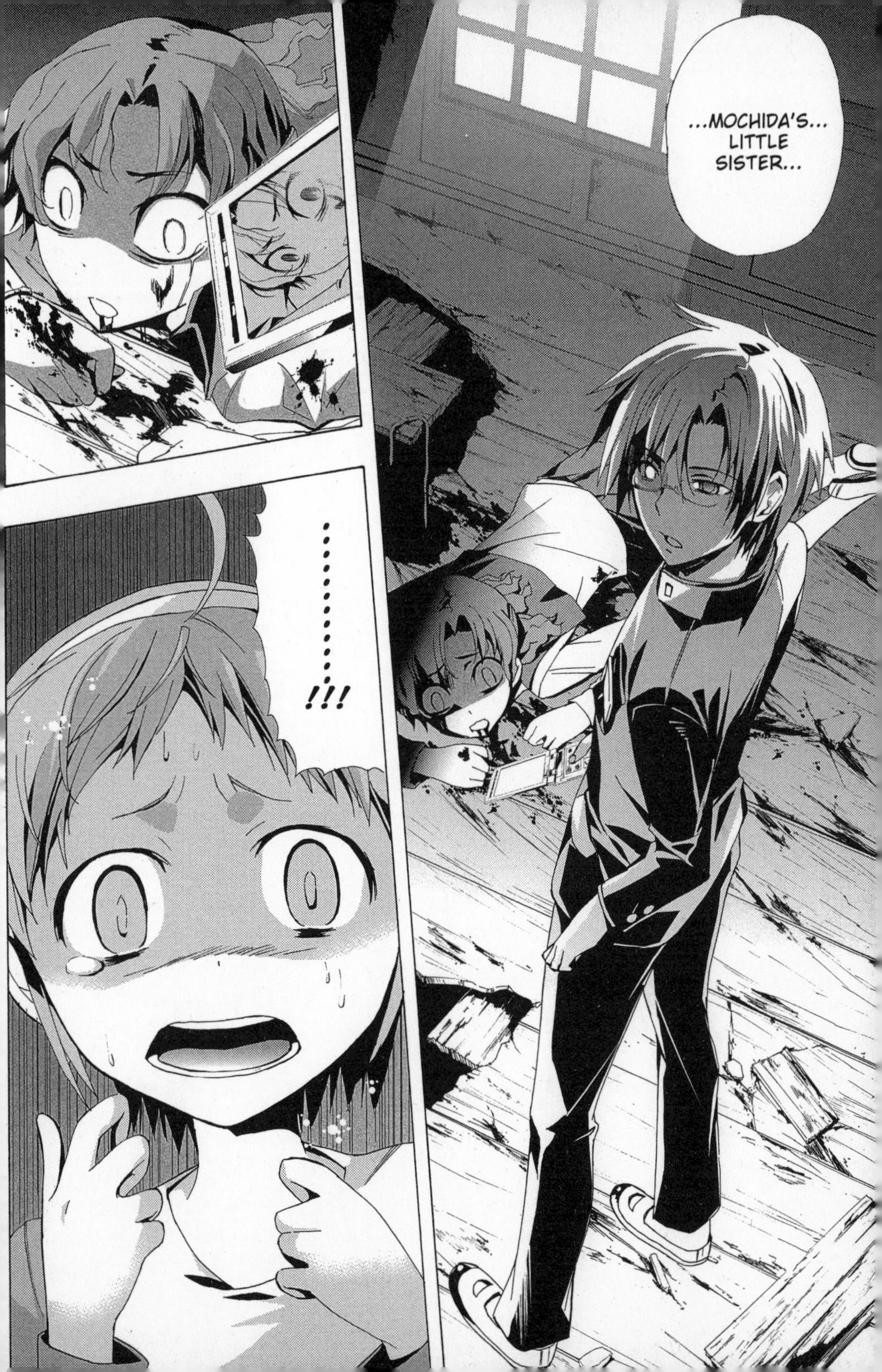
...MOCHIDA'S... LITTLE SISTER...
..........!!!

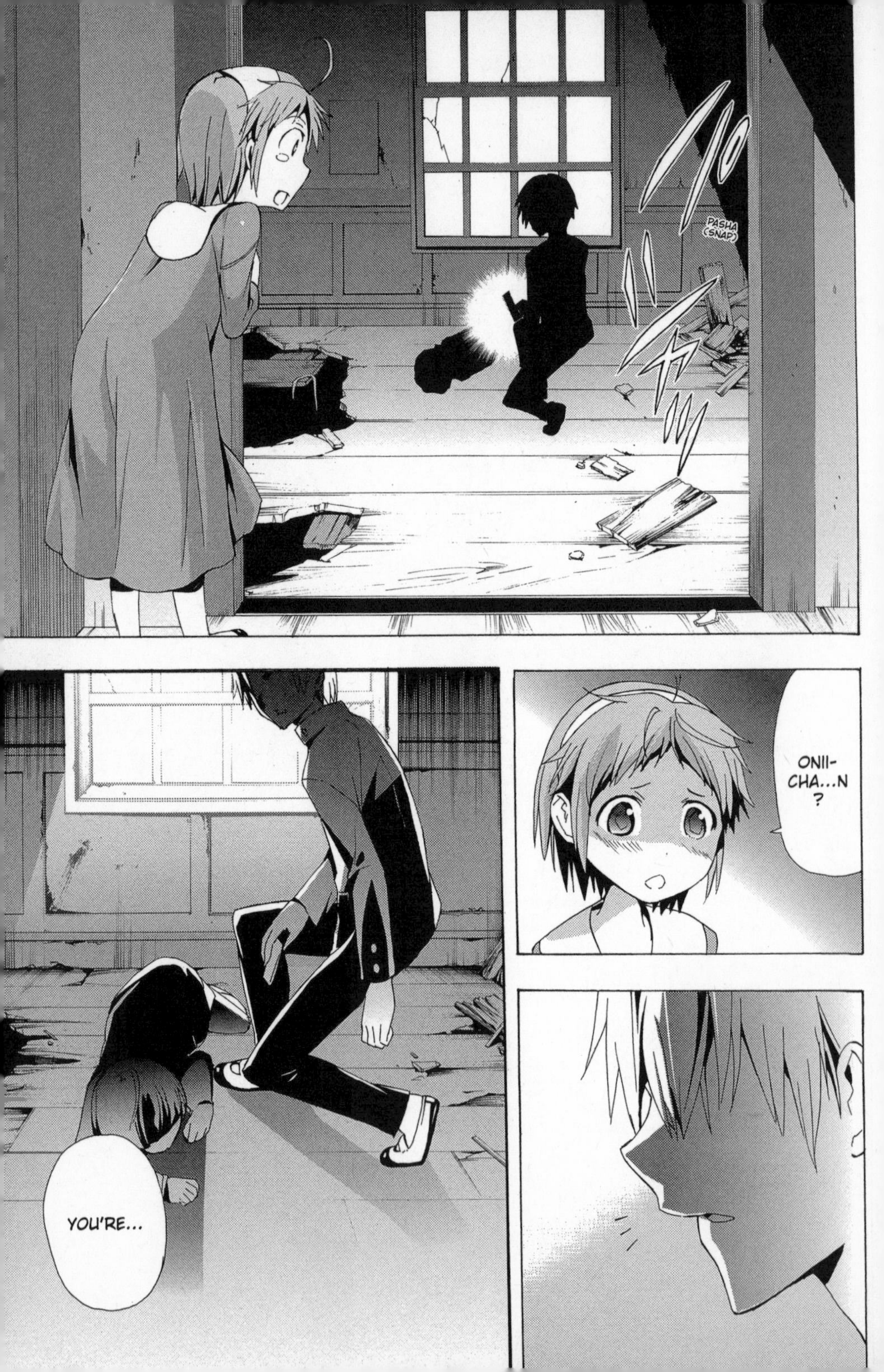
PASHA (SNAP)
ONII-CHA...N ?
YOU'RE...

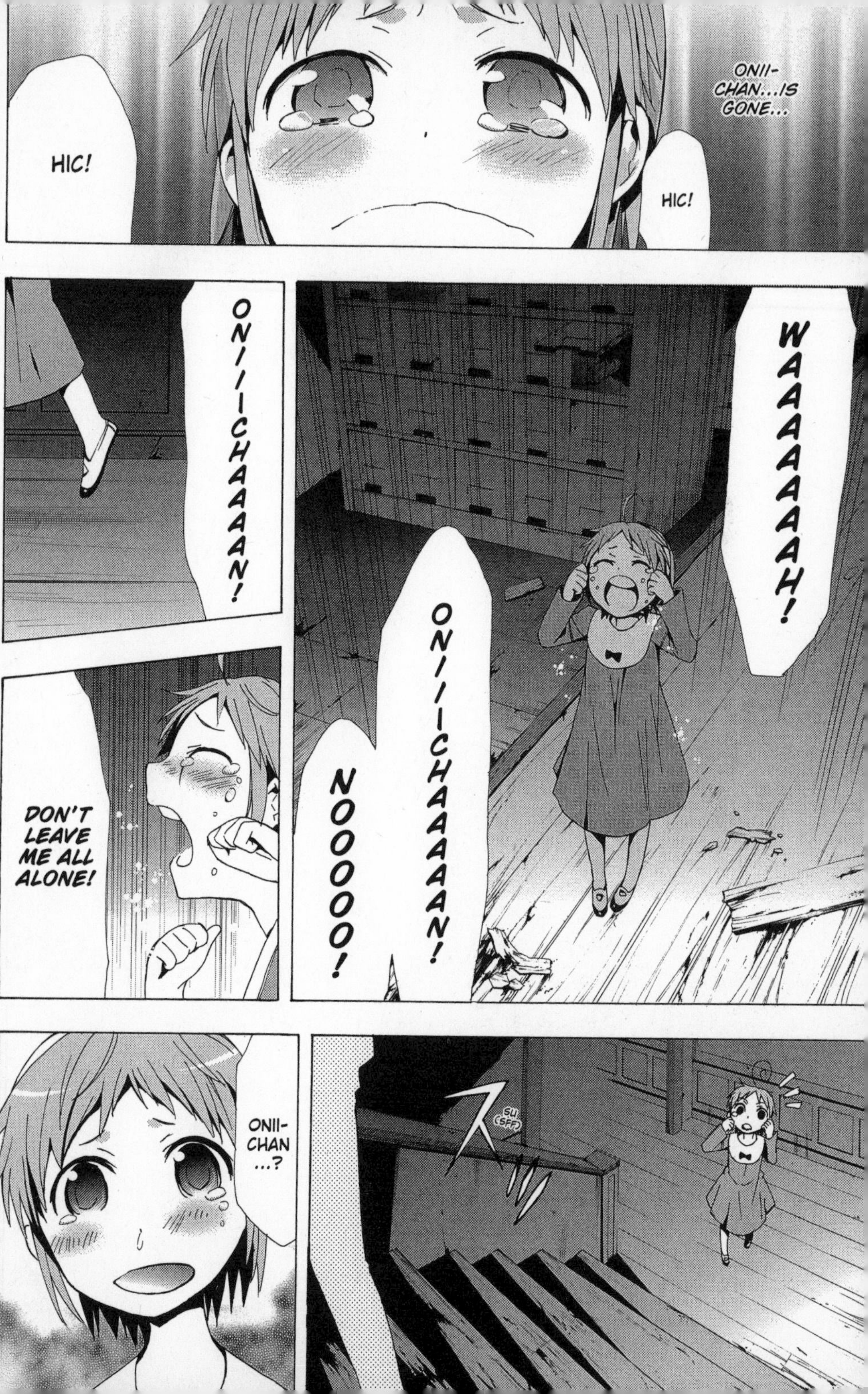
ONII-CHAN...IS GONE...
HIC!
HIC!
WAAAAAAAAH!
ONIIICHAAAAAAN!
NOOOOOO!
ONIIICHAAAAAN!
DON'T LEAVE ME ALL ALONE!
SU (SFF)
ONII-CHAN...?

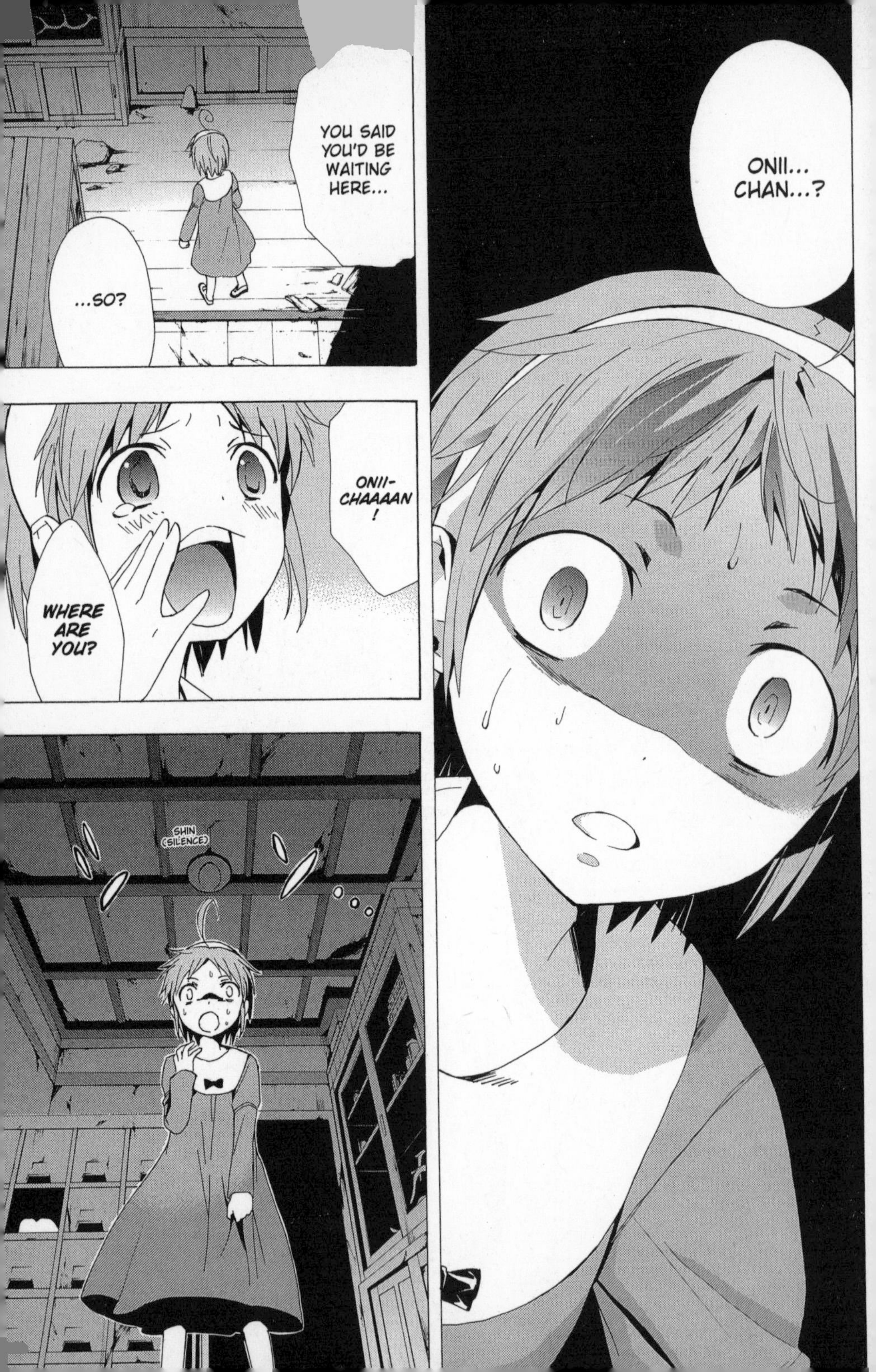
ONII... CHAN...?
YOU SAID YOU'D BE WAITING HERE...
...SO?
ONII-CHAAAAN!
WHERE ARE YOU?
SHIN (SILENCE)

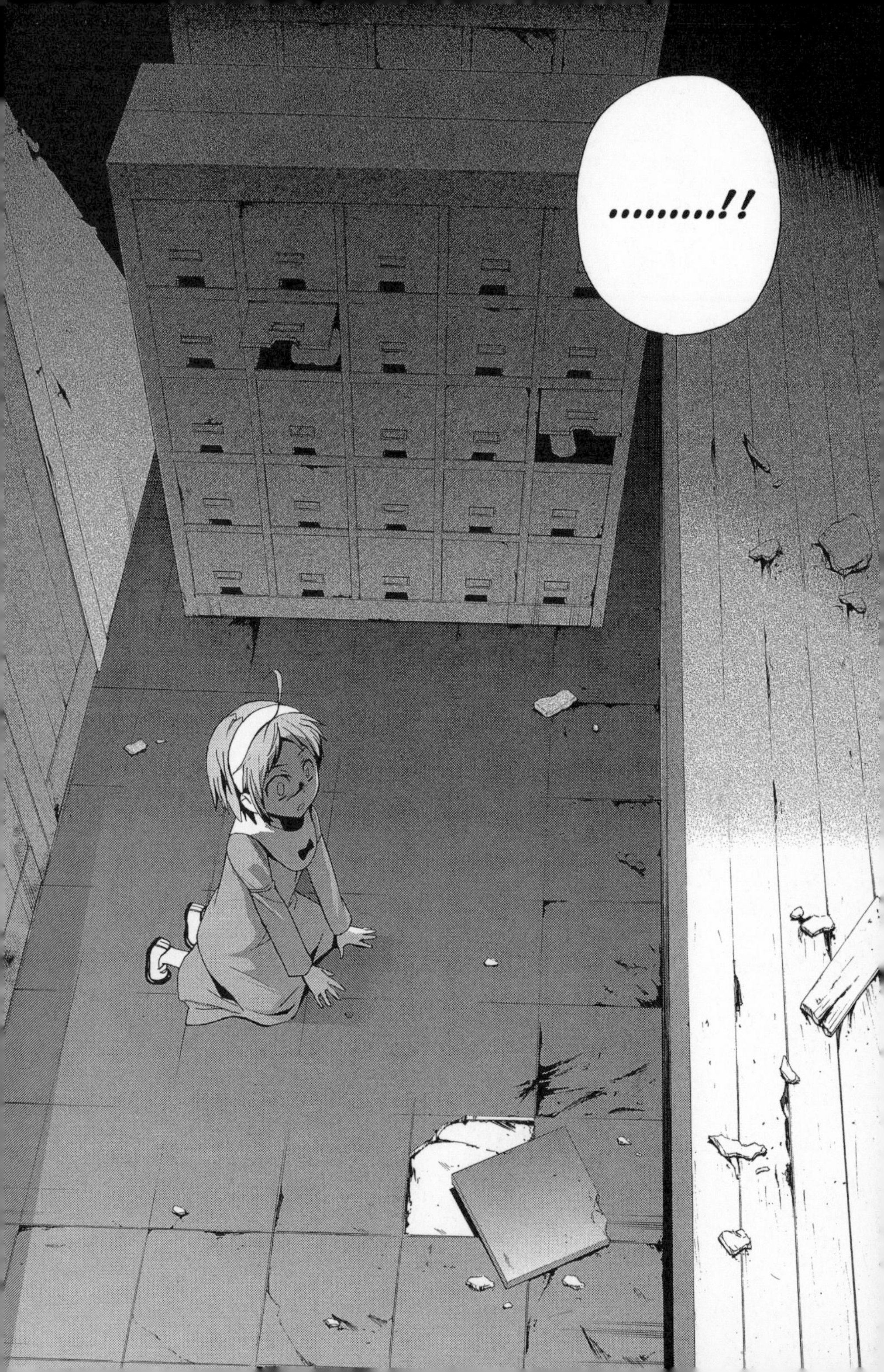

.........!!

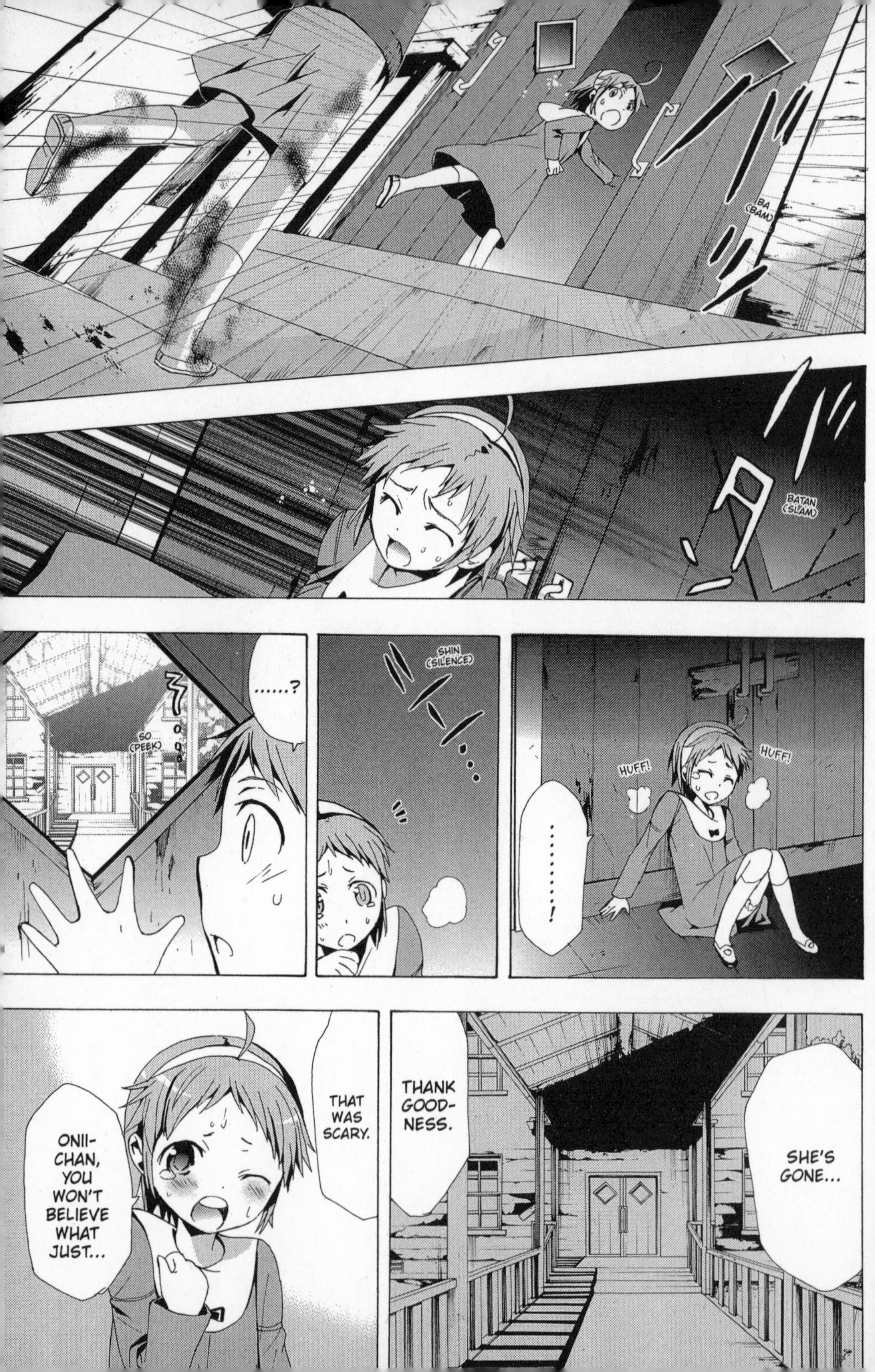
BA (BAN)
BATAN (SLAM)
HUFF!
HUFF!
........!
SHIN (SILENCE)
......?
SO (PEEK)
SHE'S GONE...
THANK GOODNESS.
THAT WAS SCARY.
ONII-CHAN, YOU WON'T BELIEVE WHAT JUST...

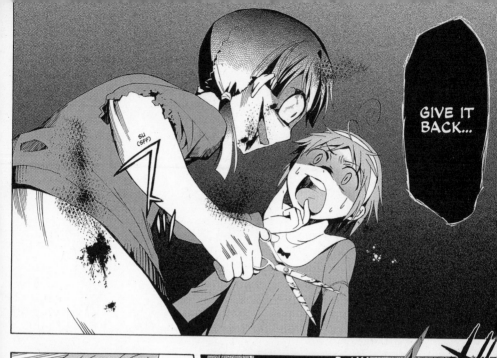

GIVE IT BACK...

EEEK!

AAAAAH!

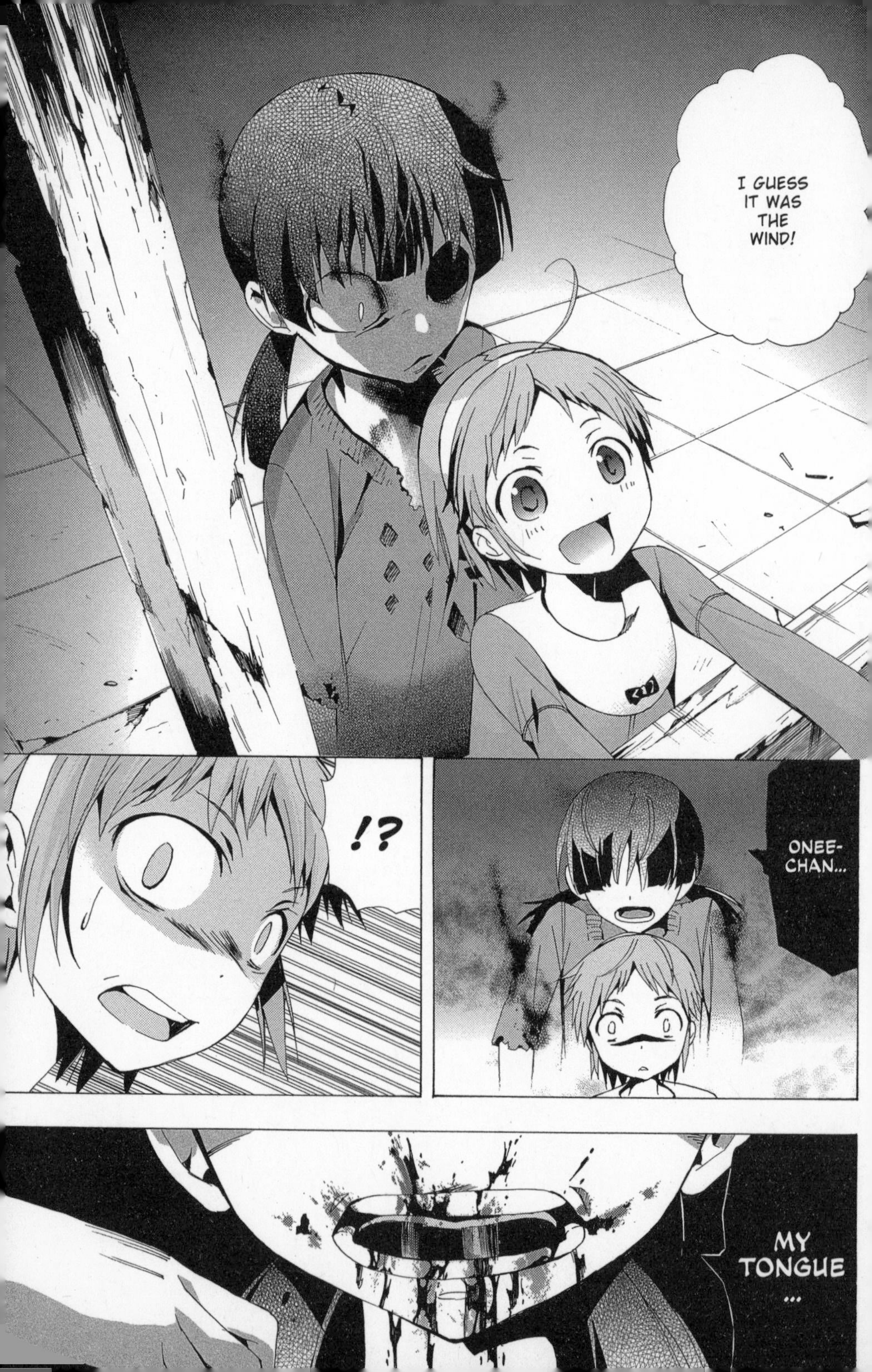
I GUESS IT WAS THE WIND!
ONEE-CHAN...
!?
MY TONGUE ...

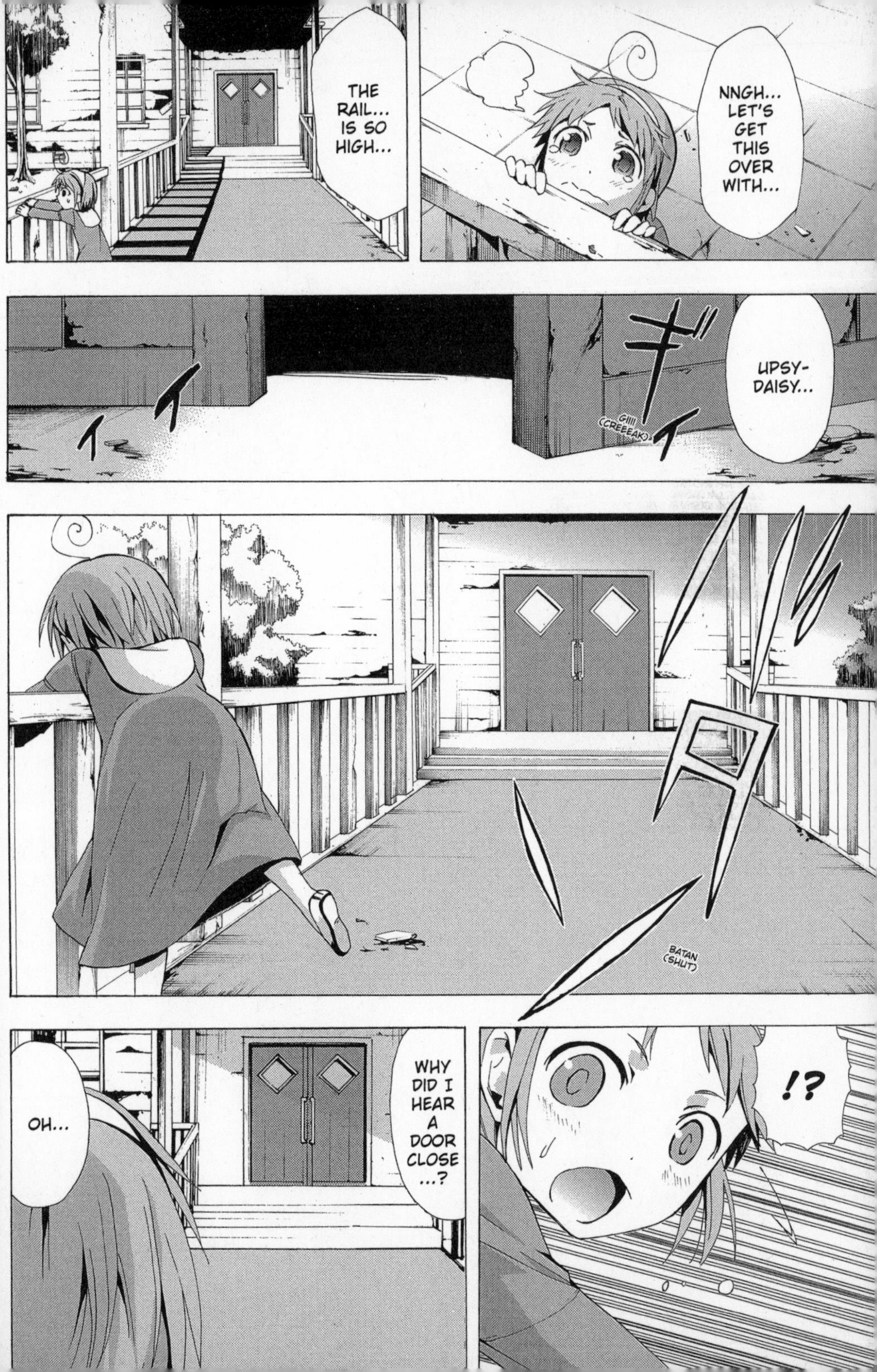
NNGH... LET'S GET THIS OVER WITH...
THE RAIL... IS SO HIGH...
UPSY-DAISY...
GIIII (CREEEAK)
BATAN (SHUT)
!?
WHY DID I HEAR A DOOR CLOSE ...?
OH...

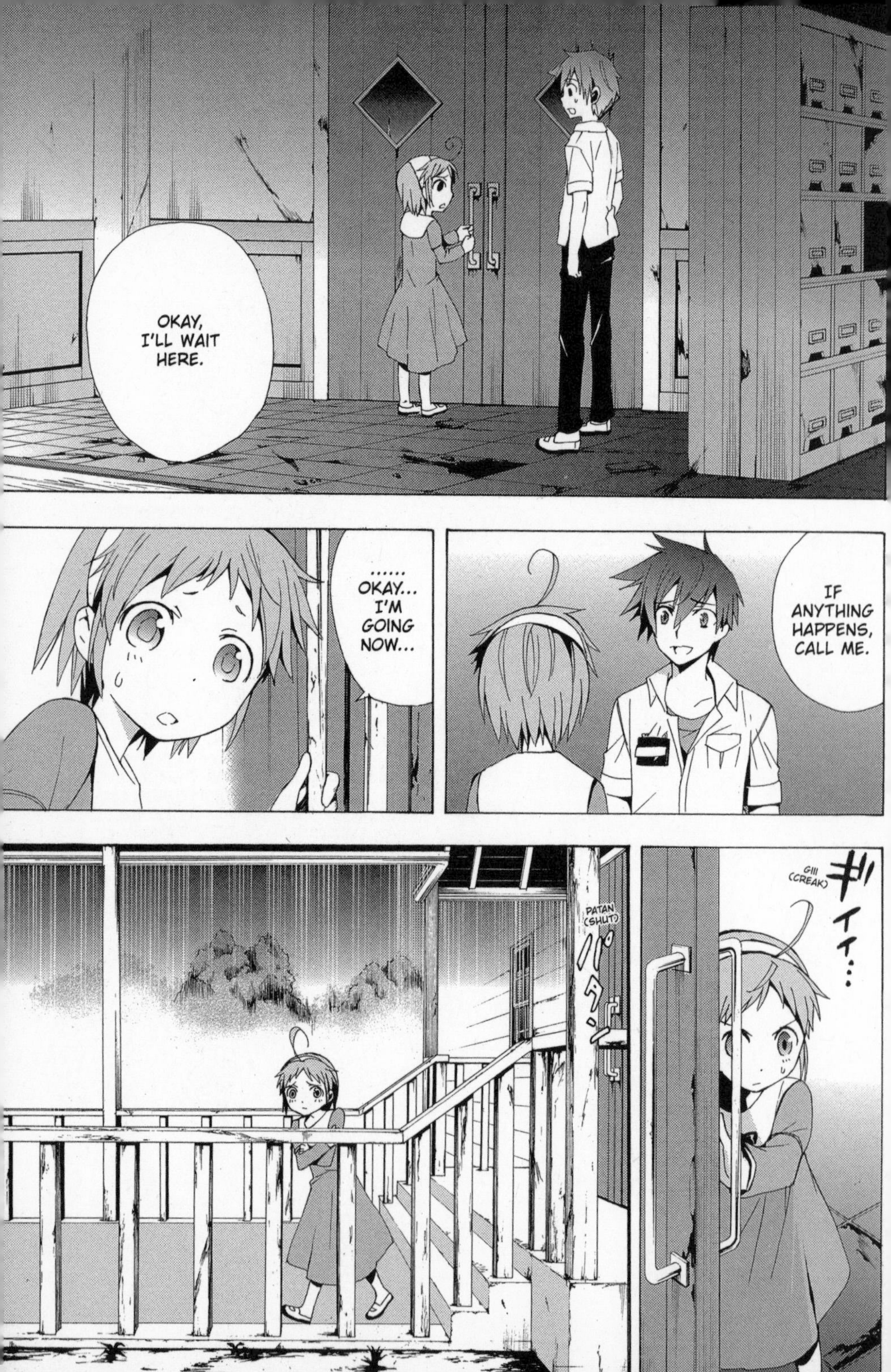
OKAY, I'LL WAIT HERE.
IF ANYTHING HAPPENS, CALL ME.
...... OKAY... I'M GOING NOW...
GIII (CREAK)
ギイイ…
PATAN (SHUT)
パタン

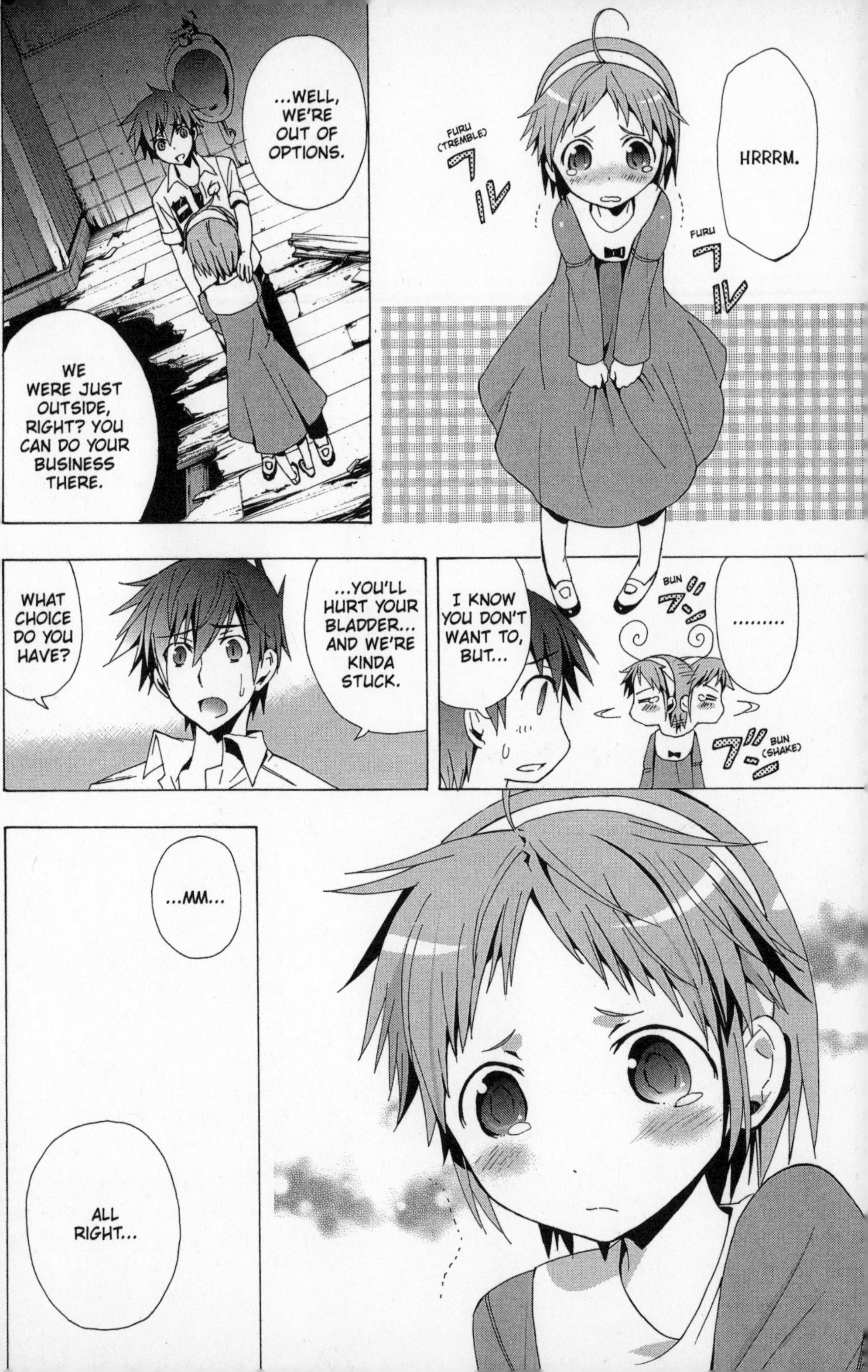
HRRRM.
FURU (TREMBLE)
FURU
...WELL, WE'RE OUT OF OPTIONS.
WE WERE JUST OUTSIDE, RIGHT? YOU CAN DO YOUR BUSINESS THERE.
....
BUN
BUN (SHAKE)
I KNOW YOU DON'T WANT TO, BUT...
...YOU'LL HURT YOUR BLADDER... AND WE'RE KINDA STUCK.
WHAT CHOICE DO YOU HAVE?
...MM...
ALL RIGHT...

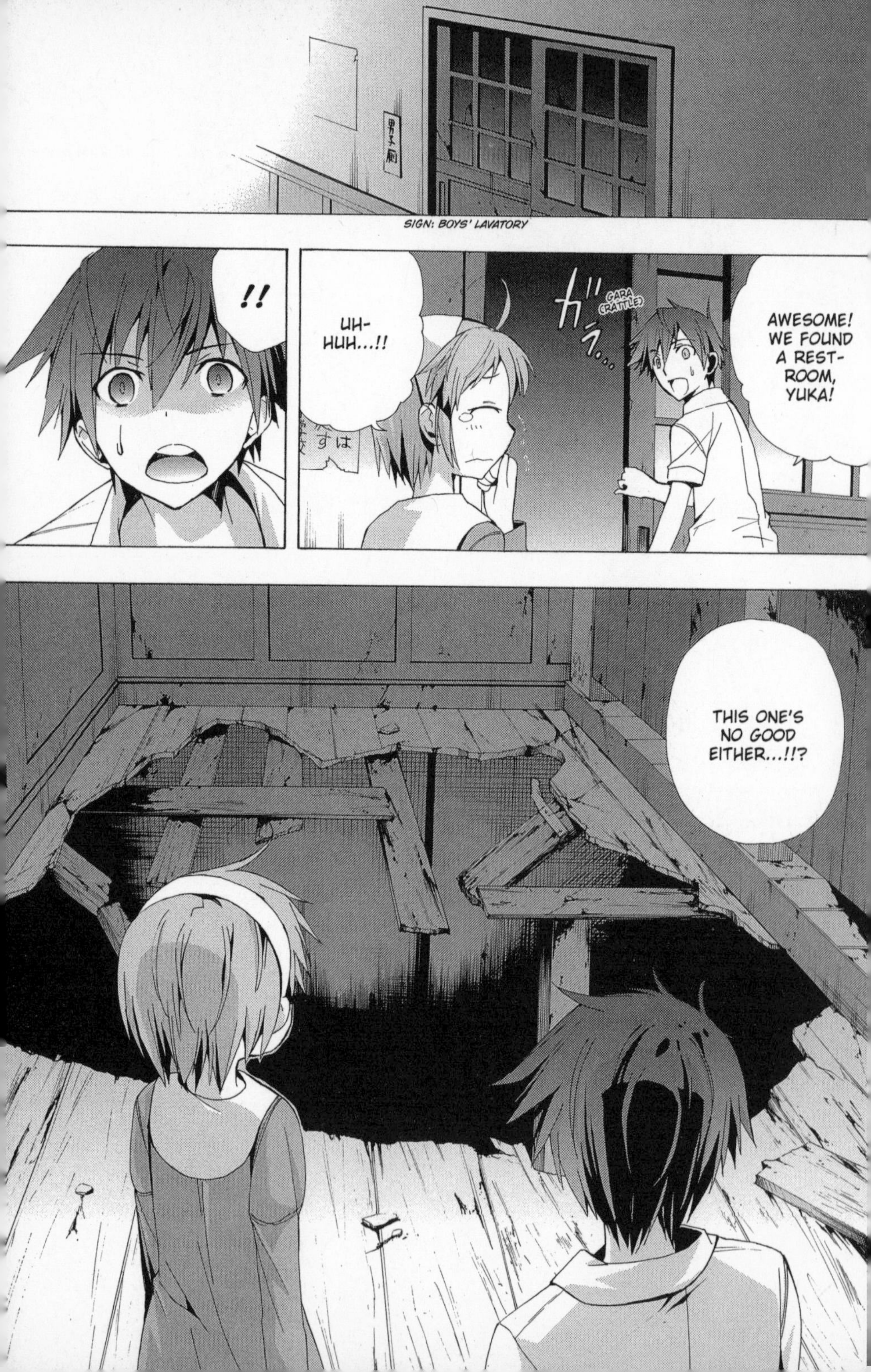
SIGN: BOYS' LAVATORY
AWESOME! WE FOUND A REST-ROOM, YUKA!
GARA (RATTLE)
UH-HUH...!!
!!
THIS ONE'S NO GOOD EITHER...!!?

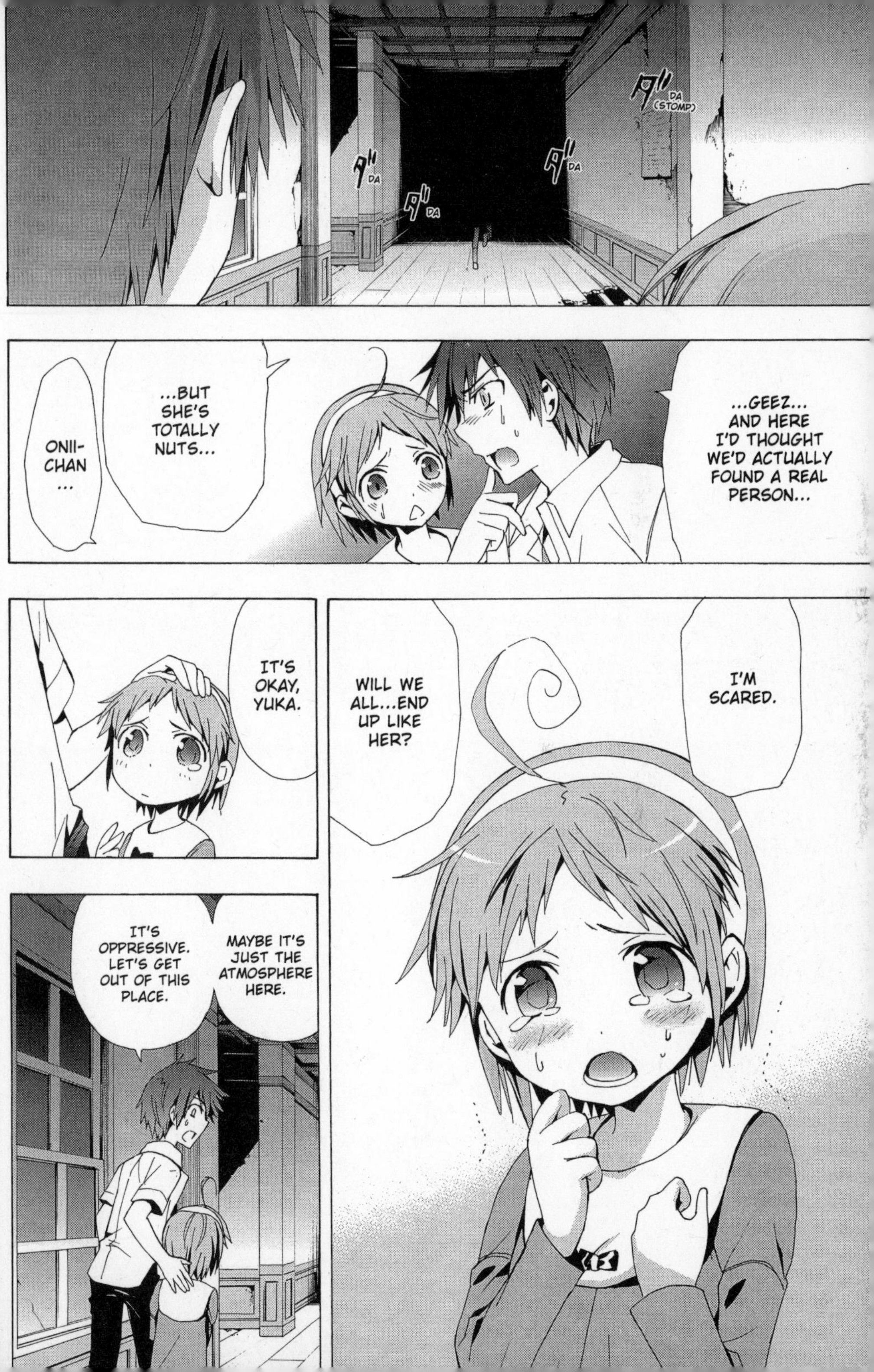
ダ DA (STOMP)
ダ DA
ダ DA
ダ DA
...GEEZ... AND HERE I'D THOUGHT WE'D ACTUALLY FOUND A REAL PERSON...
...BUT SHE'S TOTALLY NUTS...
ONII-CHAN ...
I'M SCARED.
WILL WE ALL...END UP LIKE HER?
IT'S OKAY, YUKA.
MAYBE IT'S JUST THE ATMOSPHERE HERE.
IT'S OPPRESSIVE. LET'S GET OUT OF THIS PLACE.

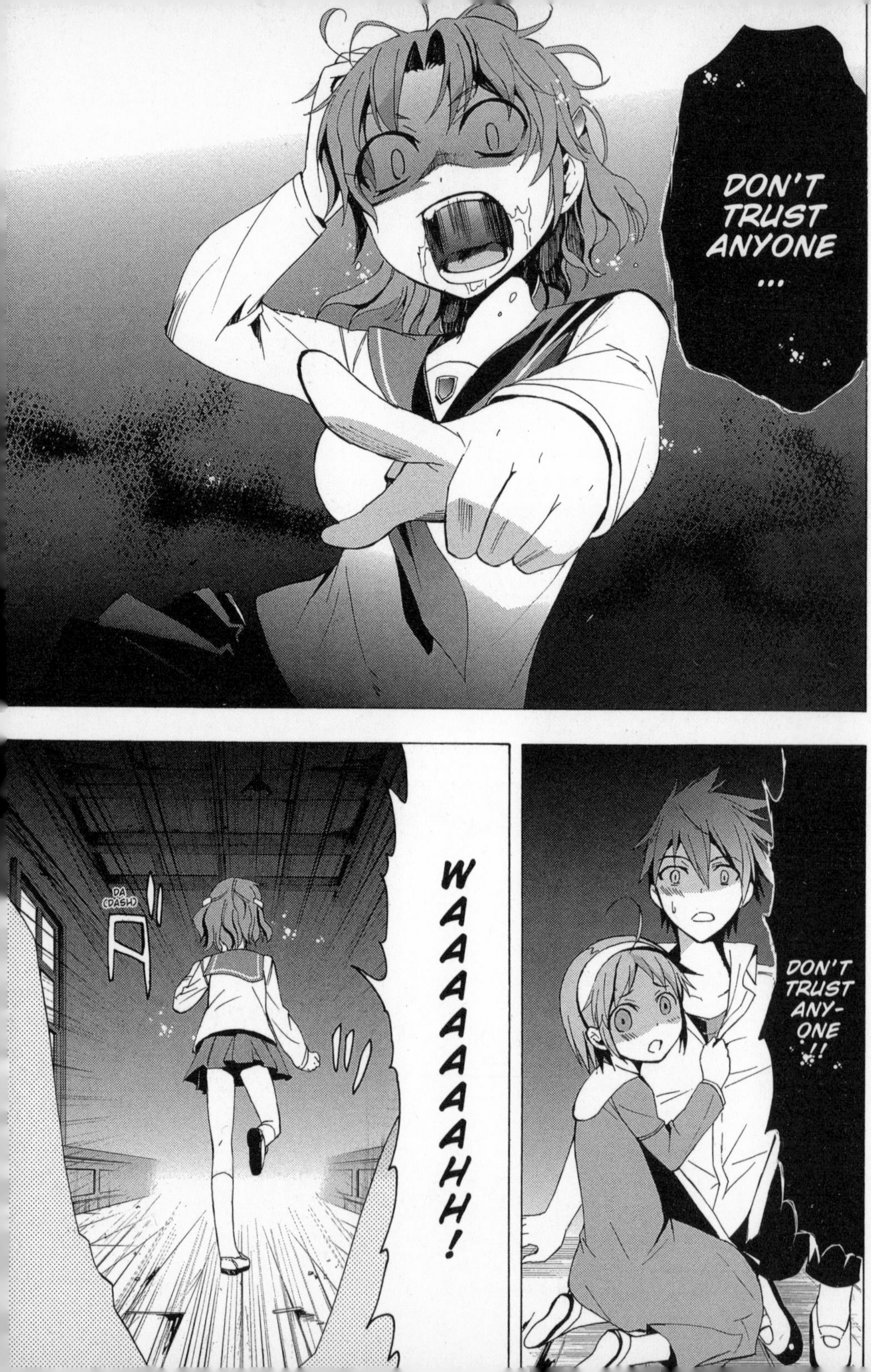
DON'T TRUST ANYONE ...
DON'T TRUST ANY-ONE !!
WAAAAAAAHH!
DA (DASH)

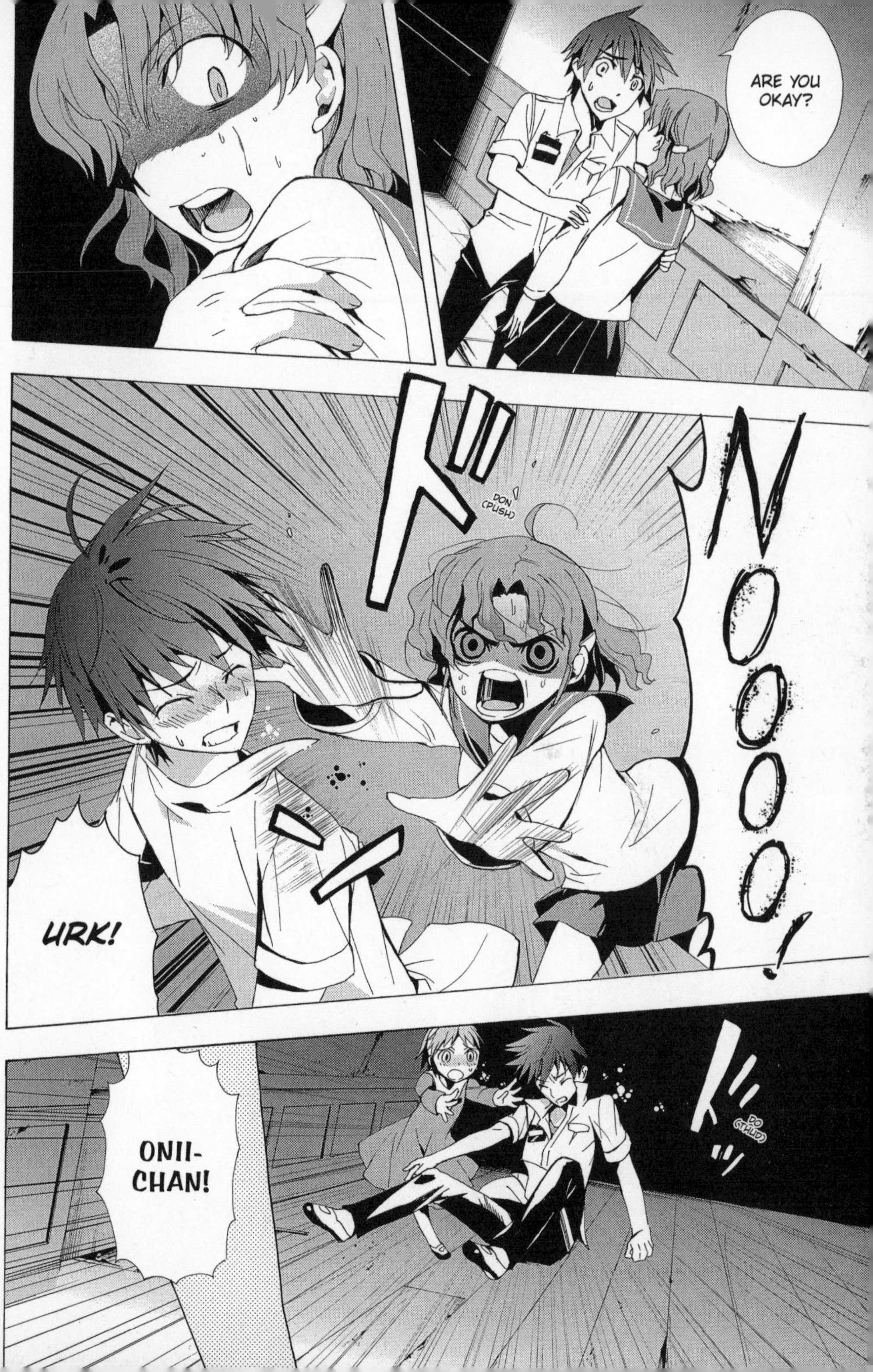
ARE YOU OKAY?
DON (PUSH)
NOOOOO!
URK!
DO (THUD)
ONII-CHAN!

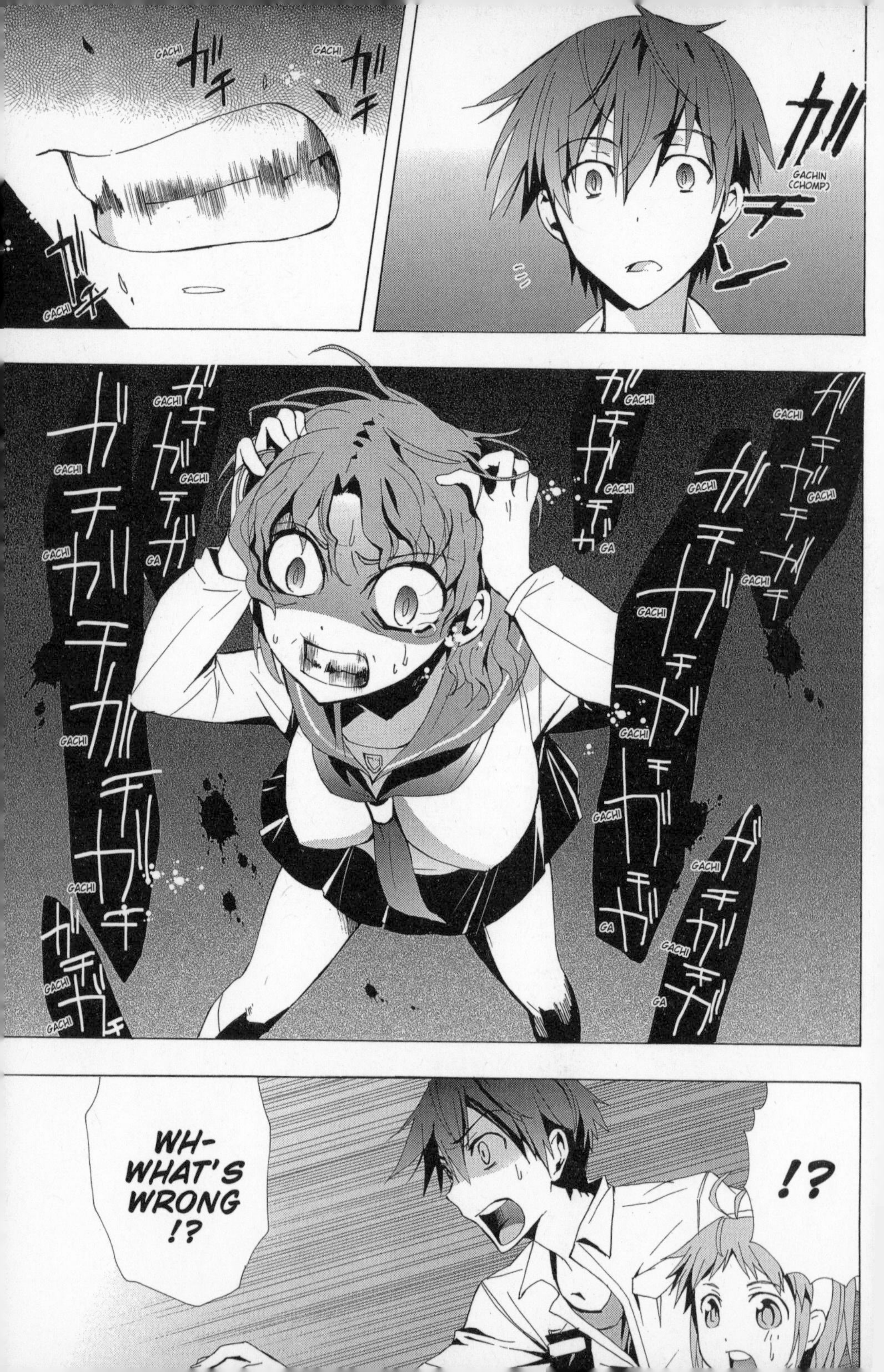
GACHIN (CHOMP)
GACHI
GACHI
GACHI
GACHI
GACHI
GACHI
GACHI
GACHI
GACHI
GACHI
GACHI
GA
GACHI
GACHI
GA
GACHI
GA
GACHI
GACHI
GACHI
GACHI
GA
GACHI
GACHI
GACHI
GACHI
GACHI
!?
WH-WHAT'S WRONG!?

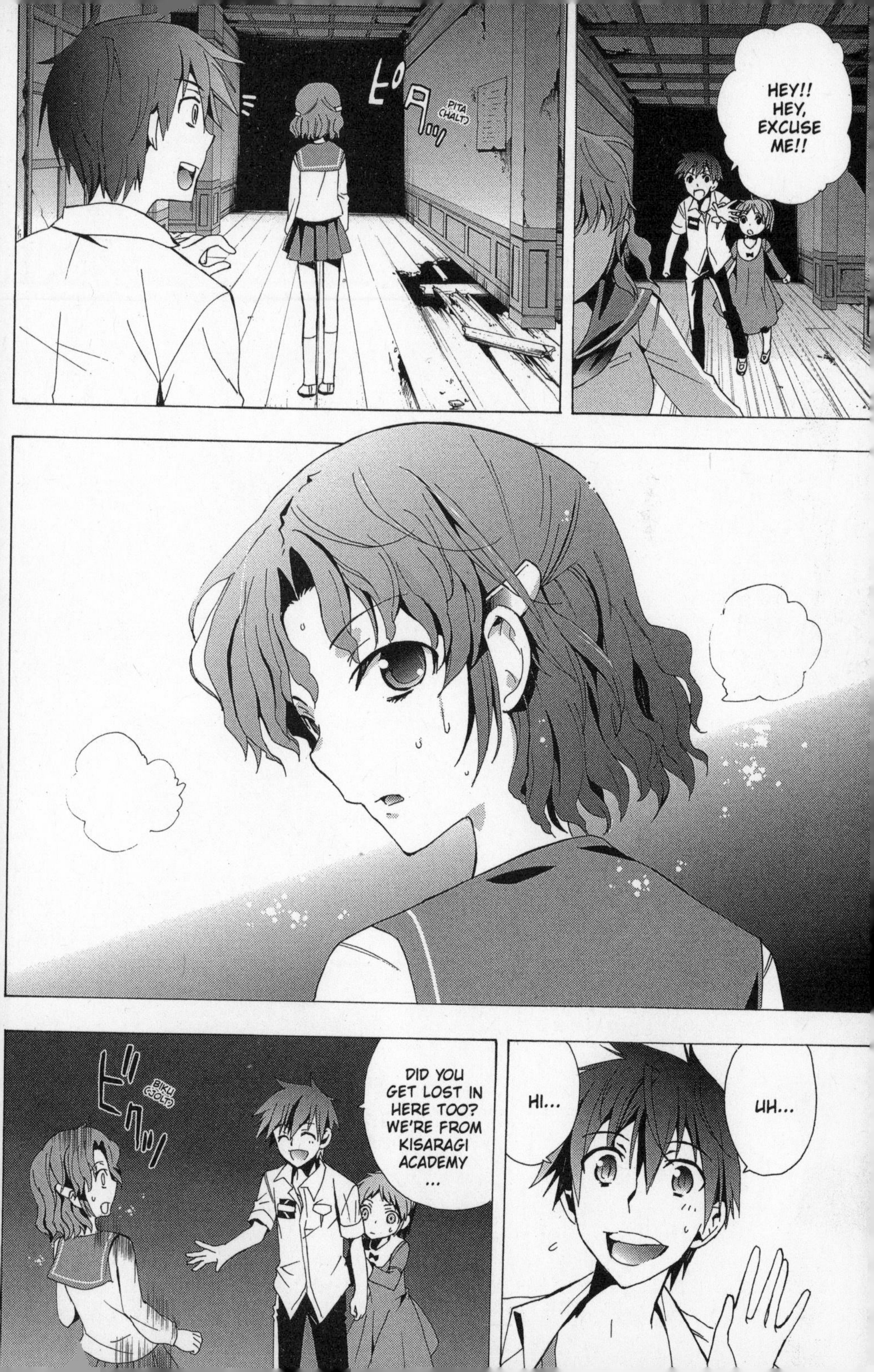
HEY!! HEY, EXCUSE ME!!
ピタッ
PITA (HALT)
UH...
HI...
DID YOU GET LOST IN HERE TOO? WE'RE FROM KISARAGI ACADEMY ...
ビクッ
BIKU (JOLT)

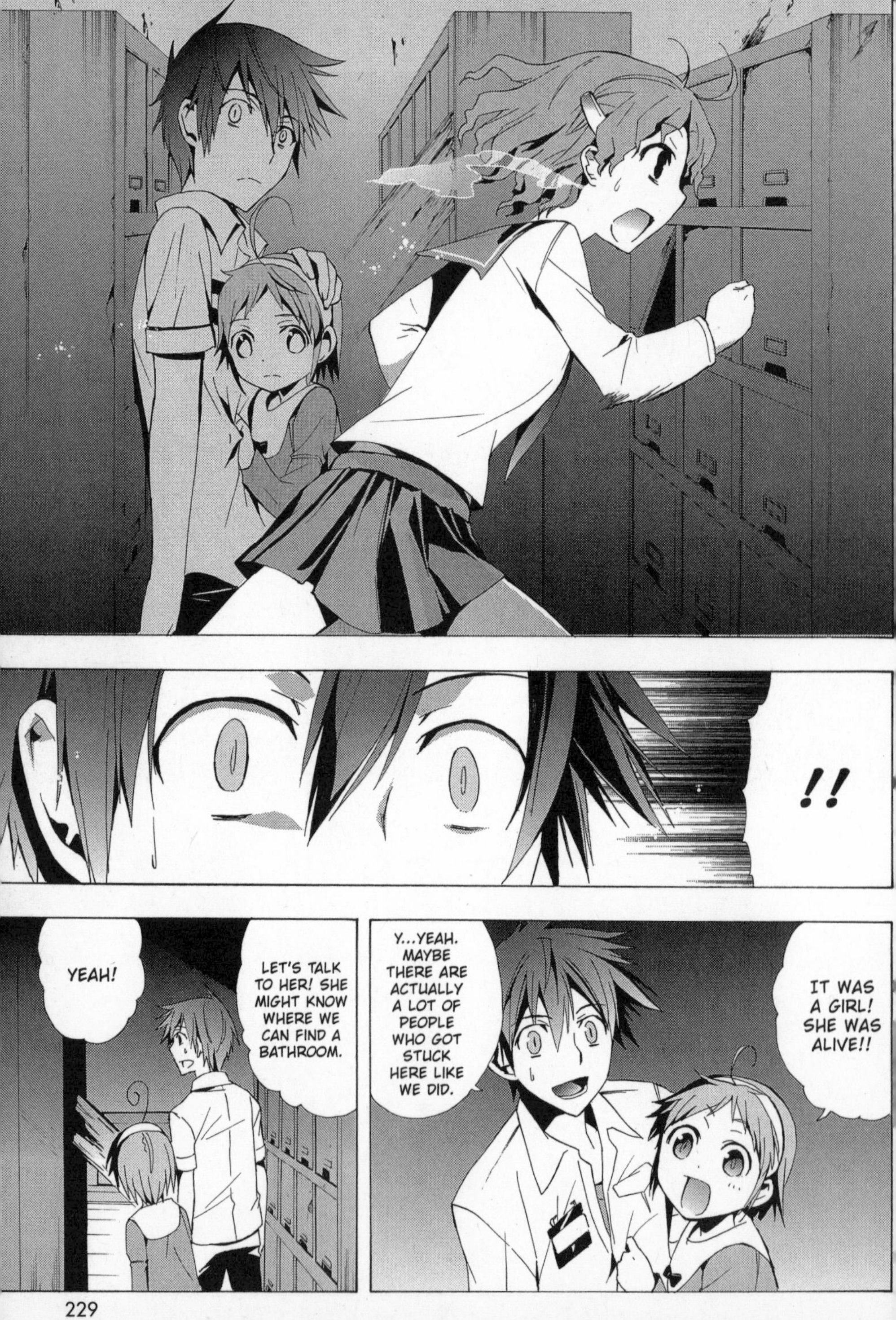
!!
IT WAS A GIRL! SHE WAS ALIVE!!
Y...YEAH. MAYBE THERE ARE ACTUALLY A LOT OF PEOPLE WHO GOT STUCK HERE LIKE WE DID.
LET'S TALK TO HER! SHE MIGHT KNOW WHERE WE CAN FIND A BATHROOM.
YEAH!

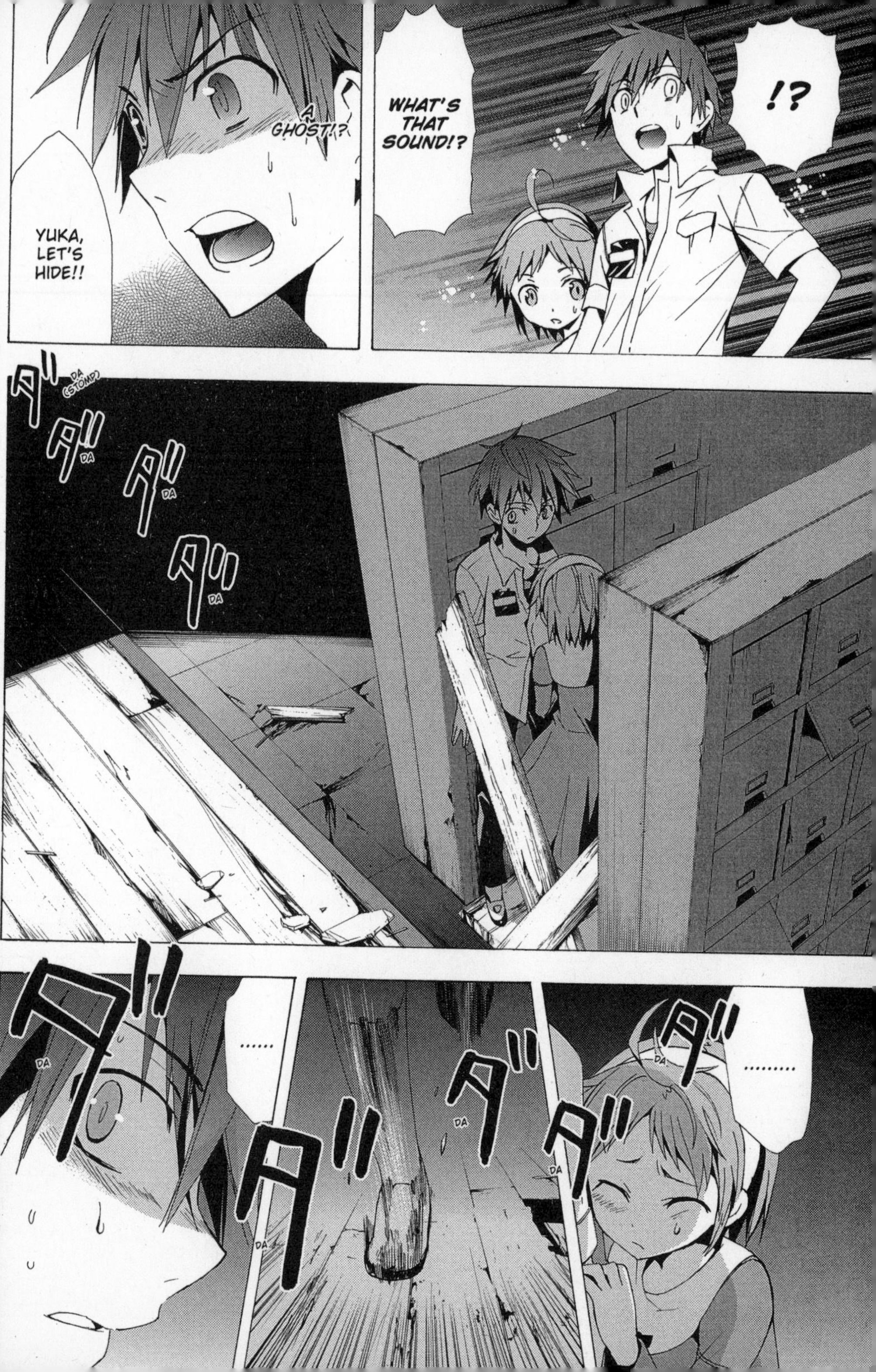

!?
WHAT'S THAT SOUND!?
A GHOST!?
YUKA, LET'S HIDE!!
ダ DA (STOMP)
ダ DA
ダ DA
ダ DA
ダ DA
....
ダ DA
ダ DA
ダ DA
ダ DA
......

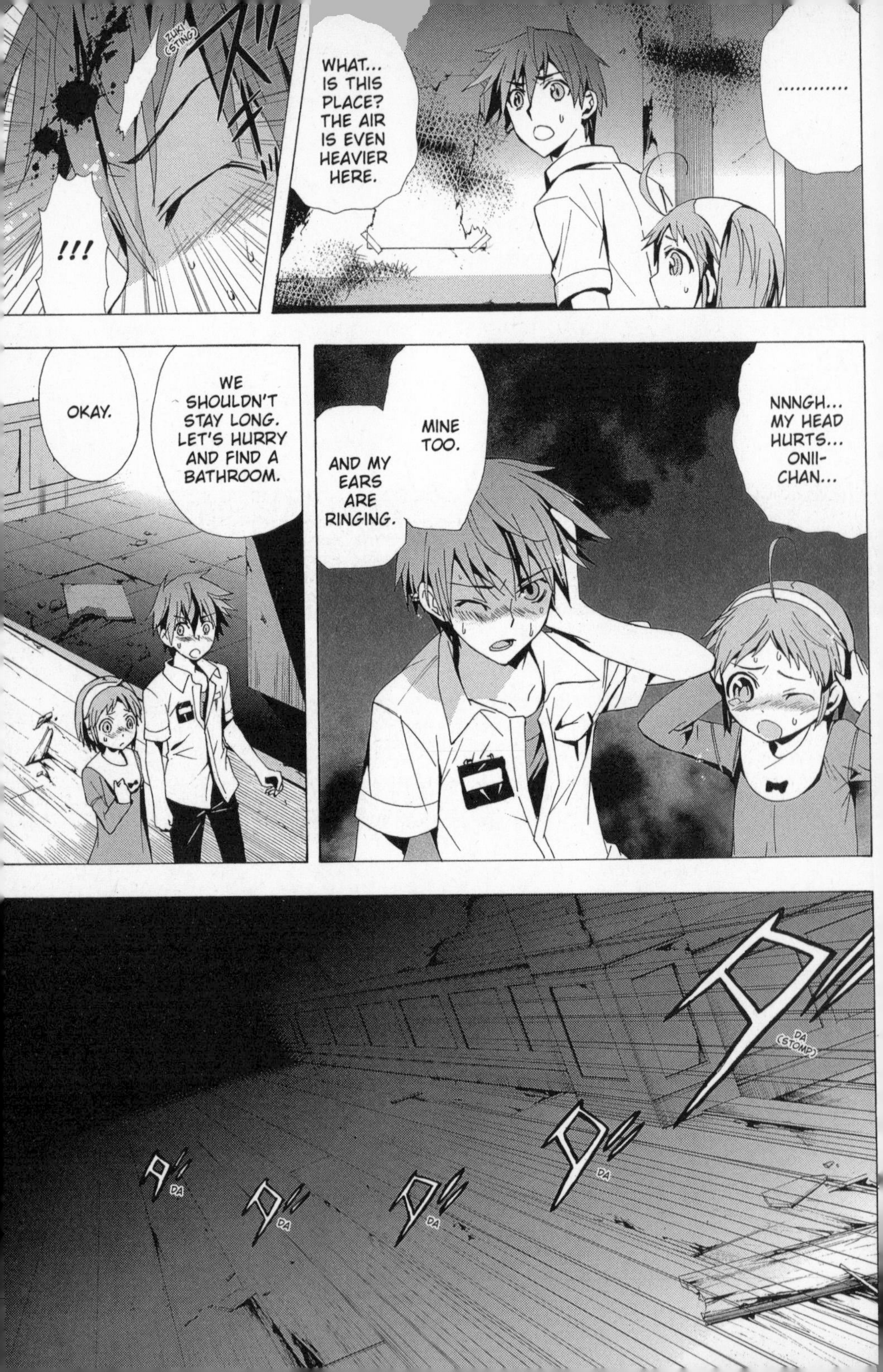
....
WHAT... IS THIS PLACE? THE AIR IS EVEN HEAVIER HERE.
ZUKI (STING)
!!!
NNNGH... MY HEAD HURTS... ONII-CHAN...
MINE TOO.
AND MY EARS ARE RINGING.
WE SHOULDN'T STAY LONG. LET'S HURRY AND FIND A BATHROOM.
OKAY.
DA (STOMP)
DA
DA
DA
DA

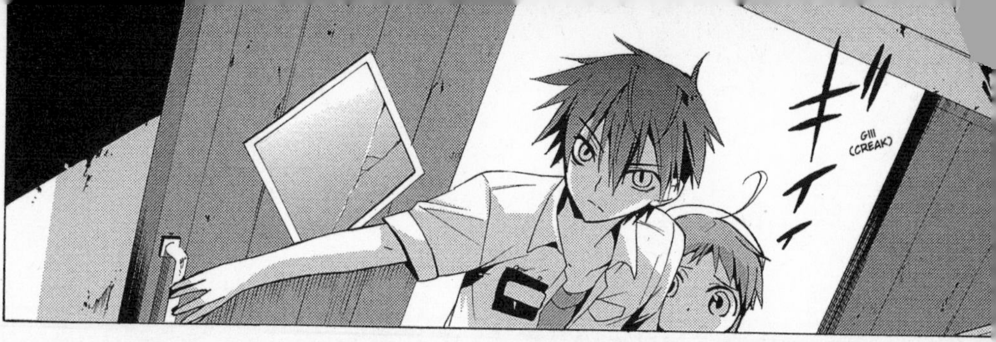
ギィィ
GIII
(CREAK)
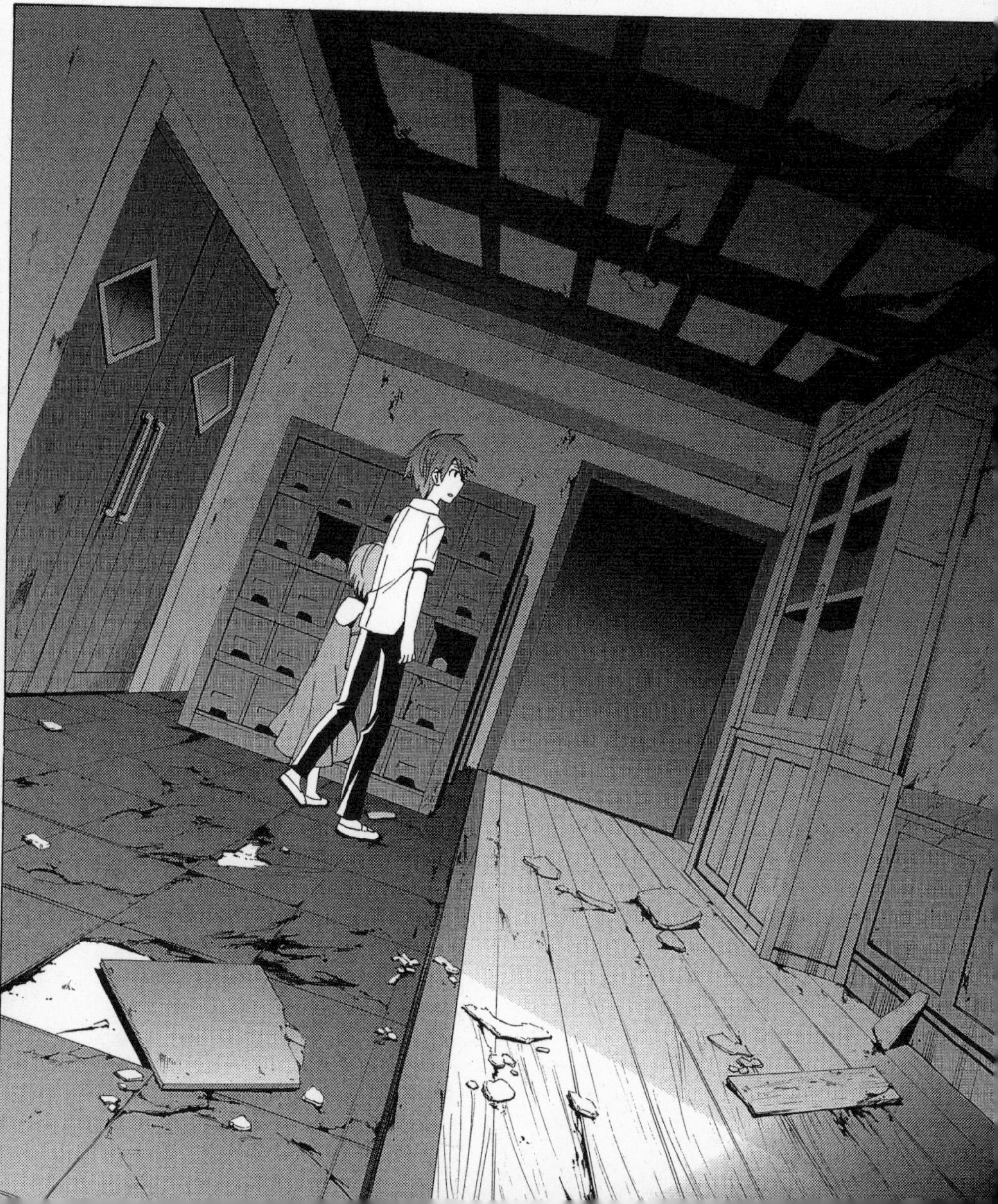

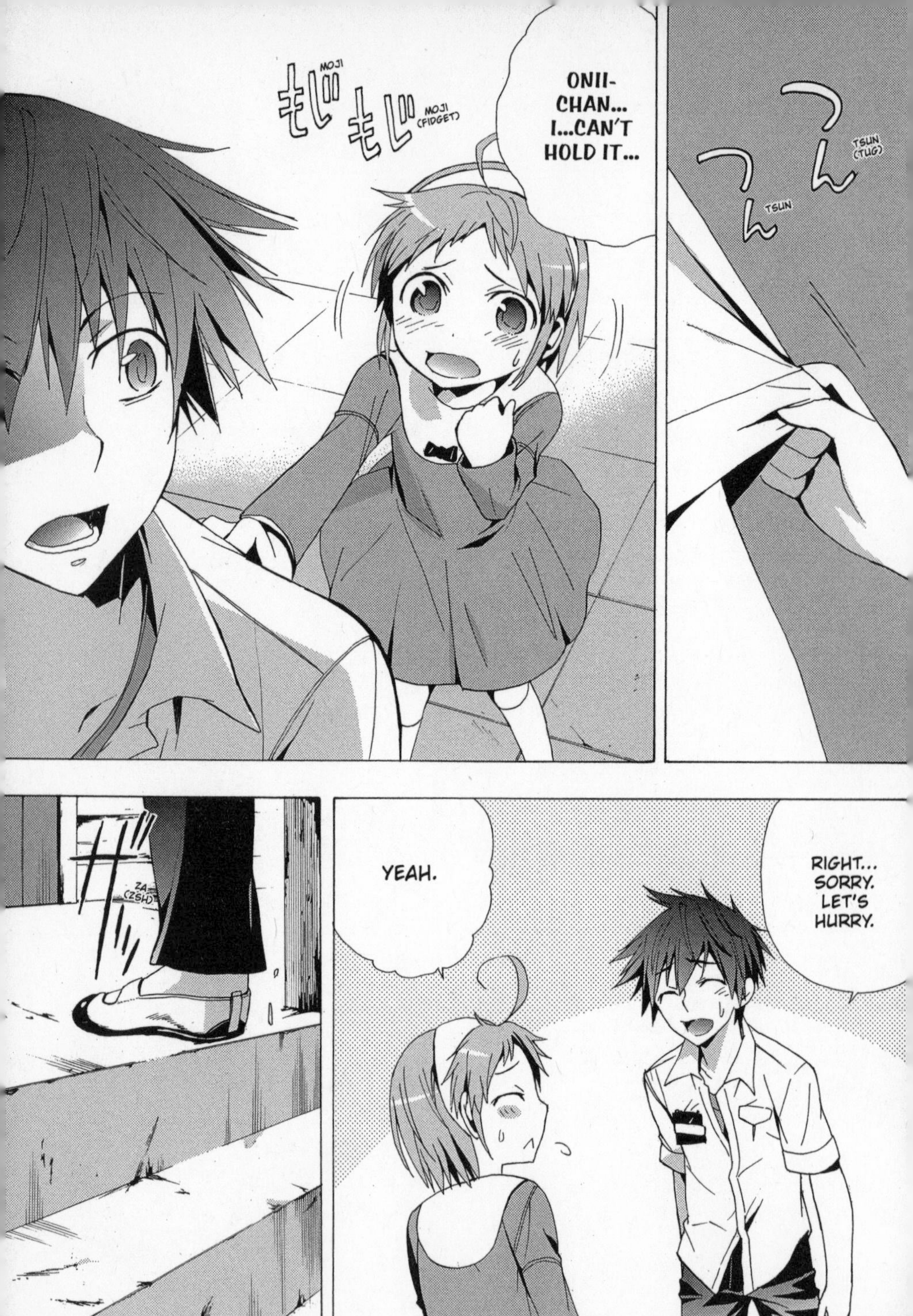
つん つん
TSUN (TUG)
TSUN
ONII-CHAN... I...CAN'T HOLD IT...
もじ もじ
MOJI
MOJI (FIDGET)
RIGHT... SORRY. LET'S HURRY.
YEAH.
ZA (ZSH)

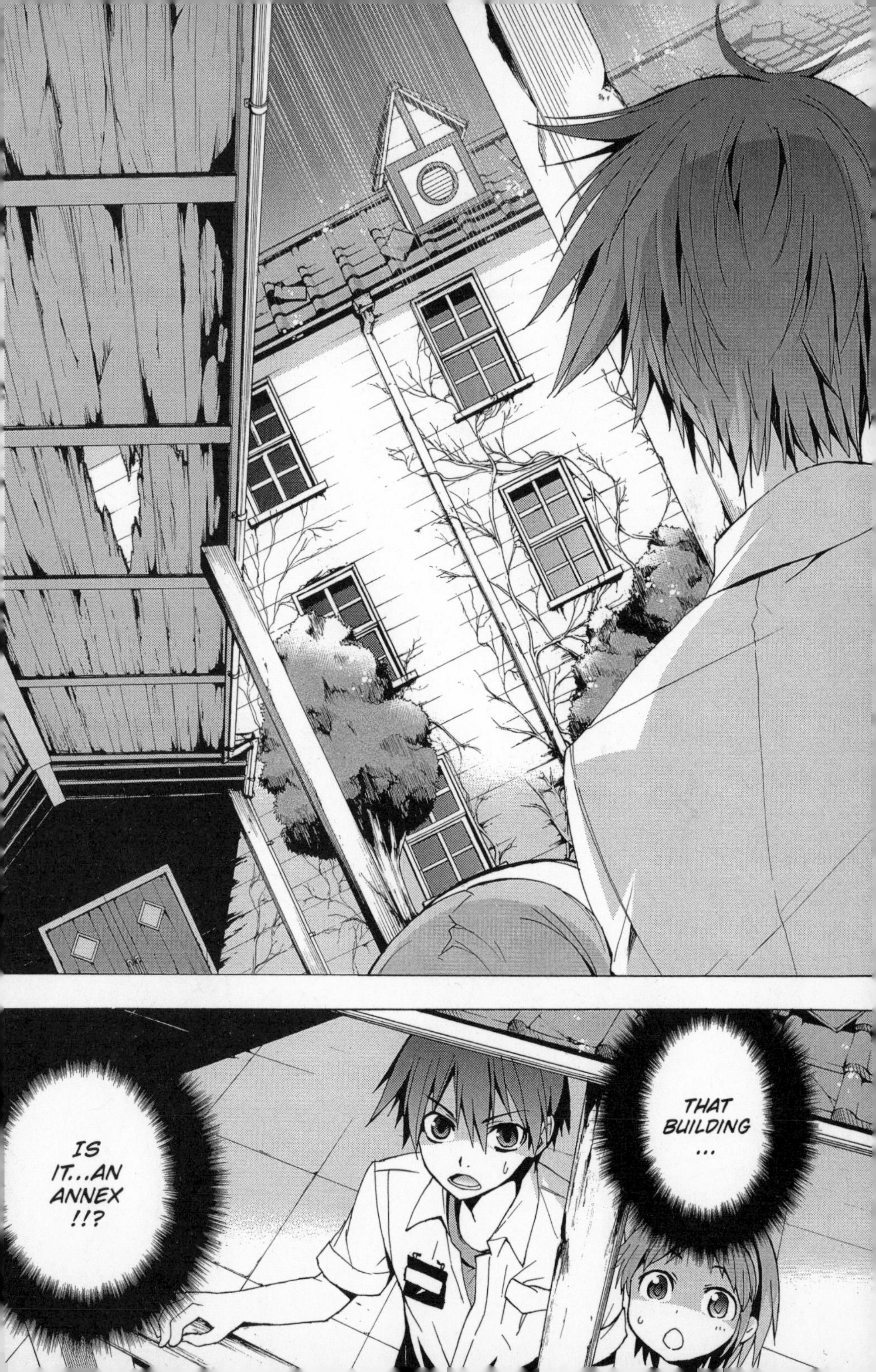
THAT BUILDING ...
IS IT...AN ANNEX !!?

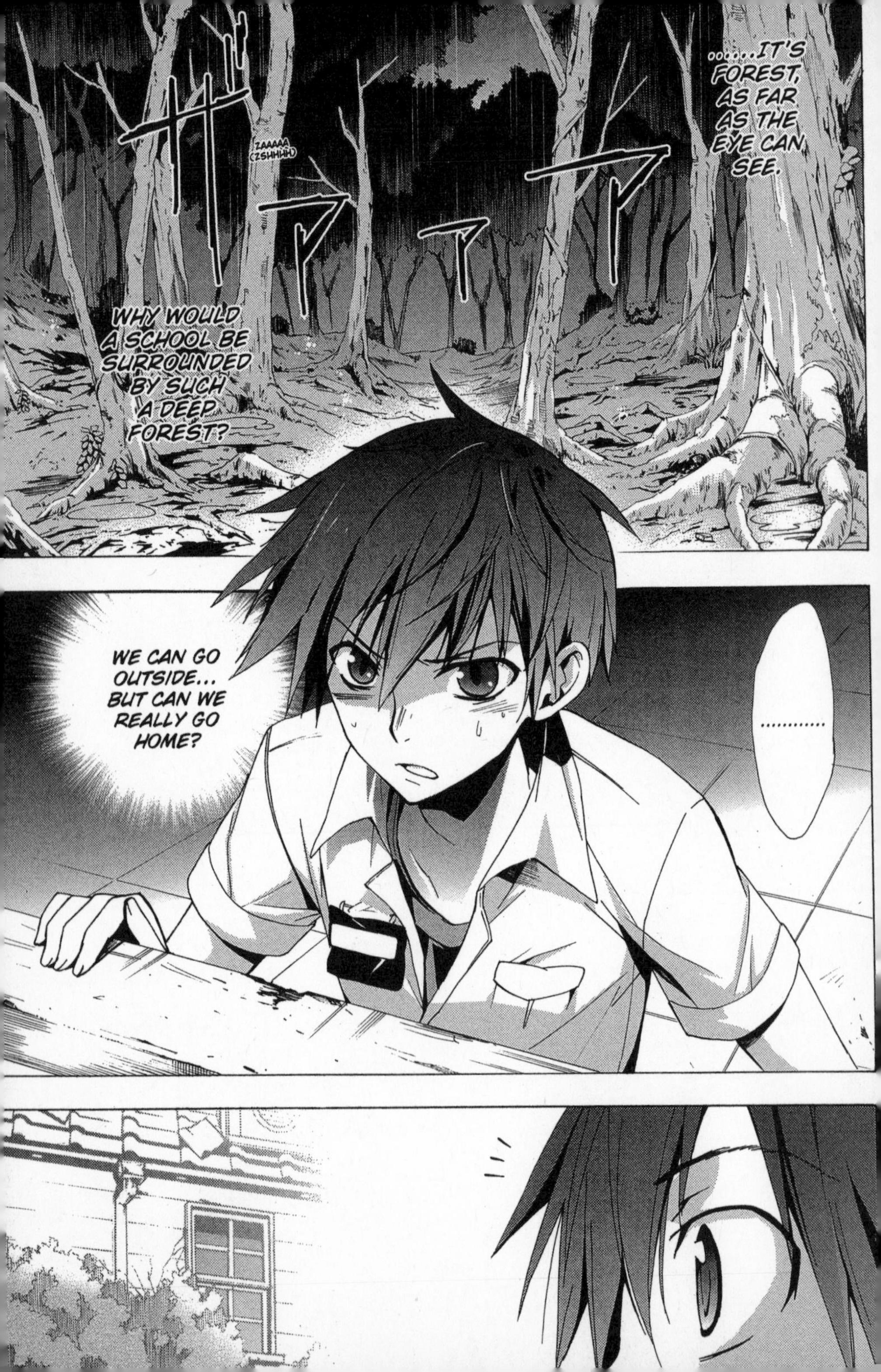
......IT'S FOREST, AS FAR AS THE EYE CAN SEE.
ZAAAAA (ZSHHHH)
WHY WOULD A SCHOOL BE SURROUNDED BY SUCH A DEEP FOREST?
....
WE CAN GO OUTSIDE... BUT CAN WE REALLY GO HOME?

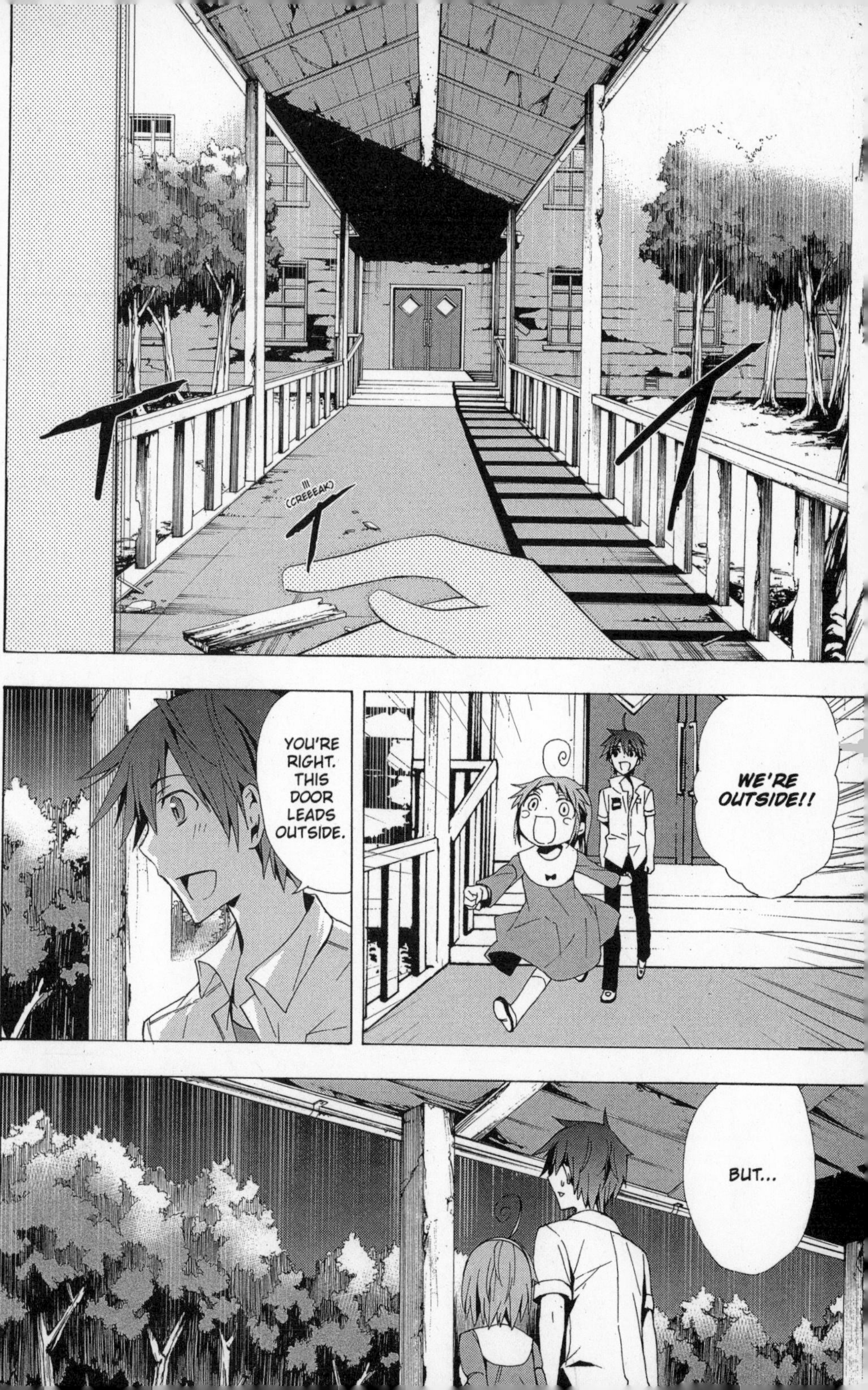
(CREEEAK)
WE'RE OUTSIDE!!
YOU'RE RIGHT. THIS DOOR LEADS OUTSIDE.
BUT...

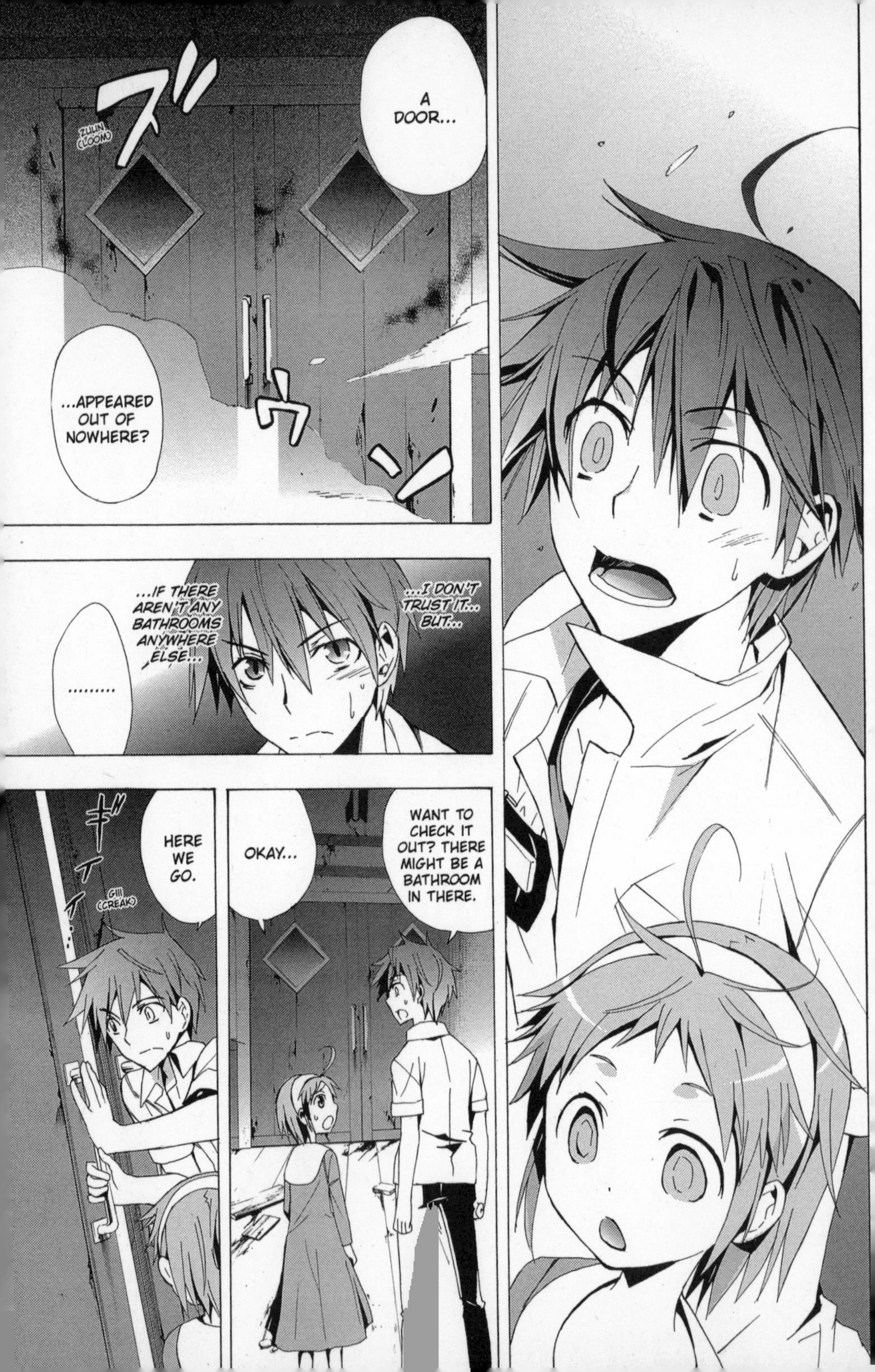
ZUUN (LOOM)
A DOOR...
...APPEARED OUT OF NOWHERE?
...I DON'T TRUST IT... BUT...
...IF THERE AREN'T ANY BATHROOMS ANYWHERE ELSE...
....
WANT TO CHECK IT OUT? THERE MIGHT BE A BATHROOM IN THERE.
OKAY...
HERE WE GO.
GIII (CREAK)

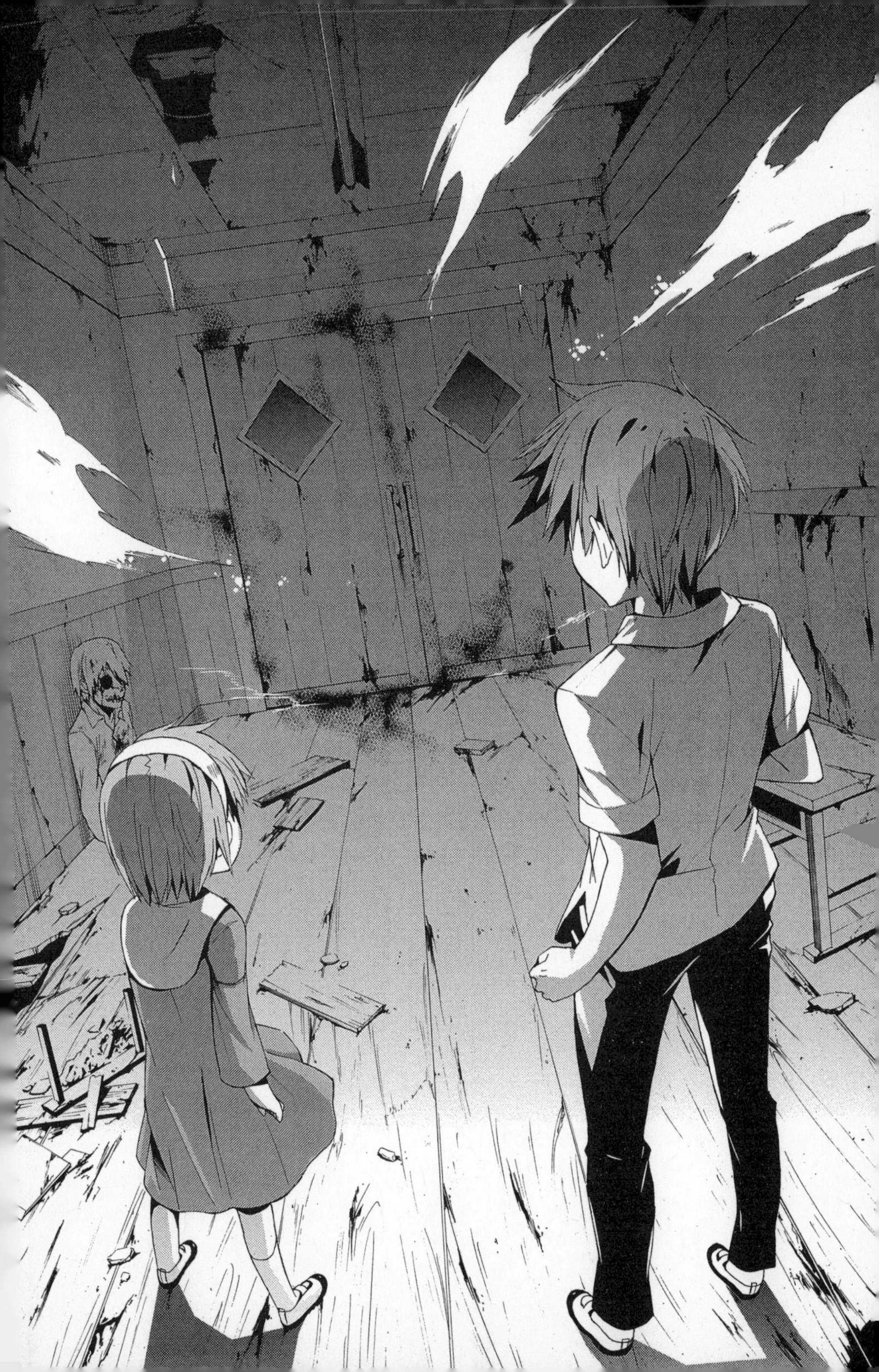

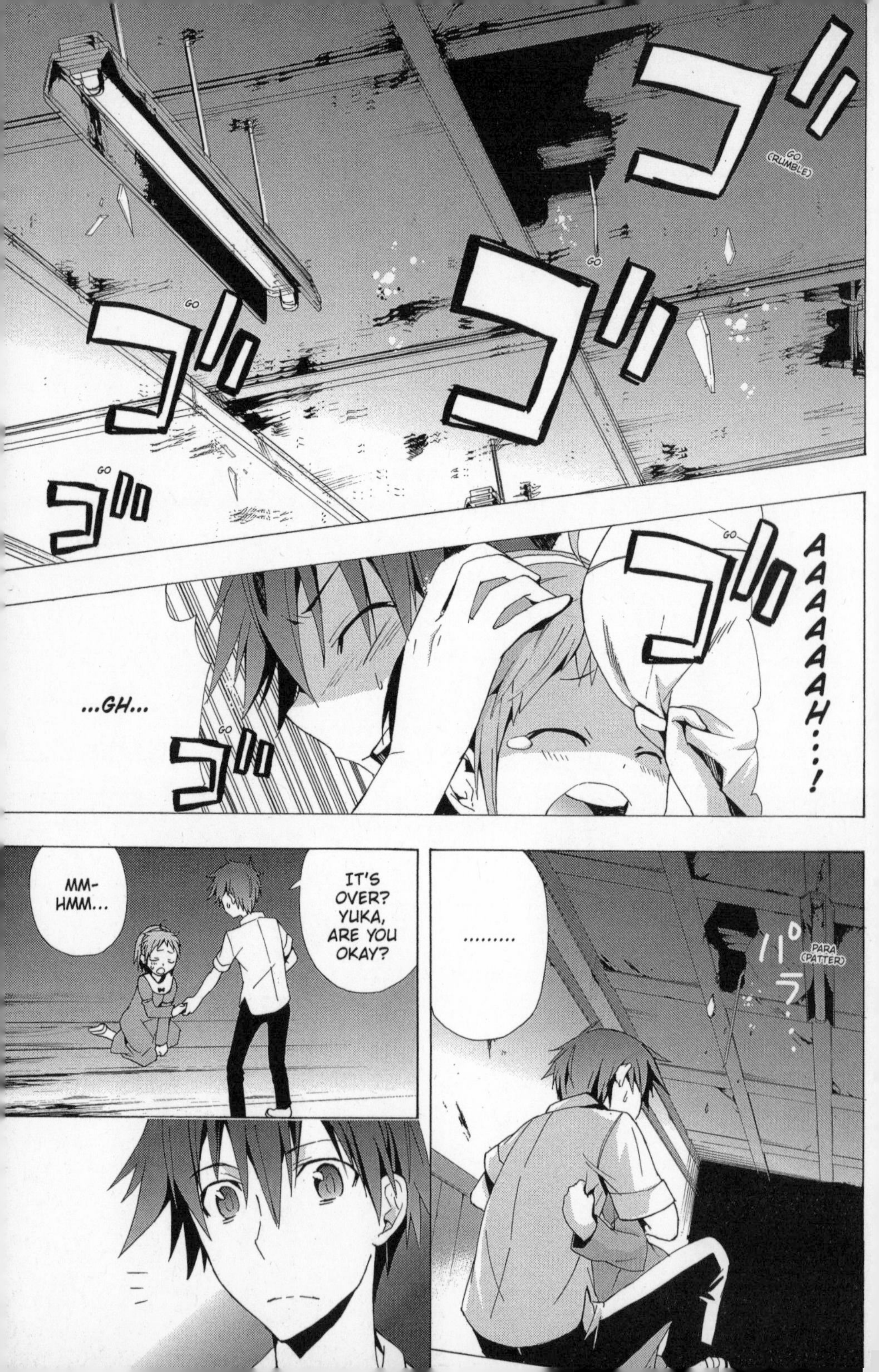
GO
(RUMBLE)
GO
GO
GO
GO
AAAAAAAH...!
...GH...
GO
....
PARA
(PATTER)
IT'S OVER? YUKA, ARE YOU OKAY?
MM-HMM...

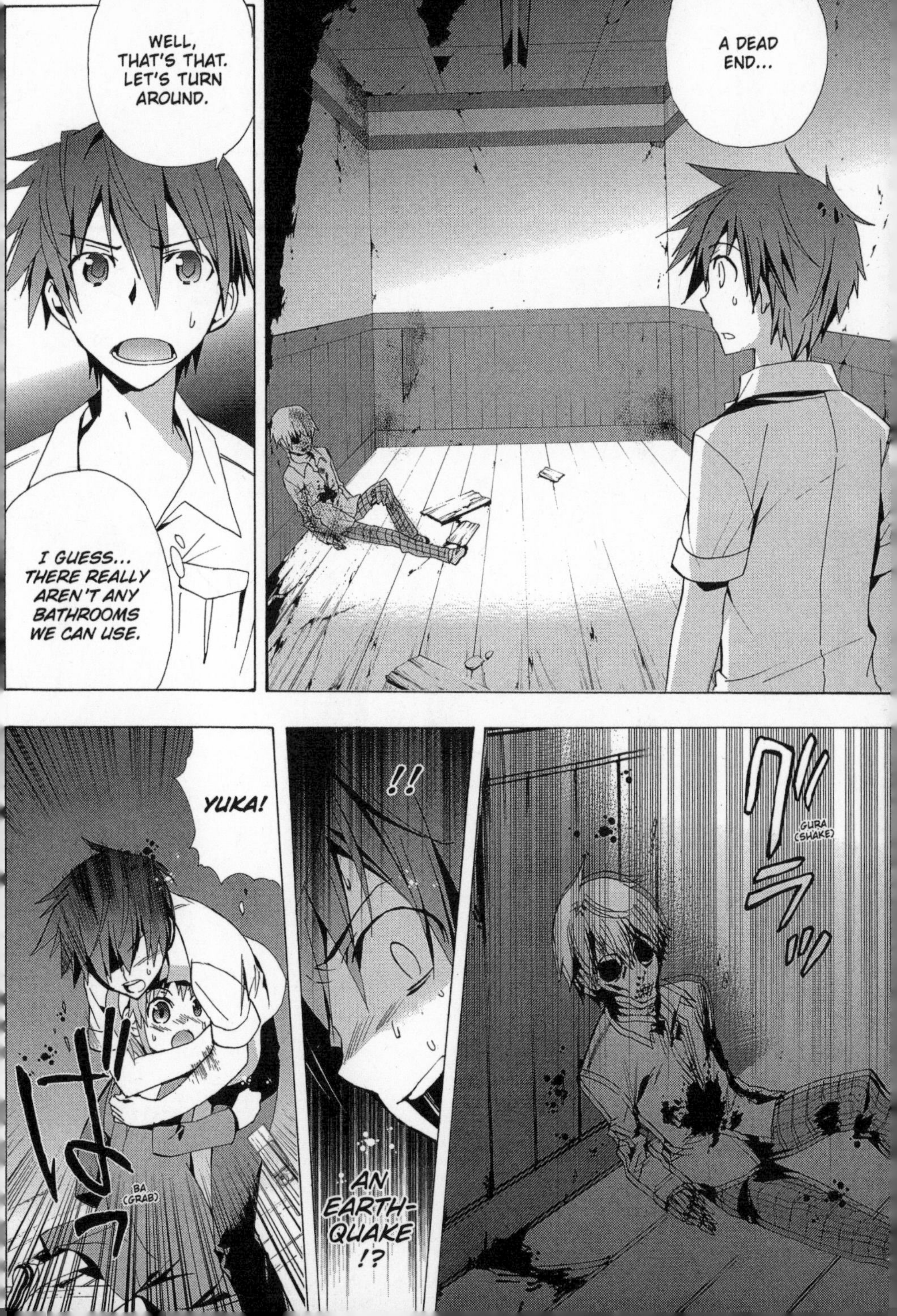
A DEAD END...
WELL, THAT'S THAT. LET'S TURN AROUND.
I GUESS... THERE REALLY AREN'T ANY BATHROOMS WE CAN USE.
GURA (SHAKE)
!!
AN EARTH-QUAKE!?
YUKA!
BA (GRAB)

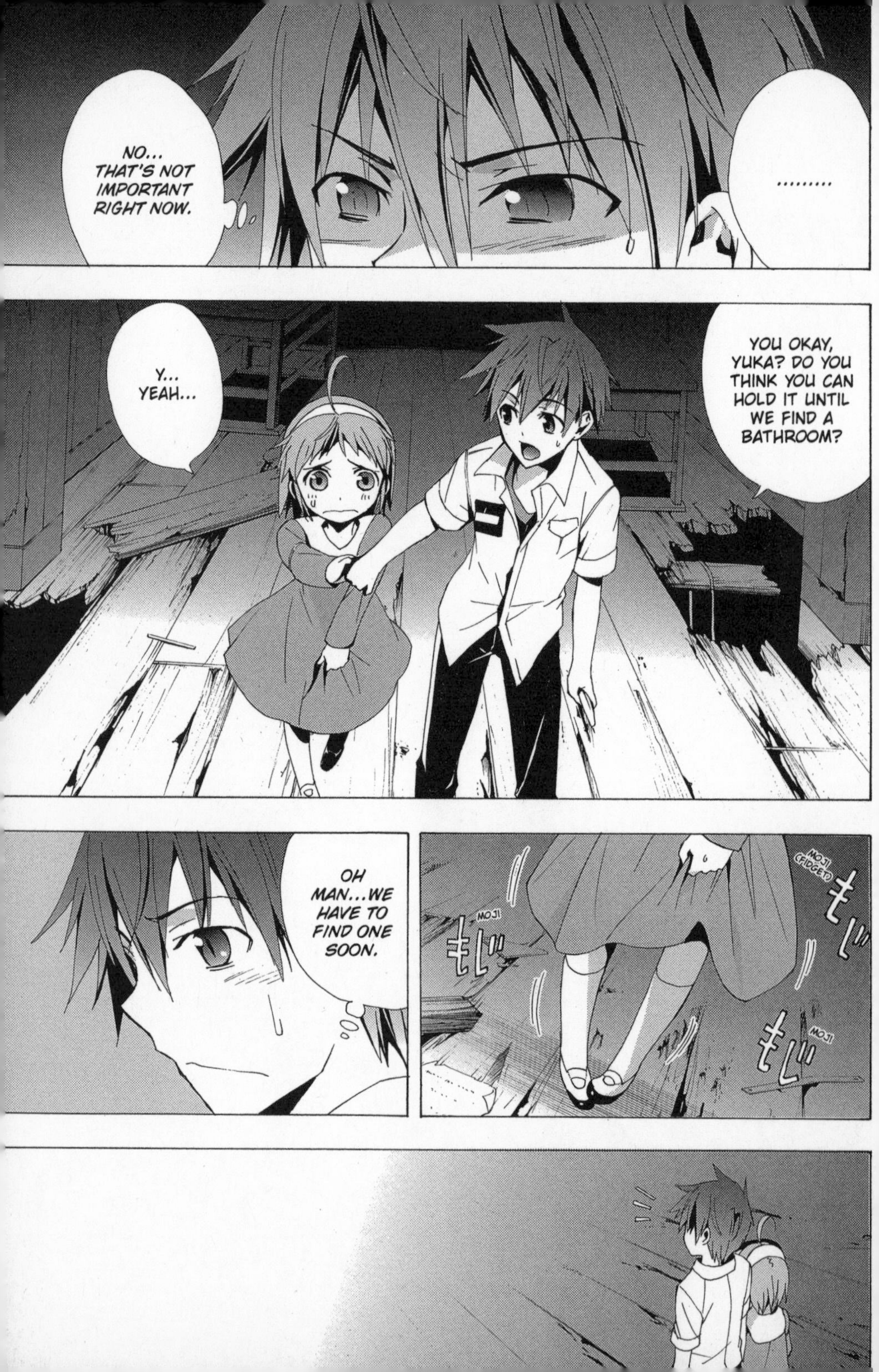
....
NO... THAT'S NOT IMPORTANT RIGHT NOW.
YOU OKAY, YUKA? DO YOU THINK YOU CAN HOLD IT UNTIL WE FIND A BATHROOM?
Y... YEAH...
MOJI (FIDGET)
もじ
MOJI
もじ
MOJI
もじ
OH MAN...WE HAVE TO FIND ONE SOON.

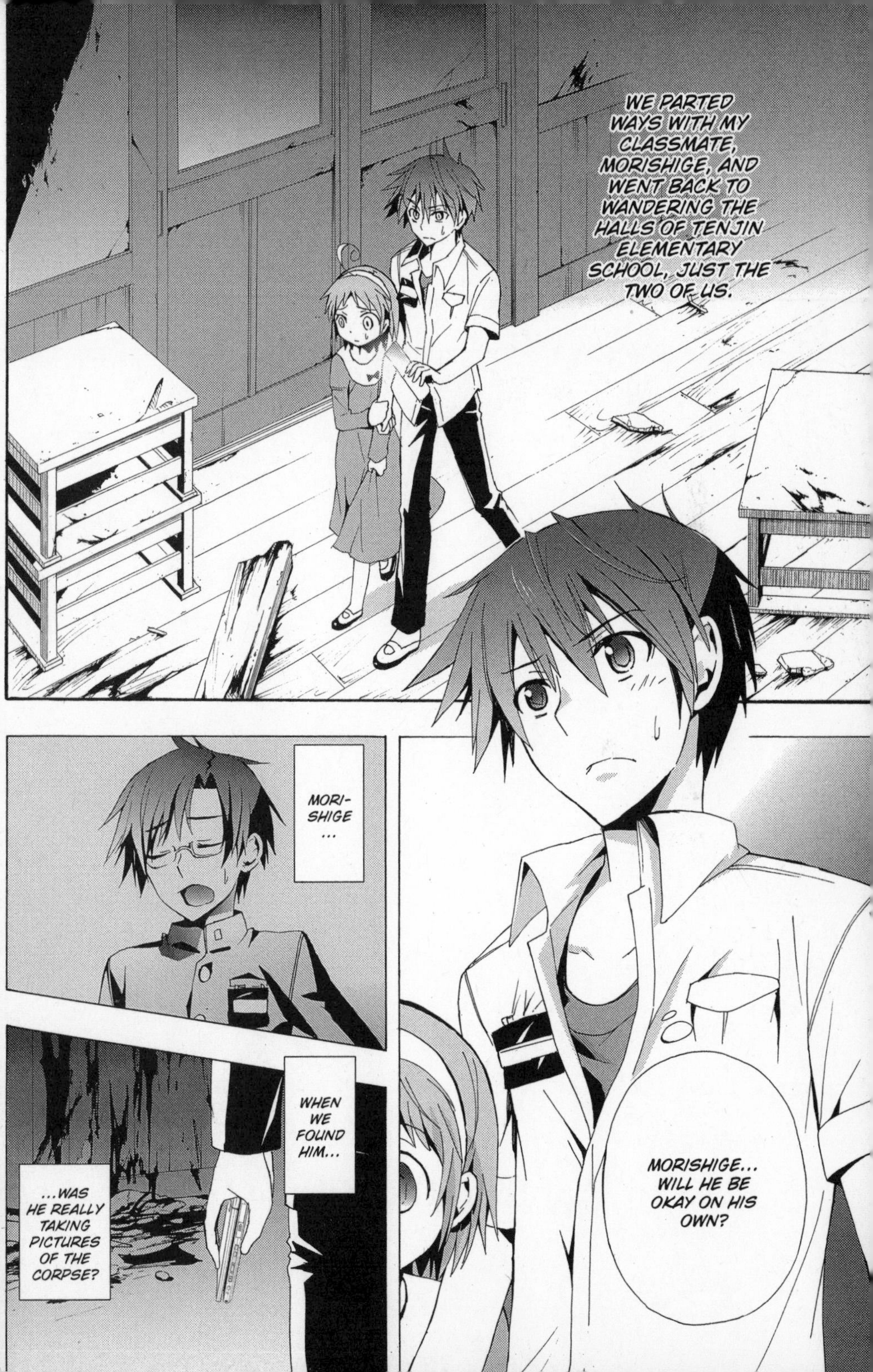
WE PARTED WAYS WITH MY CLASSMATE, MORISHIGE, AND WENT BACK TO WANDERING THE HALLS OF TENJIN ELEMENTARY SCHOOL, JUST THE TWO OF US.
MORISHIGE... WILL HE BE OKAY ON HIS OWN?
MORI-SHIGE...
WHEN WE FOUND HIM...
...WAS HE REALLY TAKING PICTURES OF THE CORPSE?

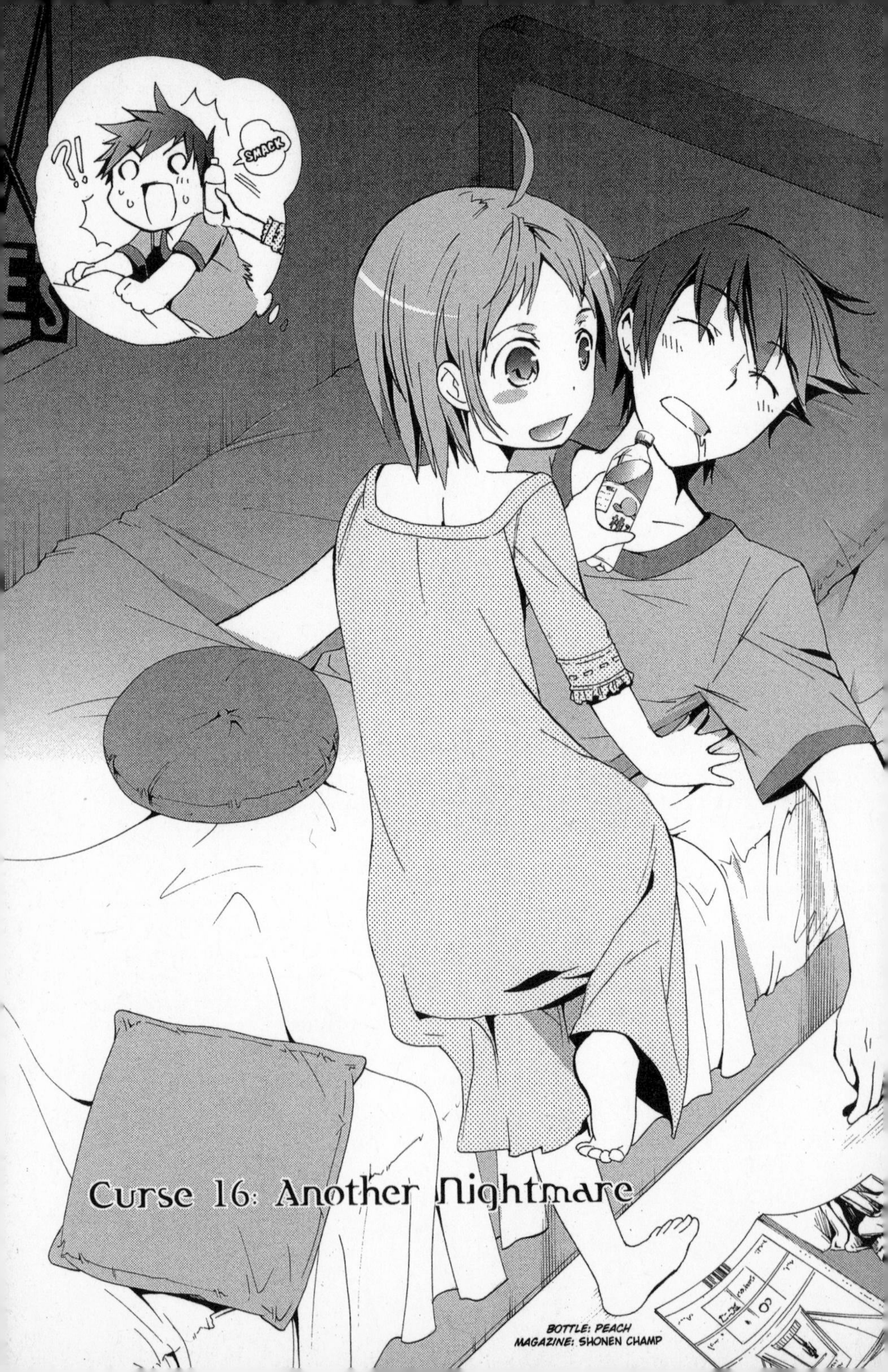
SMACK
?!
BOTTLE: PEACH
MAGAZINE: SHONEN CHAMP

Curse 16: Another Nightmare

CORPSE PARTY
Blood Covered

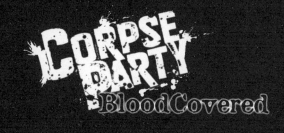

a list of hints/01

The black stain in front of the
nurse's office

A line, as if something had been
dragged across the floor, traces
the hallway until the intersection.
A pulverized female corpse is
plastered to the wall.

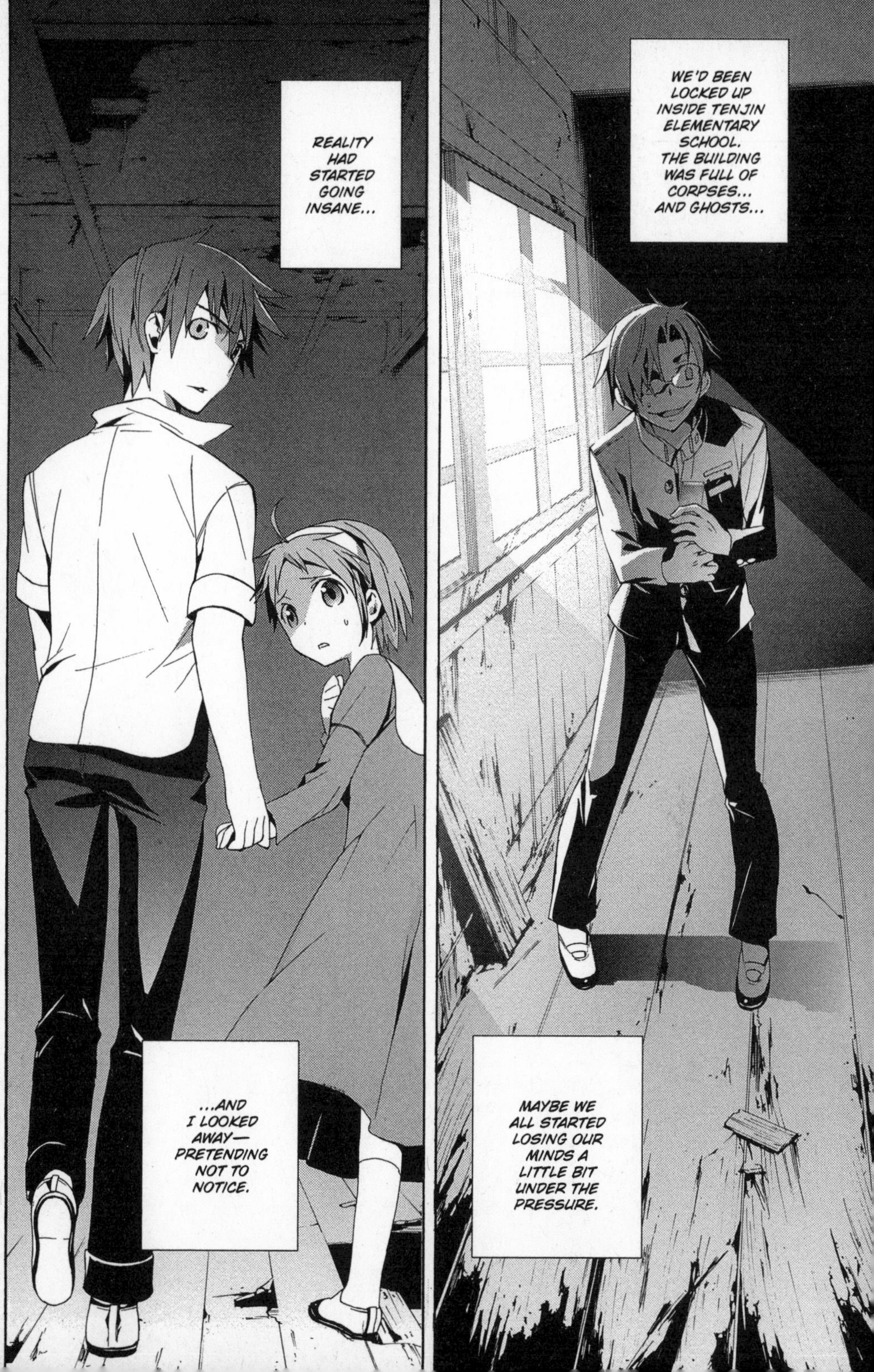
WE'D BEEN LOCKED UP INSIDE TENJIN ELEMENTARY SCHOOL. THE BUILDING WAS FULL OF CORPSES... AND GHOSTS...
MAYBE WE ALL STARTED LOSING OUR MINDS A LITTLE BIT UNDER THE PRESSURE.
REALITY HAD STARTED GOING INSANE...
...AND I LOOKED AWAY—PRETENDING NOT TO NOTICE.

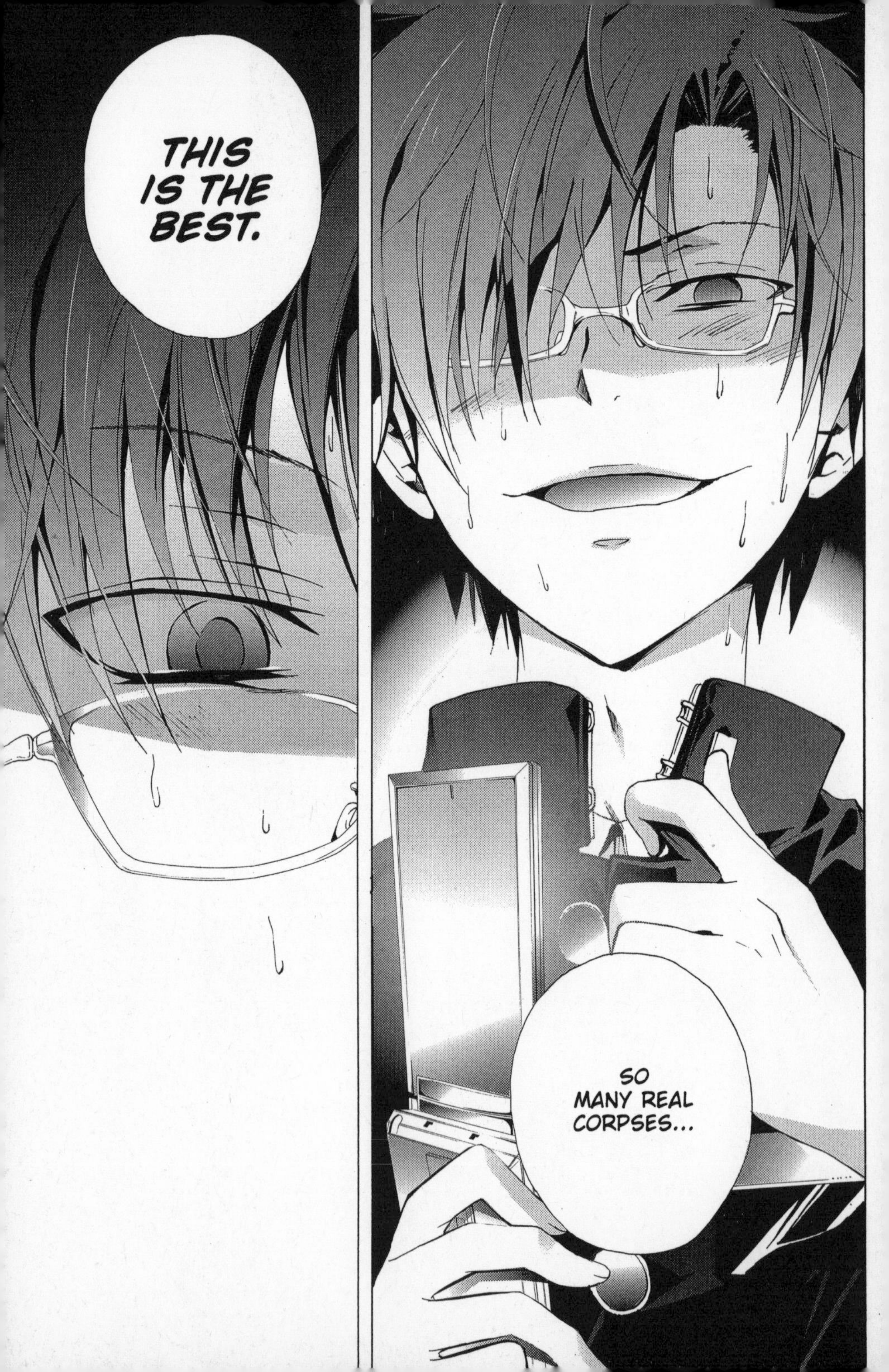
SO MANY REAL CORPSES...
THIS IS THE BEST.

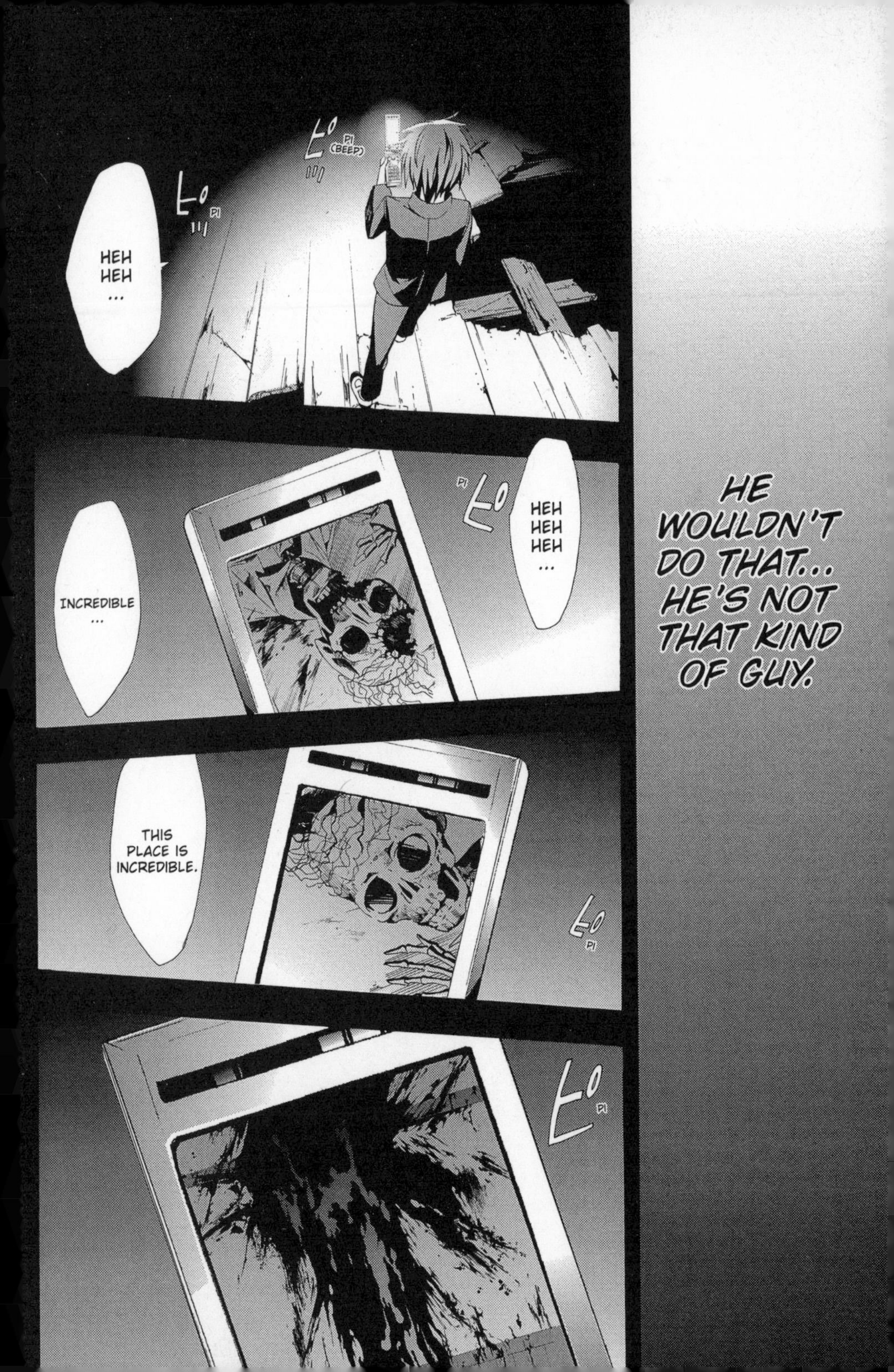
HE WOULDN'T DO THAT... HE'S NOT THAT KIND OF GUY.
ピッ PI (BEEP)
ピッ PI
HEH HEH ...
HEH HEH HEH ...
ピッ PI
INCREDIBLE ...
THIS PLACE IS INCREDIBLE.
ピッ PI
ピッ PI

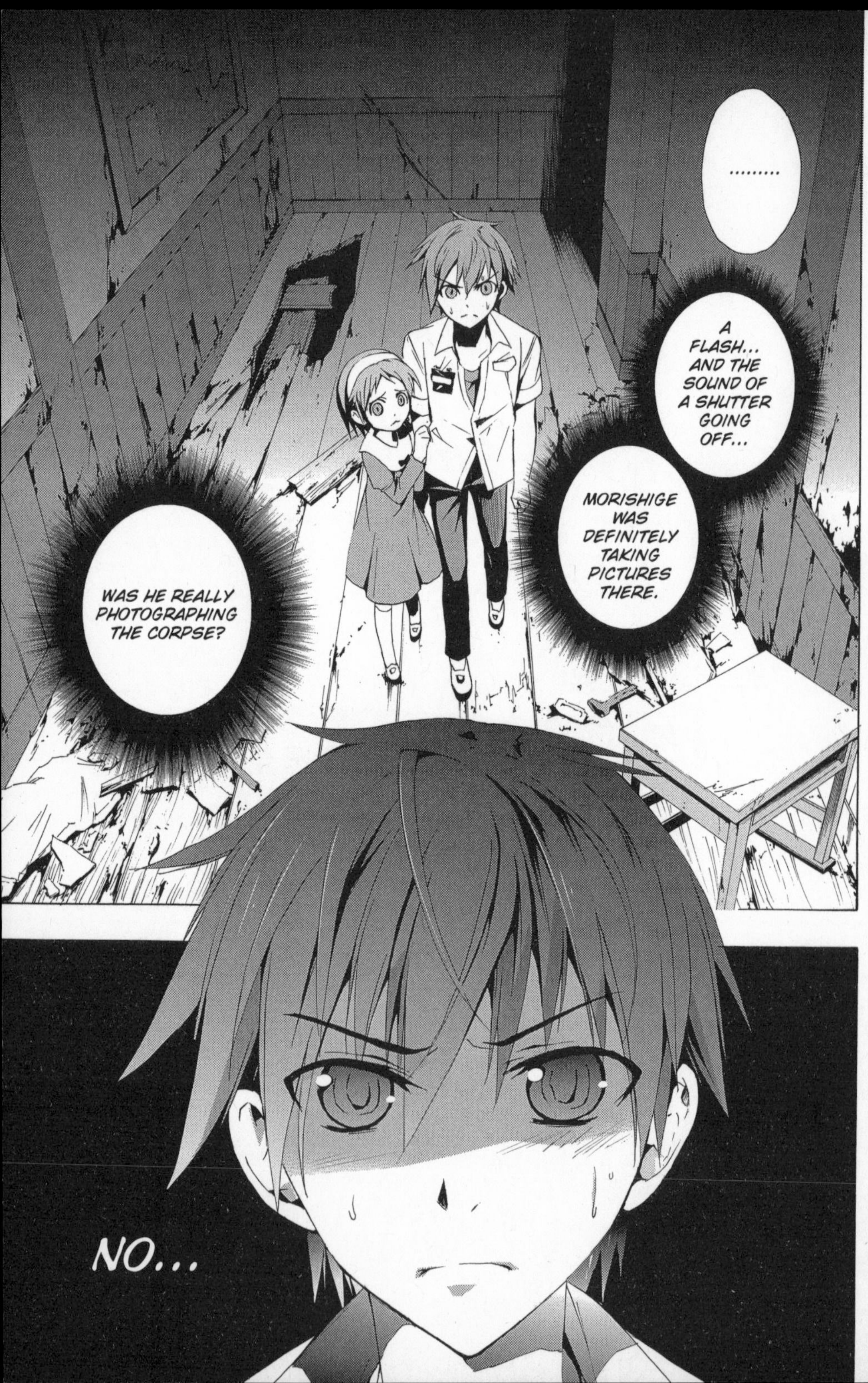
....
A FLASH... AND THE SOUND OF A SHUTTER GOING OFF...
MORISHIGE WAS DEFINITELY TAKING PICTURES THERE.
WAS HE REALLY PHOTOGRAPHING THE CORPSE?
NO...

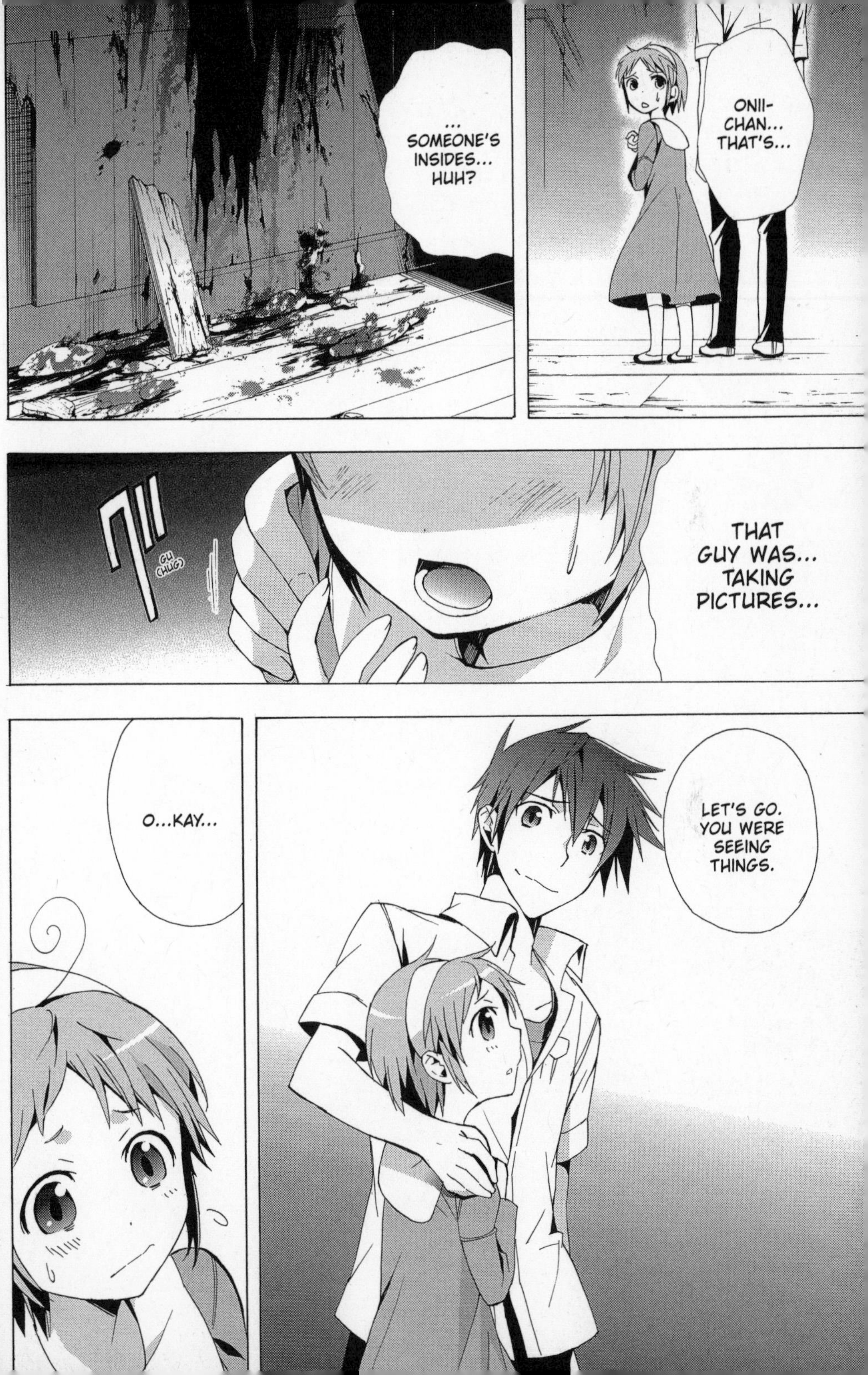
ONII-CHAN... THAT'S...
... SOMEONE'S INSIDES... HUH?
THAT GUY WAS... TAKING PICTURES...
GU (CHUG)
LET'S GO. YOU WERE SEEING THINGS.
O...KAY...

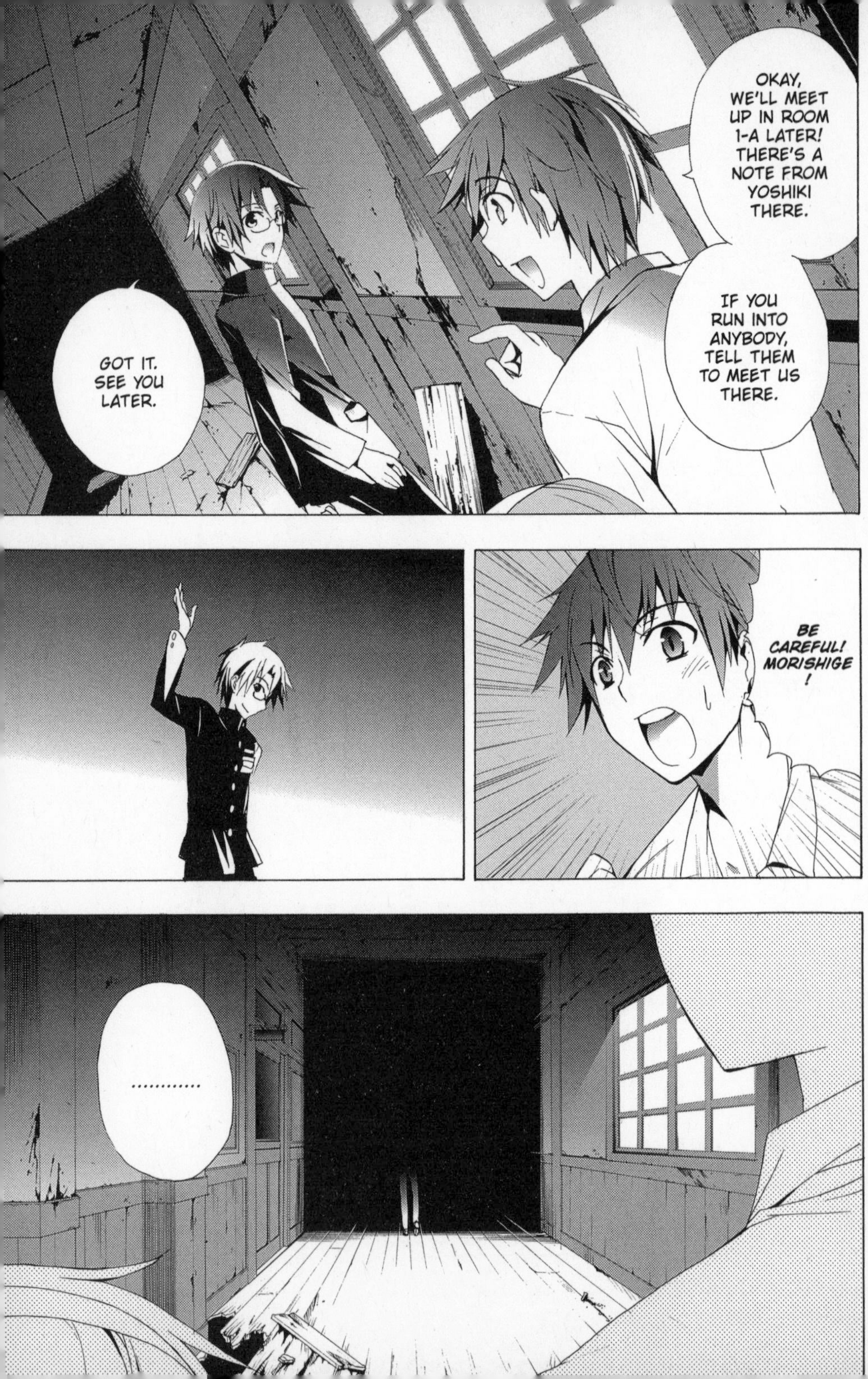
OKAY, WE'LL MEET UP IN ROOM 1-A LATER! THERE'S A NOTE FROM YOSHIKI THERE.
IF YOU RUN INTO ANYBODY, TELL THEM TO MEET US THERE.
GOT IT. SEE YOU LATER.
BE CAREFUL! MORISHIGE!
....

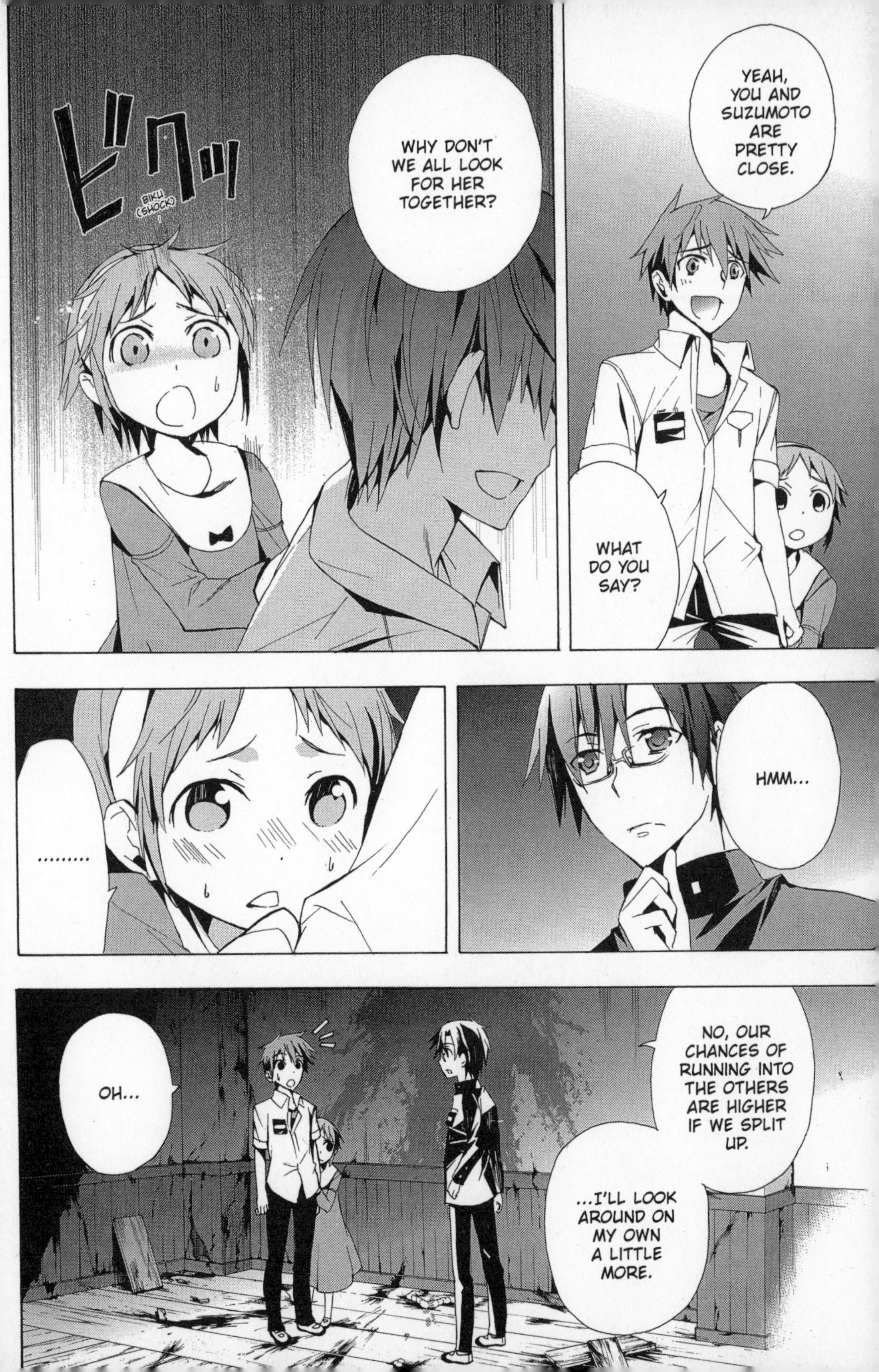
YEAH, YOU AND SUZUMOTO ARE PRETTY CLOSE.
WHAT DO YOU SAY?
WHY DON'T WE ALL LOOK FOR HER TOGETHER?
ビクッ
BIKU (SHOCK)
HMM...
....
NO, OUR CHANCES OF RUNNING INTO THE OTHERS ARE HIGHER IF WE SPLIT UP.
...I'LL LOOK AROUND ON MY OWN A LITTLE MORE.
OH...

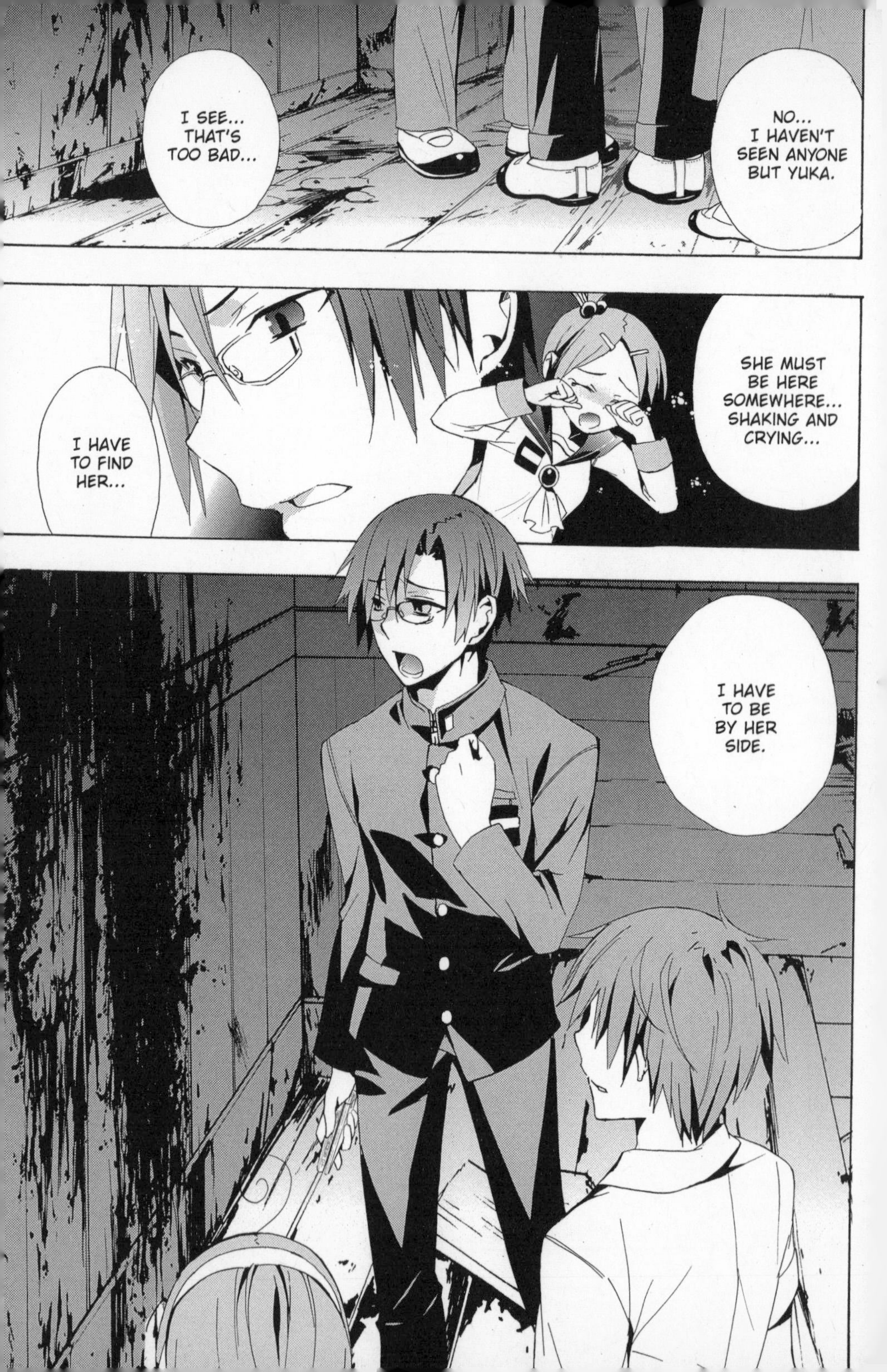
NO... I HAVEN'T SEEN ANYONE BUT YUKA.
I SEE... THAT'S TOO BAD...
SHE MUST BE HERE SOMEWHERE... SHAKING AND CRYING...
I HAVE TO FIND HER...
I HAVE TO BE BY HER SIDE.

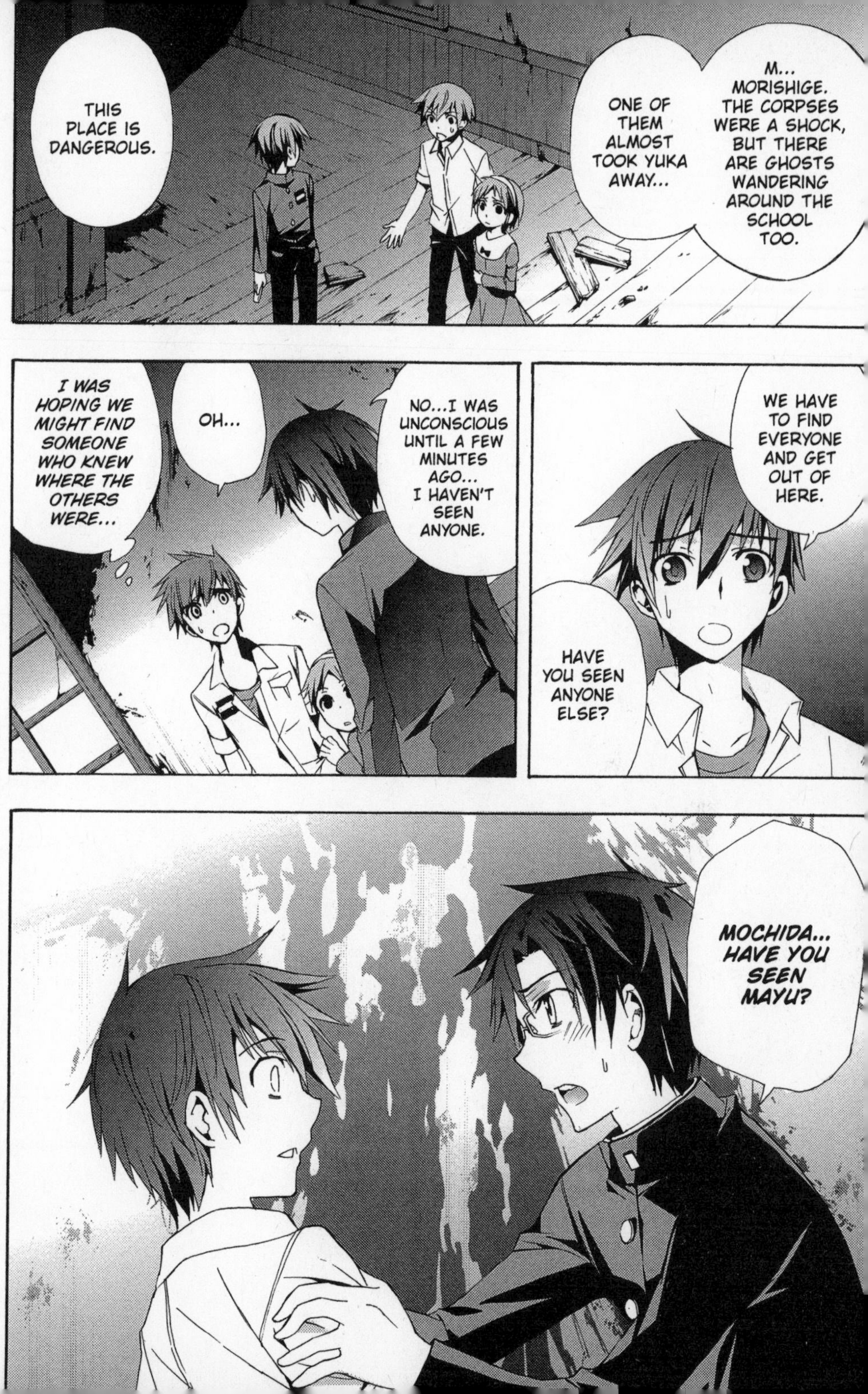
M... MORISHIGE. THE CORPSES WERE A SHOCK, BUT THERE ARE GHOSTS WANDERING AROUND THE SCHOOL TOO.
ONE OF THEM ALMOST TOOK YUKA AWAY...
THIS PLACE IS DANGEROUS.
WE HAVE TO FIND EVERYONE AND GET OUT OF HERE.
HAVE YOU SEEN ANYONE ELSE?
NO...I WAS UNCONSCIOUS UNTIL A FEW MINUTES AGO... I HAVEN'T SEEN ANYONE.
OH...
I WAS HOPING WE MIGHT FIND SOMEONE WHO KNEW WHERE THE OTHERS WERE...
MOCHIDA... HAVE YOU SEEN MAYU?

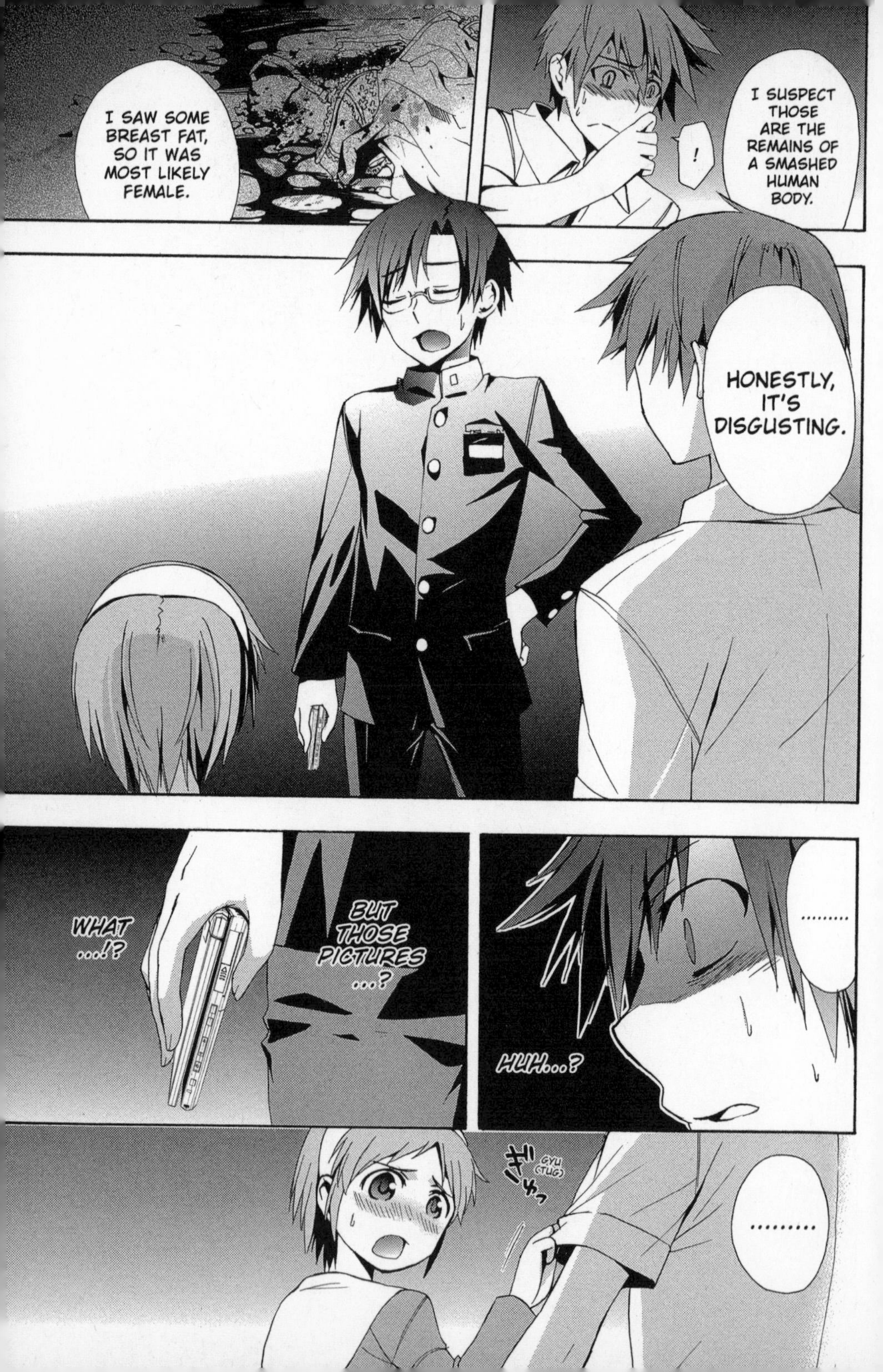
I SUSPECT THOSE ARE THE REMAINS OF A SMASHED HUMAN BODY.
!
I SAW SOME BREAST FAT, SO IT WAS MOST LIKELY FEMALE.
HONESTLY, IT'S DISGUSTING.
....
HUH...?
BUT THOSE PICTURES ...?
WHAT ...!?
GYU (TUG)
....

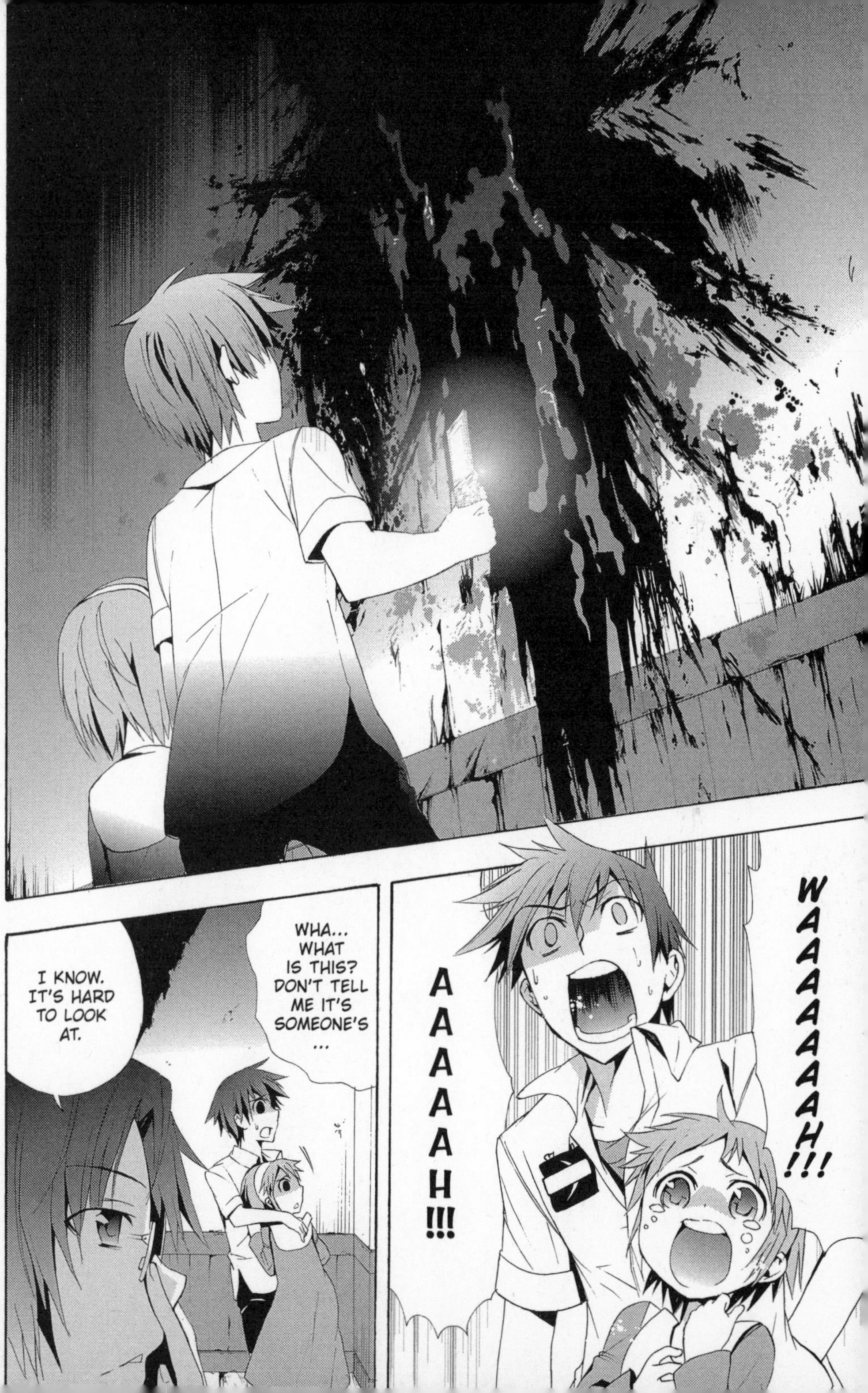
WAAAAAAAH!!!
AAAAAAH!!!
WHA... WHAT IS THIS? DON'T TELL ME IT'S SOMEONE'S...
I KNOW. IT'S HARD TO LOOK AT.

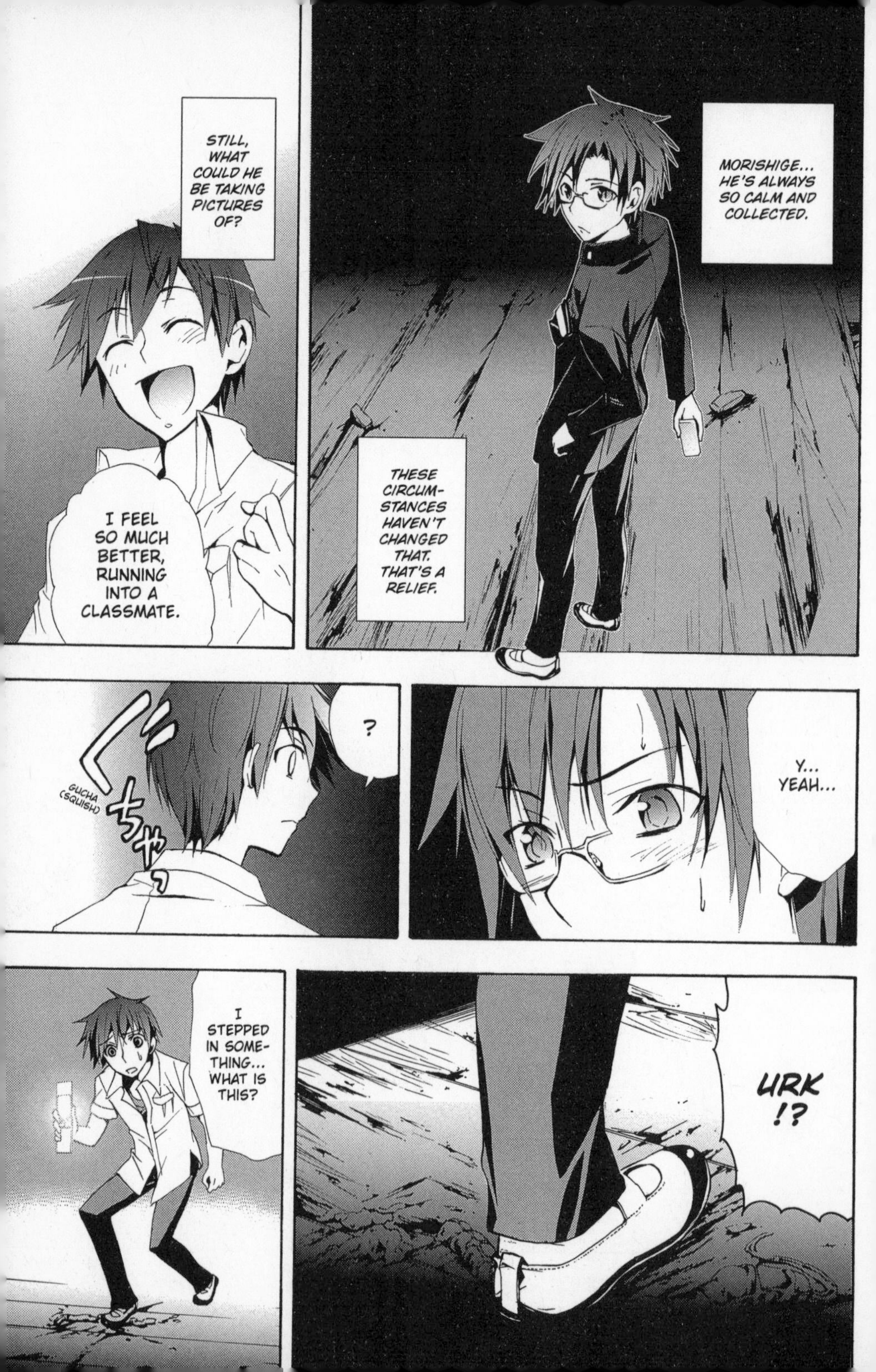

MORISHIGE... HE'S ALWAYS SO CALM AND COLLECTED.
THESE CIRCUMSTANCES HAVEN'T CHANGED THAT. THAT'S A RELIEF.
STILL, WHAT COULD HE BE TAKING PICTURES OF?
I FEEL SO MUCH BETTER, RUNNING INTO A CLASSMATE.
Y... YEAH...
?
ぐちゃっ
GUCHA (SQUISH)
URK !?
I STEPPED IN SOMETHING... WHAT IS THIS?

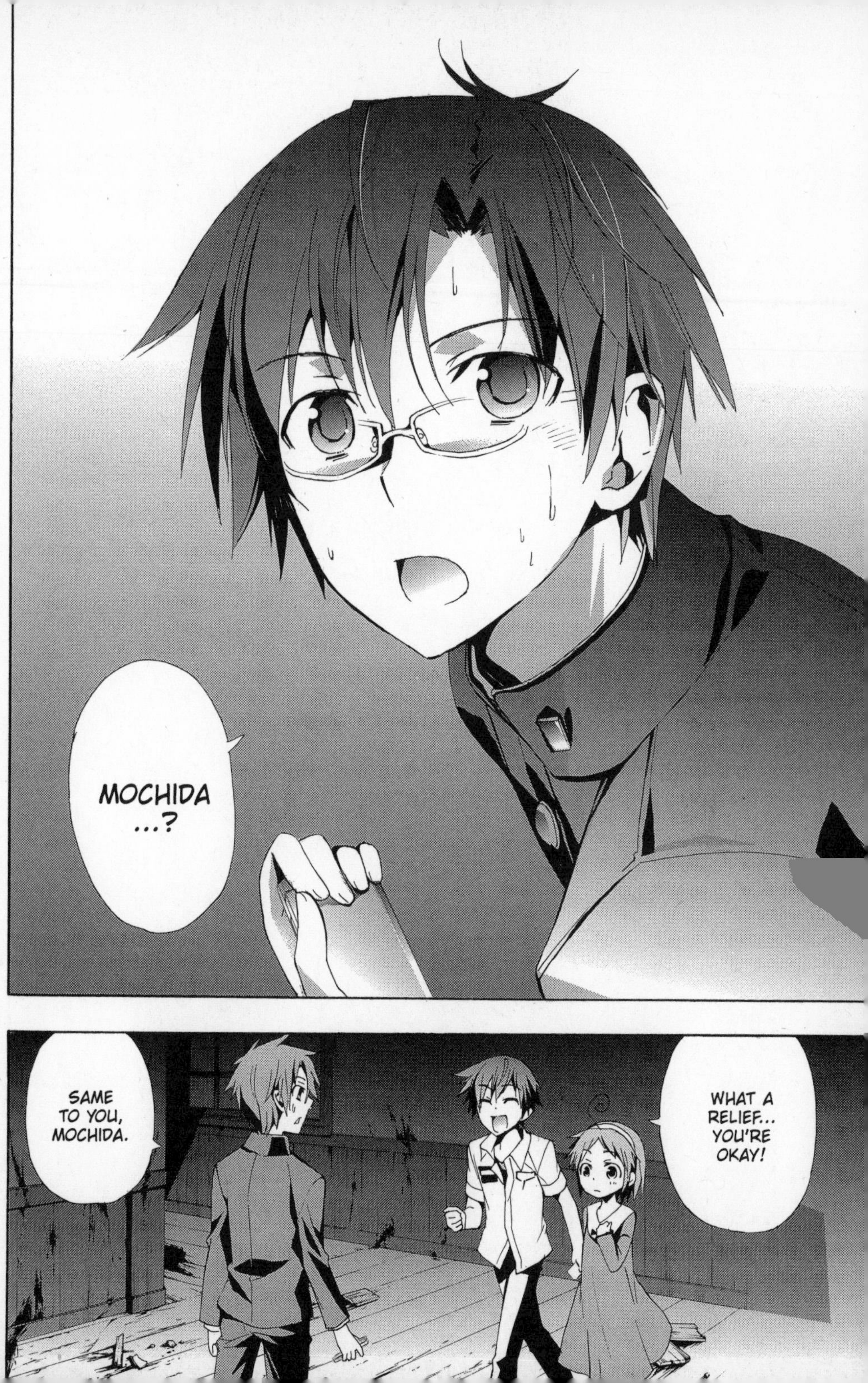
MOCHIDA ...?
WHAT A RELIEF... YOU'RE OKAY!
SAME TO YOU, MOCHIDA.

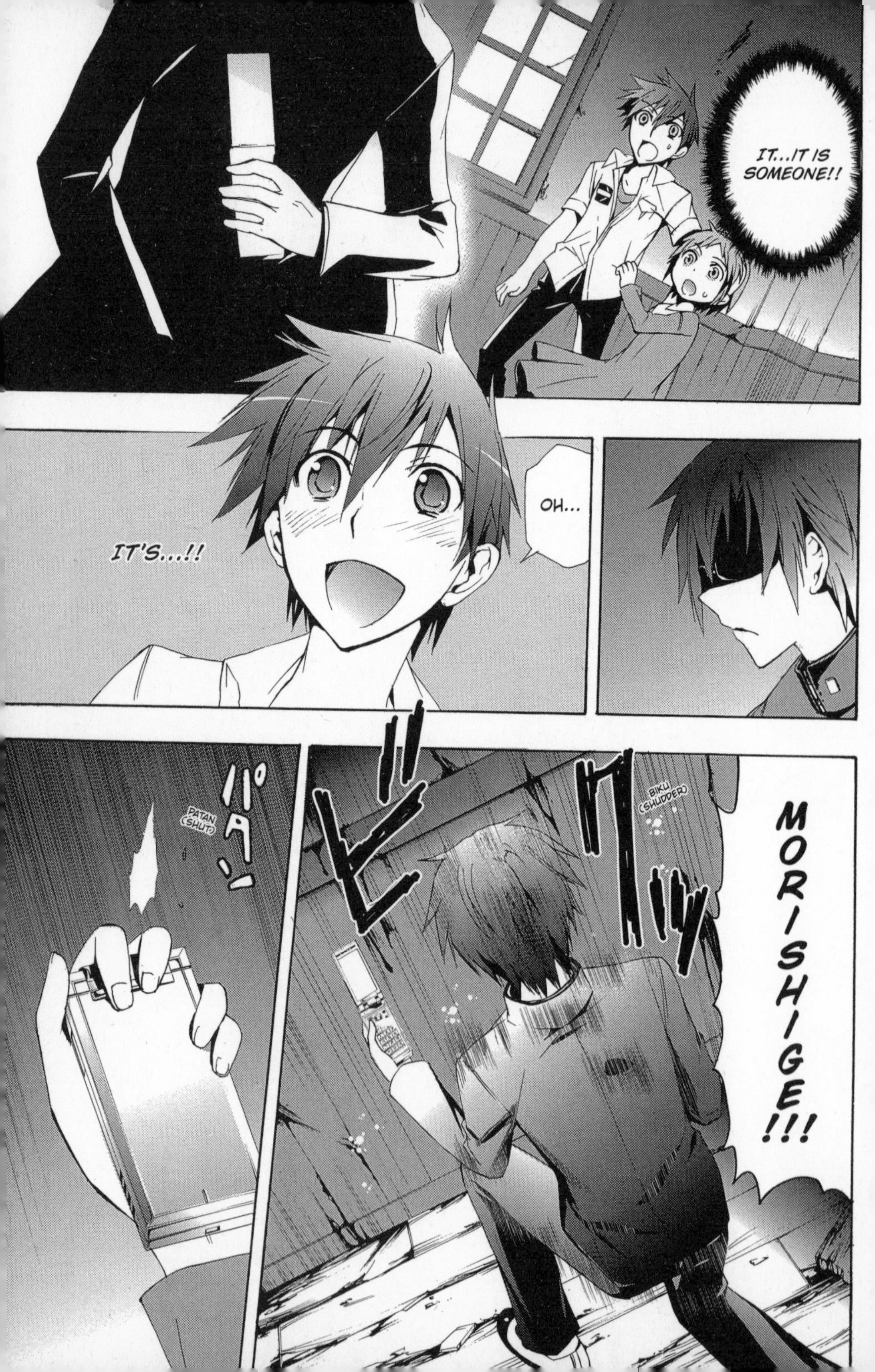
IT...IT IS SOMEONE!!
OH...
IT'S...!!
MORISHIGE!!!
BIKU (SHUDDER)
ビクッ
PATAN (SHUT)
パタン

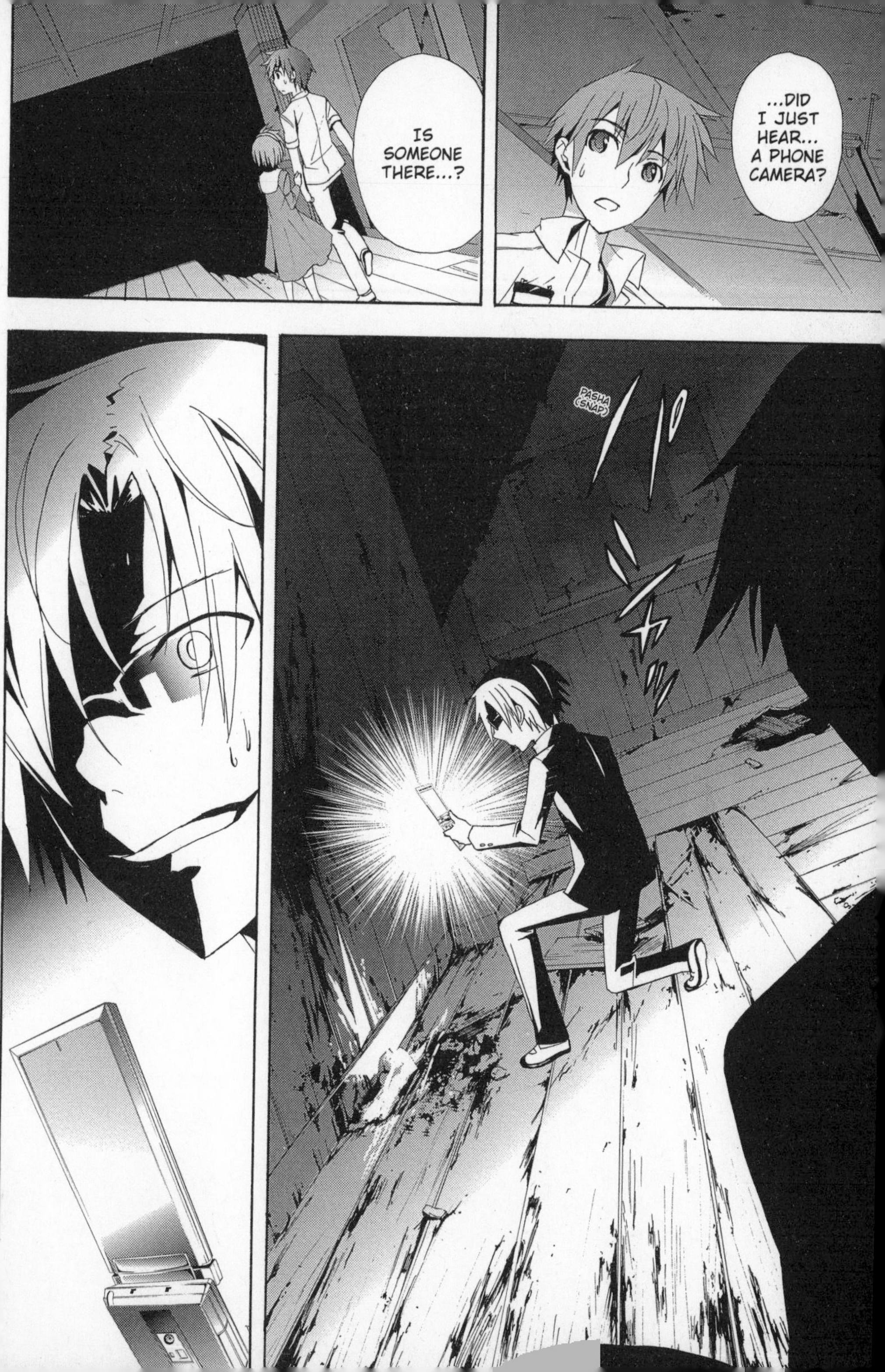
...DID I JUST HEAR... A PHONE CAMERA?
IS SOMEONE THERE...?
PASHA (SNAP)

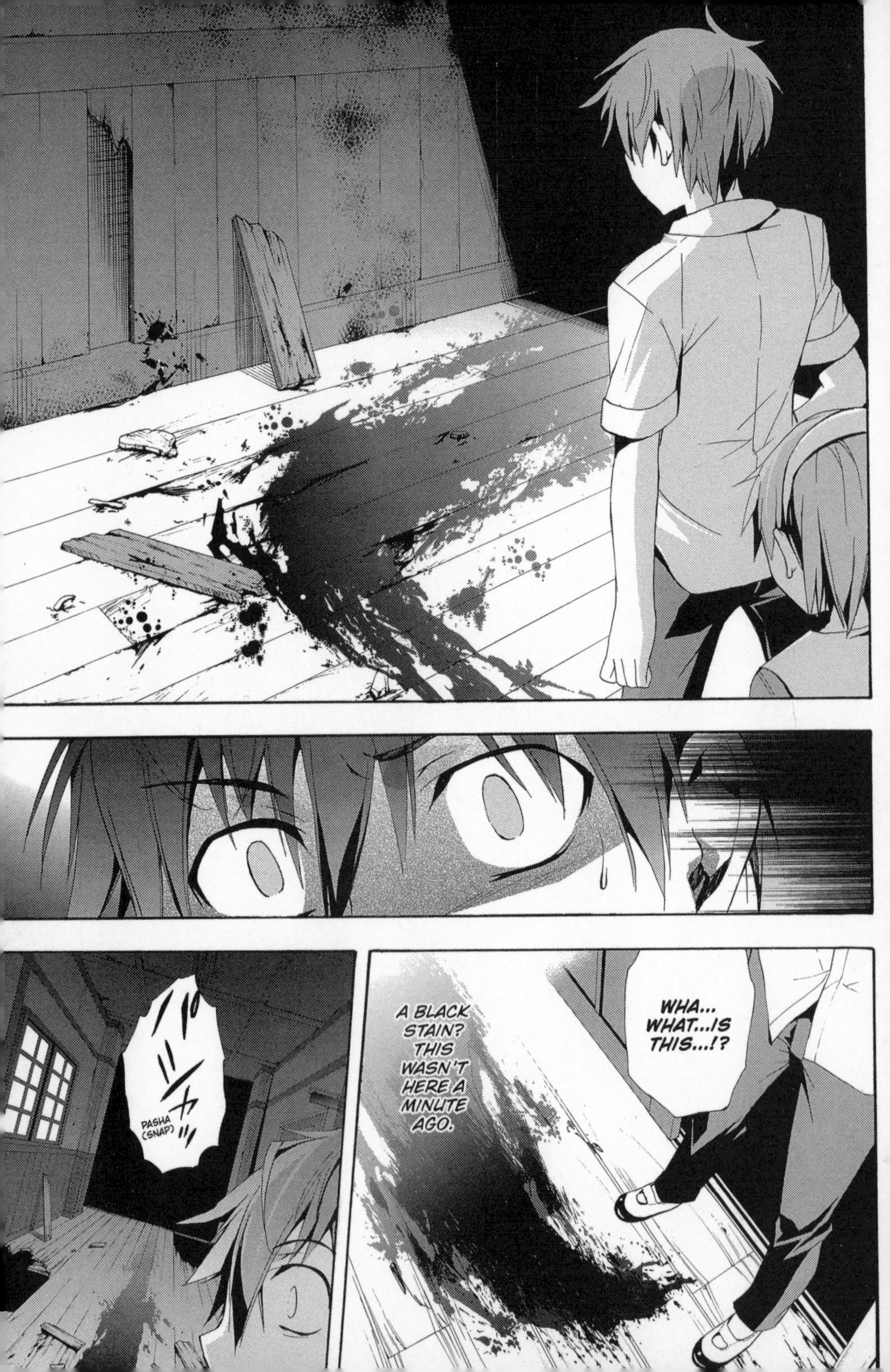
WHA... WHAT...IS THIS...!?
A BLACK STAIN? THIS WASN'T HERE A MINUTE AGO.
PASHA (SNAP)

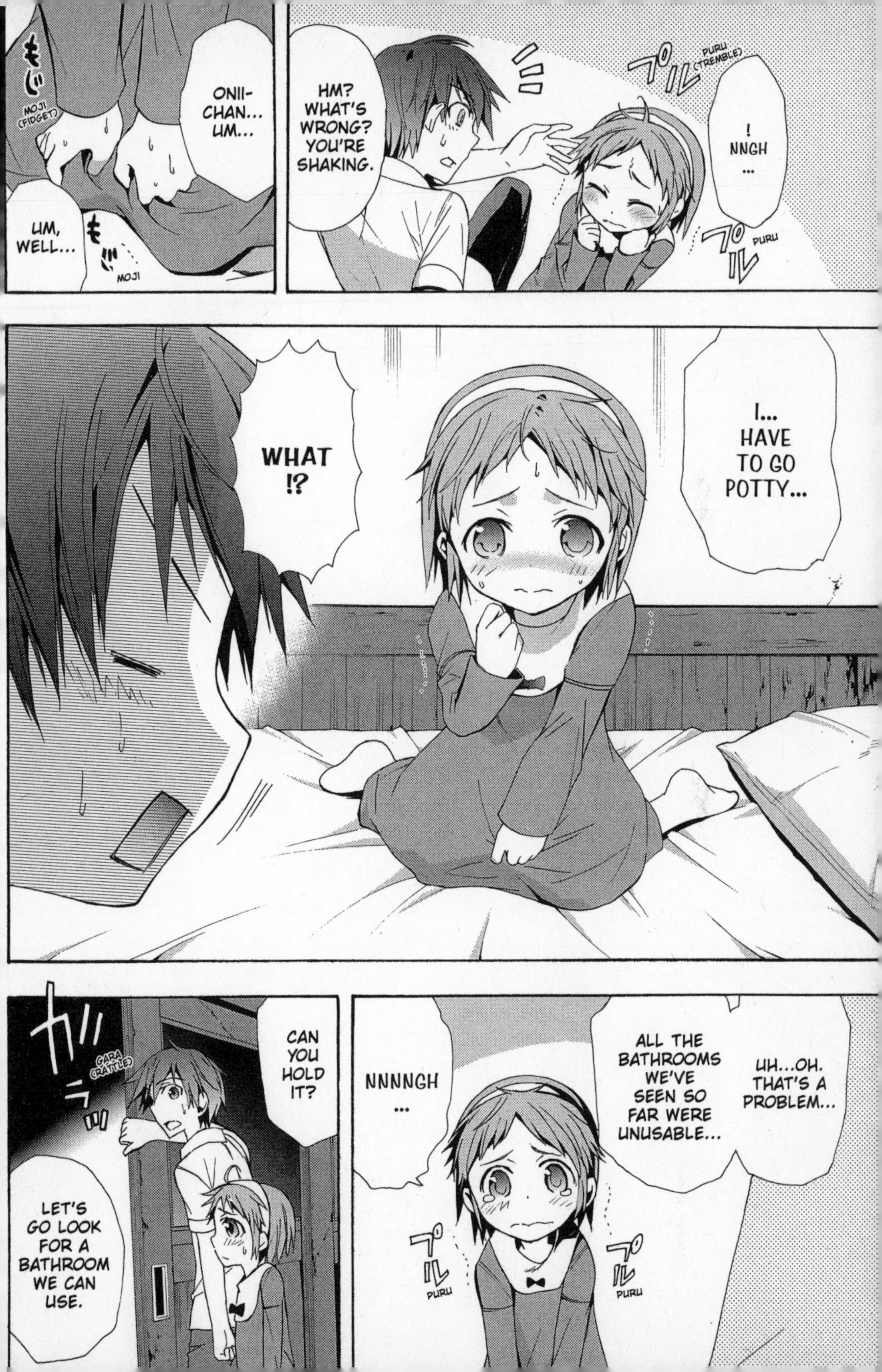
プル
PURU (TREMBLE)
! NNGH ...
HM? WHAT'S WRONG? YOU'RE SHAKING.
プル
PURU
ONII-CHAN... UM...
もじ
MOJI (FIDGET)
UM, WELL...
もじ
MOJI
I... HAVE TO GO POTTY...
WHAT !?
UH...OH. THAT'S A PROBLEM...
ALL THE BATHROOMS WE'VE SEEN SO FAR WERE UNUSABLE...
NNNNGH ...
プル
PURU
プル
PURU
CAN YOU HOLD IT?
GARA (RATTLE)
LET'S GO LOOK FOR A BATHROOM WE CAN USE.

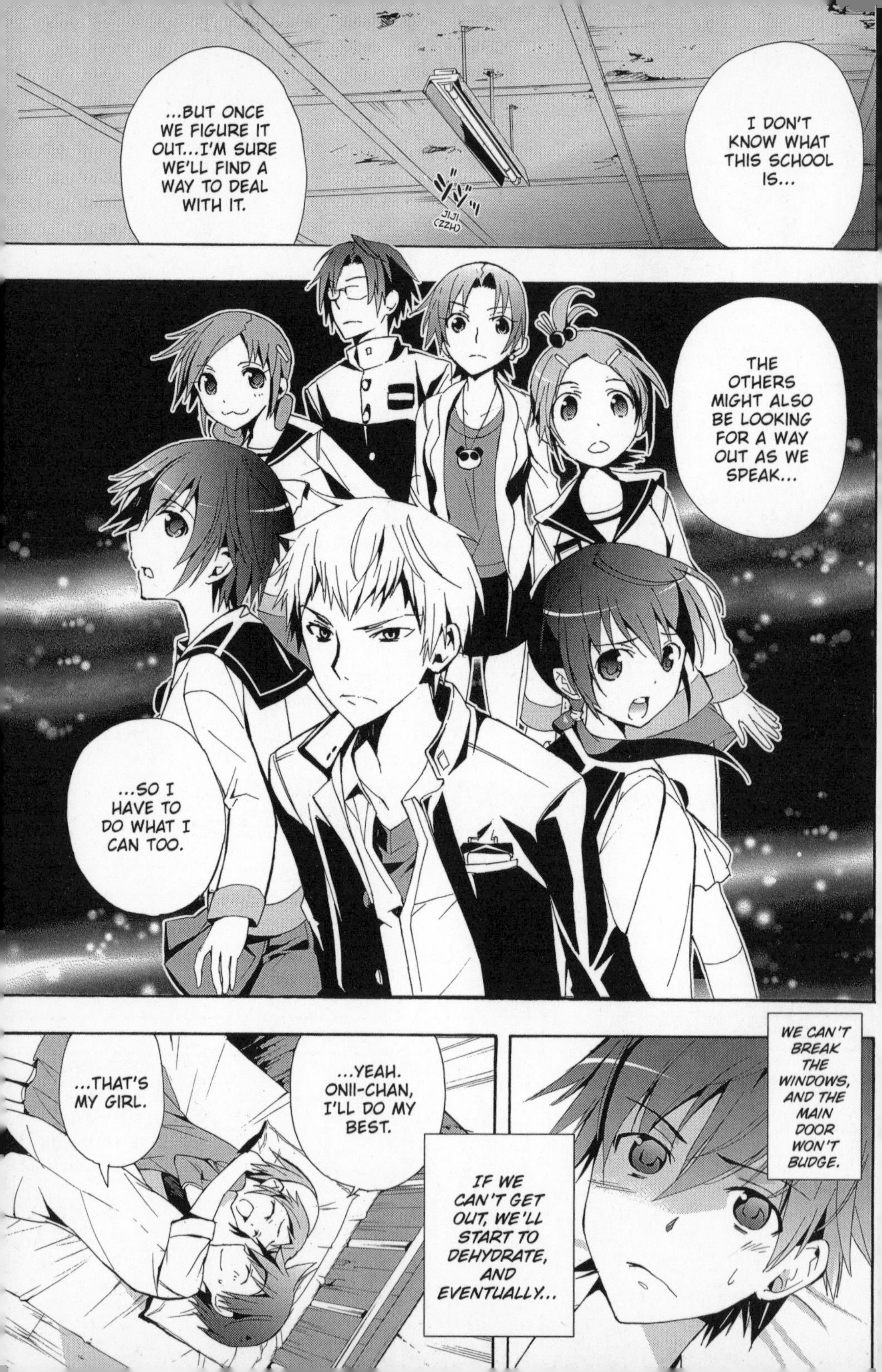

I DON'T KNOW WHAT THIS SCHOOL IS...
...BUT ONCE WE FIGURE IT OUT...I'M SURE WE'LL FIND A WAY TO DEAL WITH IT.
JIJI (ZZH)
THE OTHERS MIGHT ALSO BE LOOKING FOR A WAY OUT AS WE SPEAK...
...SO I HAVE TO DO WHAT I CAN TOO.
WE CAN'T BREAK THE WINDOWS, AND THE MAIN DOOR WON'T BUDGE.
IF WE CAN'T GET OUT, WE'LL START TO DEHYDRATE, AND EVENTUALLY...
...YEAH. ONII-CHAN, I'LL DO MY BEST.
...THAT'S MY GIRL.

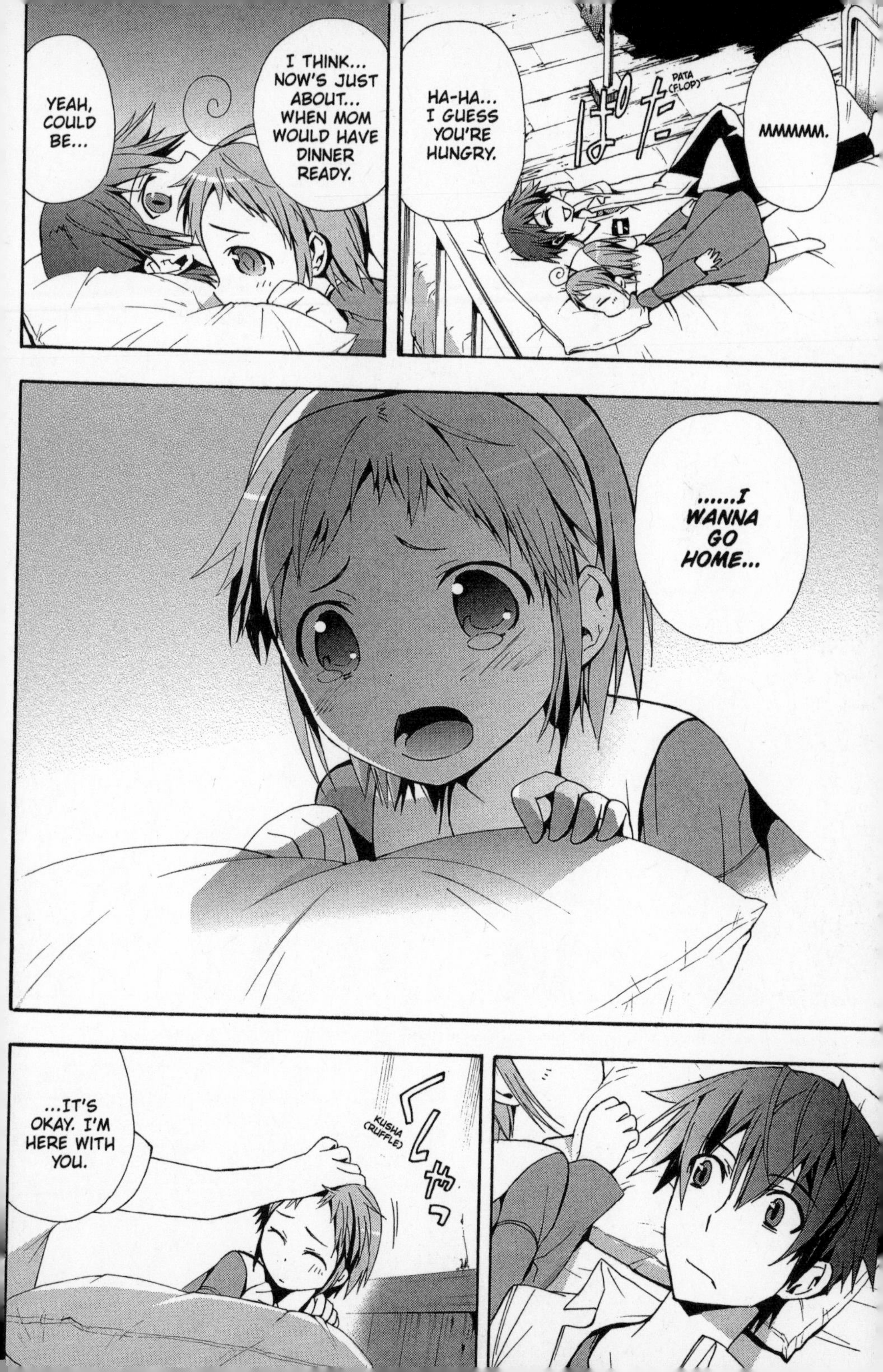
MMMMM.
ぱた
PATA (FLOP)
HA-HA... I GUESS YOU'RE HUNGRY.
I THINK... NOW'S JUST ABOUT... WHEN MOM WOULD HAVE DINNER READY.
YEAH, COULD BE...
......I WANNA GO HOME...
くしゃ
KUSHA (RUFFLE)
...IT'S OKAY. I'M HERE WITH YOU.

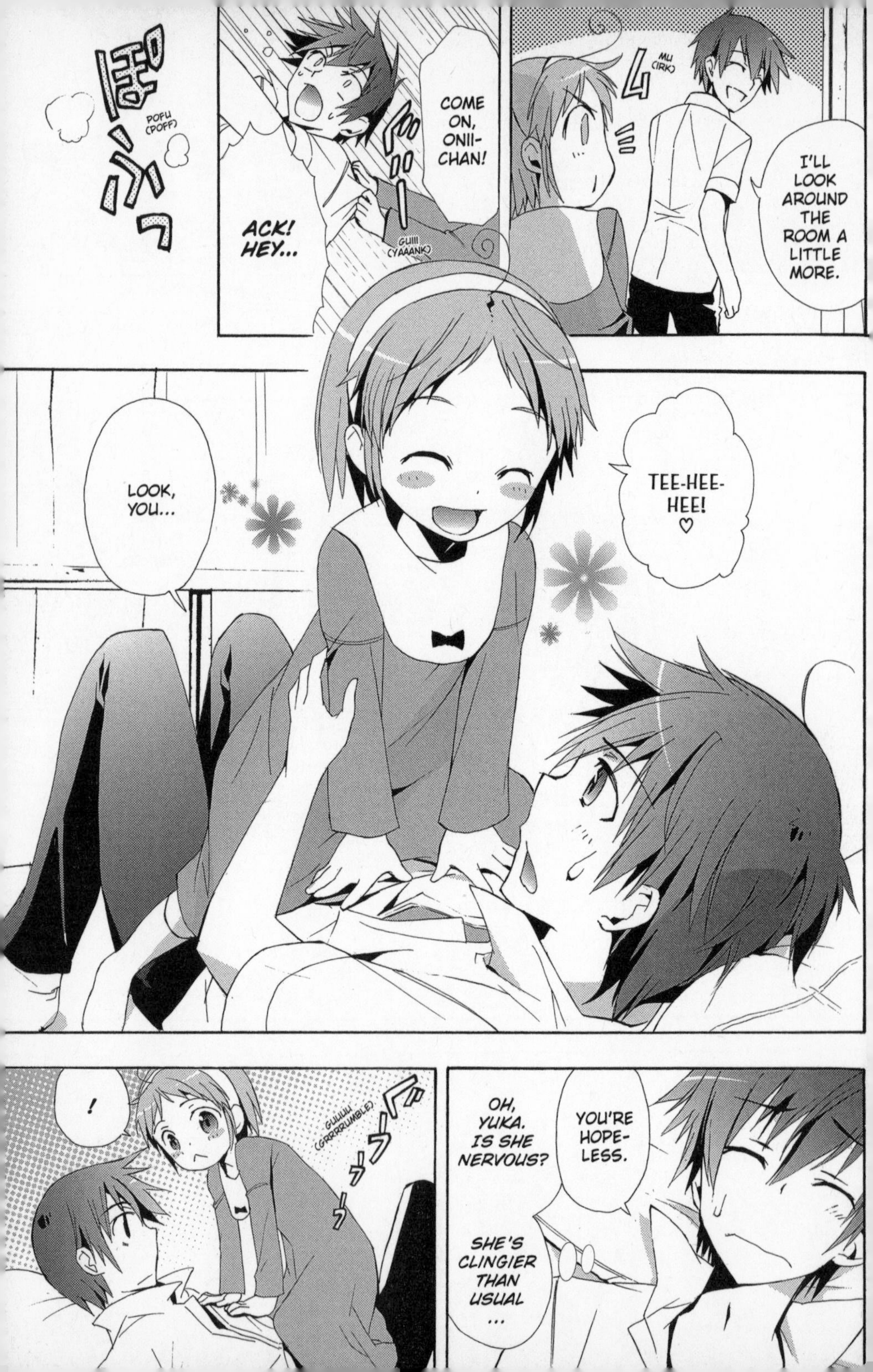
I'LL LOOK AROUND THE ROOM A LITTLE MORE.
MU (IRK)
COME ON, ONII-CHAN!
GUIII (YAAANK)
ACK! HEY...
POFU (POFF)
TEE-HEE-HEE! ♡
LOOK, YOU...
YOU'RE HOPE-LESS.
OH, YUKA. IS SHE NERVOUS?
SHE'S CLINGIER THAN USUAL ...
!
GUUUU (GRRRRUMBLE)

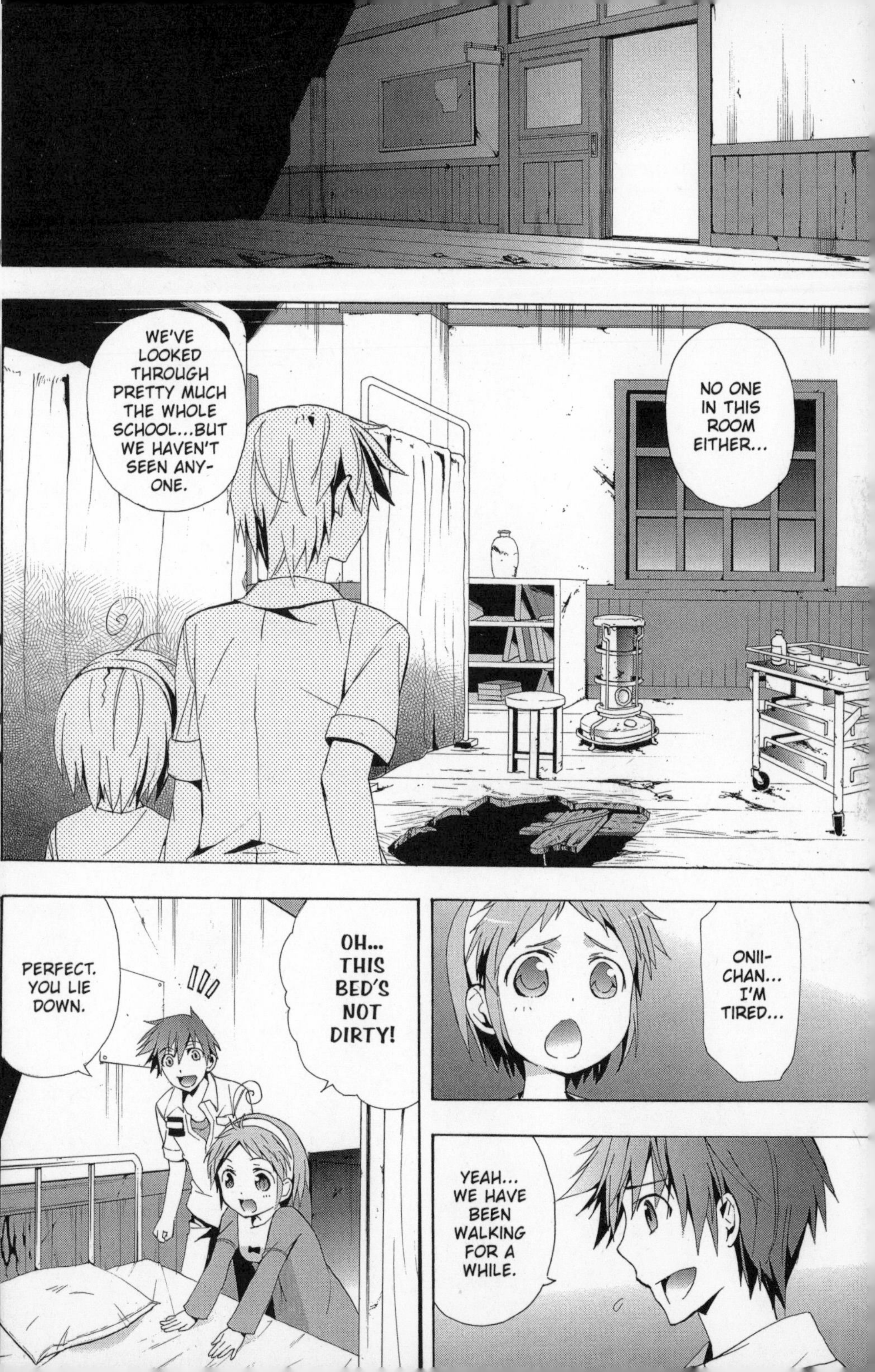
NO ONE IN THIS ROOM EITHER...
WE'VE LOOKED THROUGH PRETTY MUCH THE WHOLE SCHOOL...BUT WE HAVEN'T SEEN ANY-ONE.
ONII-CHAN... I'M TIRED...
YEAH... WE HAVE BEEN WALKING FOR A WHILE.
OH... THIS BED'S NOT DIRTY!
PERFECT. YOU LIE DOWN.

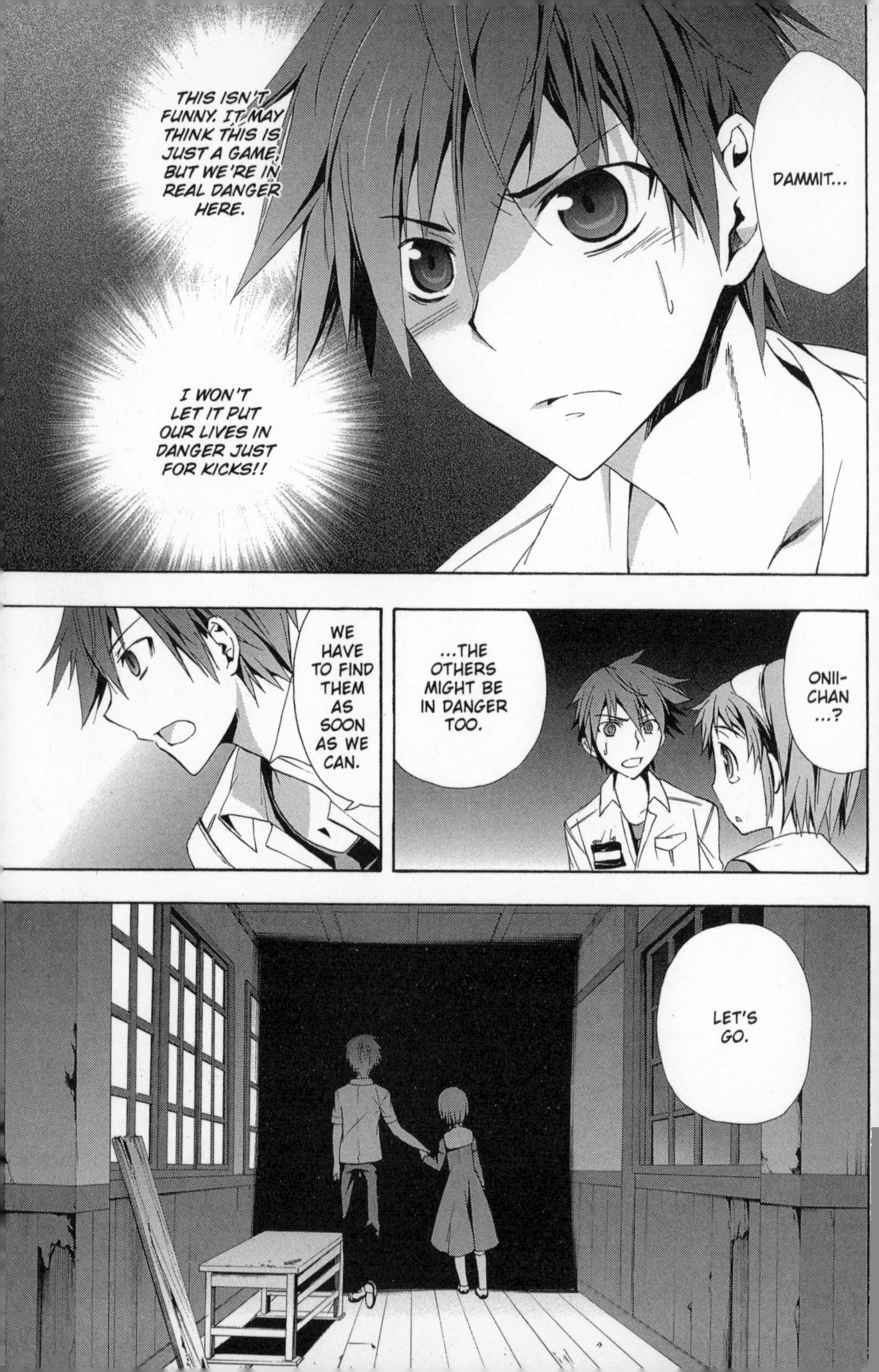
DAMMIT...
THIS ISN'T FUNNY. IT MAY THINK THIS IS JUST A GAME, BUT WE'RE IN REAL DANGER HERE.
I WON'T LET IT PUT OUR LIVES IN DANGER JUST FOR KICKS!!
ONII-CHAN ...?
...THE OTHERS MIGHT BE IN DANGER TOO.
WE HAVE TO FIND THEM AS SOON AS WE CAN.
LET'S GO.

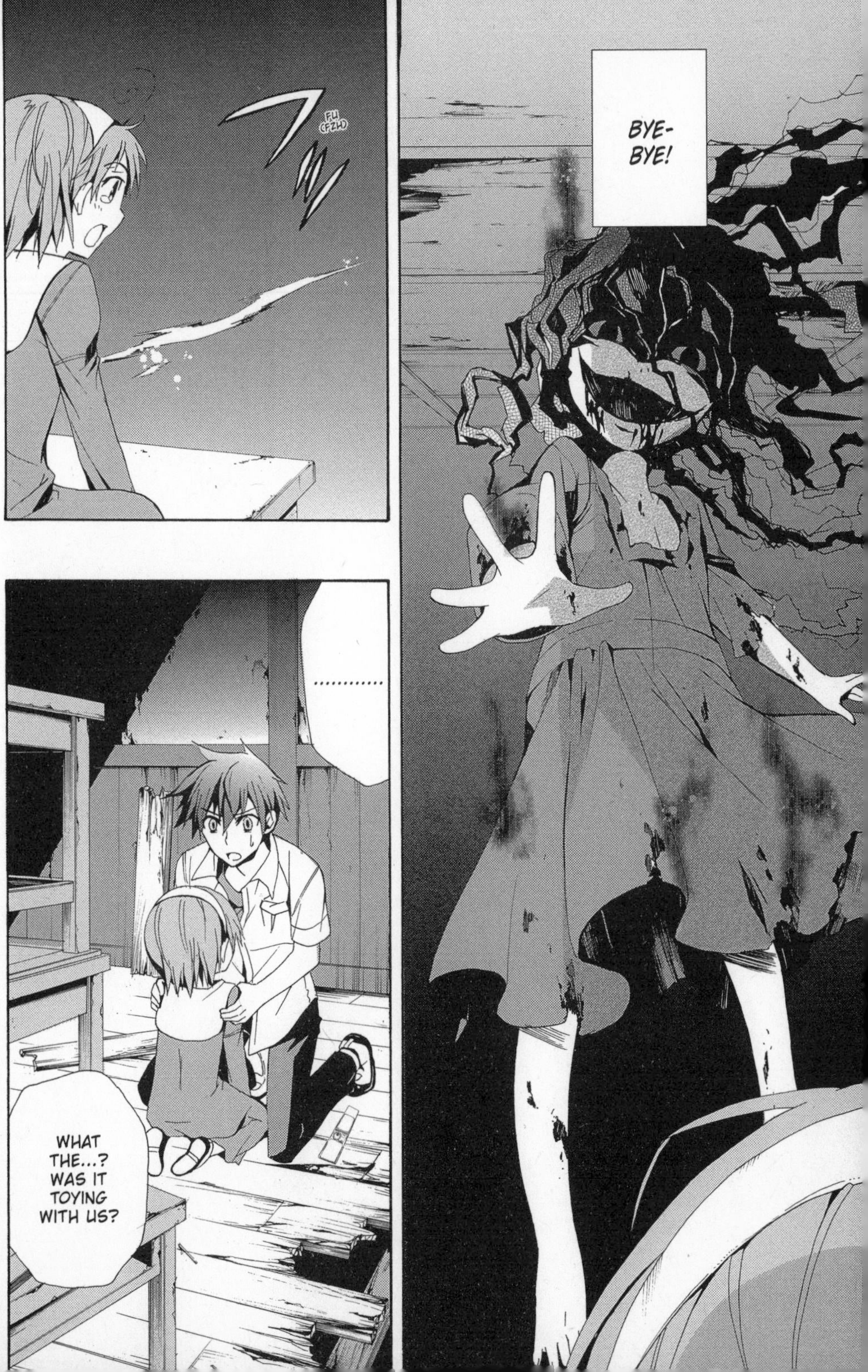
BYE-BYE!
FU (FZH)
....
WHAT THE...? WAS IT TOYING WITH US?

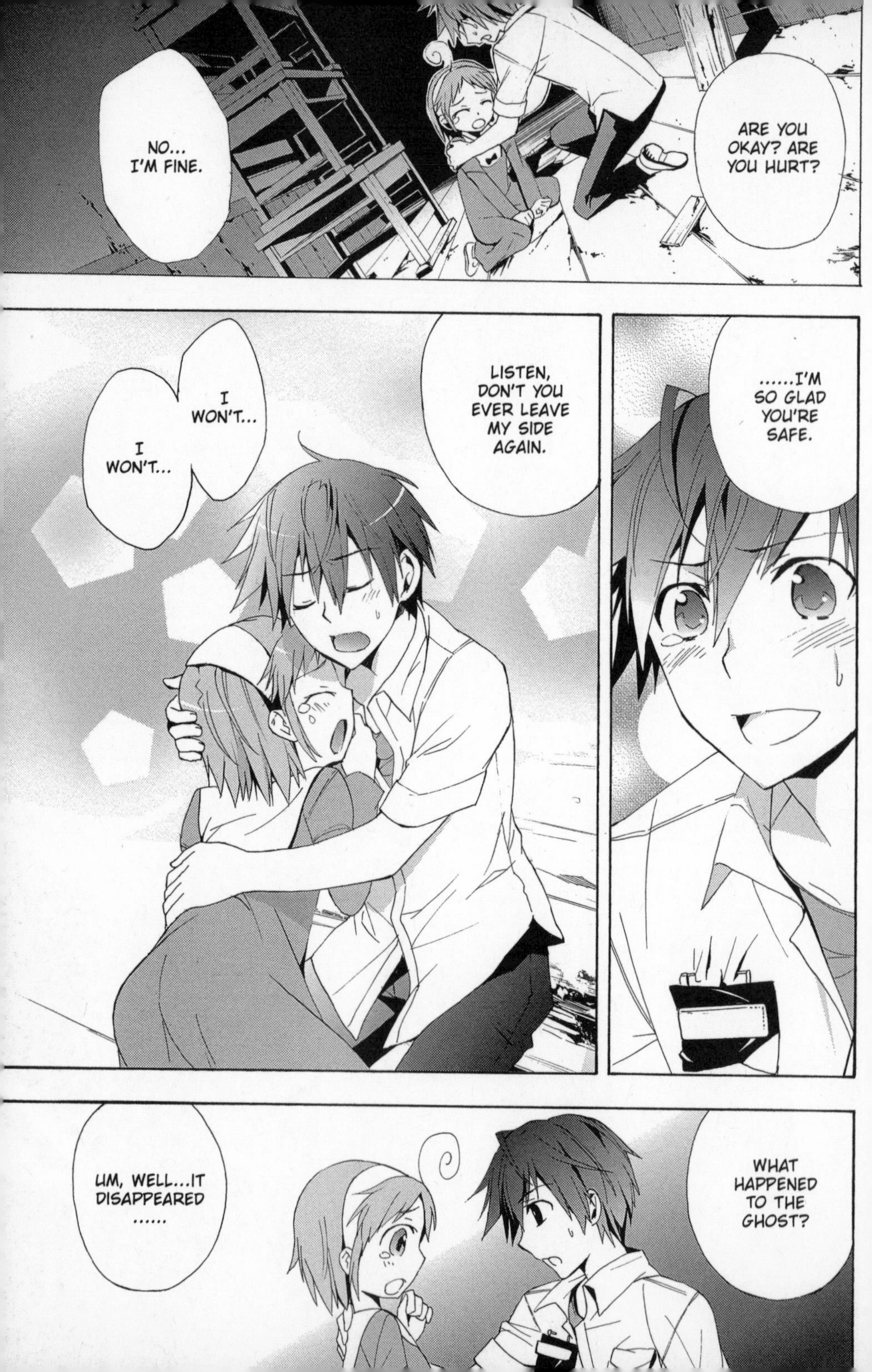
ARE YOU OKAY? ARE YOU HURT?
NO... I'M FINE.
......I'M SO GLAD YOU'RE SAFE.
LISTEN, DON'T YOU EVER LEAVE MY SIDE AGAIN.
I WON'T... I WON'T...
WHAT HAPPENED TO THE GHOST?
UM, WELL...IT DISAPPEARED ......

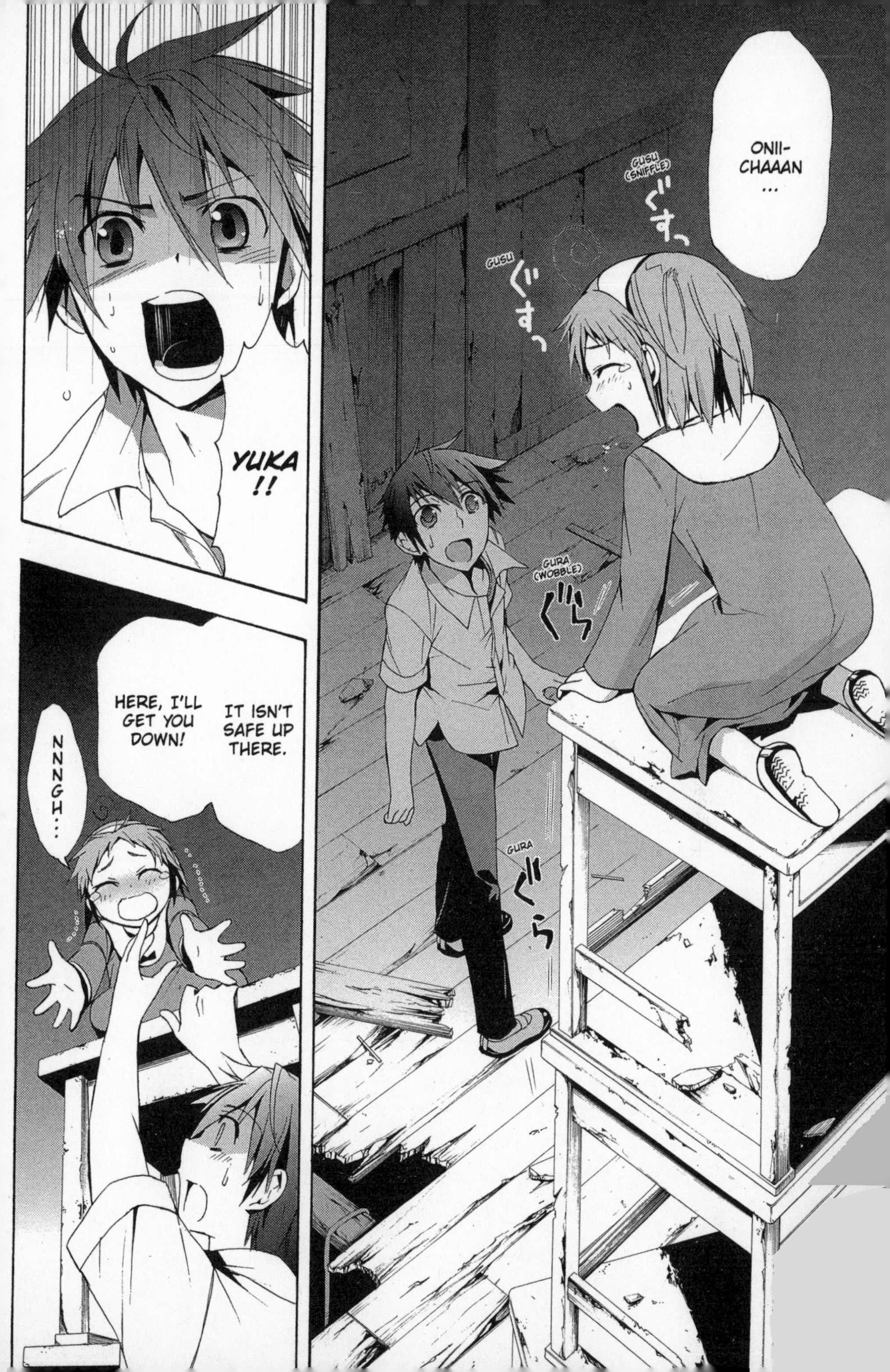
ONII-CHAAAN ...
GUSU (SNIFFLE)
ぐすっ
GUSU
ぐすっ
GURA (WOBBLE)
ぐら
GURA
ぐら
YUKA !!
IT ISN'T SAFE UP THERE.
HERE, I'LL GET YOU DOWN!
NNNGH...

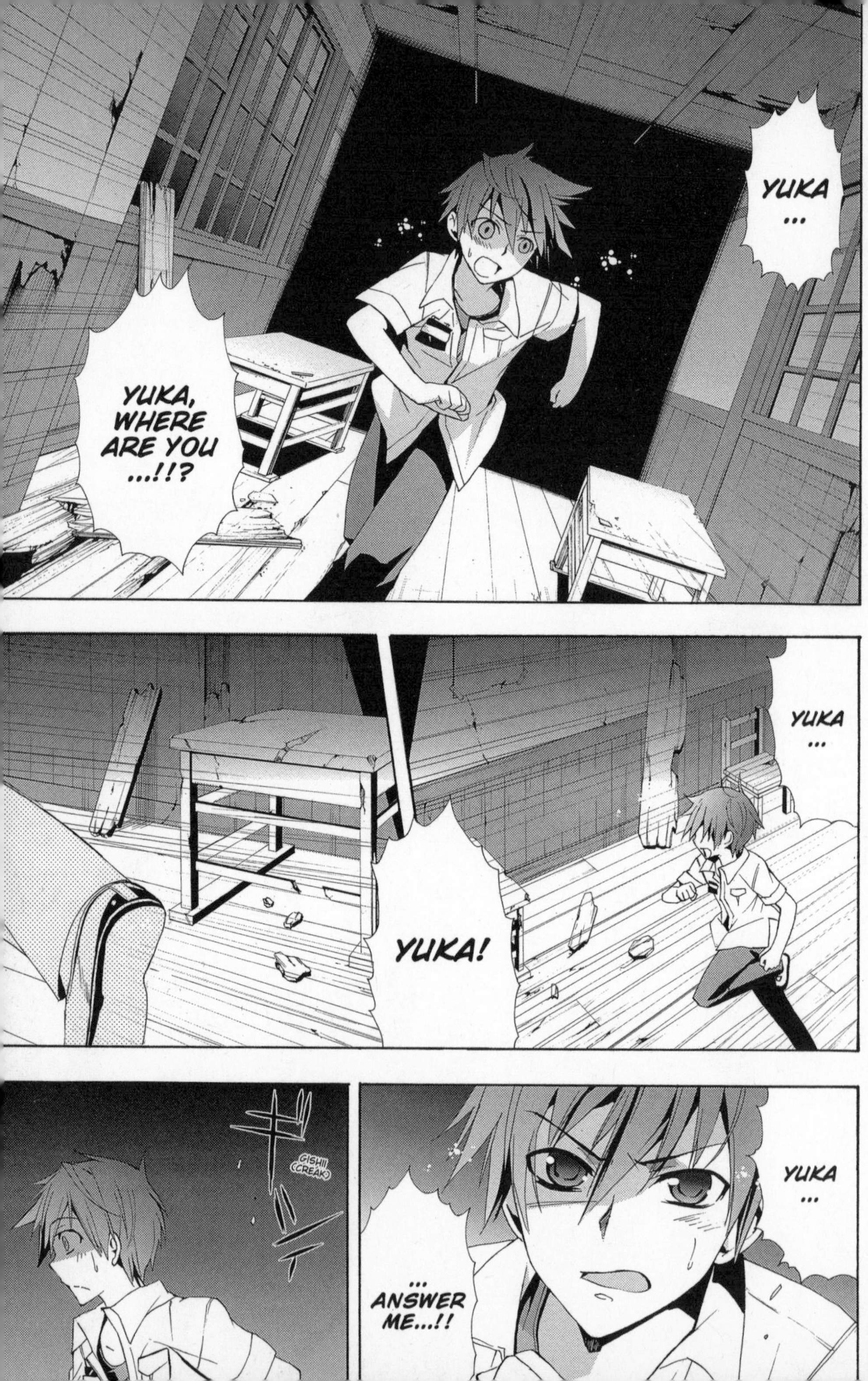
YUKA ...
YUKA, WHERE ARE YOU ...!!?
YUKA ...
YUKA!
YUKA ...
... ANSWER ME...!!
GISHII (CREAK)

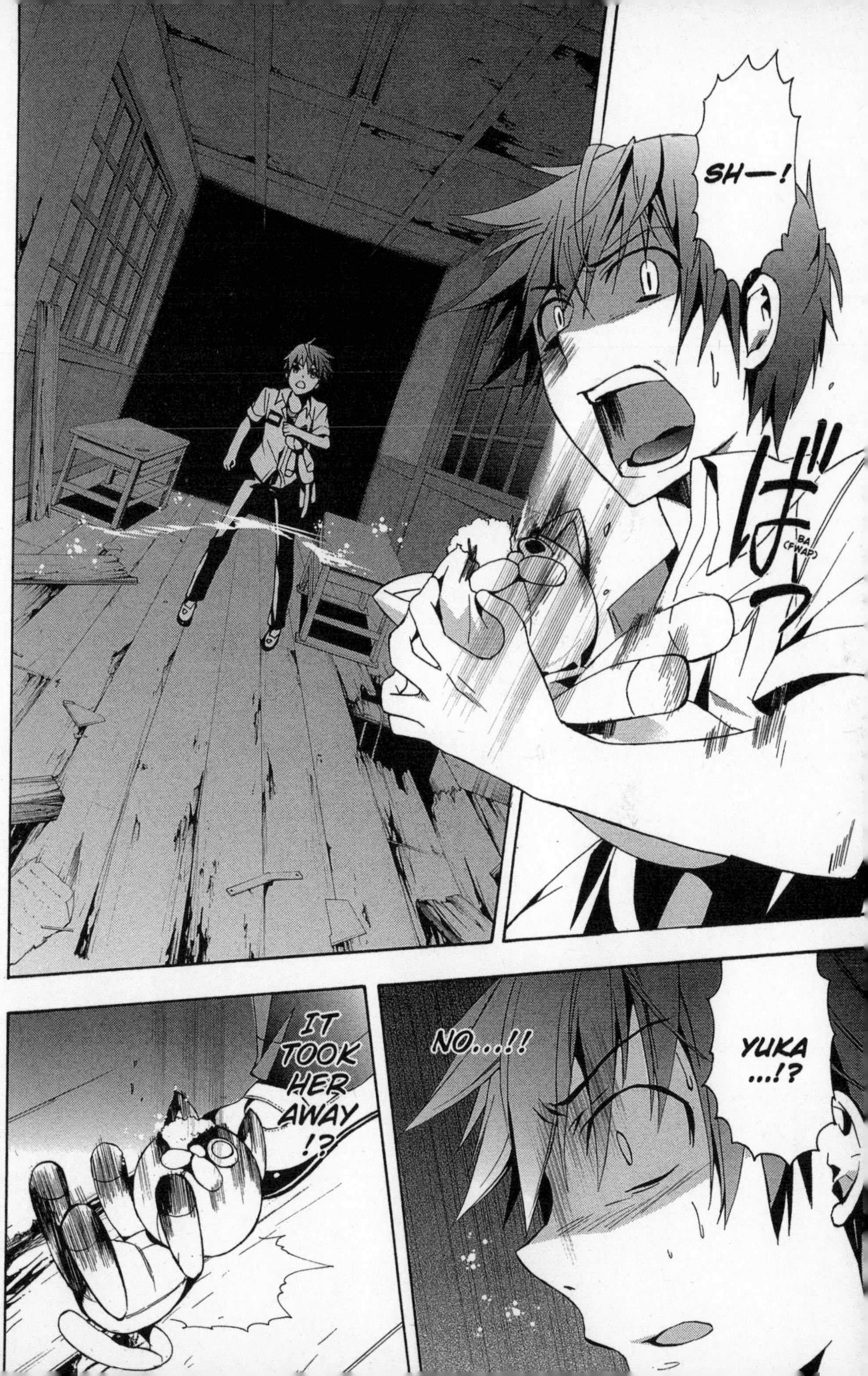
SH—!
ばっ
BA (FWAP)
YUKA ...!?
NO...!!
IT TOOK HER AWAY !?

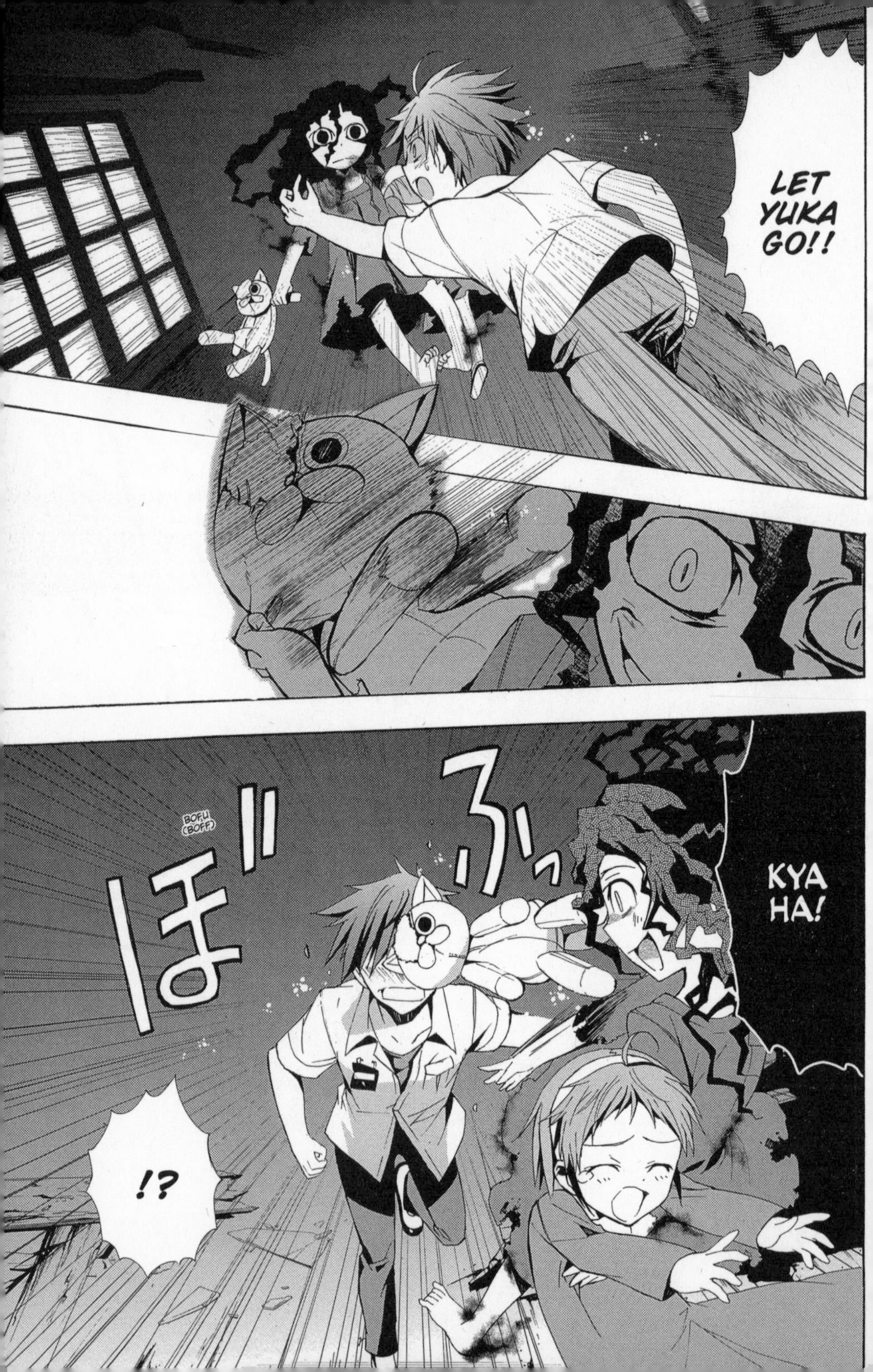
LET YUKA GO!!
KYA HA!
ふっ
BOFU (BOFF)
ぼ
!?

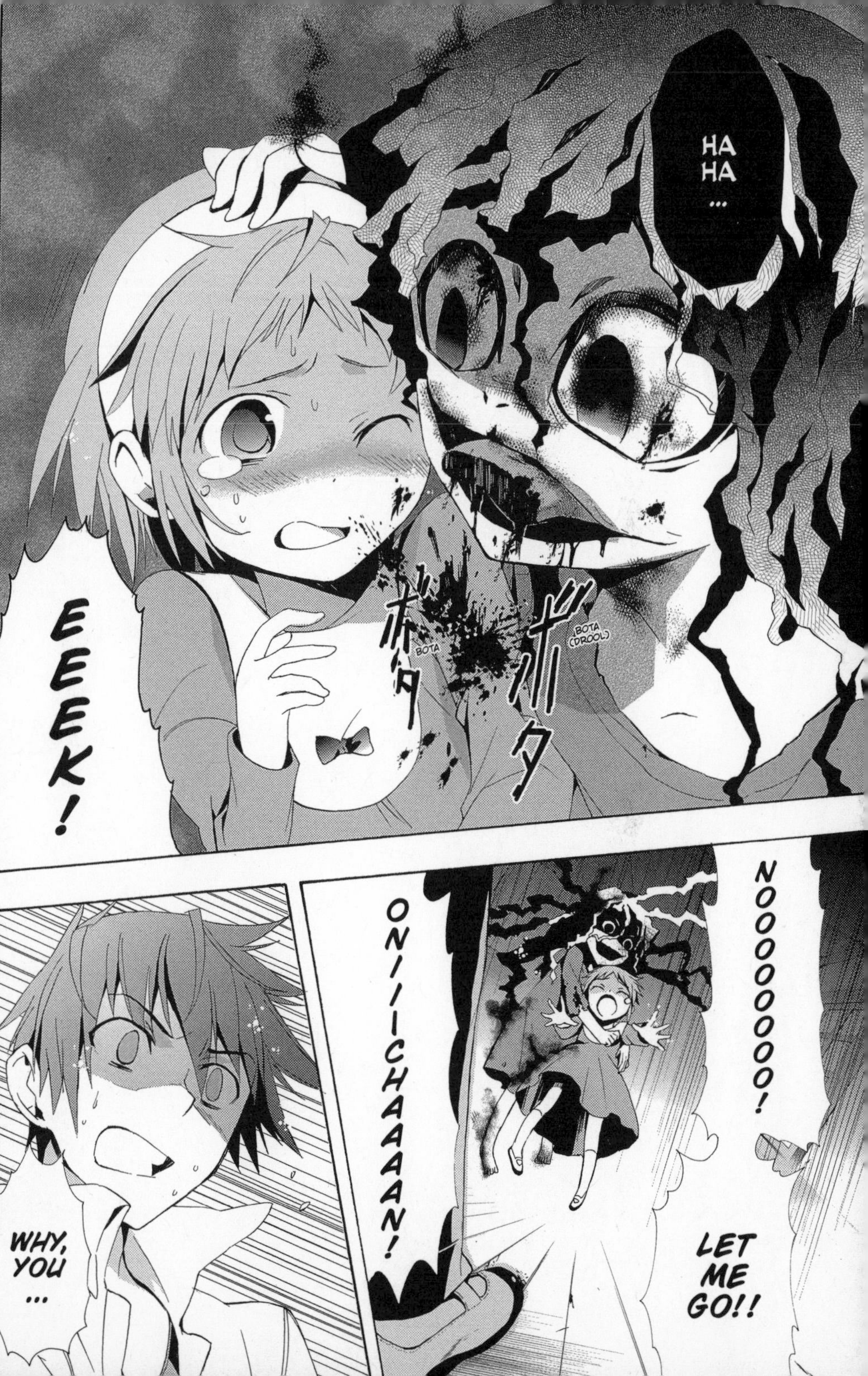
HA HA ...
BOTA (DROOL)
BOTA
EEEK!
NOOOOOOOOO!
ONIIICHAAAAN!
LET ME GO!!
WHY, YOU ...

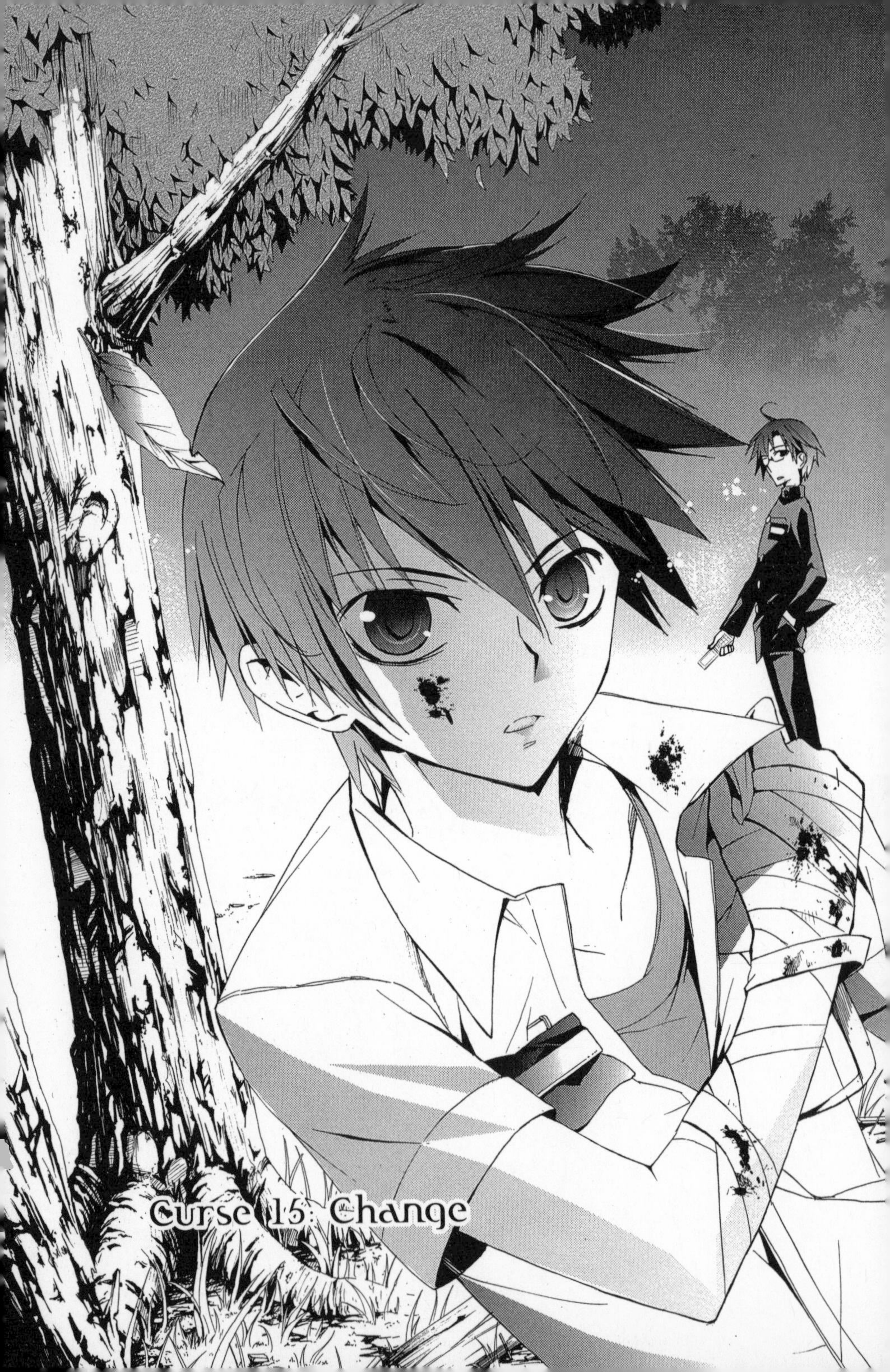
Curse 15: Change

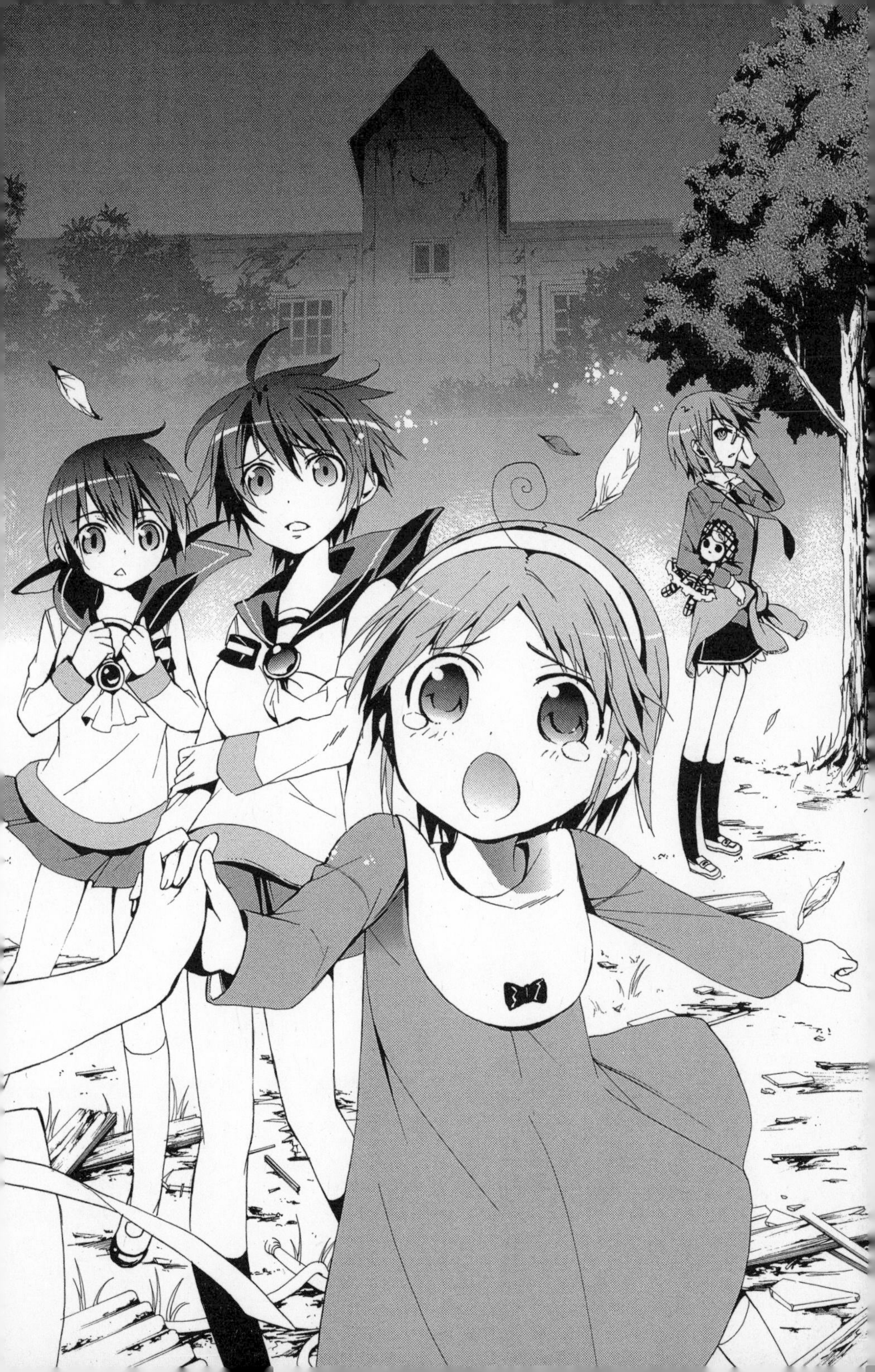

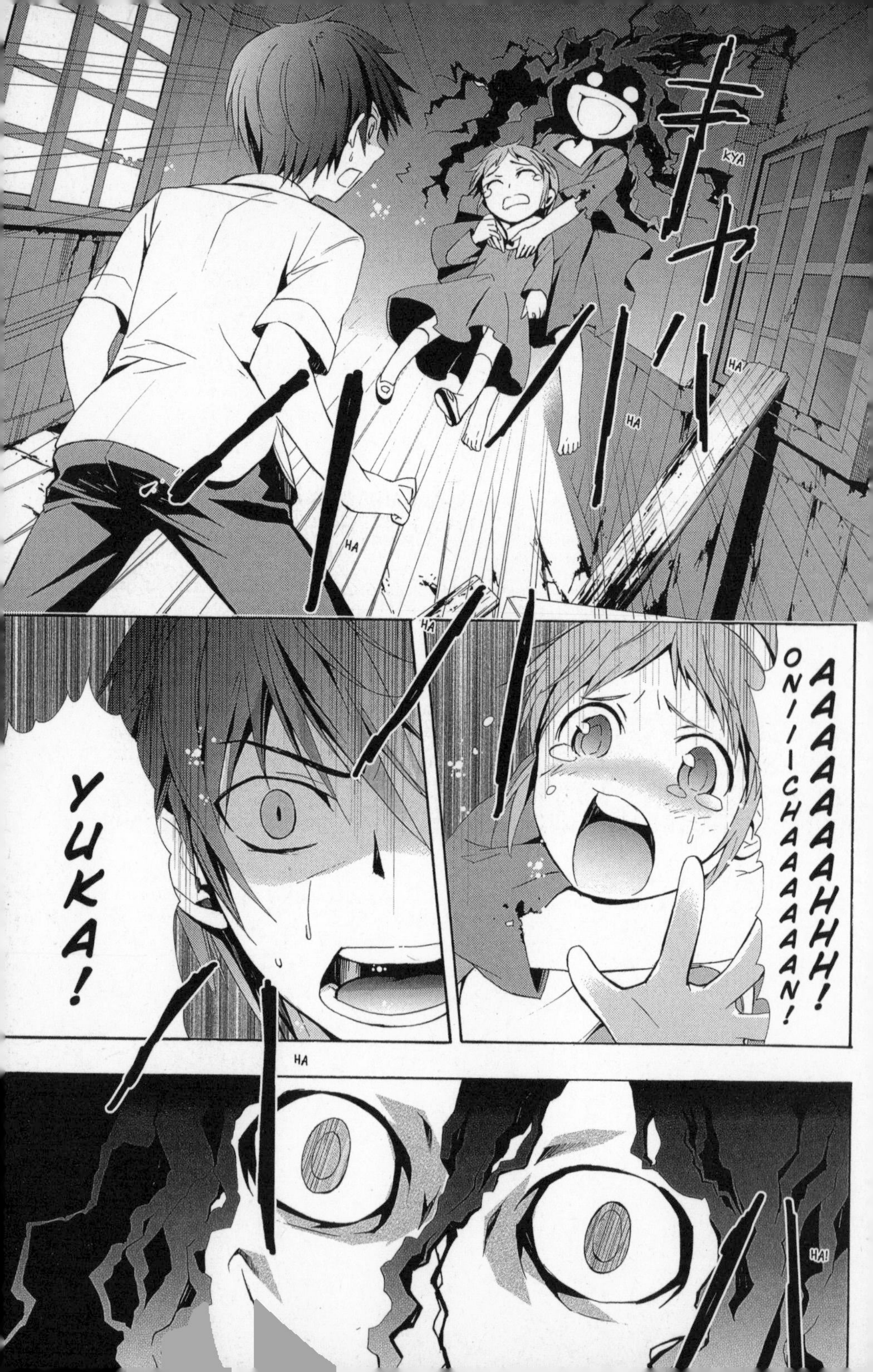
キャハハハ
KYA
HA
HA
HA
HA
AAAAAAAAHHH!
ONIIIICHAAAAAAAN!
YUKA!
HA
HA!

CORPSE PARTY
Blood Covered

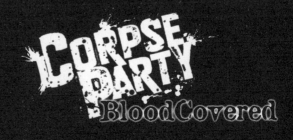

AFTERWORD

DU-DUN! KEDOUIN HERE. IT'S BEEN A LONG TIME, HASN'T IT, EVERYONE? SHINOMIYA-SENSEI, CONGRATULATIONS ON RELEASING VOLUME 3 OF THE MANGA VERSION!

THE THIRD INSTALLMENT OF OUR SADISTIC PRISON TALE FEATURES POOR LITTLE YOSHIKI-KUN AND ADORABLE AYUMI-CHAN ON THEIR TORTURE TOUR DATE.

PEOPLE CHANGE IN TEN-PLUS YEARS, AND WHEN I COMPARE THIS TO MY PREVIOUS WORK, THESE TWO LOOK ESPECIALLY MORE REFINED. WITH THE HELP OF MANY WONDERFUL ILLUSTRATIONS, STARTING WITH SHINOMIYA-SENSEI'S MANGA AND INCLUDING THE BEAUTIFUL ART POSTED BY MANY PEOPLE ON THE INTERNET, REBORN YOSHIKI AND REBORN AYUMI CONTINUE TO EVOLVE DAY BY DAY.

AYUMI, WHO LOVES ANIME, MANGA, AND LIGHT NOVELS, AND WHO IS ADDICTED TO CELL PHONE GAMES, DRAWING, AND BLOGS, WILL NEVER GIVE UP HER RULE THAT GLASSES ARE A FASHIONABLE ITEM, AND YOSHIKI, WHO PURSUES HIS OWN DREAM TO THE POINT OF CLASHING WITH HIS PARENTS, GETS DISINHERITED AND GOES OFF TO LIVE ON HIS OWN.

I THINK I WAS PROBABLY MORE SURPRISED THAN ANYONE TO SEE THAT THEY WERE SUCH GREAT KIDS! I HOPE YOU WILL CONTINUE TO LOVE THEM LONG INTO THE FUTURE.

MAKOTO KEDOUIN

CORPSEPARTY BloodCovered,

...HAS STARTED AN ACCOUNT ON THE PIXIV ONLINE ART COMMUNITY.

KEYWORDS: CORPSE BR ON PSP

HOME   WORKS   BOOKM

AYUMI SHINOZAKI VIEW PROFILE

SUBMITTED ILLUSTRATIONS

FRIENDS

LATE AYUM CHA ...

SO YOU'RE DRAWING PICTURES OF YOUR FRIENDS FROM SCHOOL?

YES!!

I DRAW **ONLY** MY FRIENDS.

ONLY YOUR FRIENDS...?

YOU HEARD HER...

HUH?

WHO ARE YOU?

GOOD LUCK.

MANGA: ALBA

Character pickup

Yuka Mochida

Born October 2, blood
type A, 140cm, 34.2kg
(4'7", 75.4lbs)

Likes: Konpeito confetti
candy, peach water
Dislikes: Raisins
Hobbies: Collecting scented
beads
Dream Career: Bride

Satoshi Mochida

Born July 4, blood
type O, 168cm, 54.2kg
(5'6", 119.5lbs)

Likes: School
Dislikes: The dark, stairs,
small places
Hobbies: Collecting CDs
Dream Career: Still looking

HELLO, EVERYONE. I AM THE ARTIST, SHINOMIYA.
NOW PRESENTING *CORPSE PARTY: BLOOD COVERED* VOLUME 3!
IN VOLUME 3, WE MEET MORE CHARACTERS WHO AREN'T FROM KISARAGI
ACADEMY, AND THE HUMAN DRAMA OF TENJIN ELEMENTARY SCHOOL
BECOMES SOMETHING TO LOOK FORWARD TO!
I HOPE YOU ENJOY IT. WHO EXACTLY IS THIS SUSPICIOUS NAHO PERSON?
AS THE ARTIST, I CAN'T WAIT TO DRAW THAT TOO!
I ALSO LOOK FORWARD TO THE CONTINUATION OF THE ORIGINAL GAME.
THANK YOU VERY MUCH FOR READING.
SEE YOU AGAIN IN VOLUME 4!

TOSHIMI SHINOMIYA

SPECIAL THANKS
M KOKKO-SAN, SHIN ARAKAWA-SAN, TAKATOSHI OGURA-SAN,
MASAKI KAWANO-SAN, TOMOHIRO IKAWA-SAN,
AND EVERYONE FROM TEAM GRISGRIS, MAKOTO KEDOUIN-SAN,
MY EDITORS, AKIYAMA-SAN AND KAWANO-SAN.

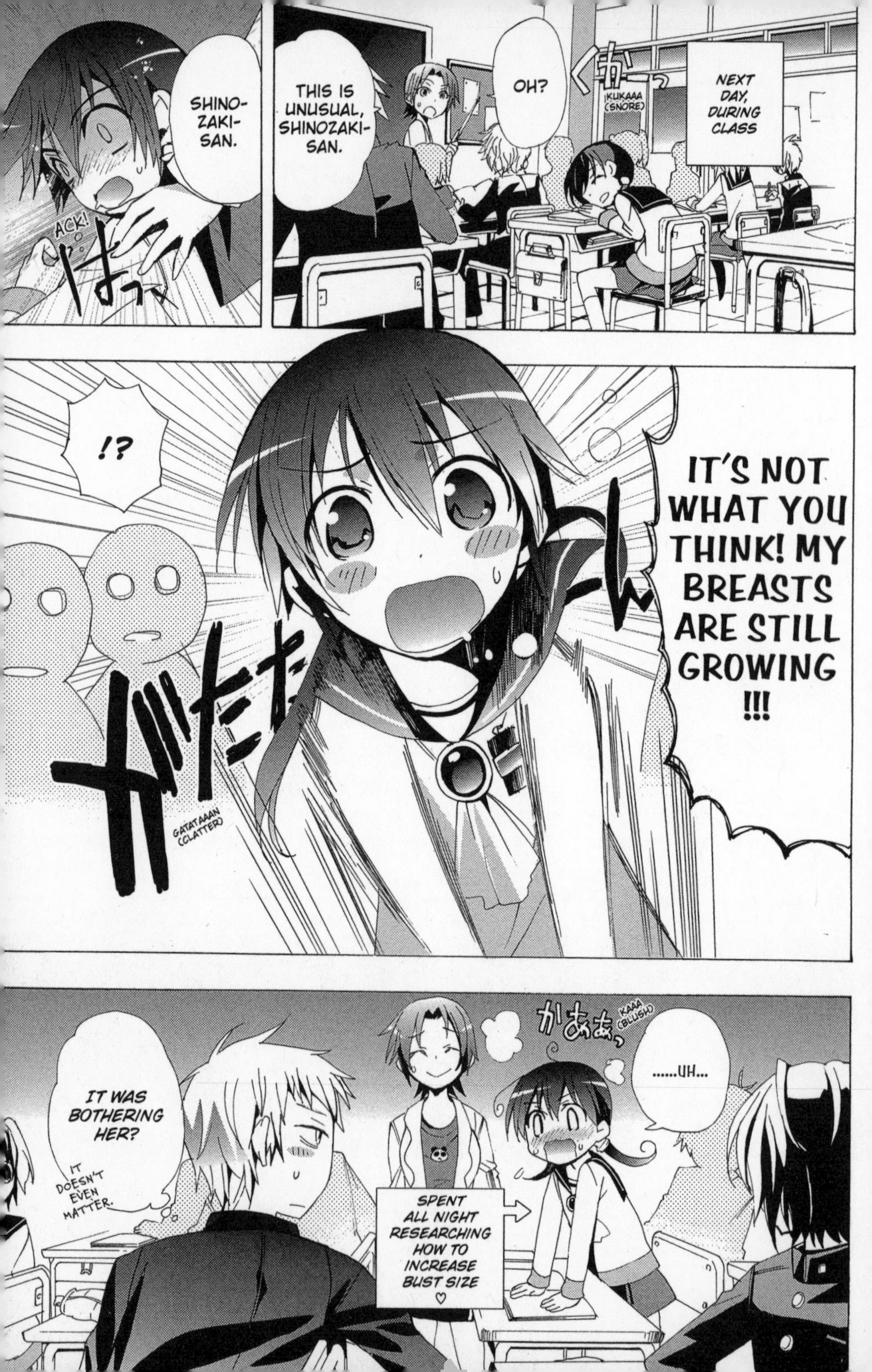
NEXT DAY, DURING CLASS
KUKAAA (SNORE)
OH?
THIS IS UNUSUAL, SHINOZAKI-SAN.
SHINO-ZAKI-SAN.
ACK!
IT'S NOT WHAT YOU THINK! MY BREASTS ARE STILL GROWING !!!
!?
GATATAAAN (CLATTER)
KAAA (BLUSH)
......UH...
SPENT ALL NIGHT RESEARCHING HOW TO INCREASE BUST SIZE ♡
IT WAS BOTHERING HER?
IT DOESN'T EVEN MATTER.

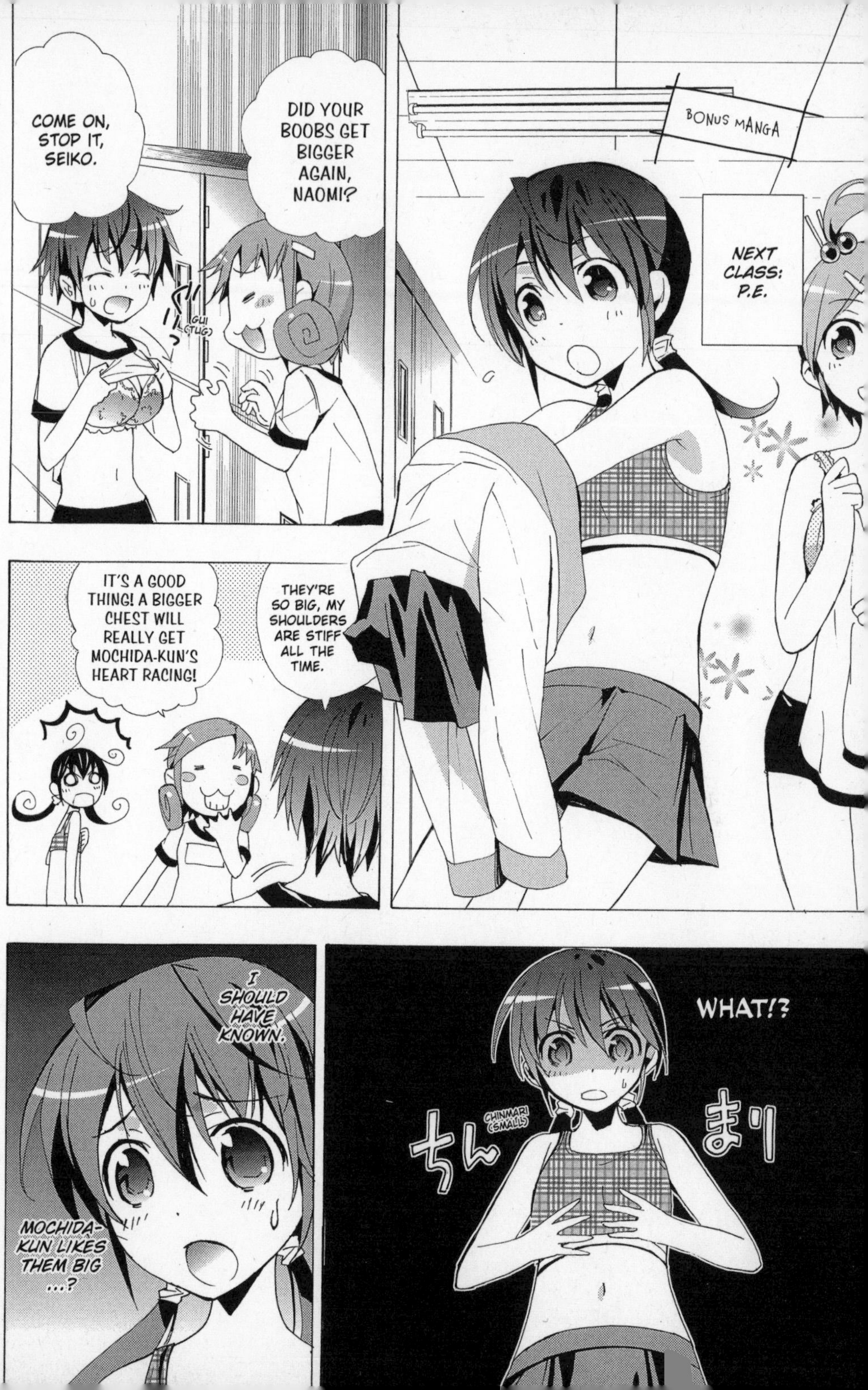

BONUS MANGA
NEXT CLASS: P.E.
DID YOUR BOOBS GET BIGGER AGAIN, NAOMI?
GUI (TUG)
COME ON, STOP IT, SEIKO.
THEY'RE SO BIG, MY SHOULDERS ARE STIFF ALL THE TIME.
IT'S A GOOD THING! A BIGGER CHEST WILL REALLY GET MOCHIDA-KUN'S HEART RACING!
WHAT!?
ちん まり
CHINMARI (SMALL)
I SHOULD HAVE KNOWN.
MOCHIDA-KUN LIKES THEM BIG ...?

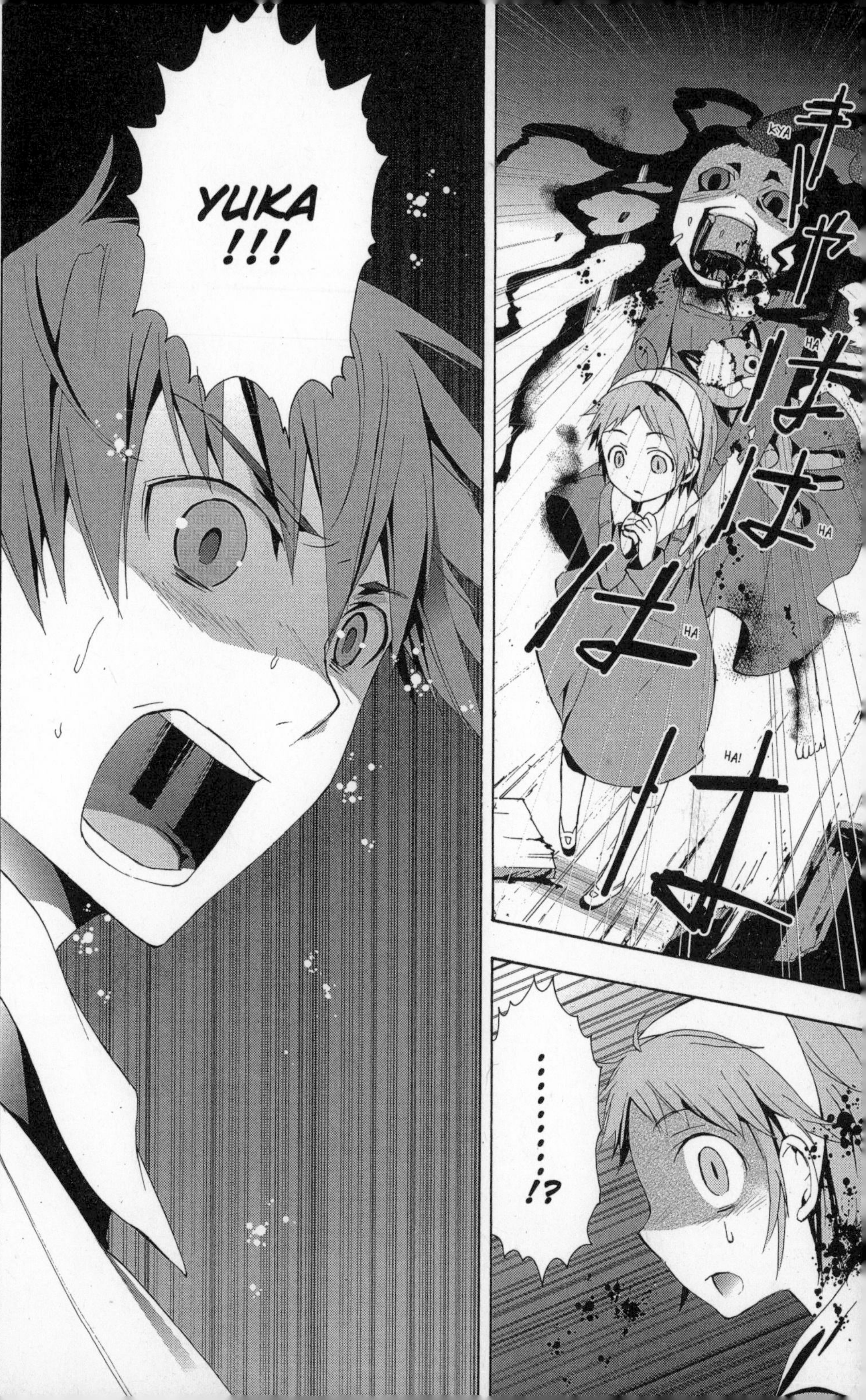
きゃははは
KYA
HA
HA
HA
HA!
......!?
YUKA
!!!

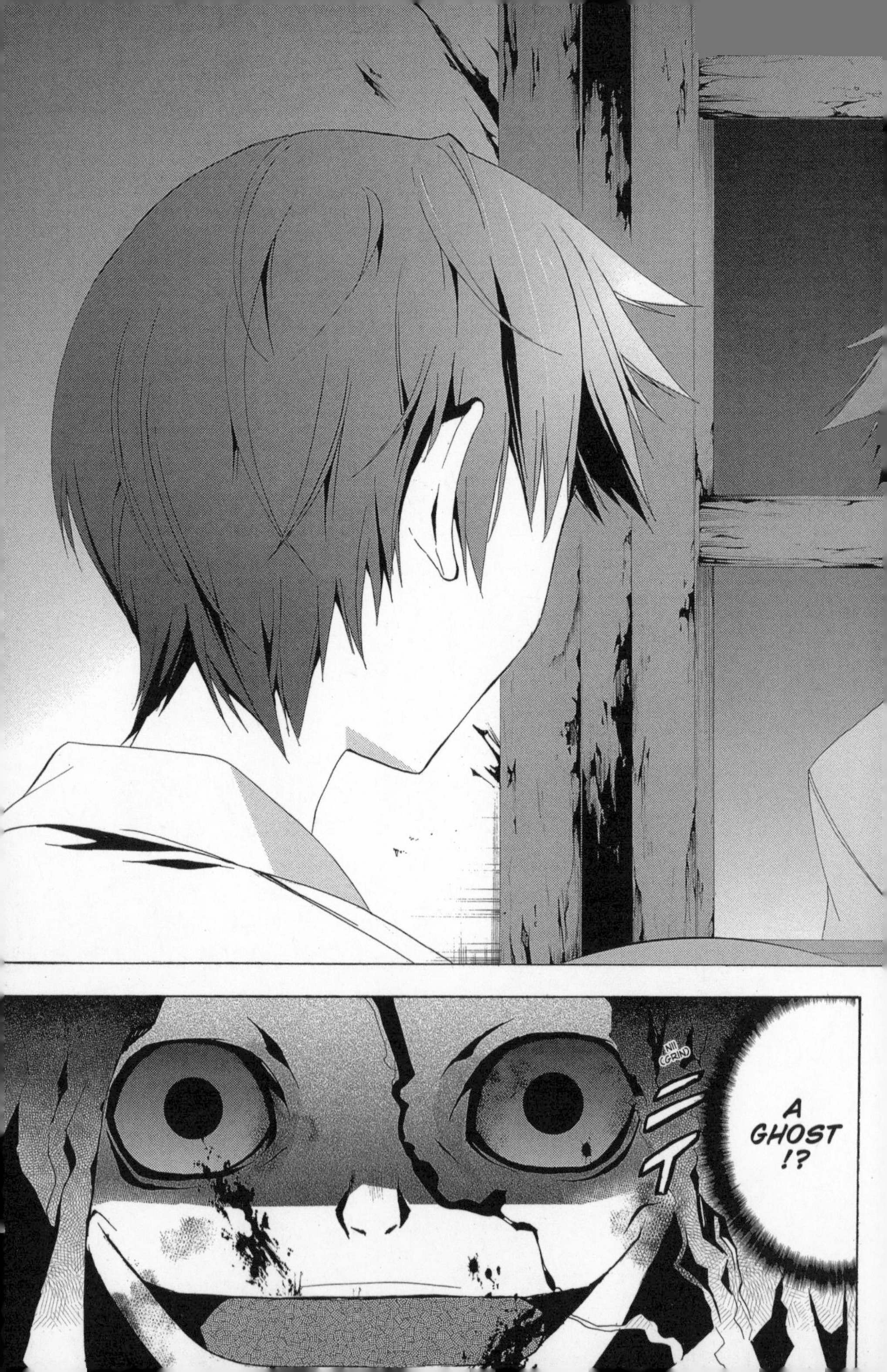
A GHOST !?
NII (GRIN)

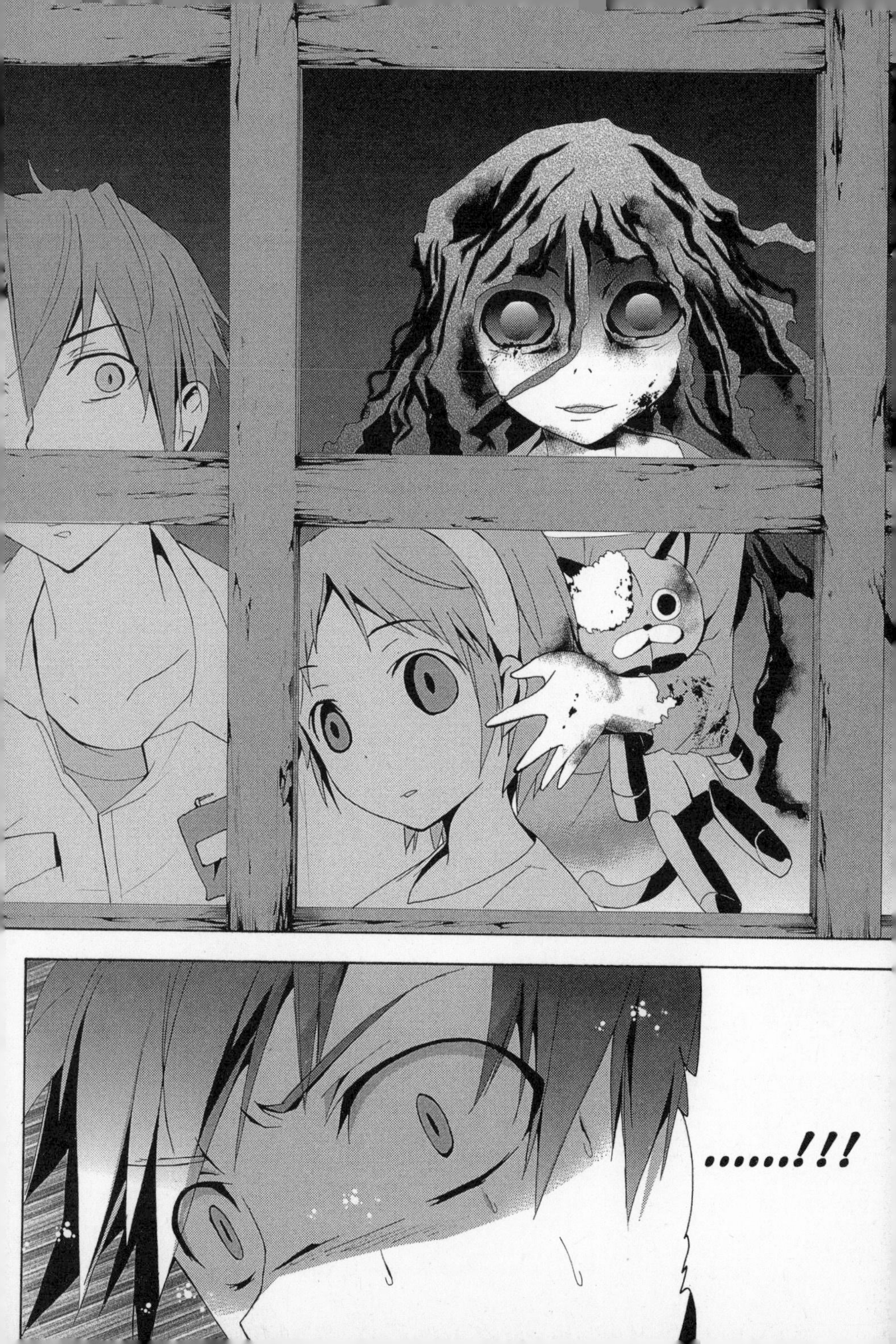
......!!!

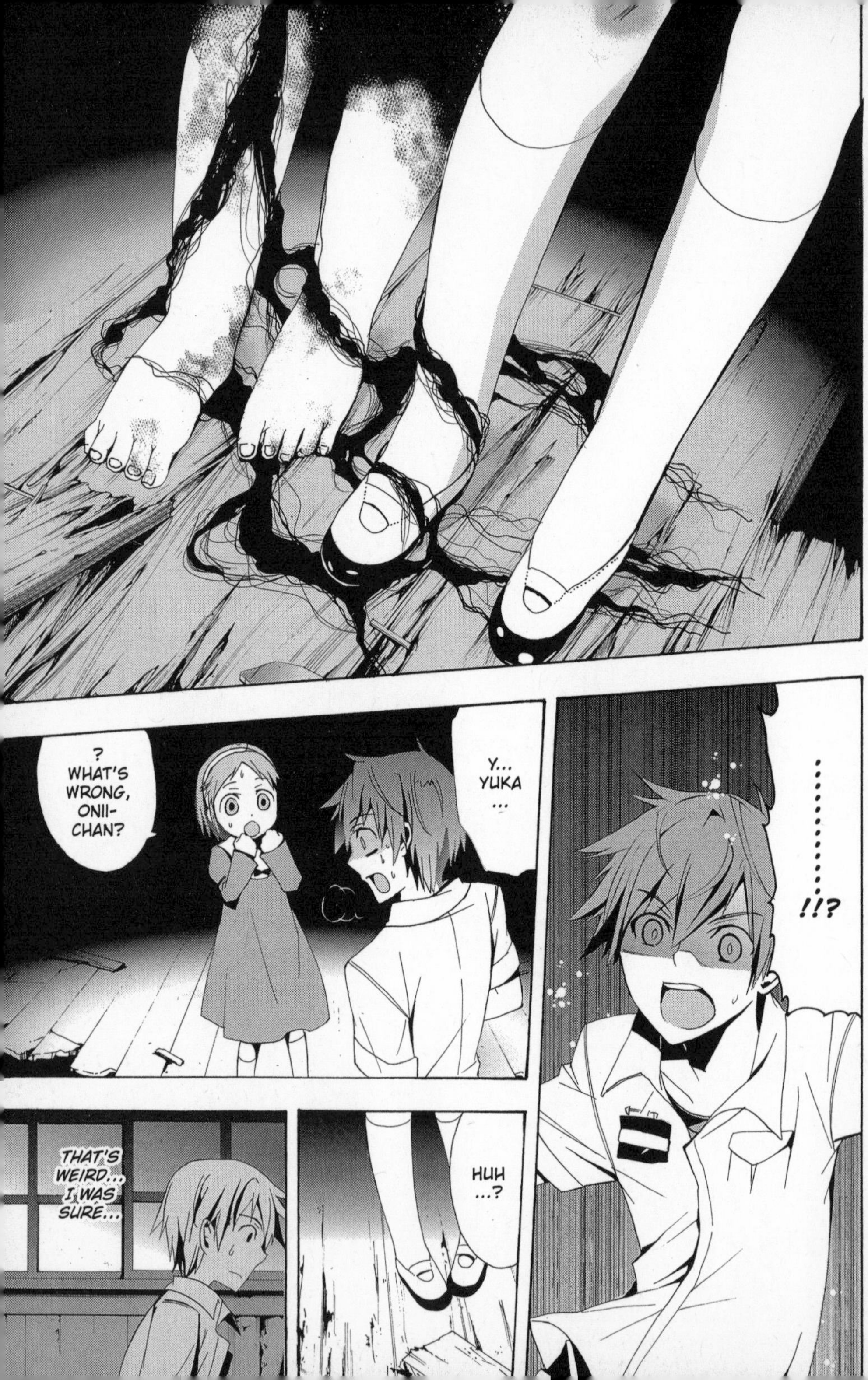
....
!!?
Y... YUKA ...
? WHAT'S WRONG, ONII-CHAN?
HUH ...?
THAT'S WEIRD... I WAS SURE...

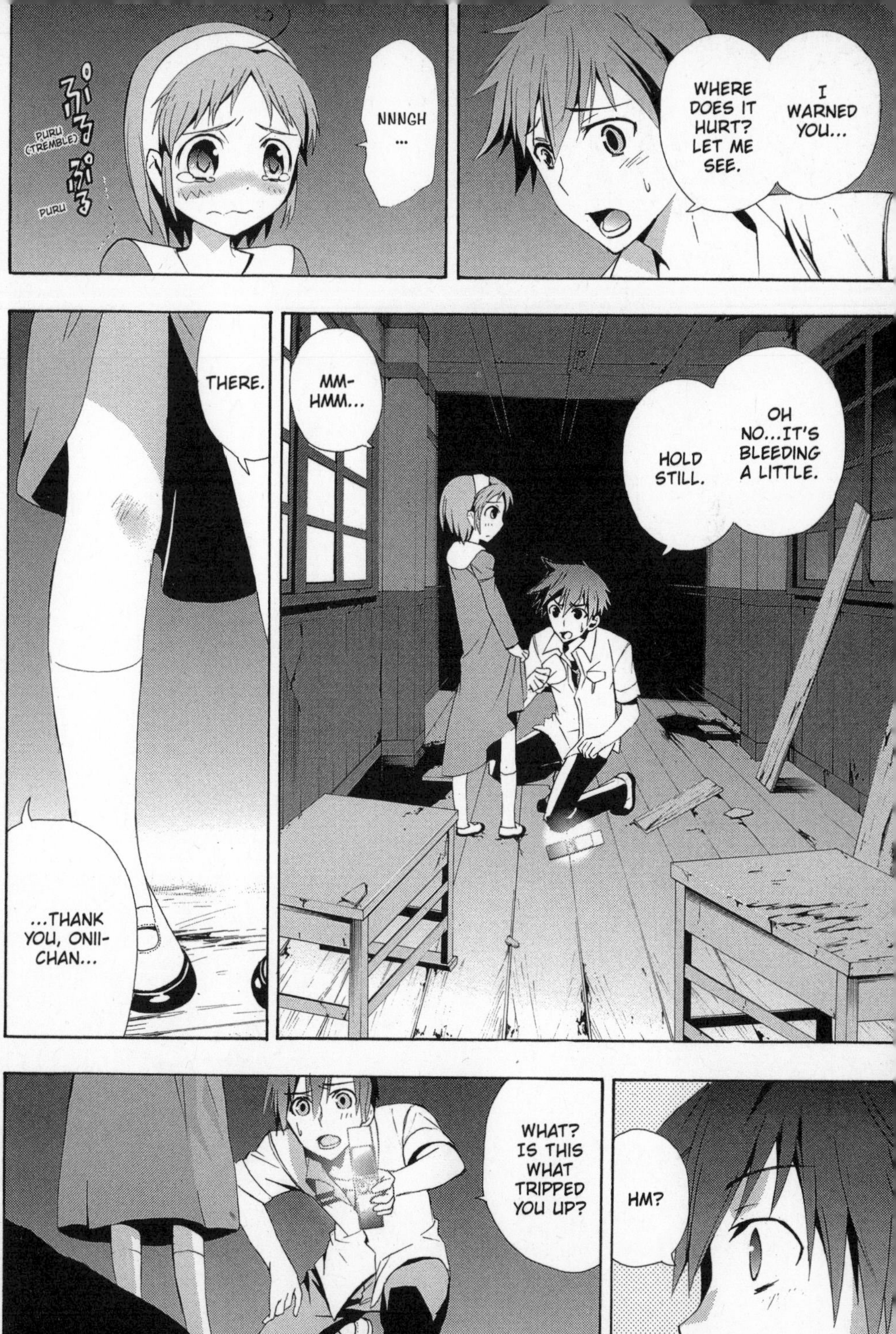
I WARNED YOU...
WHERE DOES IT HURT? LET ME SEE.
NNNGH ...
ぷるぷる
PURU (TREMBLE)
PURU
OH NO...IT'S BLEEDING A LITTLE.
HOLD STILL.
MM-HMM...
THERE.
...THANK YOU, ONII-CHAN...
HM?
WHAT? IS THIS WHAT TRIPPED YOU UP?

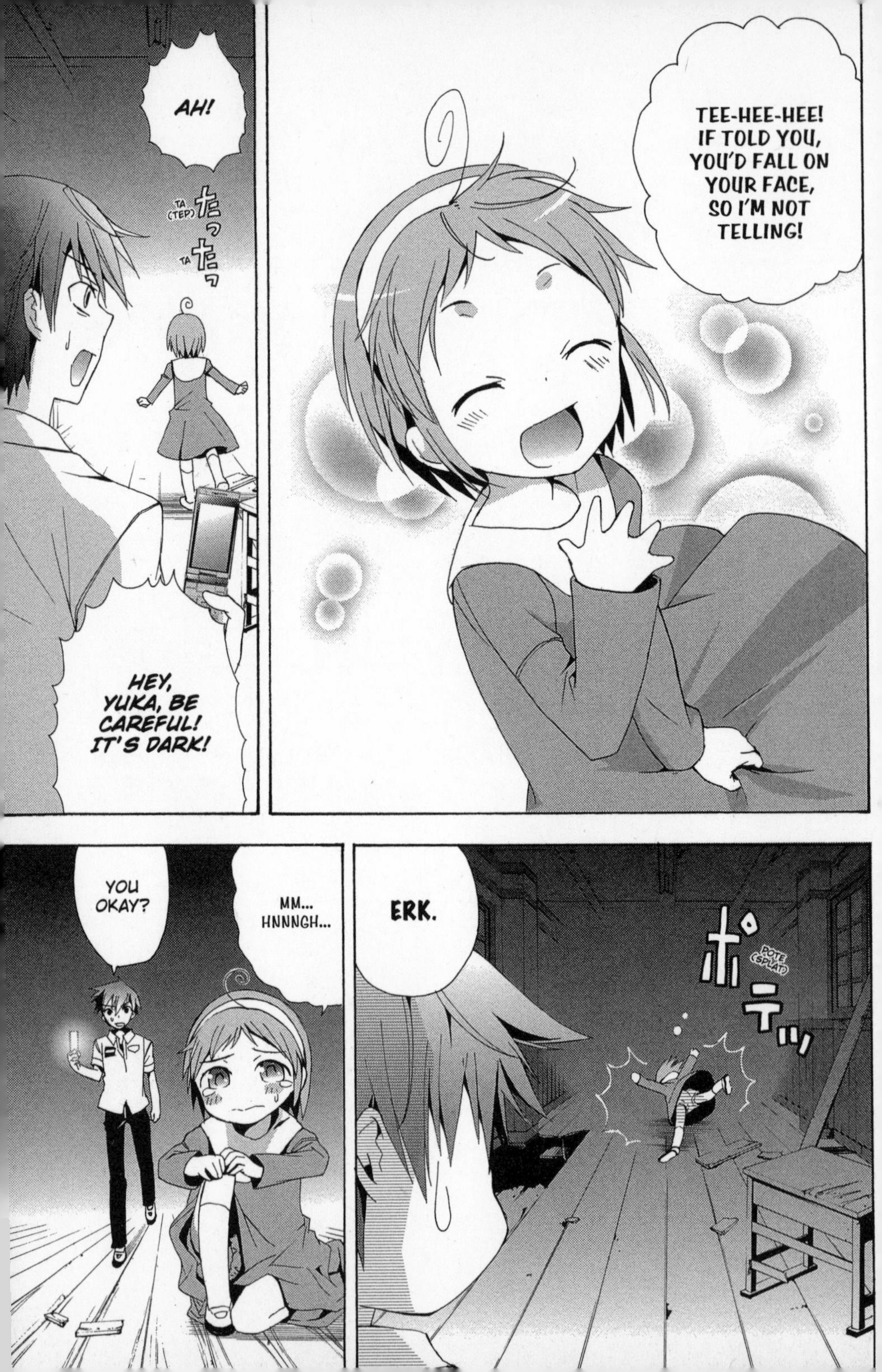
TEE-HEE-HEE! IF TOLD YOU, YOU'D FALL ON YOUR FACE, SO I'M NOT TELLING!
AH!
たっ TA (TEP)
たっ TA
HEY, YUKA, BE CAREFUL! IT'S DARK!
ERK.
ポテッ
POTE (SPLAT)
MM... HNNNGH...
YOU OKAY?

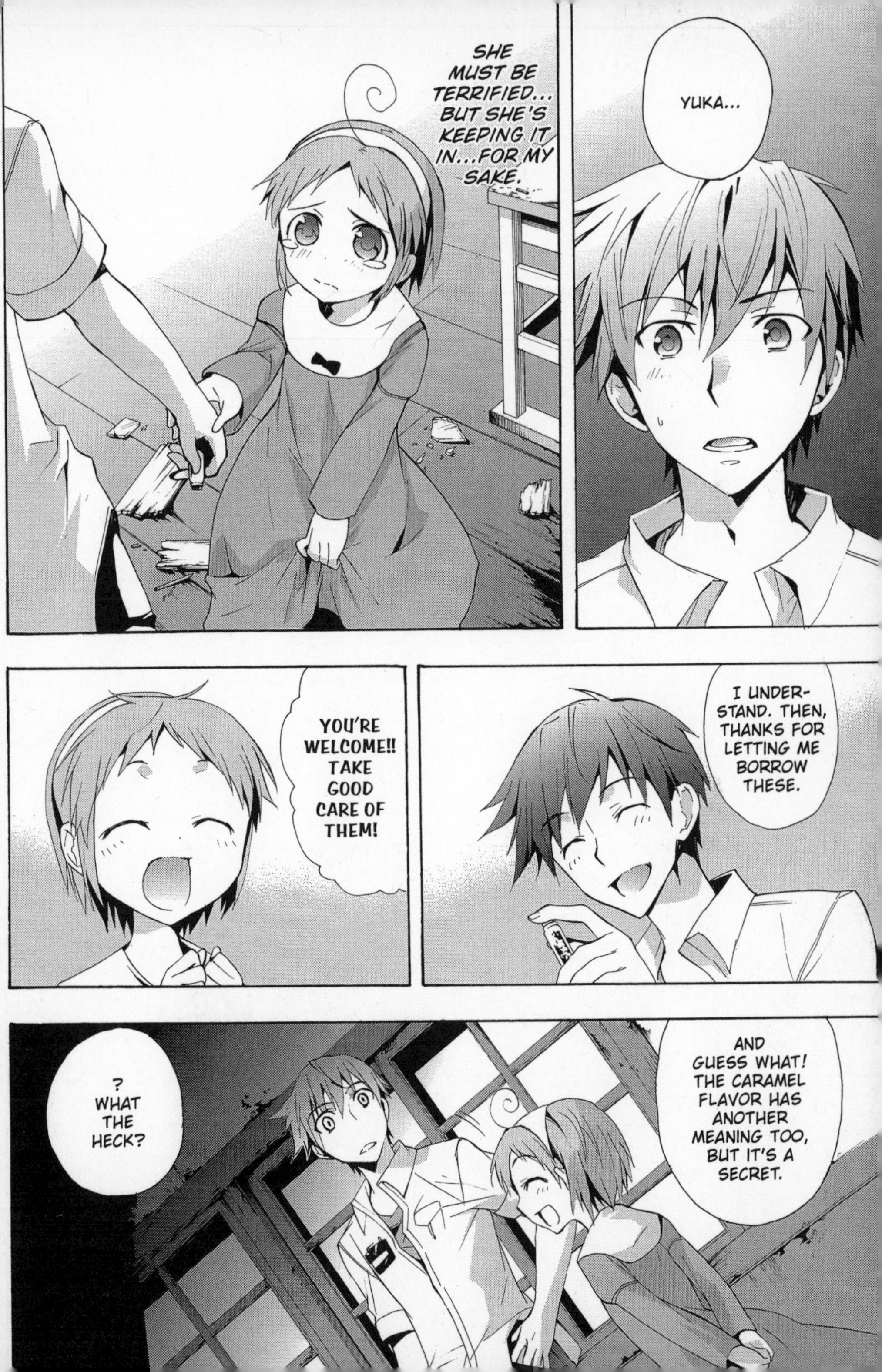
YUKA...
SHE MUST BE TERRIFIED... BUT SHE'S KEEPING IT IN...FOR MY SAKE.
I UNDER-STAND. THEN, THANKS FOR LETTING ME BORROW THESE.
YOU'RE WELCOME!! TAKE GOOD CARE OF THEM!
AND GUESS WHAT! THE CARAMEL FLAVOR HAS ANOTHER MEANING TOO, BUT IT'S A SECRET.
? WHAT THE HECK?

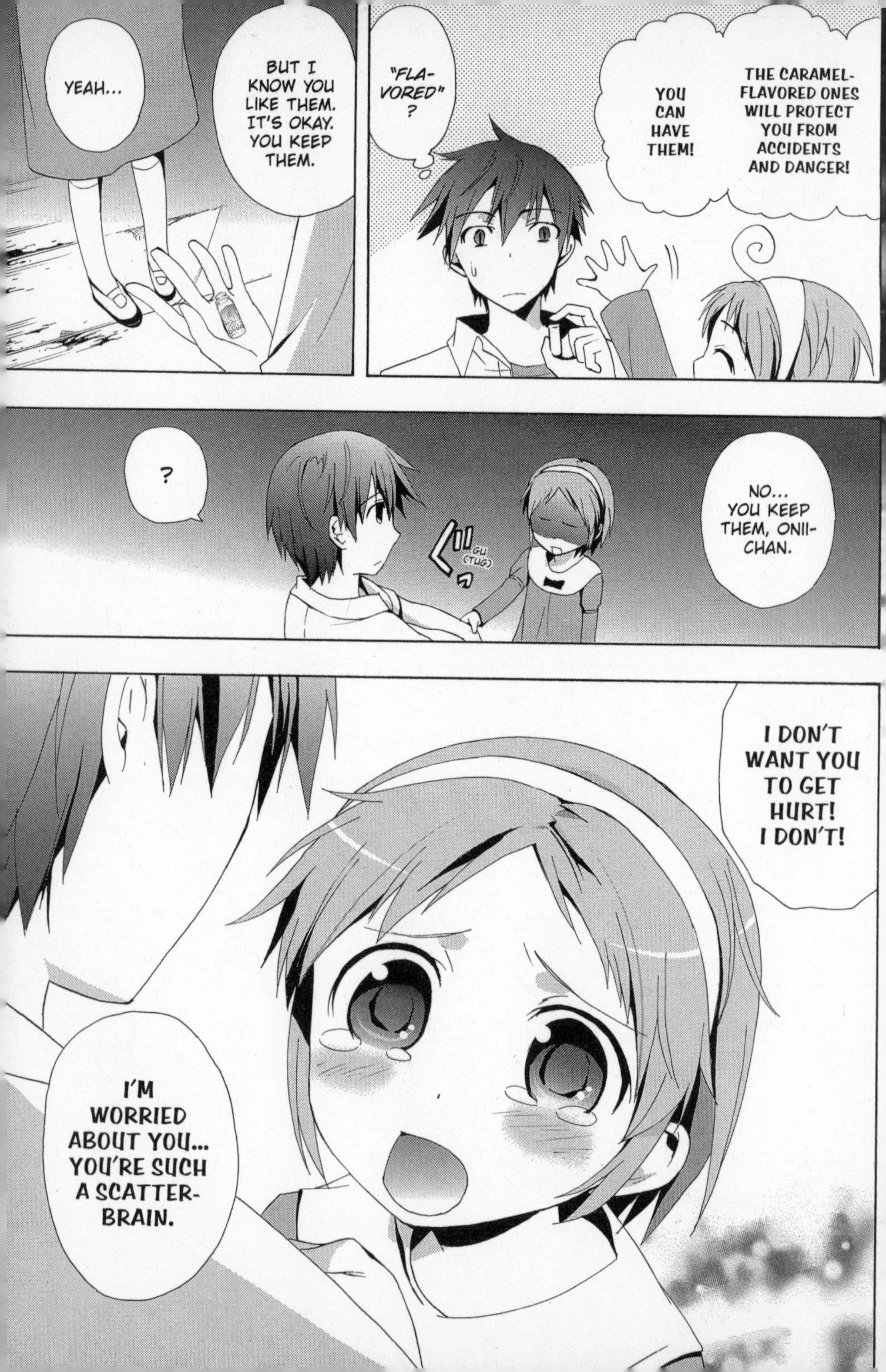
THE CARAMEL-FLAVORED ONES WILL PROTECT YOU FROM ACCIDENTS AND DANGER!
YOU CAN HAVE THEM!
"FLAVORED"?
BUT I KNOW YOU LIKE THEM. IT'S OKAY. YOU KEEP THEM.
YEAH...
NO... YOU KEEP THEM, ONII-CHAN.
GU (TUG)
?
I DON'T WANT YOU TO GET HURT! I DON'T!
I'M WORRIED ABOUT YOU... YOU'RE SUCH A SCATTER-BRAIN.

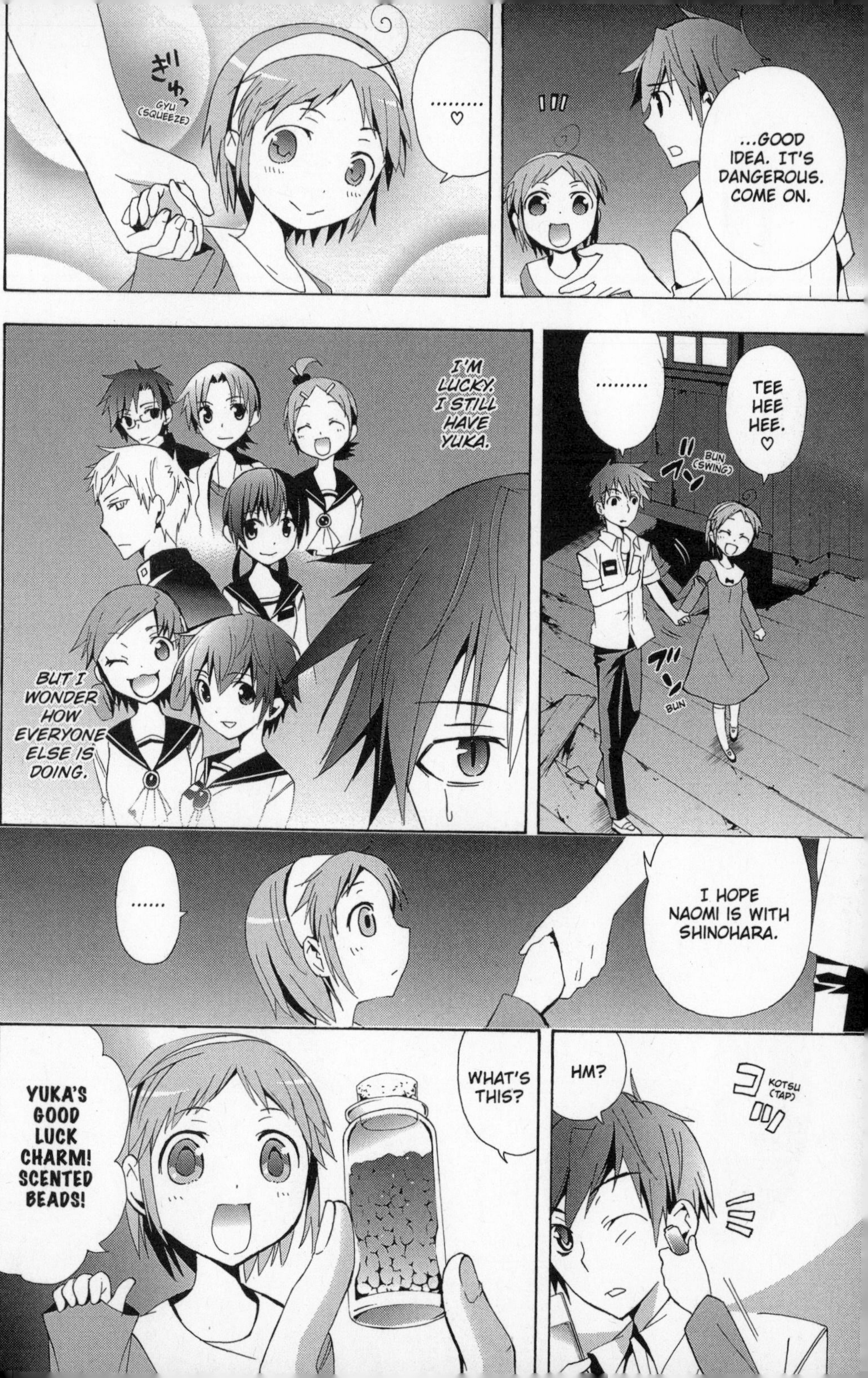
...GOOD IDEA. IT'S DANGEROUS. COME ON.
ぎゅっ
GYU (SQUEEZE)
..........♡
....
TEE HEE HEE. ♡
BUN (SWING)
BUN
I'M LUCKY. I STILL HAVE YUKA.
BUT I WONDER HOW EVERYONE ELSE IS DOING.
I HOPE NAOMI IS WITH SHINOHARA.
......
HM?
KOTSU (TAP)
WHAT'S THIS?
YUKA'S GOOD LUCK CHARM! SCENTED BEADS!

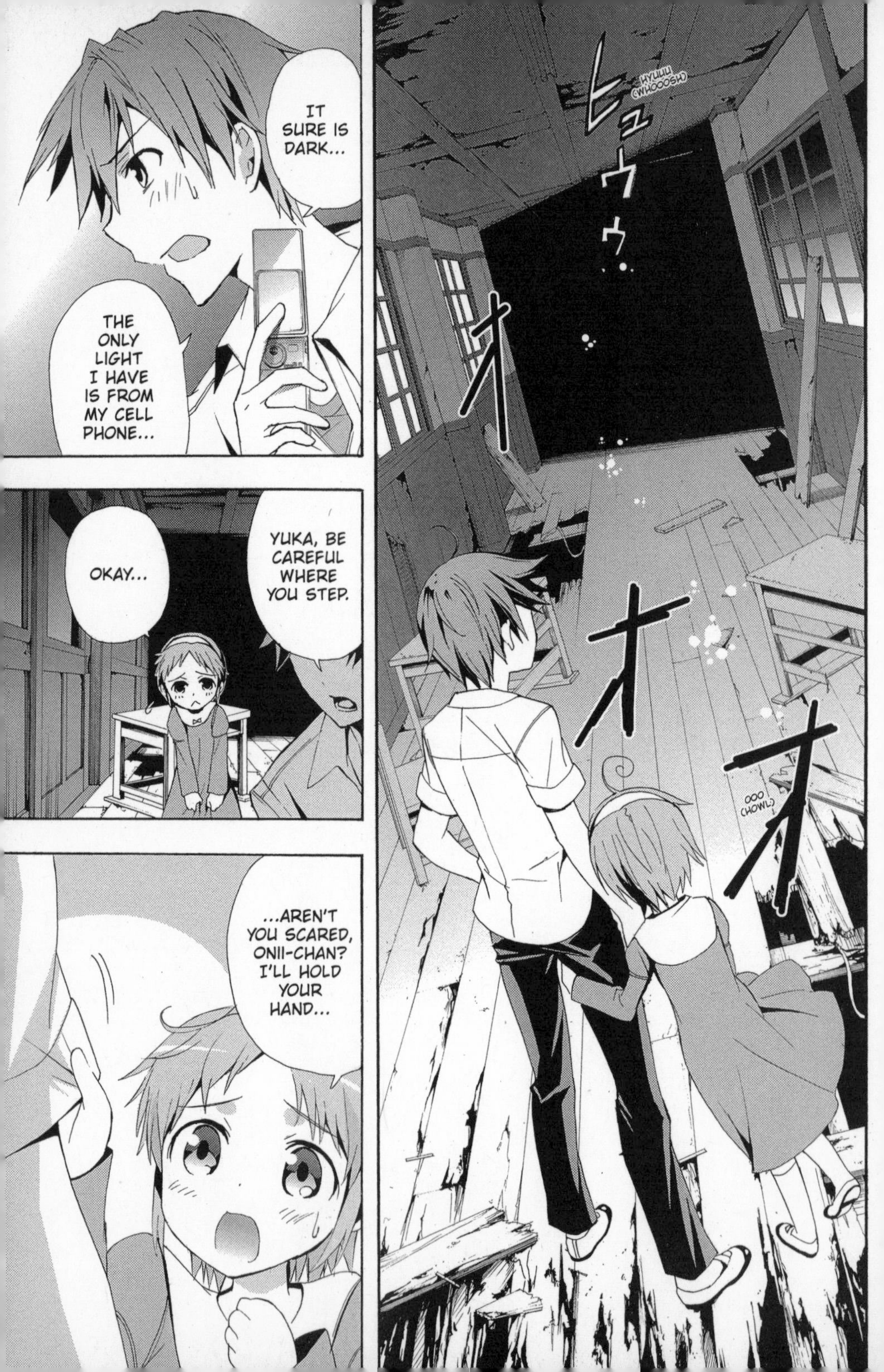
ヒュウウ
HYUUU (WHOOOSH)
オオオ
OOO (HOWL)
IT SURE IS DARK...
THE ONLY LIGHT I HAVE IS FROM MY CELL PHONE...
YUKA, BE CAREFUL WHERE YOU STEP.
OKAY...
...AREN'T YOU SCARED, ONII-CHAN? I'LL HOLD YOUR HAND...

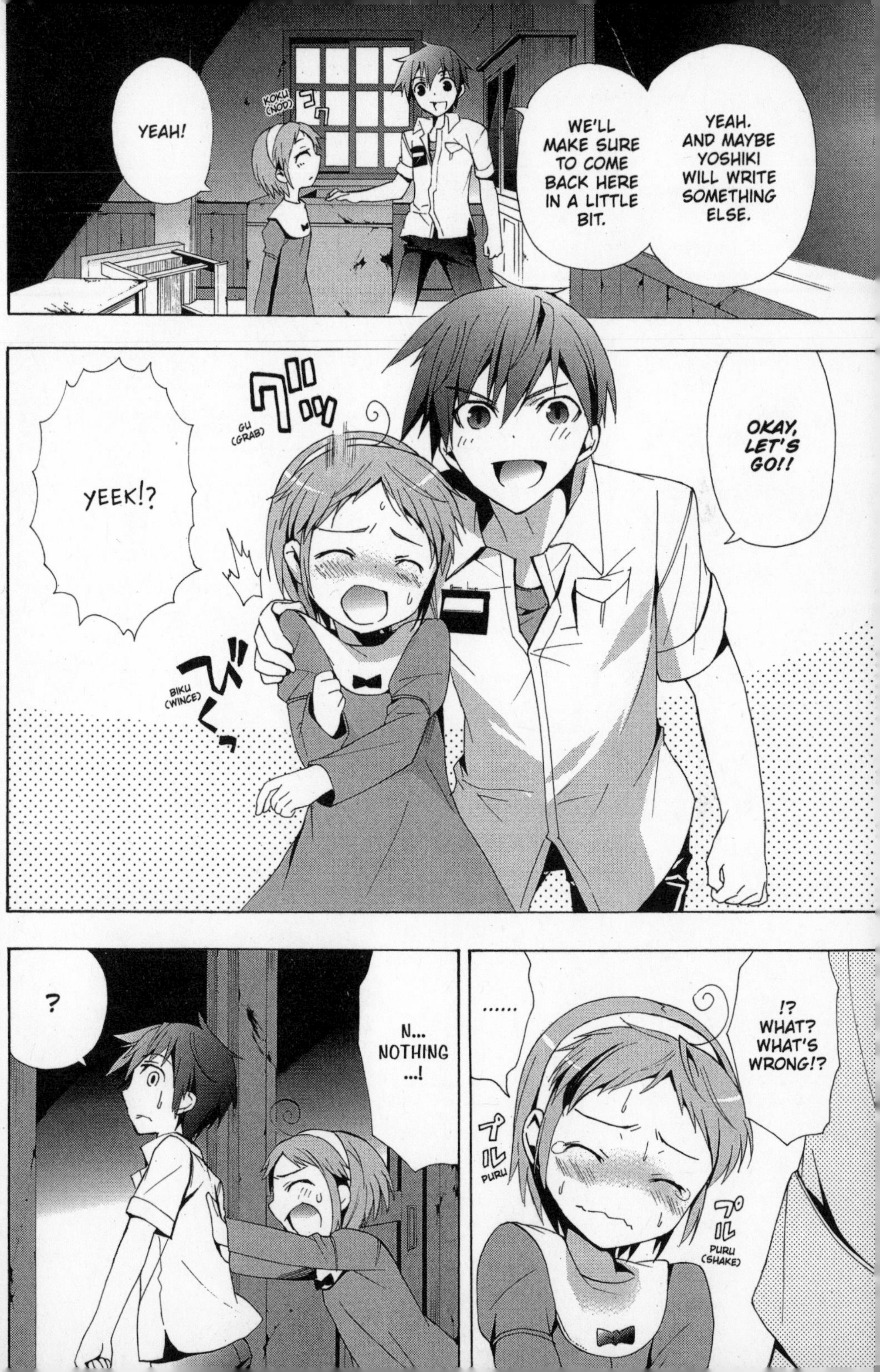
YEAH. AND MAYBE YOSHIKI WILL WRITE SOMETHING ELSE.
WE'LL MAKE SURE TO COME BACK HERE IN A LITTLE BIT.
KOKU (NOD)
YEAH!
OKAY, LET'S GO!!
GU (GRAB)
YEEK!?
BIKU (WINCE)
!? WHAT? WHAT'S WRONG!?
PURU (SHAKE)
PURU
......
N... NOTHING ...!
?

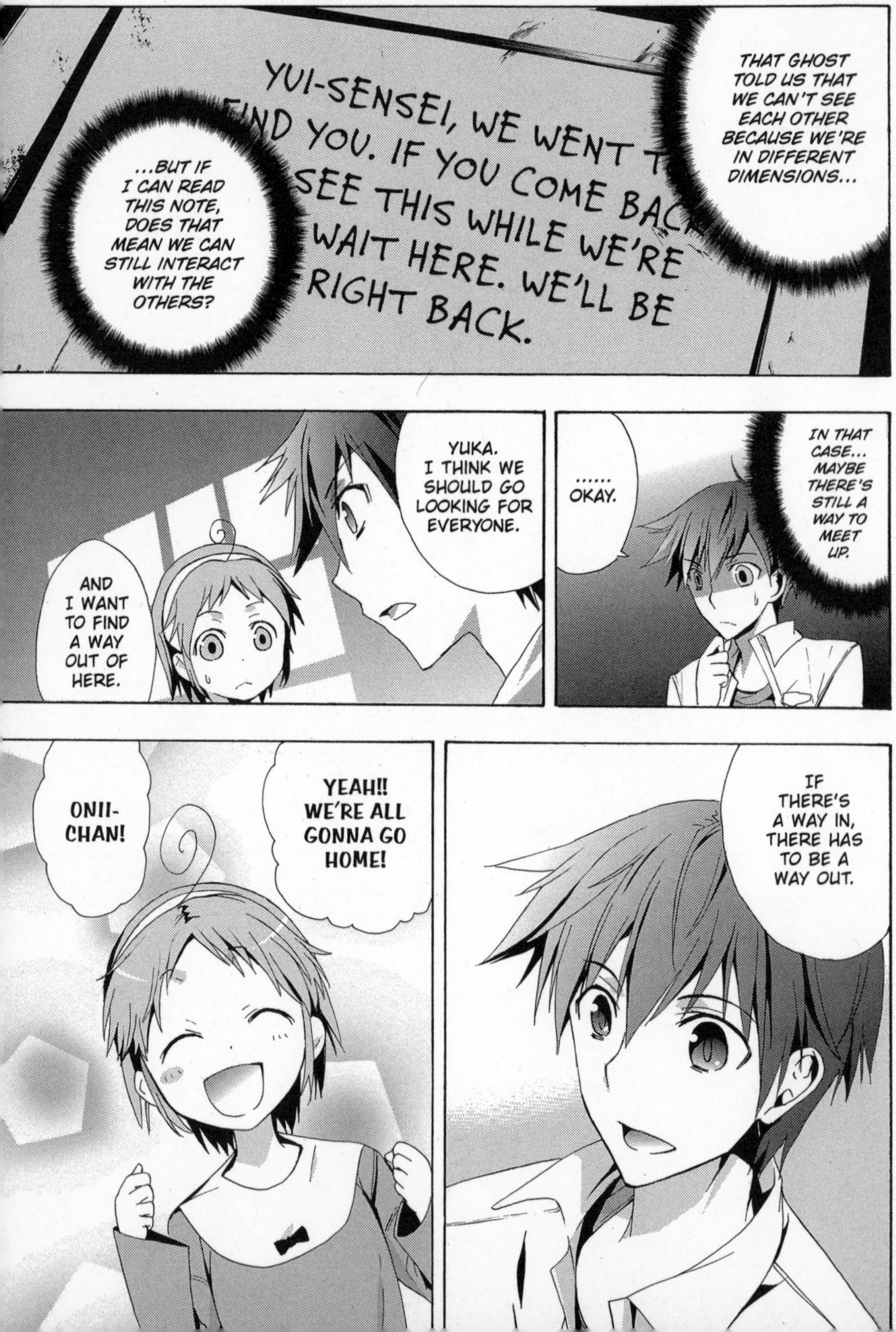
THAT GHOST TOLD US THAT WE CAN'T SEE EACH OTHER BECAUSE WE'RE IN DIFFERENT DIMENSIONS...
YUI-SENSEI, WE WENT T
IND YOU. IF YOU COME BAC
SEE THIS WHILE WE'RE
WAIT HERE. WE'LL BE
RIGHT BACK.
...BUT IF I CAN READ THIS NOTE, DOES THAT MEAN WE CAN STILL INTERACT WITH THE OTHERS?
IN THAT CASE... MAYBE THERE'S STILL A WAY TO MEET UP.
......OKAY.
YUKA. I THINK WE SHOULD GO LOOKING FOR EVERYONE.
AND I WANT TO FIND A WAY OUT OF HERE.
IF THERE'S A WAY IN, THERE HAS TO BE A WAY OUT.
YEAH!! WE'RE ALL GONNA GO HOME!
ONII-CHAN!

...THIS IS YOSHIKI'S WRITING.

ONII-CHAN, THERE'S SOMETHING WRITTEN HERE.

HUH?

WE WENT

F YOU COM

THIS

YUI-SENSEI WE WENT TO
FIND YOU. IF YOU COME B
AND SEE THIS WHILE WE
SEE WAIT HERE. WE'
RIGHT BACK.

YEAH. I'D KNOW HIS GRAFFITI ANYWHERE.

YOSHIKI-SAN'S?

OH, GOOD... AT LEAST FOR NOW, WE KNOW THOSE THREE ARE OKAY...

AND SHINOZAKI AND YUI-SENSEI ARE WITH HIM!

YUI-SENSEI WE WENT TO
ND YOU. IF YOU COME BACK
E SEE THIS WHILE WE'RE
'E WAIT HERE. WE'LL BE
RIGHT BACK.

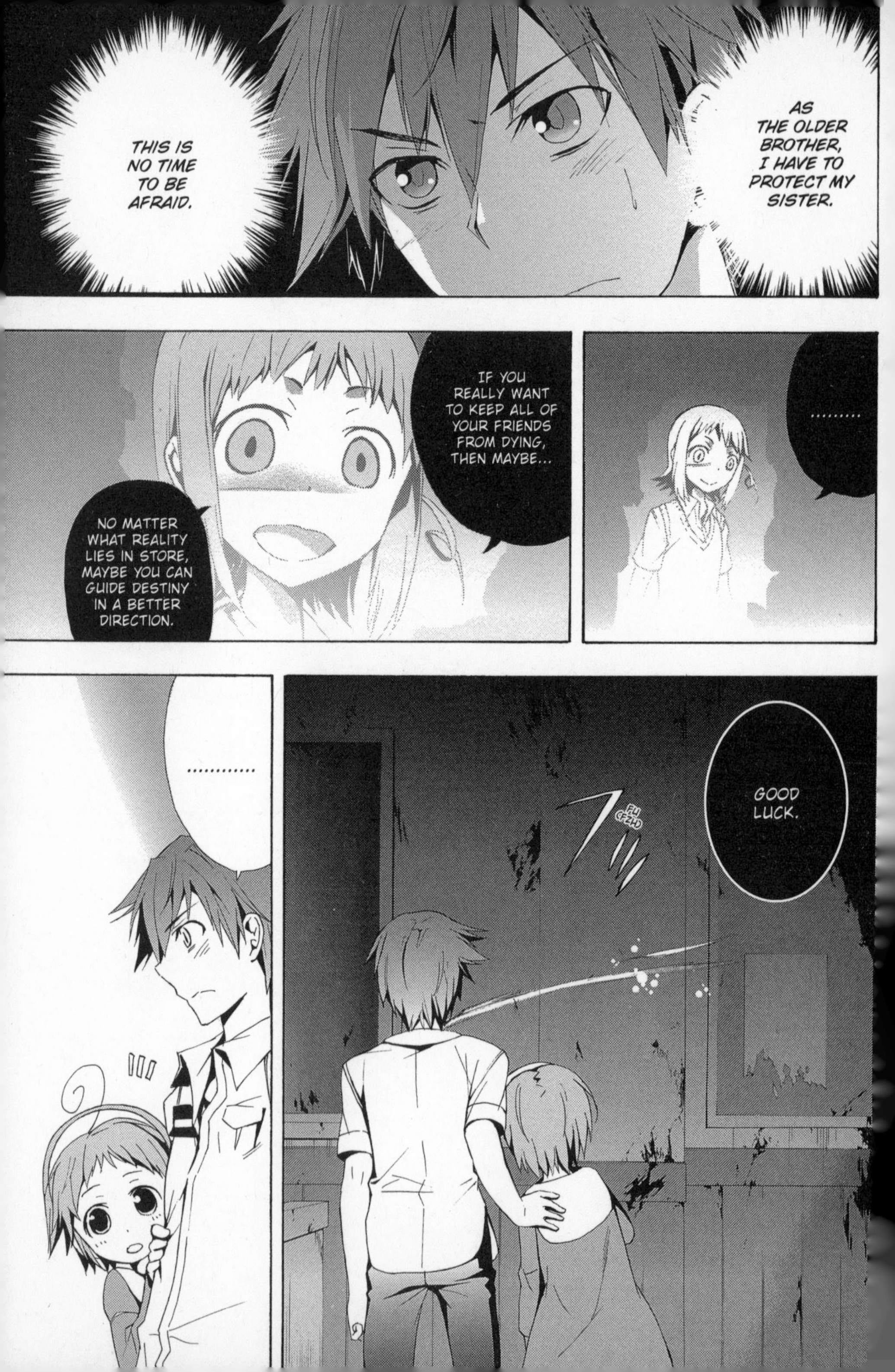
AS THE OLDER BROTHER, I HAVE TO PROTECT MY SISTER.
THIS IS NO TIME TO BE AFRAID.
....
IF YOU REALLY WANT TO KEEP ALL OF YOUR FRIENDS FROM DYING, THEN MAYBE...
NO MATTER WHAT REALITY LIES IN STORE, MAYBE YOU CAN GUIDE DESTINY IN A BETTER DIRECTION.
GOOD LUCK.
FU (FZH)
....

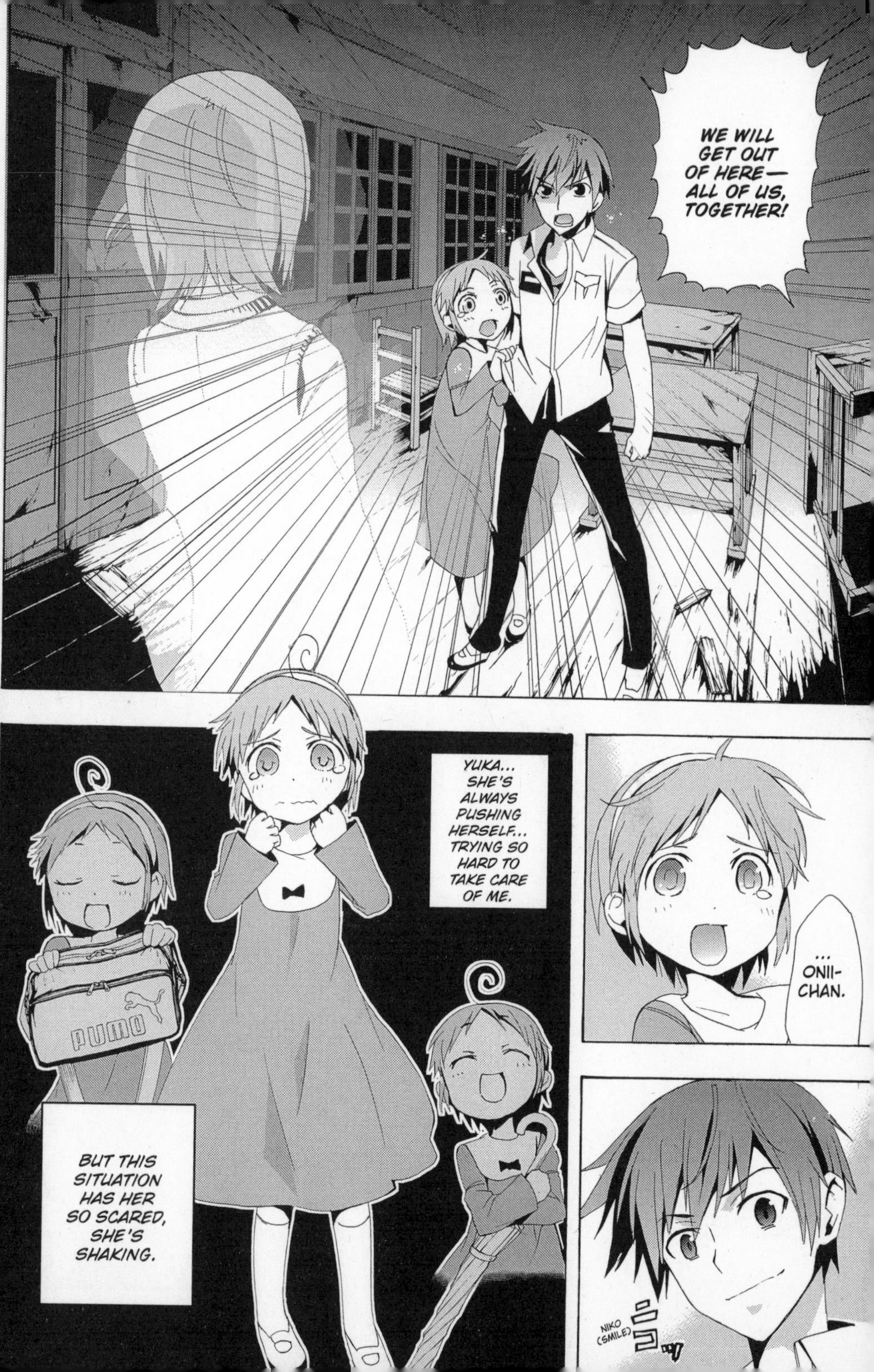
WE WILL GET OUT OF HERE—ALL OF US, TOGETHER!
...ONII-CHAN.
NIKO (SMILE)
YUKA... SHE'S ALWAYS PUSHING HERSELF... TRYING SO HARD TO TAKE CARE OF ME.
PUMO
BUT THIS SITUATION HAS HER SO SCARED, SHE'S SHAKING.

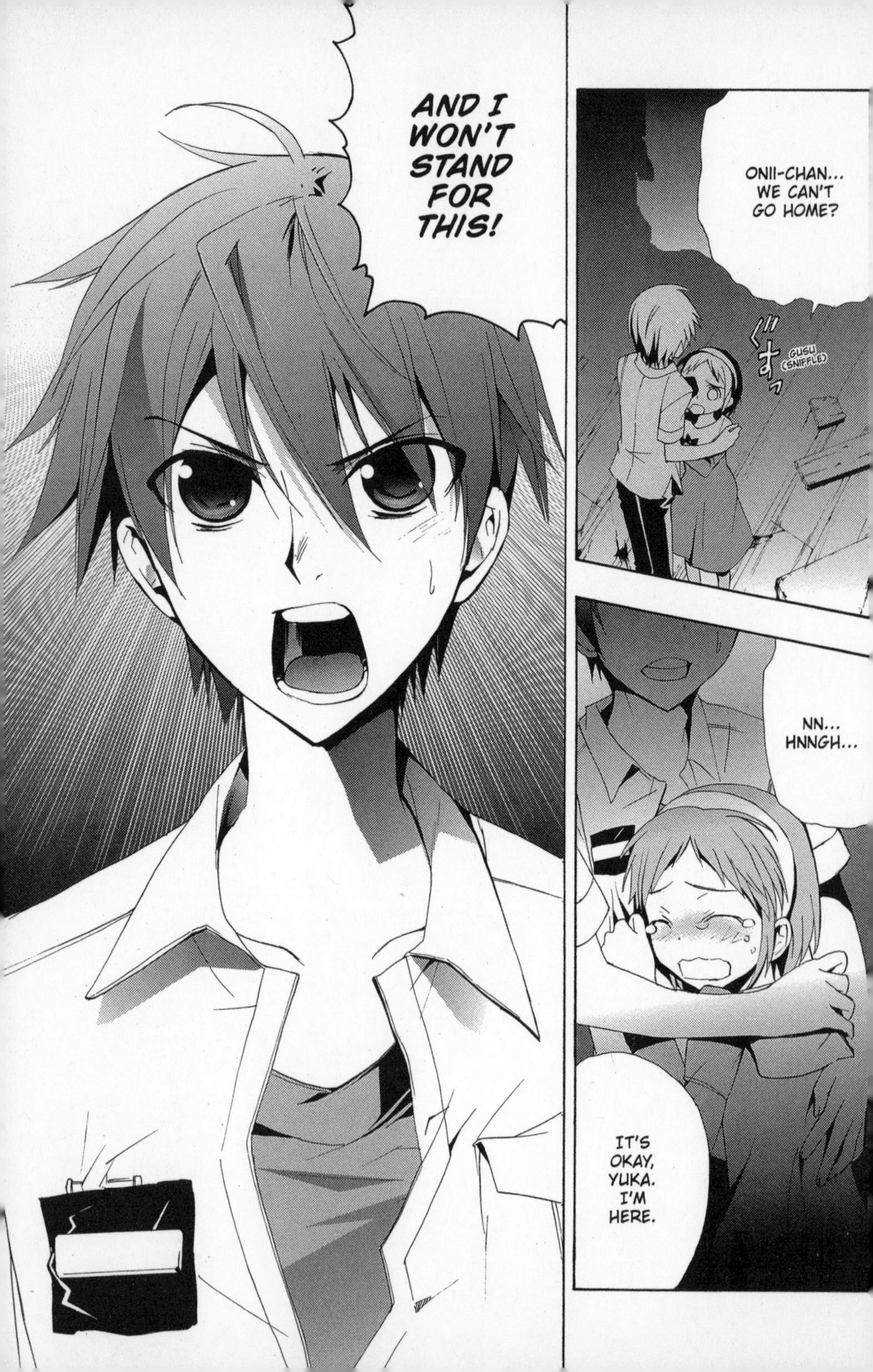
ONII-CHAN... WE CAN'T GO HOME?
ぐすっ
GUSU (SNIFFLE)
NN... HNNGH...
IT'S OKAY, YUKA. I'M HERE.
AND I WON'T STAND FOR THIS!

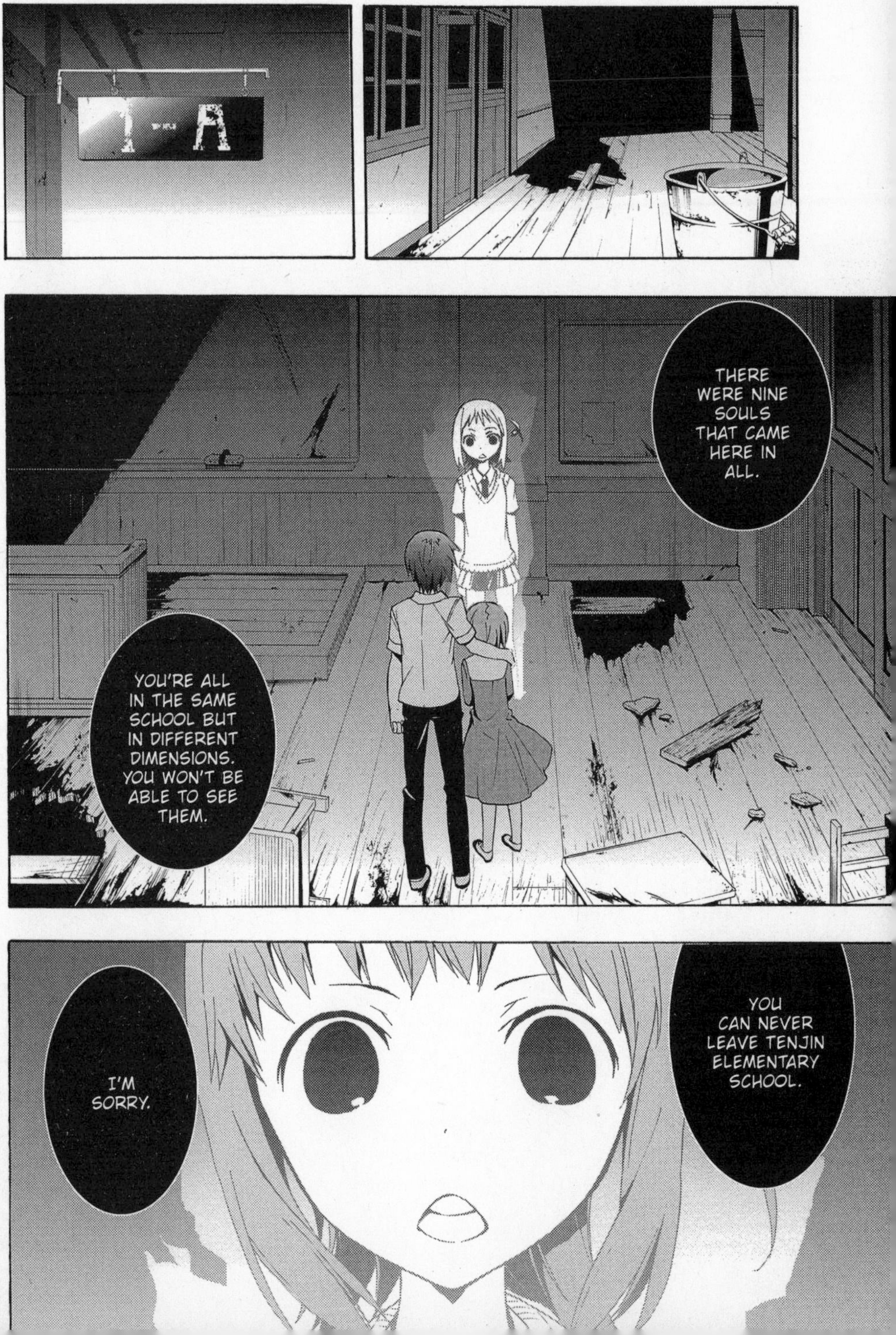
1-A
THERE WERE NINE SOULS THAT CAME HERE IN ALL.
YOU'RE ALL IN THE SAME SCHOOL BUT IN DIFFERENT DIMENSIONS. YOU WON'T BE ABLE TO SEE THEM.
YOU CAN NEVER LEAVE TENJIN ELEMENTARY SCHOOL.
I'M SORRY.

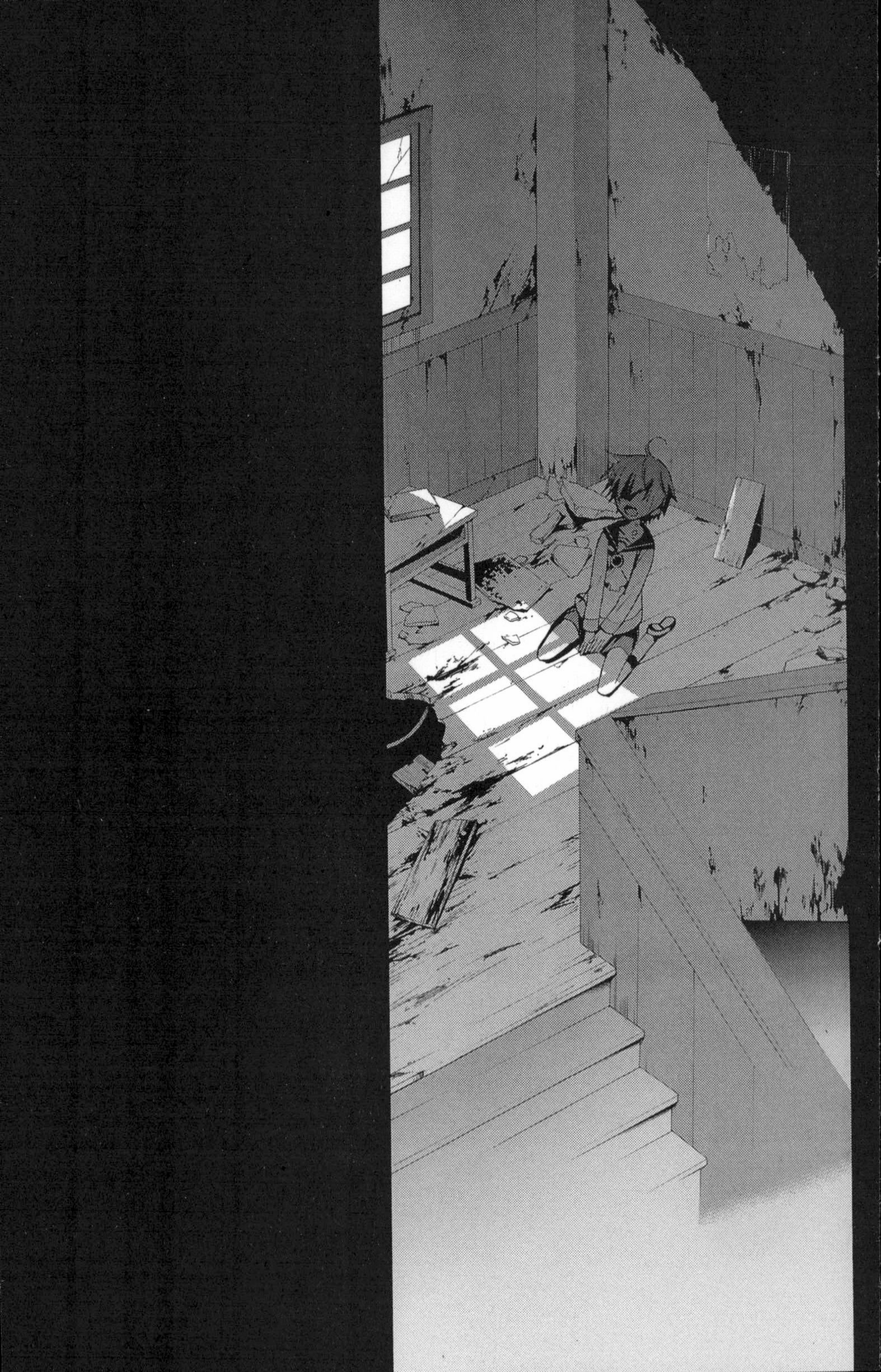

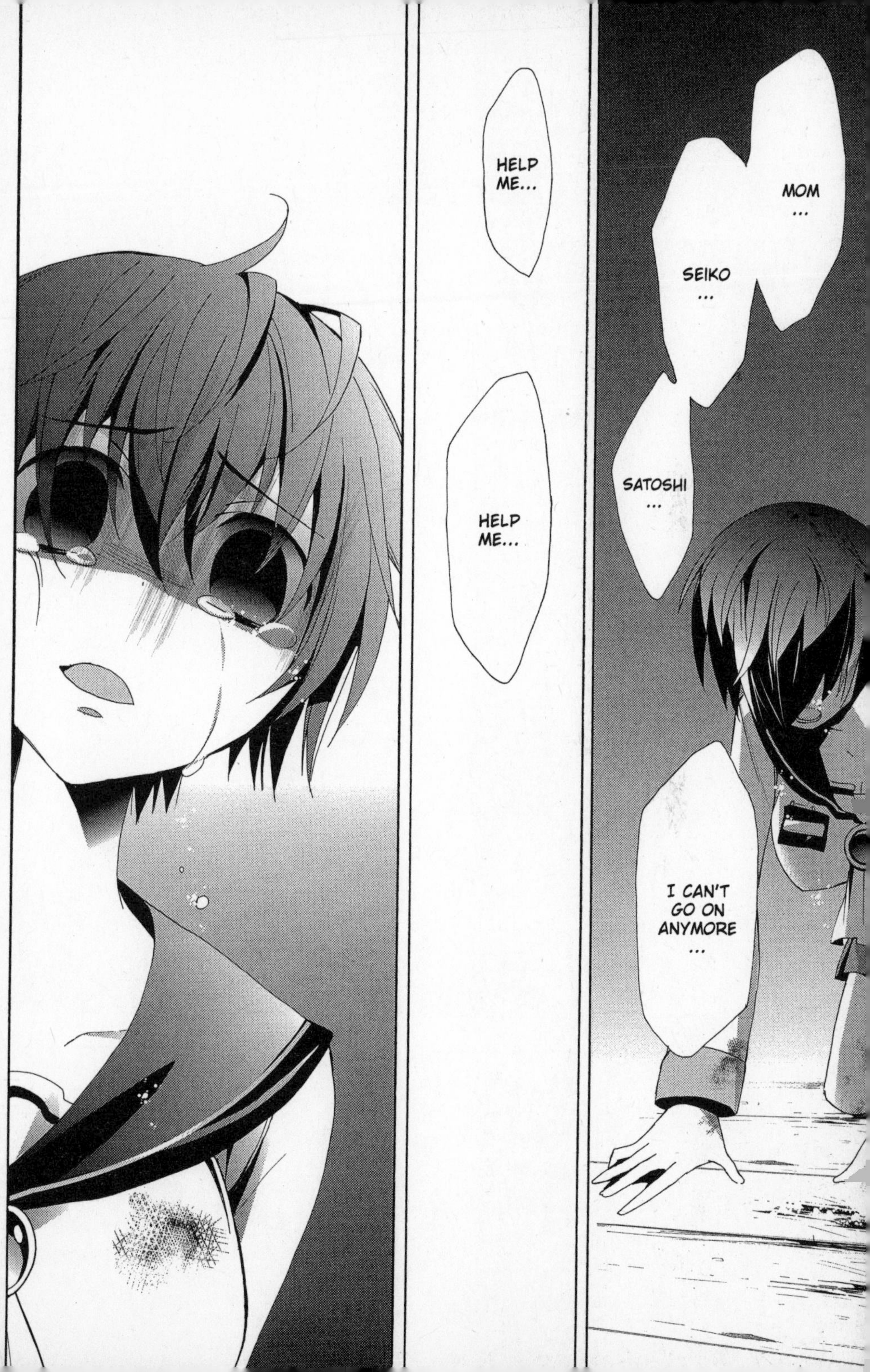
MOM ...
SEIKO ...
SATOSHI ...
I CAN'T GO ON ANYMORE ...
HELP ME...
HELP ME...

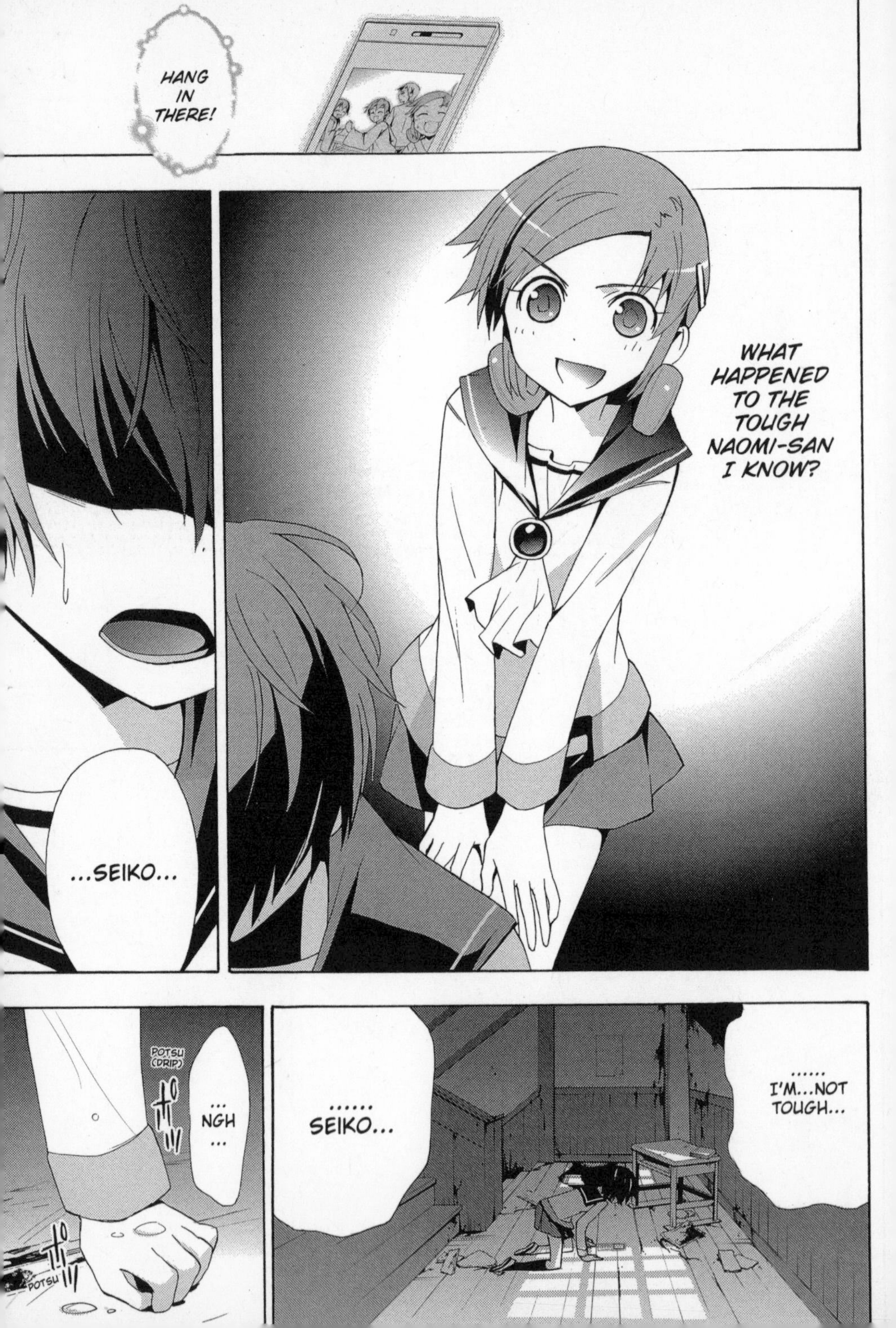
HANG IN THERE!
WHAT HAPPENED TO THE TOUGH NAOMI-SAN I KNOW?
...SEIKO...
...... I'M...NOT TOUGH...
...... SEIKO...
POTSU (DRIP)
... NGH ...
POTSU

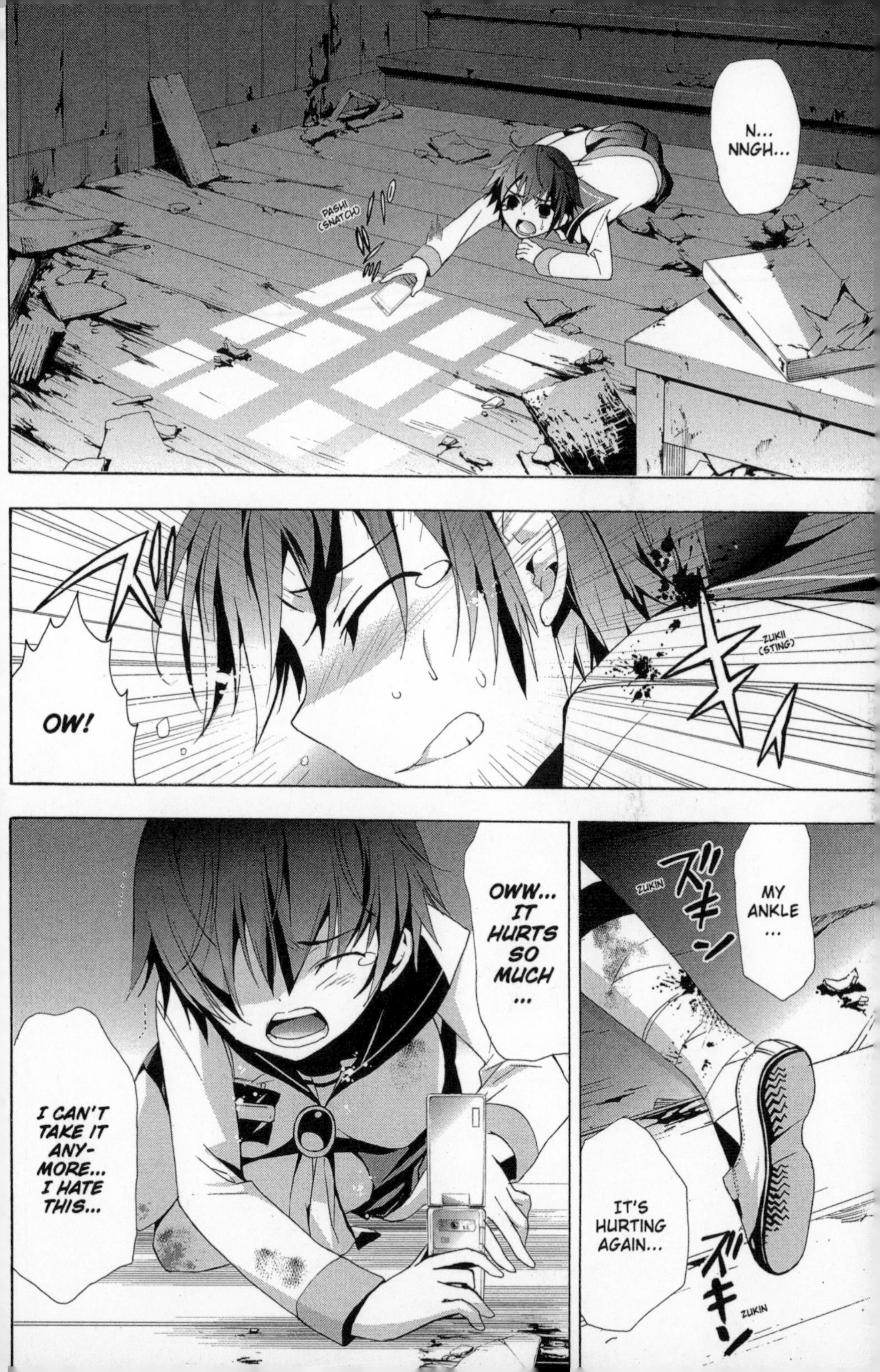
N...
NNGH...
PASHI (SNATCH)
ZUKII (STING)
OW!
ZUKIN
MY ANKLE ...
IT'S HURTING AGAIN...
ZUKIN
OWW... IT HURTS SO MUCH ...
I CAN'T TAKE IT ANYMORE... I HATE THIS...

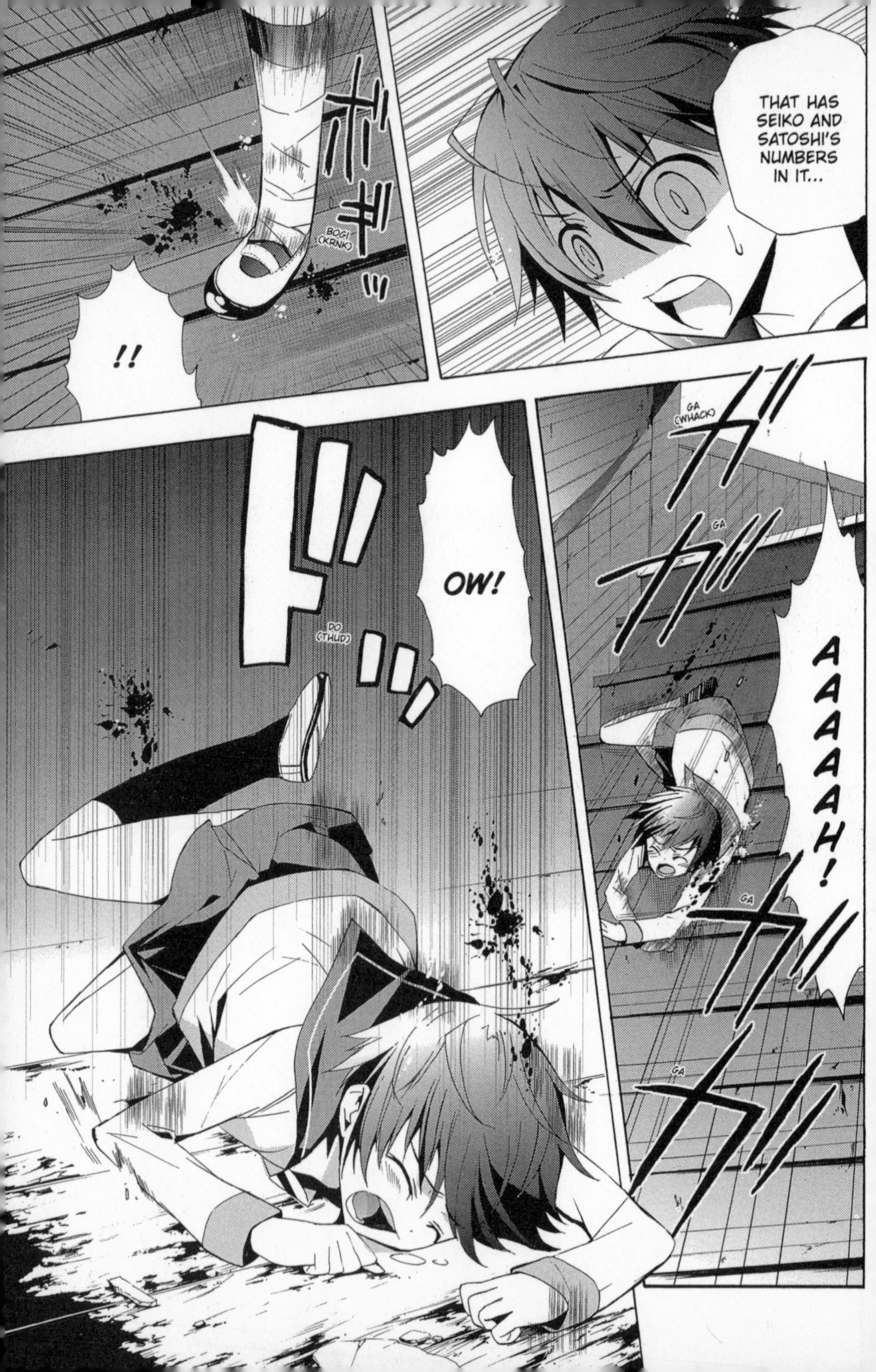
THAT HAS SEIKO AND SATOSHI'S NUMBERS IN IT...
BOGI (KRNK)
!!
GA (WHACK)
GA
AAAAAAH!
GA
GA
OW!
DO (THUD)

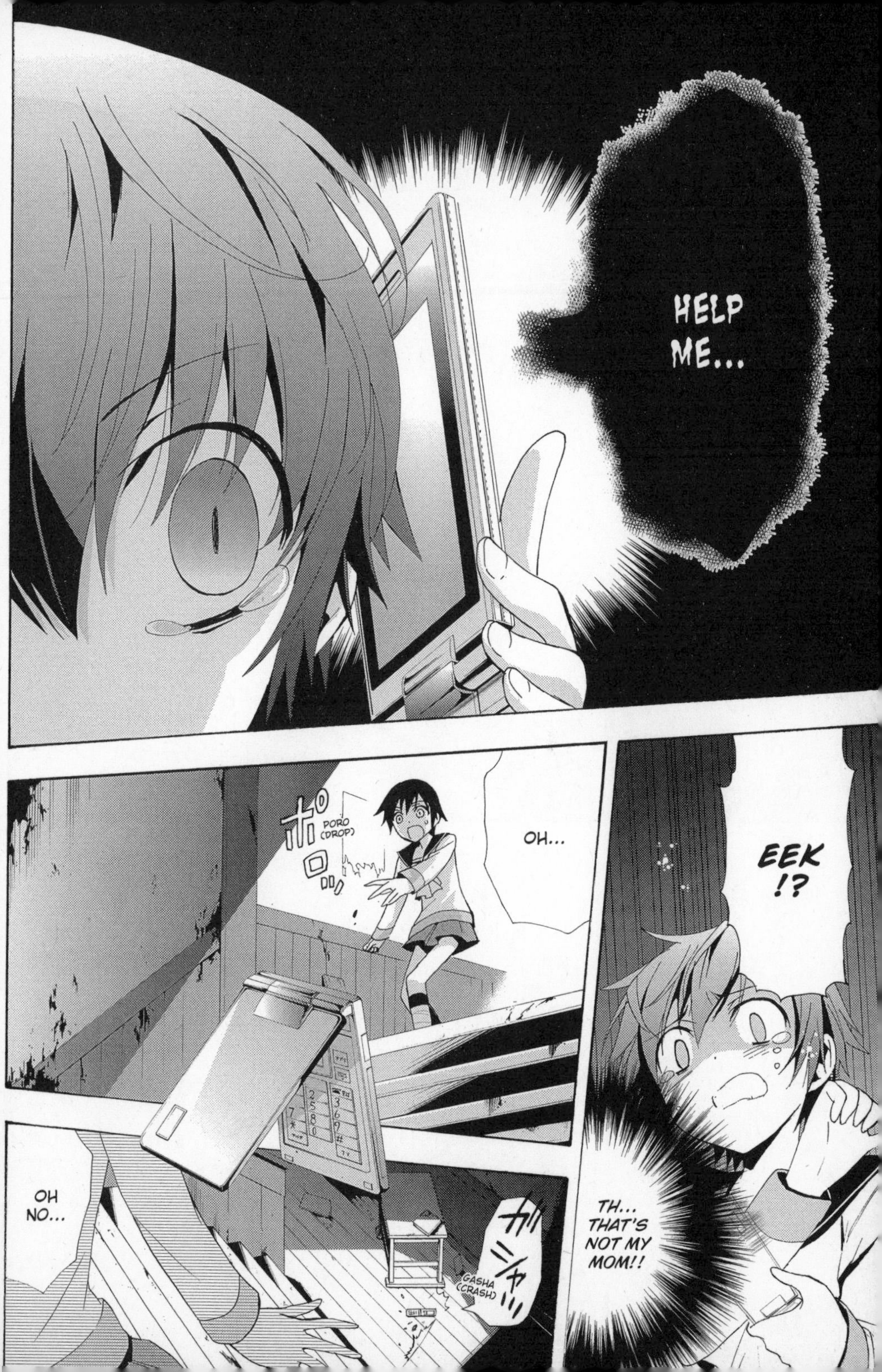
HELP ME...
EEK !?
TH... THAT'S NOT MY MOM!!
OH...
PORO (DROP)
OH NO...
GASHA (CRASH)

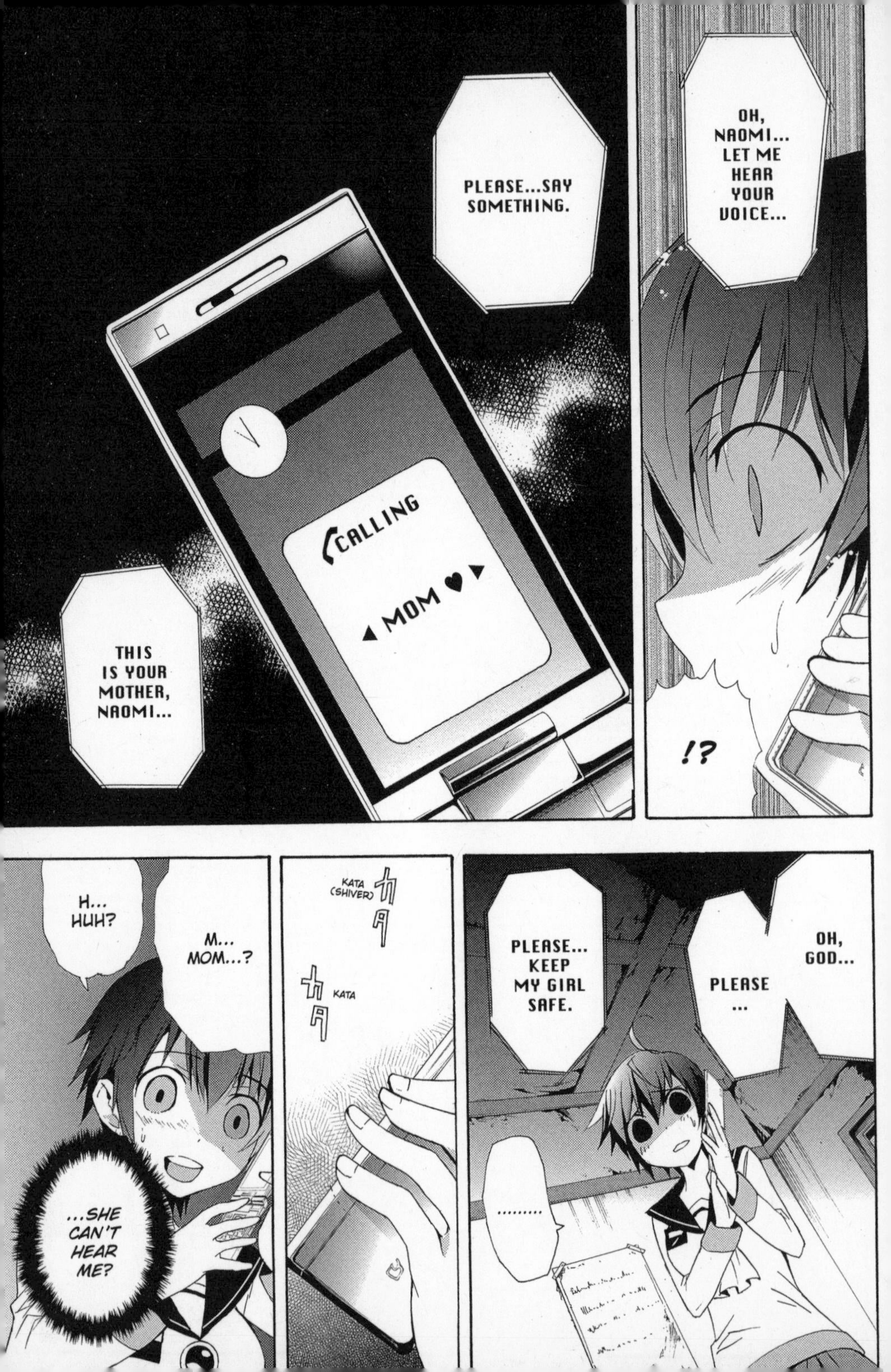
OH, NAOMI... LET ME HEAR YOUR VOICE...
!?
PLEASE...SAY SOMETHING.
CALLING
MOM ♥
THIS IS YOUR MOTHER, NAOMI...
OH, GOD...
PLEASE ...
PLEASE... KEEP MY GIRL SAFE.
....
KATA (SHIVER)
KATA
H... HUH?
M... MOM...?
...SHE CAN'T HEAR ME?

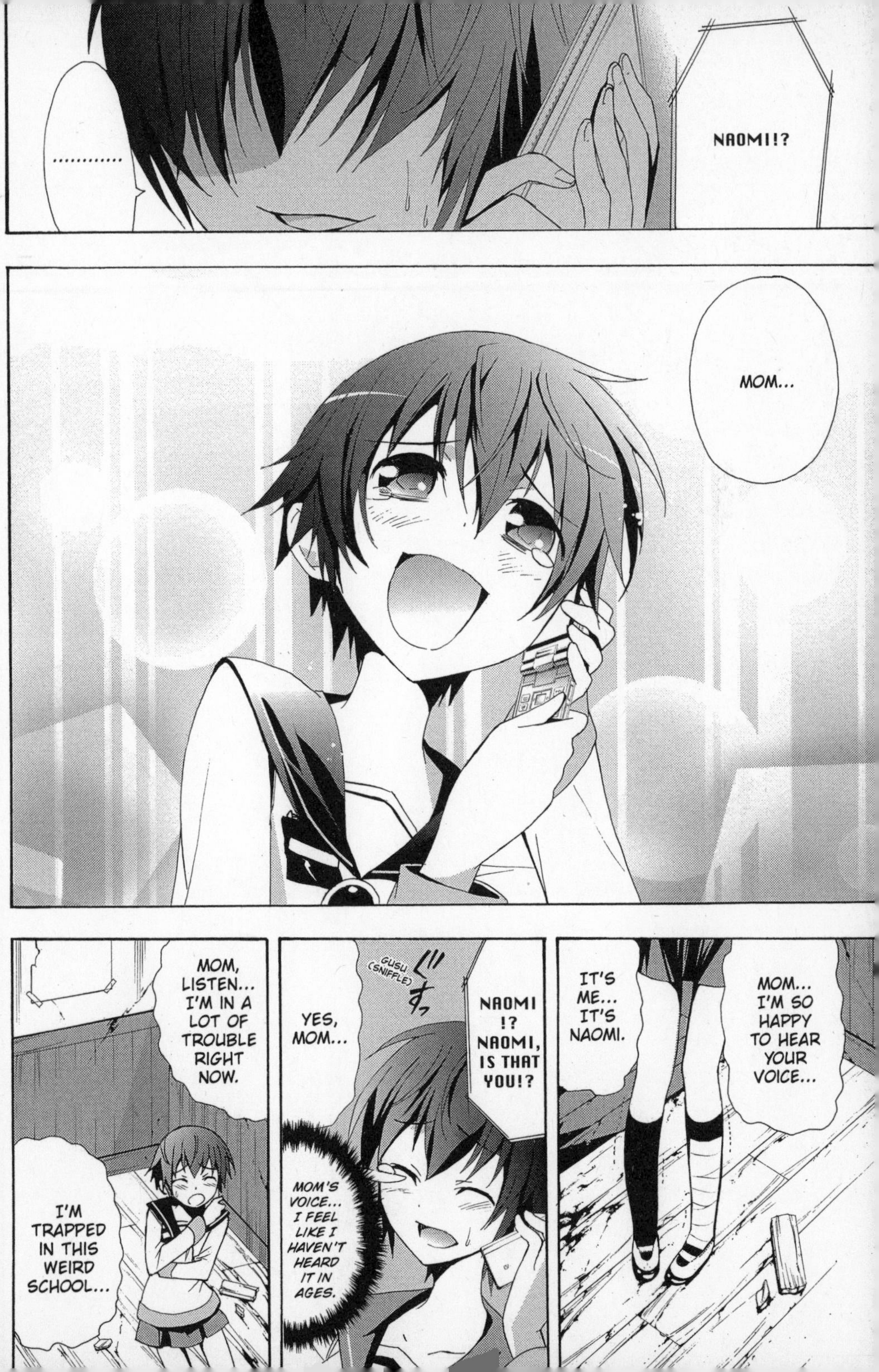
NAOMI!?
....
MOM...
MOM... I'M SO HAPPY TO HEAR YOUR VOICE...
IT'S ME... IT'S NAOMI.
NAOMI!? NAOMI, IS THAT YOU!?
GUSU (SNIFFLE)
YES, MOM...
MOM'S VOICE... I FEEL LIKE I HAVEN'T HEARD IT IN AGES.
MOM, LISTEN... I'M IN A LOT OF TROUBLE RIGHT NOW.
I'M TRAPPED IN THIS WEIRD SCHOOL...

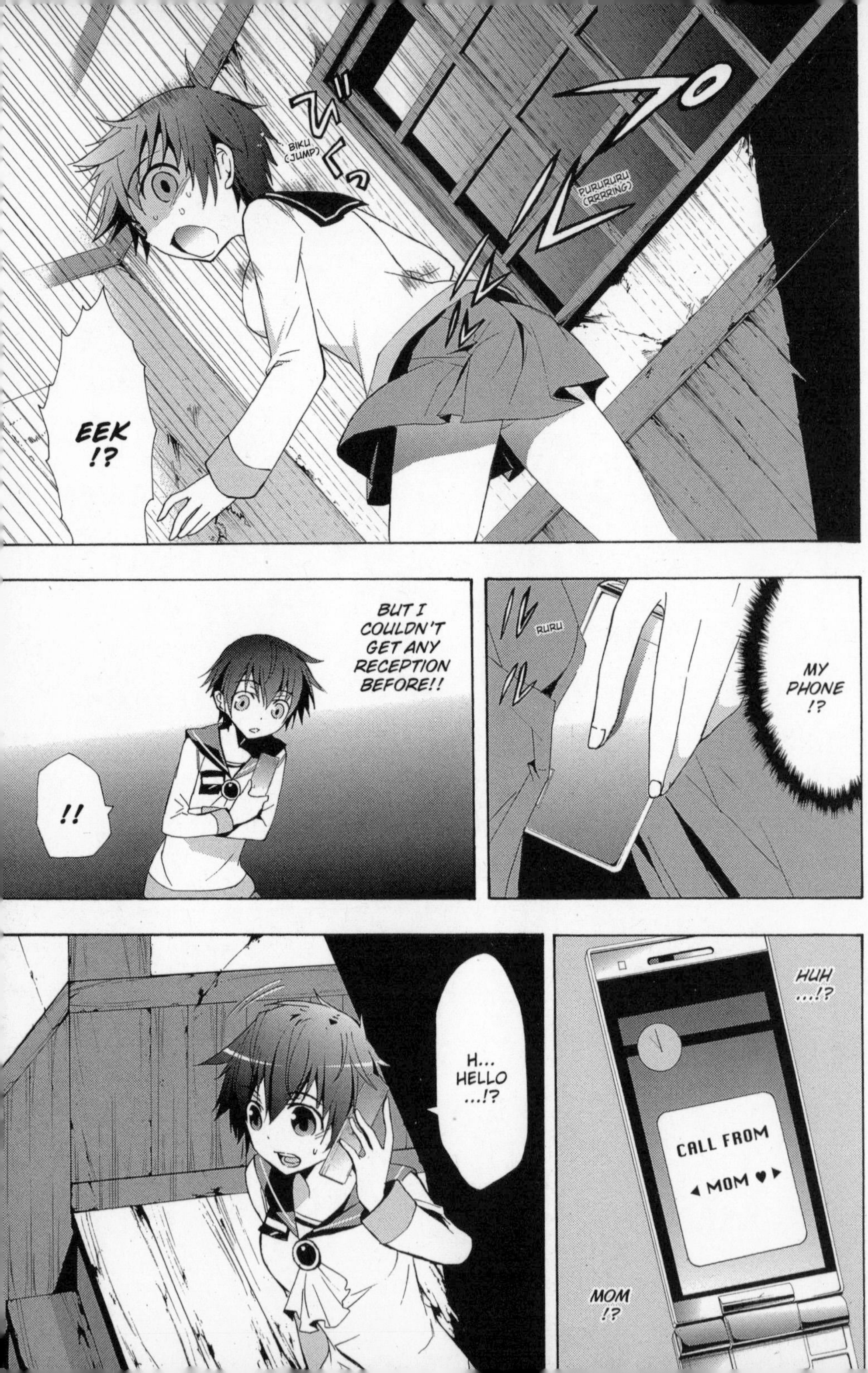
PURURURU (RRRING)
BIKU (JUMP)
EEK !?
RURU
MY PHONE !?
BUT I COULDN'T GET ANY RECEPTION BEFORE!!
!!
HUH ...!?
CALL FROM
◀ MOM ♥ ▶
MOM !?
H... HELLO ...!?

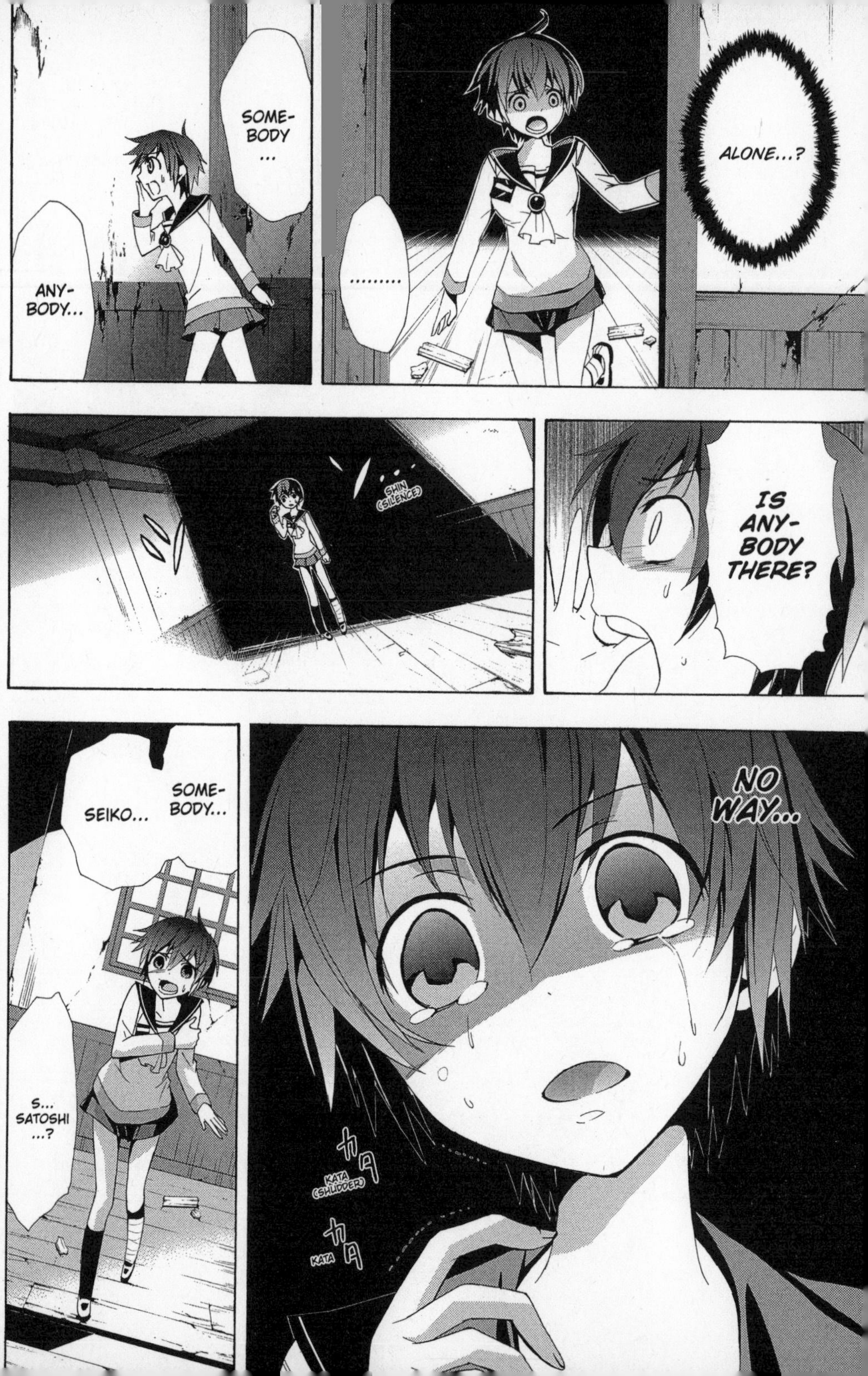
ALONE...?
....
SOME-BODY...
ANY-BODY...
IS ANY-BODY THERE?
SHIN (SILENCE)
NO WAY...
KATA (SHUDDER)
KATA
SOME-BODY...
SEIKO...
S... SATOSHI...?

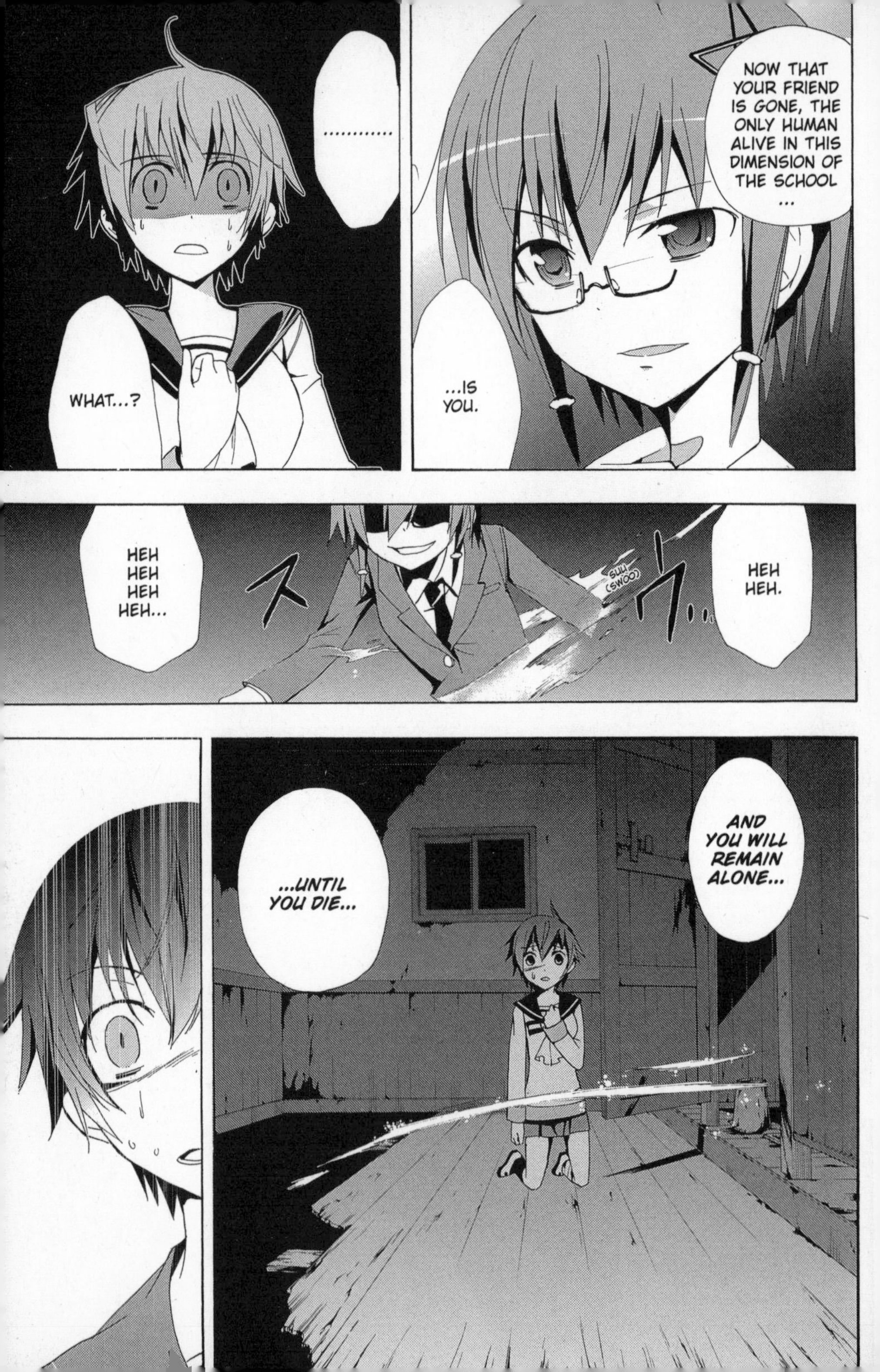
NOW THAT YOUR FRIEND IS GONE, THE ONLY HUMAN ALIVE IN THIS DIMENSION OF THE SCHOOL ...
...IS YOU.
....
WHAT...?
HEH HEH.
SUU (SWOO)
HEH HEH HEH HEH...
AND YOU WILL REMAIN ALONE...
...UNTIL YOU DIE...

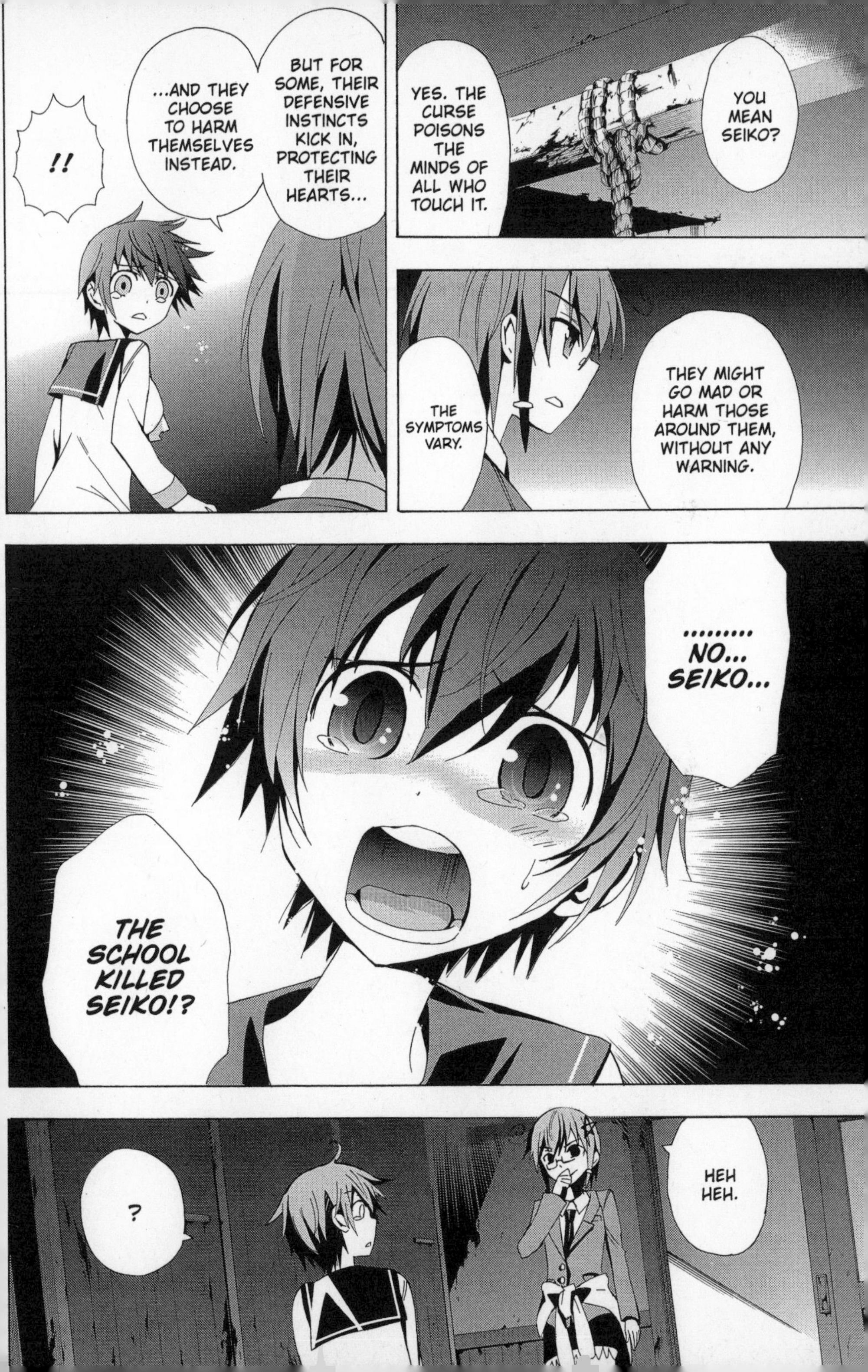
YOU MEAN SEIKO?
YES. THE CURSE POISONS THE MINDS OF ALL WHO TOUCH IT.
THE SYMPTOMS VARY.
THEY MIGHT GO MAD OR HARM THOSE AROUND THEM, WITHOUT ANY WARNING.
BUT FOR SOME, THEIR DEFENSIVE INSTINCTS KICK IN, PROTECTING THEIR HEARTS...
...AND THEY CHOOSE TO HARM THEMSELVES INSTEAD.
!!
.... NO... SEIKO...
THE SCHOOL KILLED SEIKO!?
HEH HEH.
?

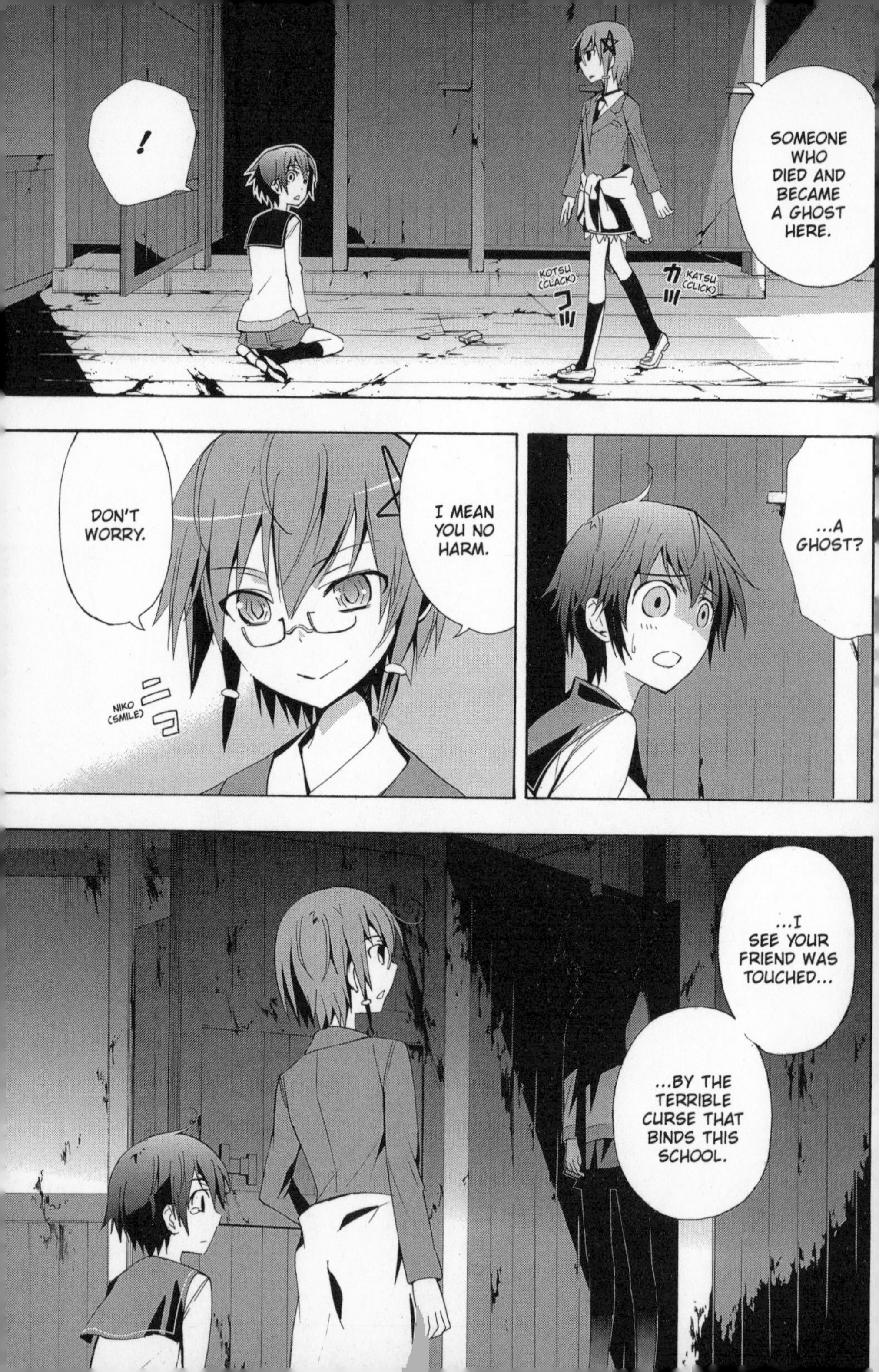

SOMEONE WHO DIED AND BECAME A GHOST HERE.
カツ
KATSU (CLICK)
コツ
KOTSU (CLACK)
!
...A GHOST?
I MEAN YOU NO HARM.
DON'T WORRY.
ニコ
NIKO (SMILE)
...I SEE YOUR FRIEND WAS TOUCHED...
...BY THE TERRIBLE CURSE THAT BINDS THIS SCHOOL.

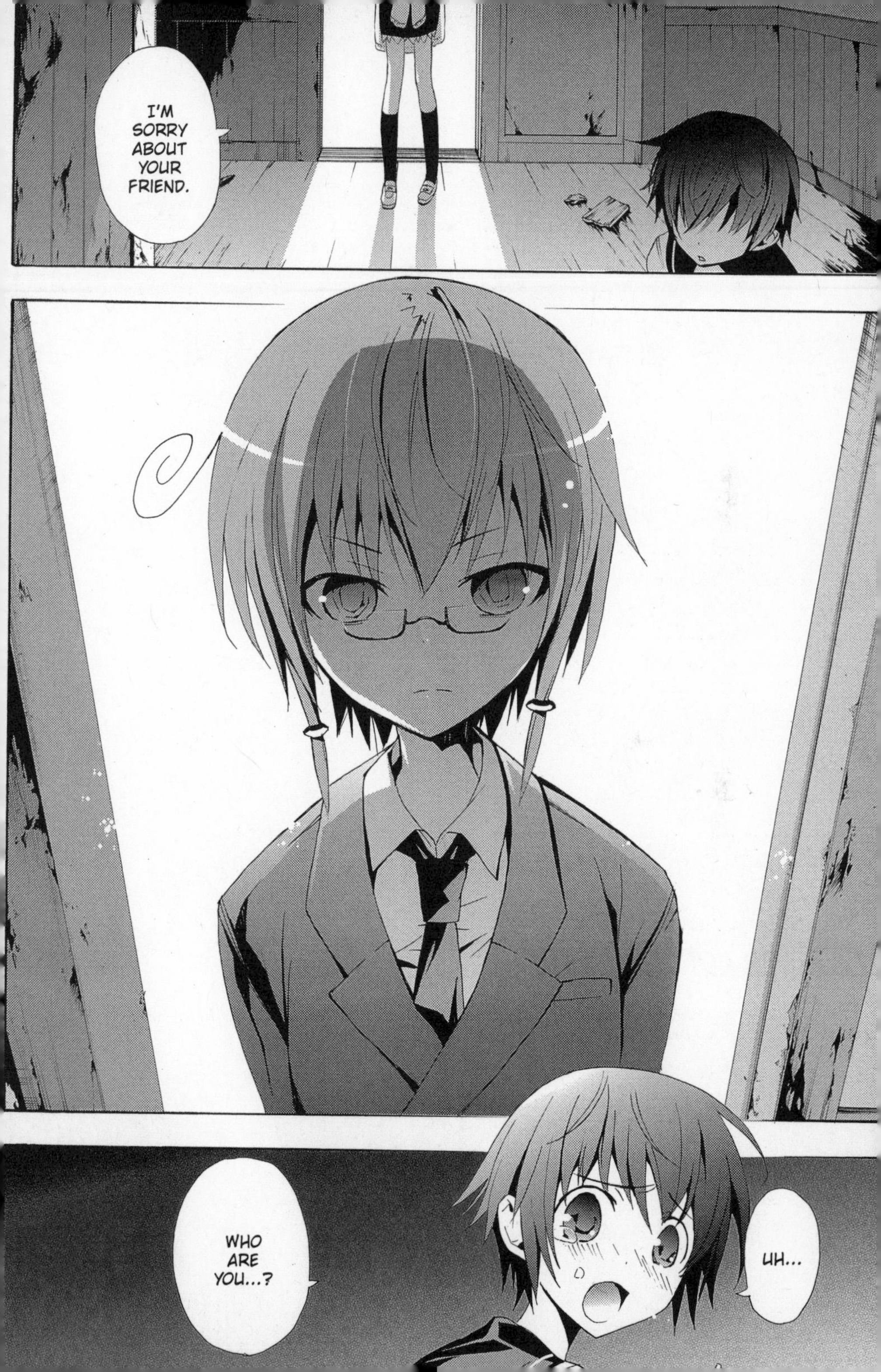
I'M SORRY ABOUT YOUR FRIEND.
UH...
WHO ARE YOU...?

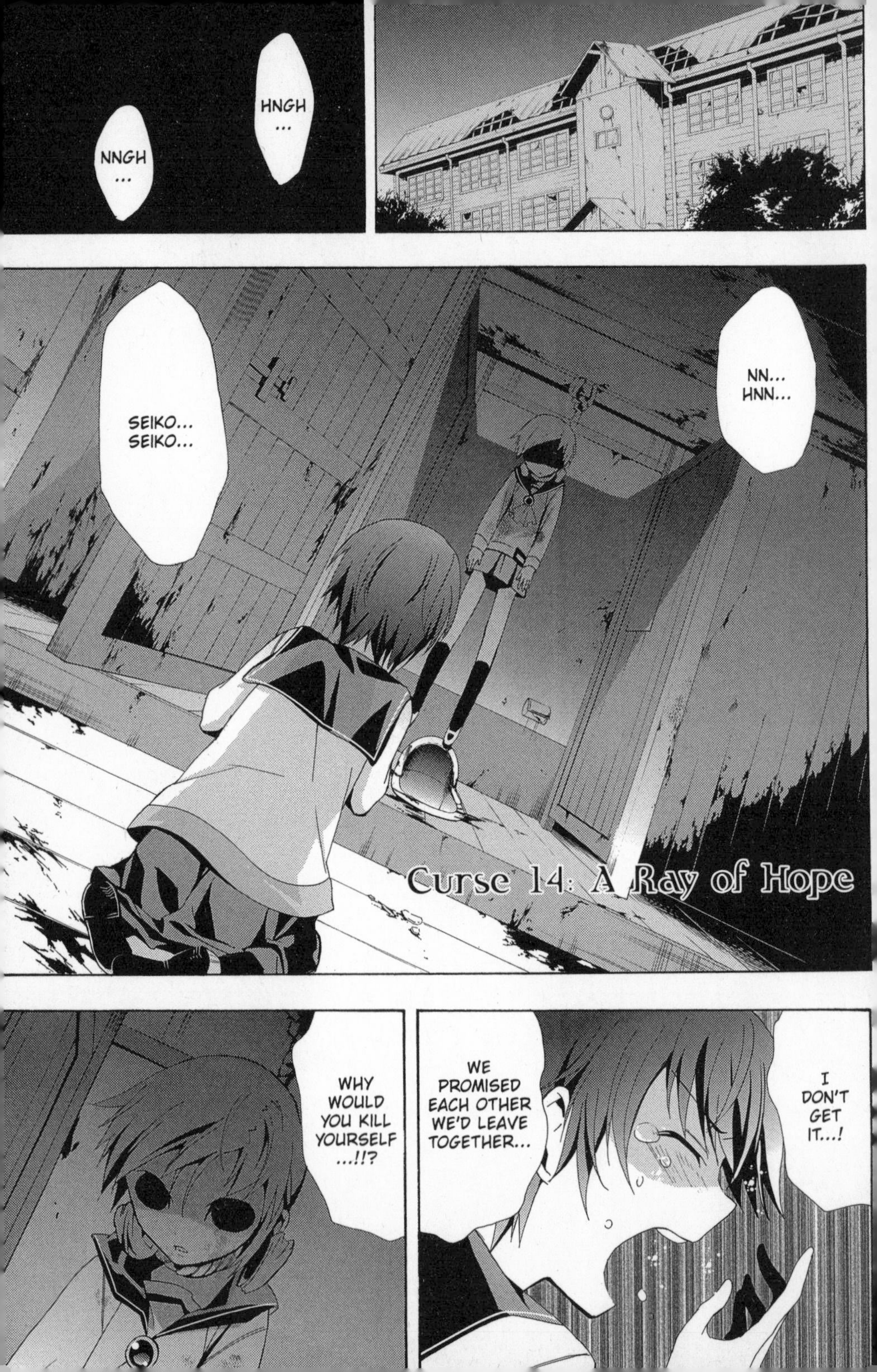
HNGH...
NNGH...
NN... HNN...
SEIKO... SEIKO...
Curse 14: A Ray of Hope
I DON'T GET IT...!
WE PROMISED EACH OTHER WE'D LEAVE TOGETHER...
WHY WOULD YOU KILL YOURSELF...!!?

a list of corpses/06

Kisaragi Academy, Class 2-9,
Mayu Suzumoto

Died when slammed against
a wall by the child ghosts.

Her remains were splattered
all over the wall.

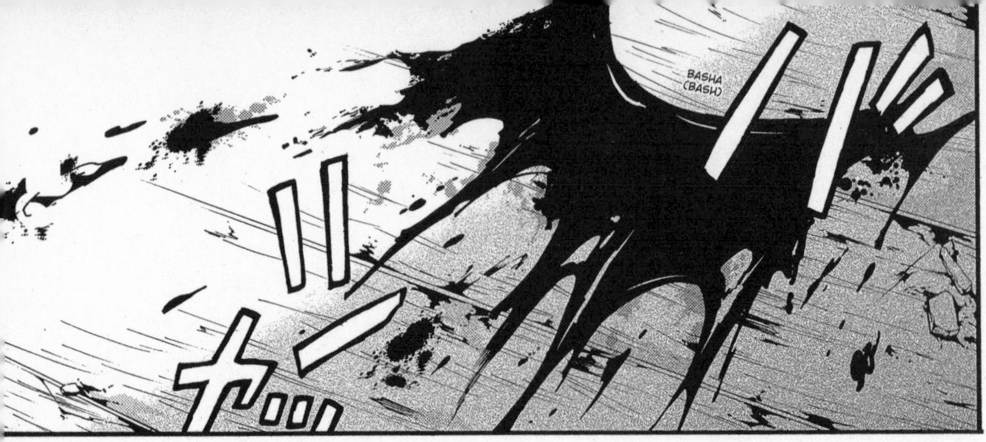
BASHA
(BASH)

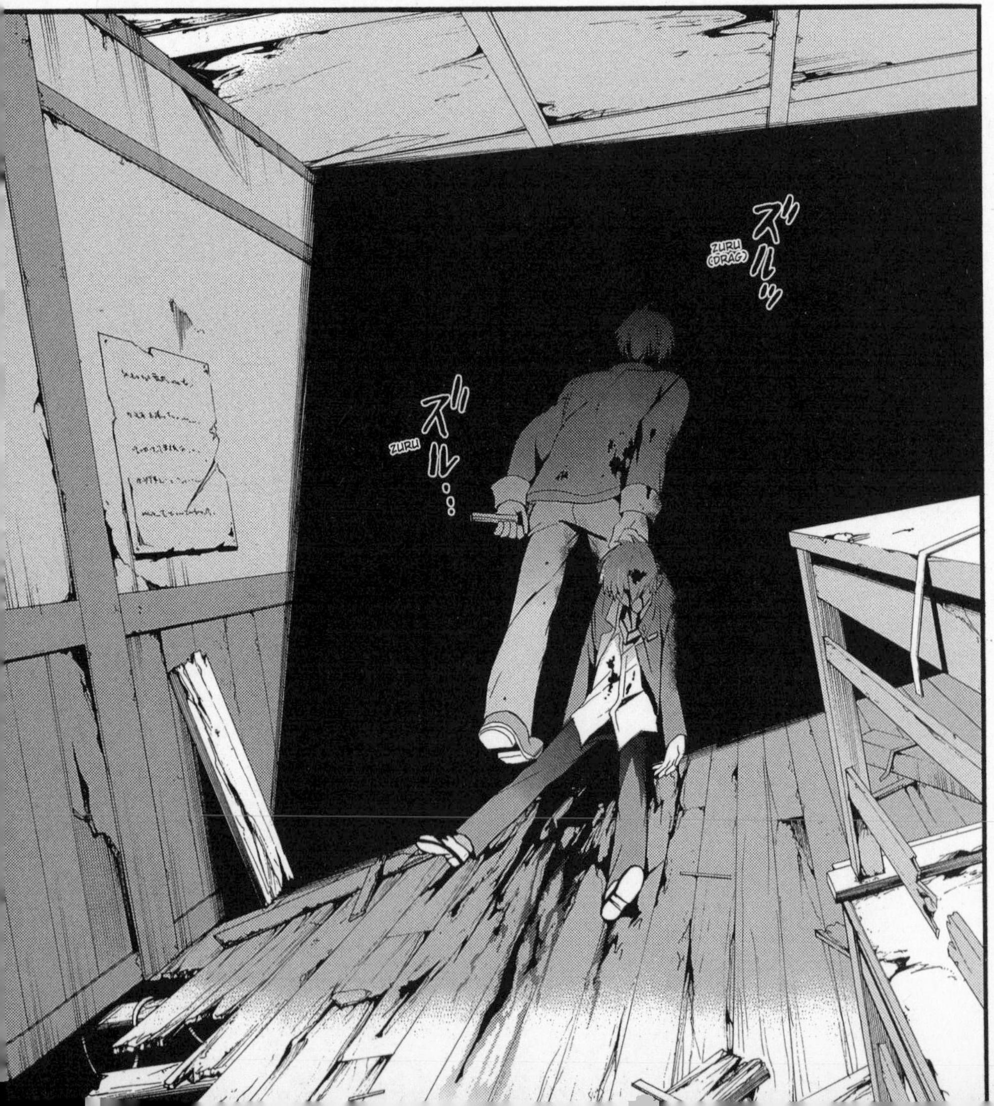
ズルッ
ZURU
(DRAG)
ズル‥
ZURU

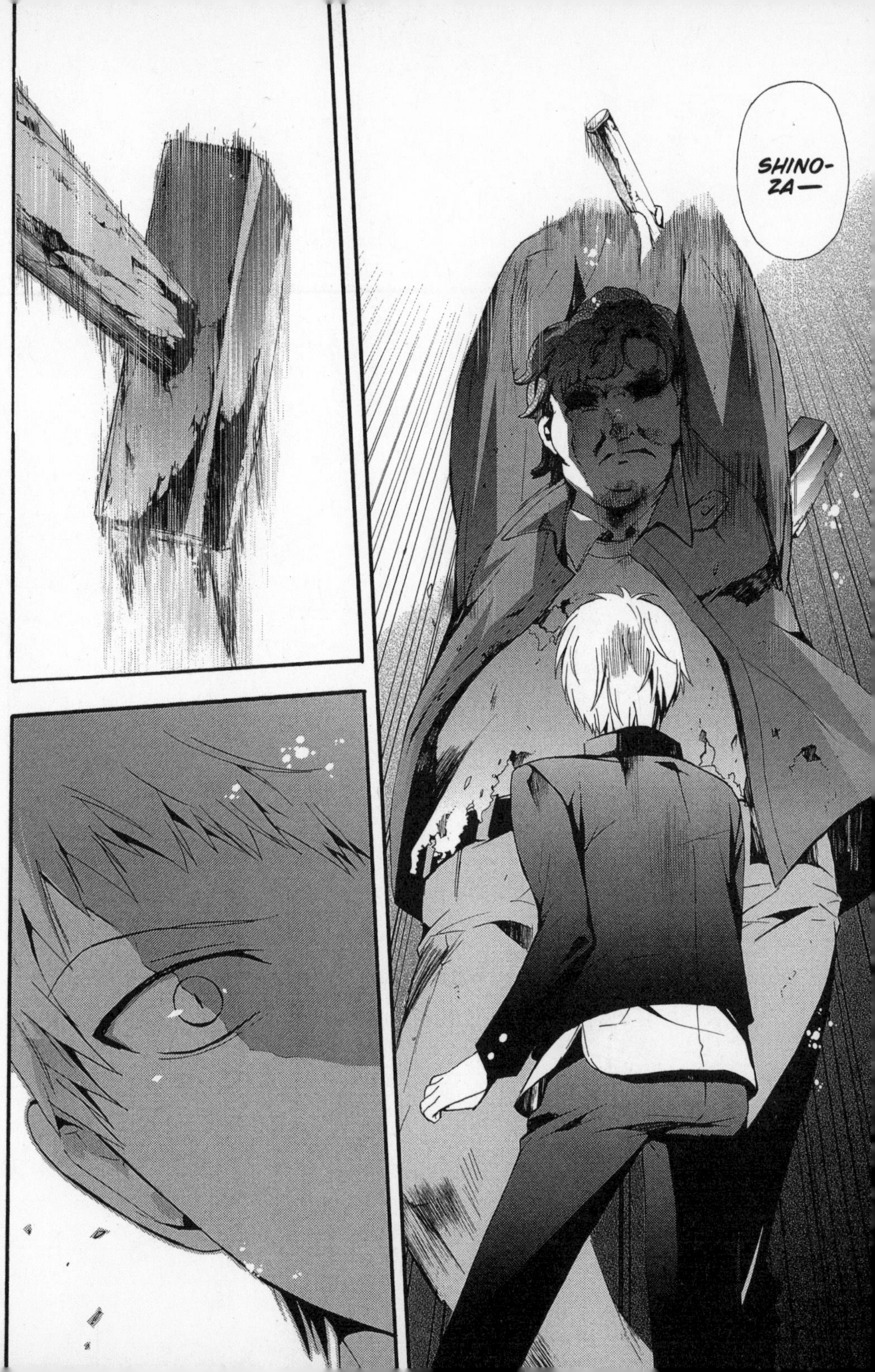
SHINO-
ZA—

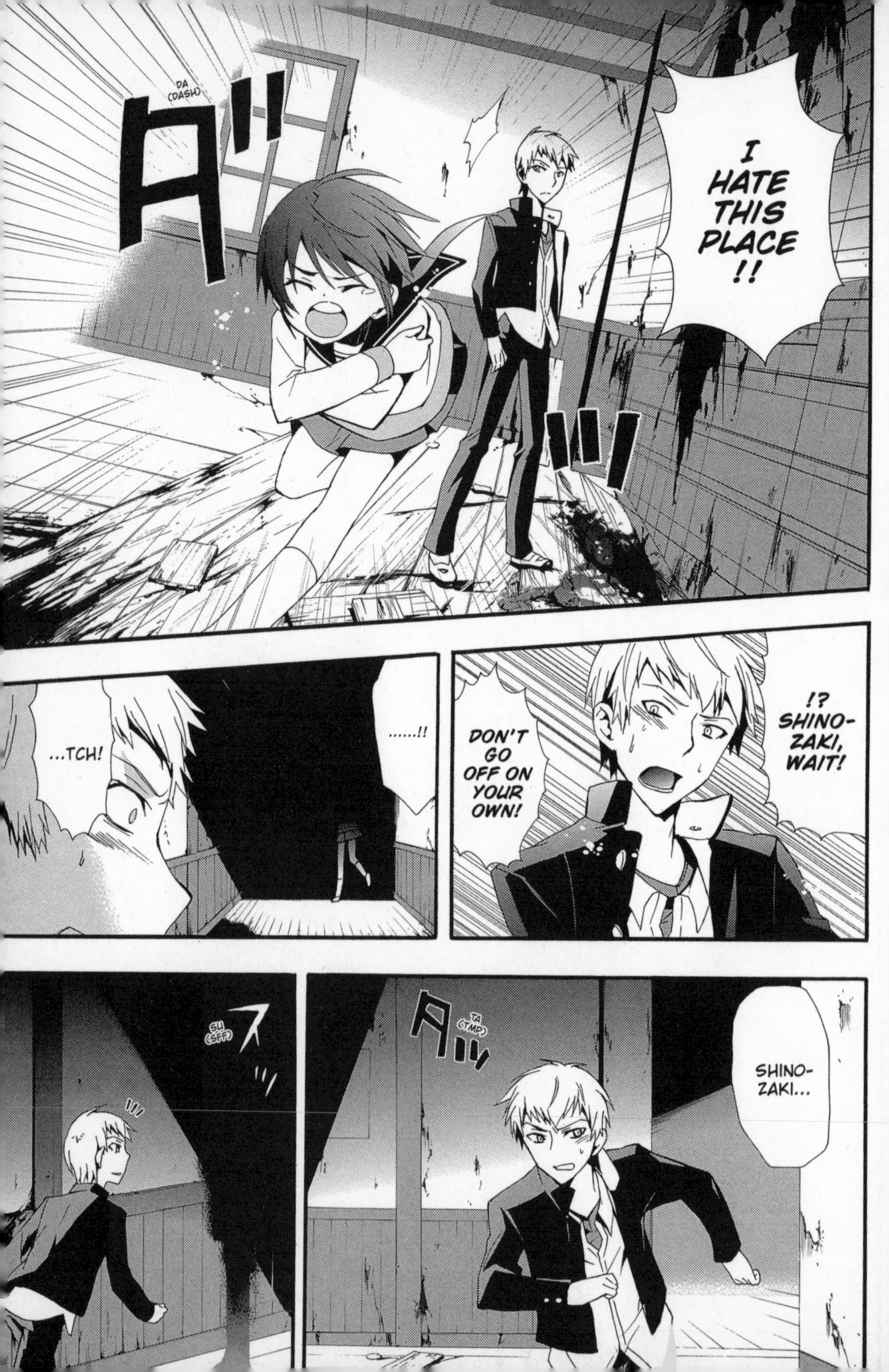
I HATE THIS PLACE !!
DA (DASH)
!? SHINO-ZAKI, WAIT!
DON'T GO OFF ON YOUR OWN!
......!!
...TCH!
SHINO-ZAKI...
TA (TMP)
SU (SFF)

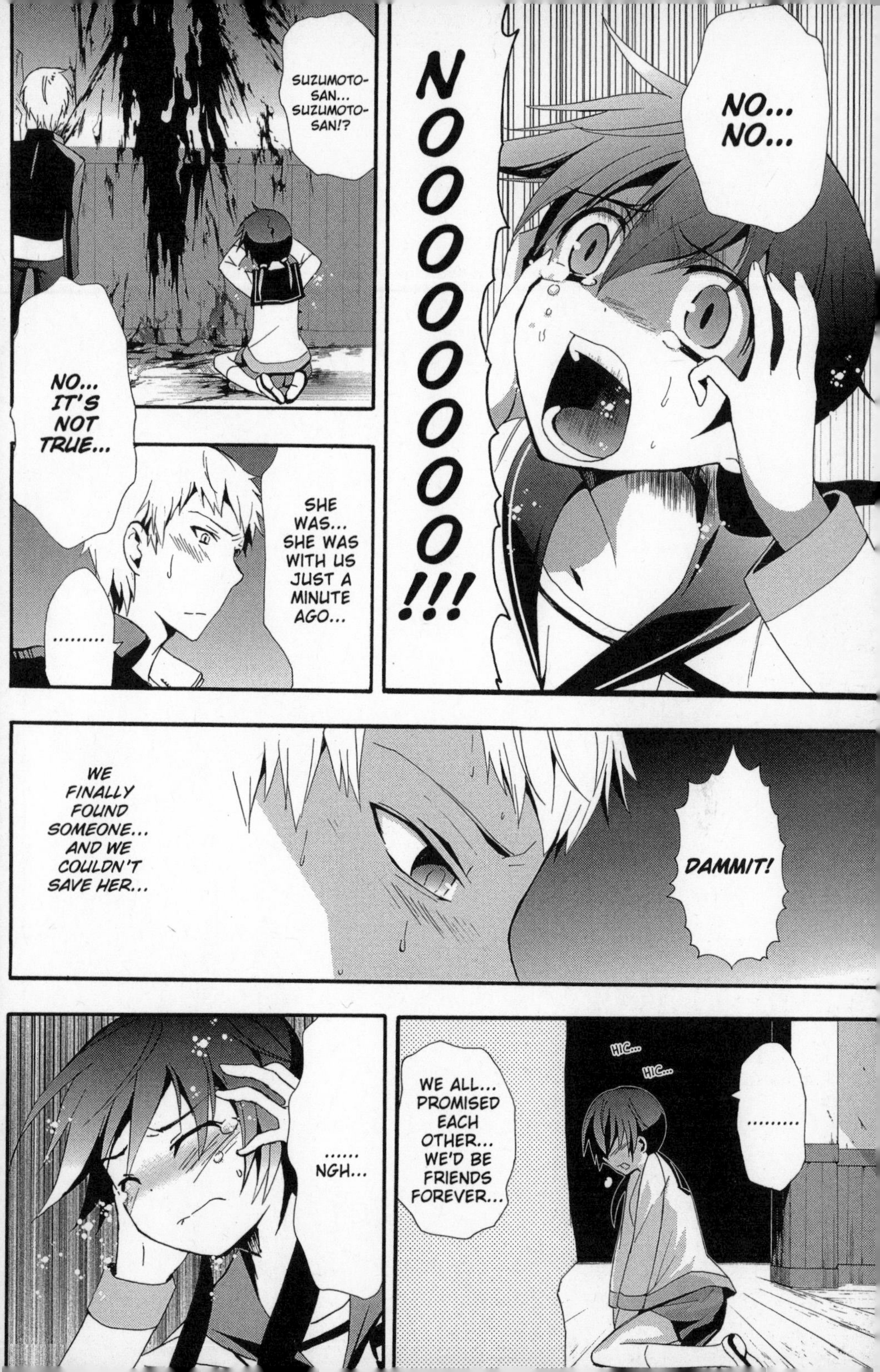
NO... NO...
NOOOOOOOOOO!!!
SUZUMOTO-SAN... SUZUMOTO-SAN!?
NO... IT'S NOT TRUE...
SHE WAS... SHE WAS WITH US JUST A MINUTE AGO...
....
DAMMIT!
WE FINALLY FOUND SOMEONE... AND WE COULDN'T SAVE HER...
....
HIC... HIC...
WE ALL... PROMISED EACH OTHER... WE'D BE FRIENDS FOREVER...
...... NGH...

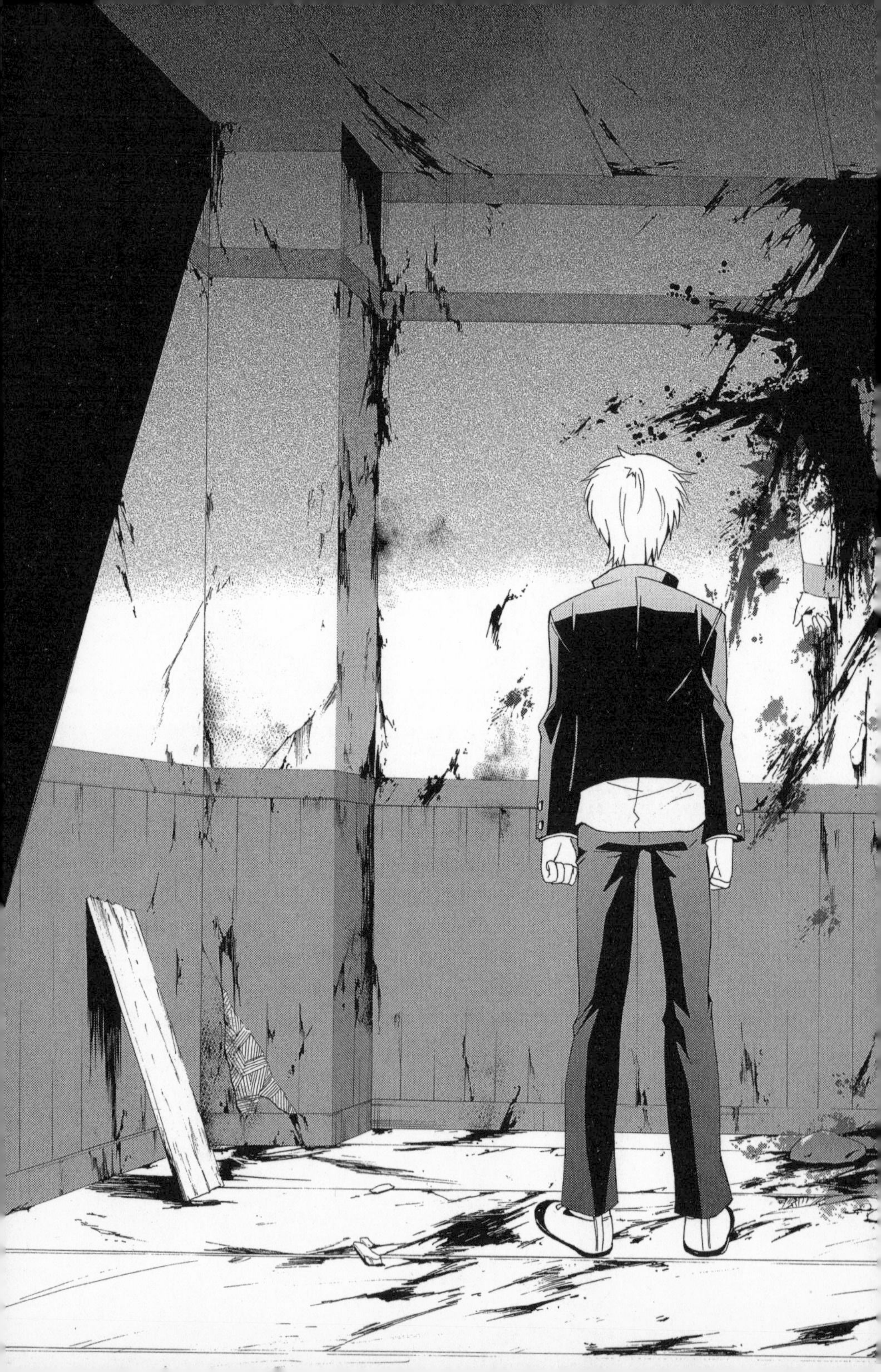

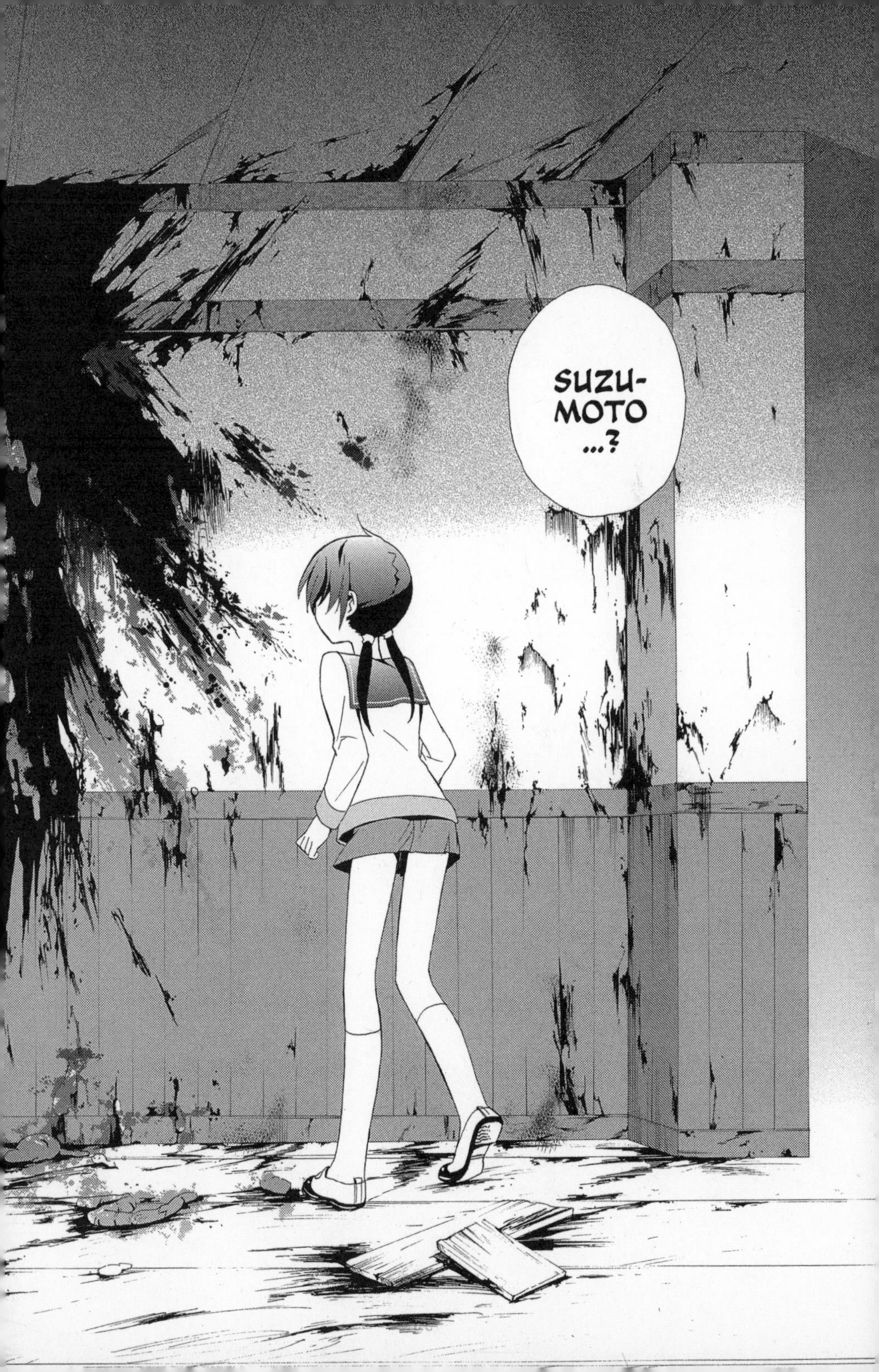
SUZU-MOTO ...?

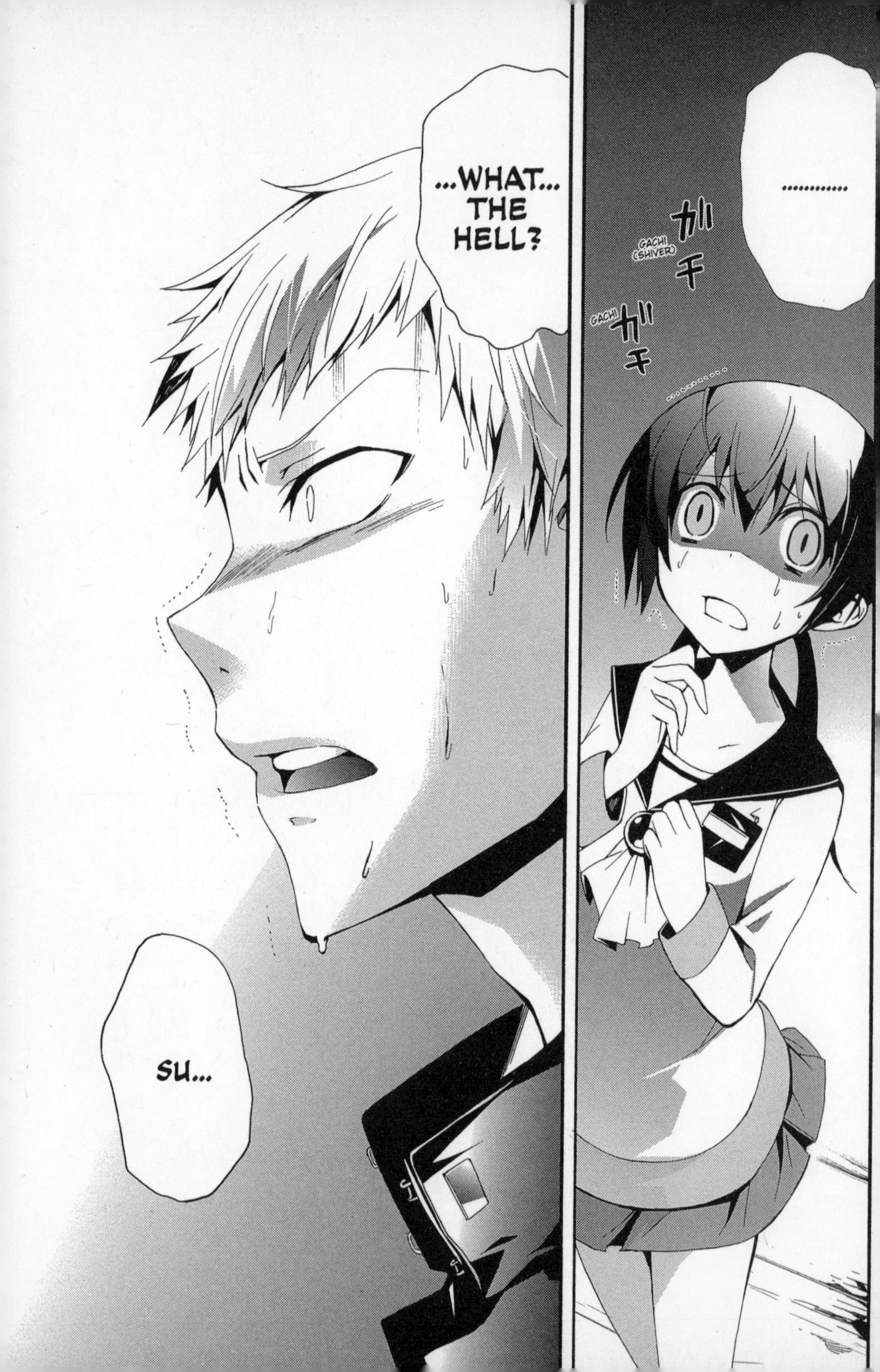

....
ガチ
GACHI (SHIVER)
ガチ
GACHI
...WHAT... THE HELL?
SU...

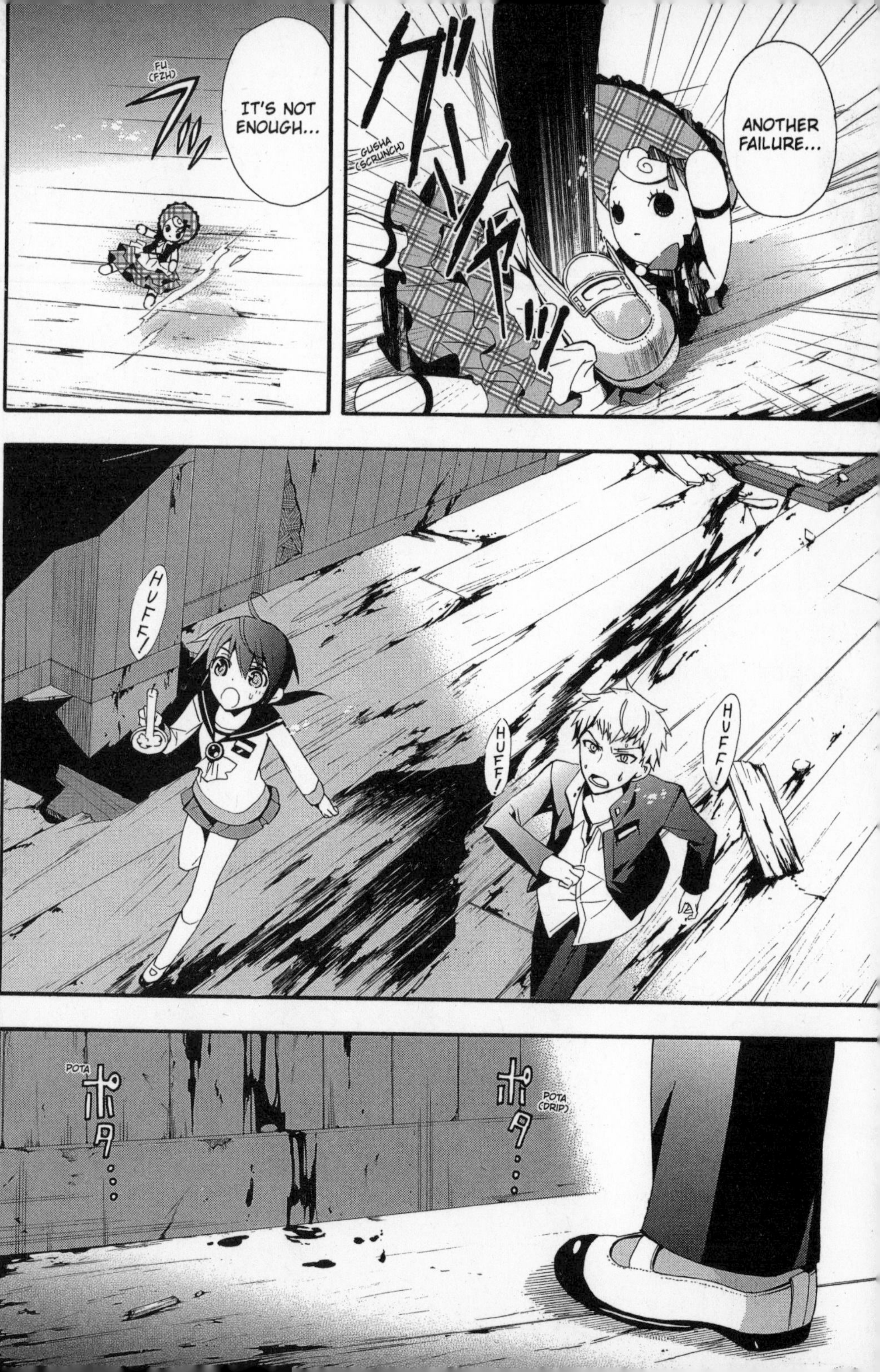
ANOTHER FAILURE...
GUSHA (SCRUNCH)
FU (FZH)
IT'S NOT ENOUGH...
HUFF!
HUFF!
HUFF!
ポタ...
POTA (DRIP)
ポタ...
POTA

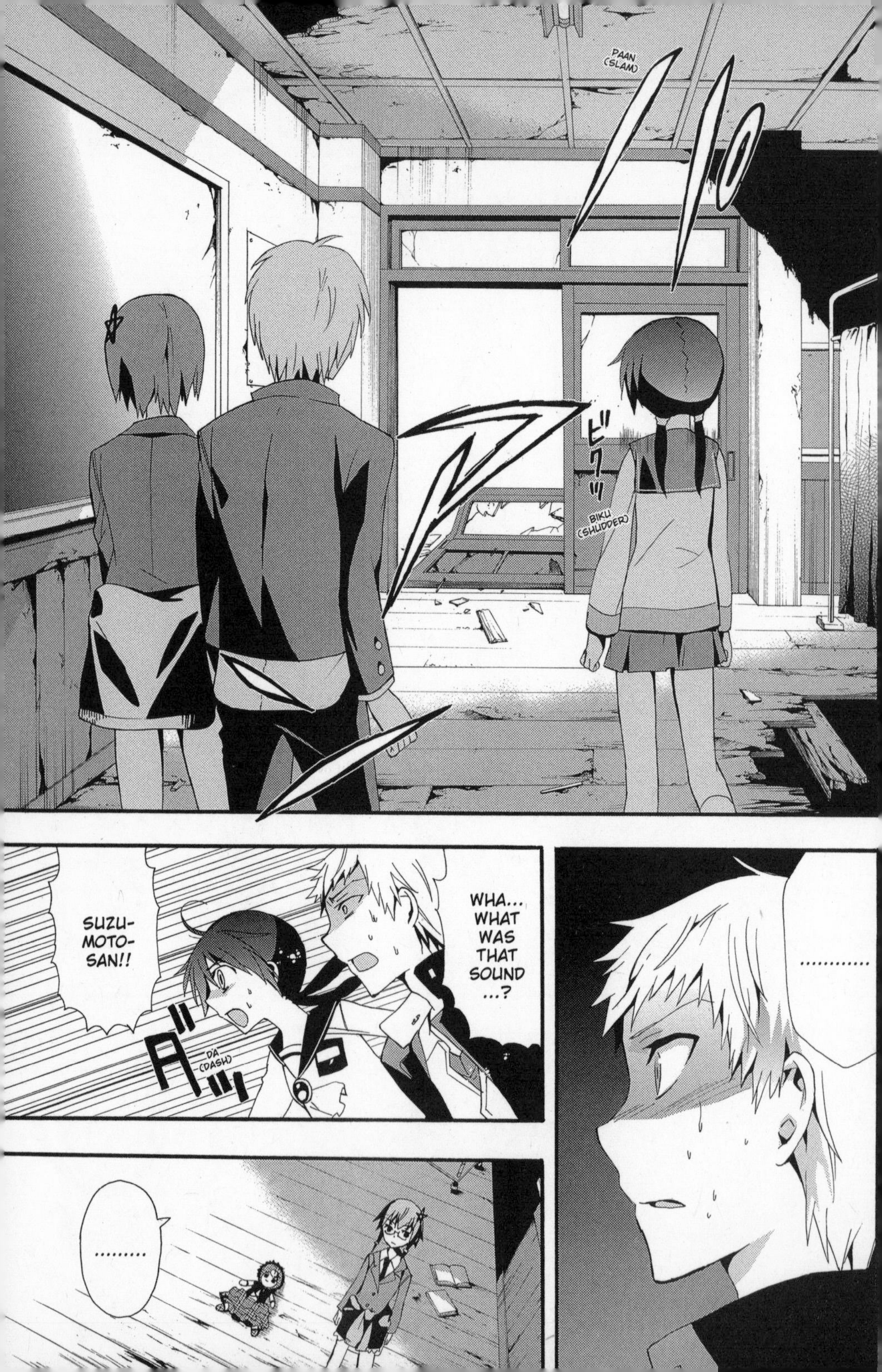
PAAN (SLAM)
BIKU (SHUDDER)
....
WHA... WHAT WAS THAT SOUND ...?
SUZU-MOTO-SAN!!
DA (DASH)
....

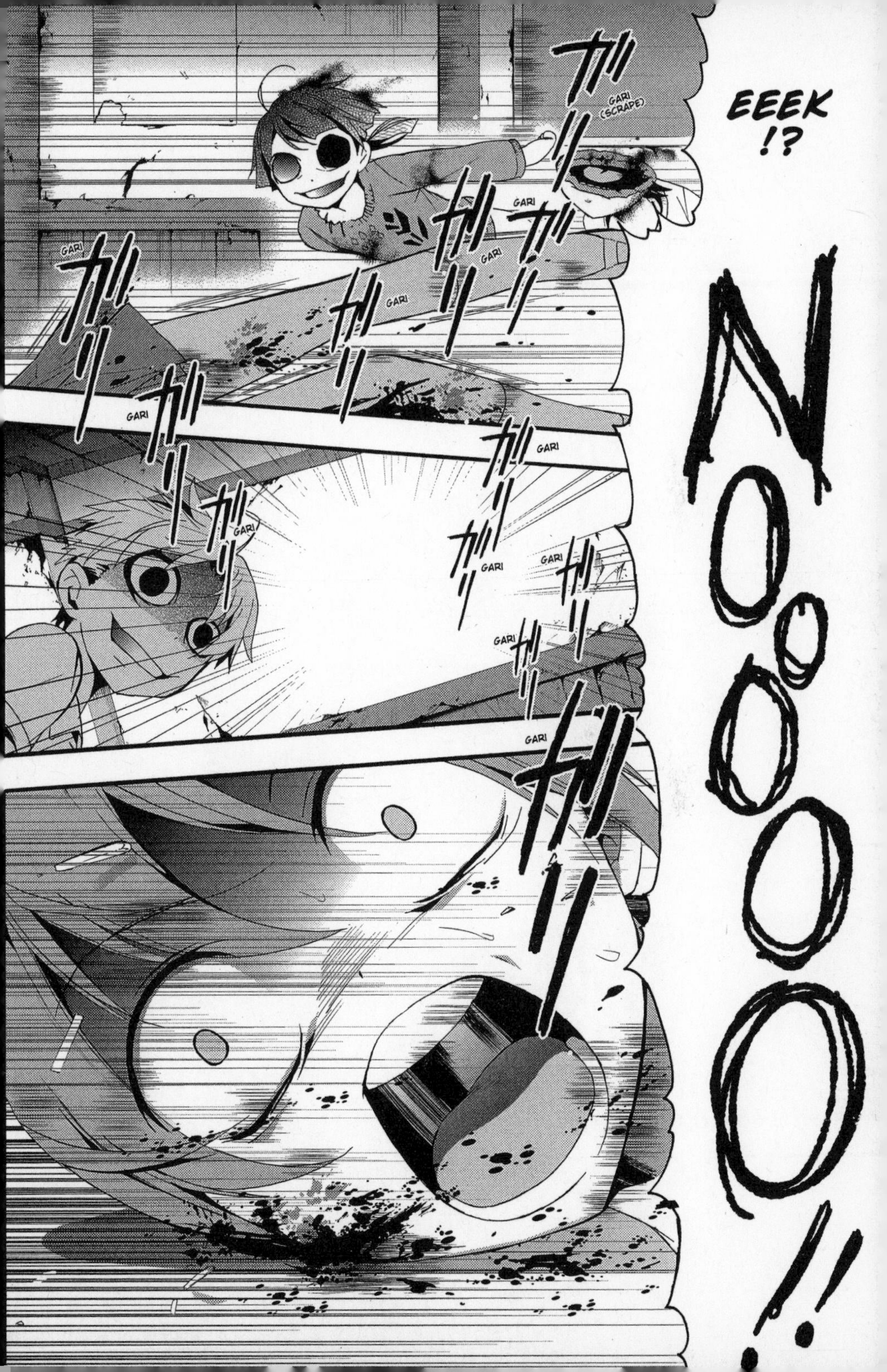
EEEK !?
NOOOOO!!
GARI (SCRAPE)
GARI
GARI
GARI
GARI
GARI
GARI
GARI
GARI
GARI
GARI
GARI

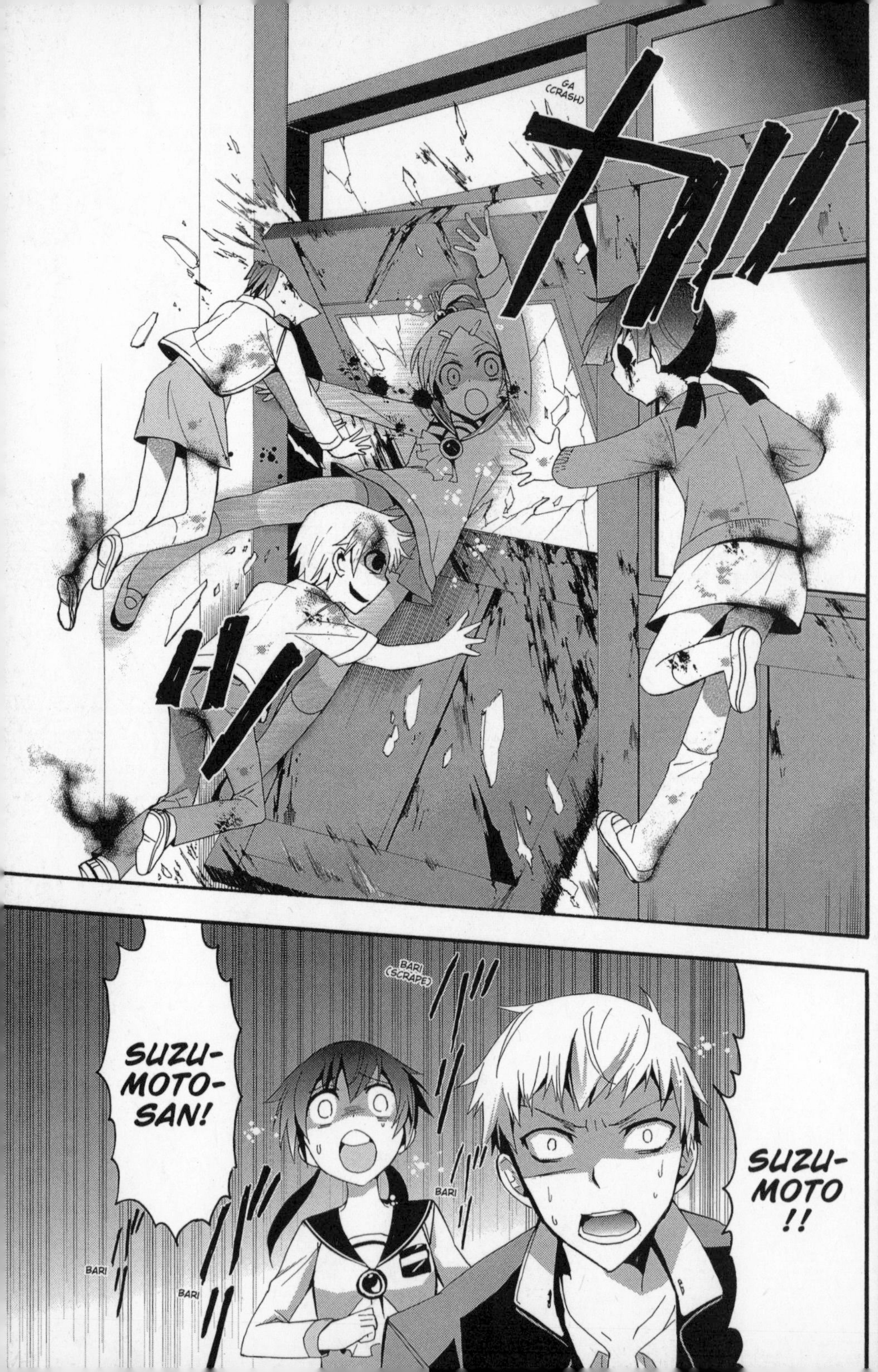
GA (CRASH)
BARI (SCRAPE)
SUZU-MOTO!!
SUZU-MOTO-SAN!
BARI
BARI
BARI

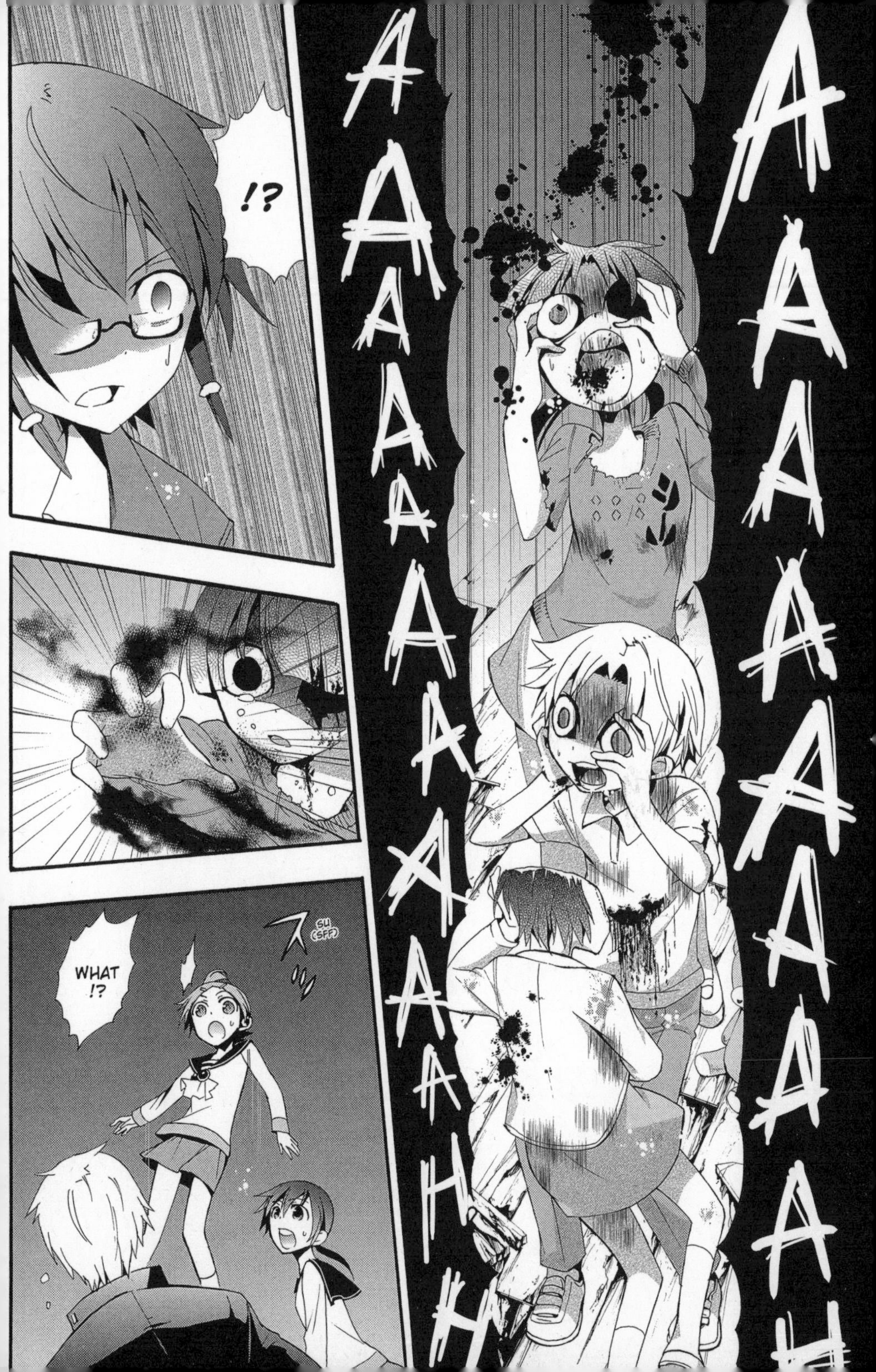

AAAAAAAAAAAAAAH
AAAAAAAAAAAAAAAAAH
!?
SU (SFF)
WHAT !?

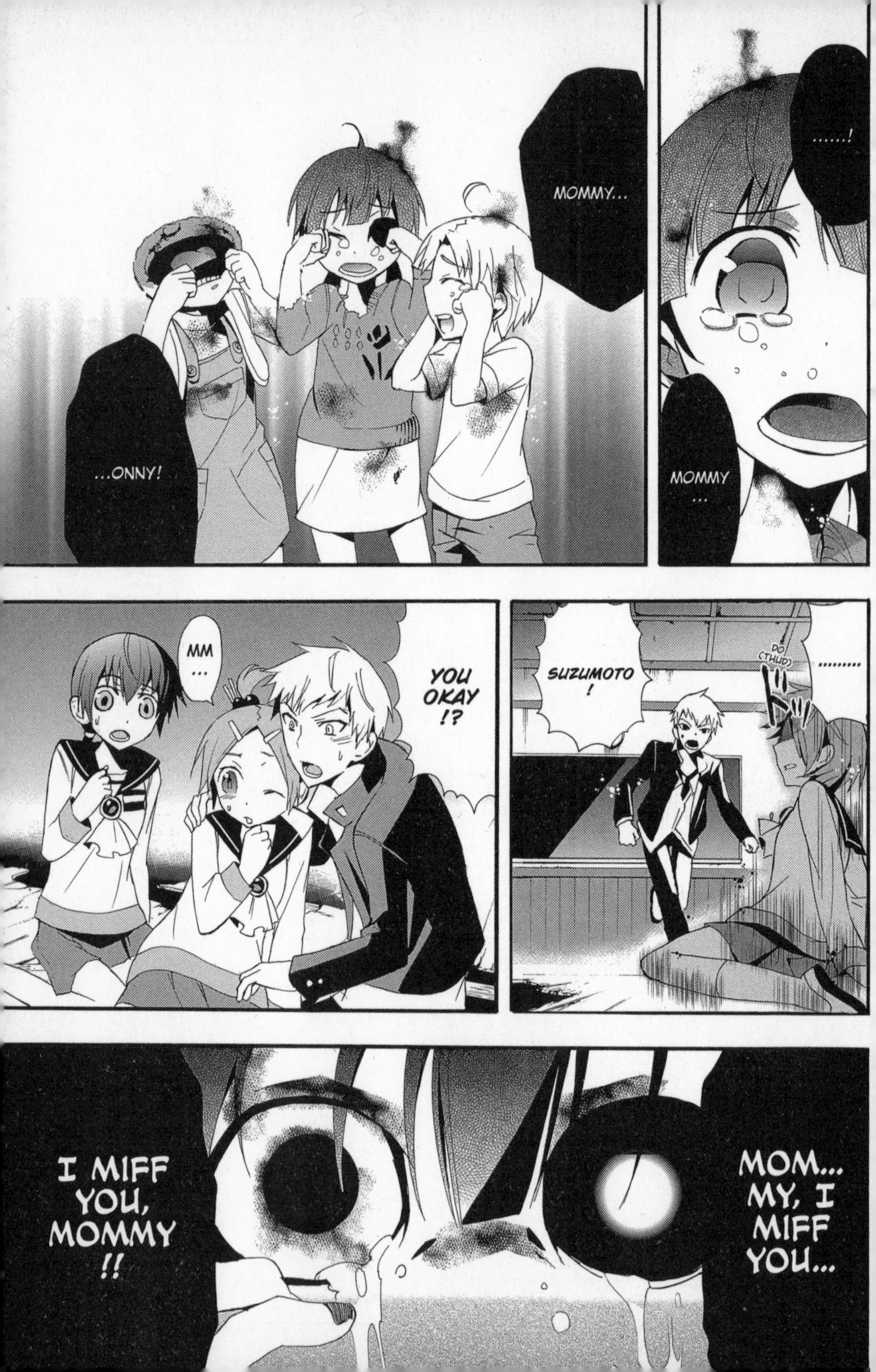
......!
MOMMY ...
MOMMY...
...ONNY!
....
DO (THUD)
SUZUMOTO !
YOU OKAY !?
MM ...
MOM... MY, I MIFF YOU...
I MIFF YOU, MOMMY !!

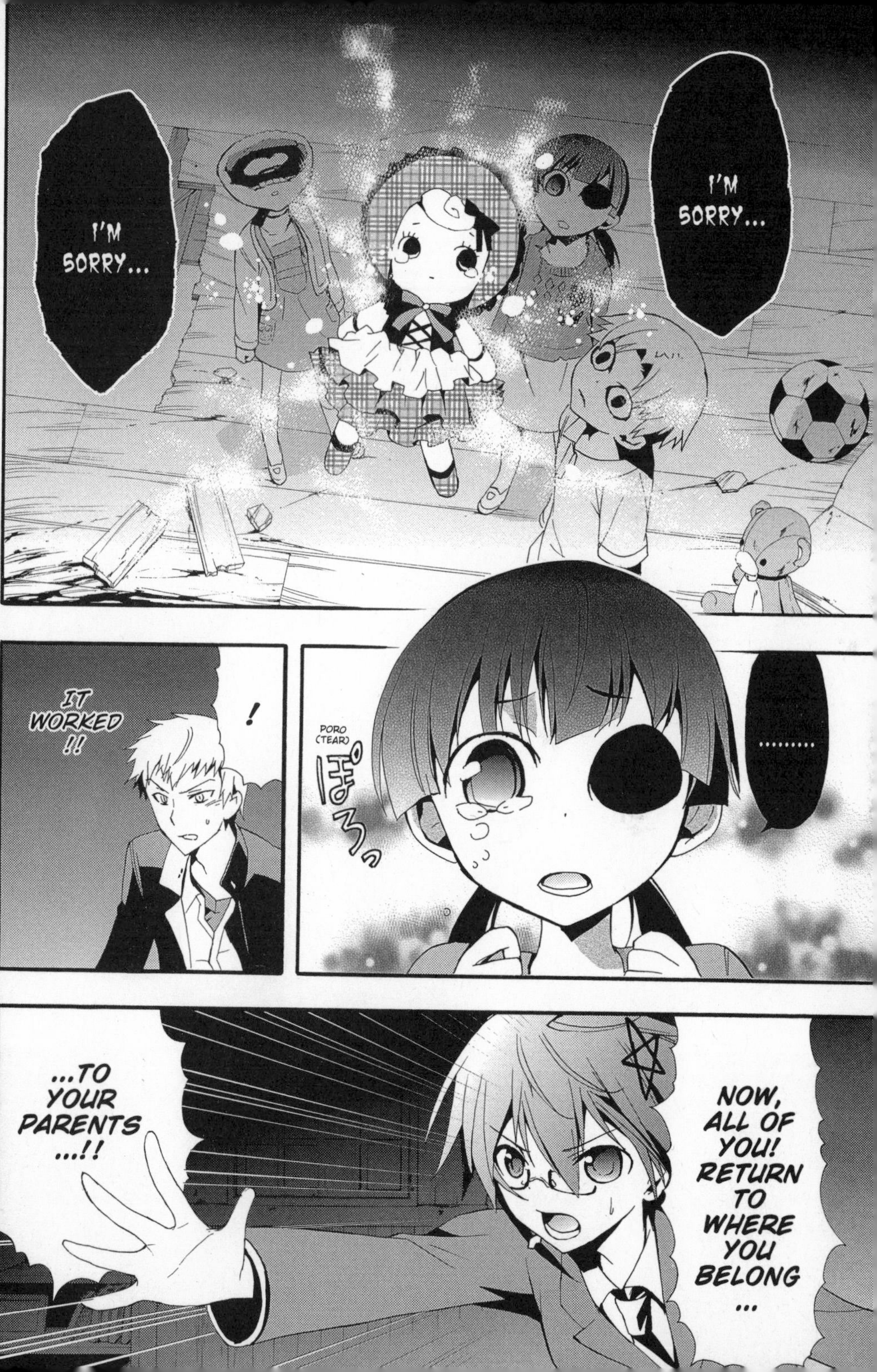
I'M SORRY...
I'M SORRY...
....
PORO (TEAR)
ぽろっ
!
IT WORKED!!
NOW, ALL OF YOU! RETURN TO WHERE YOU BELONG...
...TO YOUR PARENTS...!!

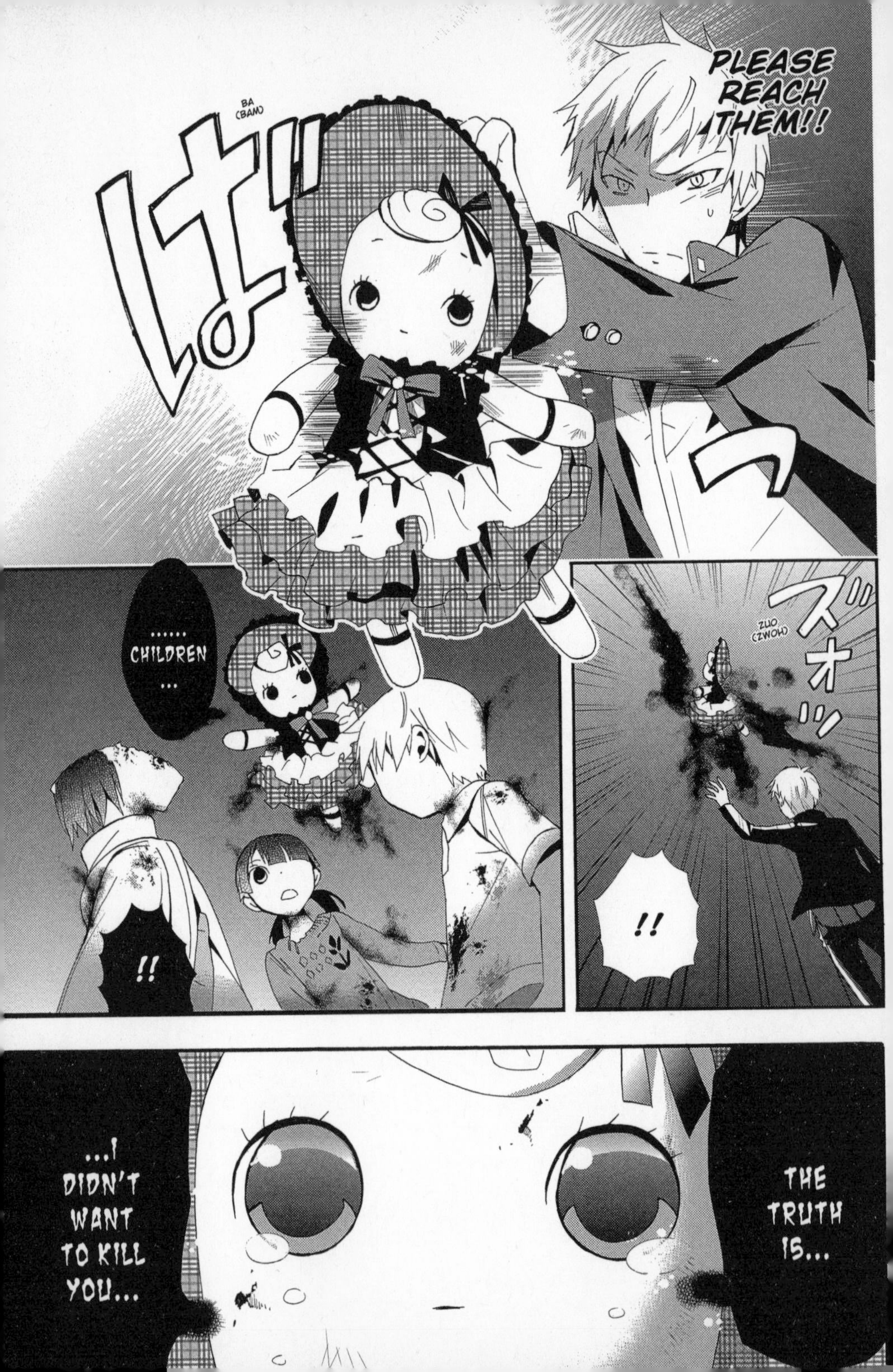
PLEASE REACH THEM!!
BA (BAM)
ZUO (ZWOH)
!!
...... CHILDREN ...
!!
THE TRUTH IS...
...I DIDN'T WANT TO KILL YOU...

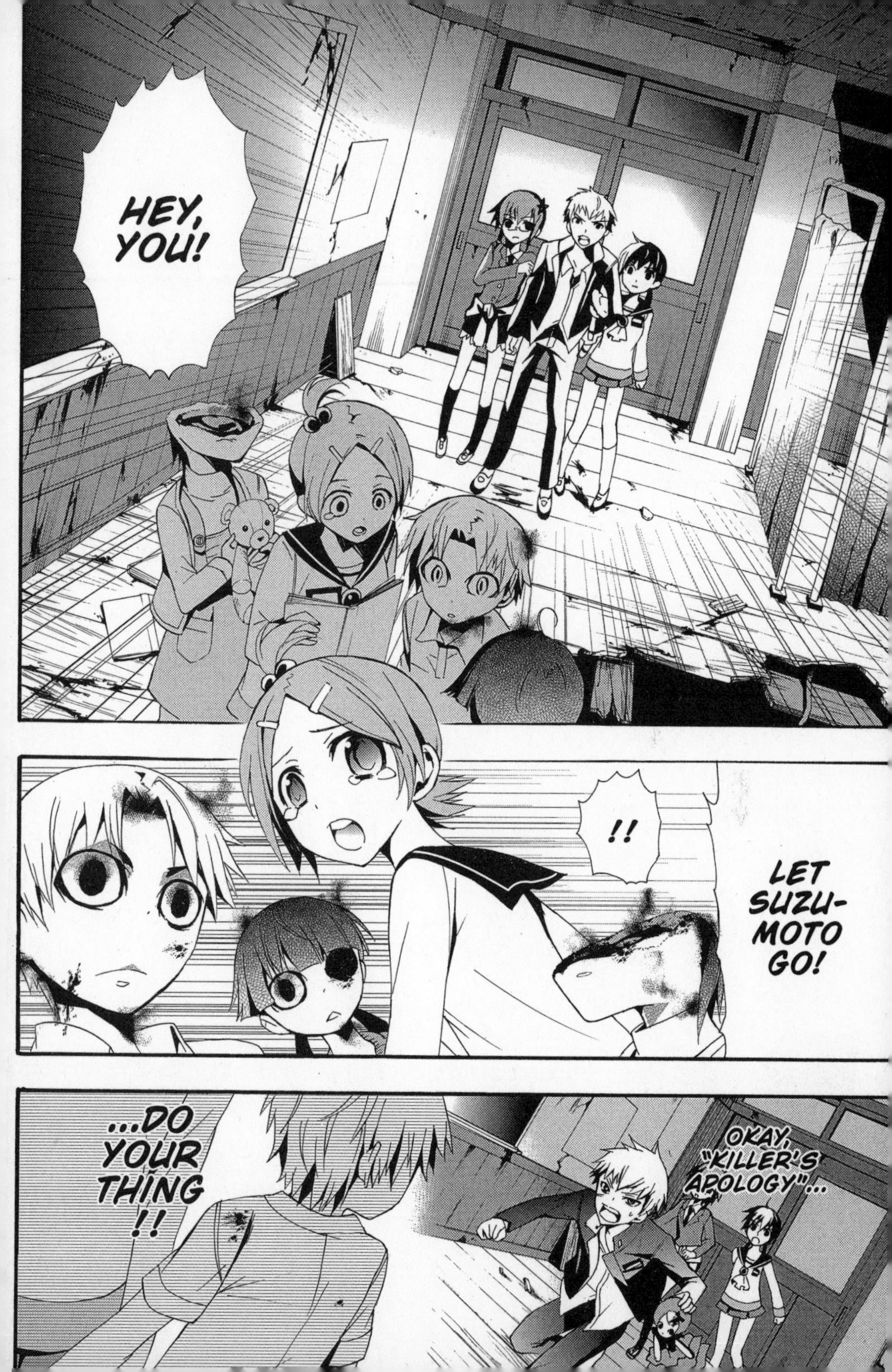
HEY, YOU!
LET SUZU-MOTO GO!
!!
OKAY, "KILLER'S APOLOGY"...
...DO YOUR THING!!

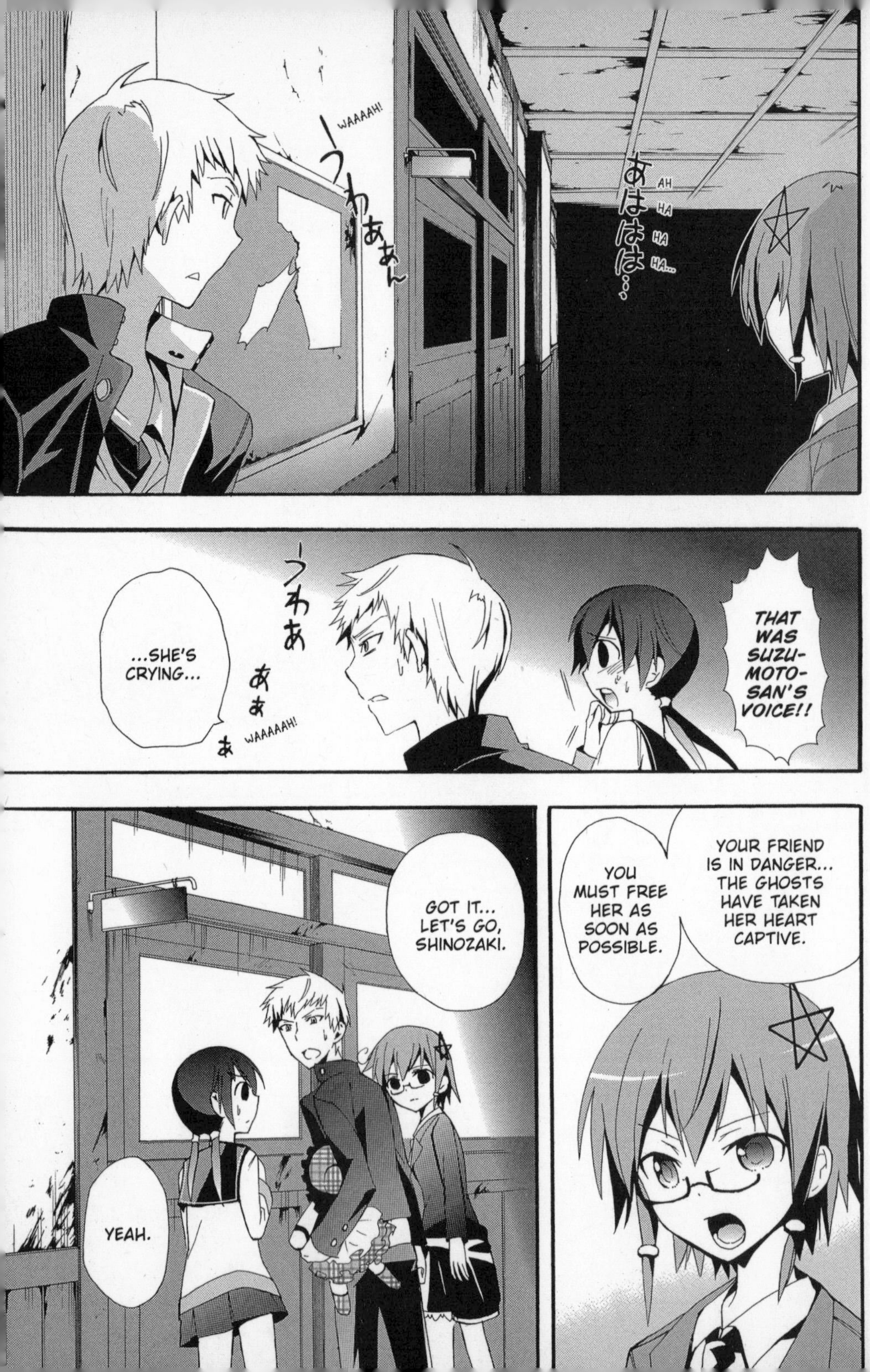
あははは…
AH HA HA HA...
うわああん
WAAAAH!
THAT WAS SUZU-MOTO-SAN'S VOICE!!
うわあああ
WAAAAAH!
...SHE'S CRYING...
YOUR FRIEND IS IN DANGER... THE GHOSTS HAVE TAKEN HER HEART CAPTIVE.
YOU MUST FREE HER AS SOON AS POSSIBLE.
GOT IT... LET'S GO, SHINOZAKI.
YEAH.

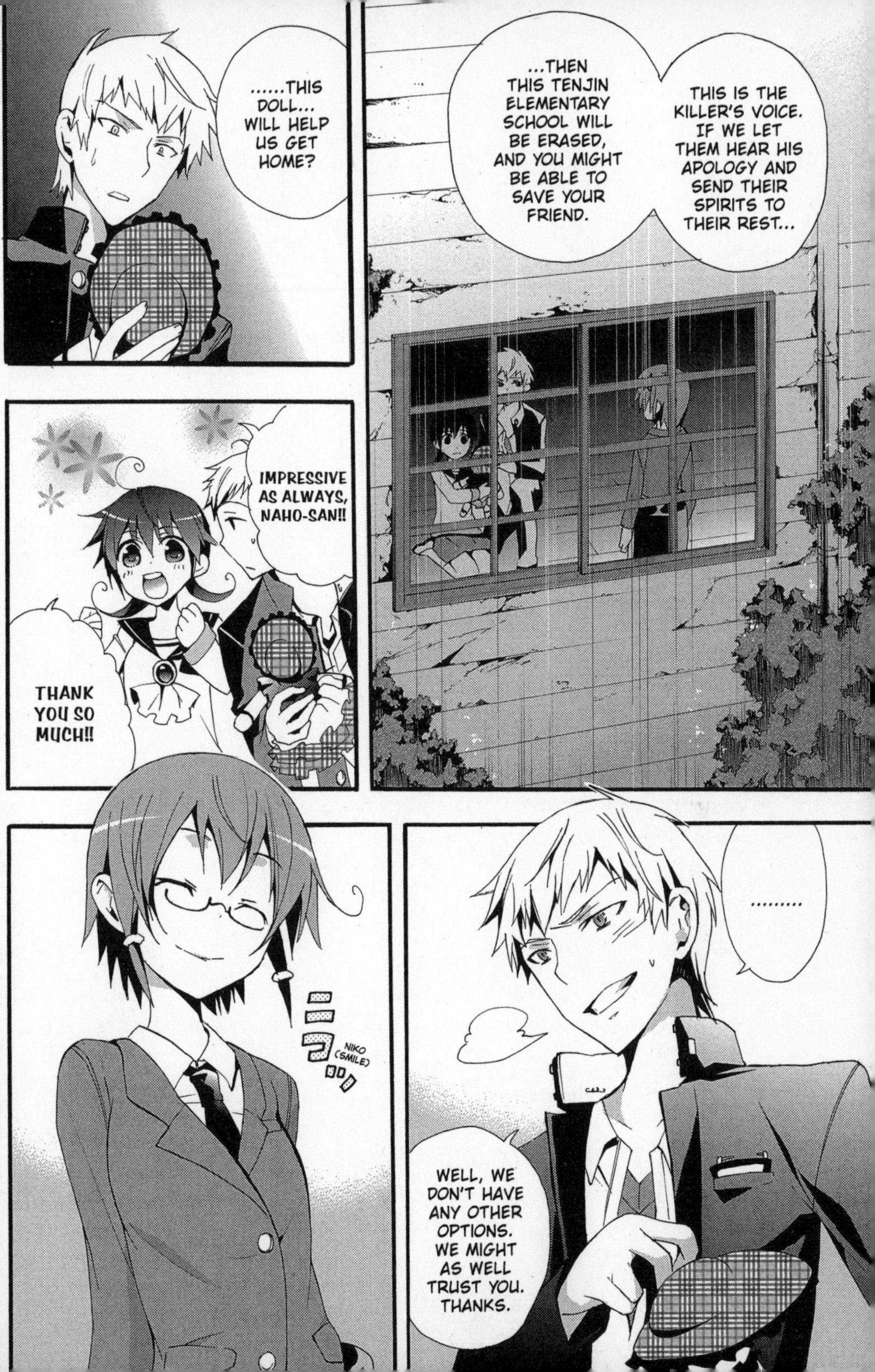

THIS IS THE KILLER'S VOICE. IF WE LET THEM HEAR HIS APOLOGY AND SEND THEIR SPIRITS TO THEIR REST...
...THEN THIS TENJIN ELEMENTARY SCHOOL WILL BE ERASED, AND YOU MIGHT BE ABLE TO SAVE YOUR FRIEND.
......THIS DOLL... WILL HELP US GET HOME?
IMPRESSIVE AS ALWAYS, NAHO-SAN!!
THANK YOU SO MUCH!!
....
WELL, WE DON'T HAVE ANY OTHER OPTIONS. WE MIGHT AS WELL TRUST YOU. THANKS.
NIKO (SMILE)

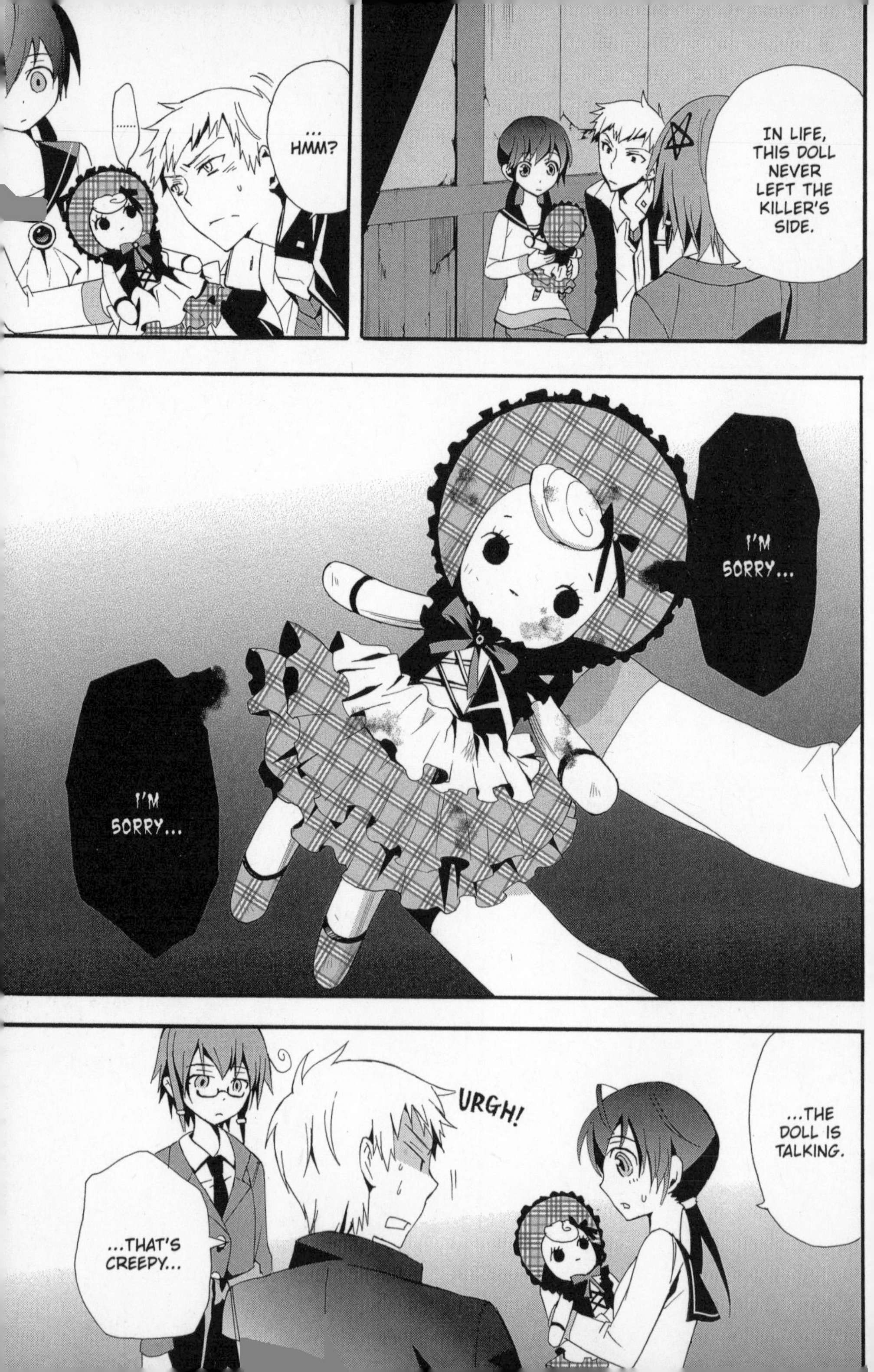
IN LIFE, THIS DOLL NEVER LEFT THE KILLER'S SIDE.
... HMM?
......
I'M SORRY...
I'M SORRY...
...THE DOLL IS TALKING.
URGH!
...THAT'S CREEPY...

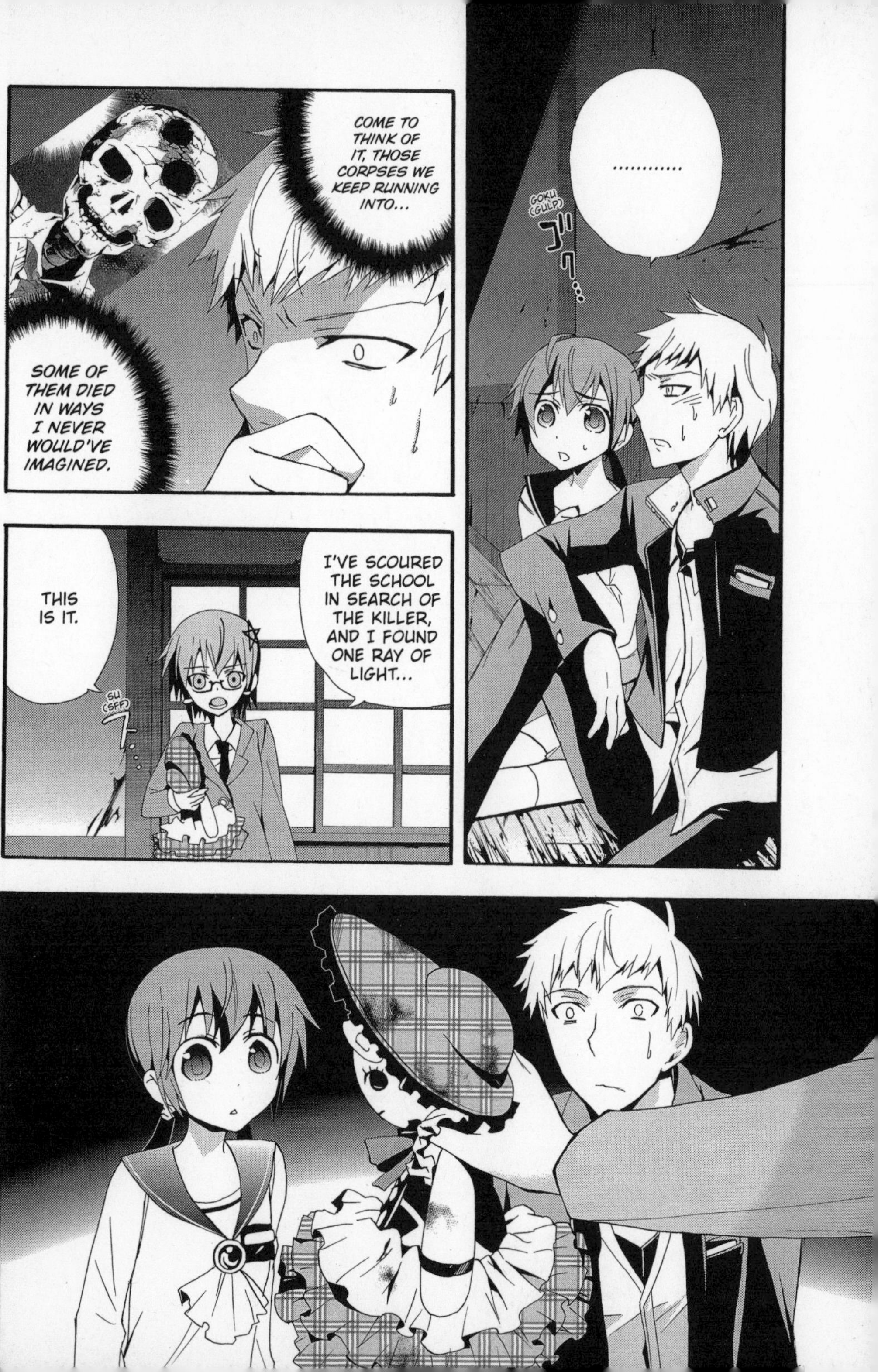
....
GOKU (GULP)
COME TO THINK OF IT, THOSE CORPSES WE KEEP RUNNING INTO...
SOME OF THEM DIED IN WAYS I NEVER WOULD'VE IMAGINED.
I'VE SCOURED THE SCHOOL IN SEARCH OF THE KILLER, AND I FOUND ONE RAY OF LIGHT...
THIS IS IT.
SU (SFF)

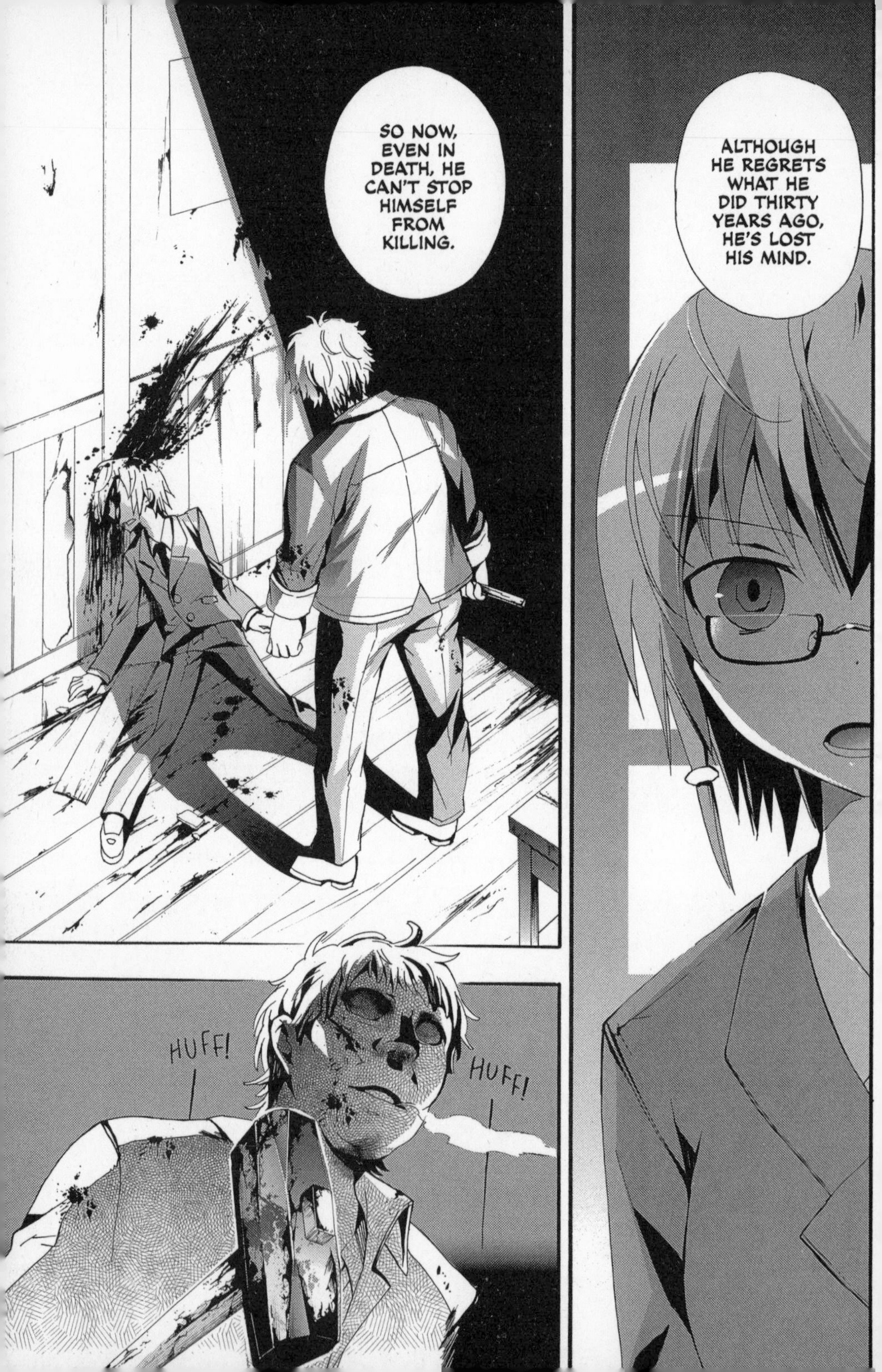
ALTHOUGH HE REGRETS WHAT HE DID THIRTY YEARS AGO, HE'S LOST HIS MIND.
SO NOW, EVEN IN DEATH, HE CAN'T STOP HIMSELF FROM KILLING.
HUFF!
HUFF!

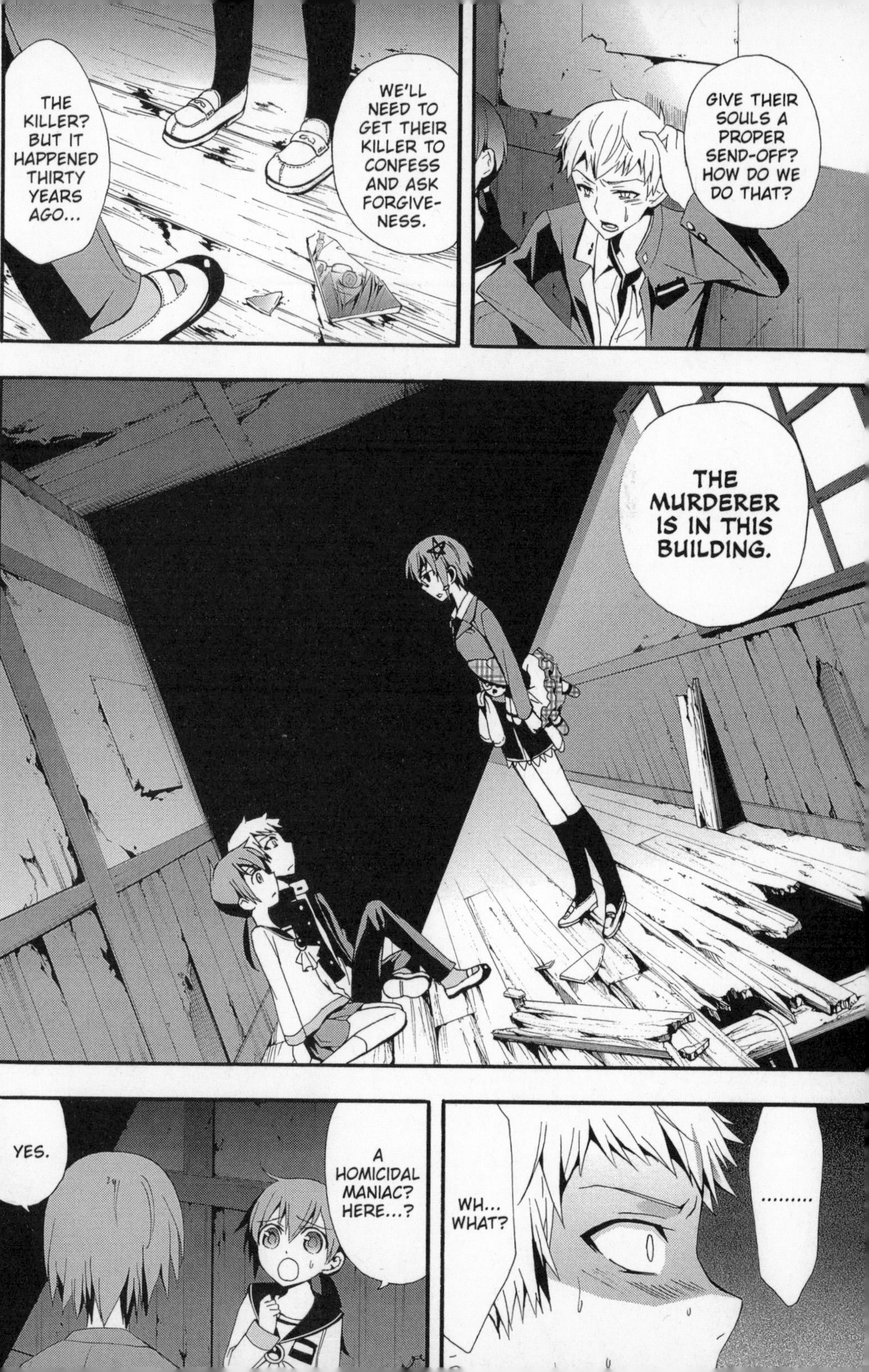
GIVE THEIR SOULS A PROPER SEND-OFF? HOW DO WE DO THAT?
WE'LL NEED TO GET THEIR KILLER TO CONFESS AND ASK FORGIVE-NESS.
THE KILLER? BUT IT HAPPENED THIRTY YEARS AGO...
THE MURDERER IS IN THIS BUILDING.
....
WH... WHAT?
A HOMICIDAL MANIAC? HERE...?
YES.

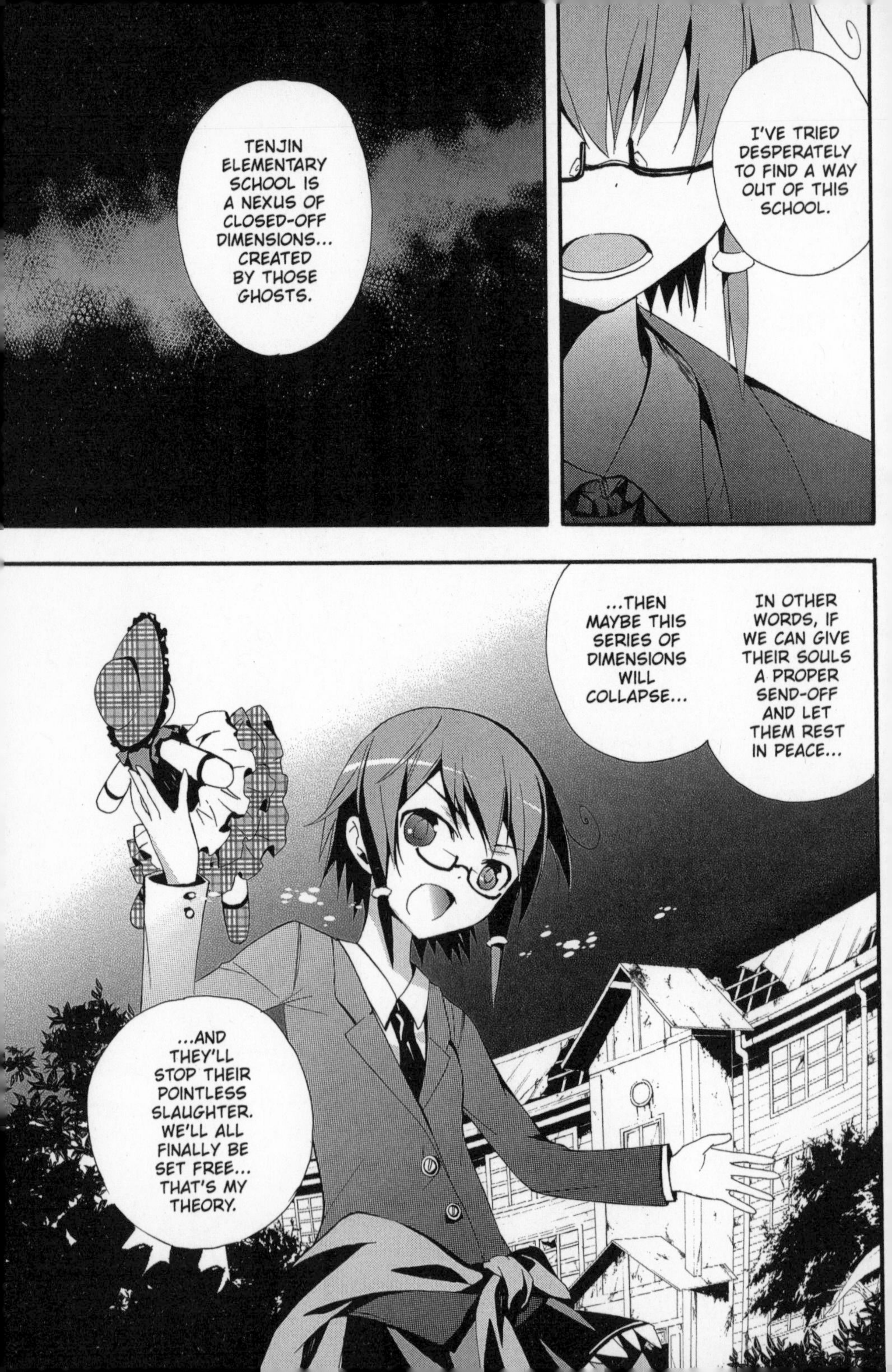
I'VE TRIED DESPERATELY TO FIND A WAY OUT OF THIS SCHOOL.
TENJIN ELEMENTARY SCHOOL IS A NEXUS OF CLOSED-OFF DIMENSIONS... CREATED BY THOSE GHOSTS.
IN OTHER WORDS, IF WE CAN GIVE THEIR SOULS A PROPER SEND-OFF AND LET THEM REST IN PEACE...
...THEN MAYBE THIS SERIES OF DIMENSIONS WILL COLLAPSE...
...AND THEY'LL STOP THEIR POINTLESS SLAUGHTER. WE'LL ALL FINALLY BE SET FREE... THAT'S MY THEORY.

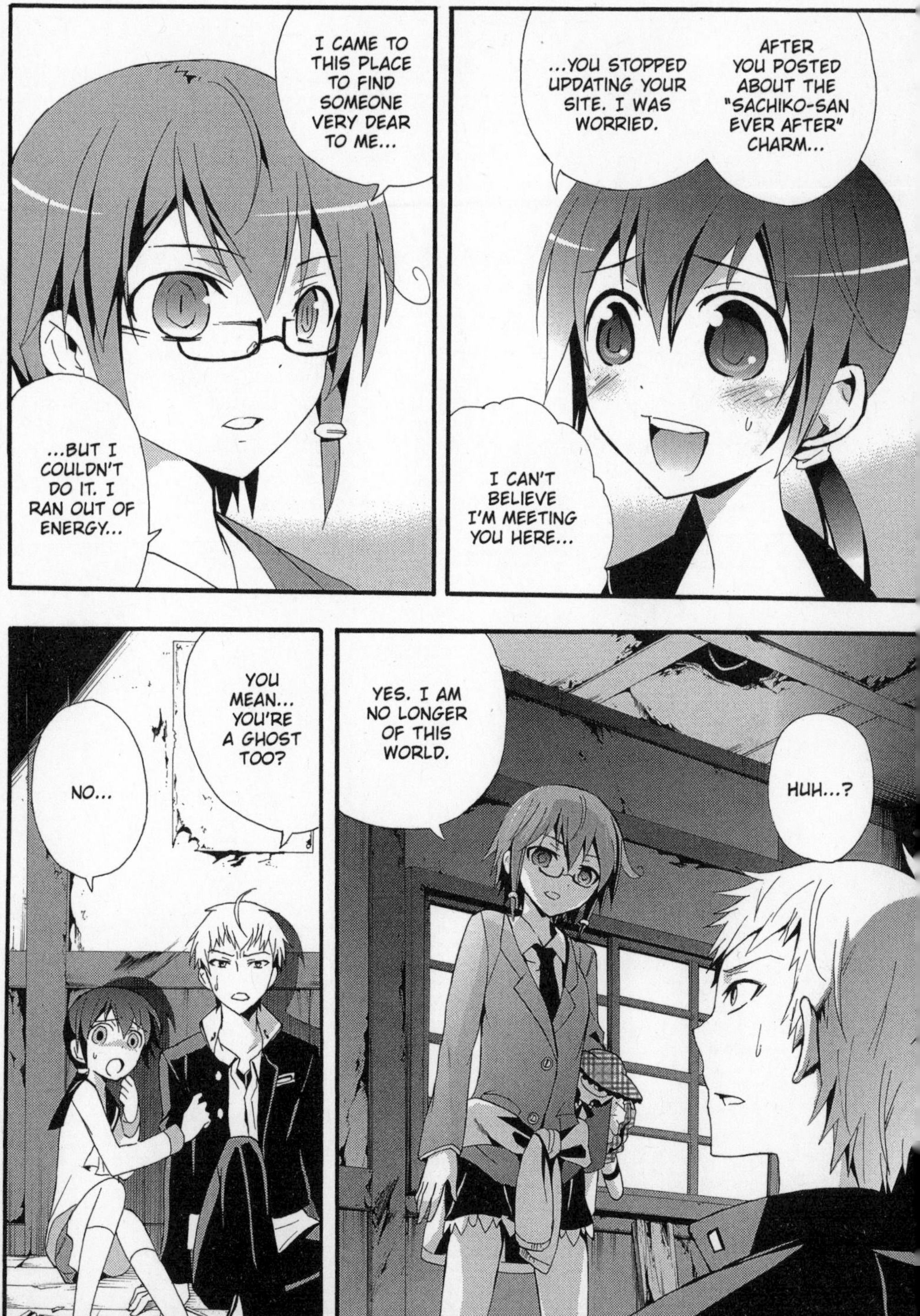
AFTER YOU POSTED ABOUT THE "SACHIKO-SAN EVER AFTER" CHARM...
...YOU STOPPED UPDATING YOUR SITE. I WAS WORRIED.
I CAN'T BELIEVE I'M MEETING YOU HERE...
I CAME TO THIS PLACE TO FIND SOMEONE VERY DEAR TO ME...
...BUT I COULDN'T DO IT. I RAN OUT OF ENERGY...
HUH...?
YES. I AM NO LONGER OF THIS WORLD.
YOU MEAN... YOU'RE A GHOST TOO?
NO...

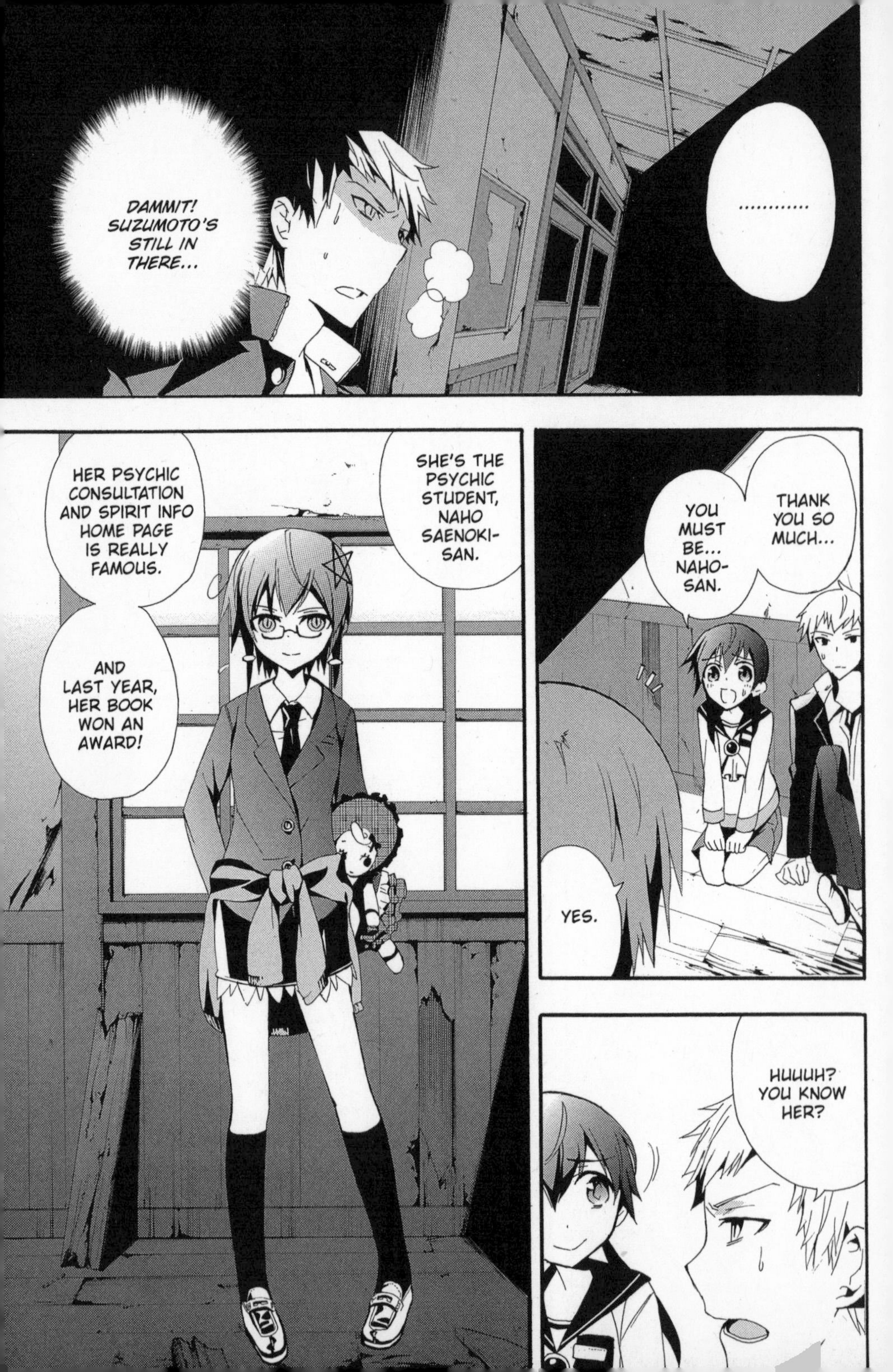
....
DAMMIT! SUZUMOTO'S STILL IN THERE...
THANK YOU SO MUCH...
YOU MUST BE... NAHO-SAN.
YES.
HUUUH? YOU KNOW HER?
SHE'S THE PSYCHIC STUDENT, NAHO SAENOKI-SAN.
HER PSYCHIC CONSULTATION AND SPIRIT INFO HOME PAGE IS REALLY FAMOUS.
AND LAST YEAR, HER BOOK WON AN AWARD!

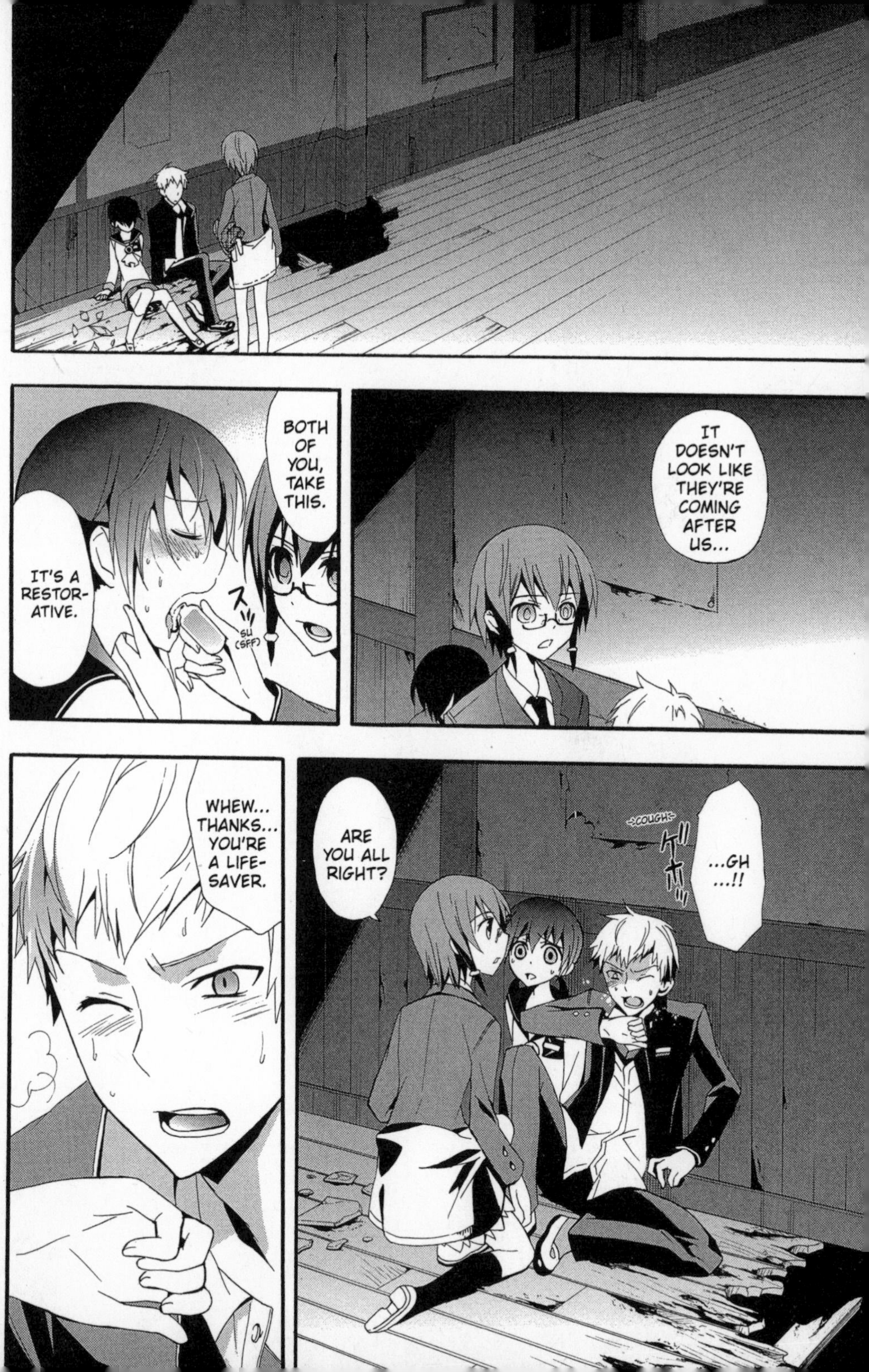
IT DOESN'T LOOK LIKE THEY'RE COMING AFTER US...
BOTH OF YOU, TAKE THIS.
ス
SU (SFF)
IT'S A RESTORATIVE.
...GH ...!!
ゲホッ
COUGH
ARE YOU ALL RIGHT?
WHEW... THANKS... YOU'RE A LIFE-SAVER.

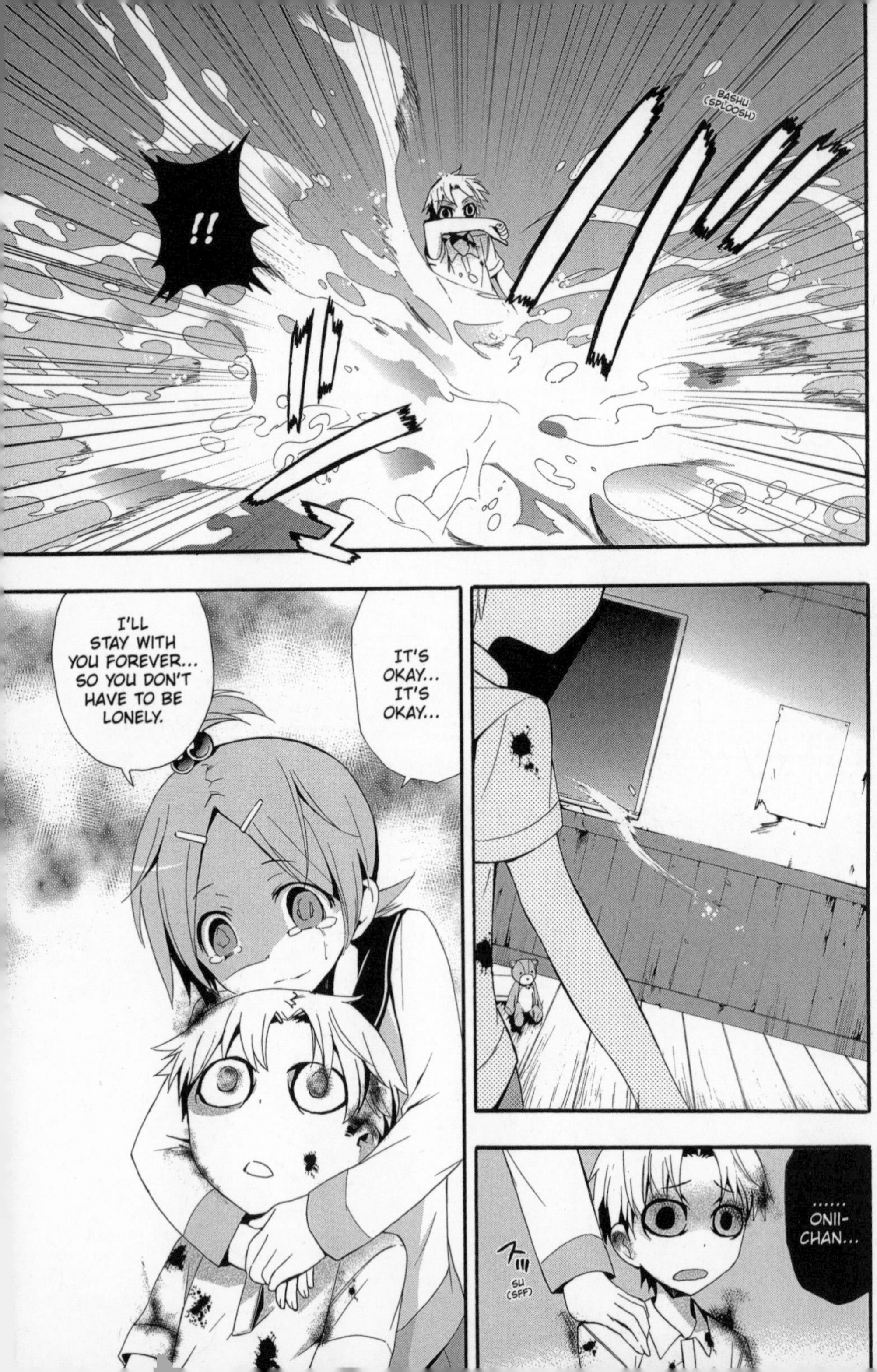
BASHU
(SPLOOSH)
!!
IT'S OKAY... IT'S OKAY...
I'LL STAY WITH YOU FOREVER... SO YOU DON'T HAVE TO BE LONELY.
...... ONII-CHAN...
SU
(SFF)

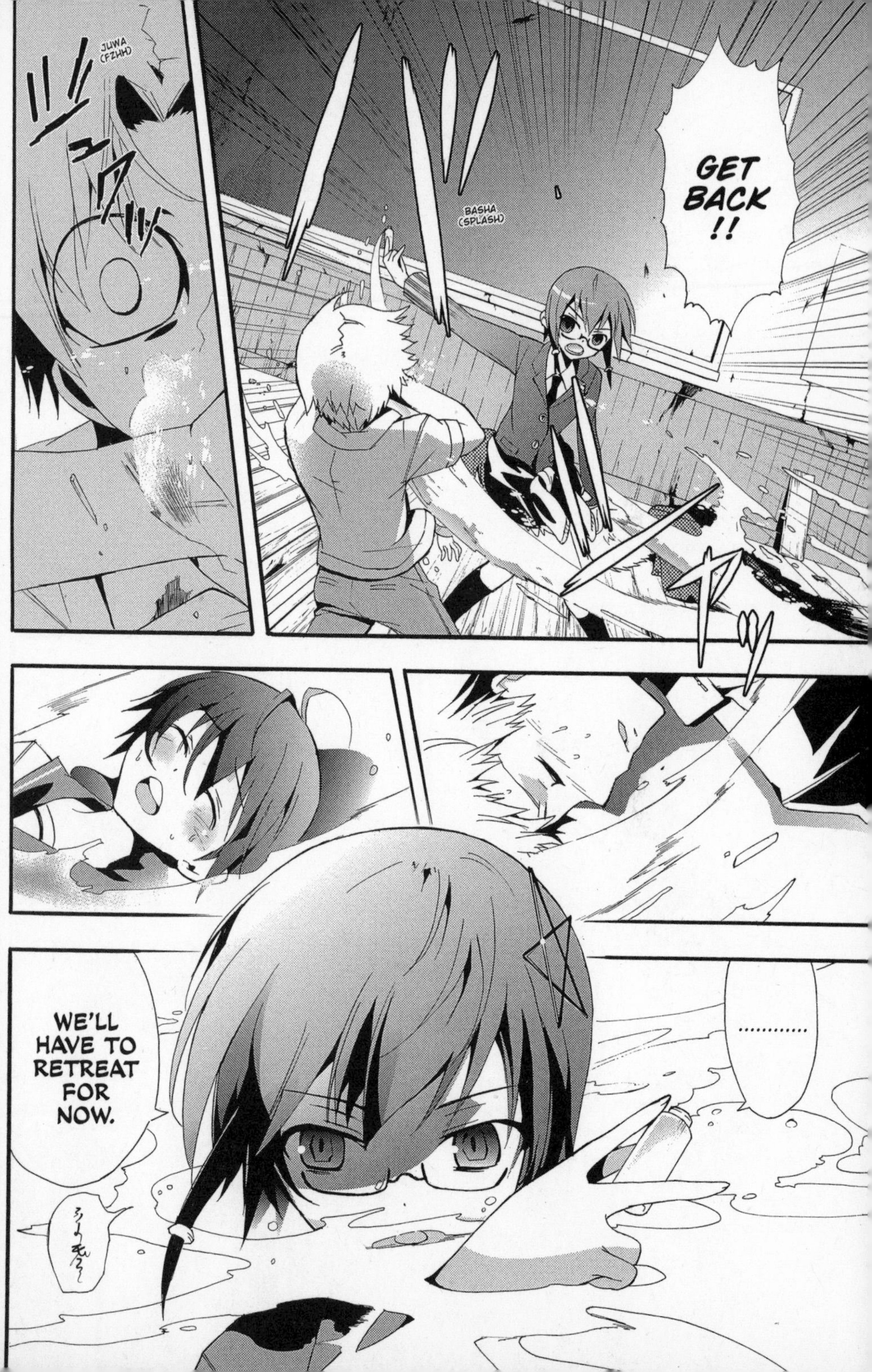
GET BACK !!
BASHA (SPLASH)
JUWA (FZHH)
....
WE'LL HAVE TO RETREAT FOR NOW.

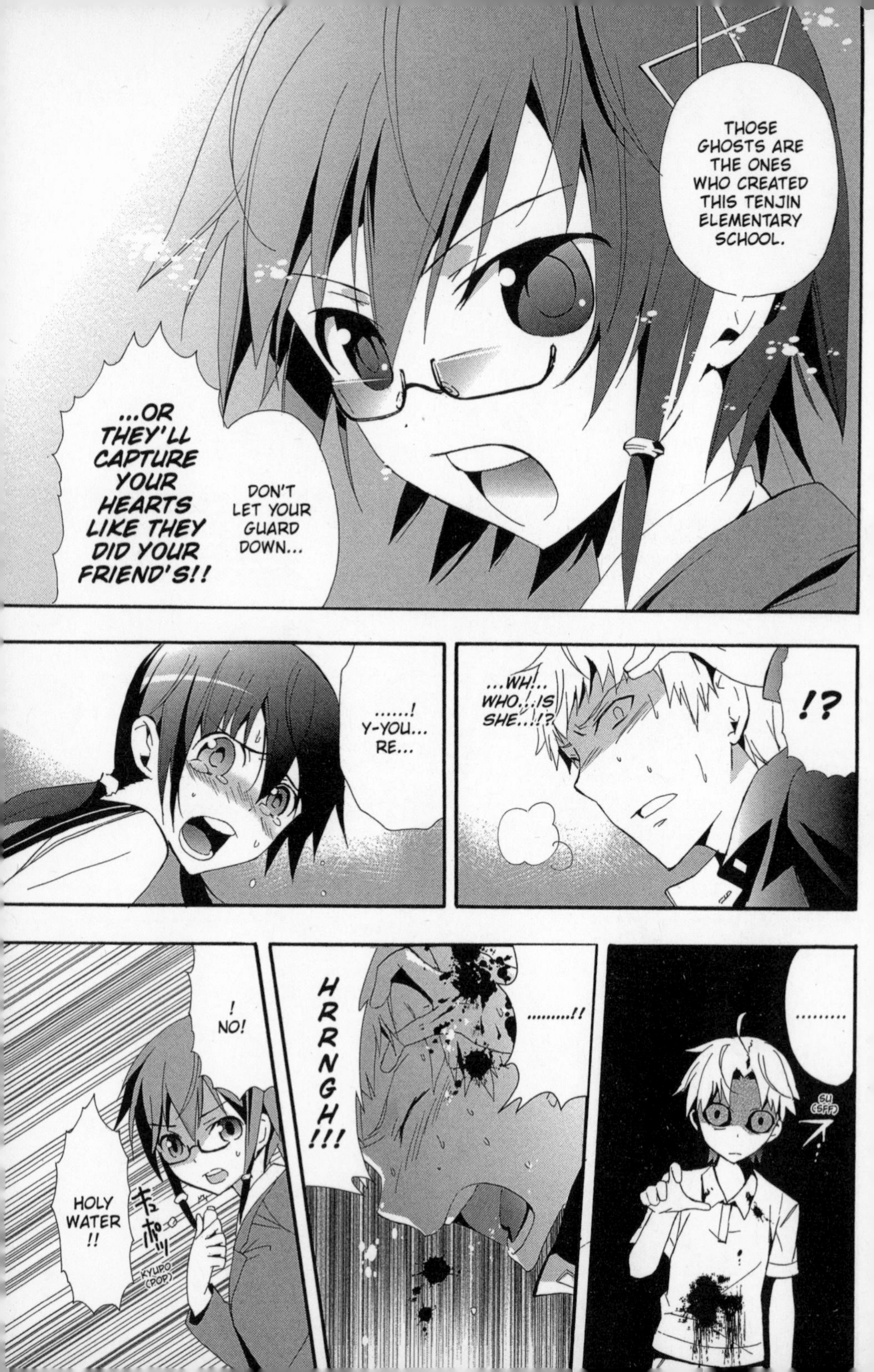
THOSE GHOSTS ARE THE ONES WHO CREATED THIS TENJIN ELEMENTARY SCHOOL.
DON'T LET YOUR GUARD DOWN...
...OR THEY'LL CAPTURE YOUR HEARTS LIKE THEY DID YOUR FRIEND'S!!
!?
...WH!.. WHO..!..IS SHE...!?
......! Y-YOU... RE...
....
SU (SFFF)
........!!
HRRNGH!!!
! NO!
HOLY WATER !!
キュポッ
KYUPO (POP)

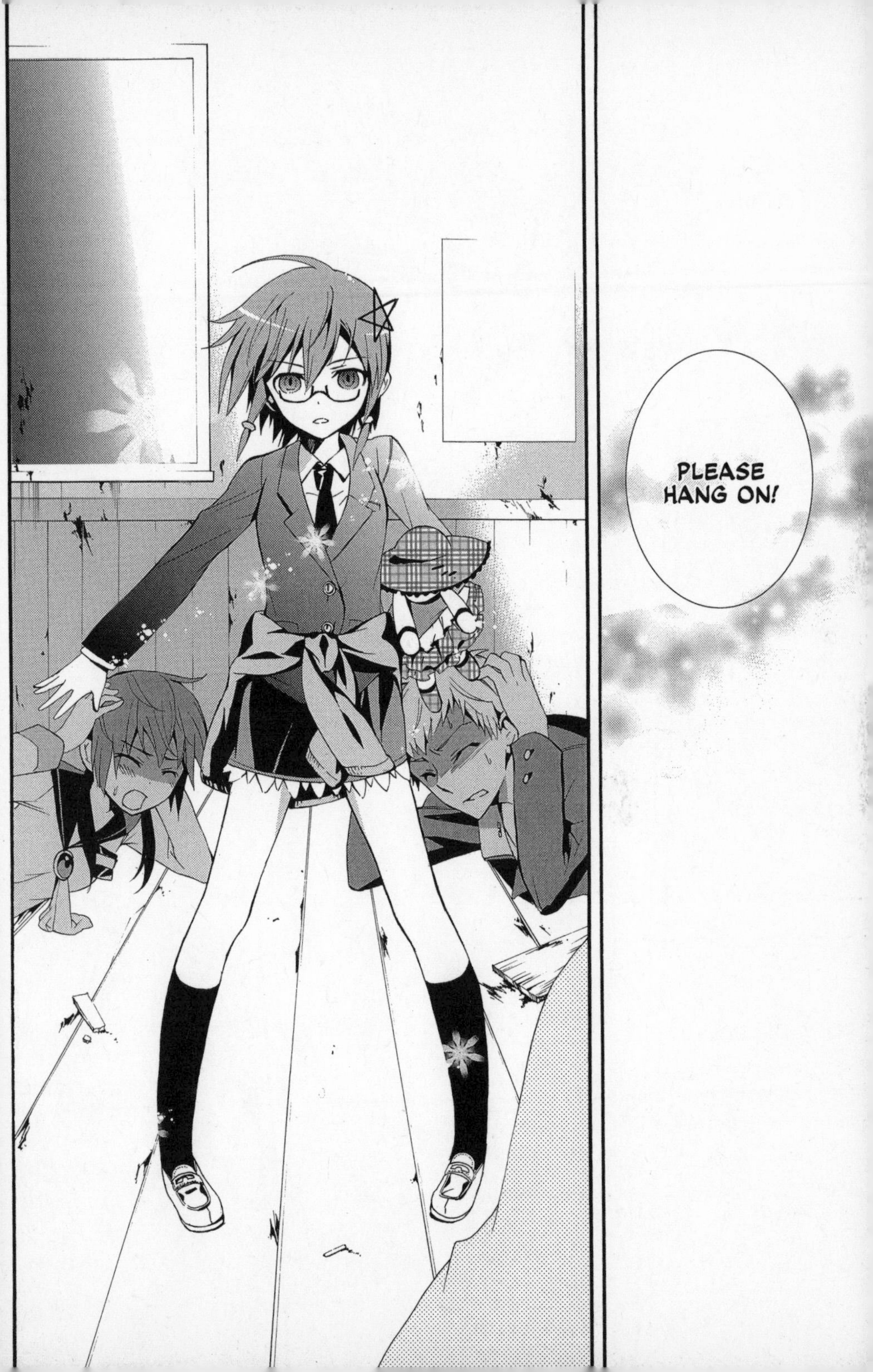
PLEASE HANG ON!

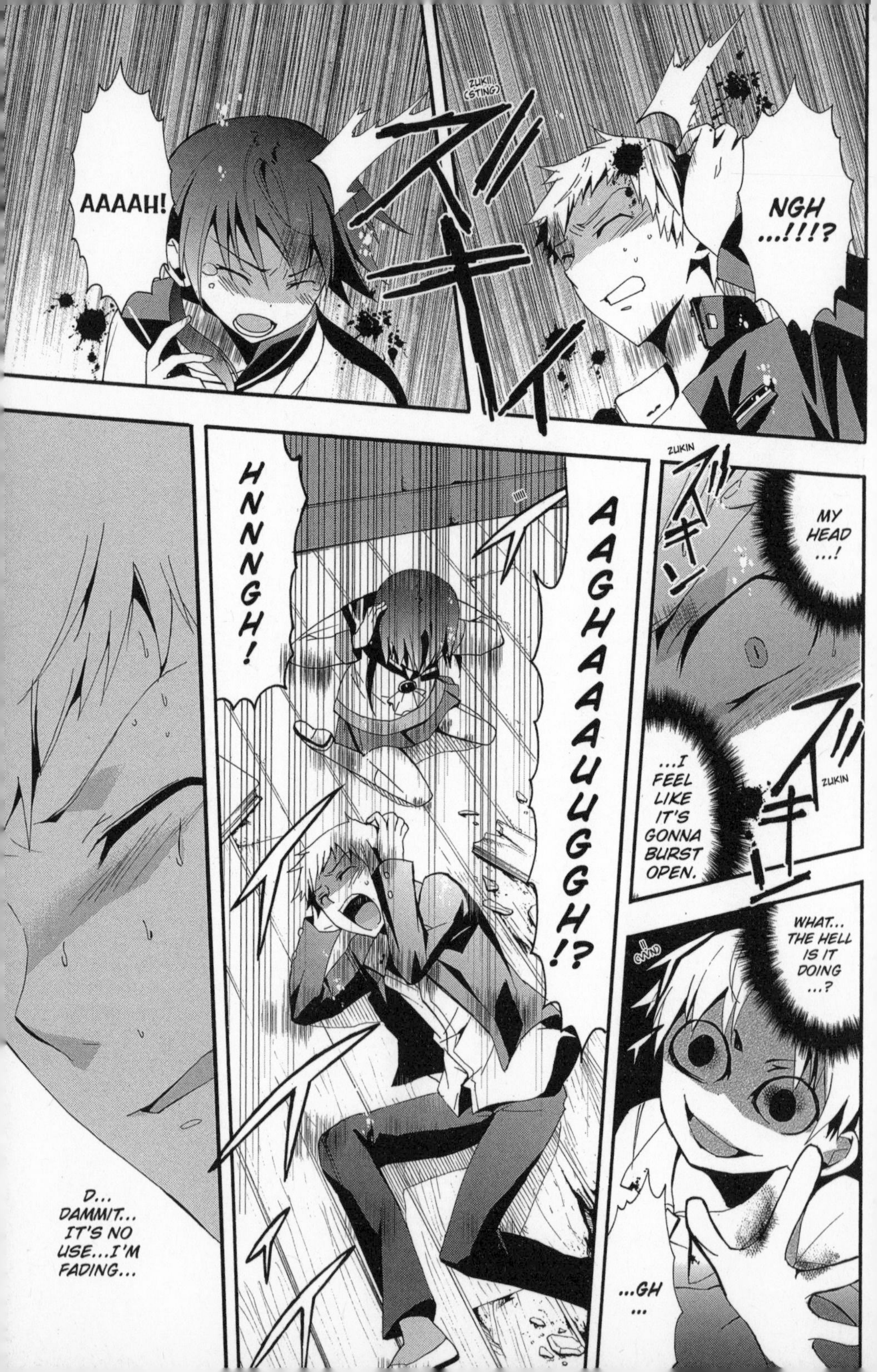
NGH ...!!!?
ZUKI (STING)
AAAAH!
ZUKIN
MY HEAD ...!
...I FEEL LIKE IT'S GONNA BURST OPEN.
ZUKIN
WHAT... THE HELL IS IT DOING ...?
...GH ...
AAGHAAAAAUUGGGH!?
HNNNGH!
D... DAMMIT... IT'S NO USE...I'M FADING...

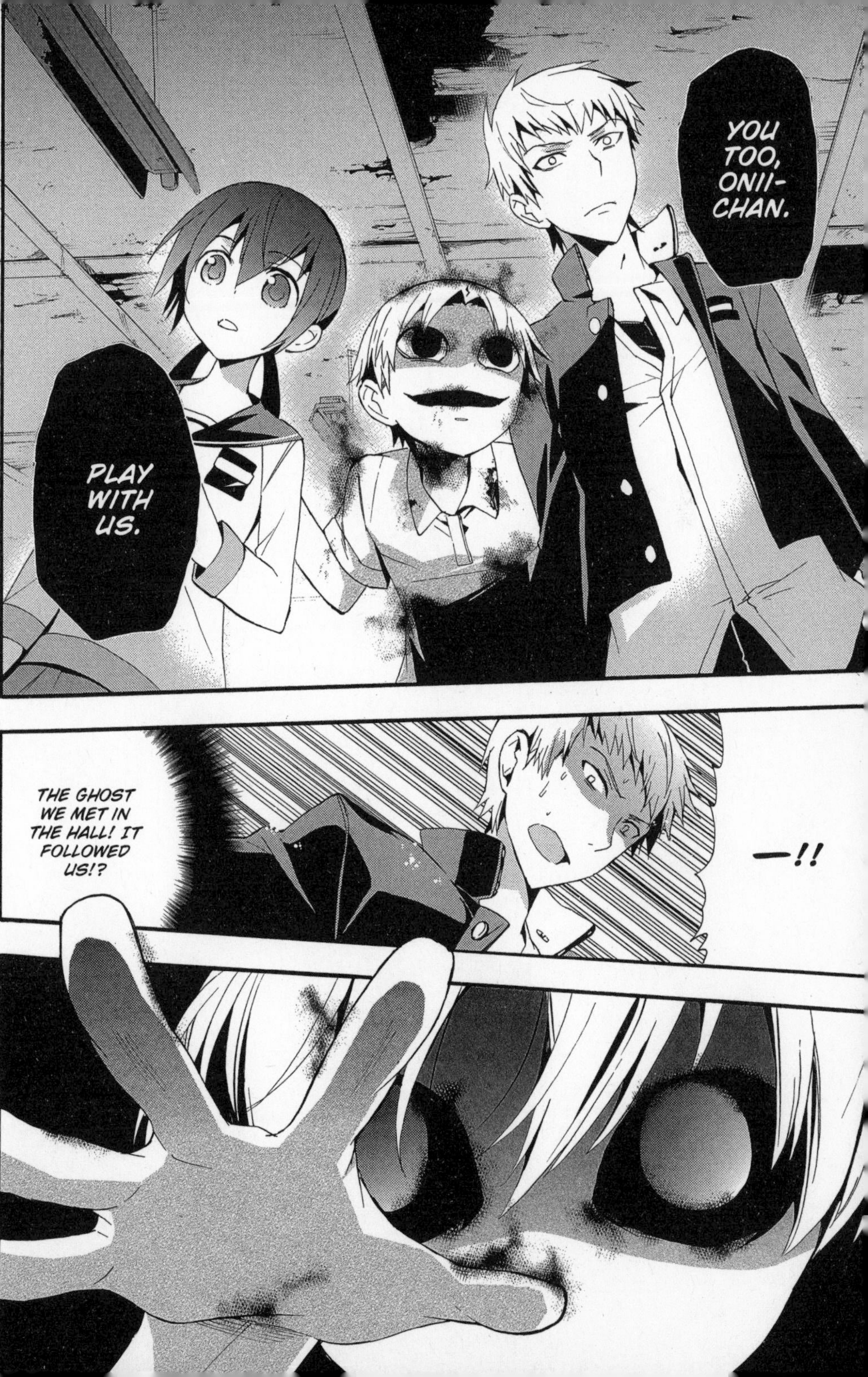
YOU TOO, ONII-CHAN.
PLAY WITH US.
—!!
THE GHOST WE MET IN THE HALL! IT FOLLOWED US!?

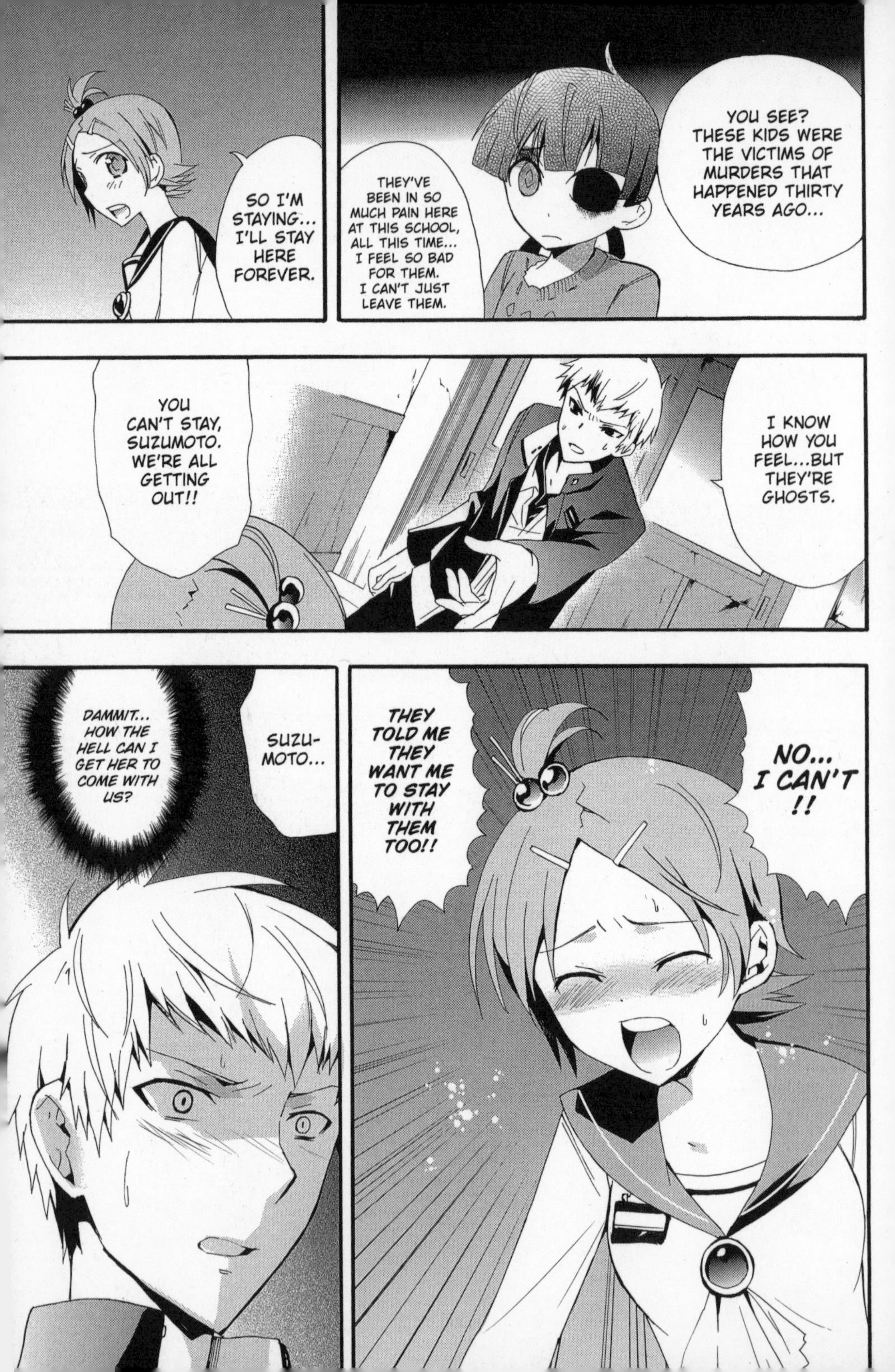
YOU SEE? THESE KIDS WERE THE VICTIMS OF MURDERS THAT HAPPENED THIRTY YEARS AGO...
THEY'VE BEEN IN SO MUCH PAIN HERE AT THIS SCHOOL, ALL THIS TIME... I FEEL SO BAD FOR THEM. I CAN'T JUST LEAVE THEM.
SO I'M STAYING... I'LL STAY HERE FOREVER.
I KNOW HOW YOU FEEL...BUT THEY'RE GHOSTS.
YOU CAN'T STAY, SUZUMOTO. WE'RE ALL GETTING OUT!!
NO... I CAN'T !!
THEY TOLD ME THEY WANT ME TO STAY WITH THEM TOO!!
SUZU-MOTO...
DAMMIT... HOW THE HELL CAN I GET HER TO COME WITH US?

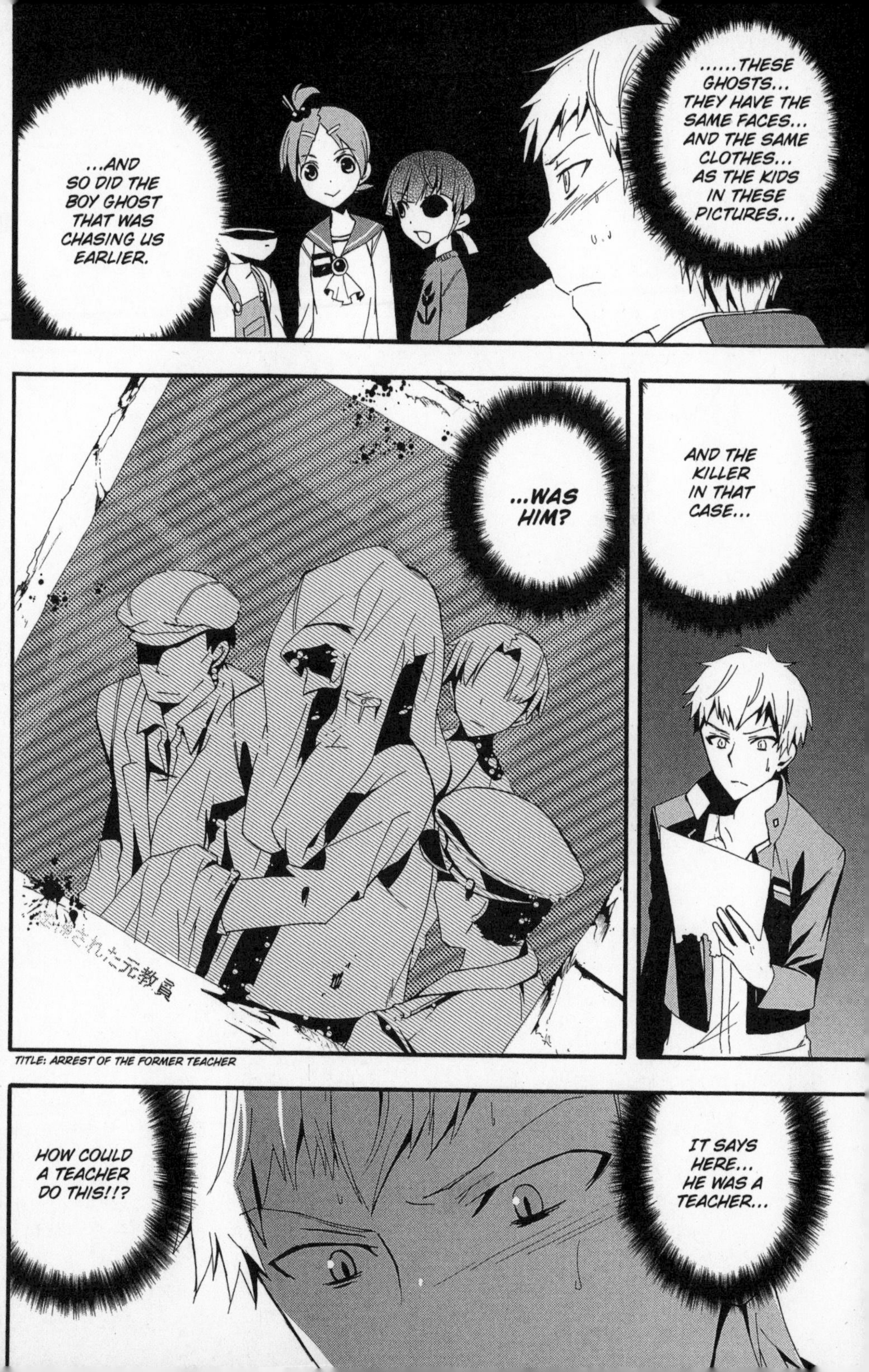
......THESE GHOSTS... THEY HAVE THE SAME FACES... AND THE SAME CLOTHES... AS THE KIDS IN THESE PICTURES...
...AND SO DID THE BOY GHOST THAT WAS CHASING US EARLIER.
AND THE KILLER IN THAT CASE...
...WAS HIM?
された元教員
TITLE: ARREST OF THE FORMER TEACHER
IT SAYS HERE... HE WAS A TEACHER...
HOW COULD A TEACHER DO THIS!!?

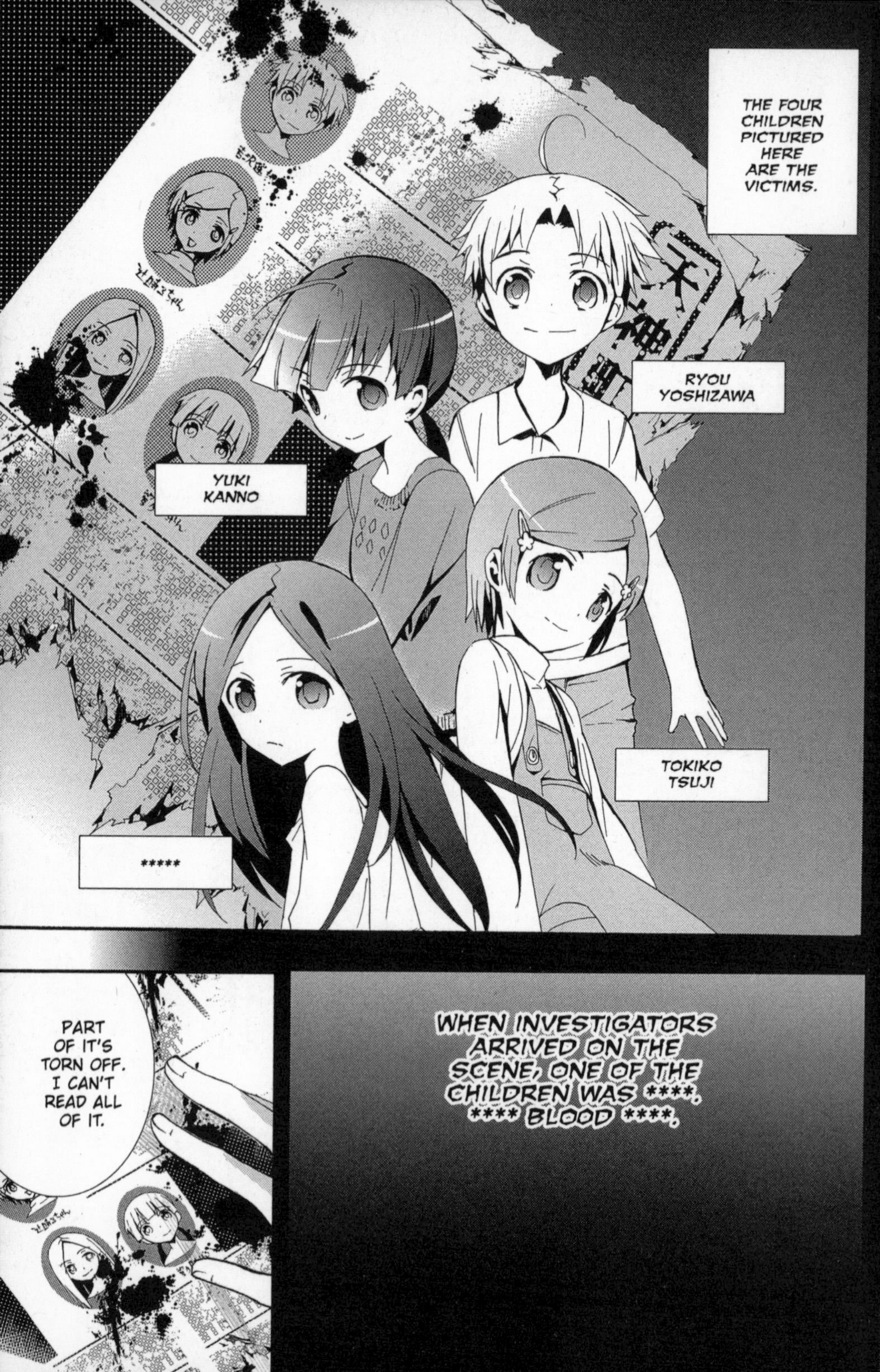
THE FOUR CHILDREN PICTURED HERE ARE THE VICTIMS.
RYOU YOSHIZAWA
YUKI KANNO
TOKIKO TSUJI
*****
WHEN INVESTIGATORS ARRIVED ON THE SCENE, ONE OF THE CHILDREN WAS ****. **** BLOOD ****.
PART OF IT'S TORN OFF. I CAN'T READ ALL OF IT.

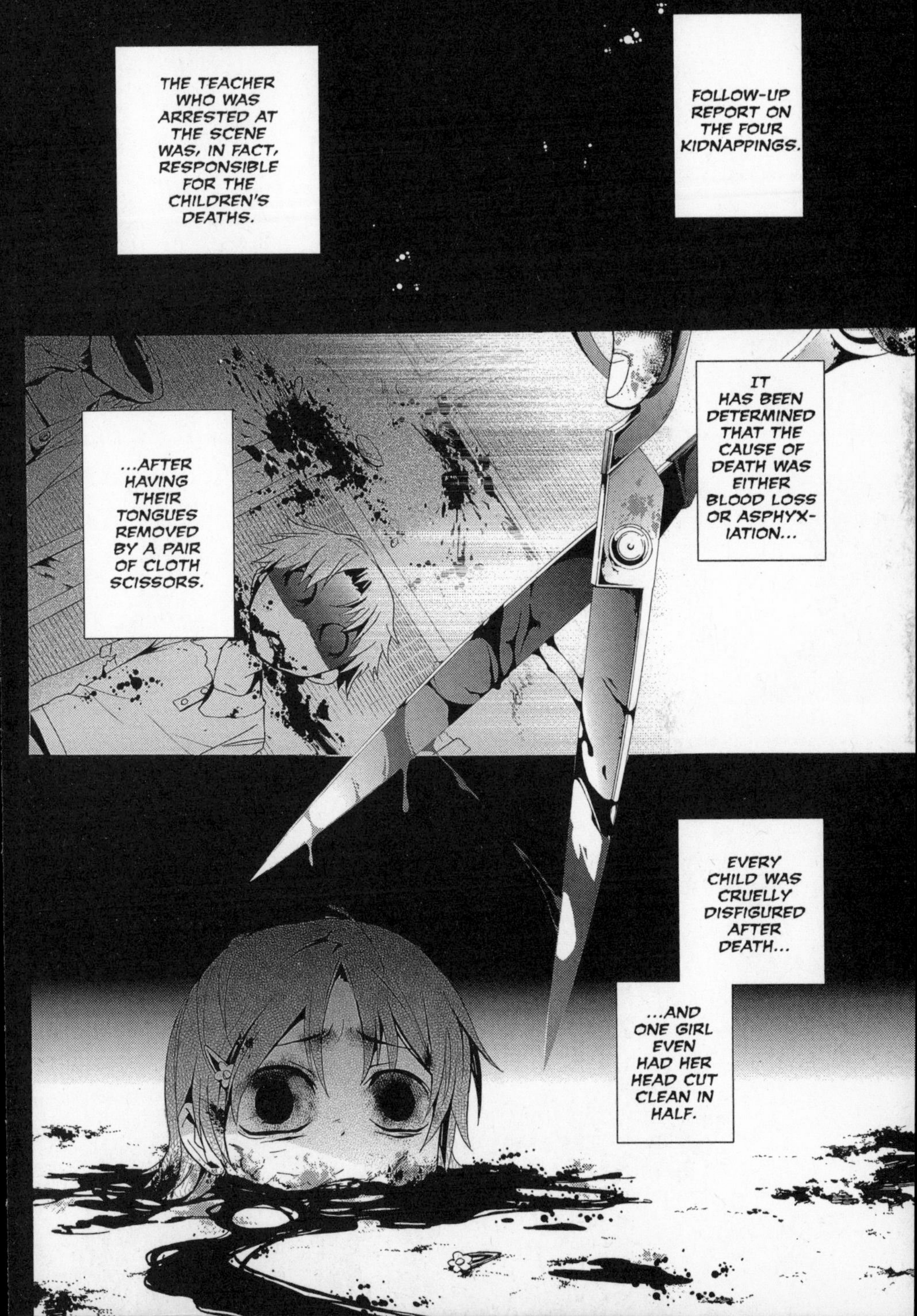
FOLLOW-UP REPORT ON THE FOUR KIDNAPPINGS.
THE TEACHER WHO WAS ARRESTED AT THE SCENE WAS, IN FACT, RESPONSIBLE FOR THE CHILDREN'S DEATHS.
IT HAS BEEN DETERMINED THAT THE CAUSE OF DEATH WAS EITHER BLOOD LOSS OR ASPHYX-IATION...
...AFTER HAVING THEIR TONGUES REMOVED BY A PAIR OF CLOTH SCISSORS.
EVERY CHILD WAS CRUELLY DISFIGURED AFTER DEATH...
...AND ONE GIRL EVEN HAD HER HEAD CUT CLEAN IN HALF.

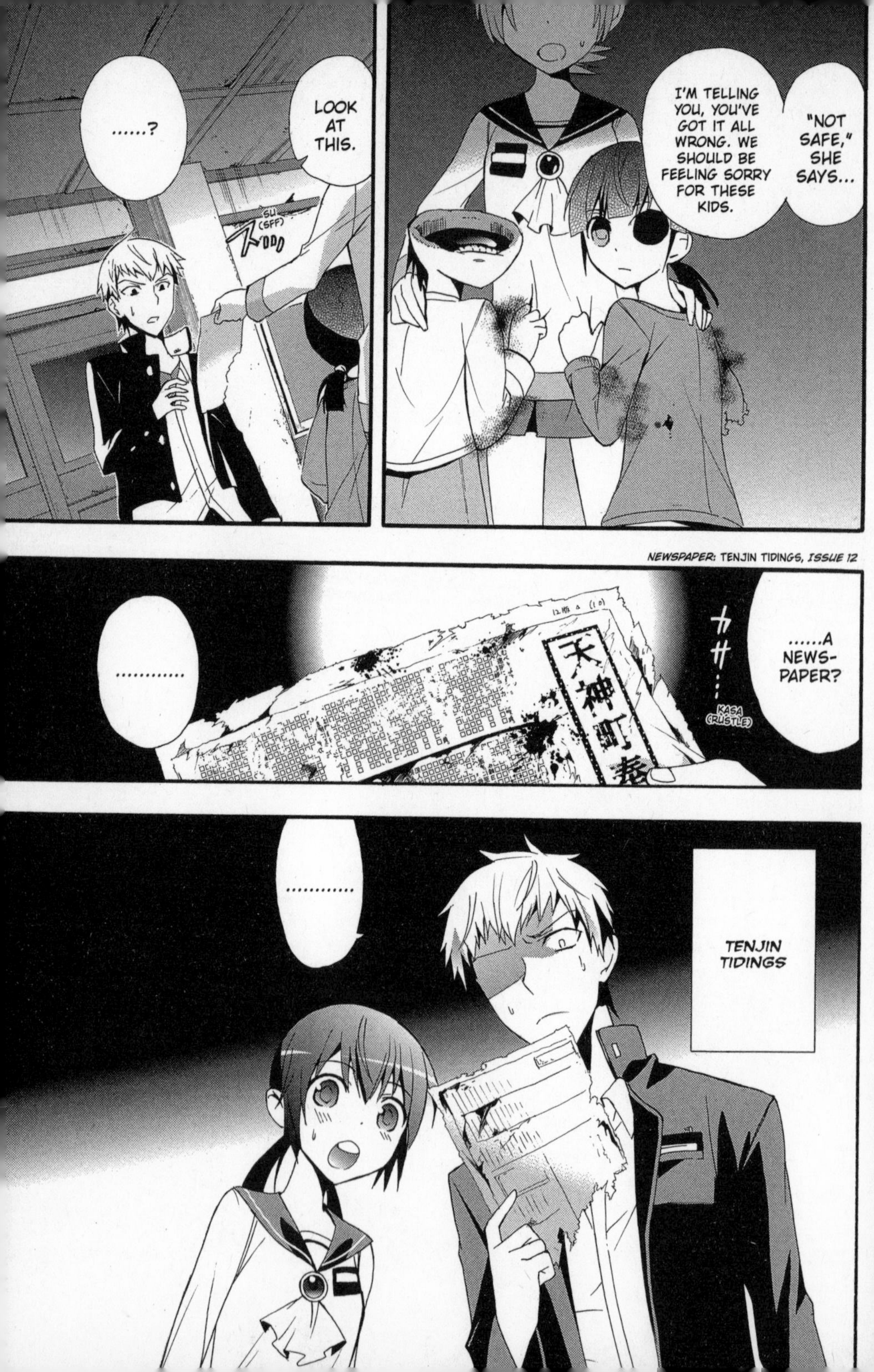

"NOT SAFE," SHE SAYS...
I'M TELLING YOU, YOU'VE GOT IT ALL WRONG. WE SHOULD BE FEELING SORRY FOR THESE KIDS.
LOOK AT THIS.
SU (SFF)
......?
NEWSPAPER: TENJIN TIDINGS, ISSUE 12
......A NEWS-PAPER?
KASA (RUSTLE)
....
TENJIN TIDINGS
....

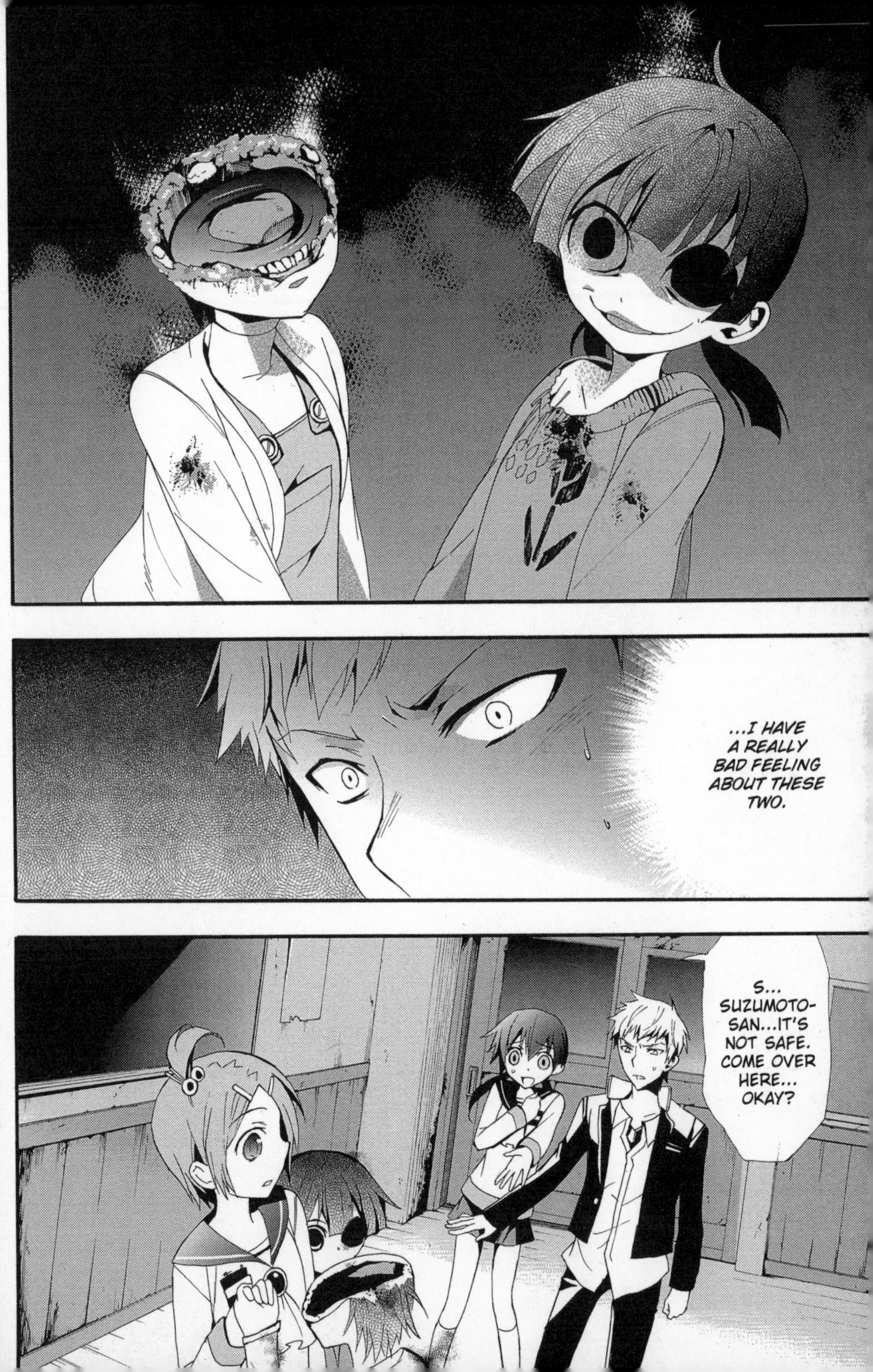
...I HAVE A REALLY BAD FEELING ABOUT THESE TWO.
S... SUZUMOTO-SAN...IT'S NOT SAFE. COME OVER HERE... OKAY?

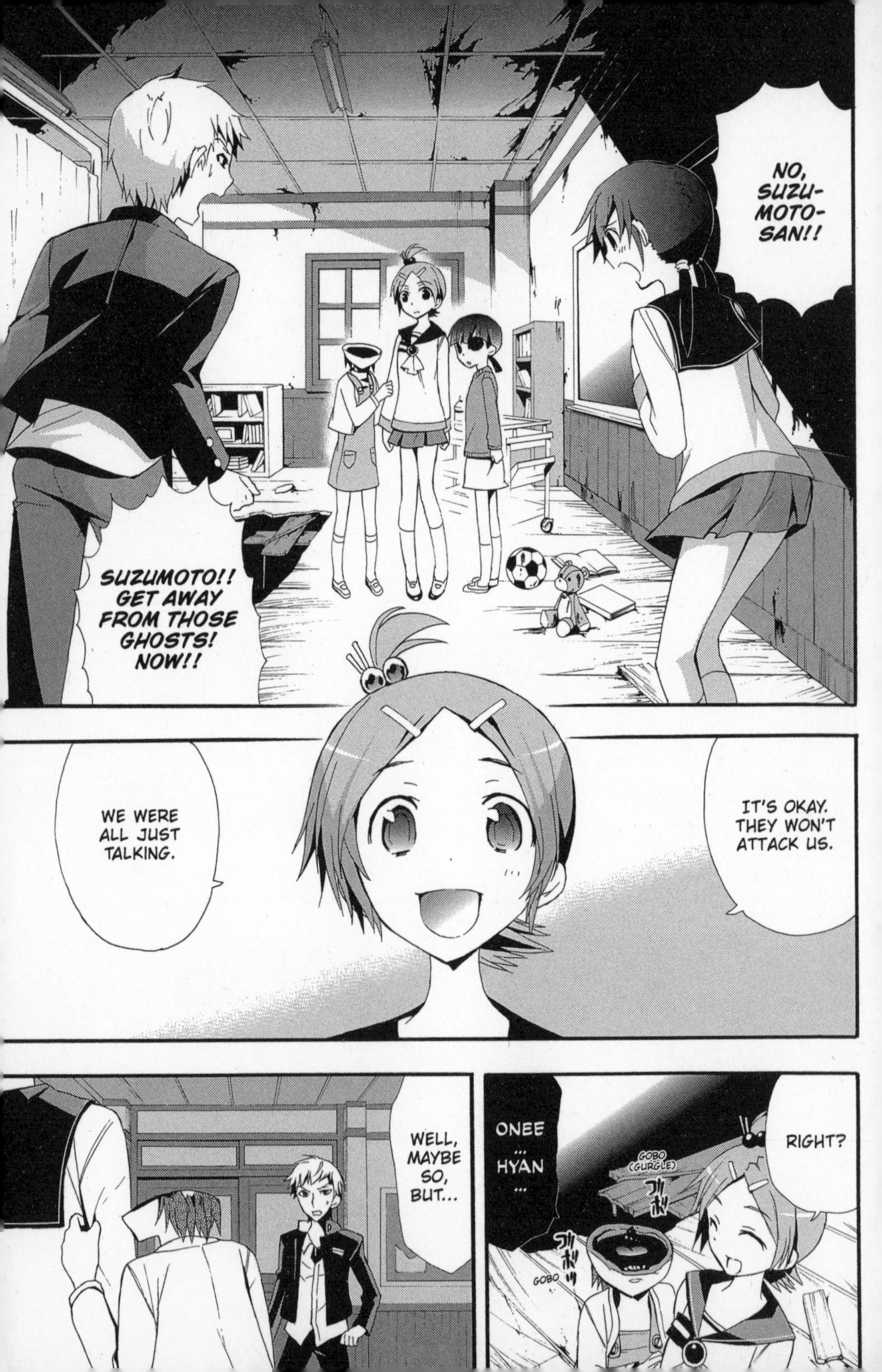
NO, SUZU-MOTO-SAN!!
SUZUMOTO!! GET AWAY FROM THOSE GHOSTS! NOW!!
IT'S OKAY. THEY WON'T ATTACK US.
WE WERE ALL JUST TALKING.
RIGHT?
GOBO (GURGLE)
GOBO
ONEE ... HYAN ...
WELL, MAYBE SO, BUT...

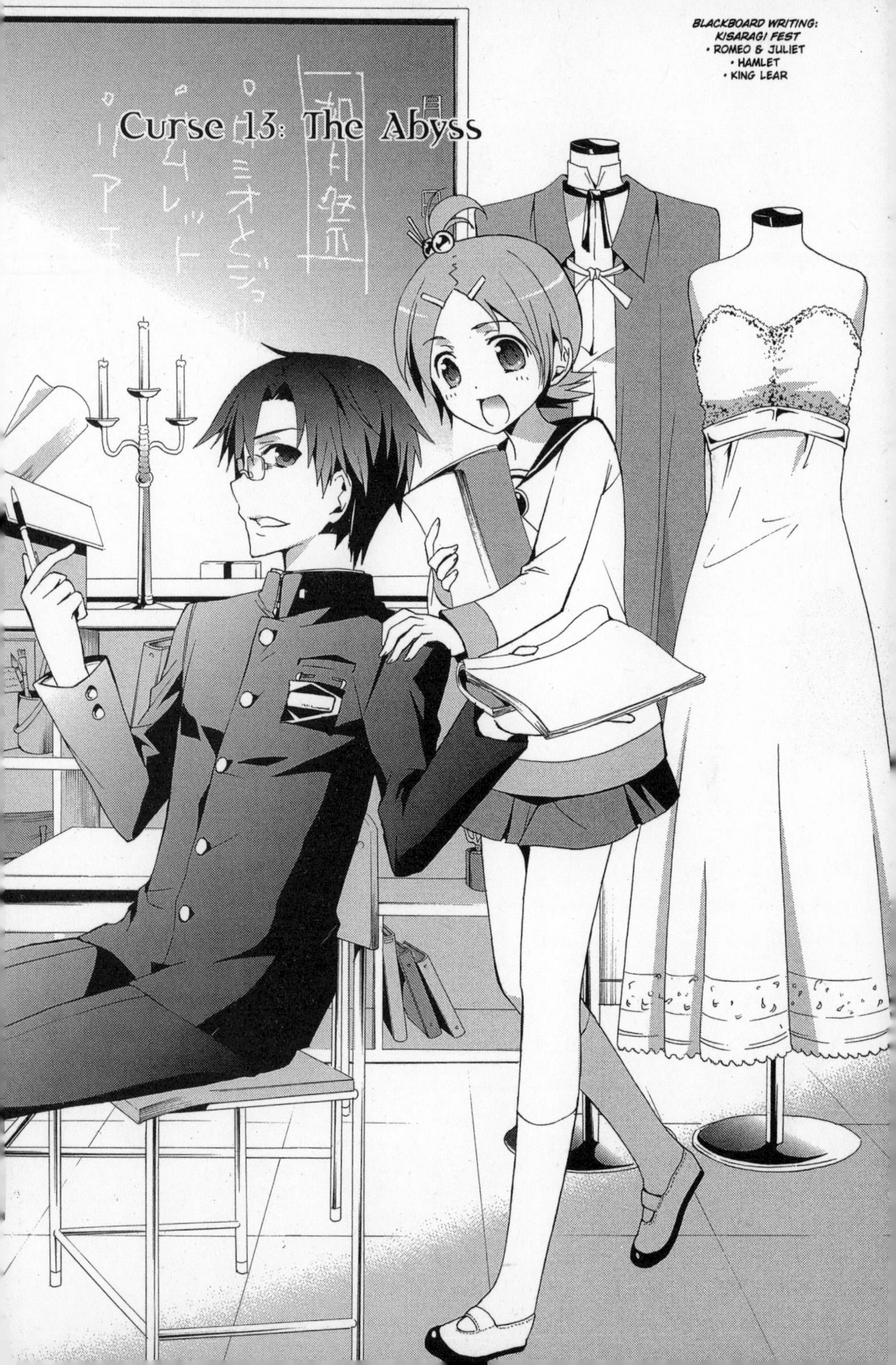
Curse 13: The Abyss
BLACKBOARD WRITING:
KISARAGI FEST
• ROMEO & JULIET
• HAMLET
• KING LEAR

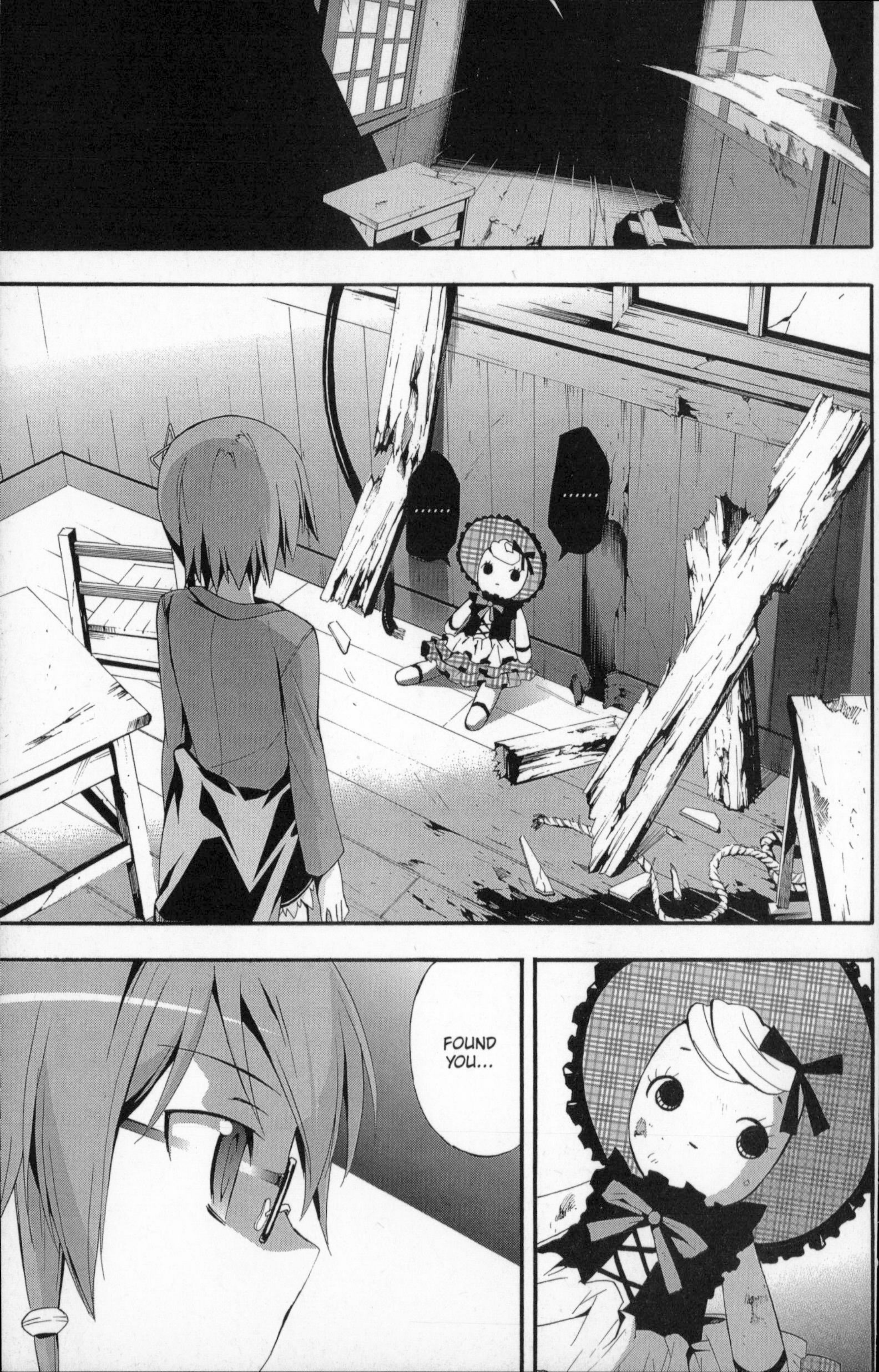
......
......
FOUND YOU...

a list of ghosts/06

Tokiko Tsuji

One of the child ghosts who have taken up residence at Tenjin Elementary School.

She is missing her head from the tongue up. She met Yoshiki and Ayumi while hanging out with Mayu.

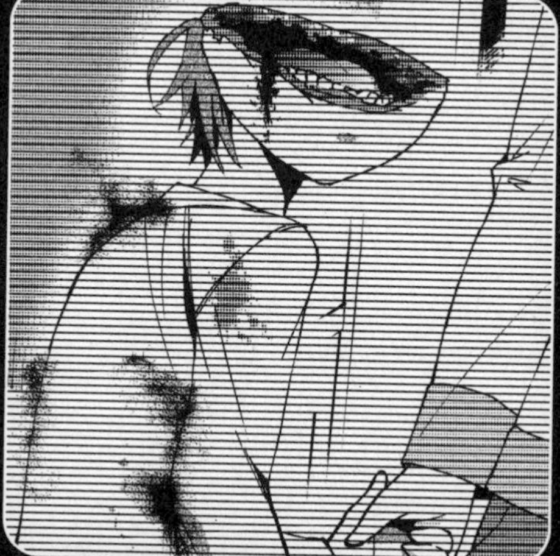

a list of ghosts/05

Yuki Kanno

One of the child ghosts who have taken up residence at Tenjin Elementary School.

Has no tongue or left eye. She met Yoshiki and Ayumi while hanging out with Mayu.

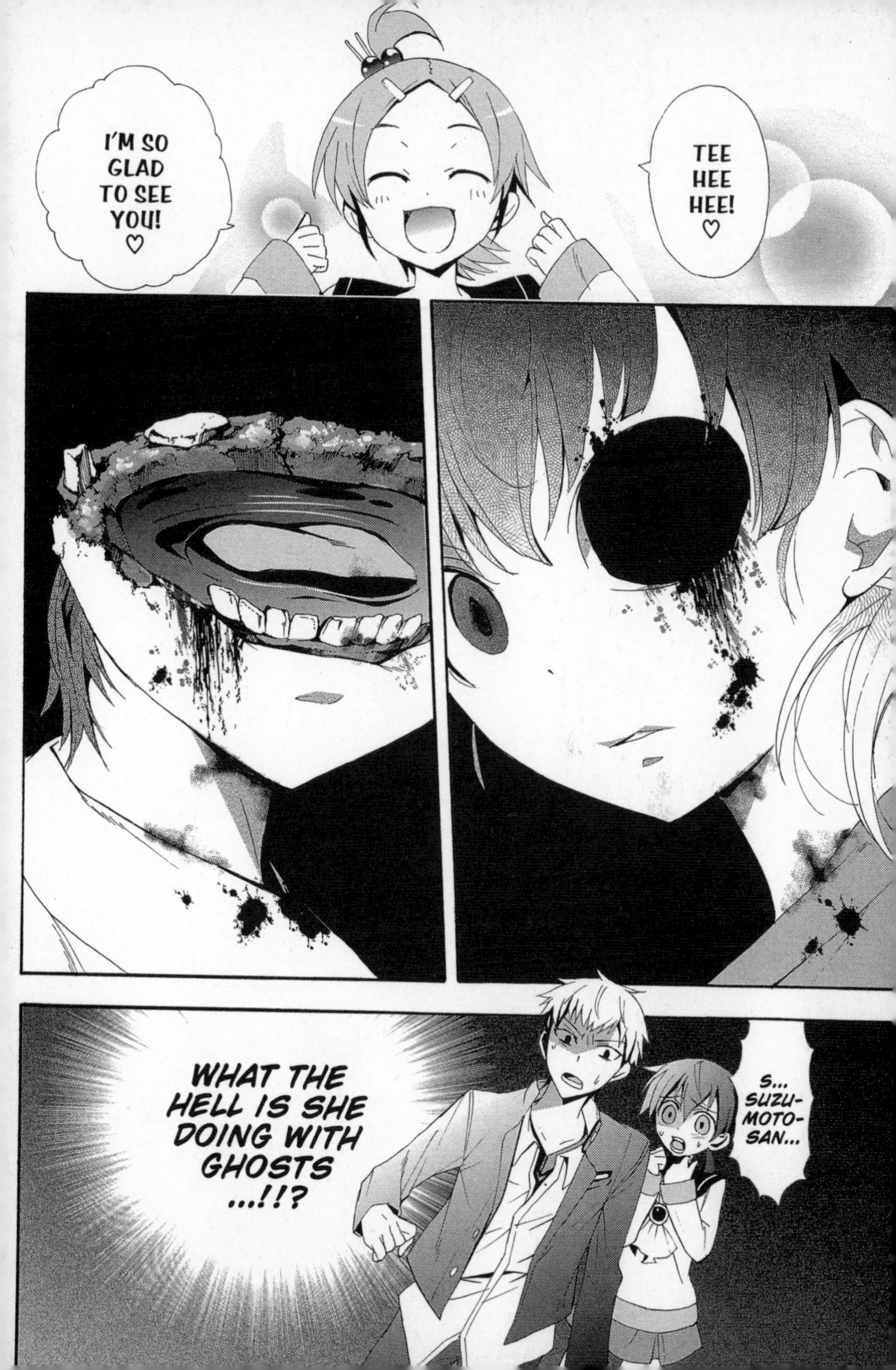
TEE HEE HEE! ♡
I'M SO GLAD TO SEE YOU! ♡
S... SUZU-MOTO-SAN...
WHAT THE HELL IS SHE DOING WITH GHOSTS ...!!?

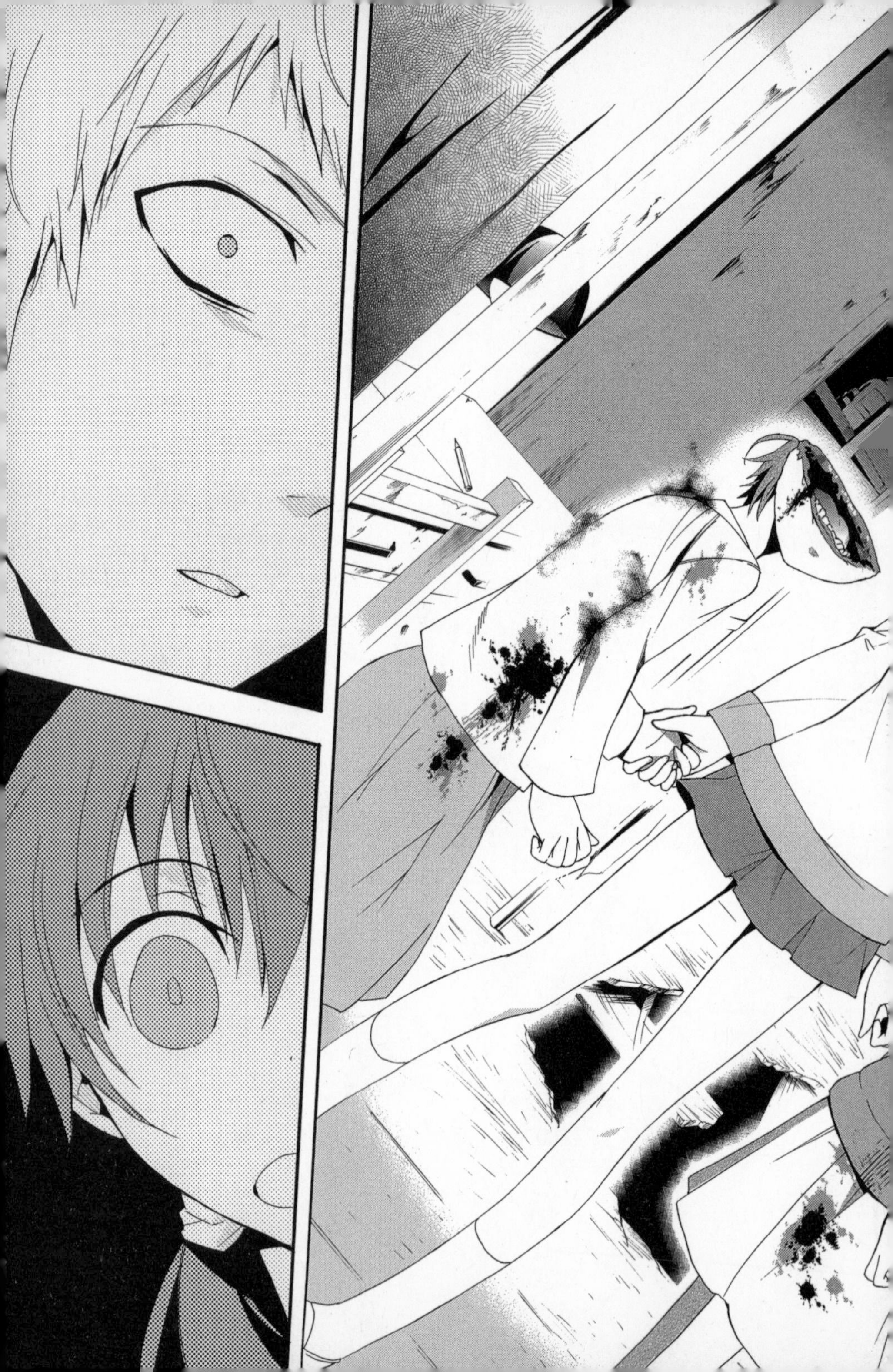

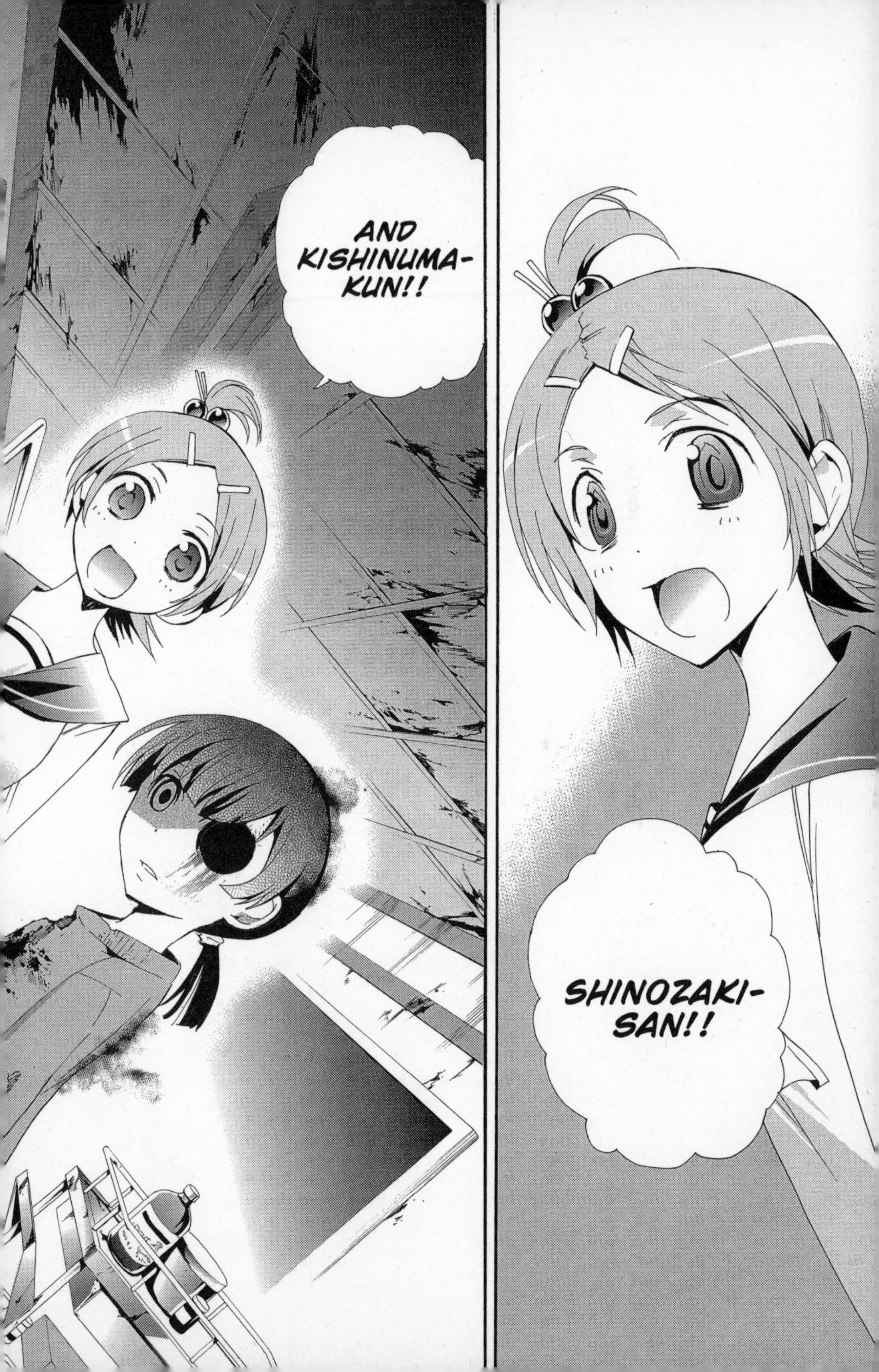
SHINOZAKI-SAN!!
AND KISHINUMA-KUN!!

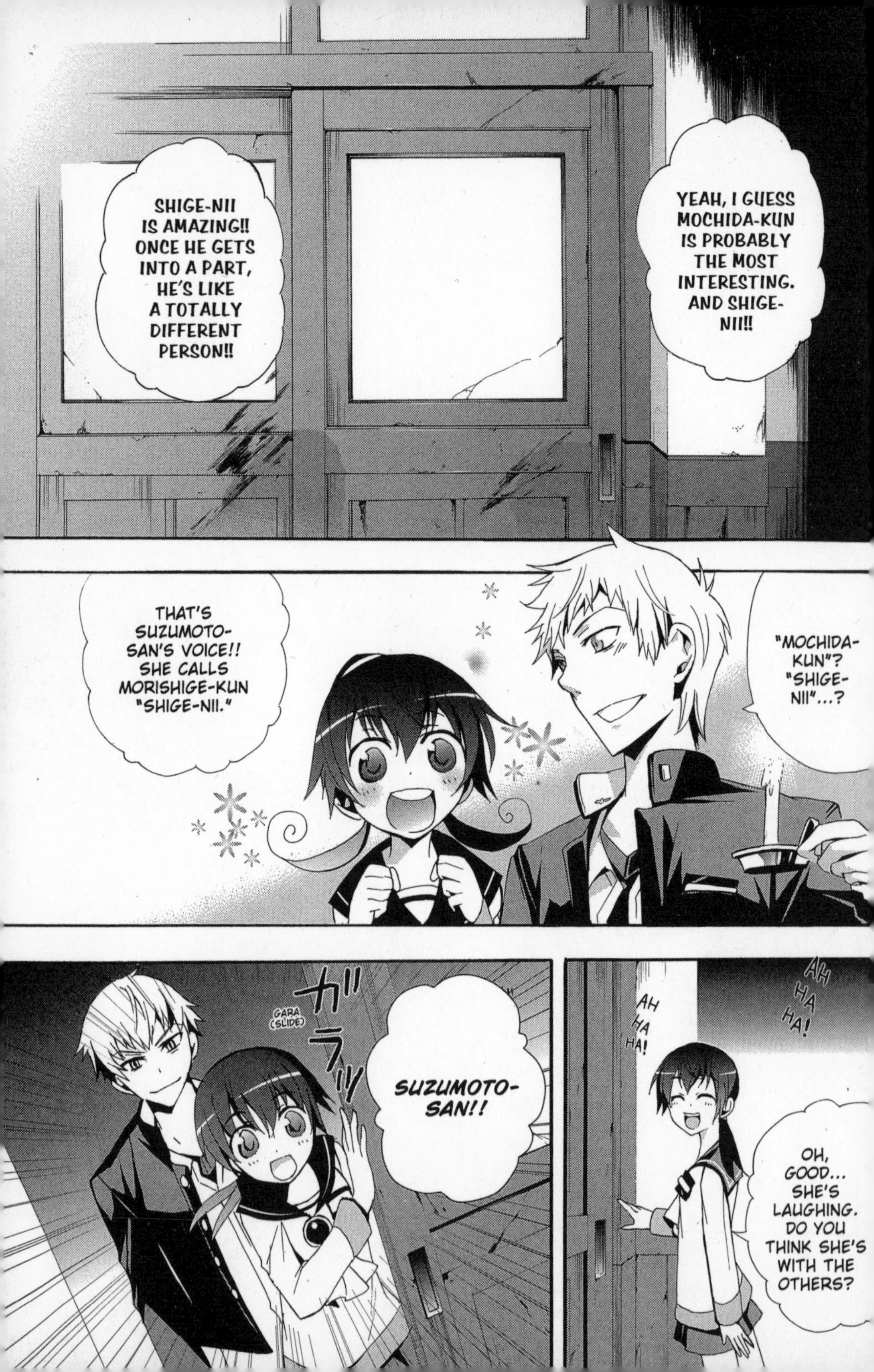
YEAH, I GUESS MOCHIDA-KUN IS PROBABLY THE MOST INTERESTING. AND SHIGE-NII!!
SHIGE-NII IS AMAZING!! ONCE HE GETS INTO A PART, HE'S LIKE A TOTALLY DIFFERENT PERSON!!
"MOCHIDA-KUN"? "SHIGE-NII"...?
THAT'S SUZUMOTO-SAN'S VOICE!! SHE CALLS MORISHIGE-KUN "SHIGE-NII."
AH HA HA!
AH HA HA!
OH, GOOD... SHE'S LAUGHING. DO YOU THINK SHE'S WITH THE OTHERS?
SUZUMOTO-SAN!!
GARA (SLIDE)

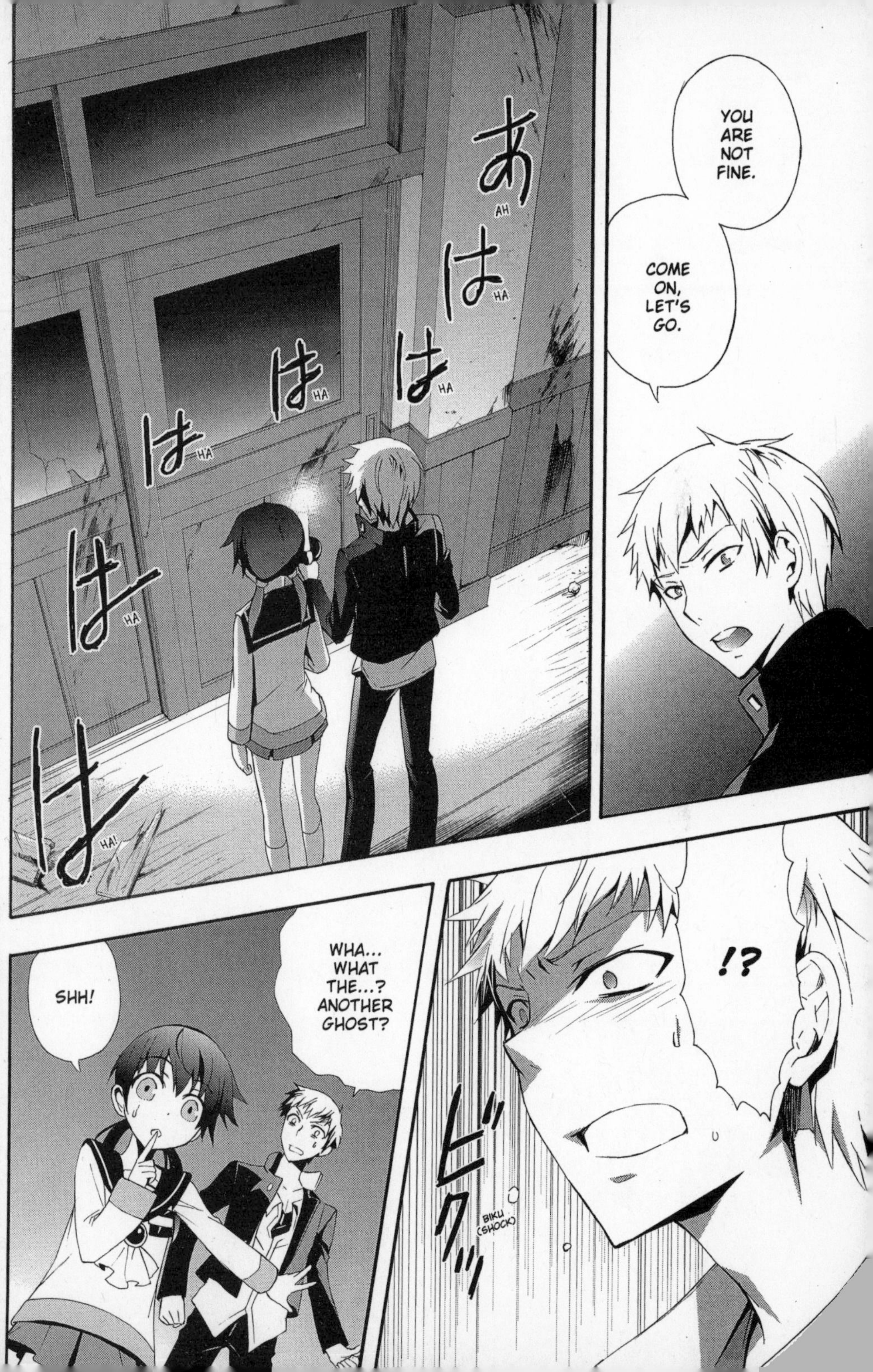
YOU ARE NOT FINE.
COME ON, LET'S GO.
あ AH
は HA
は HA
は HA
は HA
は HA
は HA!
!?
ビクッ
BIKU (SHOCK)
WHA... WHAT THE...? ANOTHER GHOST?
SHH!

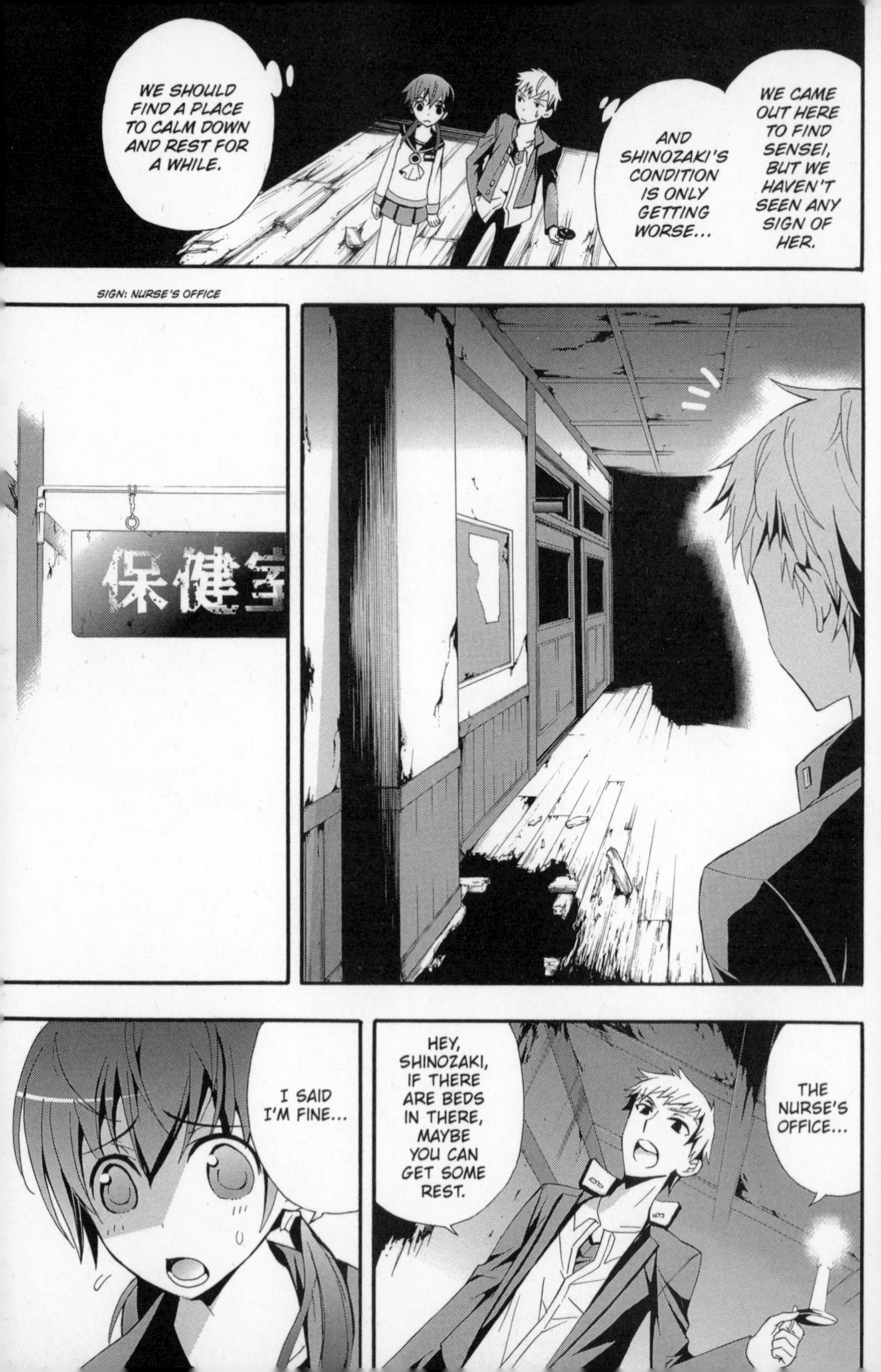
WE CAME OUT HERE TO FIND SENSEI, BUT WE HAVEN'T SEEN ANY SIGN OF HER.
AND SHINOZAKI'S CONDITION IS ONLY GETTING WORSE...
WE SHOULD FIND A PLACE TO CALM DOWN AND REST FOR A WHILE.
SIGN: NURSE'S OFFICE
THE NURSE'S OFFICE...
HEY, SHINOZAKI, IF THERE ARE BEDS IN THERE, MAYBE YOU CAN GET SOME REST.
I SAID I'M FINE...

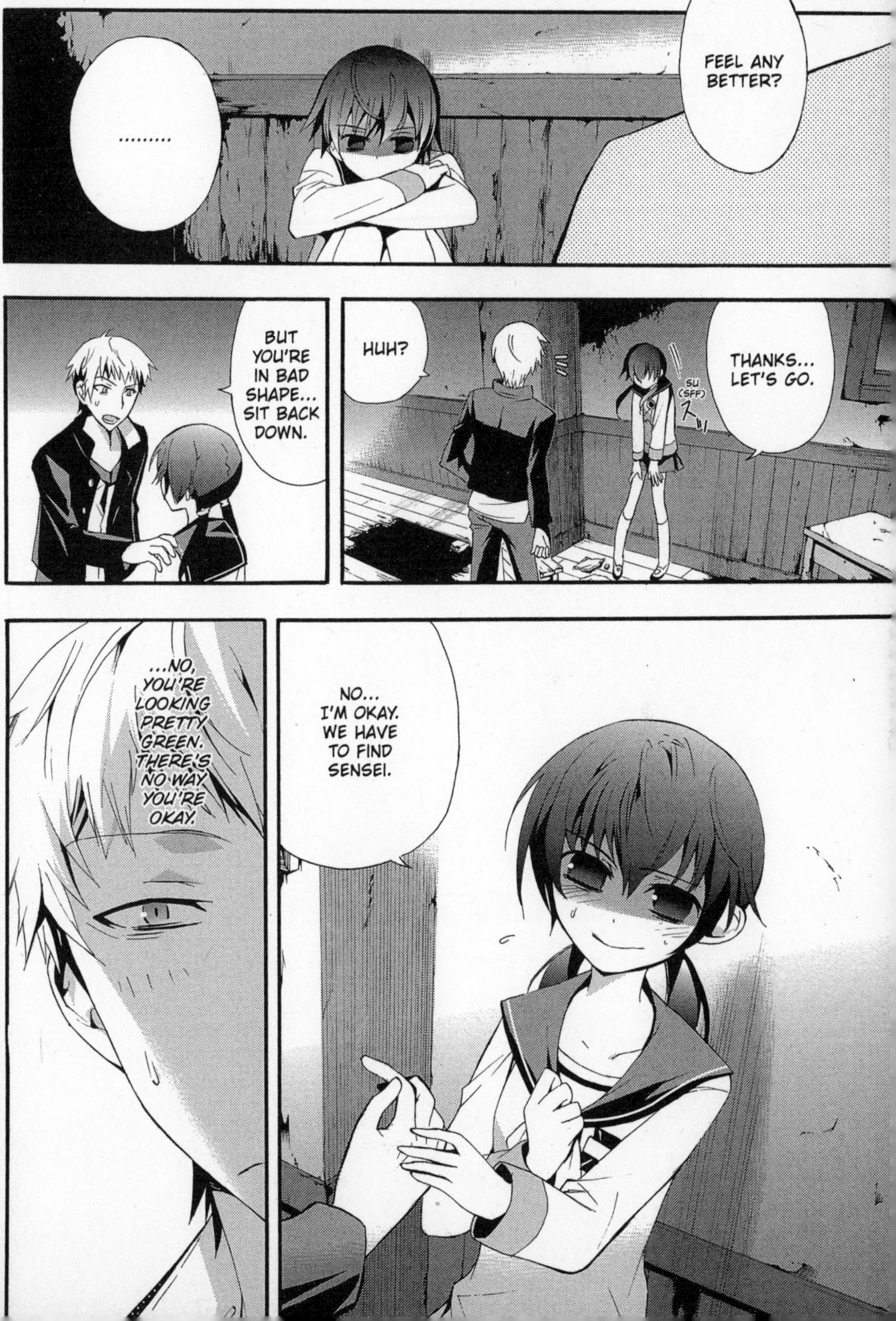
FEEL ANY BETTER?
....
THANKS... LET'S GO.
SU (SFF)
HUH?
BUT YOU'RE IN BAD SHAPE... SIT BACK DOWN.
NO... I'M OKAY. WE HAVE TO FIND SENSEI.
...NO, YOU'RE LOOKING PRETTY GREEN. THERE'S NO WAY YOU'RE OKAY.

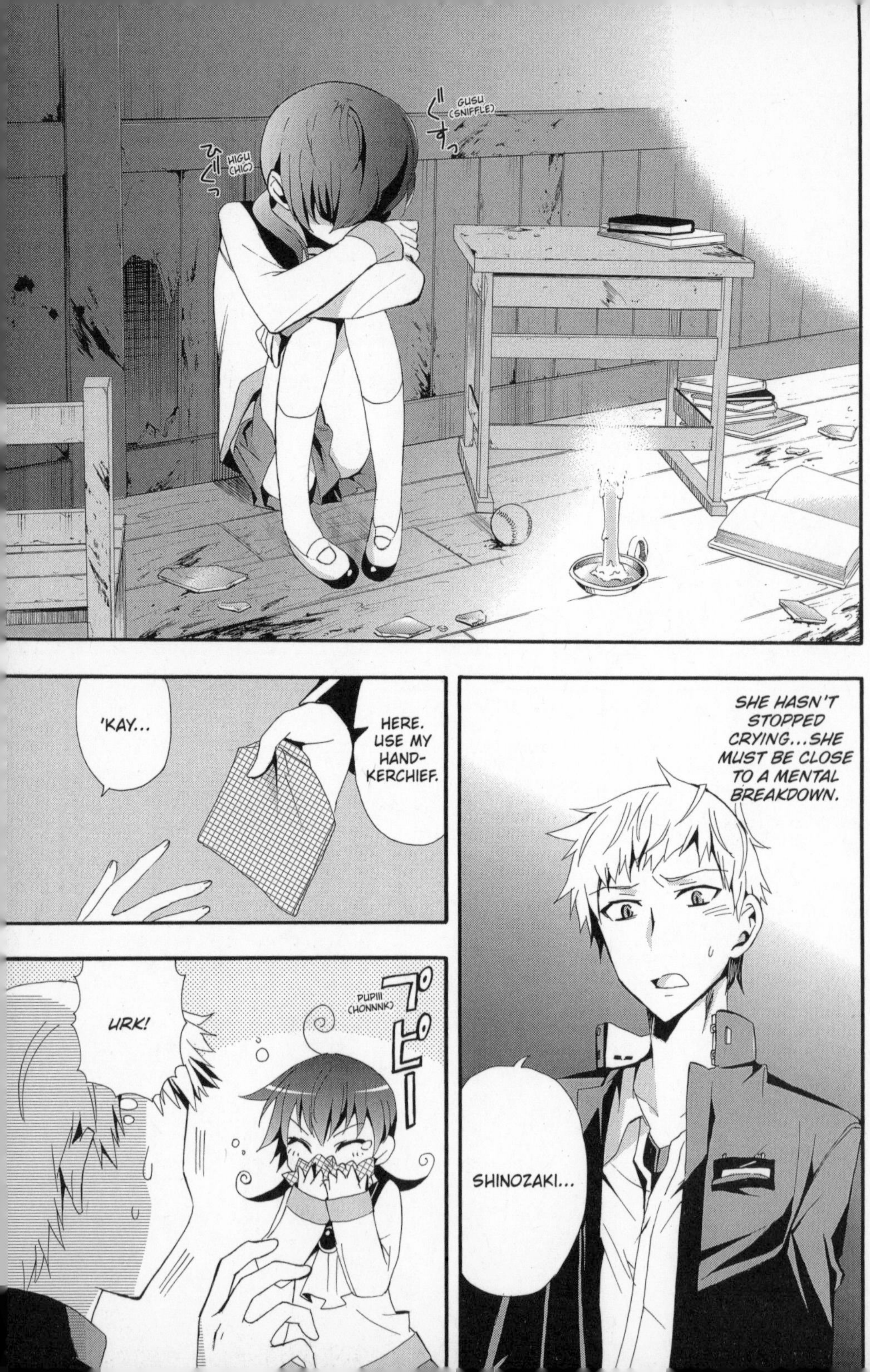
ぐすっ
GUSU (SNIFFLE)
HIGU (HIC)
SHE HASN'T STOPPED CRYING...SHE MUST BE CLOSE TO A MENTAL BREAKDOWN.
SHINOZAKI...
HERE. USE MY HAND-KERCHIEF.
'KAY...
プピー
PUPIII (HONNNK)
URK!

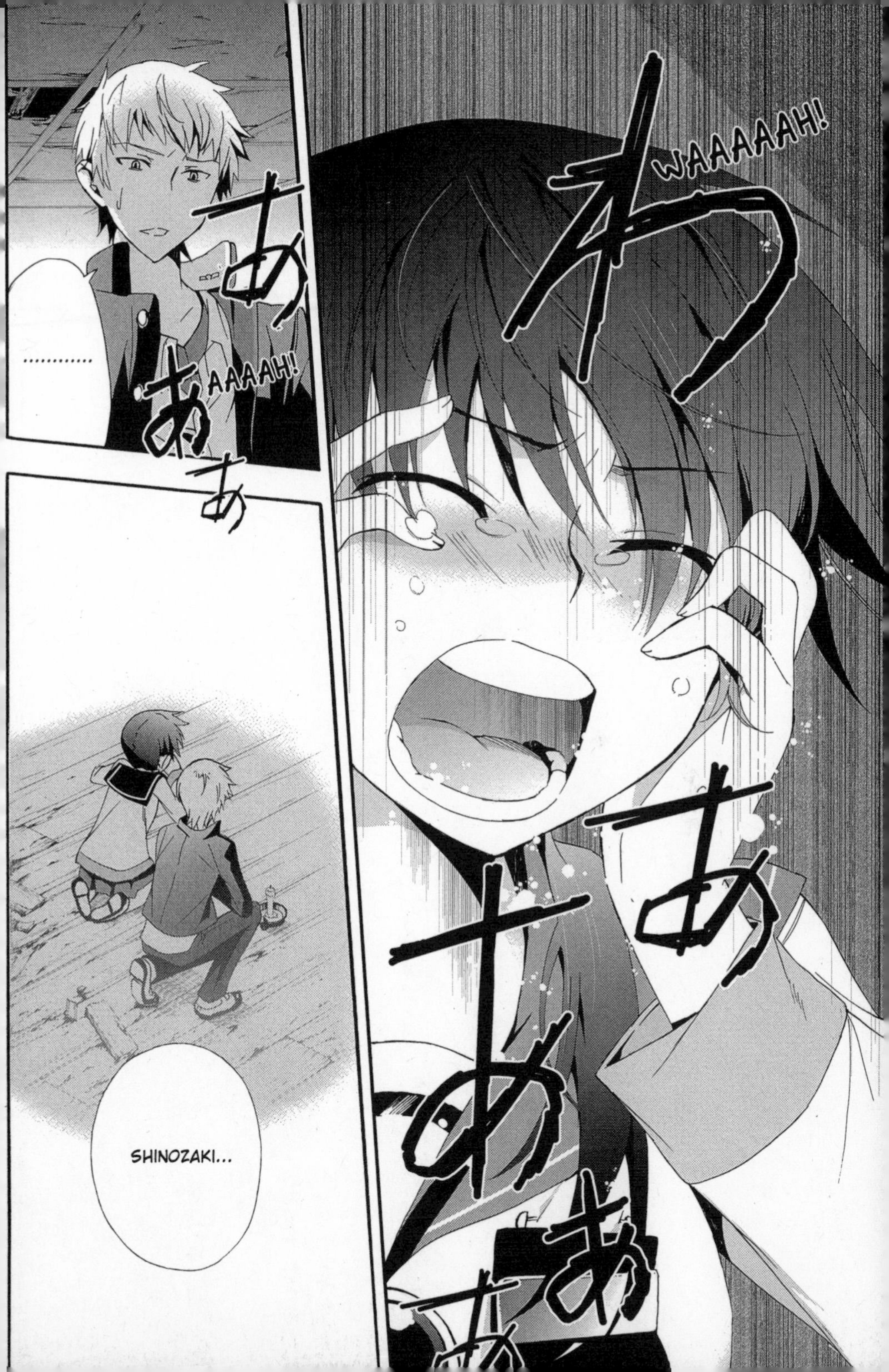

わあああ
WAAAAAAH!
あああ
AAAAH!
....
SHINOZAKI...

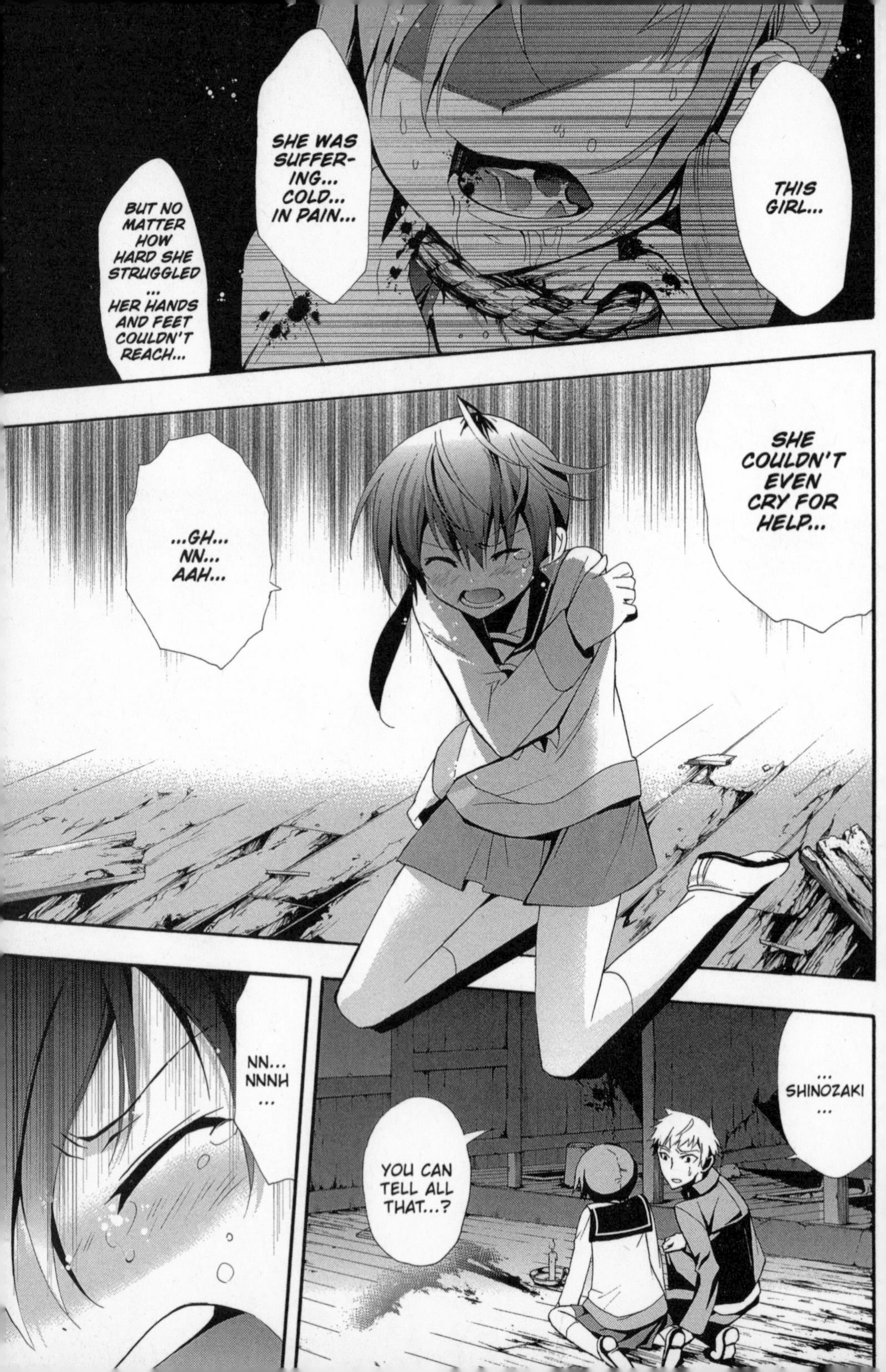
THIS GIRL...
SHE WAS SUFFER-ING... COLD... IN PAIN...
BUT NO MATTER HOW HARD SHE STRUGGLED ... HER HANDS AND FEET COULDN'T REACH...
SHE COULDN'T EVEN CRY FOR HELP...
...GH... NN... AAH...
... SHINOZAKI ...
YOU CAN TELL ALL THAT...?
NN... NNNH ...

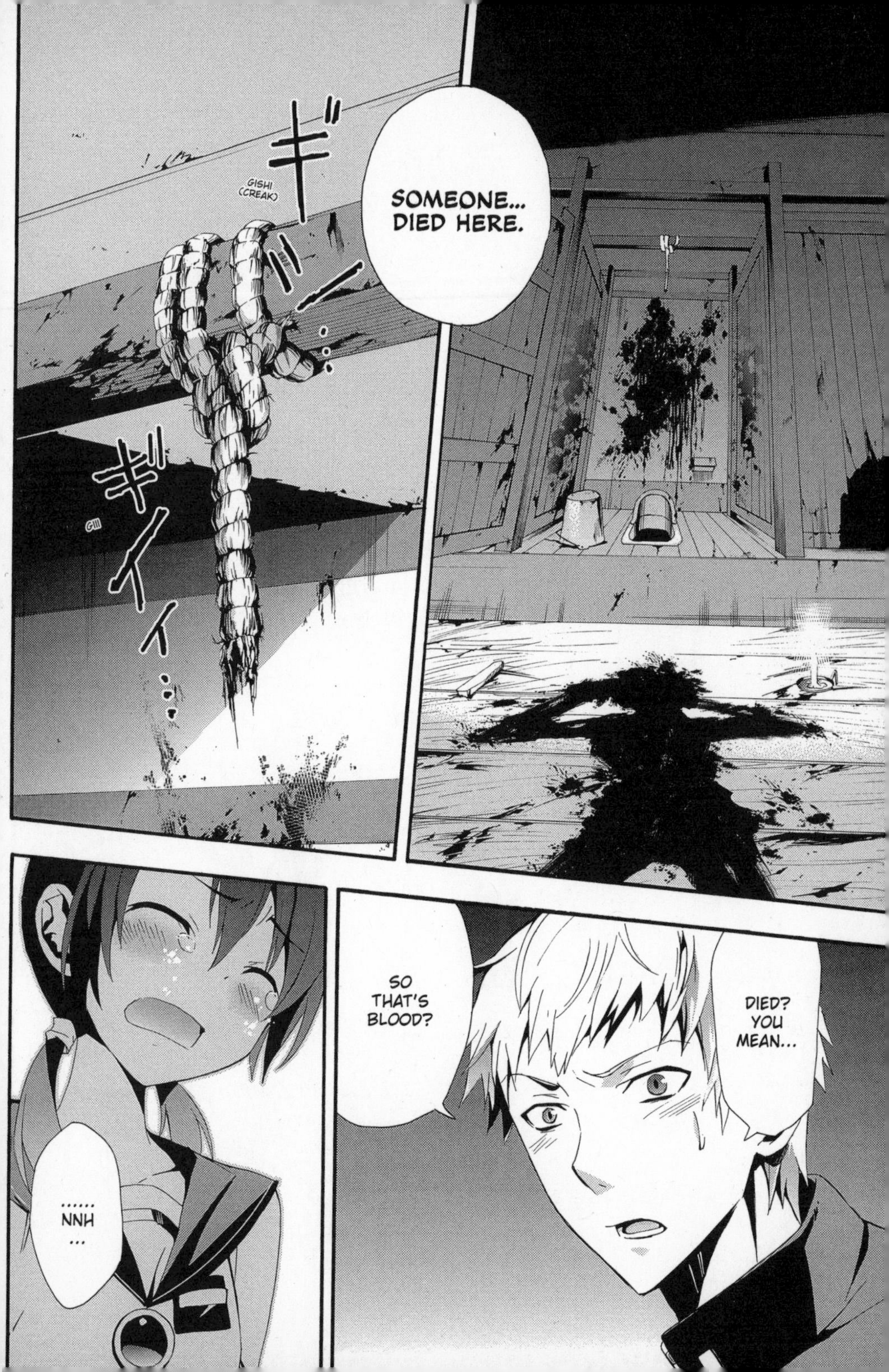
SOMEONE... DIED HERE.
GISHI (CREAK)
GIII
DIED? YOU MEAN...
SO THAT'S BLOOD?
...... NNH ...

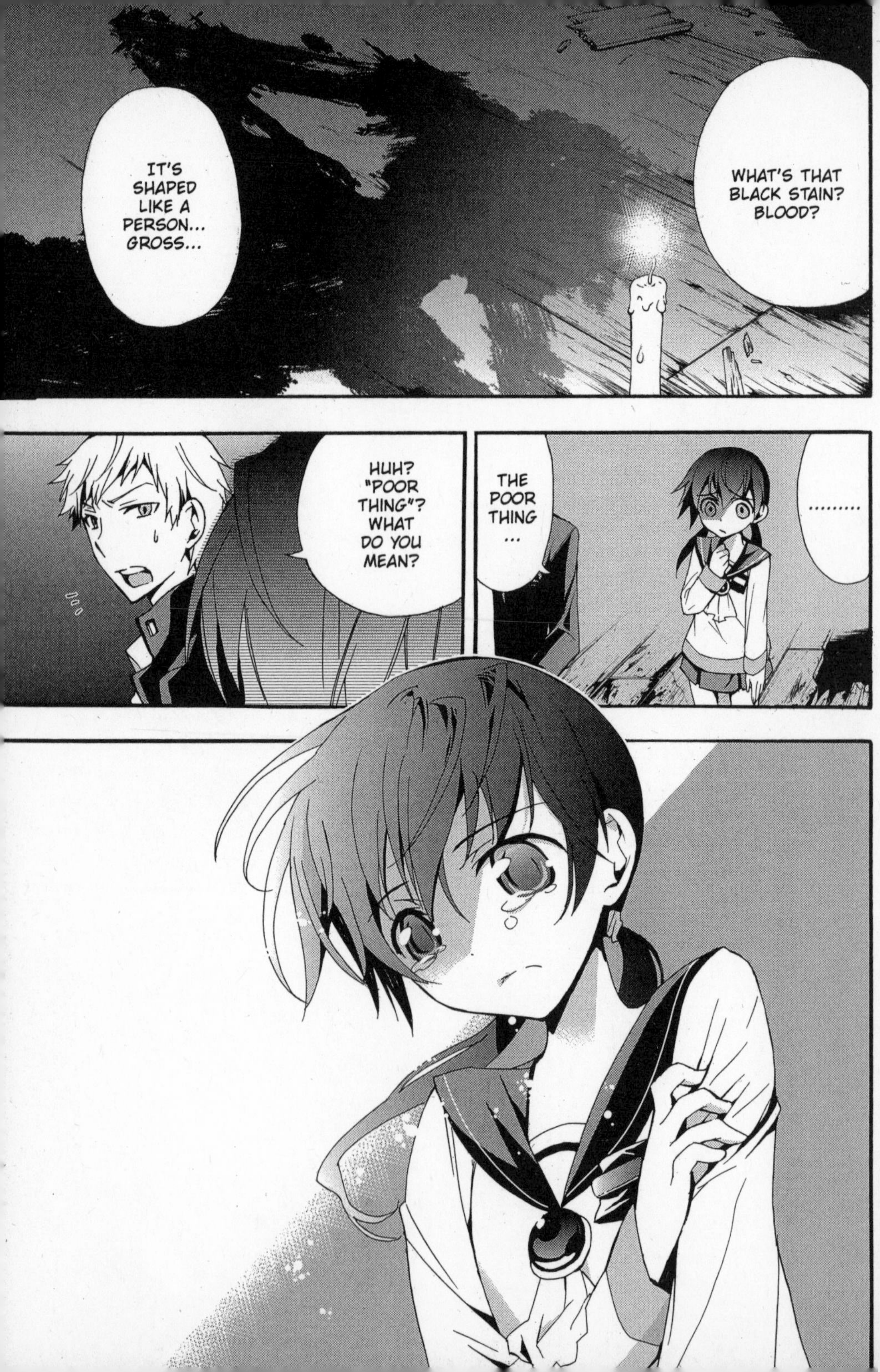
WHAT'S THAT BLACK STAIN? BLOOD?
IT'S SHAPED LIKE A PERSON... GROSS...
....
THE POOR THING...
HUH? "POOR THING"? WHAT DO YOU MEAN?

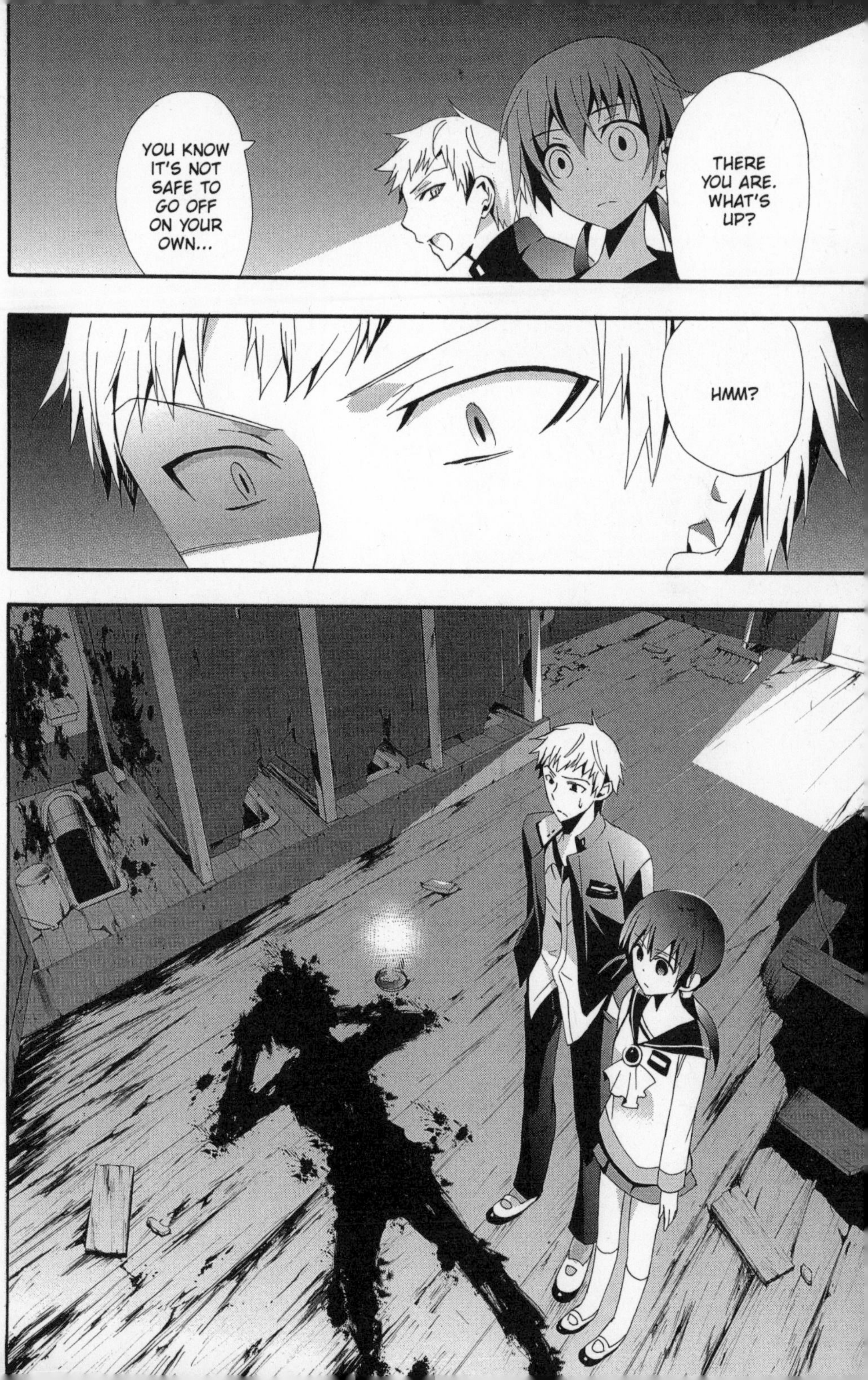
THERE YOU ARE. WHAT'S UP?
YOU KNOW IT'S NOT SAFE TO GO OFF ON YOUR OWN...
HMM?

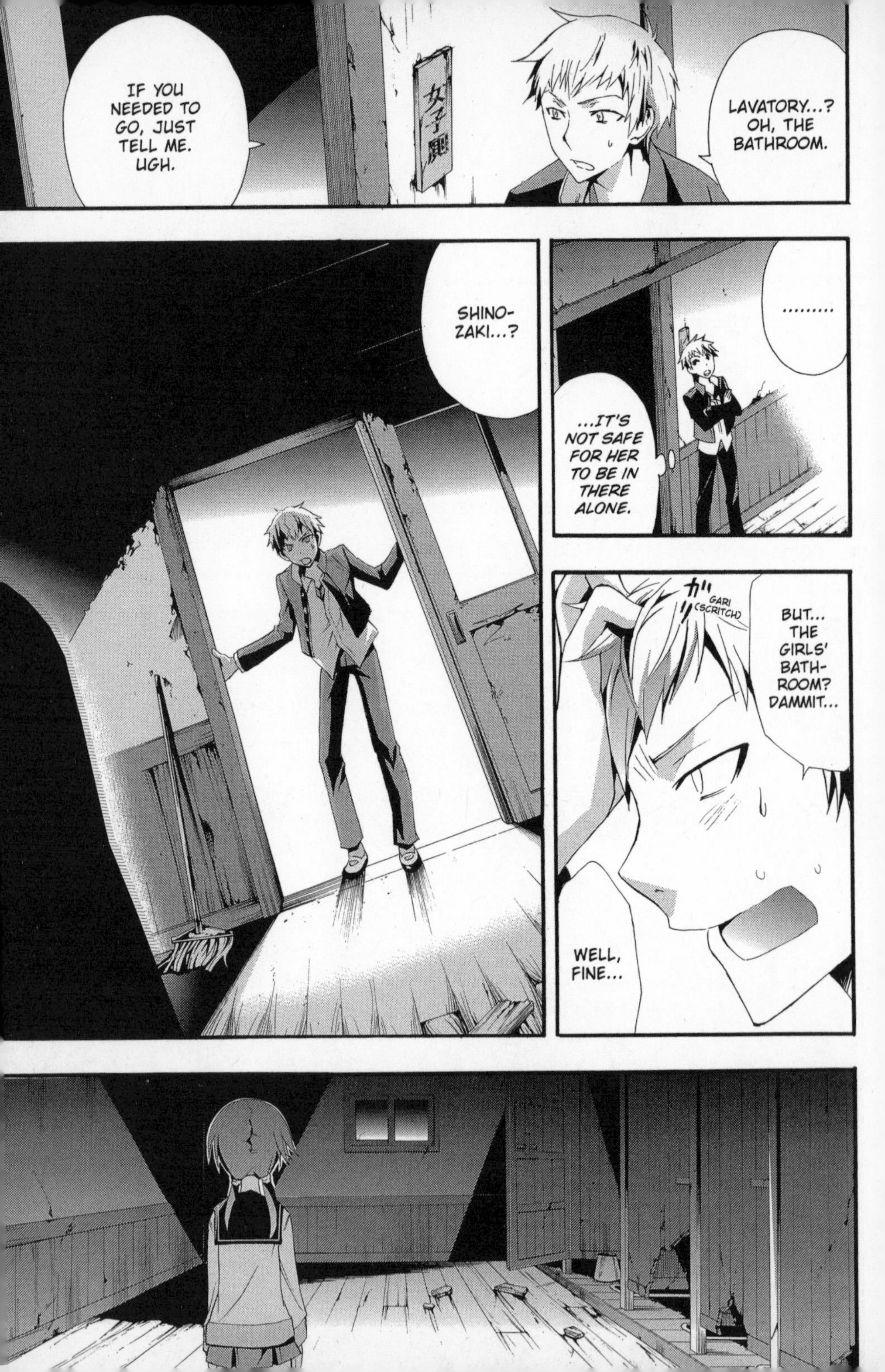
LAVATORY...? OH, THE BATHROOM.
IF YOU NEEDED TO GO, JUST TELL ME. UGH.
....
...IT'S NOT SAFE FOR HER TO BE IN THERE ALONE.
ガリ
GARI (SCRITCH)
BUT... THE GIRLS' BATH-ROOM? DAMMIT...
WELL, FINE...
SHINO-ZAKI...?

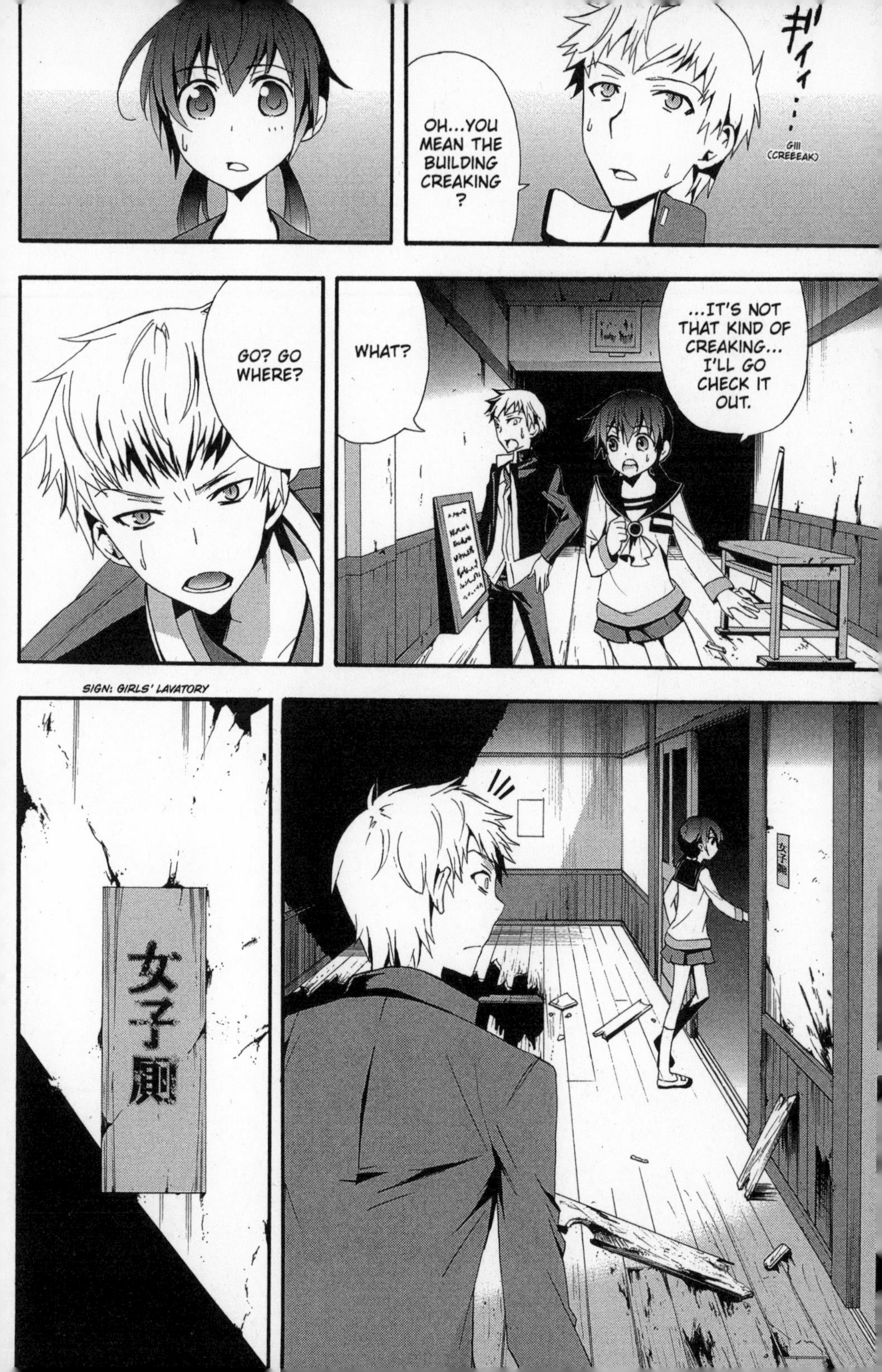
ギィィ・・・
GIII (CREEEAK)
OH...YOU MEAN THE BUILDING CREAKING ?
...IT'S NOT THAT KIND OF CREAKING... I'LL GO CHECK IT OUT.
WHAT?
GO? GO WHERE?
SIGN: GIRLS' LAVATORY
女子厠

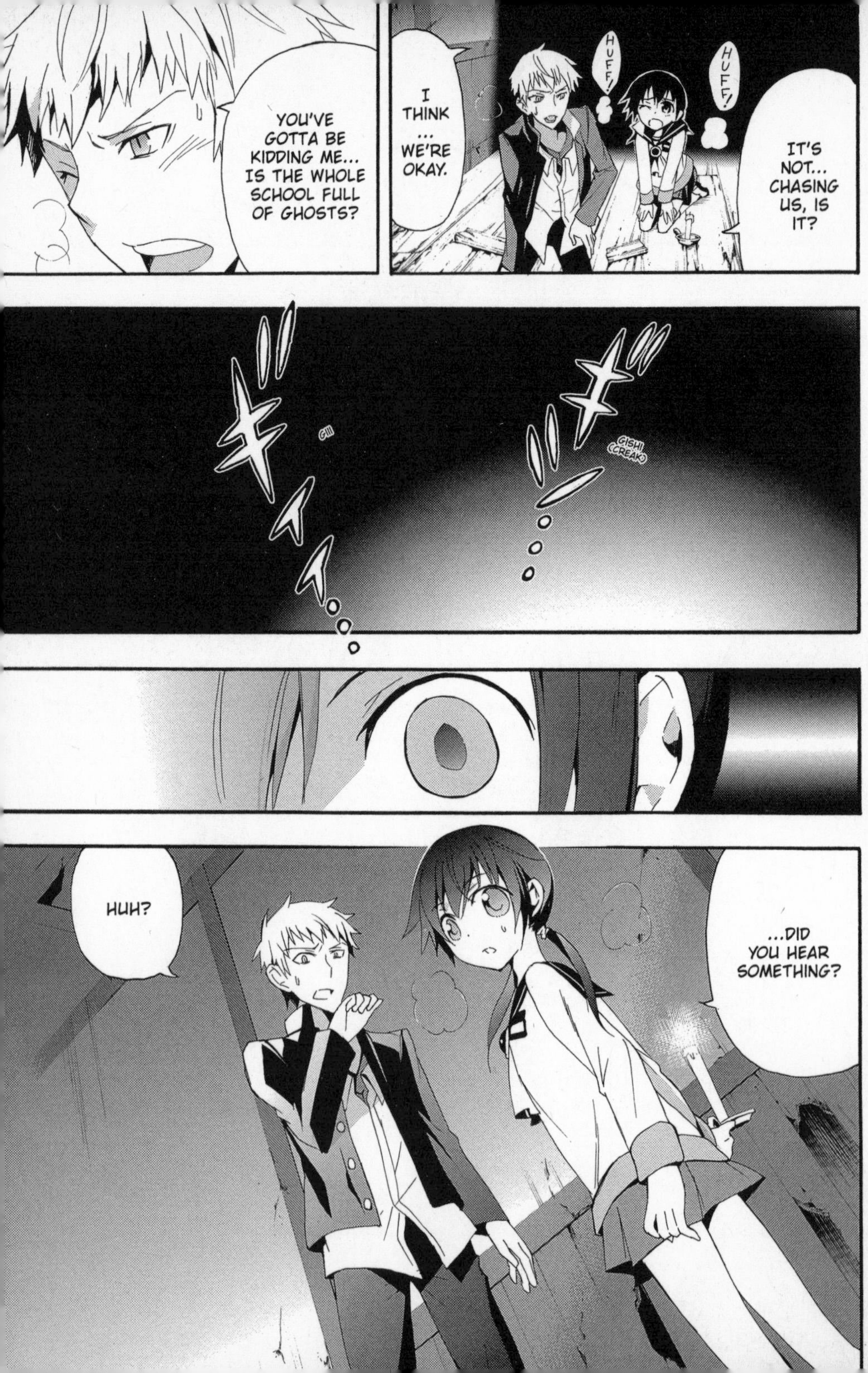
HUFF!
IT'S NOT... CHASING US, IS IT?
HUFF!
I THINK ... WE'RE OKAY.
YOU'VE GOTTA BE KIDDING ME... IS THE WHOLE SCHOOL FULL OF GHOSTS?
GISHI (CREAK)
GIII
...DID YOU HEAR SOMETHING?
HUH?

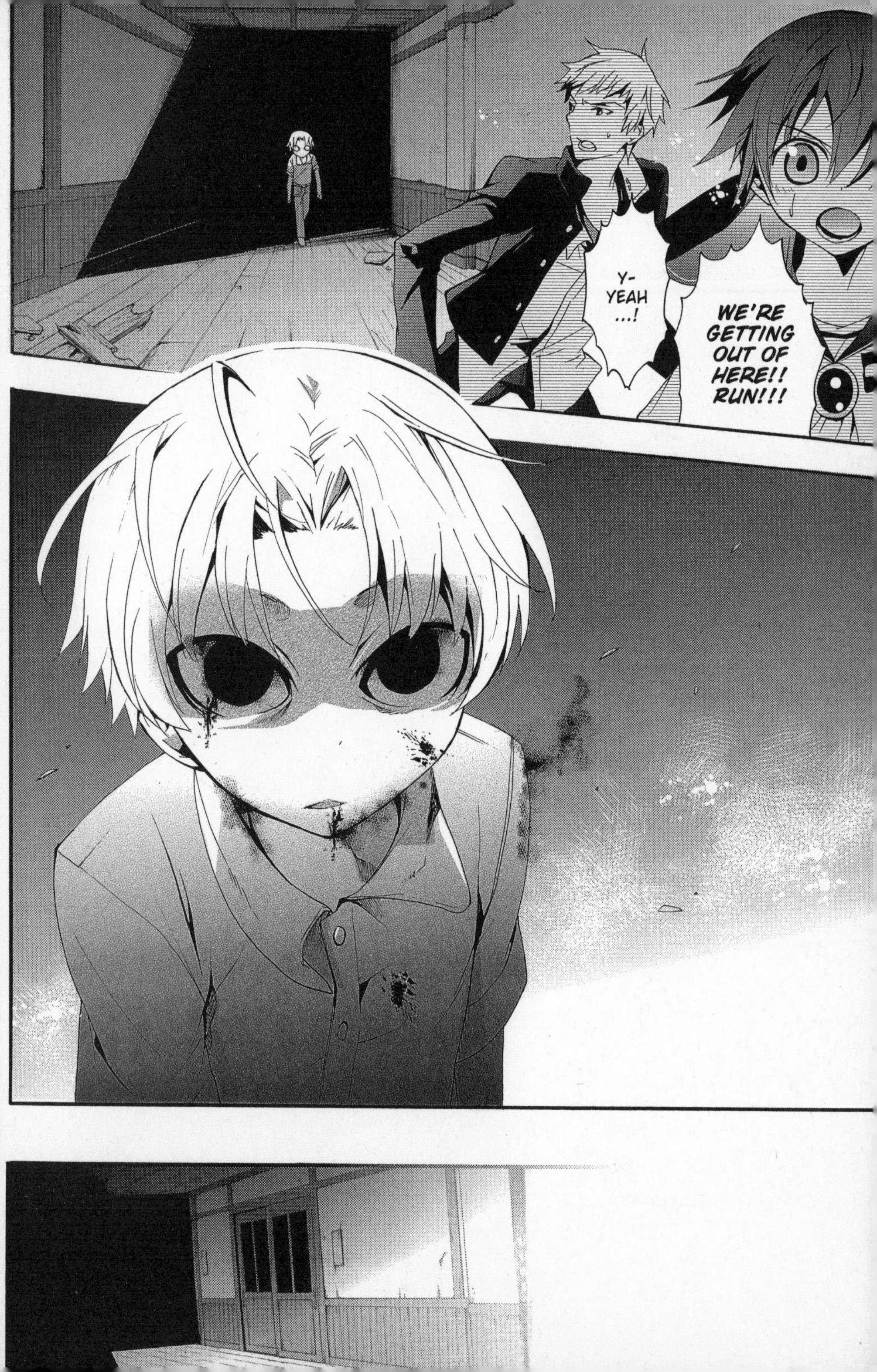
WE'RE GETTING OUT OF HERE!! RUN!!!
Y-YEAH ...!

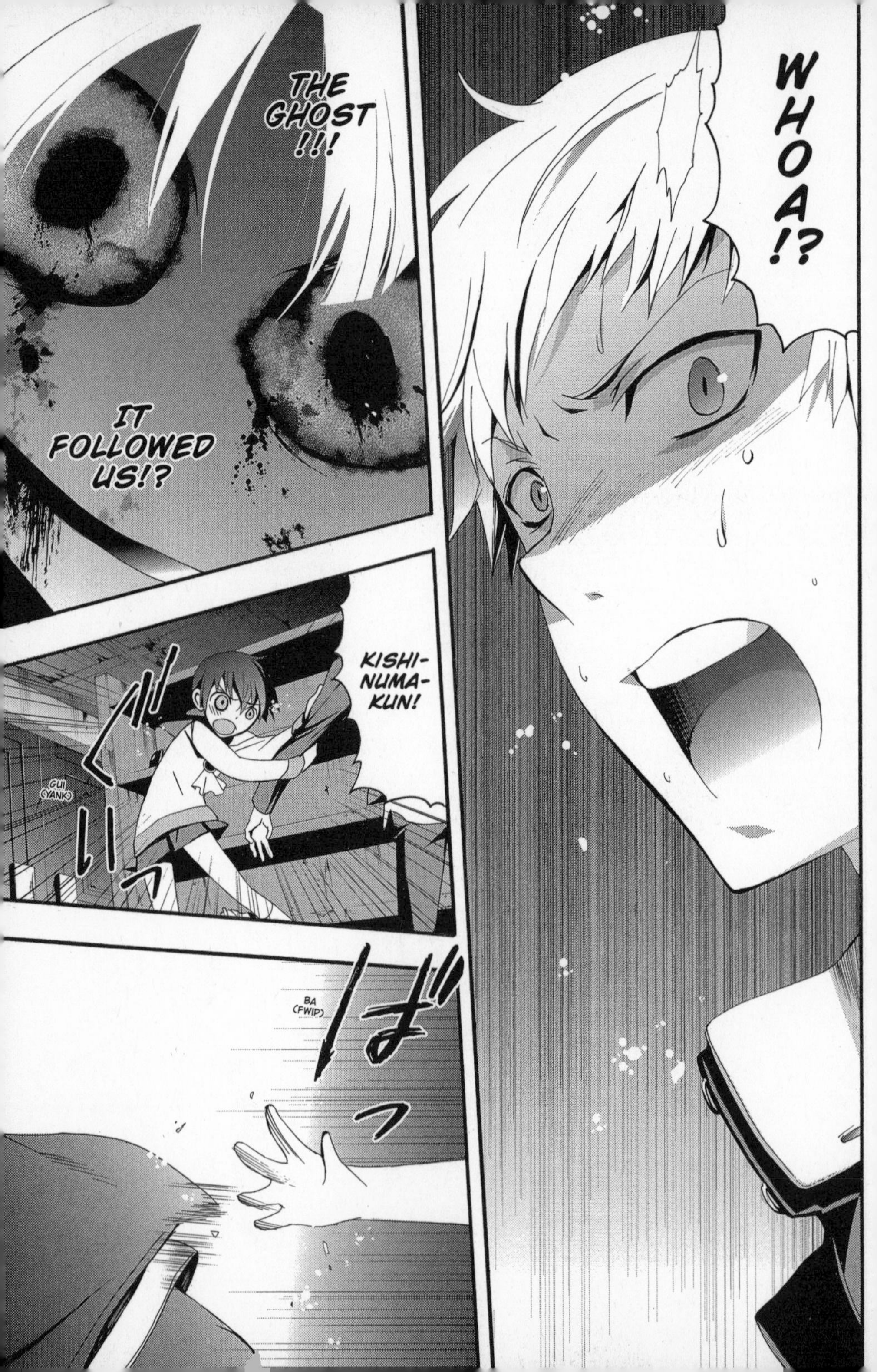
WHOA!?
THE GHOST!!!
IT FOLLOWED US!?
KISHI-NUMA-KUN!
GUI (YANK)
BA (FWIP)

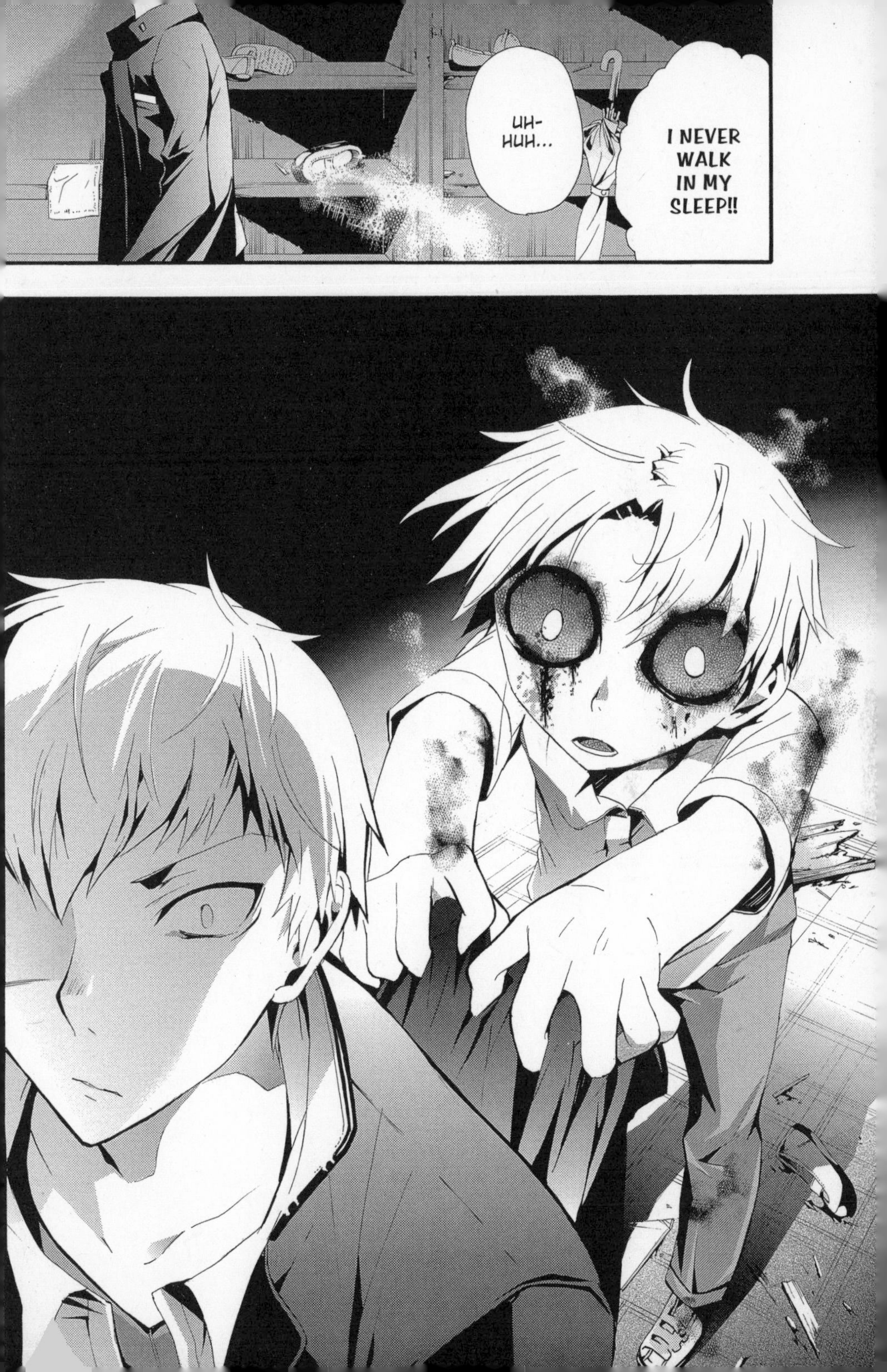
I NEVER WALK IN MY SLEEP!!
UH-HUH...

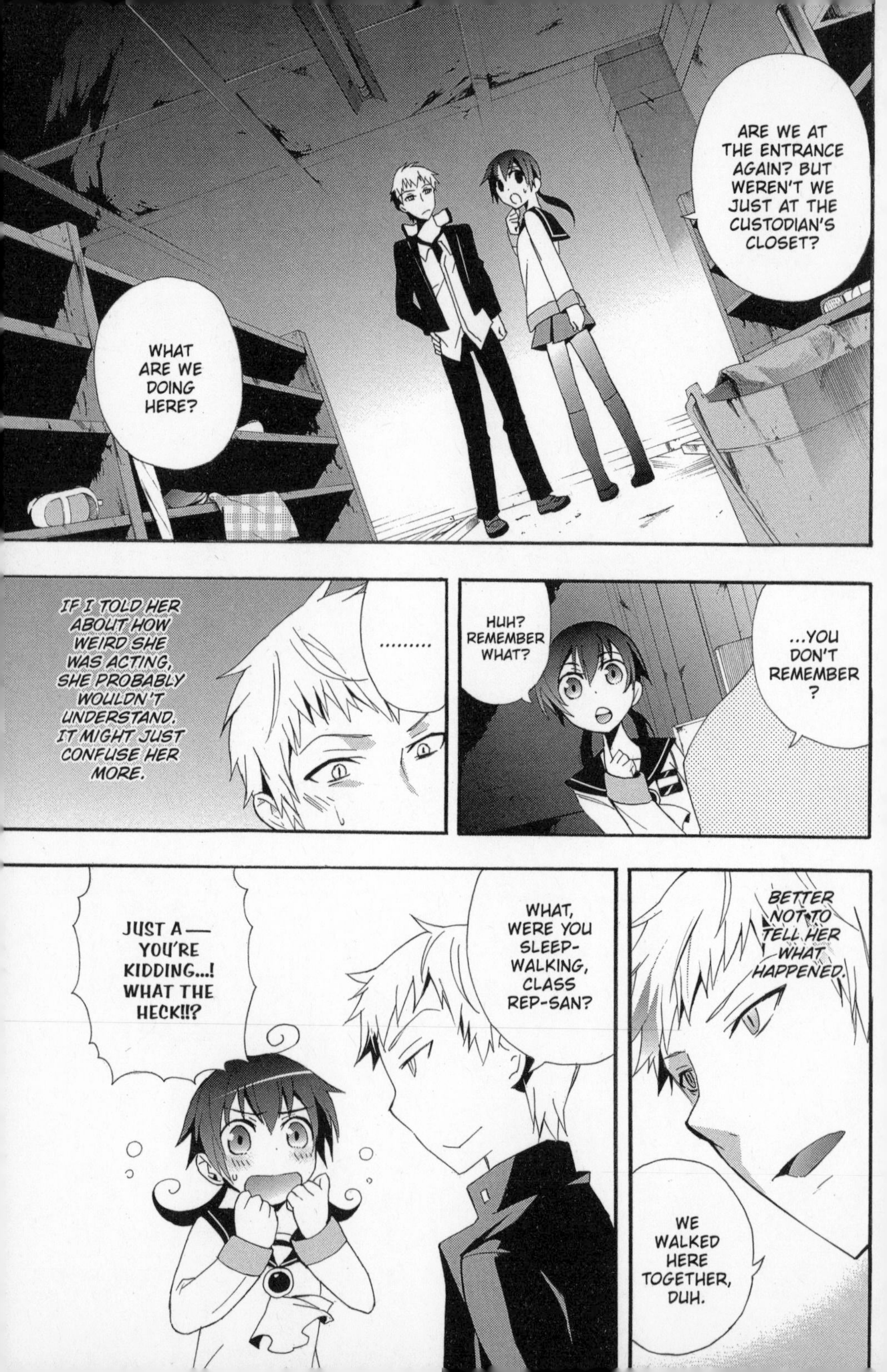
ARE WE AT THE ENTRANCE AGAIN? BUT WEREN'T WE JUST AT THE CUSTODIAN'S CLOSET?
WHAT ARE WE DOING HERE?
...YOU DON'T REMEMBER ?
HUH? REMEMBER WHAT?
....
IF I TOLD HER ABOUT HOW WEIRD SHE WAS ACTING, SHE PROBABLY WOULDN'T UNDERSTAND. IT MIGHT JUST CONFUSE HER MORE.
BETTER NOT TO TELL HER WHAT HAPPENED.
WE WALKED HERE TOGETHER, DUH.
WHAT, WERE YOU SLEEP-WALKING, CLASS REP-SAN?
JUST A— YOU'RE KIDDING...! WHAT THE HECK!!?

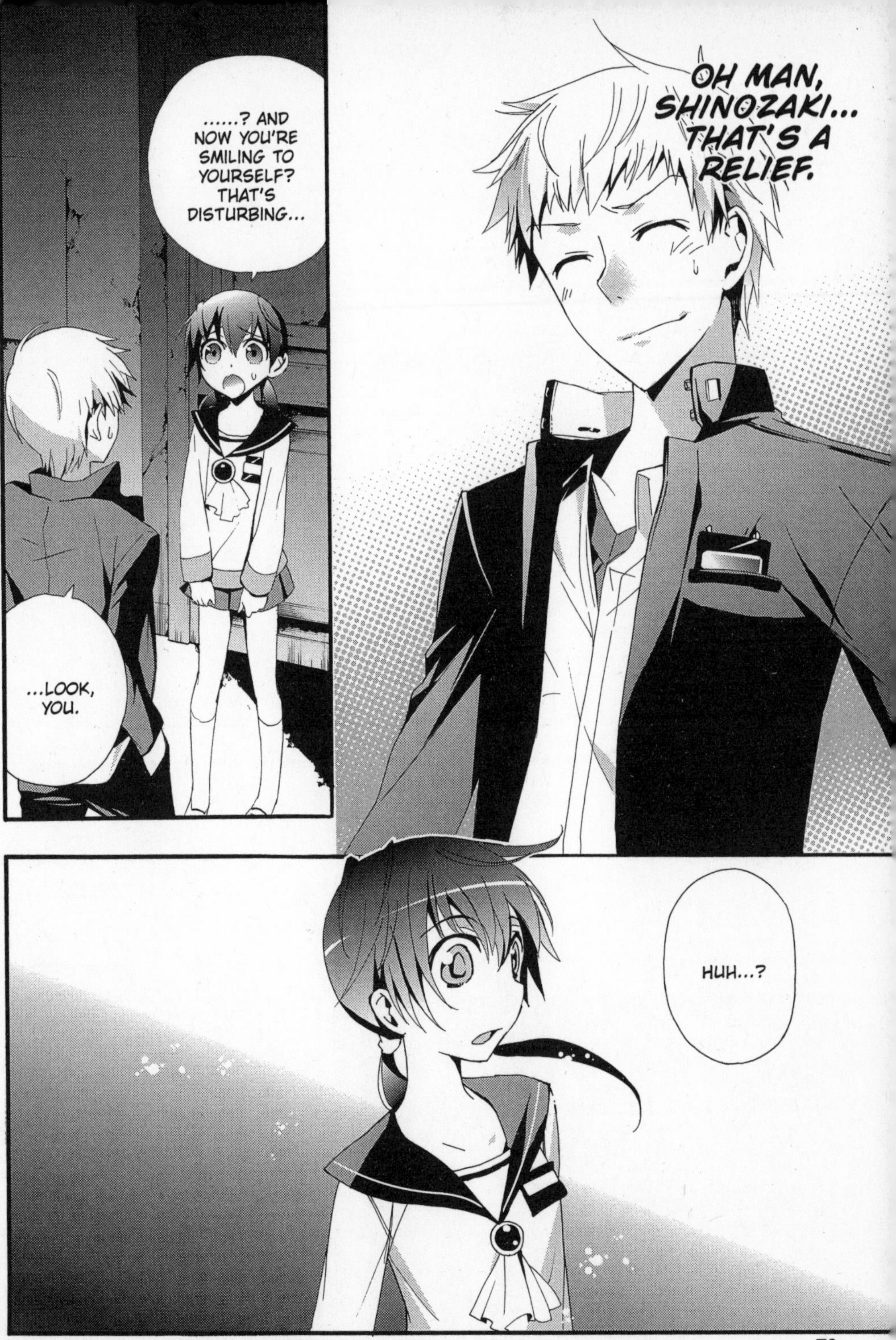
OH MAN, SHINOZAKI... THAT'S A RELIEF.
......? AND NOW YOU'RE SMILING TO YOURSELF? THAT'S DISTURBING...
...LOOK, YOU.
HUH...?

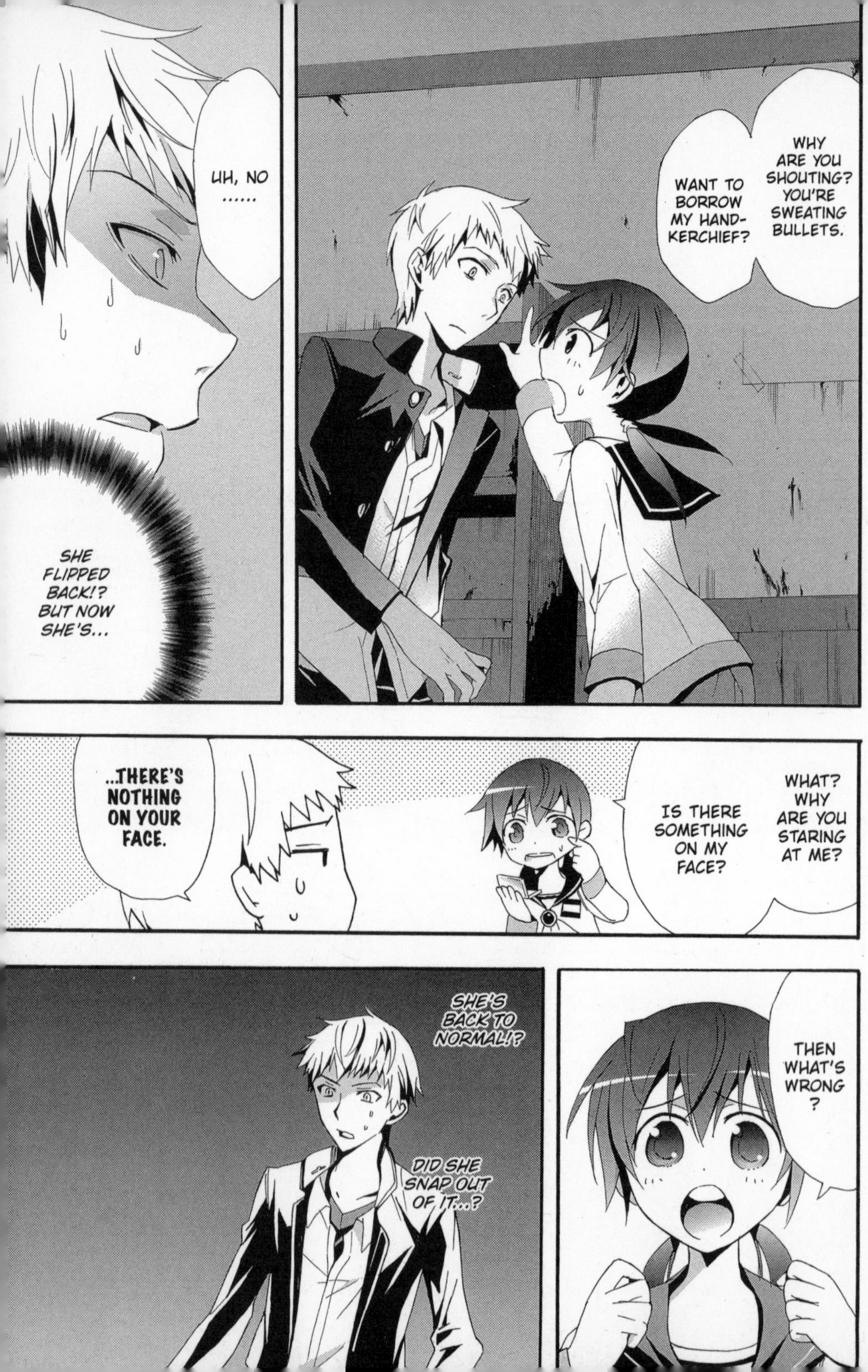
WHY ARE YOU SHOUTING? YOU'RE SWEATING BULLETS.
WANT TO BORROW MY HAND-KERCHIEF?
UH, NO ......
SHE FLIPPED BACK!? BUT NOW SHE'S...
WHAT? WHY ARE YOU STARING AT ME?
IS THERE SOMETHING ON MY FACE?
...THERE'S NOTHING ON YOUR FACE.
THEN WHAT'S WRONG?
SHE'S BACK TO NORMAL!?
DID SHE SNAP OUT OF IT...?

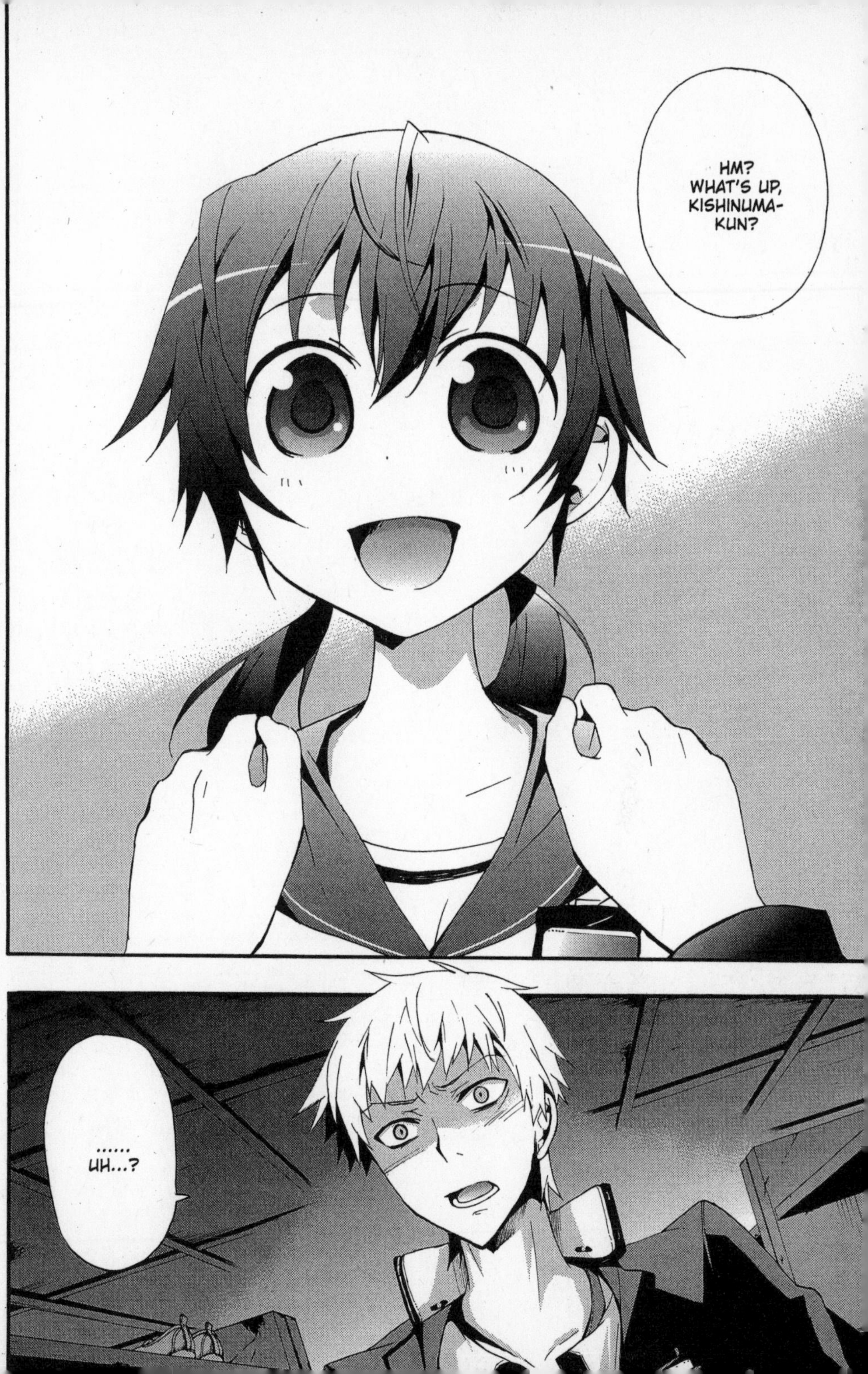
HM? WHAT'S UP, KISHINUMA-KUN?
...... UH...?

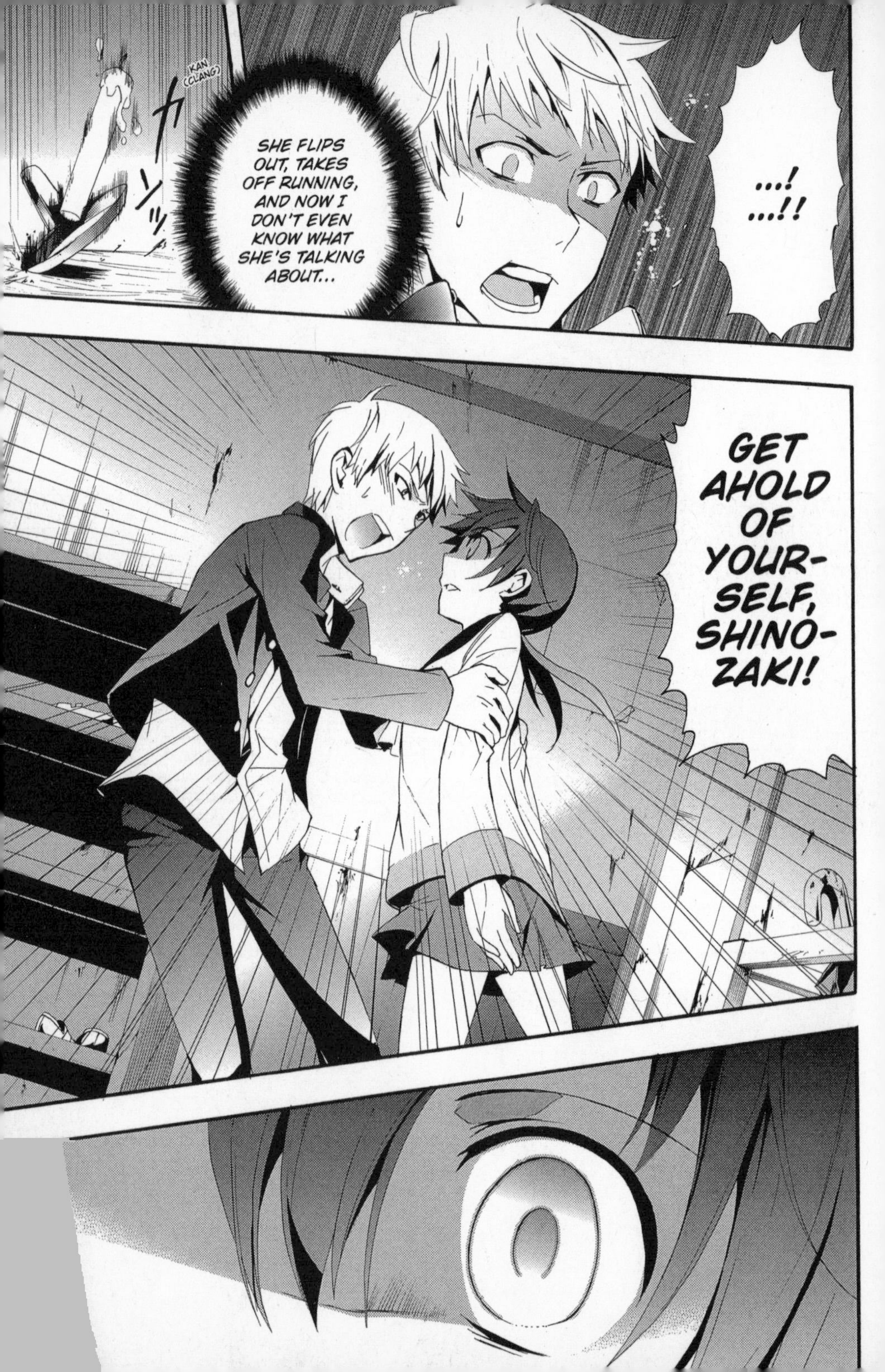
...!
...!!
SHE FLIPS OUT, TAKES OFF RUNNING, AND NOW I DON'T EVEN KNOW WHAT SHE'S TALKING ABOUT...
KAN (CLANG)
GET AHOLD OF YOUR-SELF, SHINO-ZAKI!

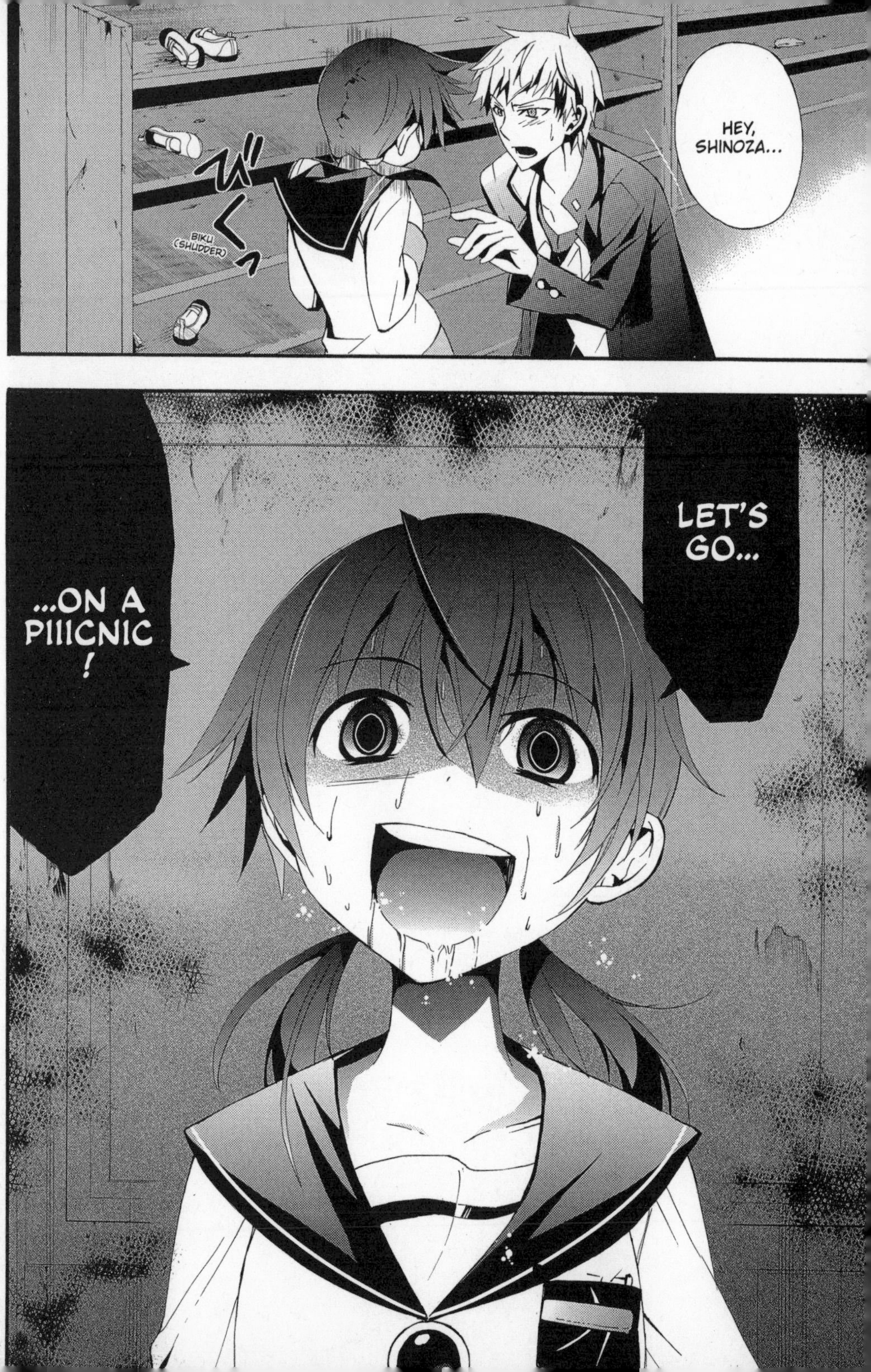
HEY, SHINOZA...
ビくっ
BIKU (SHUDDER)
LET'S GO...
...ON A PIIICNIC!

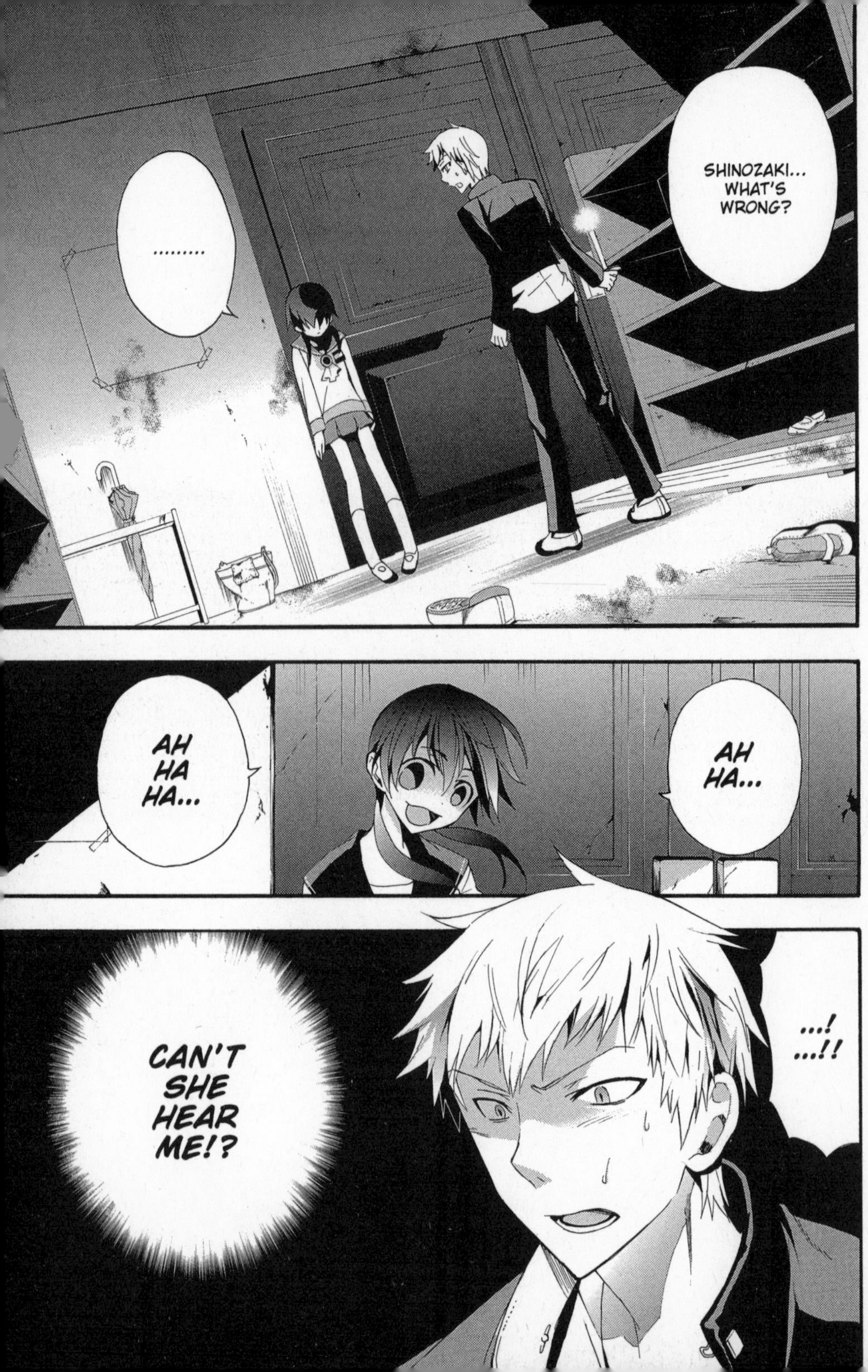
SHINOZAKI... WHAT'S WRONG?
....
AH HA...
AH HA HA...
...!
...!!
CAN'T SHE HEAR ME!?

CORPSE PARTY
BloodCovered

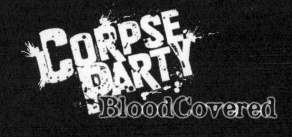

Curse 12: The Last Memory Seen

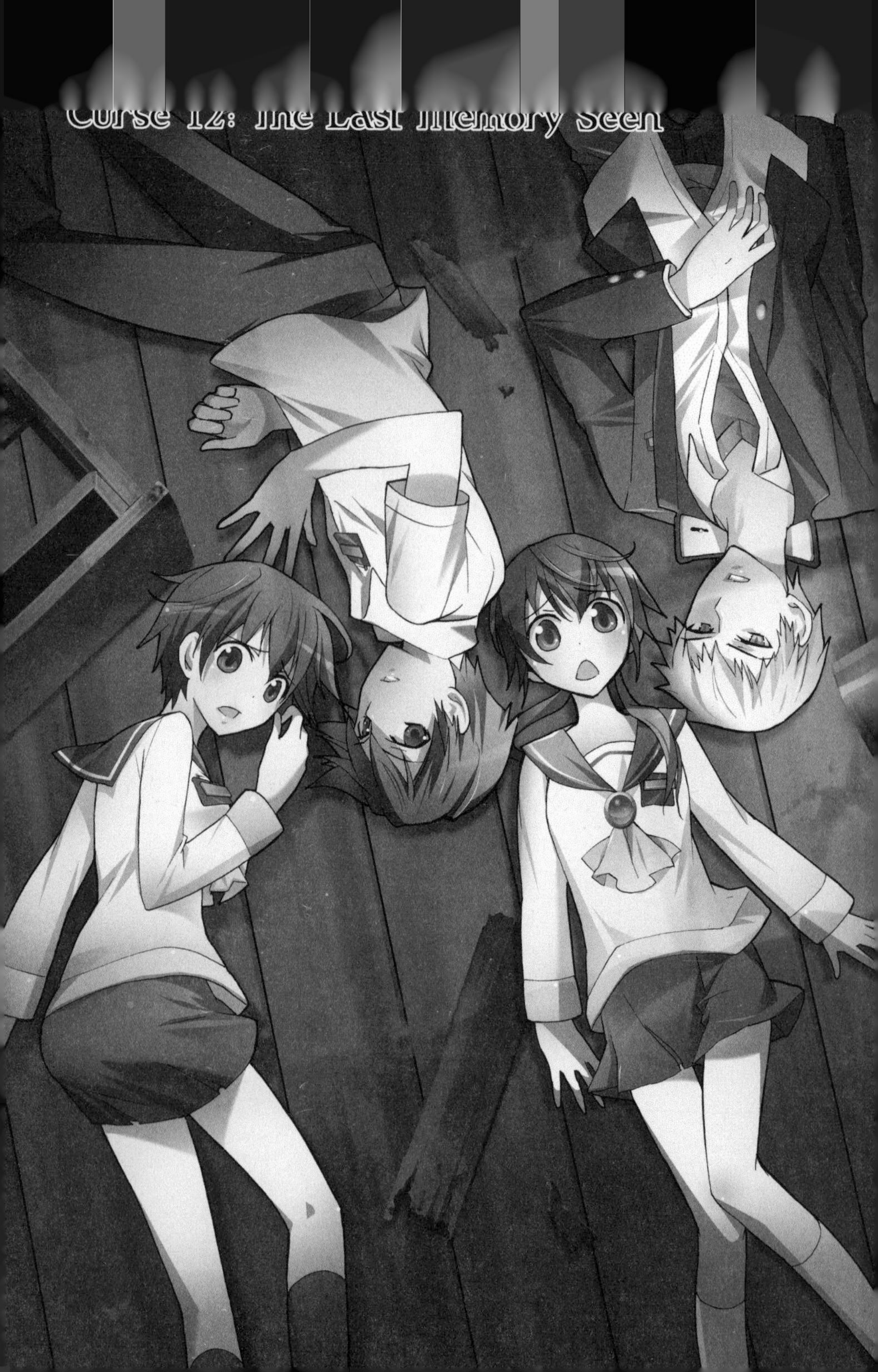

CORPSE PARTY
Blood Covered

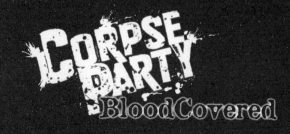

a list of ghosts/04

Ryou Yoshizawa

One of the child ghosts who have taken
up residence at Tenjin Elementary School.

With no tongue and profuse bleeding
from his abdomen, he must have died
a gruesome death.

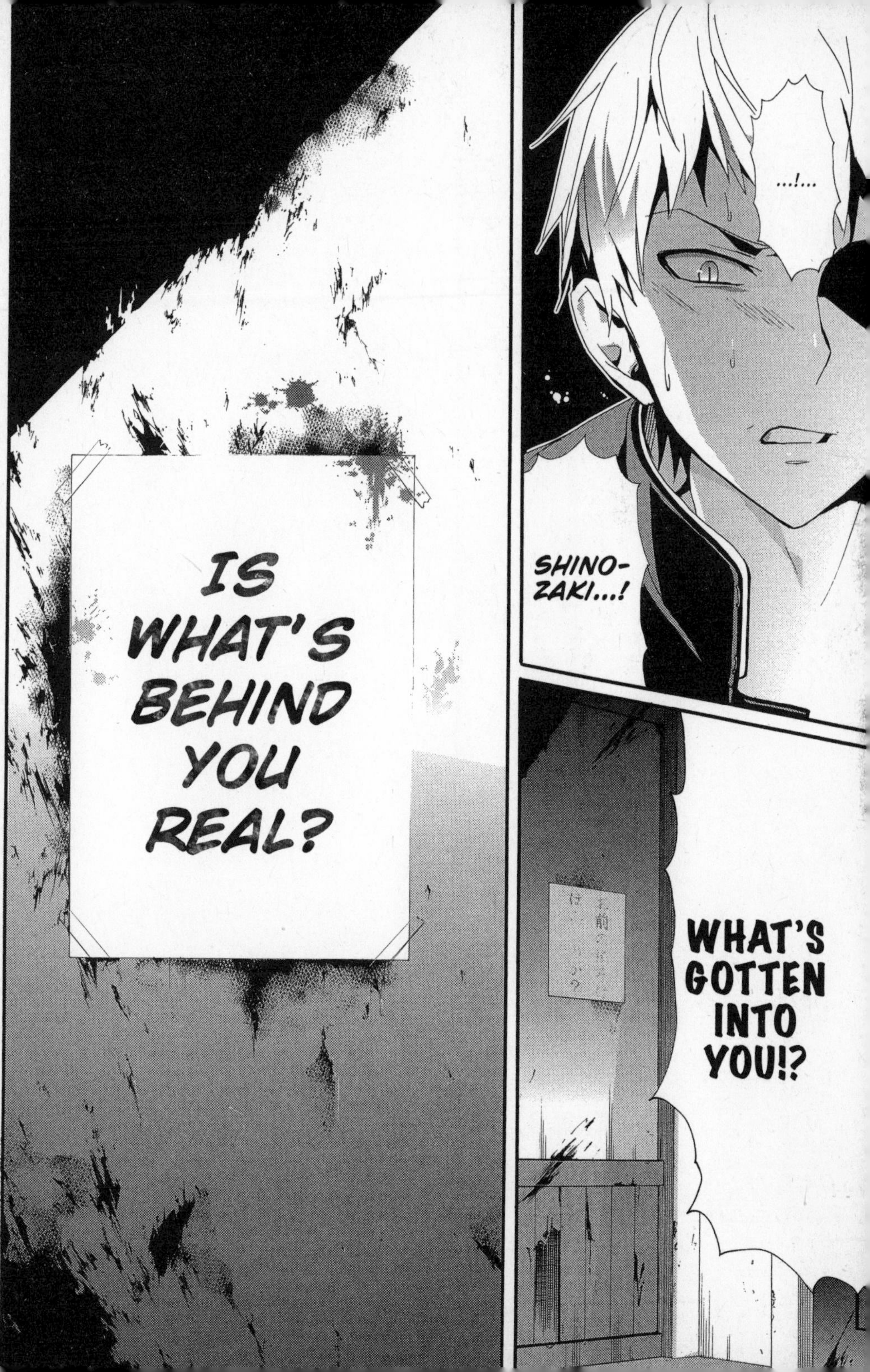
...!...
SHINO-ZAKI...!
WHAT'S GOTTEN INTO YOU!?
IS WHAT'S BEHIND YOU REAL?

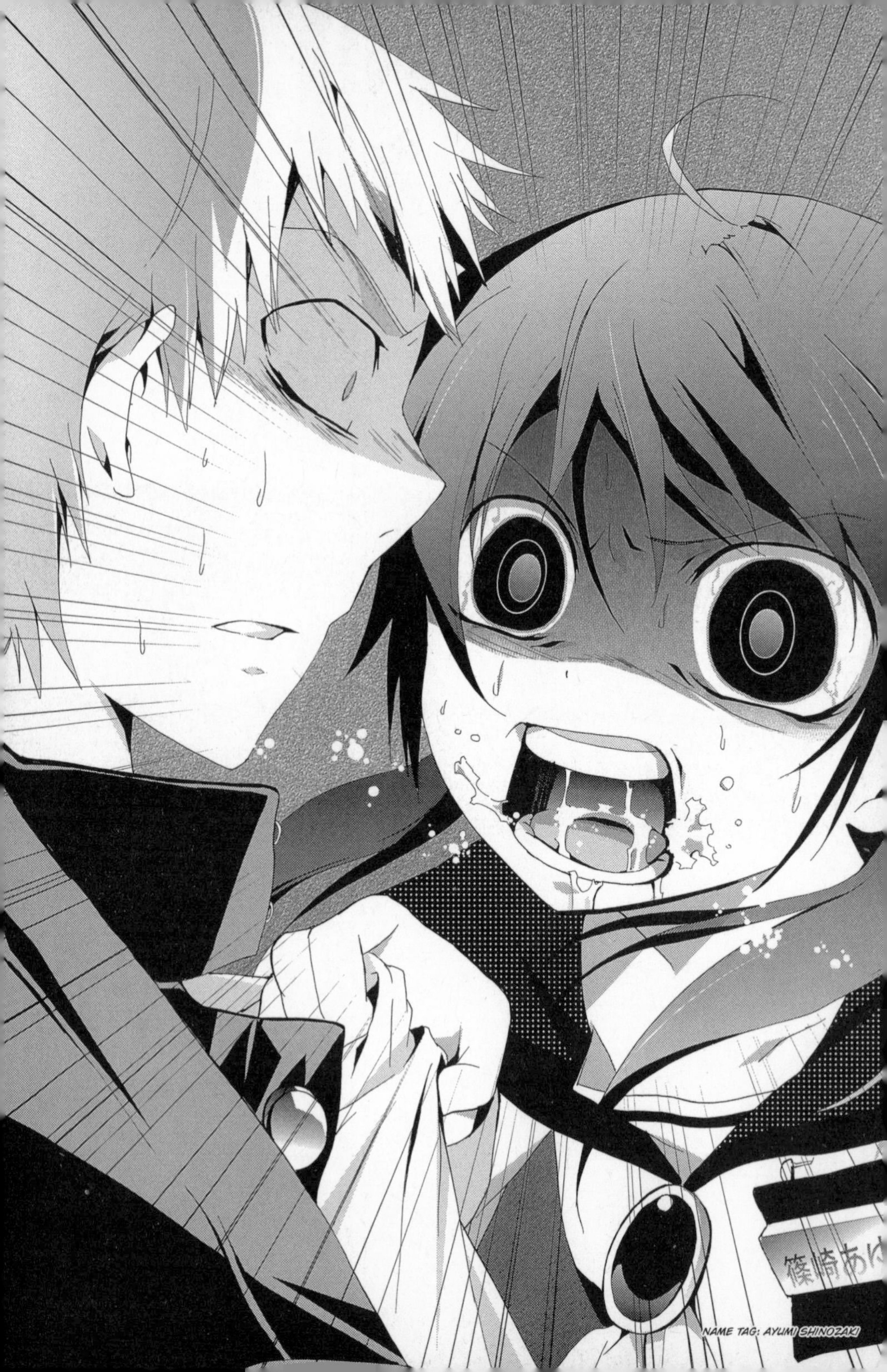
篠崎あゆ
NAME TAG: AYUMI SHINOZAKI

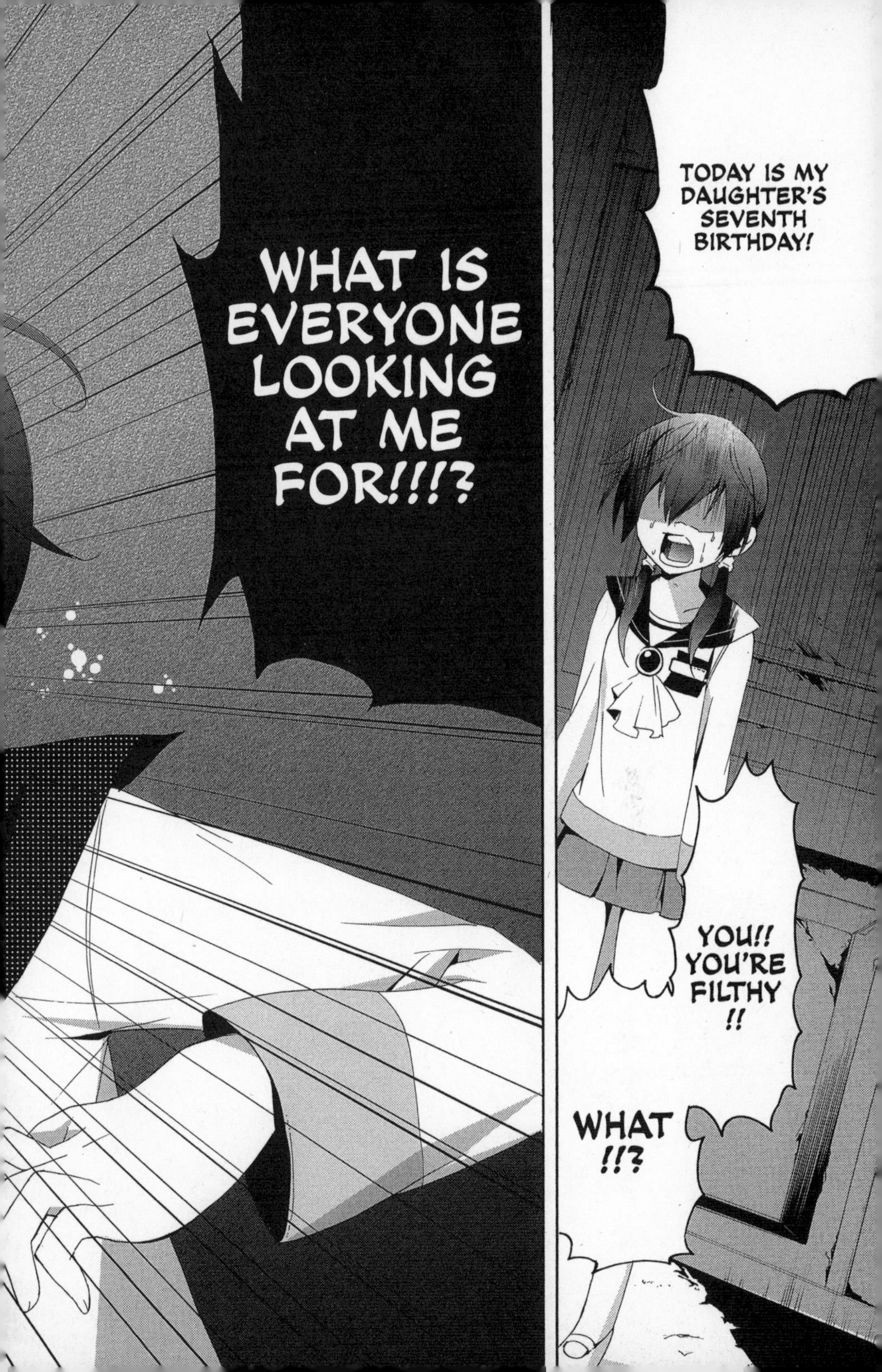
TODAY IS MY DAUGHTER'S SEVENTH BIRTHDAY!
YOU!! YOU'RE FILTHY !!
WHAT !!?
WHAT IS EVERYONE LOOKING AT ME FOR!!!?

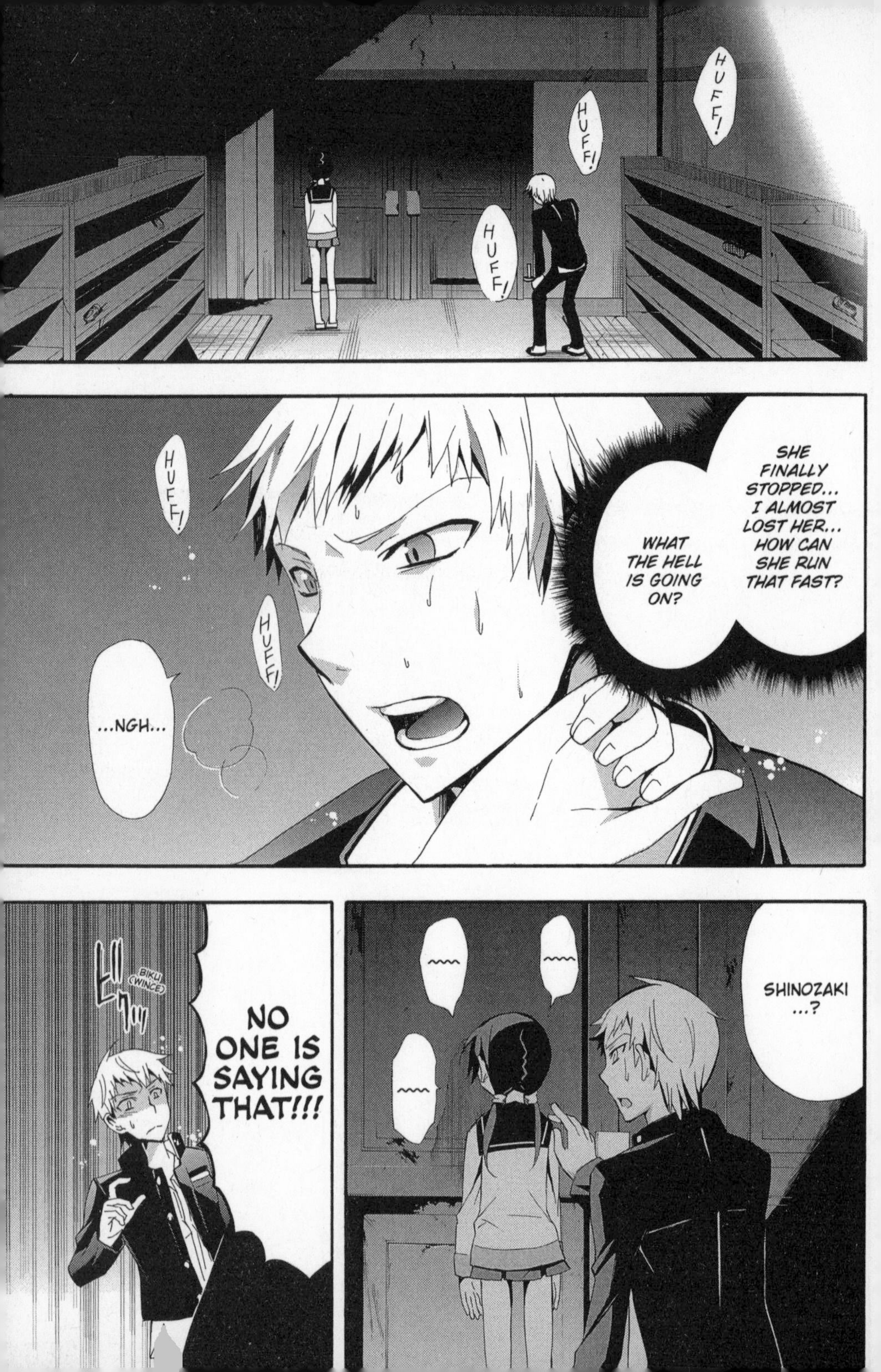
HUFF!
HUFF!
HUFF!
SHE FINALLY STOPPED... I ALMOST LOST HER... HOW CAN SHE RUN THAT FAST?
WHAT THE HELL IS GOING ON?
HUFF!
HUFF!
...NGH...
SHINOZAKI ...?
~~~
~~~
~~~
NO ONE IS SAYING THAT!!!
ビクッ
BIKU (WINCE)
~~~

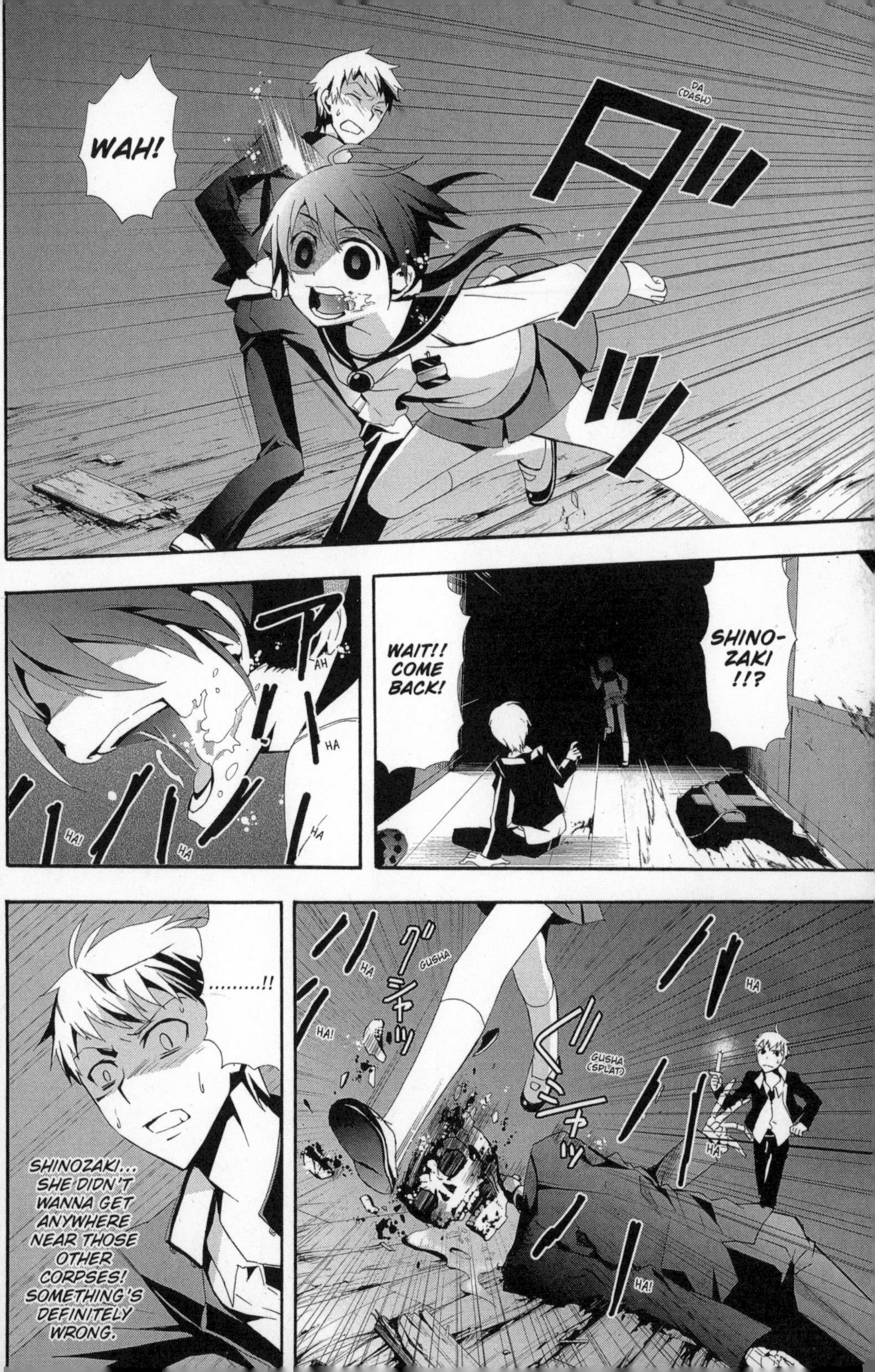
DA (DASH)
WAH!
SHINO-ZAKI !!?
WAIT!! COME BACK!
AH
HA
HA
HA
HA!
HA
GUSHA (SPLAT)
HA
HA!
GUSHA
HA
HA!
.........!!
SHINOZAKI... SHE DIDN'T WANNA GET ANYWHERE NEAR THOSE OTHER CORPSES! SOMETHING'S DEFINITELY WRONG.

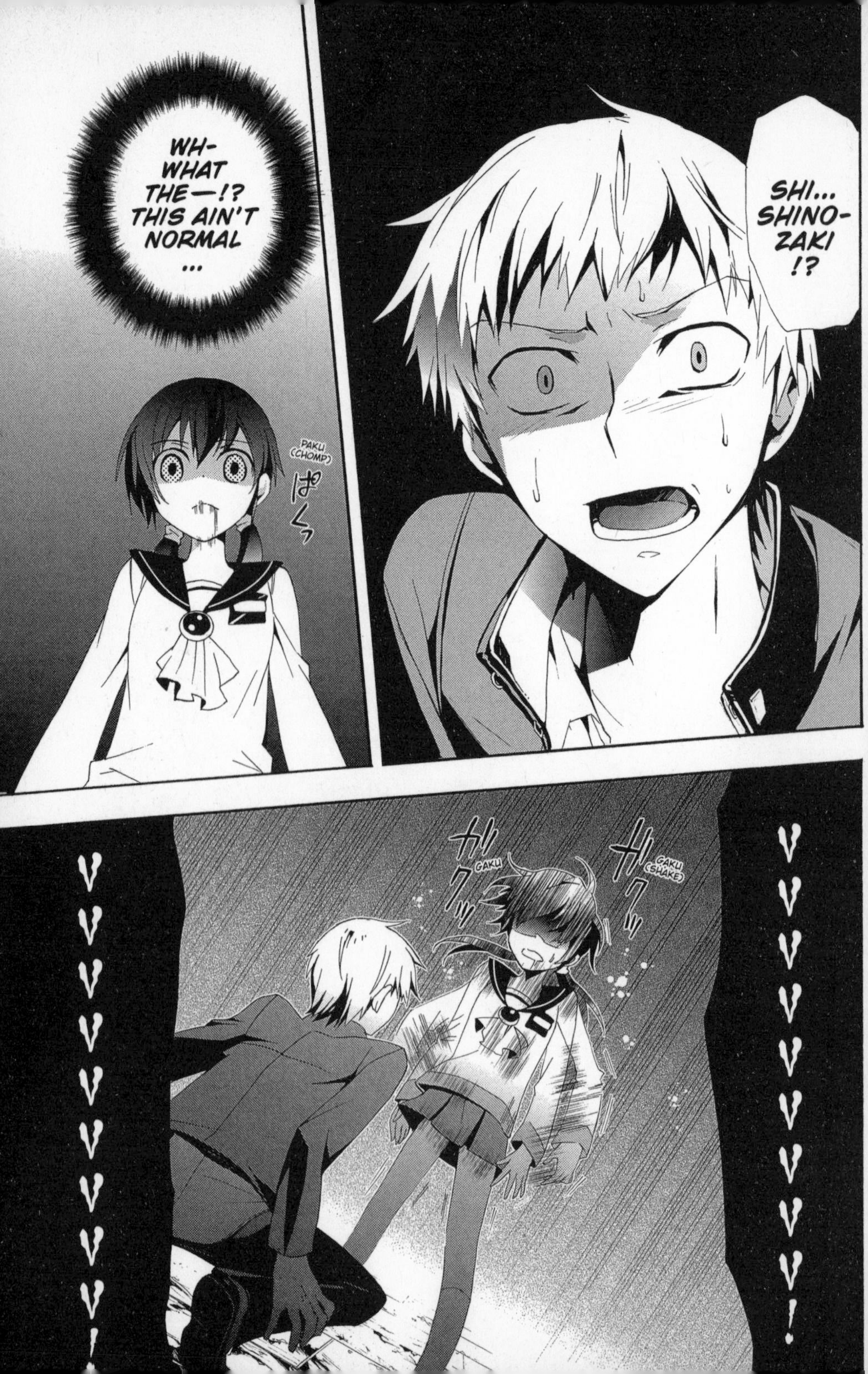
SHI... SHINOZAKI!?
WH-WHAT THE—!? THIS AIN'T NORMAL...
PAKU (CHOMP)
ぱくっ
VVVVVVVVVVVVVV!
GAKU (SHAKE)
GAKU
VVVVVVVVVVVV!

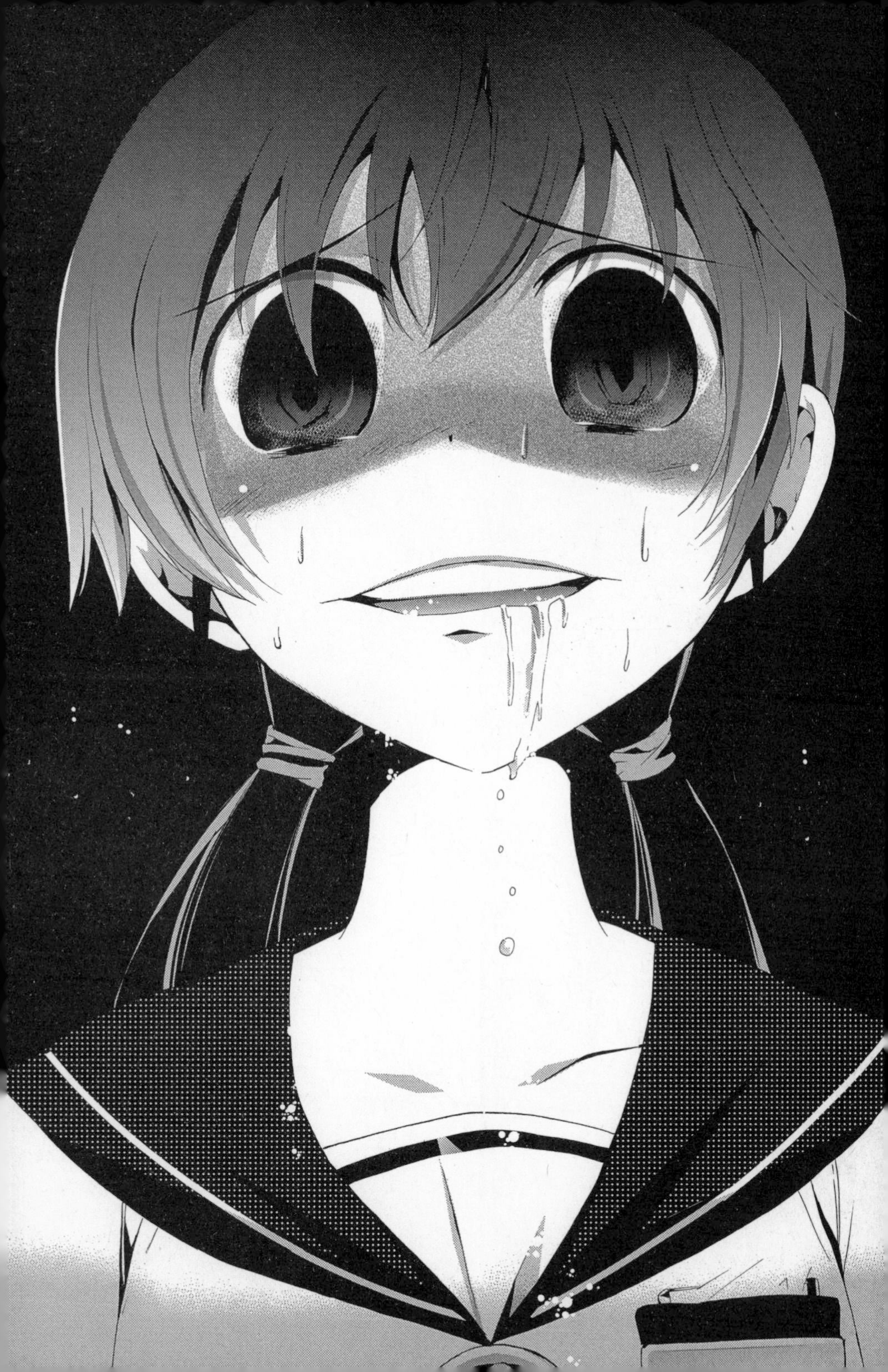

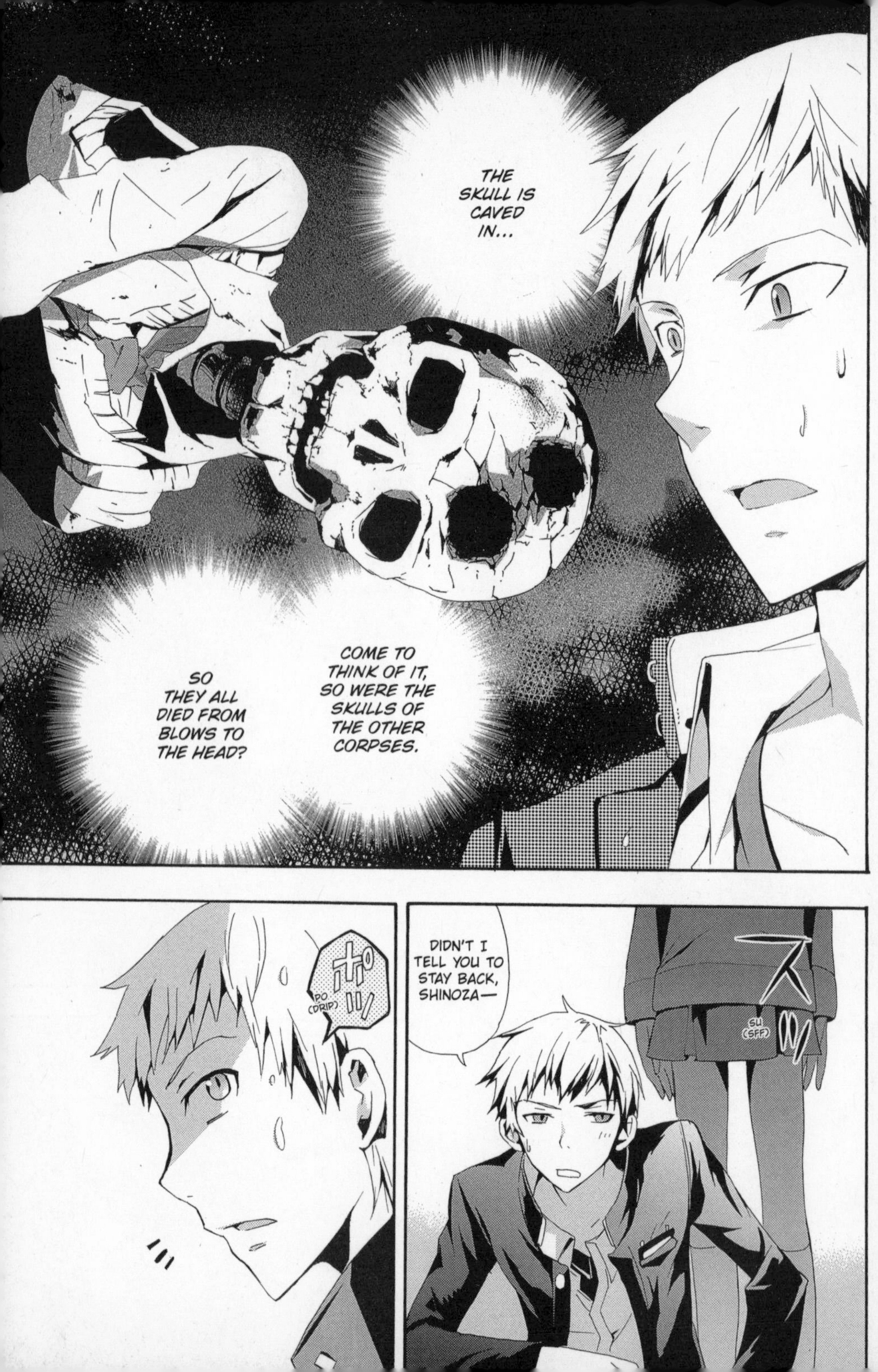
THE SKULL IS CAVED IN...
COME TO THINK OF IT, SO WERE THE SKULLS OF THE OTHER CORPSES.
SO THEY ALL DIED FROM BLOWS TO THE HEAD?
SU (SFF)
DIDN'T I TELL YOU TO STAY BACK, SHINOZA—
PO (DRIP)

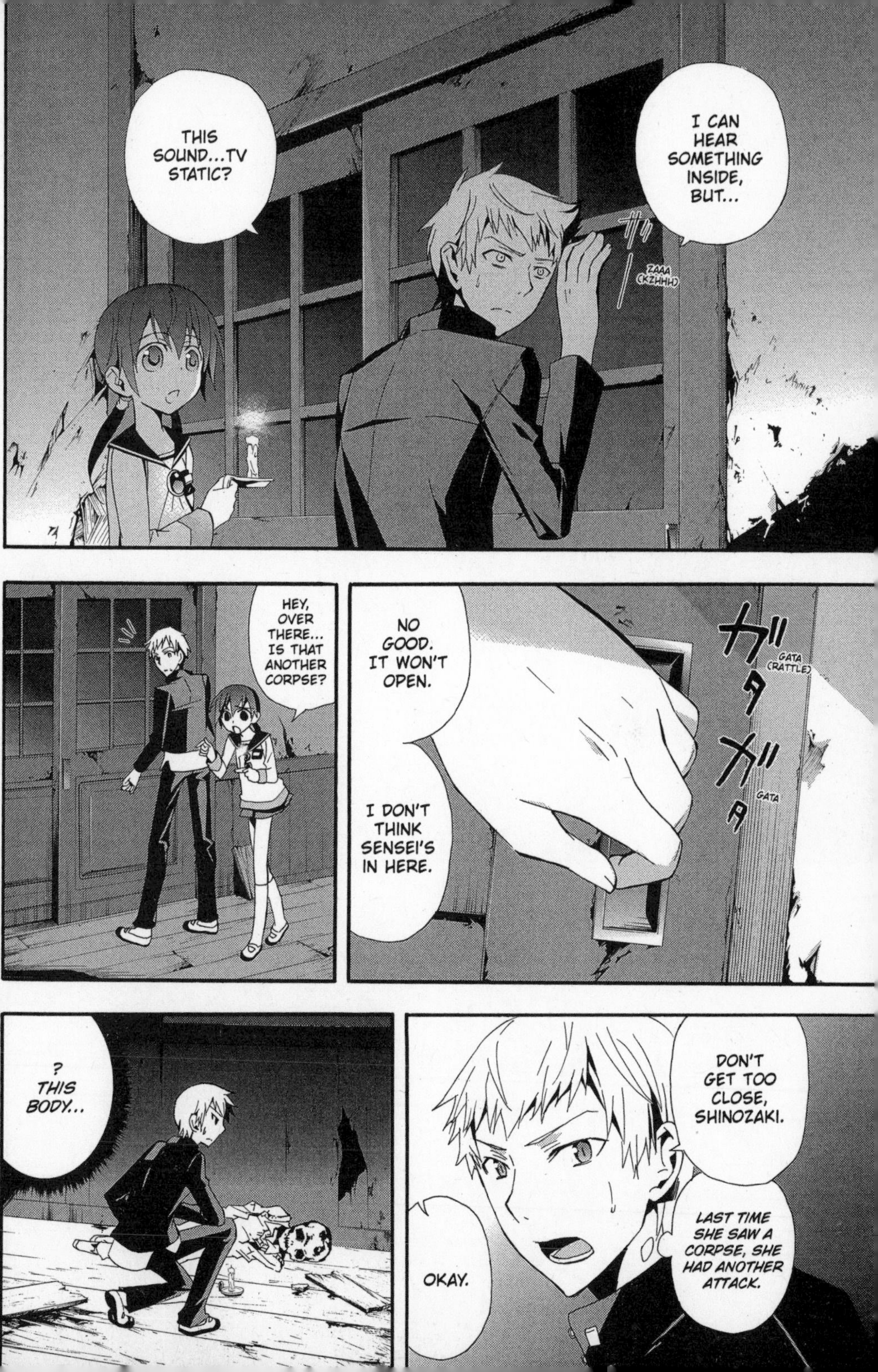
I CAN HEAR SOMETHING INSIDE, BUT...
ZAAA (KZHHH)
THIS SOUND...TV STATIC?
NO GOOD. IT WON'T OPEN.
GATA (RATTLE)
GATA
I DON'T THINK SENSEI'S IN HERE.
HEY, OVER THERE... IS THAT ANOTHER CORPSE?
DON'T GET TOO CLOSE, SHINOZAKI.
LAST TIME SHE SAW A CORPSE, SHE HAD ANOTHER ATTACK.
OKAY.
? THIS BODY...

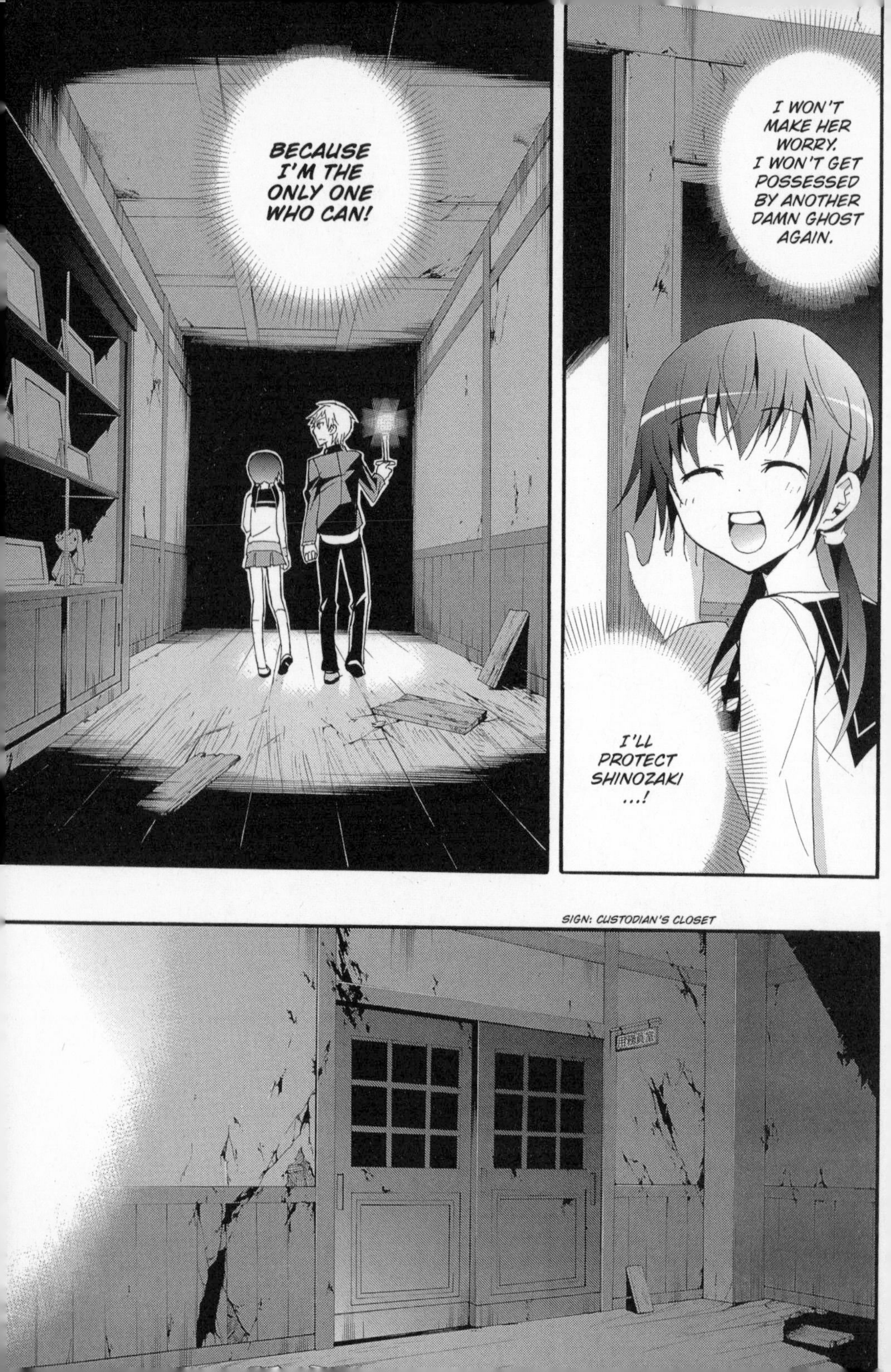
I WON'T MAKE HER WORRY. I WON'T GET POSSESSED BY ANOTHER DAMN GHOST AGAIN.
I'LL PROTECT SHINOZAKI ...!
BECAUSE I'M THE ONLY ONE WHO CAN!
SIGN: CUSTODIAN'S CLOSET

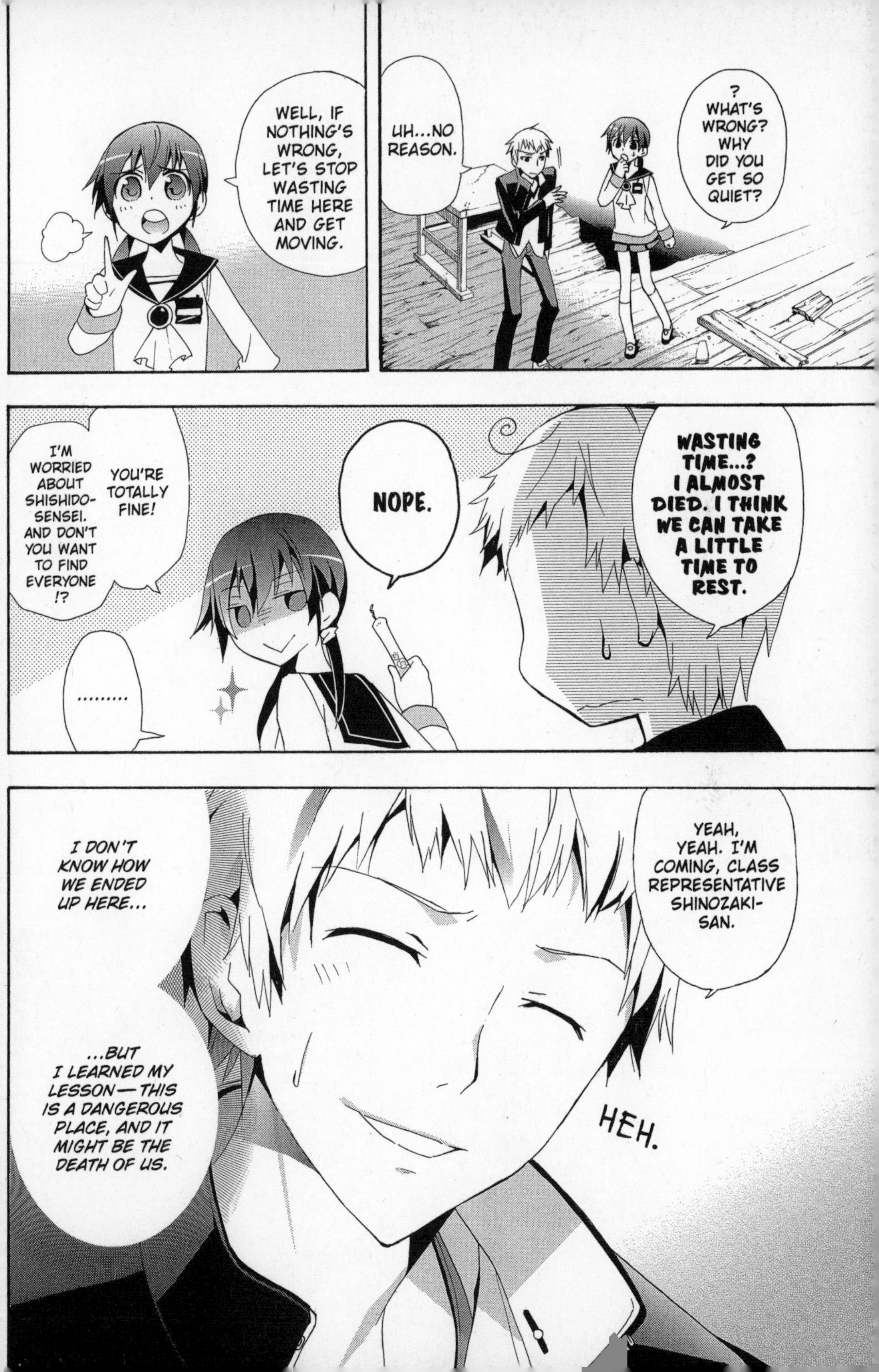
? WHAT'S WRONG? WHY DID YOU GET SO QUIET?
UH...NO REASON.
WELL, IF NOTHING'S WRONG, LET'S STOP WASTING TIME HERE AND GET MOVING.
WASTING TIME...? I ALMOST DIED. I THINK WE CAN TAKE A LITTLE TIME TO REST.
NOPE.
YOU'RE TOTALLY FINE!
I'M WORRIED ABOUT SHISHIDO-SENSEI. AND DON'T YOU WANT TO FIND EVERYONE!?
....
YEAH, YEAH. I'M COMING, CLASS REPRESENTATIVE SHINOZAKI-SAN.
HEH.
I DON'T KNOW HOW WE ENDED UP HERE...
...BUT I LEARNED MY LESSON—THIS IS A DANGEROUS PLACE, AND IT MIGHT BE THE DEATH OF US.

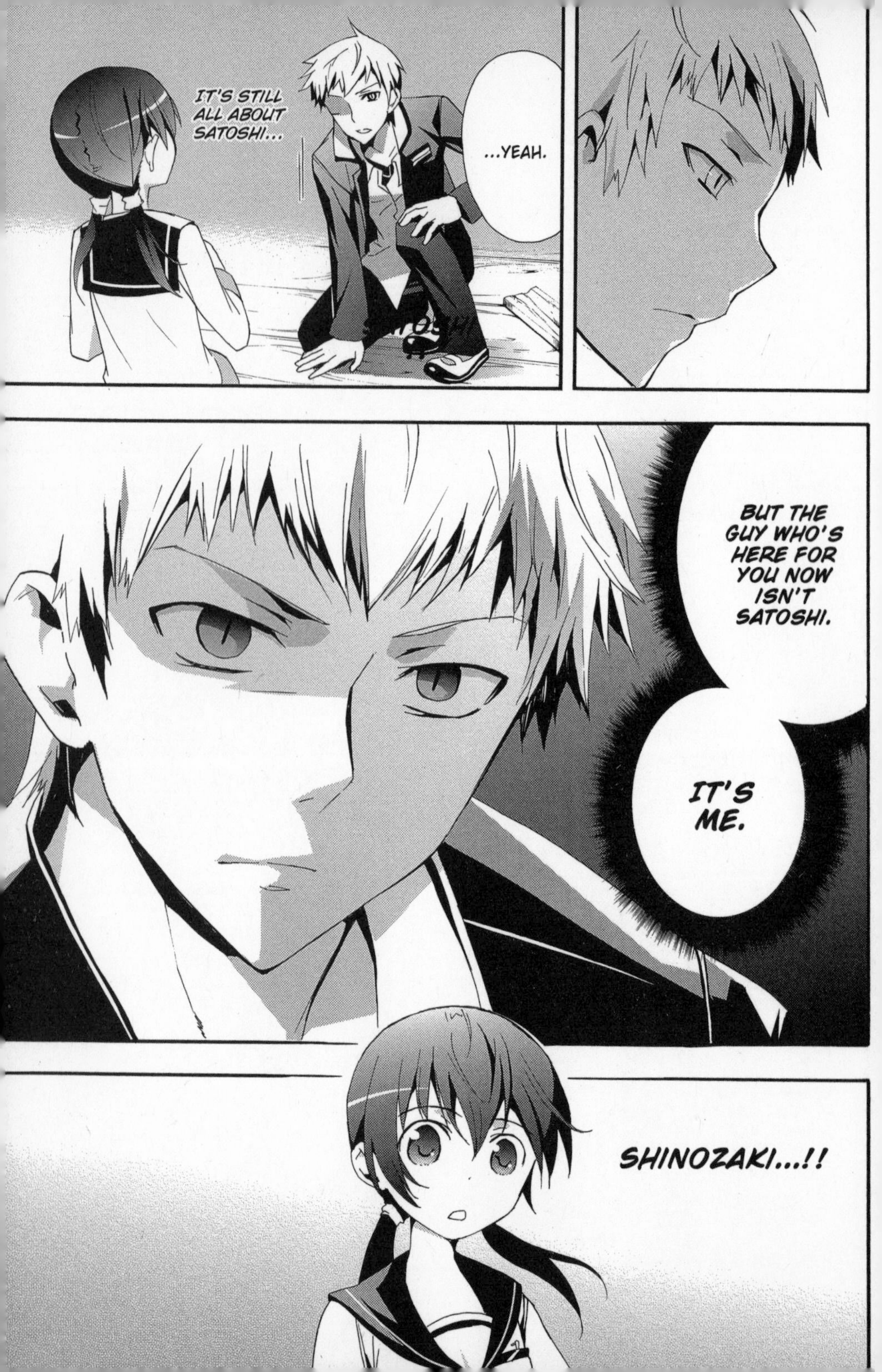
IT'S STILL ALL ABOUT SATOSHI...
...YEAH.
BUT THE GUY WHO'S HERE FOR YOU NOW ISN'T SATOSHI.
IT'S ME.
SHINOZAKI...!!

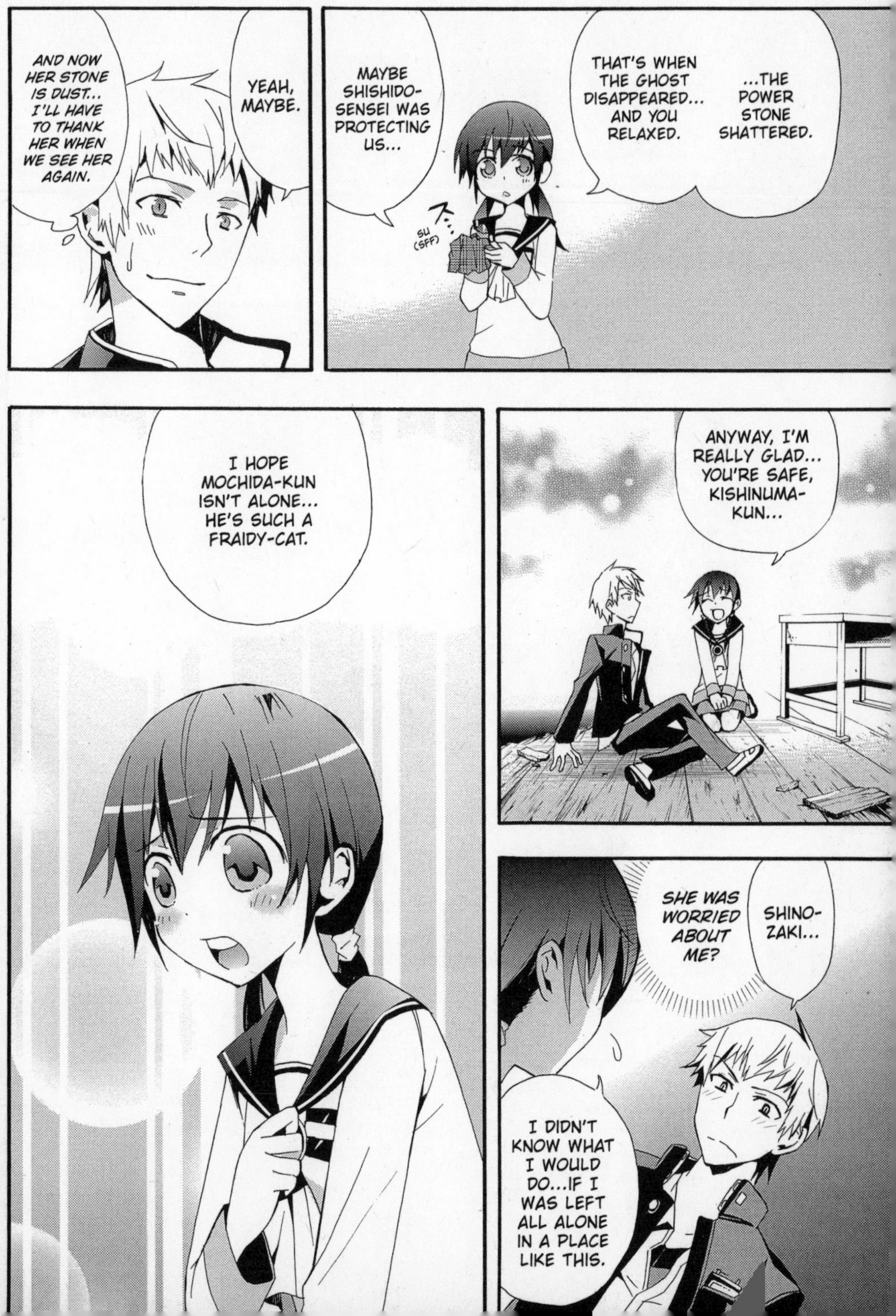
THAT'S WHEN THE GHOST DISAPPEARED... AND YOU RELAXED.
...THE POWER STONE SHATTERED.
MAYBE SHISHIDO-SENSEI WAS PROTECTING US...
SU (SFF)
YEAH, MAYBE.
AND NOW HER STONE IS DUST... I'LL HAVE TO THANK HER WHEN WE SEE HER AGAIN.
ANYWAY, I'M REALLY GLAD... YOU'RE SAFE, KISHINUMA-KUN...
SHINO-ZAKI...
SHE WAS WORRIED ABOUT ME?
I DIDN'T KNOW WHAT I WOULD DO...IF I WAS LEFT ALL ALONE IN A PLACE LIKE THIS.
I HOPE MOCHIDA-KUN ISN'T ALONE... HE'S SUCH A FRAIDY-CAT.

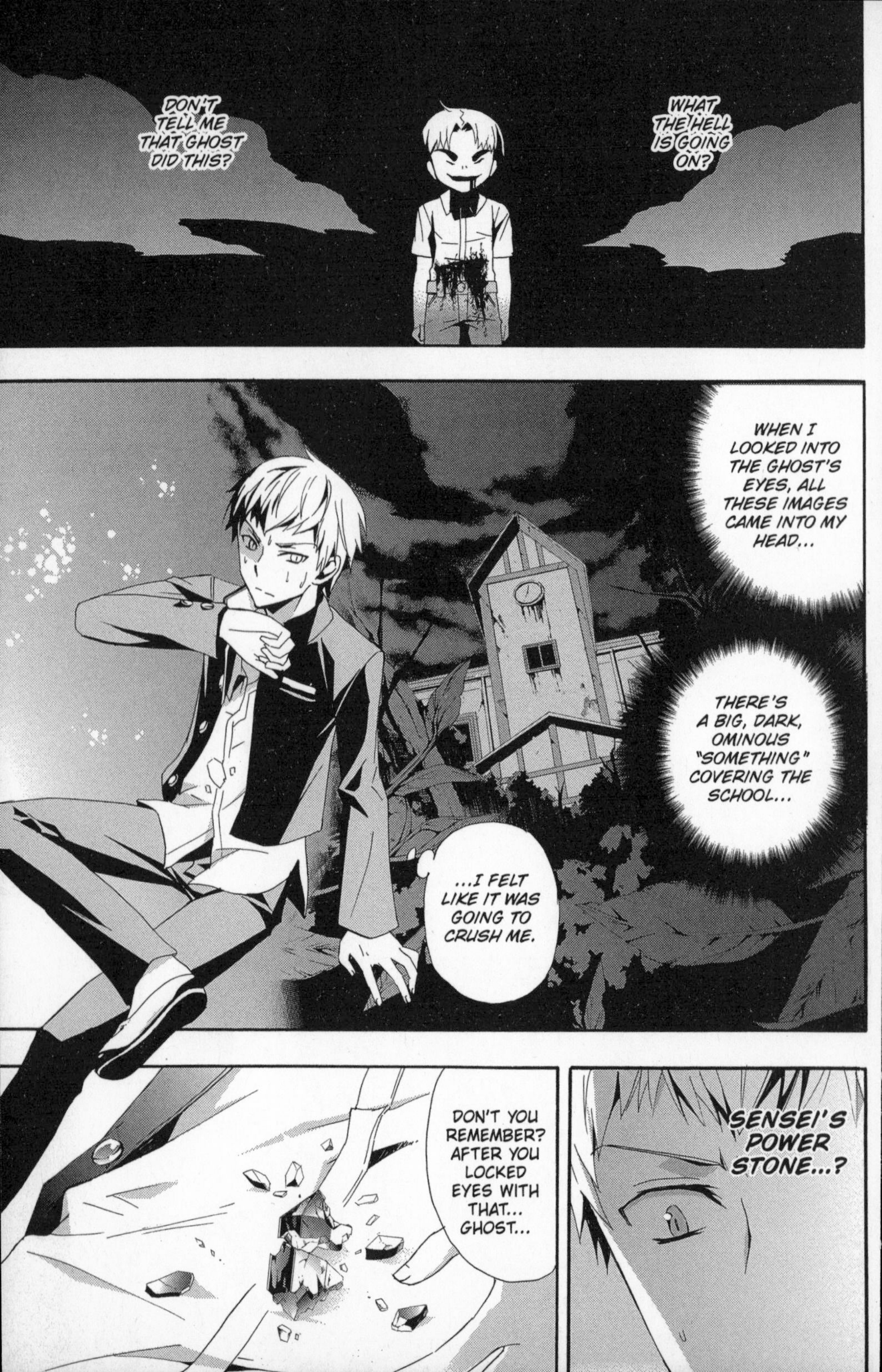
WHAT THE HELL IS GOING ON?
DON'T TELL ME THAT GHOST DID THIS?
WHEN I LOOKED INTO THE GHOST'S EYES, ALL THESE IMAGES CAME INTO MY HEAD...
THERE'S A BIG, DARK, OMINOUS "SOMETHING" COVERING THE SCHOOL...
...I FELT LIKE IT WAS GOING TO CRUSH ME.
SENSEI'S POWER STONE...?
DON'T YOU REMEMBER? AFTER YOU LOCKED EYES WITH THAT... GHOST...

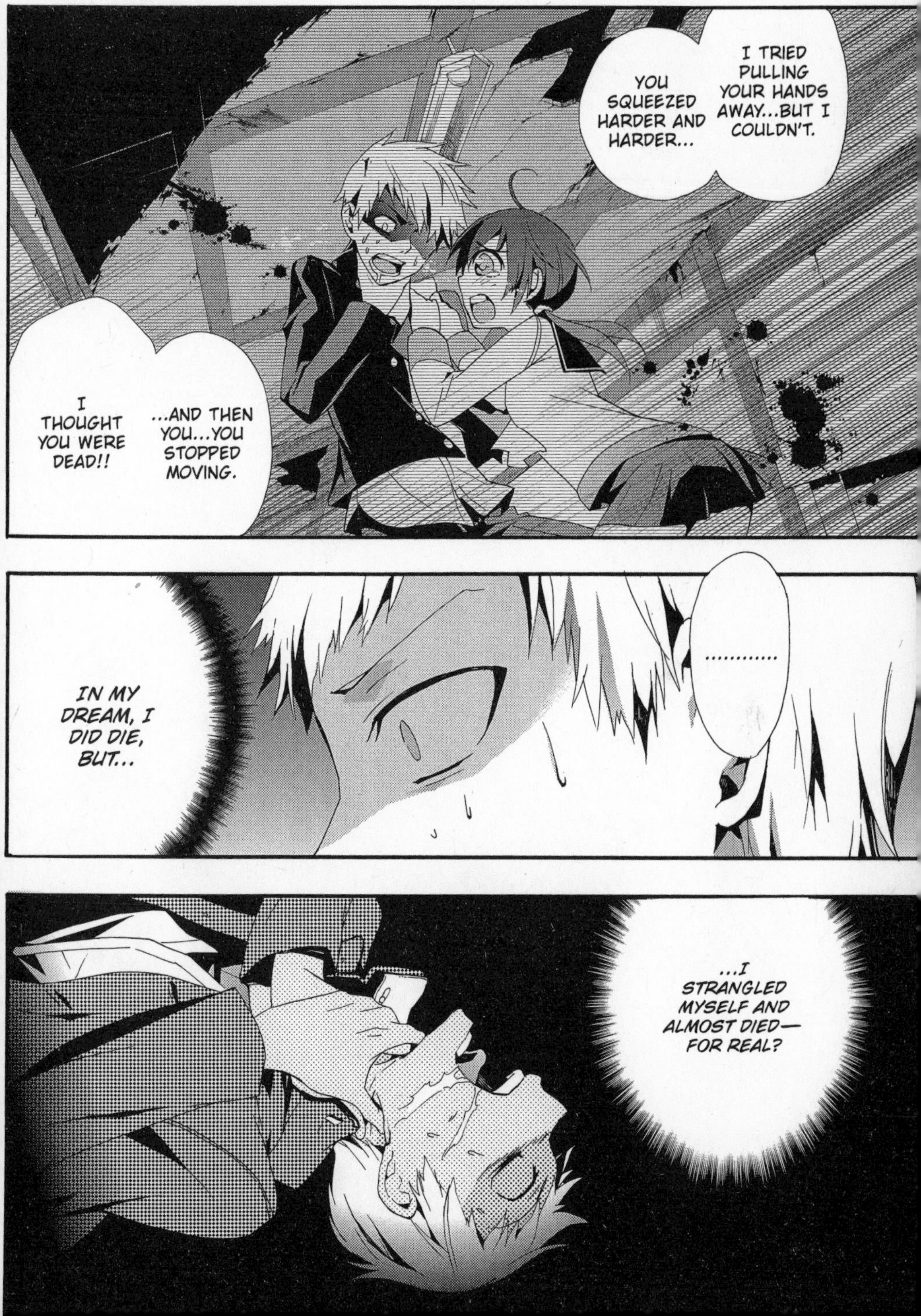
I TRIED PULLING YOUR HANDS AWAY...BUT I COULDN'T.
YOU SQUEEZED HARDER AND HARDER...
...AND THEN YOU...YOU STOPPED MOVING.
I THOUGHT YOU WERE DEAD!!
....
IN MY DREAM, I DID DIE, BUT...
...I STRANGLED MYSELF AND ALMOST DIED— FOR REAL?

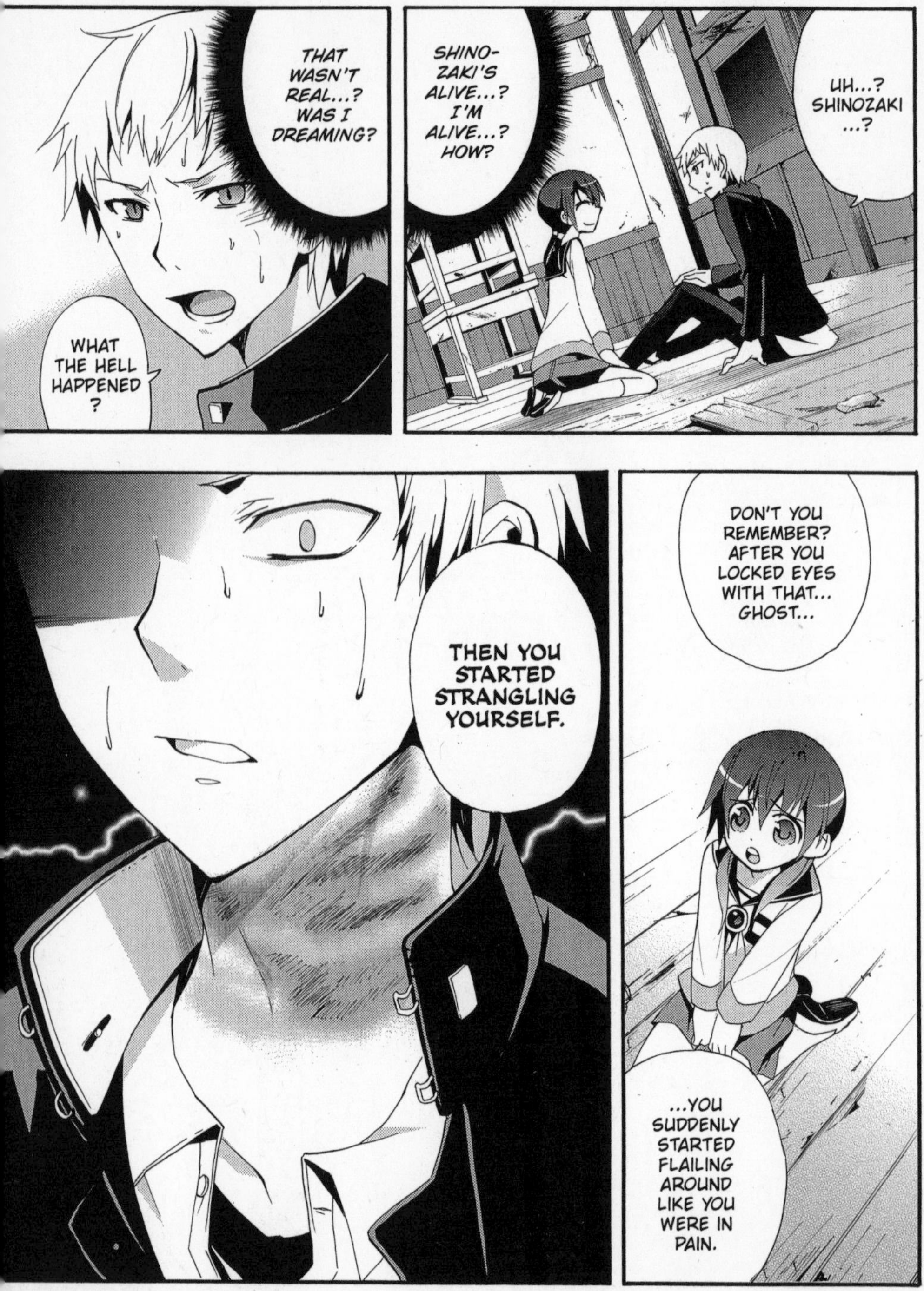
UH...? SHINOZAKI ...?
SHINO-ZAKI'S ALIVE...? I'M ALIVE...? HOW?
THAT WASN'T REAL...? WAS I DREAMING?
WHAT THE HELL HAPPENED ?
DON'T YOU REMEMBER? AFTER YOU LOCKED EYES WITH THAT... GHOST...
...YOU SUDDENLY STARTED FLAILING AROUND LIKE YOU WERE IN PAIN.
THEN YOU STARTED STRANGLING YOURSELF.

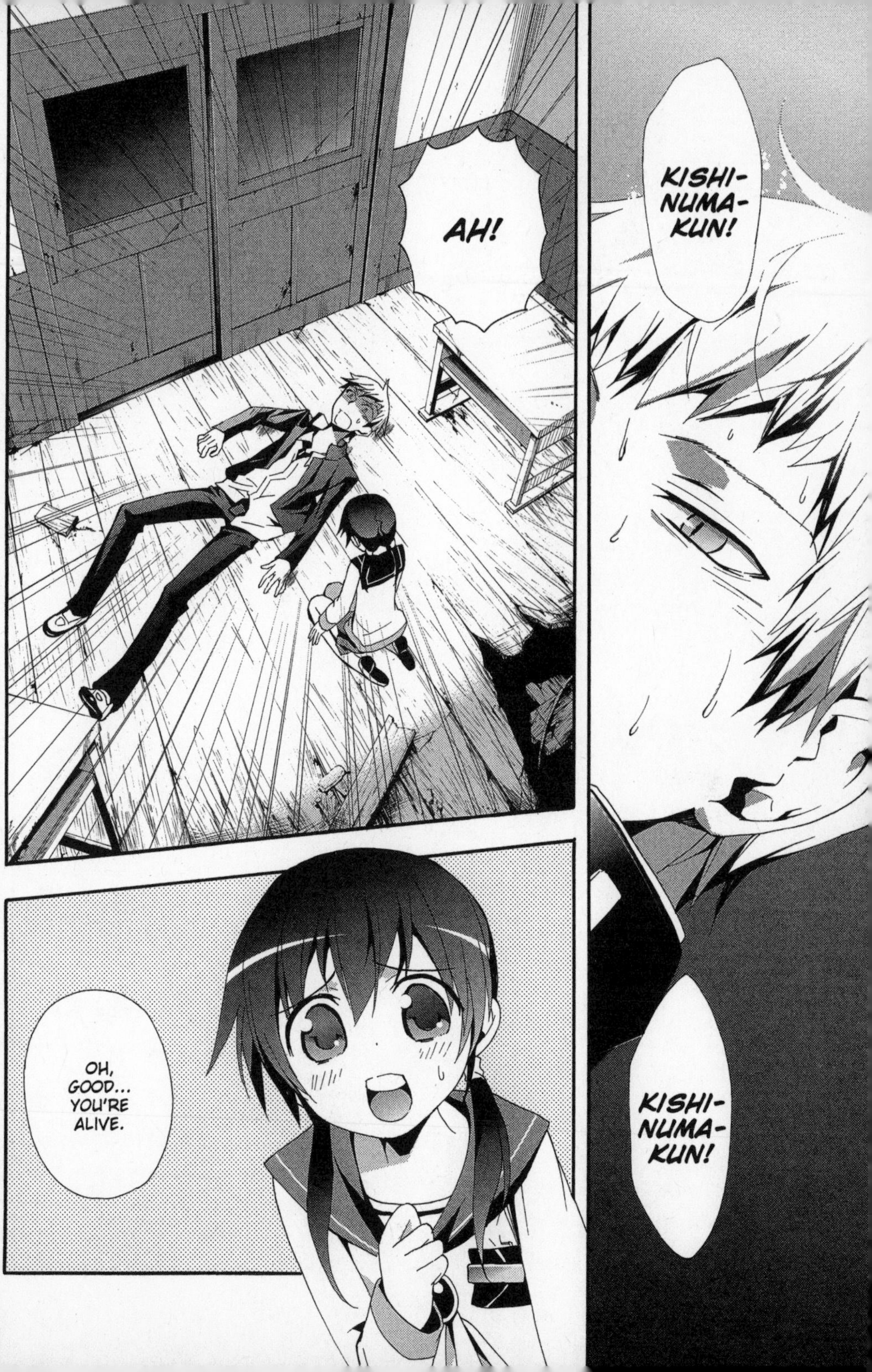
KISHI-NUMA-KUN!
KISHI-NUMA-KUN!
AH!
OH, GOOD... YOU'RE ALIVE.

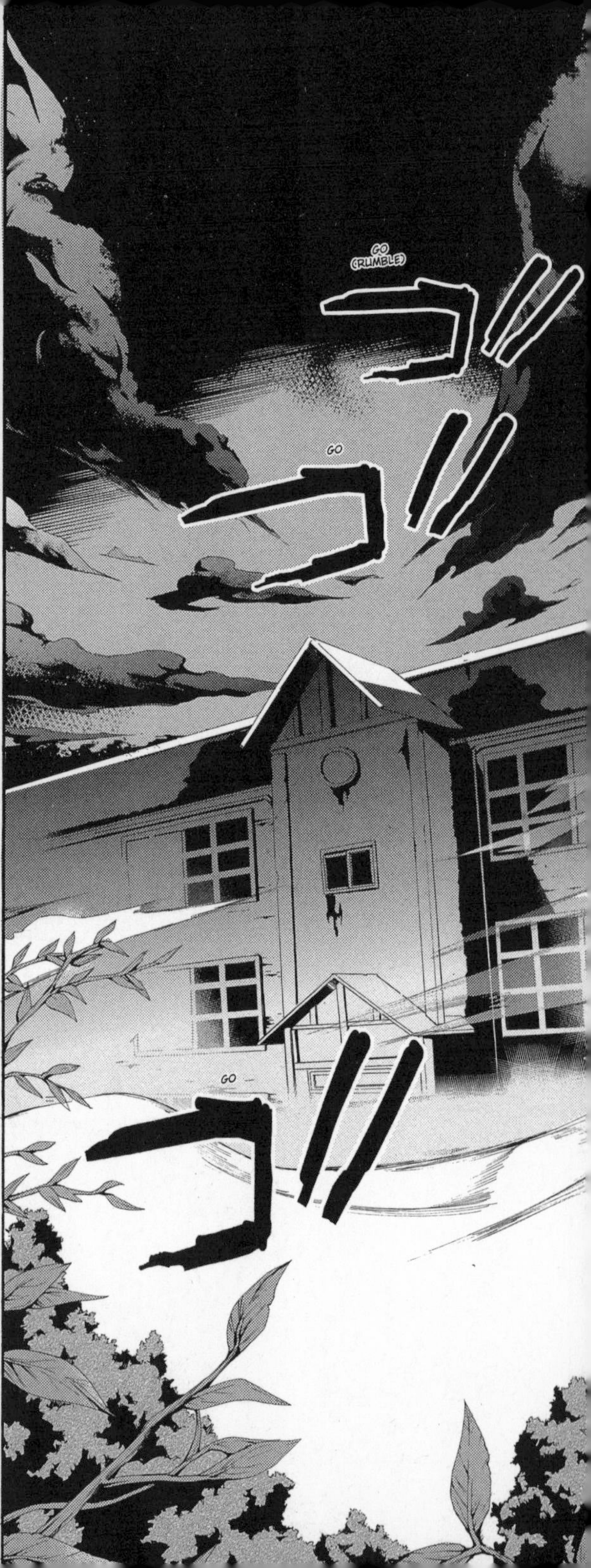
ゴ
GO
(RUMBLE)
ゴ
GO
ゴ
GO

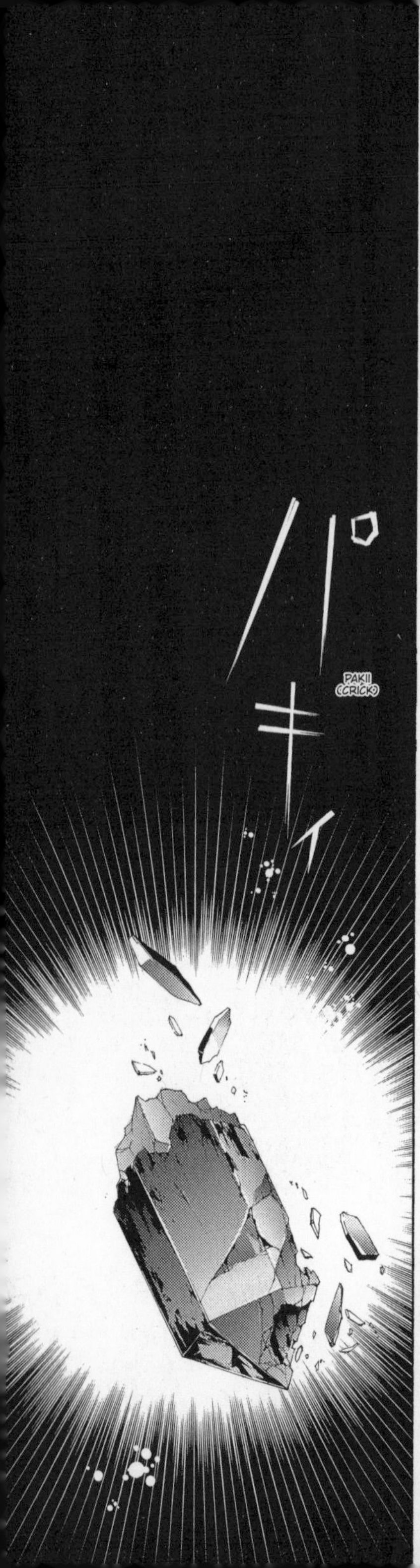
パキィ
PAKII
(CRICK)

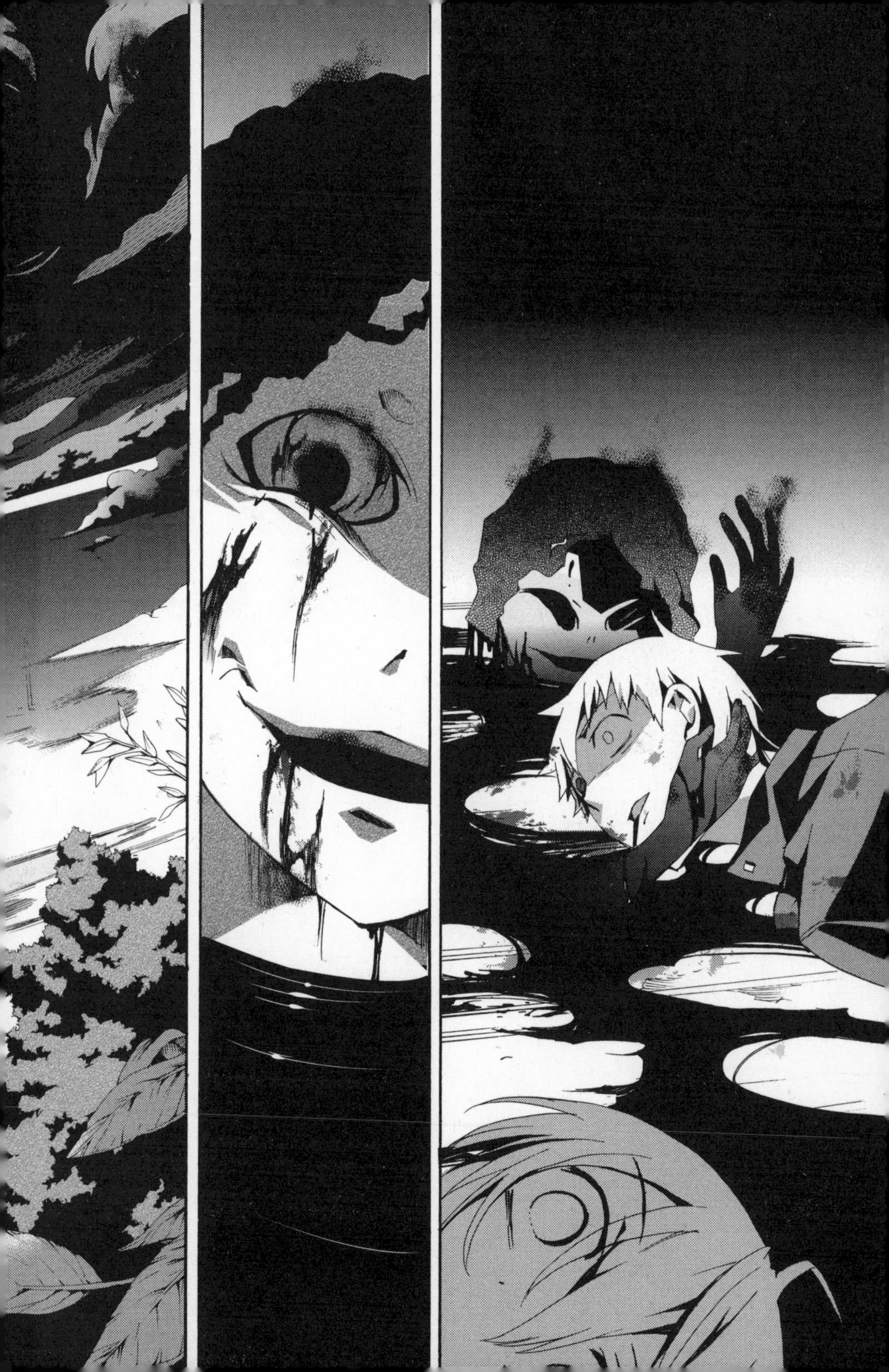

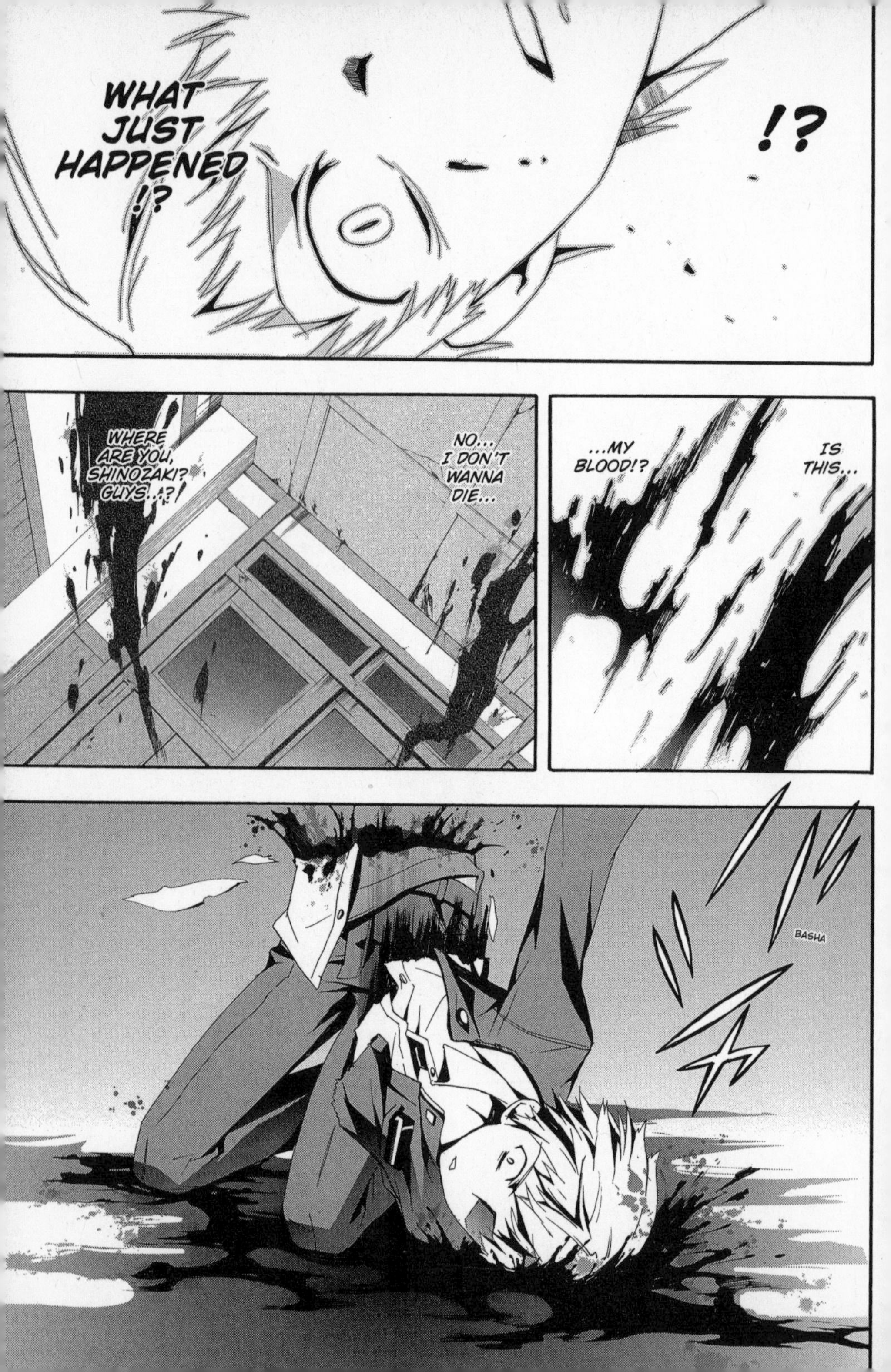
!?
WHAT JUST HAPPENED !?
IS THIS...
...MY BLOOD!?
NO... I DON'T WANNA DIE...
WHERE ARE YOU, SHINOZAKI? GUYS...?
BASHA

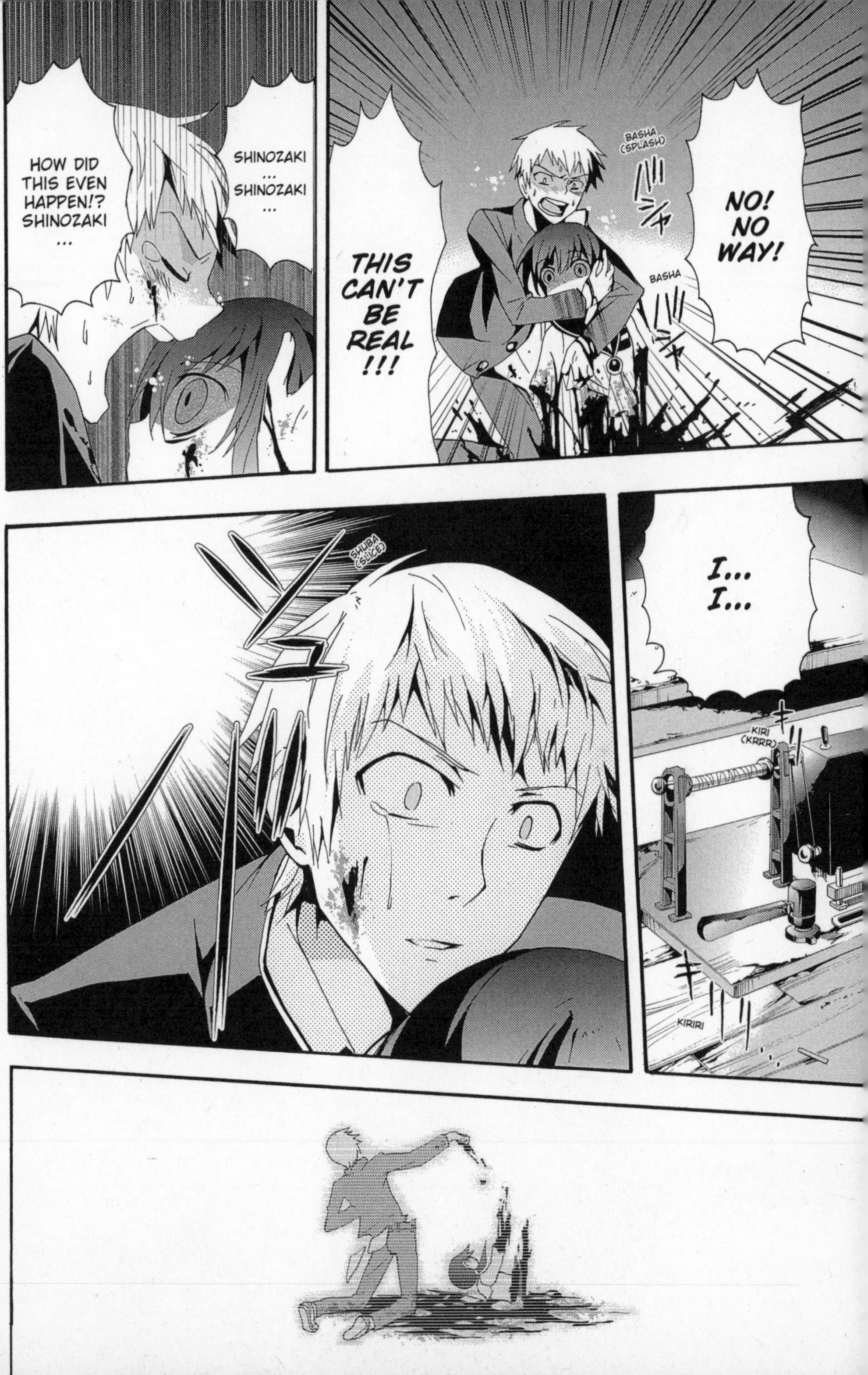
NO! NO WAY!
BASHA (SPLASH)
バシャ
BASHA
THIS CAN'T BE REAL!!!
SHINOZAKI ... SHINOZAKI ...
HOW DID THIS EVEN HAPPEN!? SHINOZAKI ...
I... I...
KIRI (KRRR)
KIRIRI
SHUBA (SLICE)

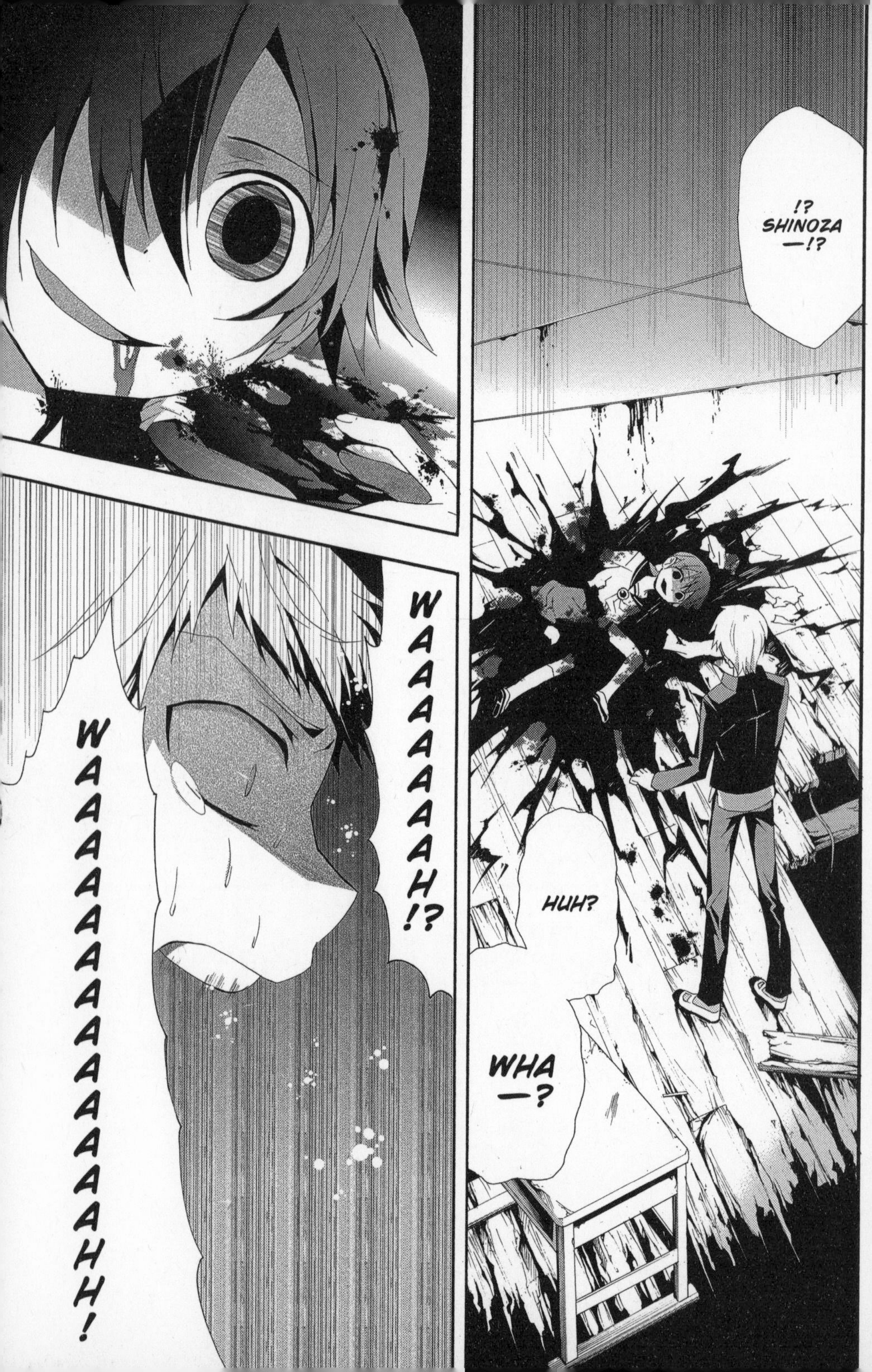
!? SHINOZA—!?
HUH?
WHA—?
WAAAAAAAAH!?
WAAAAAAAAAAAAAAAAHH!

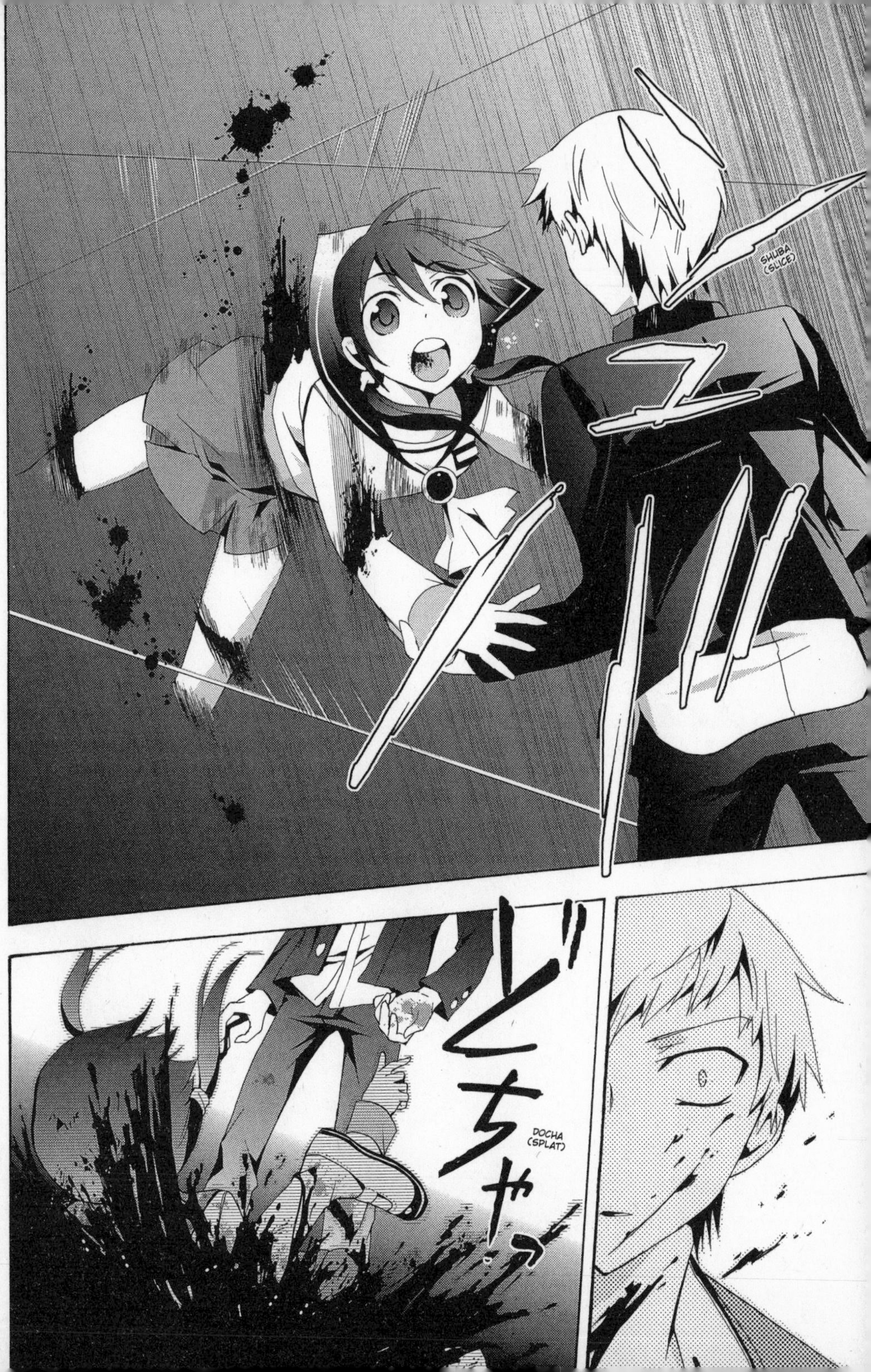
SHUBA
(SLICE)
DOCHA
(SPLAT)

GACHIN
(KACLANK)

WHAT'S THAT SOUND!?

HUH?

? WHAT'S THIS...?

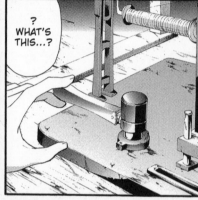

KIRIRIRIRI
(KRRRR)

IS THAT...

...PIANO WIRE...?

KIRA
(GLINT)

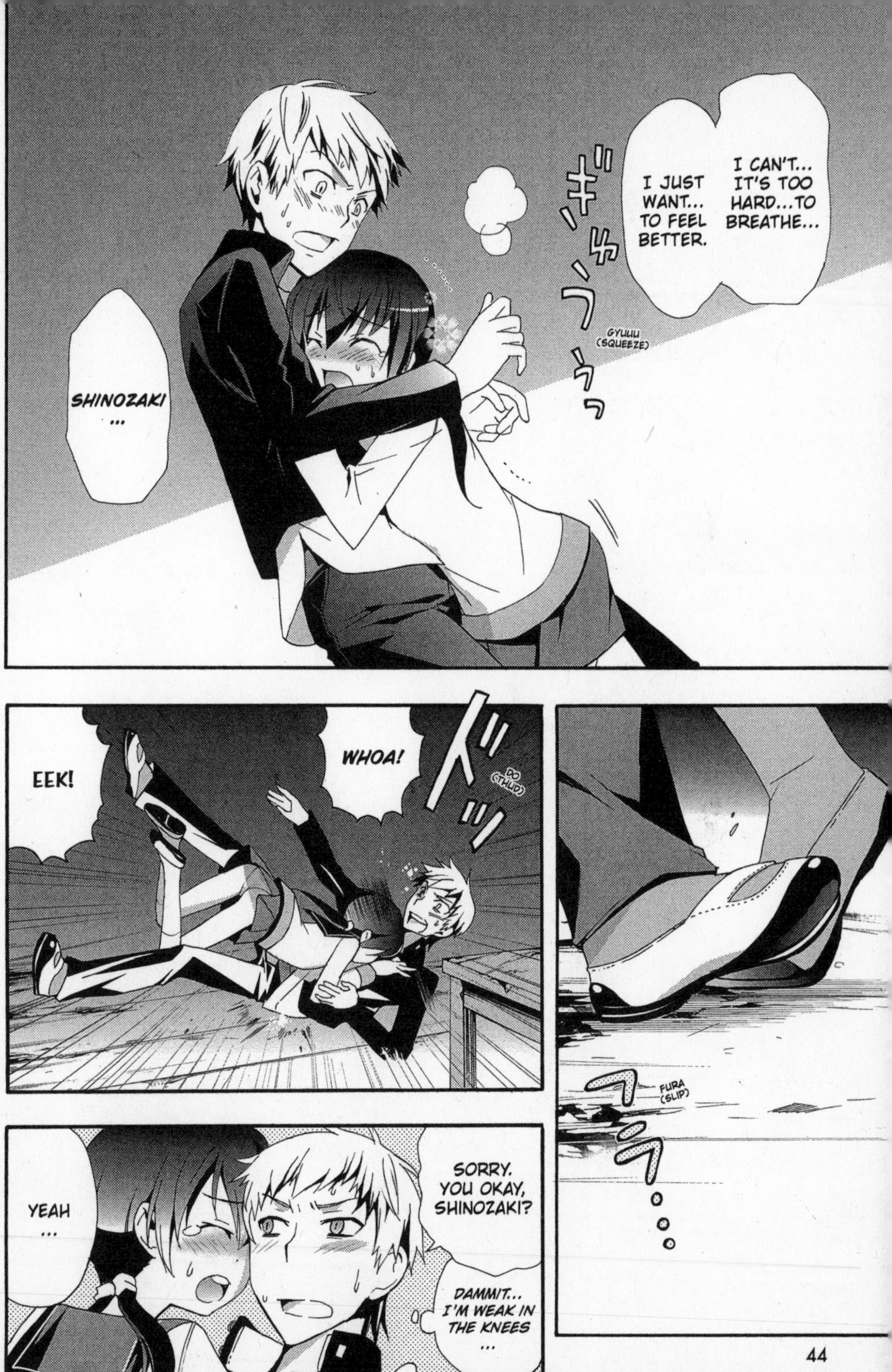
I CAN'T... IT'S TOO HARD...TO BREATHE...
I JUST WANT... TO FEEL BETTER.
GYUUU (SQUEEZE)
SHINOZAKI ...
FURA (SLIP)
WHOA!
DO (THUD)
EEK!
SORRY. YOU OKAY, SHINOZAKI?
DAMMIT... I'M WEAK IN THE KNEES ...
YEAH ...

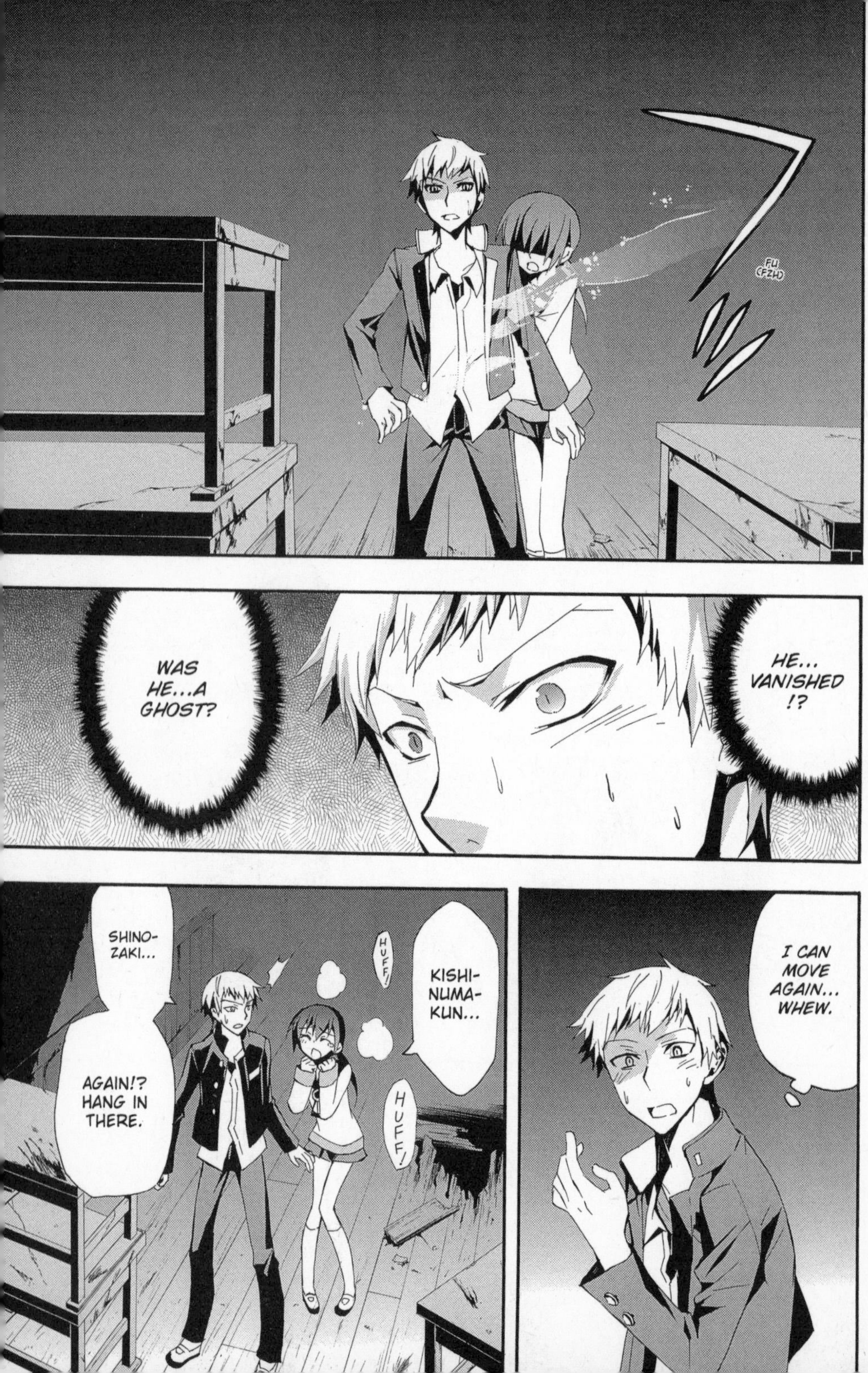
FU (FZH)
HE... VANISHED!?
WAS HE...A GHOST?
I CAN MOVE AGAIN... WHEW.
KISHI-NUMA-KUN...
HUFF!
HUFF!
SHINO-ZAKI...
AGAIN!? HANG IN THERE.

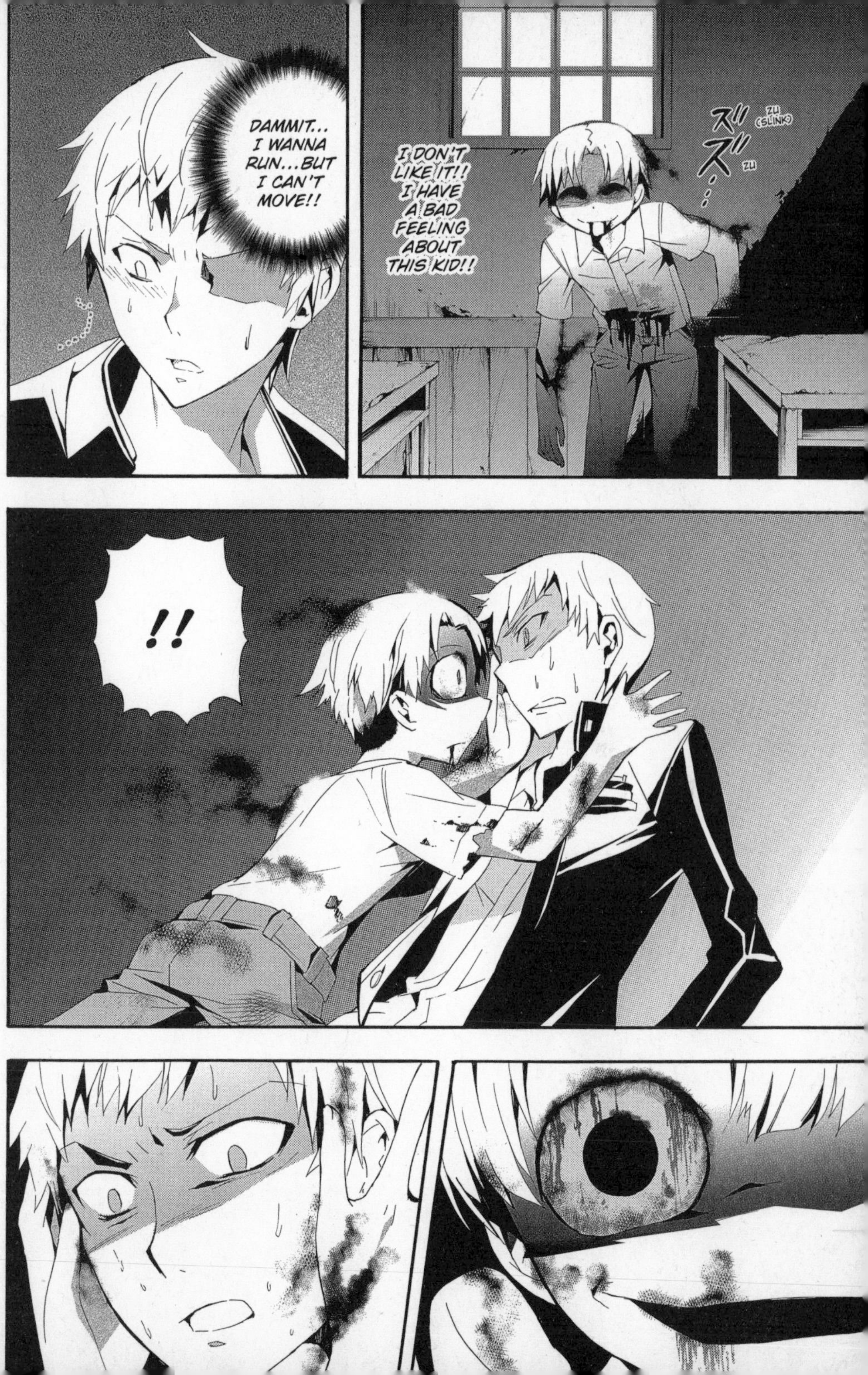
I DON'T LIKE IT!! I HAVE A BAD FEELING ABOUT THIS KID!!
ZU (SLINK)
ZU
DAMMIT... I WANNA RUN...BUT I CAN'T MOVE!!
!!

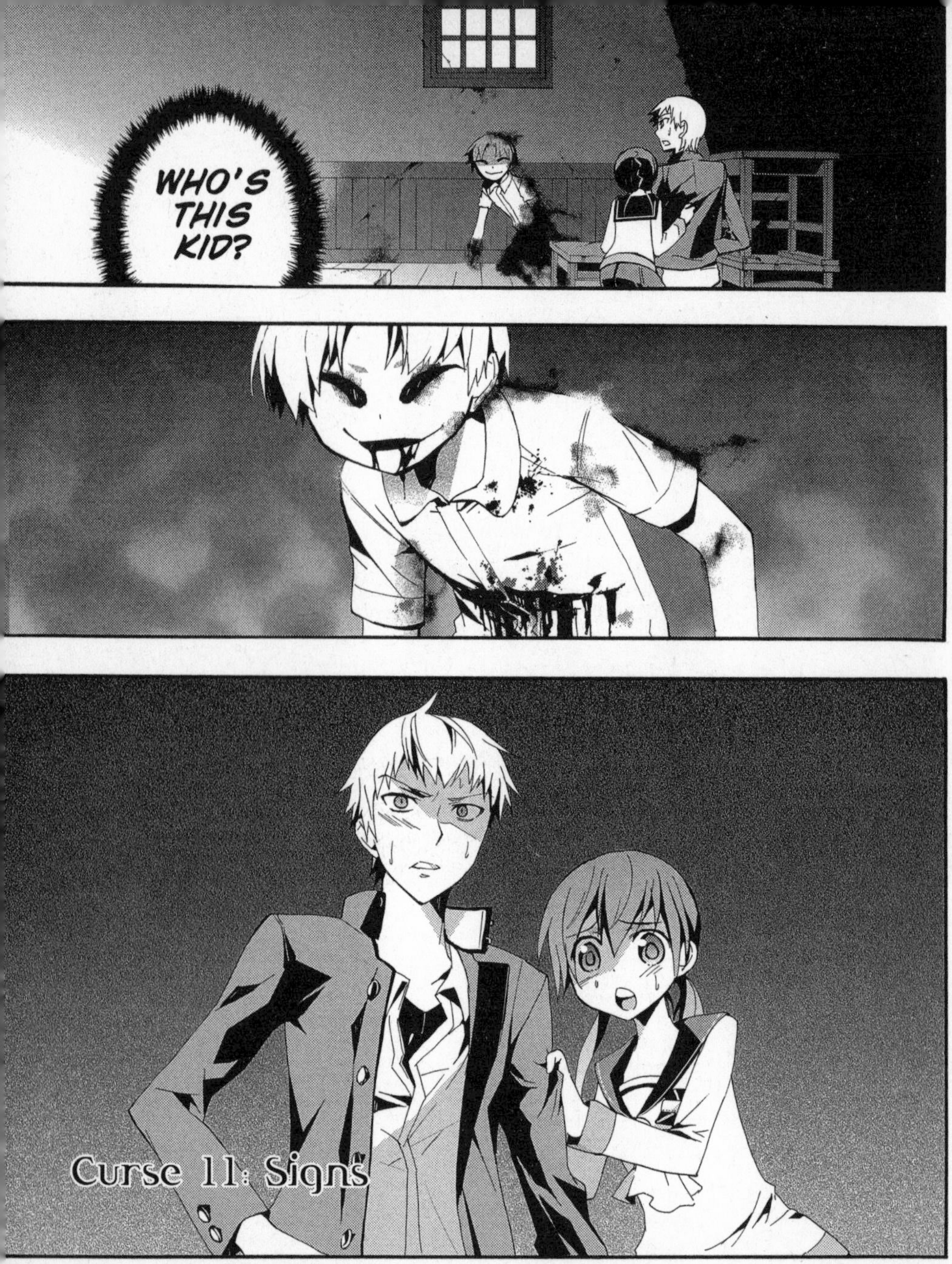
WHO'S THIS KID?
Curse 11: Signs

a list of corpses/05

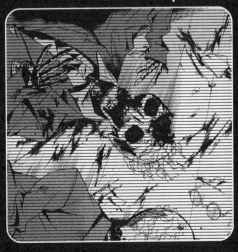

Musashigawa Girls' Junior High, Class 1-2
Female student

Byakudan Senior High School, Class 2-4
Kai Shimada
Tomohiro Ohkawa
Masato Fukuroi

Based on their name tags, it is apparent that
the three boys are classmates. The damage to
each of the corpses is severe, and they seem to
have died due to some kind of an attack.

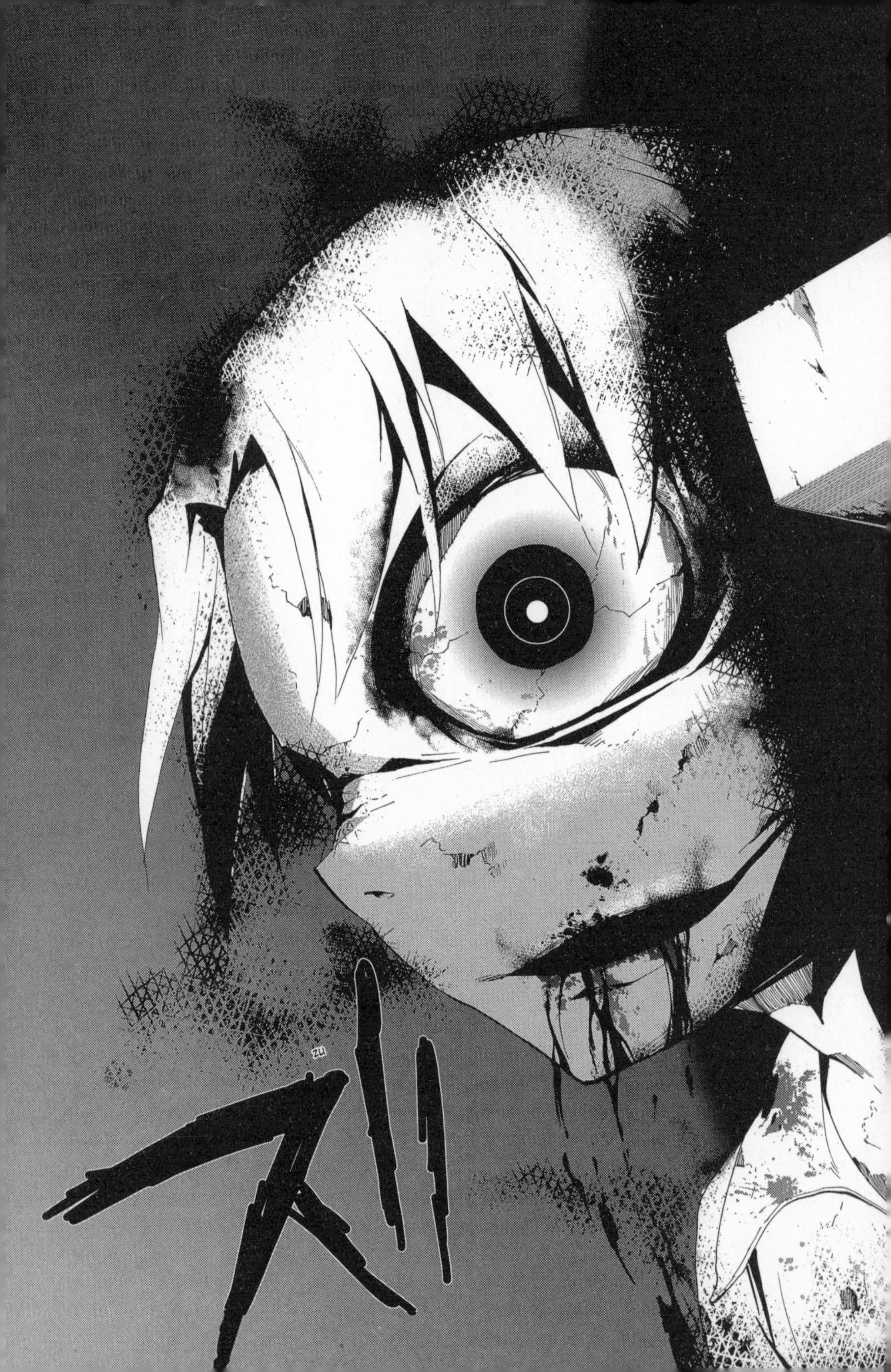
ズリ
ZU

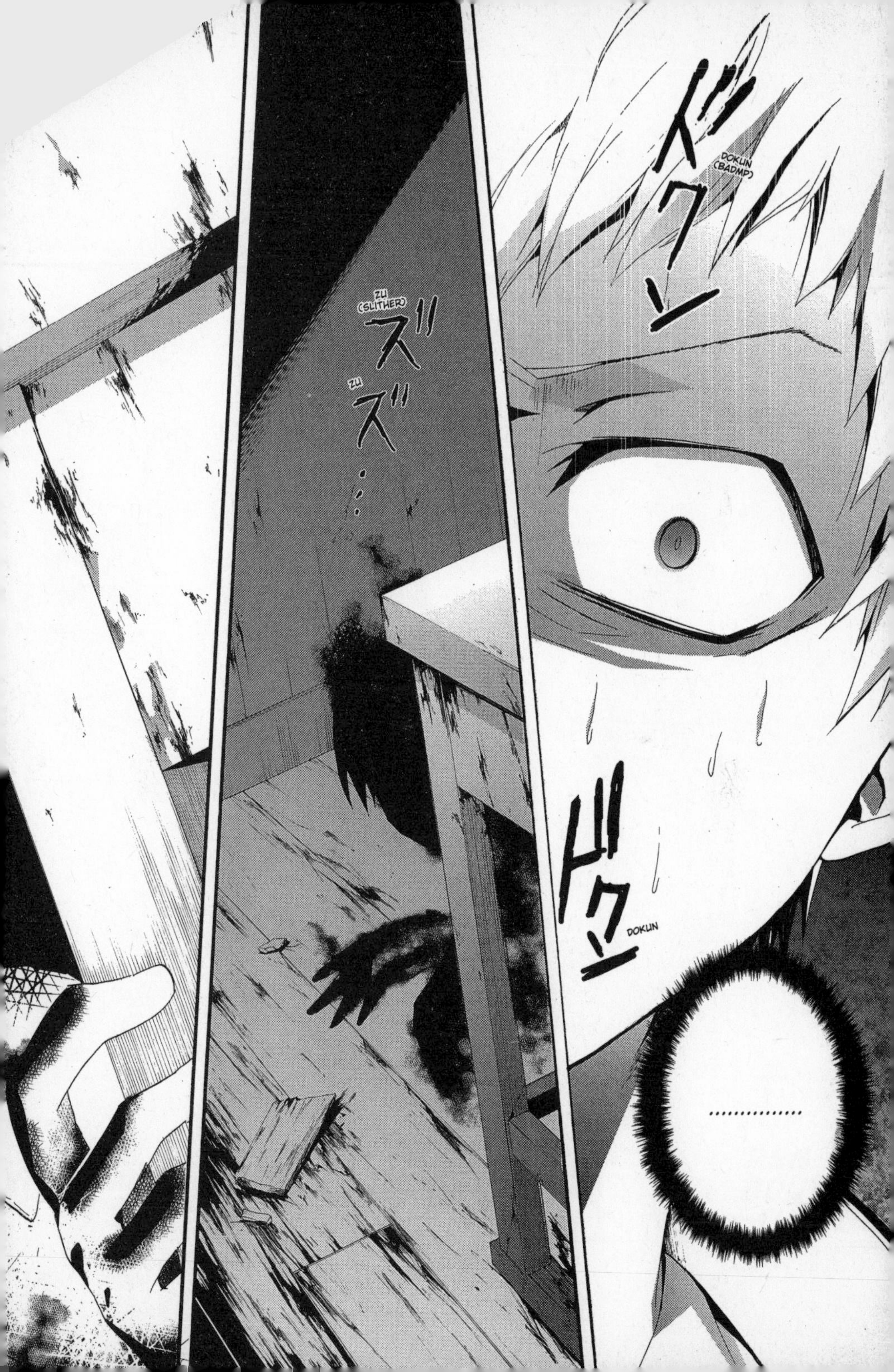
ドクン
DOKUN (BADMP)
ドクン
DOKUN
....
ズ
ZU (SLITHER)
ズ…
ZU

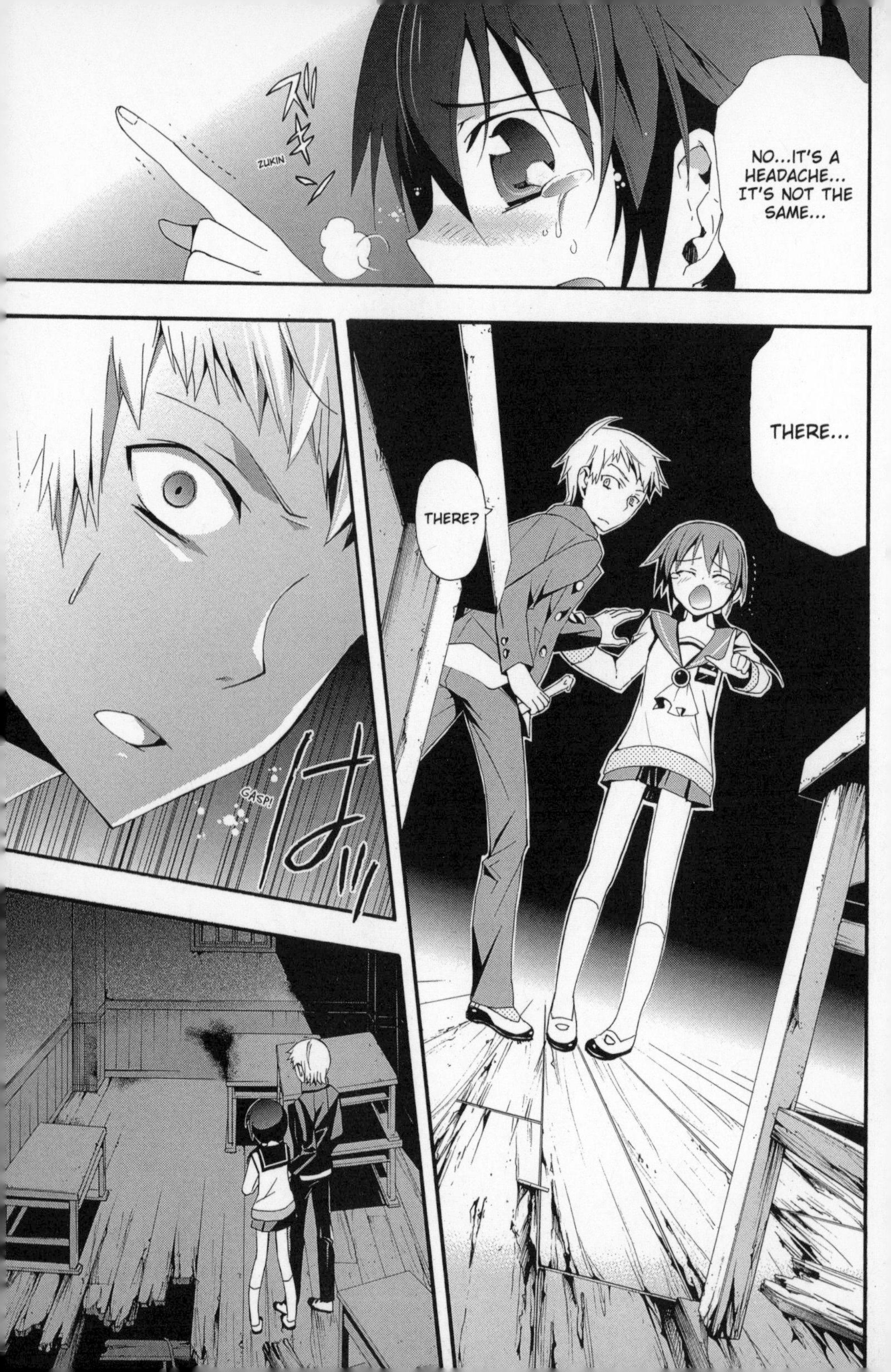
NO...IT'S A HEADACHE... IT'S NOT THE SAME...
ZUKIN
THERE...
THERE?
GASP!

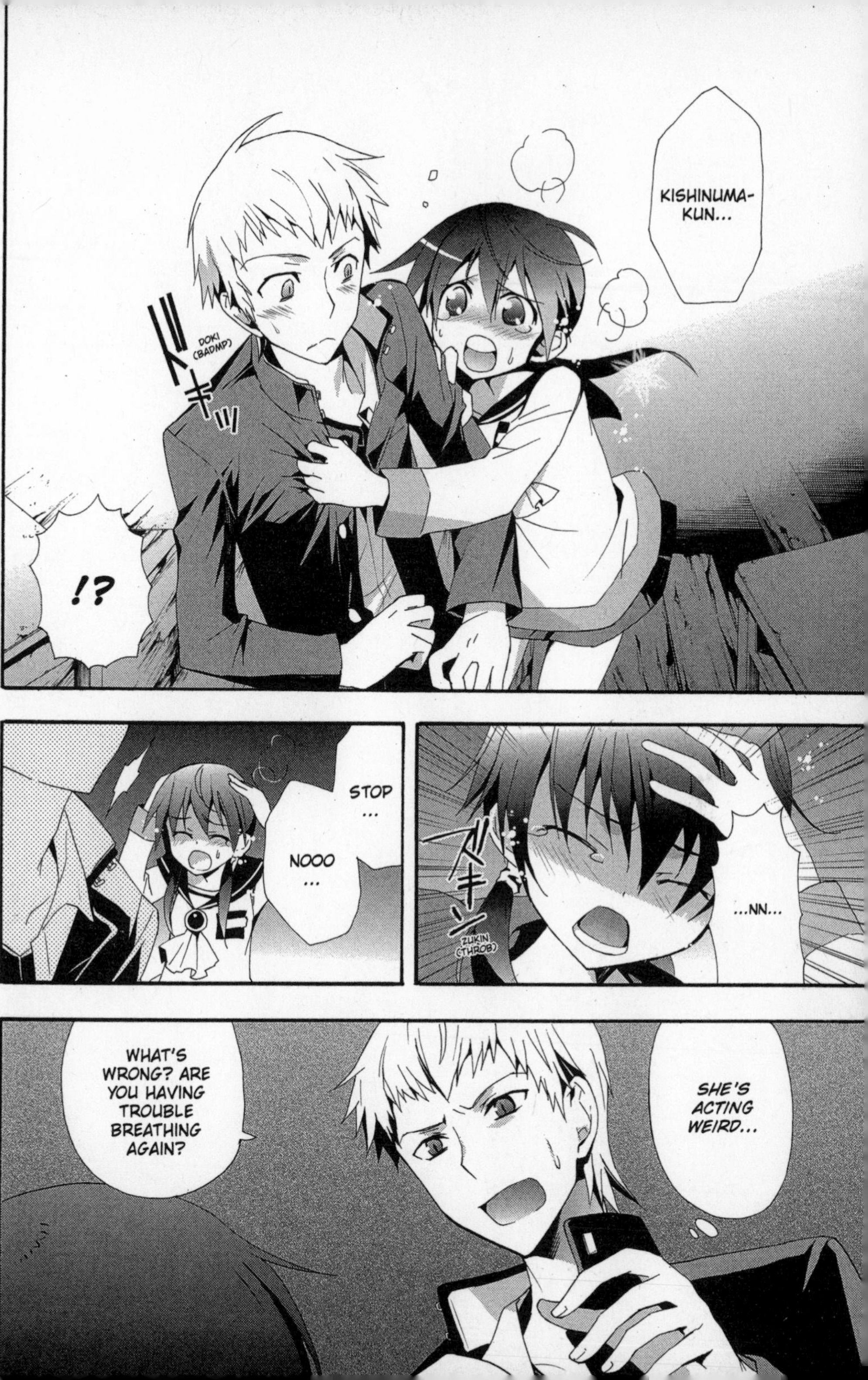
KISHINUMA-KUN...
DOKI (BADMP)
!?
...NN...
ZUKIN (THROB)
STOP ...
NOOO ...
SHE'S ACTING WEIRD...
WHAT'S WRONG? ARE YOU HAVING TROUBLE BREATHING AGAIN?

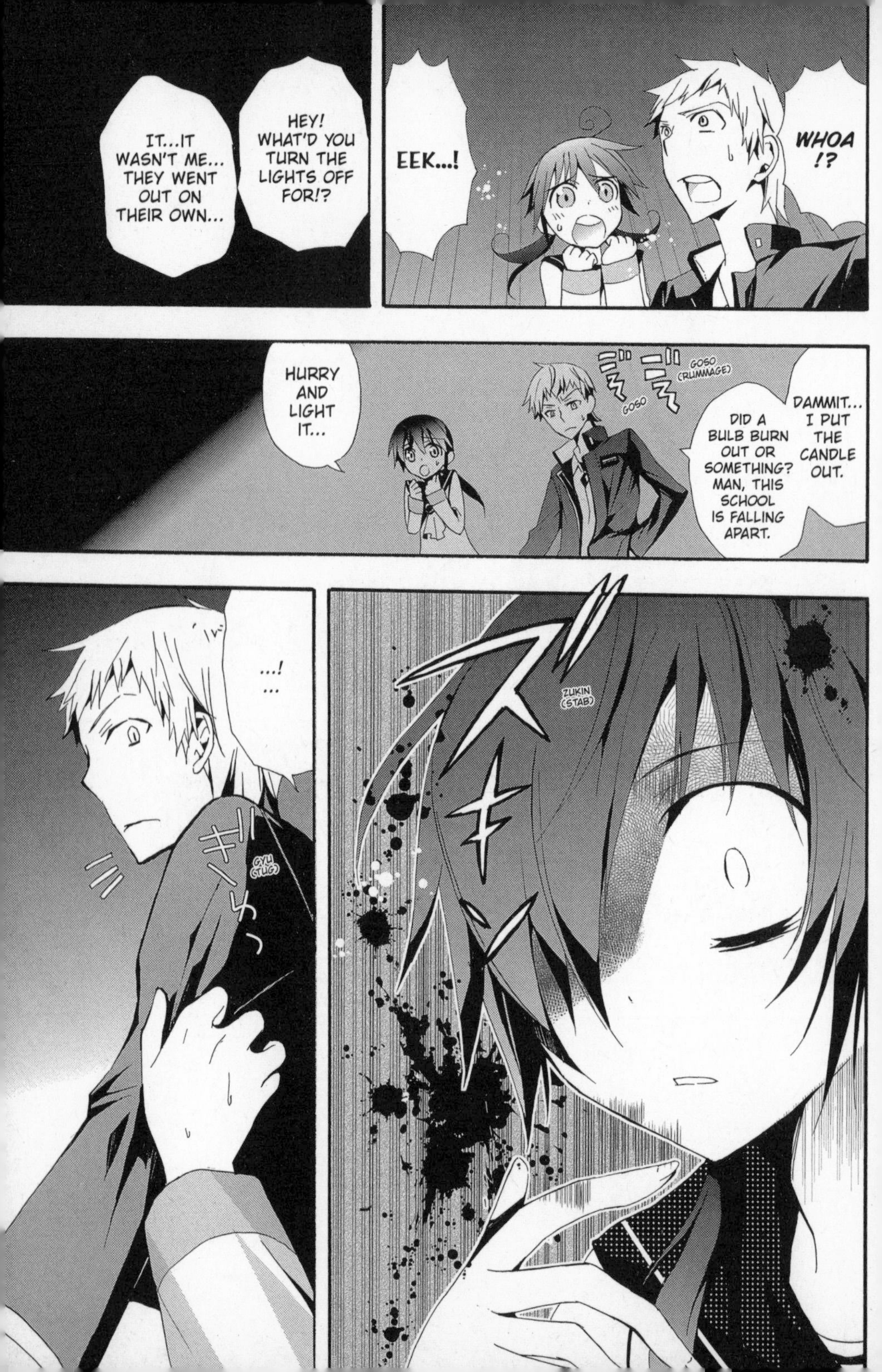
WHOA !?
EEK...!
HEY! WHAT'D YOU TURN THE LIGHTS OFF FOR!?
IT...IT WASN'T ME... THEY WENT OUT ON THEIR OWN...
DAMMIT... I PUT THE CANDLE OUT.
GOSO (RUMMAGE)
GOSO
DID A BULB BURN OUT OR SOMETHING? MAN, THIS SCHOOL IS FALLING APART.
HURRY AND LIGHT IT...
ZUKIN (STAB)
...! ...
GYU (TUG)

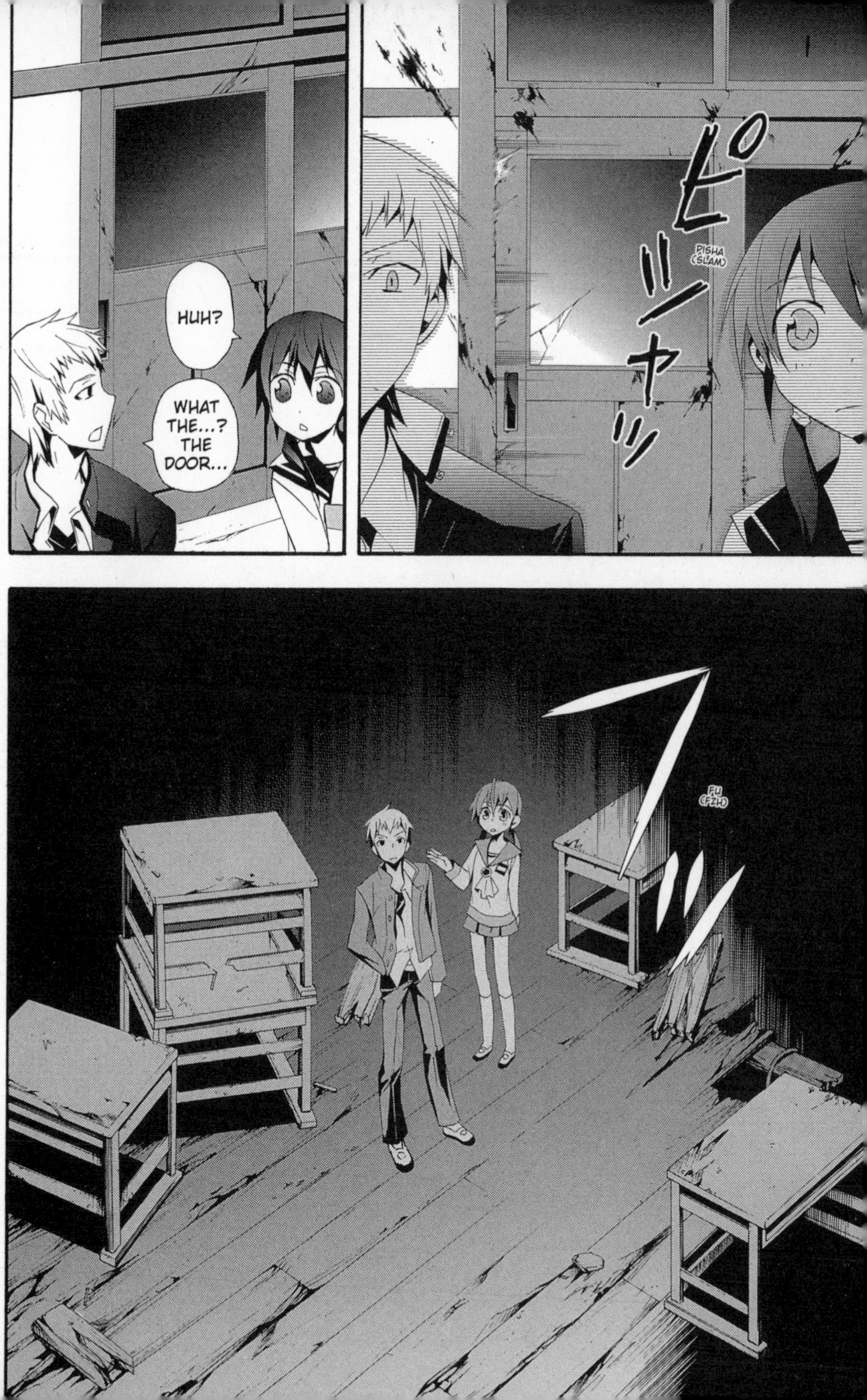
PISHA (SLAM)
HUH?
WHAT THE...? THE DOOR...
FU (FZHD)

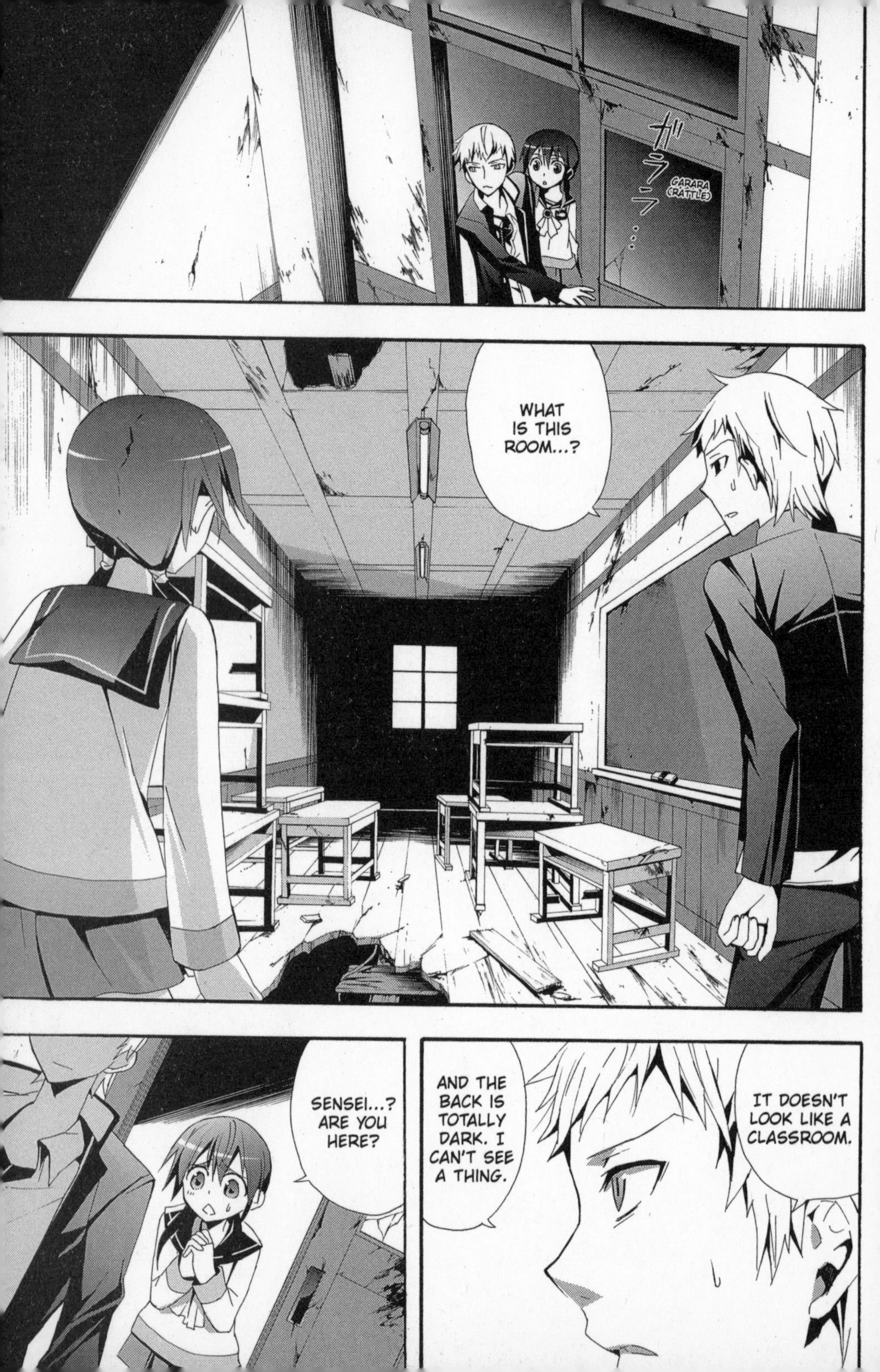
ガラララ…
GARARA (RATTLE)
WHAT IS THIS ROOM...?
IT DOESN'T LOOK LIKE A CLASSROOM.
AND THE BACK IS TOTALLY DARK. I CAN'T SEE A THING.
SENSEI...? ARE YOU HERE?

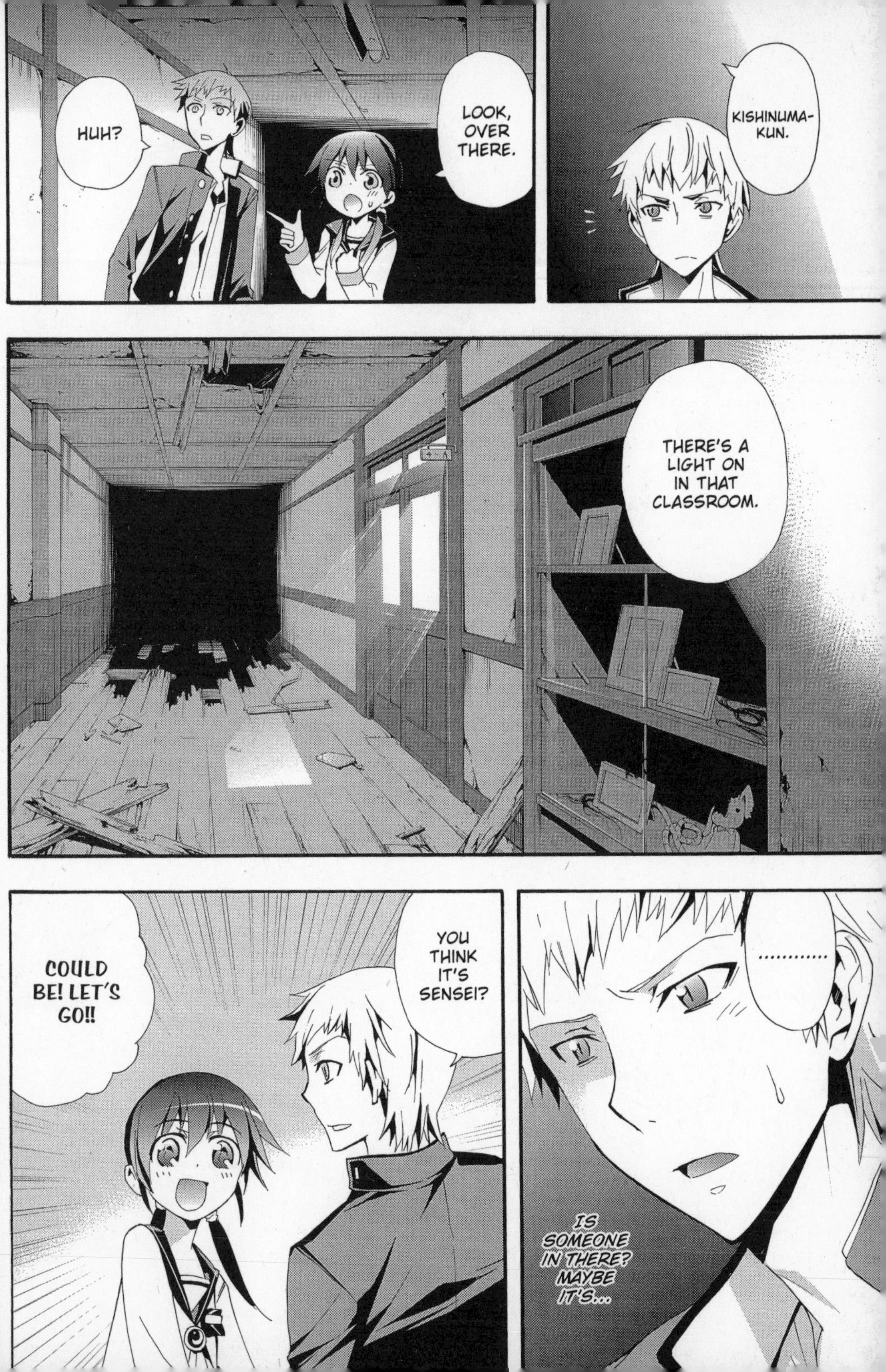
KISHINUMA-KUN.
LOOK, OVER THERE.
HUH?
THERE'S A LIGHT ON IN THAT CLASSROOM.
....
IS SOMEONE IN THERE? MAYBE IT'S...
YOU THINK IT'S SENSEI?
COULD BE! LET'S GO!!

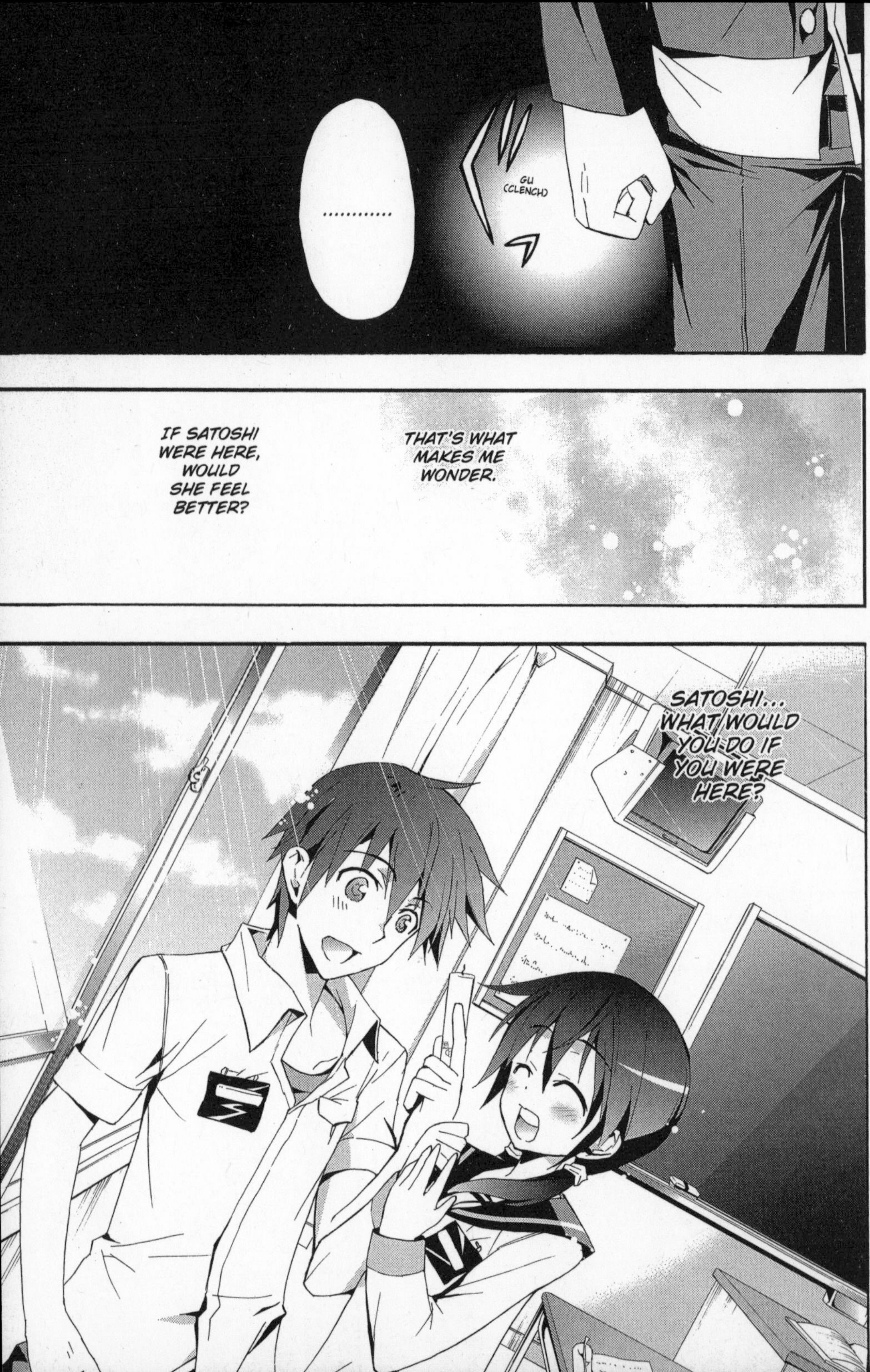
GU (CLENCH)
....
THAT'S WHAT MAKES ME WONDER.
IF SATOSHI WERE HERE, WOULD SHE FEEL BETTER?
SATOSHI... WHAT WOULD YOU DO IF YOU WERE HERE?

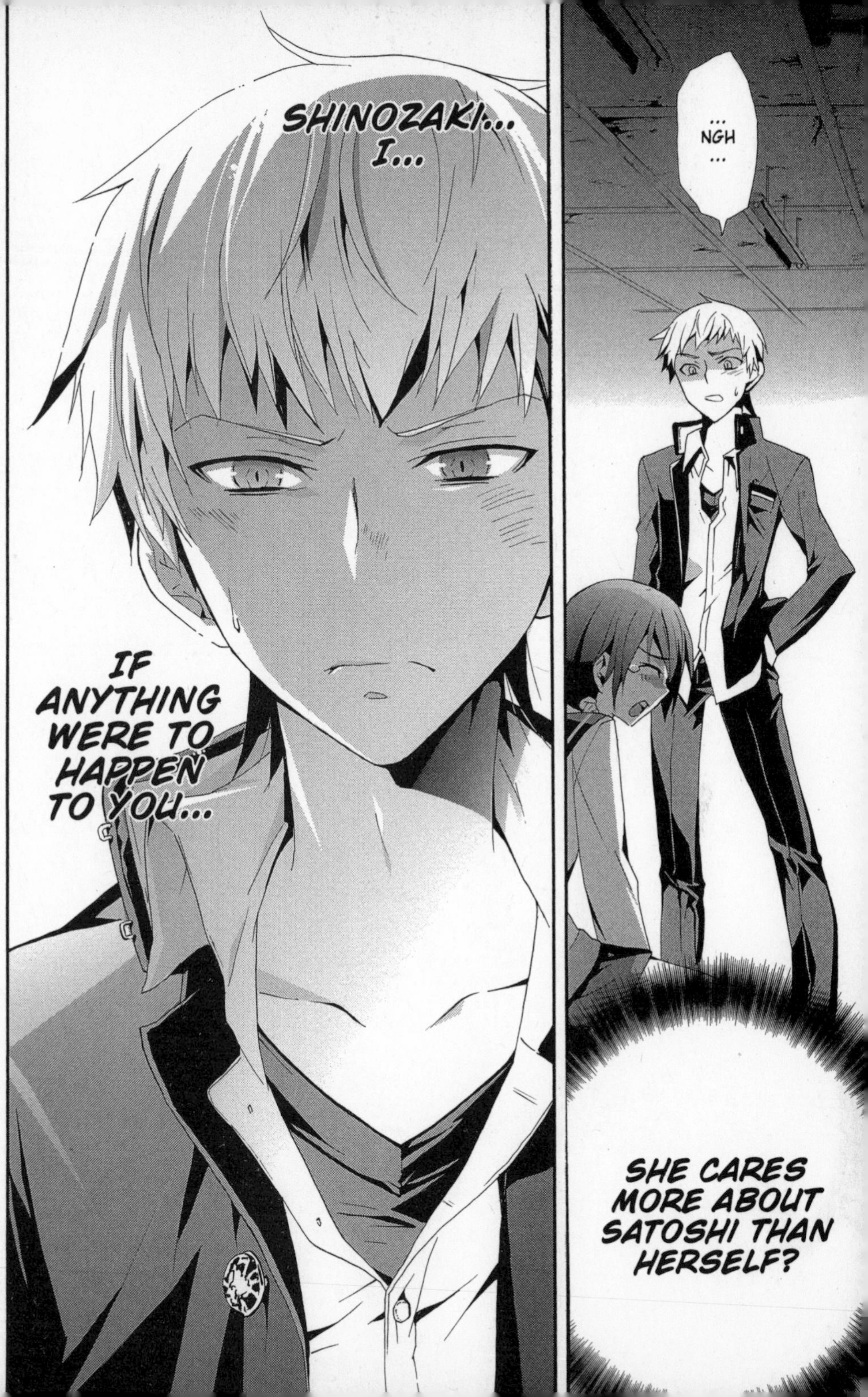
...NGH...
SHE CARES MORE ABOUT SATOSHI THAN HERSELF?
SHINOZAKI... I...
IF ANYTHING WERE TO HAPPEN TO YOU...

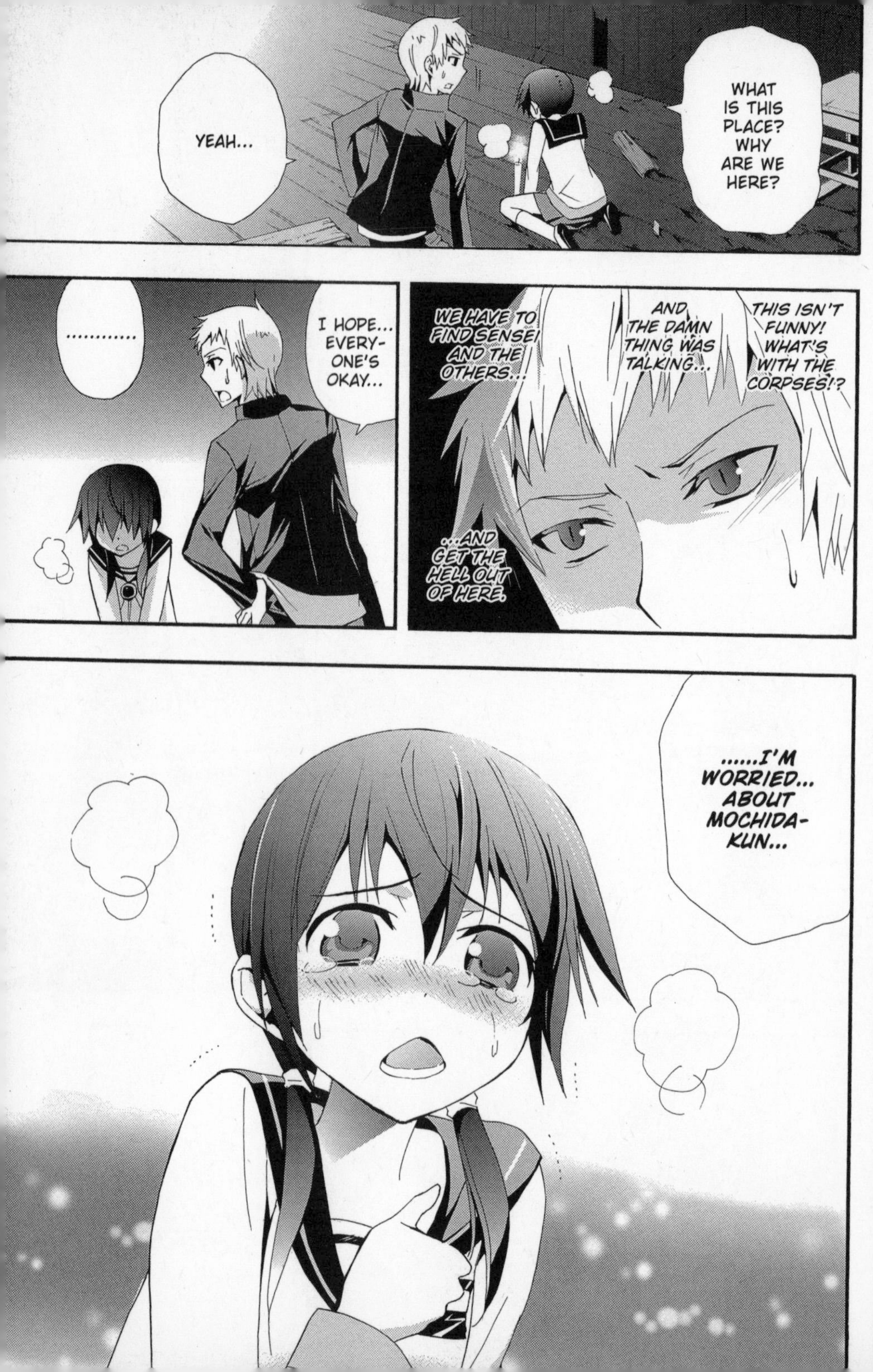
WHAT IS THIS PLACE? WHY ARE WE HERE?
YEAH...
THIS ISN'T FUNNY! WHAT'S WITH THE CORPSES!?
AND THE DAMN THING WAS TALKING...
WE HAVE TO FIND SENSEI AND THE OTHERS...
...AND GET THE HELL OUT OF HERE.
I HOPE... EVERY-ONE'S OKAY...
....
......I'M WORRIED... ABOUT MOCHIDA-KUN...

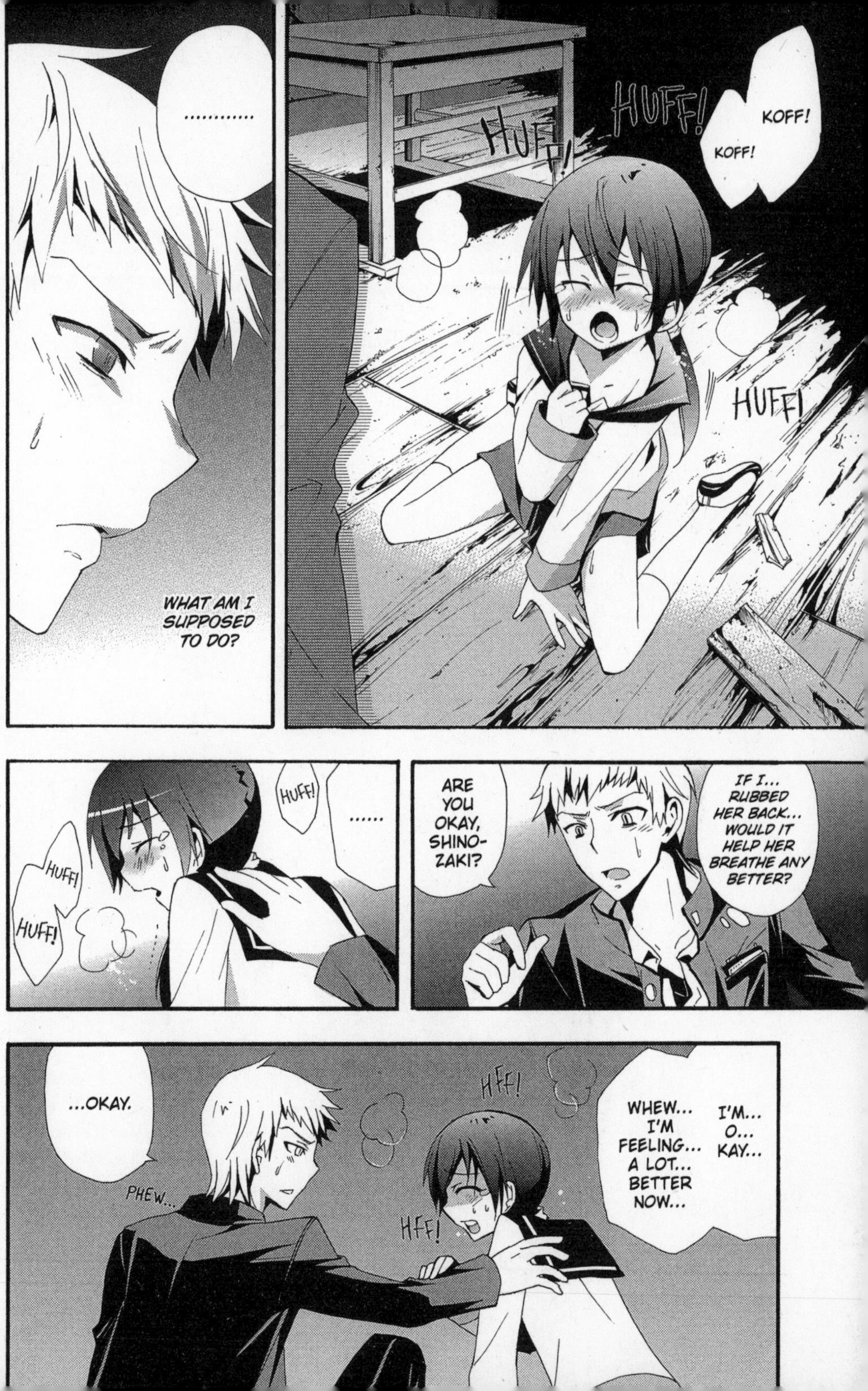
KOFF!
KOFF!
HUFF!
HUFF!
HUFF!
....
WHAT AM I SUPPOSED TO DO?
IF I... RUBBED HER BACK... WOULD IT HELP HER BREATHE ANY BETTER?
ARE YOU OKAY, SHINO-ZAKI?
......
HUFF!
HUFF!
HUFF!
I'M... O... KAY...
WHEW... I'M FEELING... A LOT... BETTER NOW...
HFF!
HFF!
...OKAY.
PHEW...

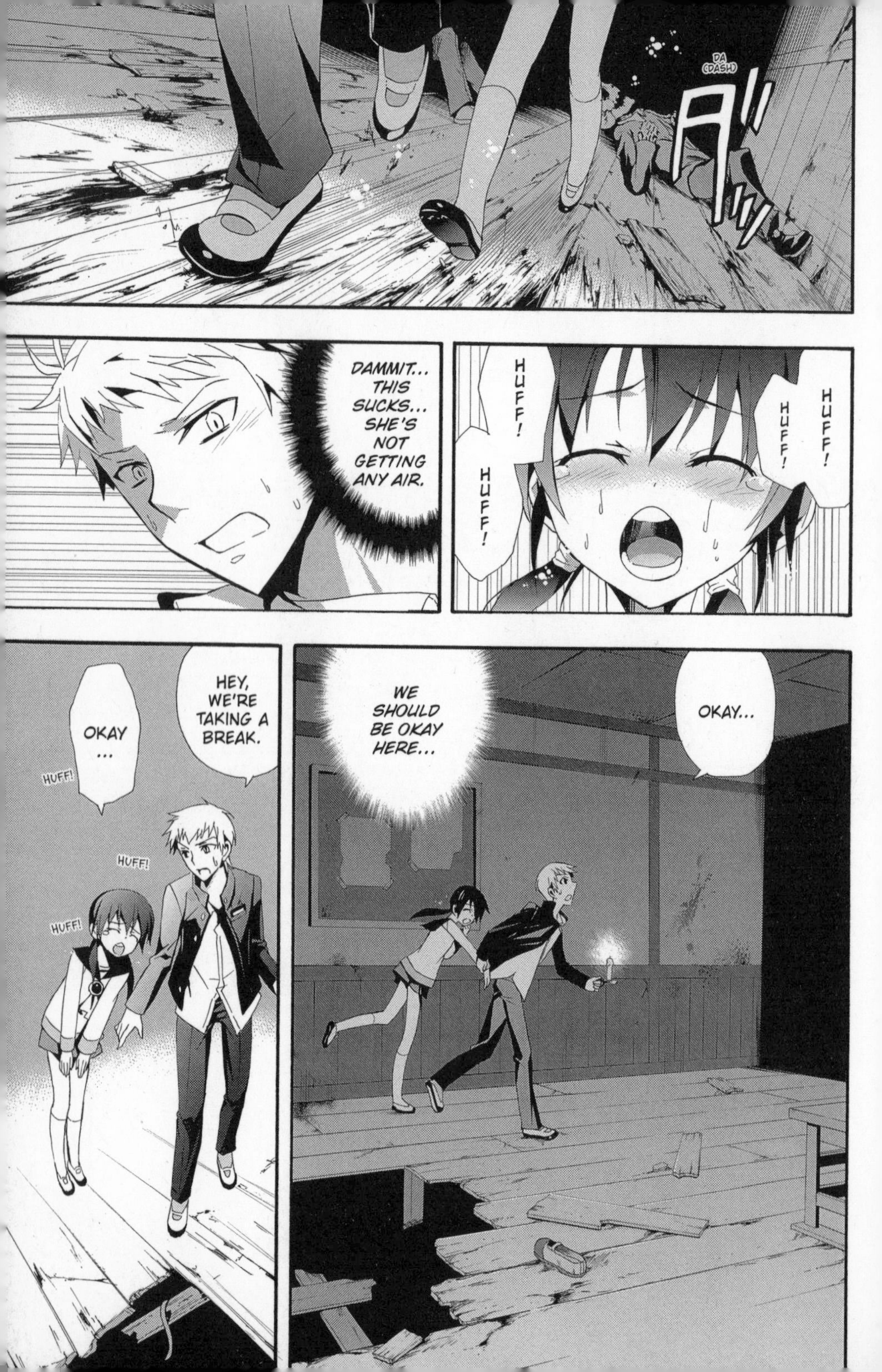

DA (DASH)
HUFF! HUFF!
HUFF! HUFF!
DAMMIT... THIS SUCKS... SHE'S NOT GETTING ANY AIR.
OKAY...
WE SHOULD BE OKAY HERE...
HEY, WE'RE TAKING A BREAK.
OKAY ...
HUFF!
HUFF!
HUFF!

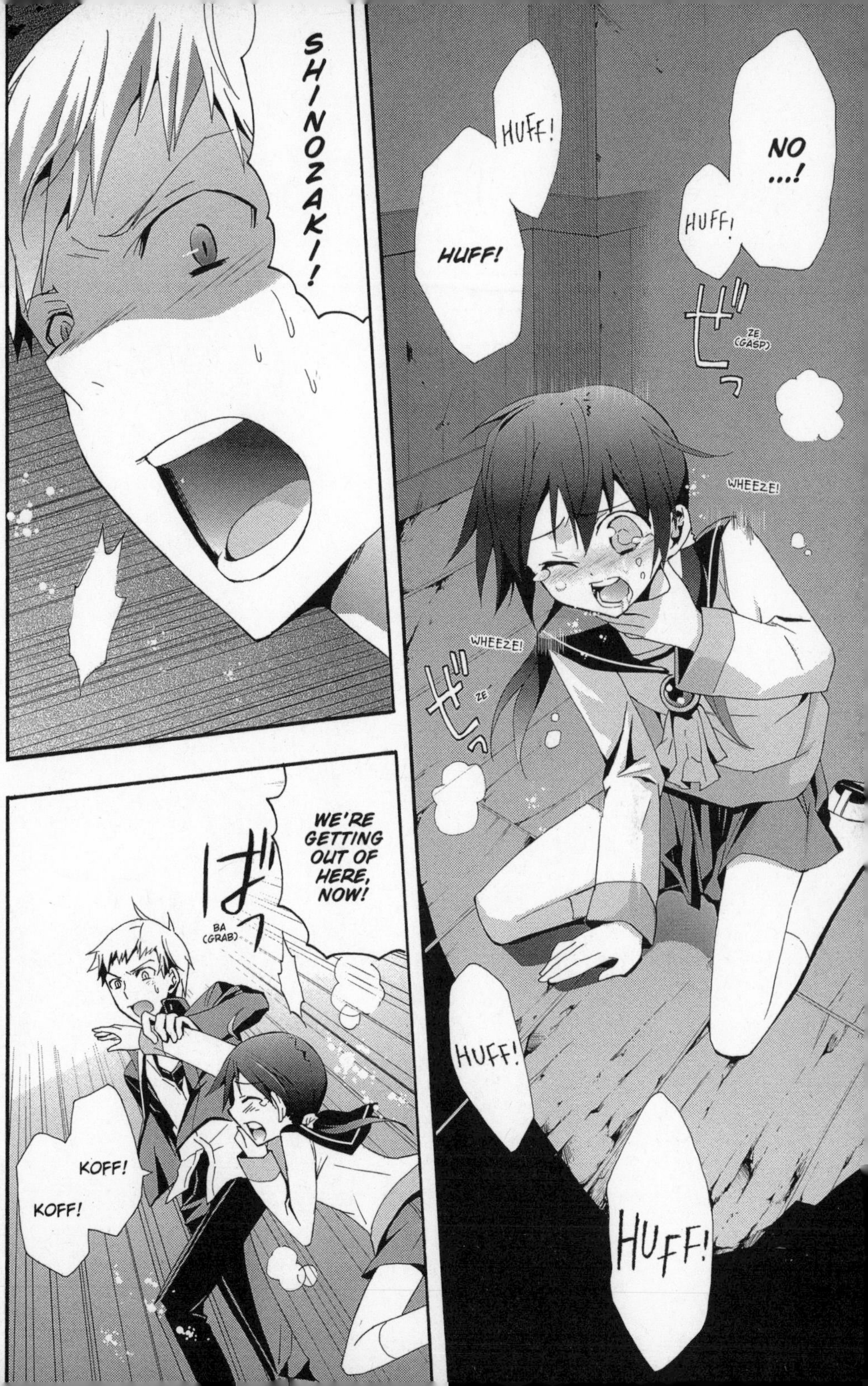
NO ...!
HUFF!
HUFF!
HUFF!
ぜっ
ZE (GASP)
WHEEZE!
WHEEZE!
ぜっ
ZE
HUFF!
HUFF!
SHINOZAKI!!
WE'RE GETTING OUT OF HERE, NOW!
ばっ
BA (GRAB)
KOFF!
KOFF!

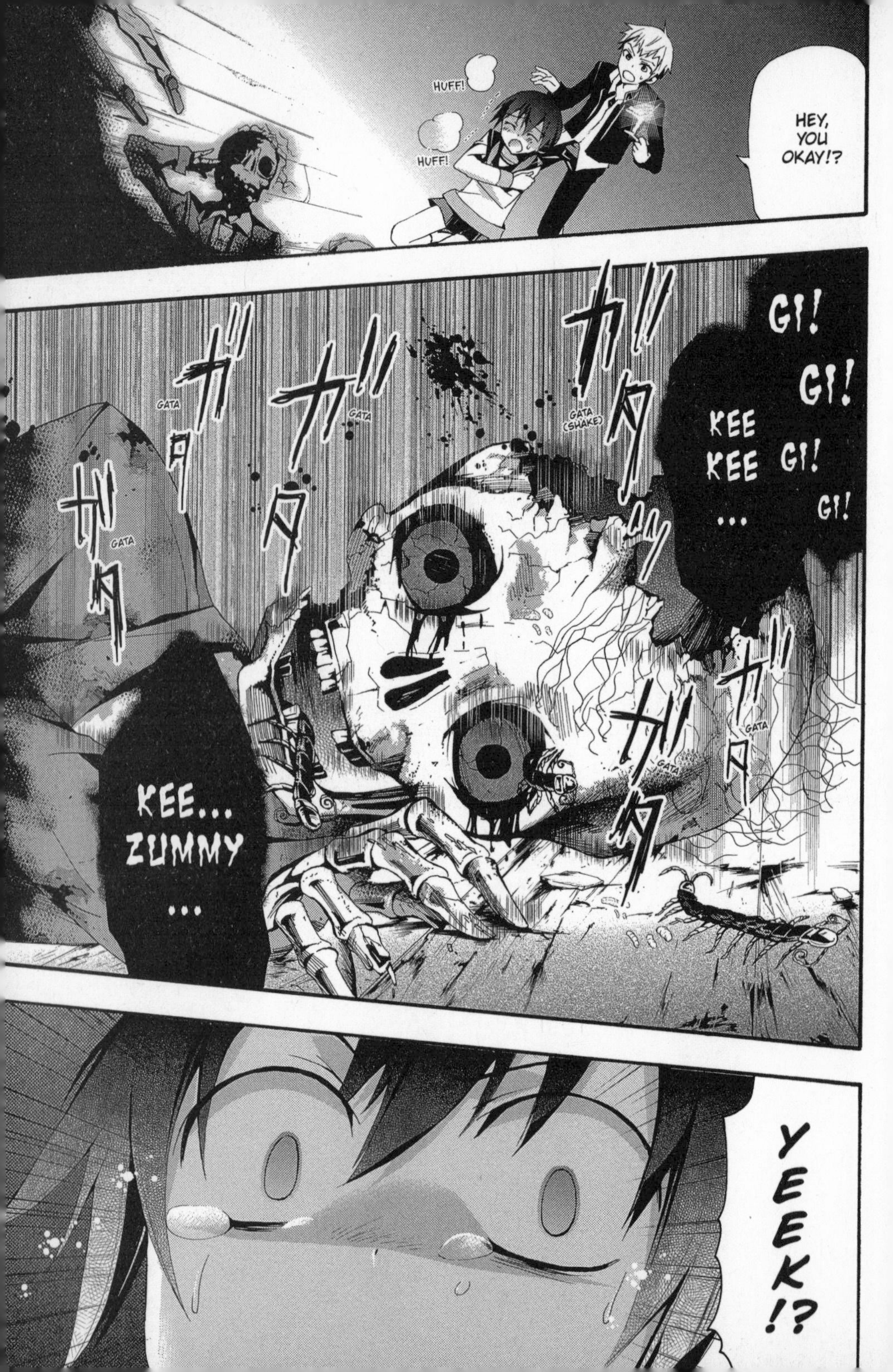

HEY, YOU OKAY!?
HUFF!
HUFF!
GI! GI! KEE KEE GI! ... GI!
GATA (SHAKE)
GATA
GATA
GATA
GATA
GATA
KEE... ZUMMY ...
YEEK!?

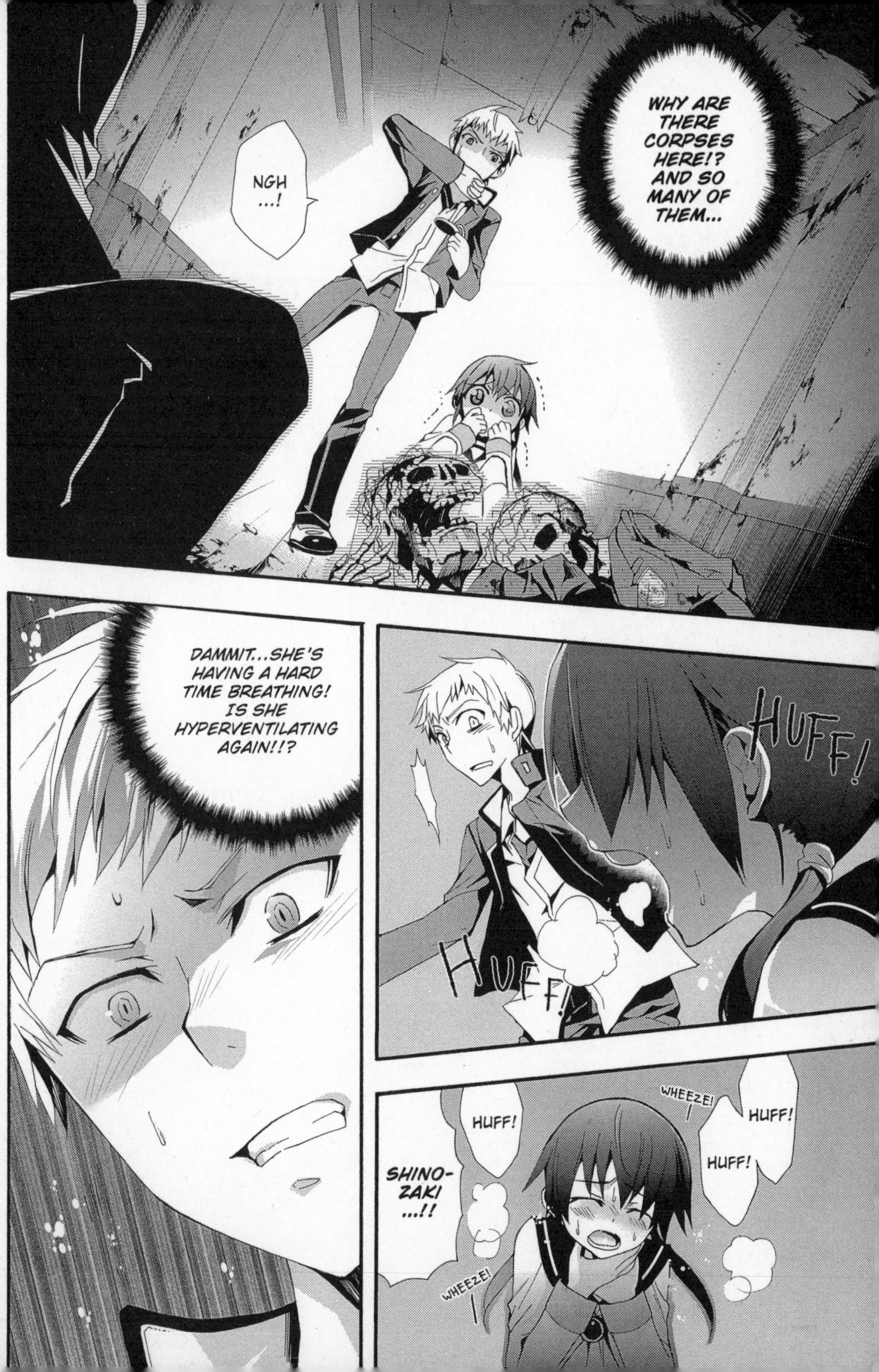
WHY ARE THERE CORPSES HERE!? AND SO MANY OF THEM...
NGH ...!
HUFF!
HUFF!
WHEEZE!
HUFF!
HUFF!
HUFF!
SHINOZAKI ...!!
WHEEZE!
DAMMIT...SHE'S HAVING A HARD TIME BREATHING! IS SHE HYPERVENTILATING AGAIN!!?

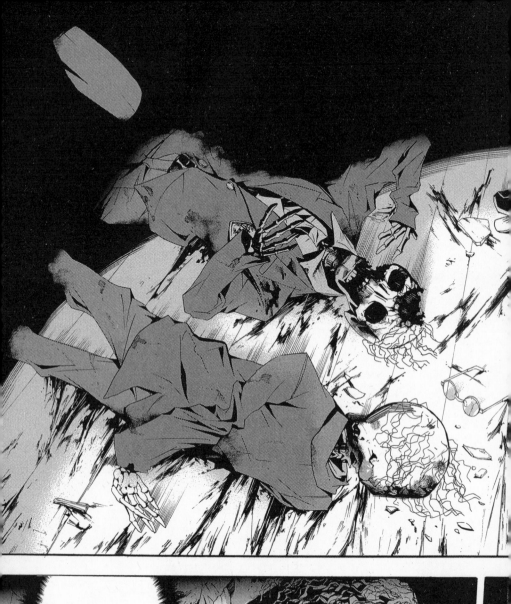

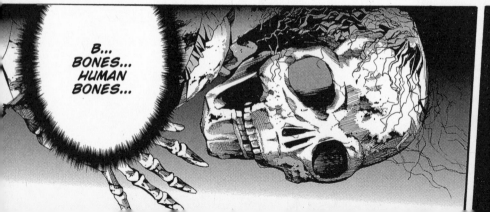

B... BONES... HUMAN BONES...

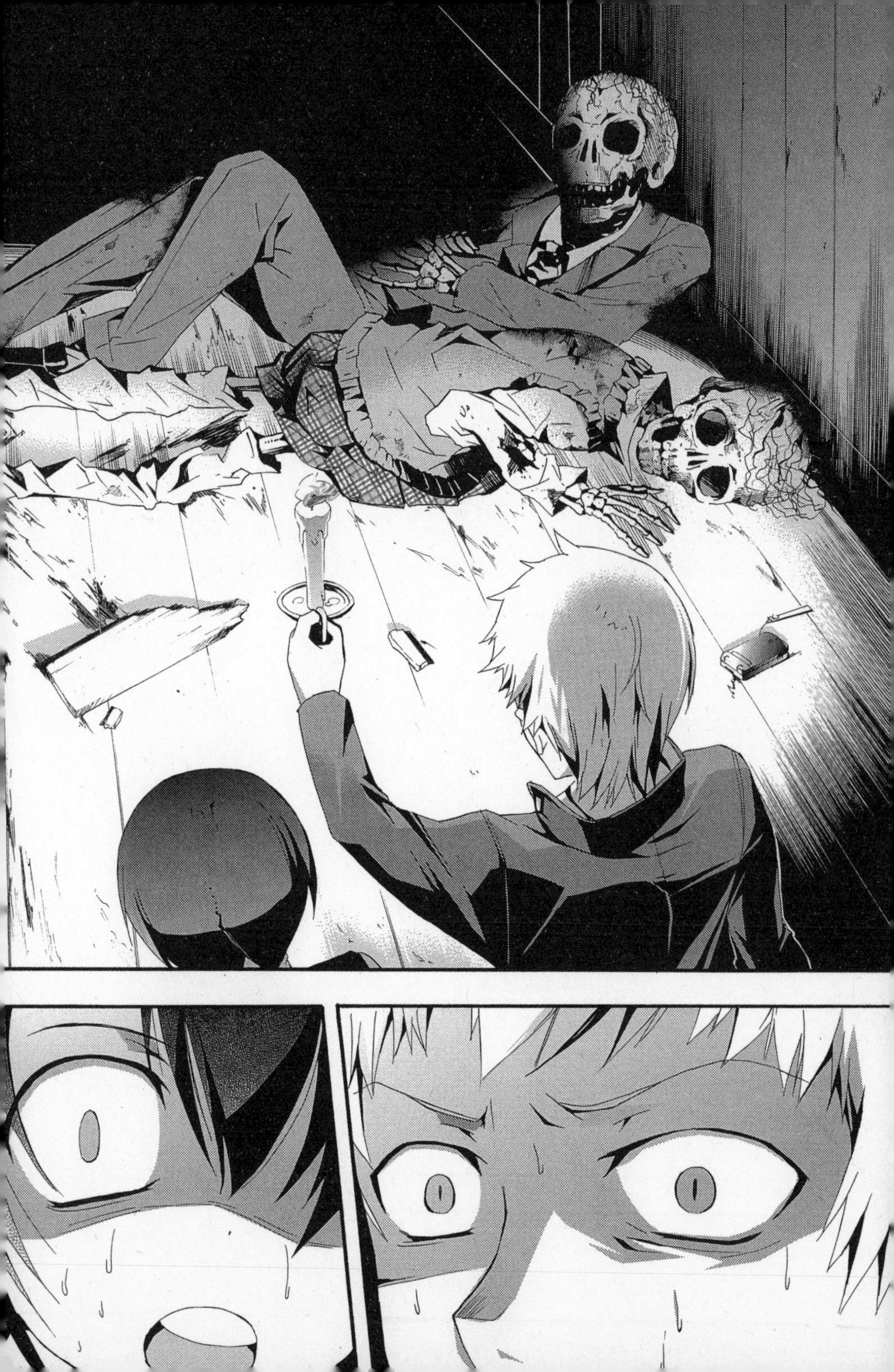

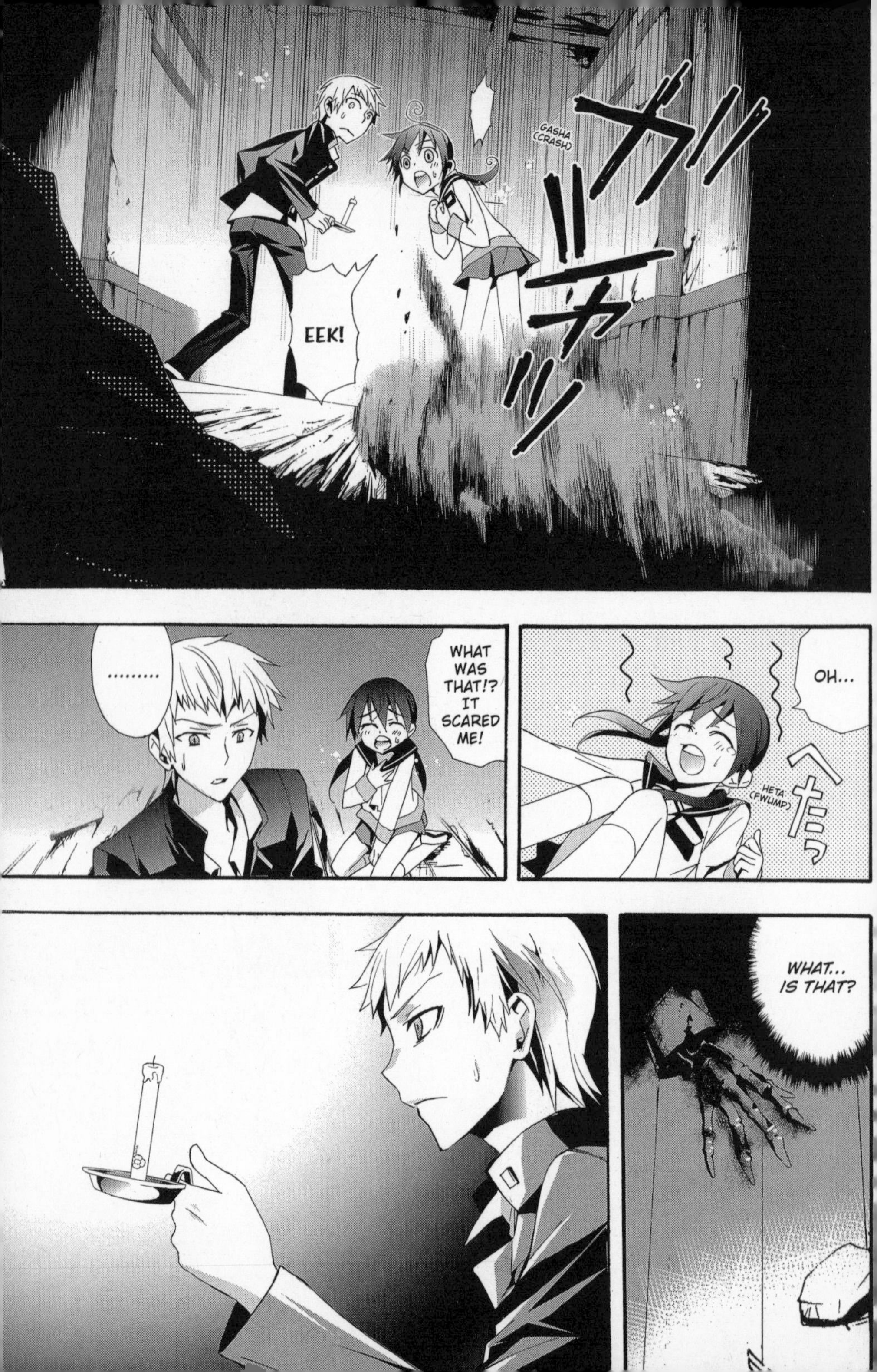
GASHA (CRASH)
EEK!
OH...
HETA (FWUMP)
WHAT WAS THAT!? IT SCARED ME!
....
WHAT... IS THAT?

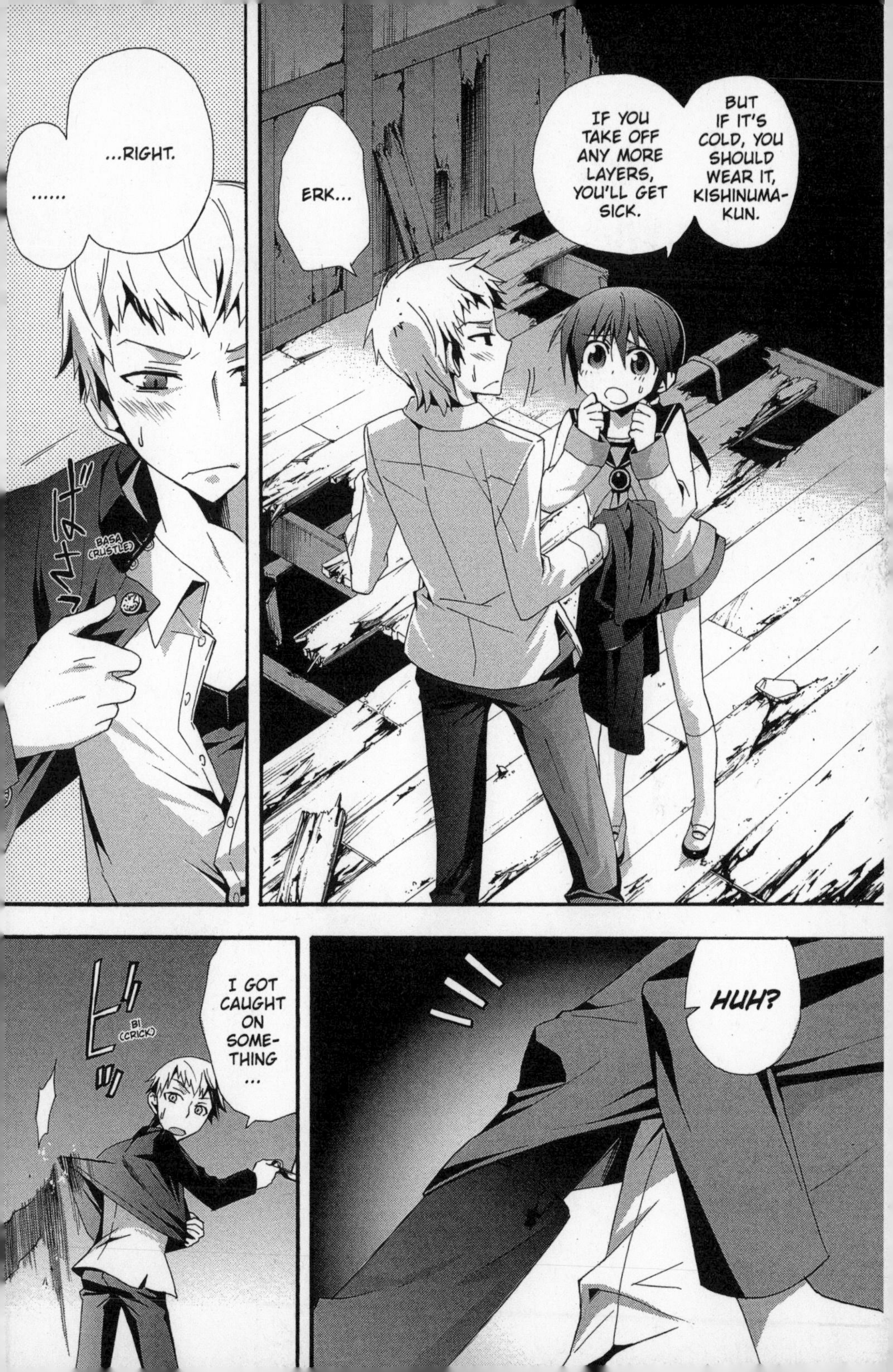
BUT IF IT'S COLD, YOU SHOULD WEAR IT, KISHINUMA-KUN.
IF YOU TAKE OFF ANY MORE LAYERS, YOU'LL GET SICK.
ERK...
...RIGHT.
......
BASA (RUSTLE)
HUH?
I GOT CAUGHT ON SOME-THING ...
BI (CRICK)

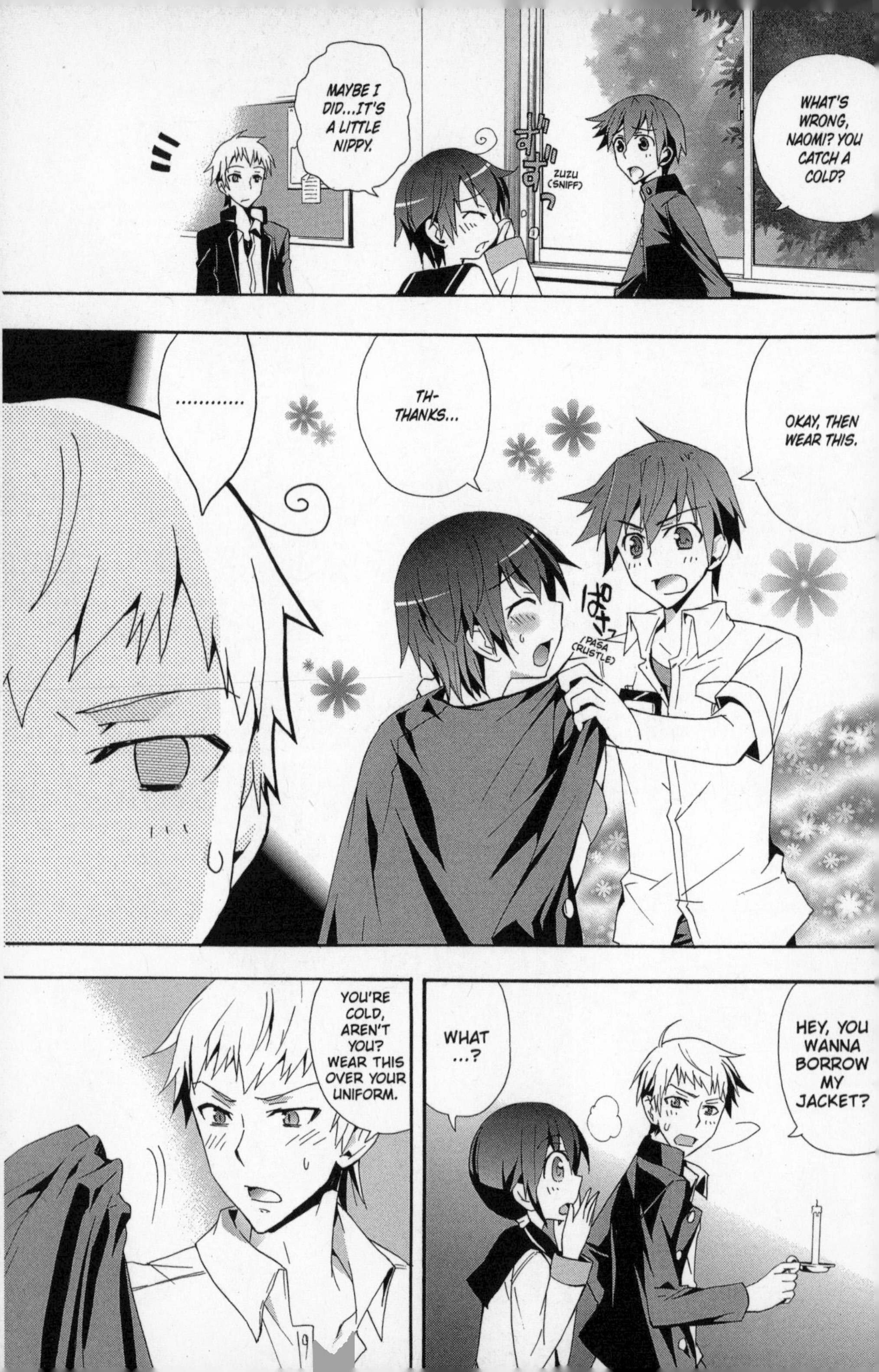
WHAT'S WRONG, NAOMI? YOU CATCH A COLD?
ZUZU (SNIFF)
MAYBE I DID...IT'S A LITTLE NIPPY.
OKAY, THEN WEAR THIS.
PASA (RUSTLE)
TH- THANKS...
....
HEY, YOU WANNA BORROW MY JACKET?
WHAT ...?
YOU'RE COLD, AREN'T YOU? WEAR THIS OVER YOUR UNIFORM.

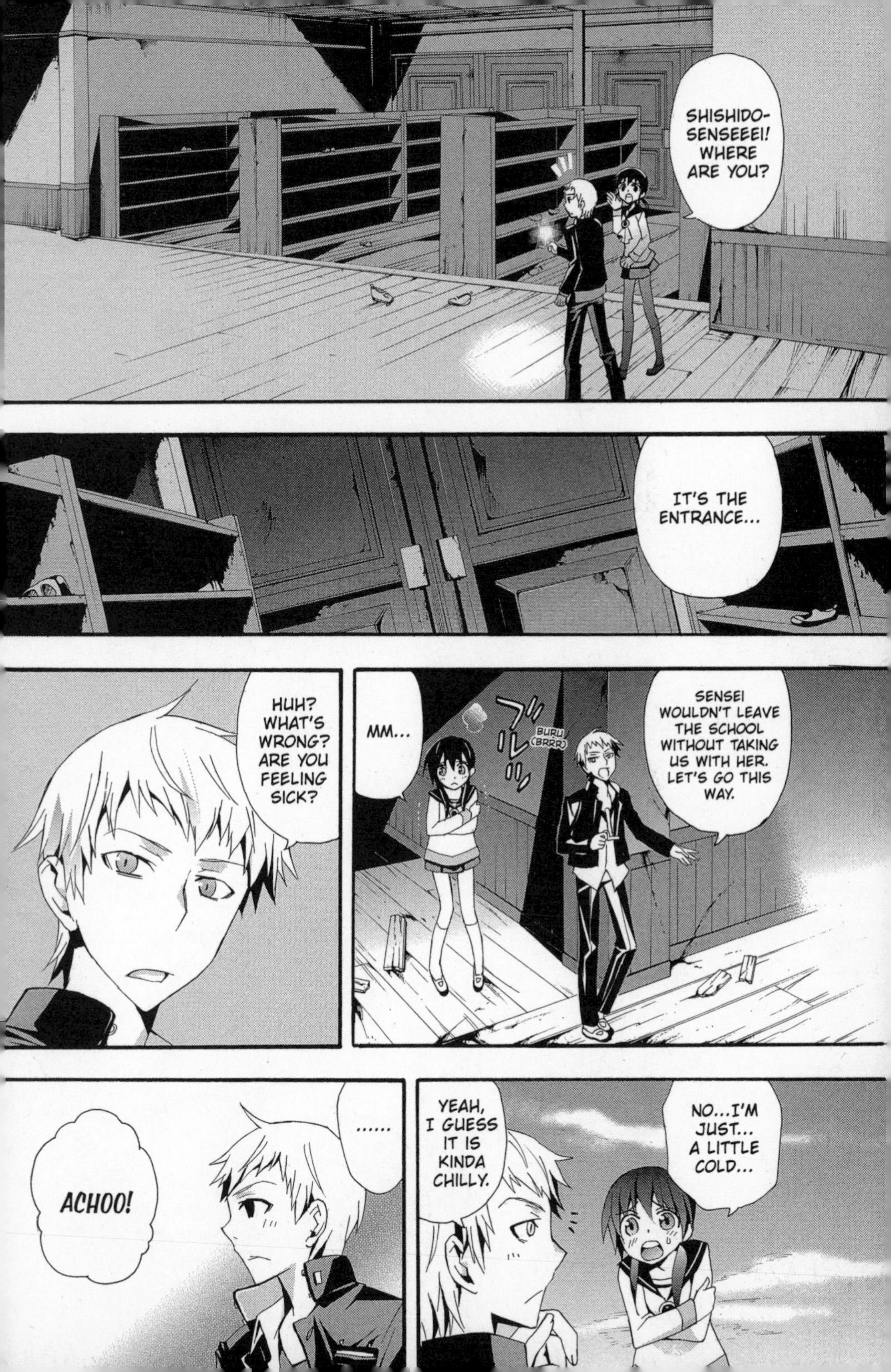
SHISHIDO-SENSEEEI! WHERE ARE YOU?
IT'S THE ENTRANCE...
SENSEI WOULDN'T LEAVE THE SCHOOL WITHOUT TAKING US WITH HER. LET'S GO THIS WAY.
BURU (BRRR)
MM...
HUH? WHAT'S WRONG? ARE YOU FEELING SICK?
NO...I'M JUST... A LITTLE COLD...
YEAH, I GUESS IT IS KINDA CHILLY.
......
ACHOO!

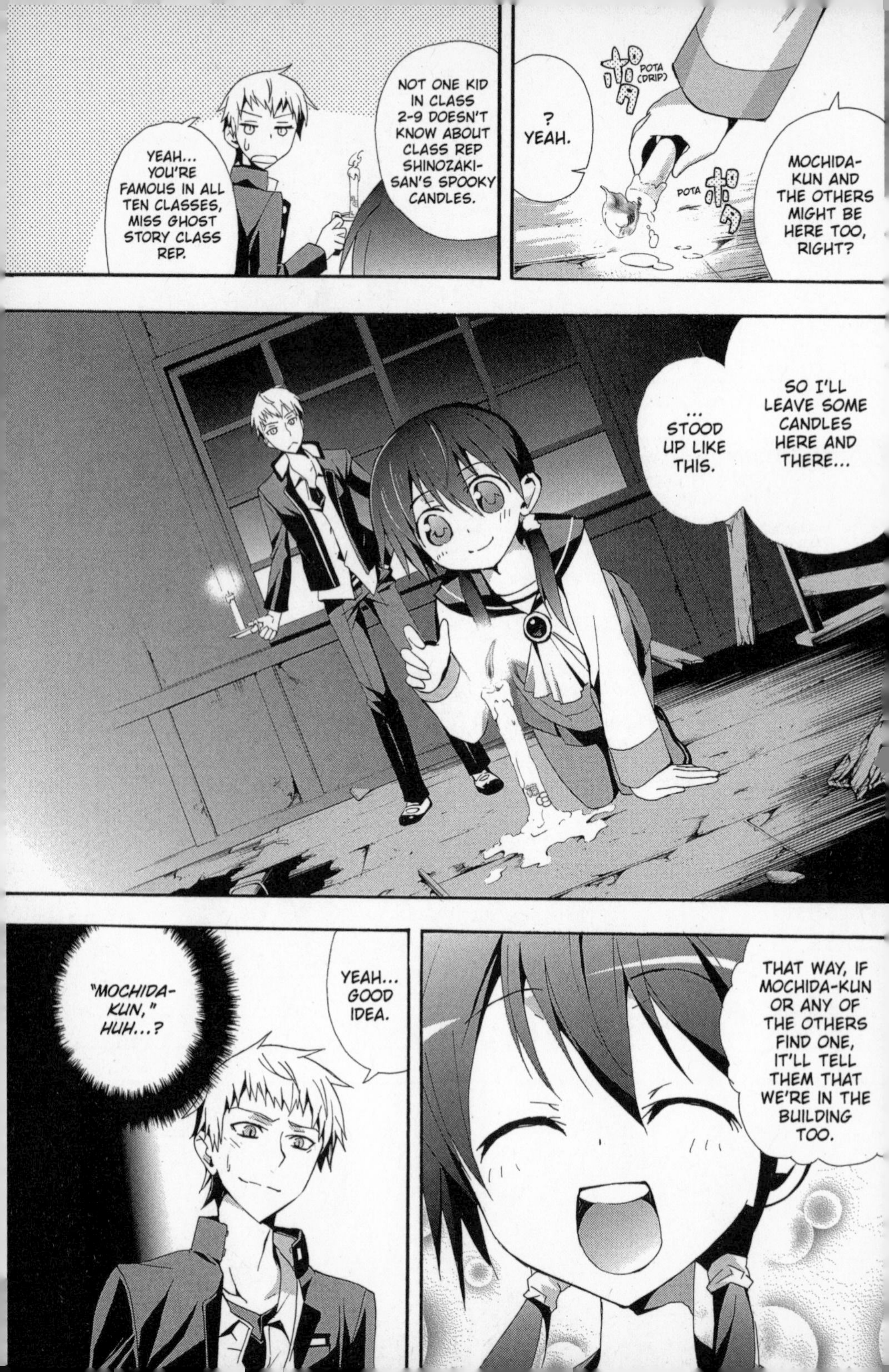
POTA (DRIP)
MOCHIDA-KUN AND THE OTHERS MIGHT BE HERE TOO, RIGHT?
POTA
? YEAH.
NOT ONE KID IN CLASS 2-9 DOESN'T KNOW ABOUT CLASS REP SHINOZAKI-SAN'S SPOOKY CANDLES.
YEAH... YOU'RE FAMOUS IN ALL TEN CLASSES, MISS GHOST STORY CLASS REP.
SO I'LL LEAVE SOME CANDLES HERE AND THERE...
... STOOD UP LIKE THIS.
THAT WAY, IF MOCHIDA-KUN OR ANY OF THE OTHERS FIND ONE, IT'LL TELL THEM THAT WE'RE IN THE BUILDING TOO.
YEAH... GOOD IDEA.
"MOCHIDA-KUN," HUH...?

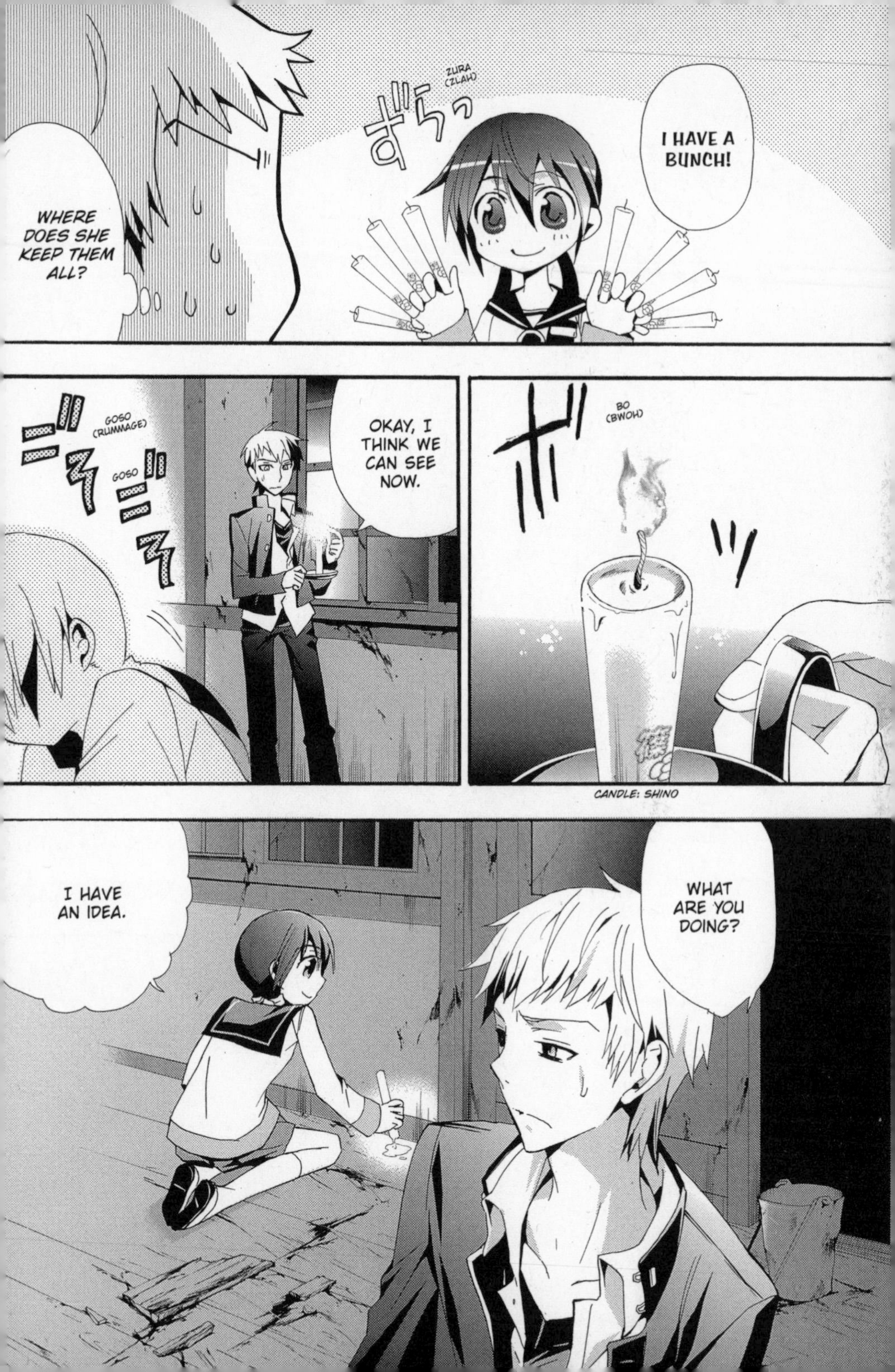
I HAVE A BUNCH!
ZURA (ZLAH)
WHERE DOES SHE KEEP THEM ALL?
BO (BWOH)
CANDLE: SHINO
OKAY, I THINK WE CAN SEE NOW.
GOSO (RUMMAGE)
GOSO
WHAT ARE YOU DOING?
I HAVE AN IDEA.

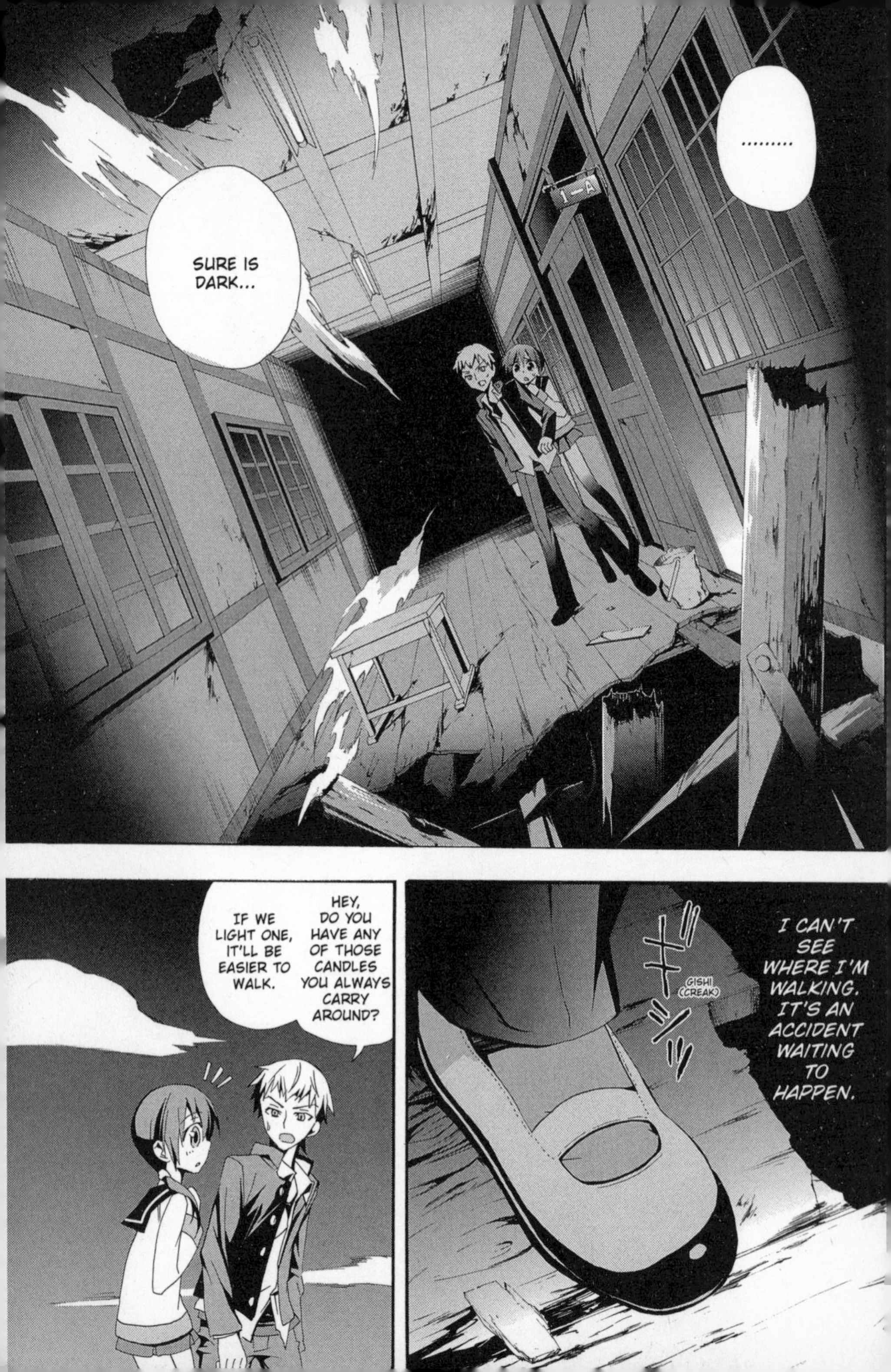
....
1—A
SURE IS DARK...
I CAN'T SEE WHERE I'M WALKING. IT'S AN ACCIDENT WAITING TO HAPPEN.
GISHI (CREAK)
HEY, DO YOU HAVE ANY OF THOSE CANDLES YOU ALWAYS CARRY AROUND?
IF WE LIGHT ONE, IT'LL BE EASIER TO WALK.

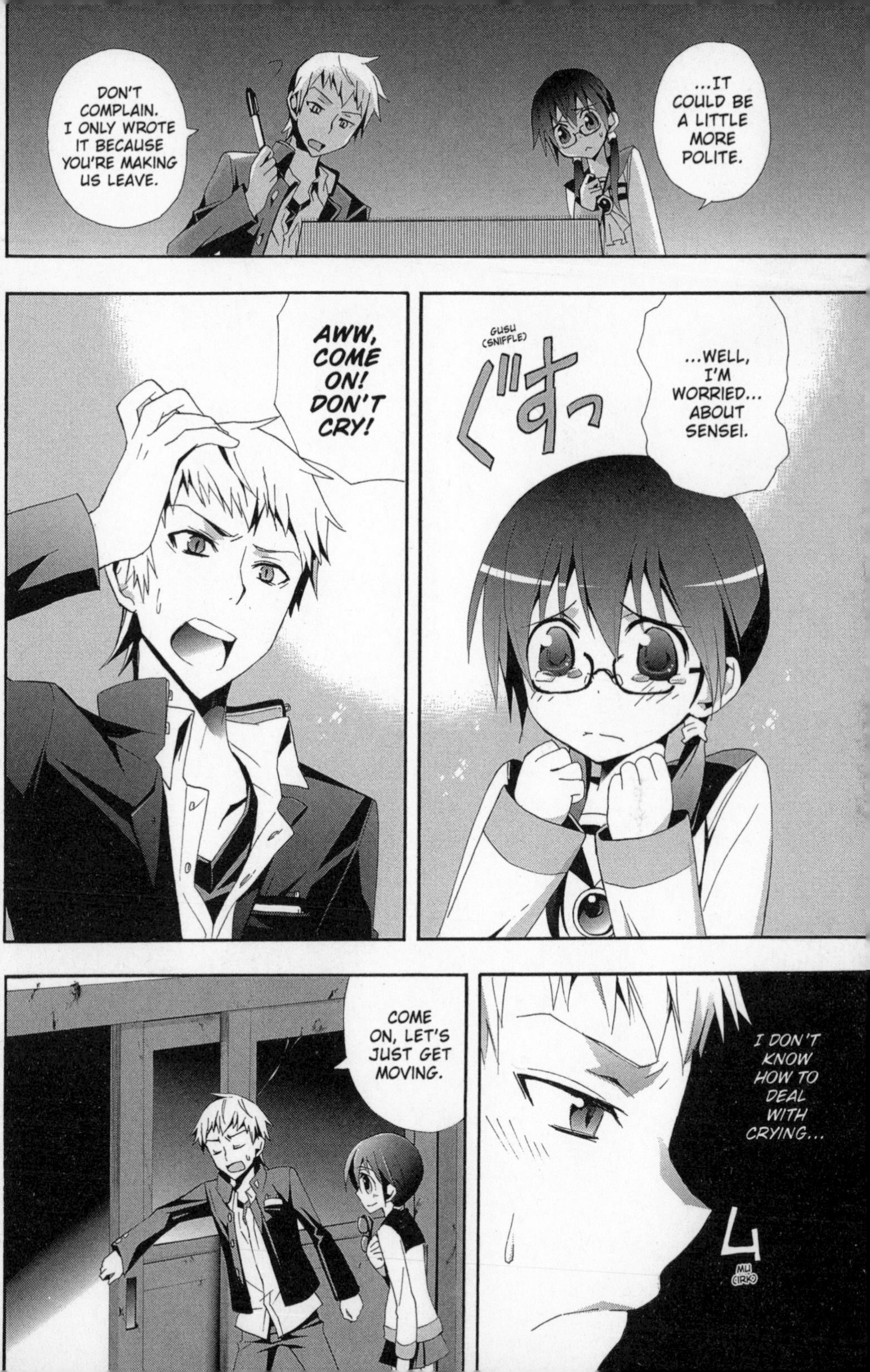
...IT COULD BE A LITTLE MORE POLITE.
DON'T COMPLAIN. I ONLY WROTE IT BECAUSE YOU'RE MAKING US LEAVE.
GUSU (SNIFFLE)
ぐすっ
...WELL, I'M WORRIED... ABOUT SENSEI.
AWW, COME ON! DON'T CRY!
I DON'T KNOW HOW TO DEAL WITH CRYING...
ム
MU (IRK)
COME ON, LET'S JUST GET MOVING.

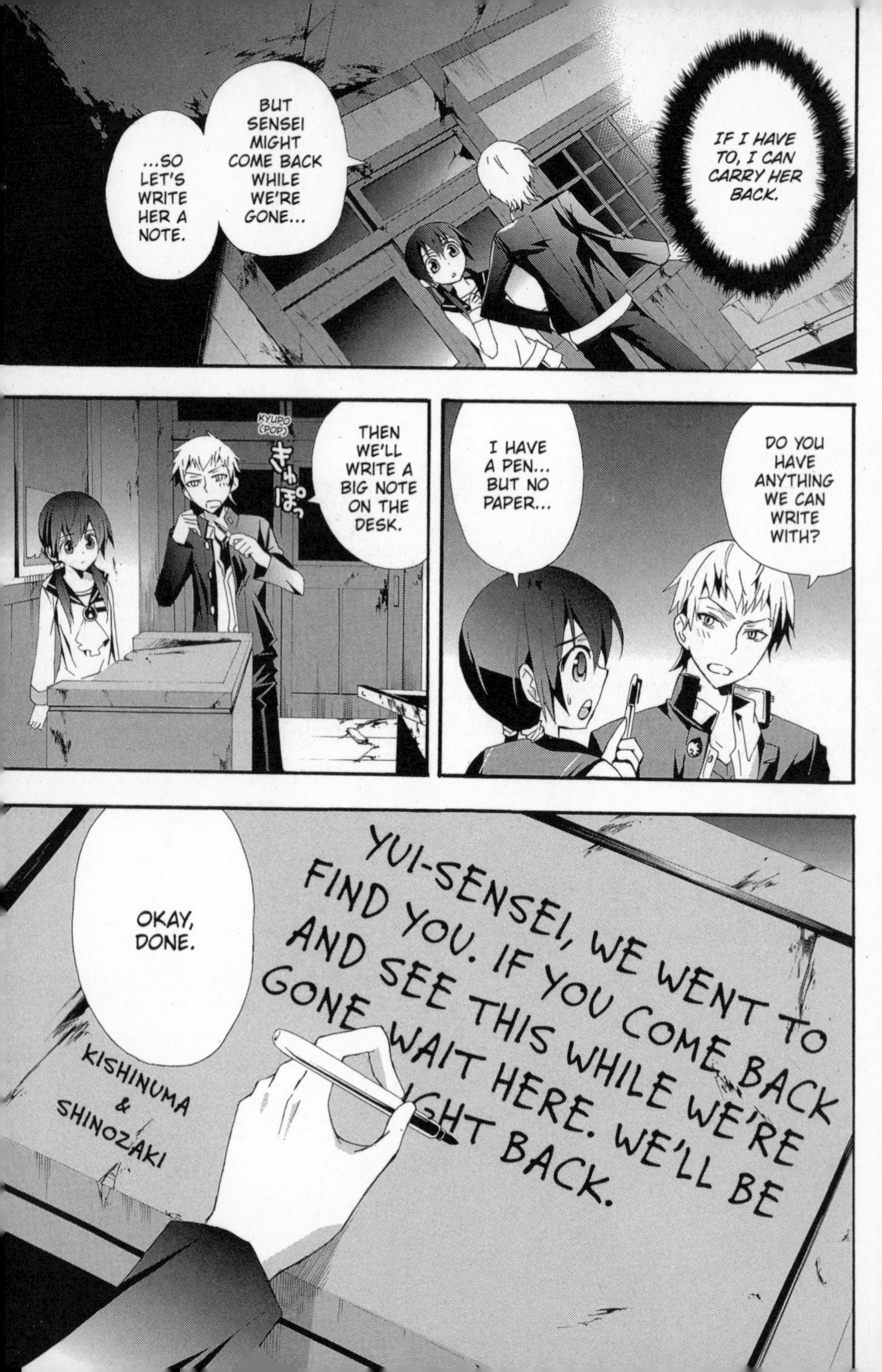
IF I HAVE TO, I CAN CARRY HER BACK.
BUT SENSEI MIGHT COME BACK WHILE WE'RE GONE...
...SO LET'S WRITE HER A NOTE.
DO YOU HAVE ANYTHING WE CAN WRITE WITH?
I HAVE A PEN... BUT NO PAPER...
THEN WE'LL WRITE A BIG NOTE ON THE DESK.
KYUPO (POP)
きゅぽっ
YUI-SENSEI, WE WENT TO FIND YOU. IF YOU COME BACK AND SEE THIS WHILE WE'RE GONE WAIT HERE. WE'LL BE
GHT BACK.
KISHINUMA & SHINOZAKI
OKAY, DONE.

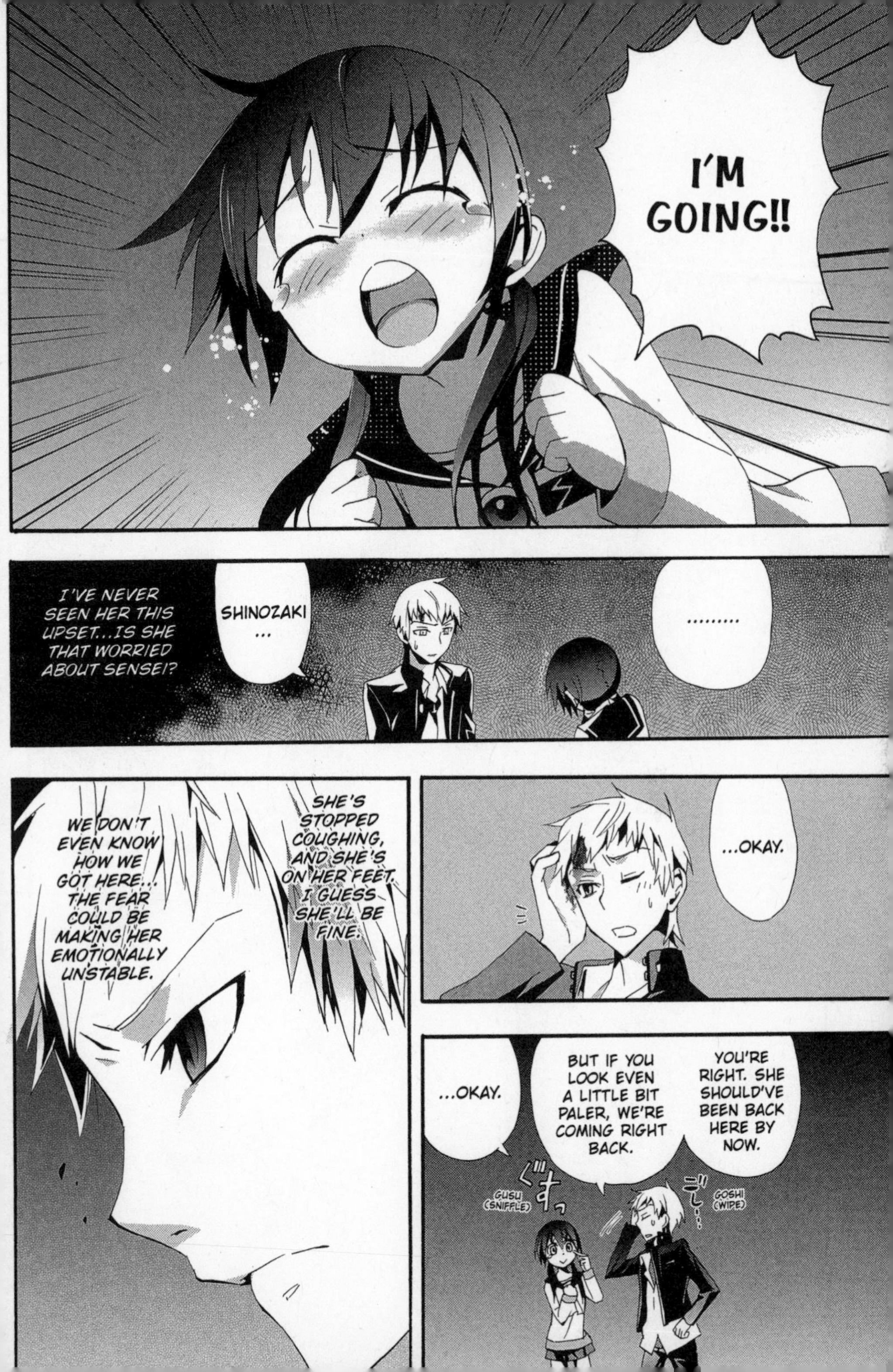
I'M GOING!!
....
SHINOZAKI ...
I'VE NEVER SEEN HER THIS UPSET...IS SHE THAT WORRIED ABOUT SENSEI?
...OKAY.
YOU'RE RIGHT. SHE SHOULD'VE BEEN BACK HERE BY NOW.
BUT IF YOU LOOK EVEN A LITTLE BIT PALER, WE'RE COMING RIGHT BACK.
...OKAY.
GOSHI (WIPE)
ぐすっ
GUSU (SNIFFLE)
SHE'S STOPPED COUGHING, AND SHE'S ON HER FEET. I GUESS SHE'LL BE FINE.
WE DON'T EVEN KNOW HOW WE GOT HERE... THE FEAR COULD BE MAKING HER EMOTIONALLY UNSTABLE.

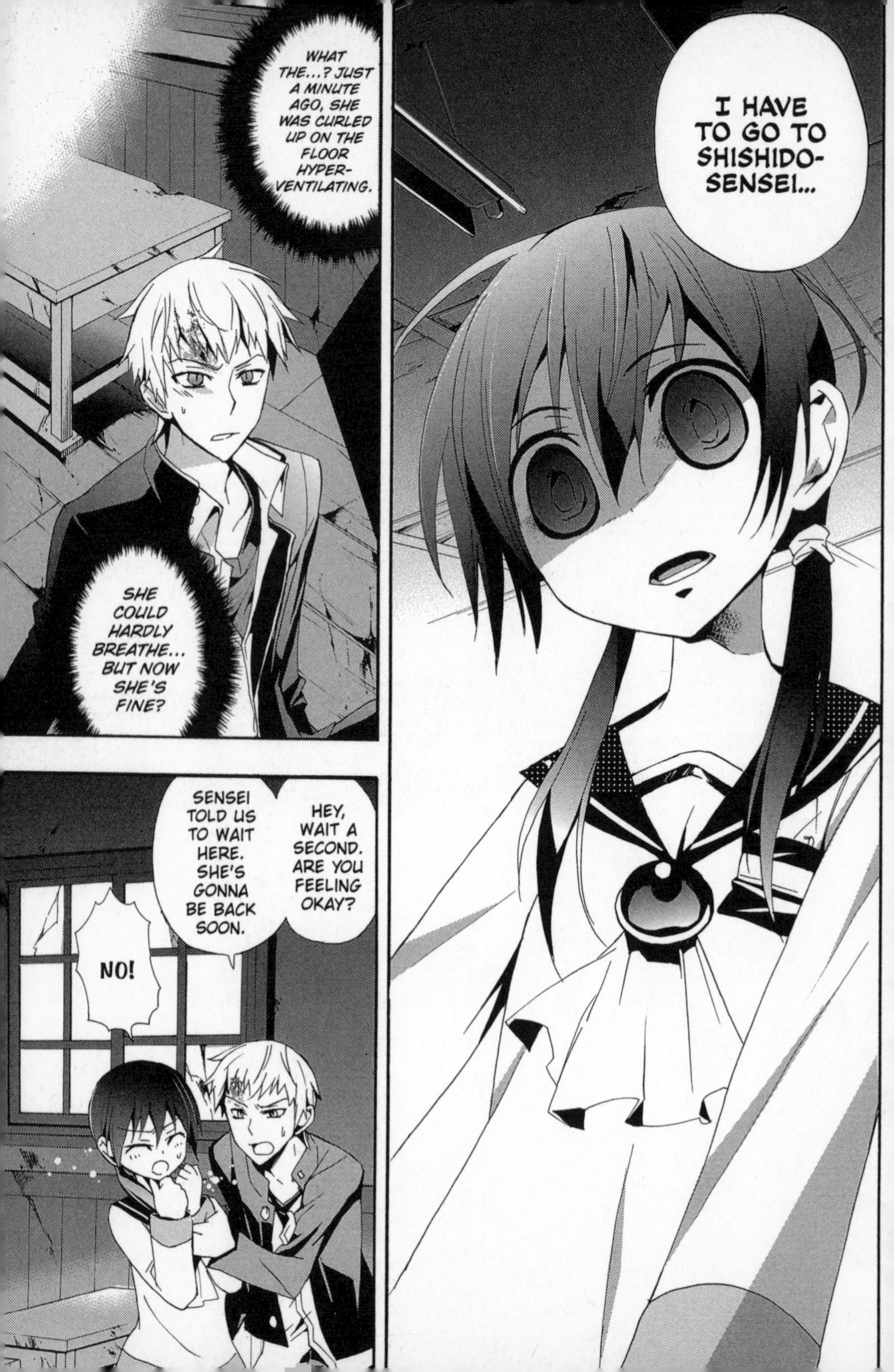
I HAVE TO GO TO SHISHIDO-SENSEI...
WHAT THE...? JUST A MINUTE AGO, SHE WAS CURLED UP ON THE FLOOR HYPER-VENTILATING.
SHE COULD HARDLY BREATHE... BUT NOW SHE'S FINE?
HEY, WAIT A SECOND. ARE YOU FEELING OKAY?
SENSEI TOLD US TO WAIT HERE. SHE'S GONNA BE BACK SOON.
NO!

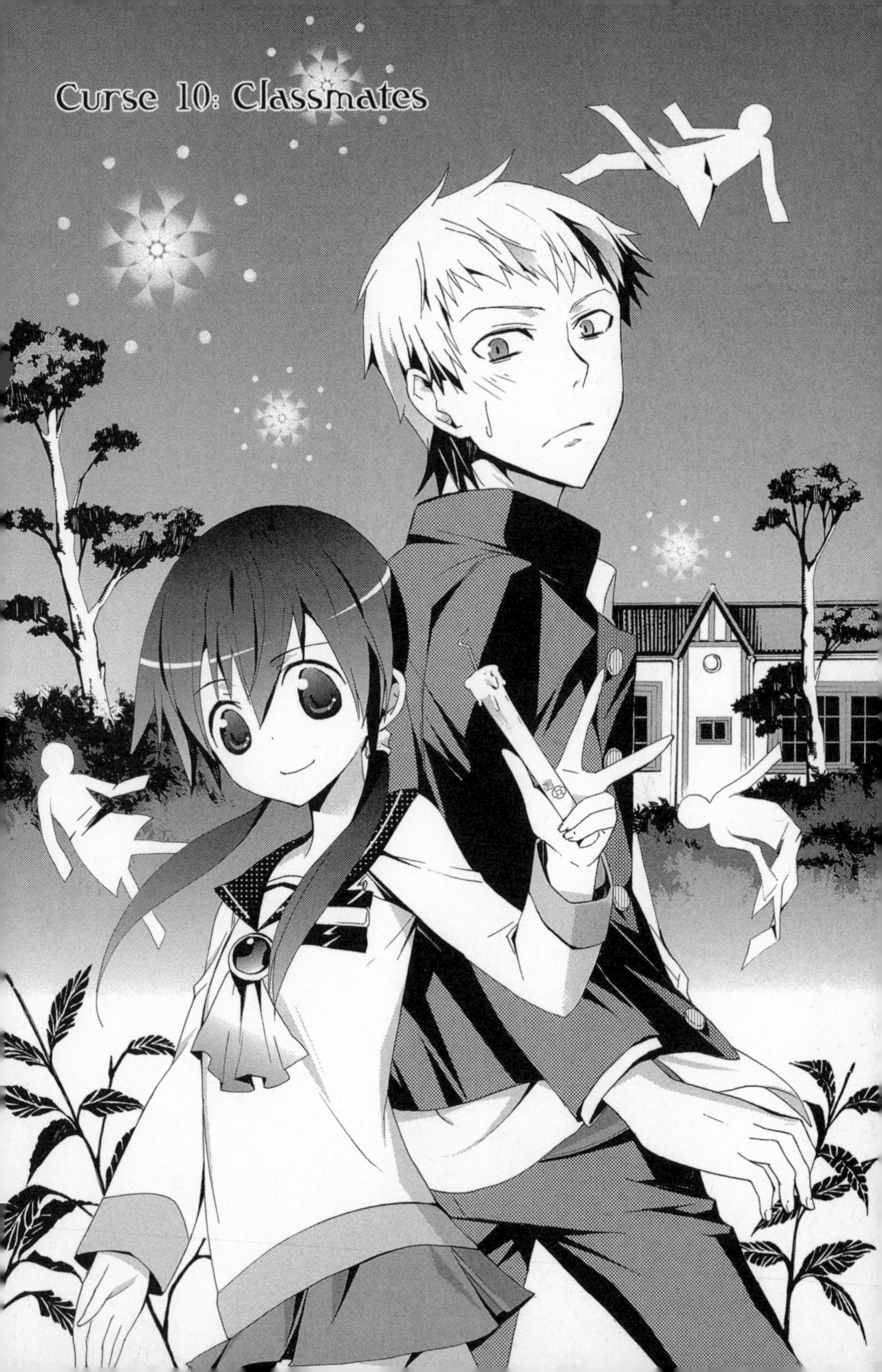
Curse 10: Classmates

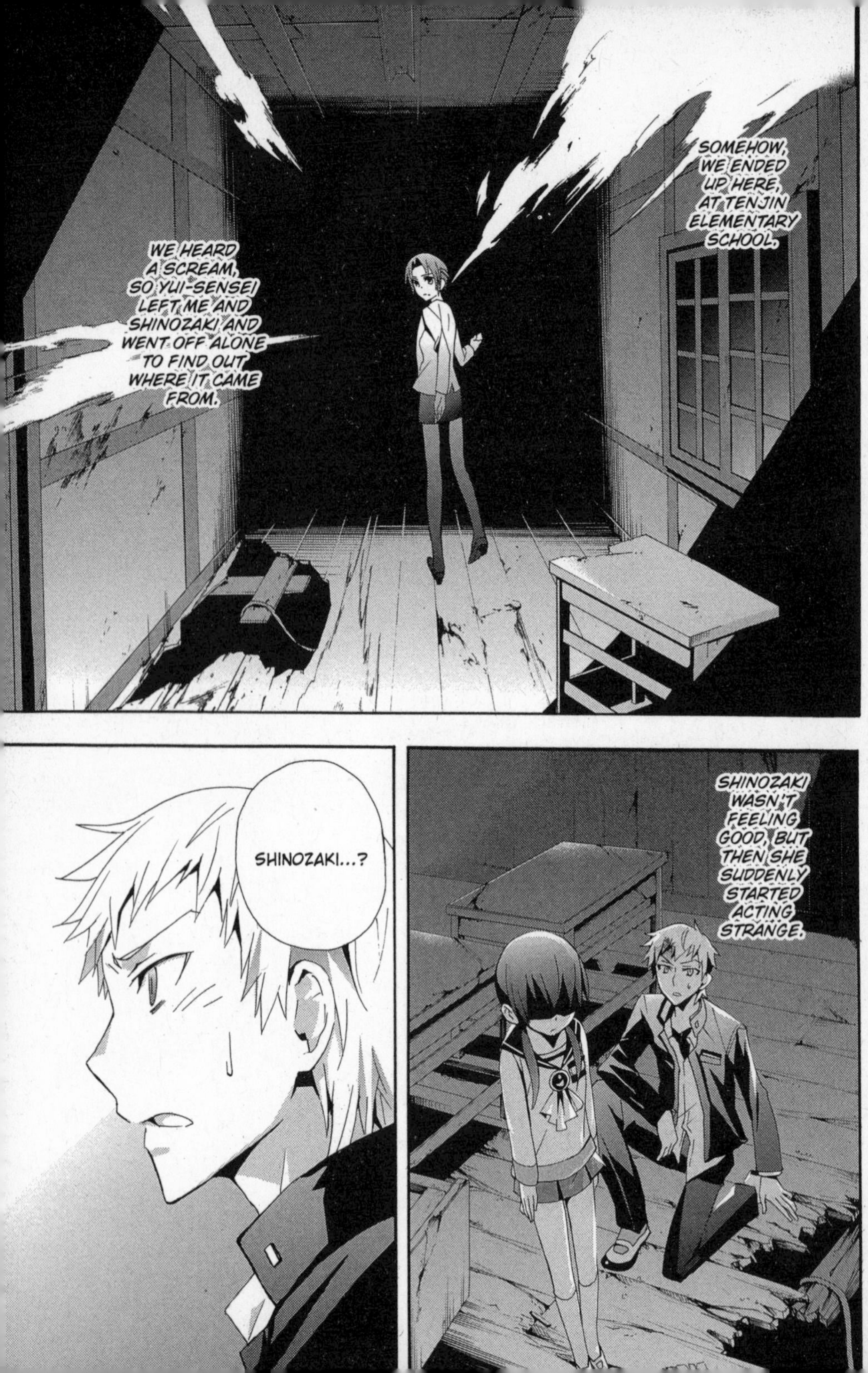
SOMEHOW, WE ENDED UP HERE, AT TENJIN ELEMENTARY SCHOOL.
WE HEARD A SCREAM, SO YUI-SENSEI LEFT ME AND SHINOZAKI AND WENT OFF ALONE TO FIND OUT WHERE IT CAME FROM.
SHINOZAKI WASN'T FEELING GOOD, BUT THEN SHE SUDDENLY STARTED ACTING STRANGE.
SHINOZAKI...?

CORPSE PARTY
BloodCovered

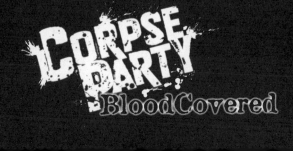

NAOMI NAKASHIMA

SHE ACTS COMPETITIVE AND TOUGH, BUT SHE ALSO HAS A SECRET ROMANTIC SIDE...

YUKA MOCHIDA

A SECOND-YEAR IN JUNIOR HIGH AND SATOSHI'S LITTLE SISTER. SHE ADORES HER BIG BROTHER!!

SATOSHI MOCHIDA

A SCAREDY-CAT WHO CAN BE RELIABLE NONETHELESS. THE HERO OF OUR STORY.

YOSHIKI KISHINUMA

A REBEL WHO'S A SURPRISINGLY NICE GUY DEEP DOWN...?

AYUMI SHINOZAKI

THE CLASS REPRESENTATIVE. A LOVER OF GHOST STORIES WHO ALWAYS HAS CANDLES ON HAND.

SEIKO SHINOHARA

NAOMI'S BEST FRIEND. HANGED TO DEATH IN THE RESTROOM.

YUI SHISHIDO

THE ASSISTANT HOMEROOM TEACHER. A NATURAL AIRHEAD WHO IS LOVED BY ALL HER STUDENTS.

SAKUTARO MORISHIGE

A GOOD FRIEND OF MAYU. THE TWO ARE LIKE BROTHER AND SISTER.

MAYU SUZUMOTO

A BRIGHT, PEPPY GIRL WHO IS ARGUABLY THE MOST POPULAR GIRL IN HER SCHOOL YEAR.

Story

THE CLASSMATES OF KISARAGI ACADEMY'S CLASS 2-9 HAVE JUST FINISHED AN ENJOYABLE SCHOOL FESTIVAL. HOWEVER, WHEN THEY PERFORM THE "SACHIKO-SAN EVER AFTER" CHARM, THEY ARE INEXPLICABLY IMPRISONED AT TENJIN ELEMENTARY SCHOOL. FEAR DESCENDS UPON THEM. CAN THEY REALLY MAKE IT OUT ALIVE!?

BloodCovered Contents

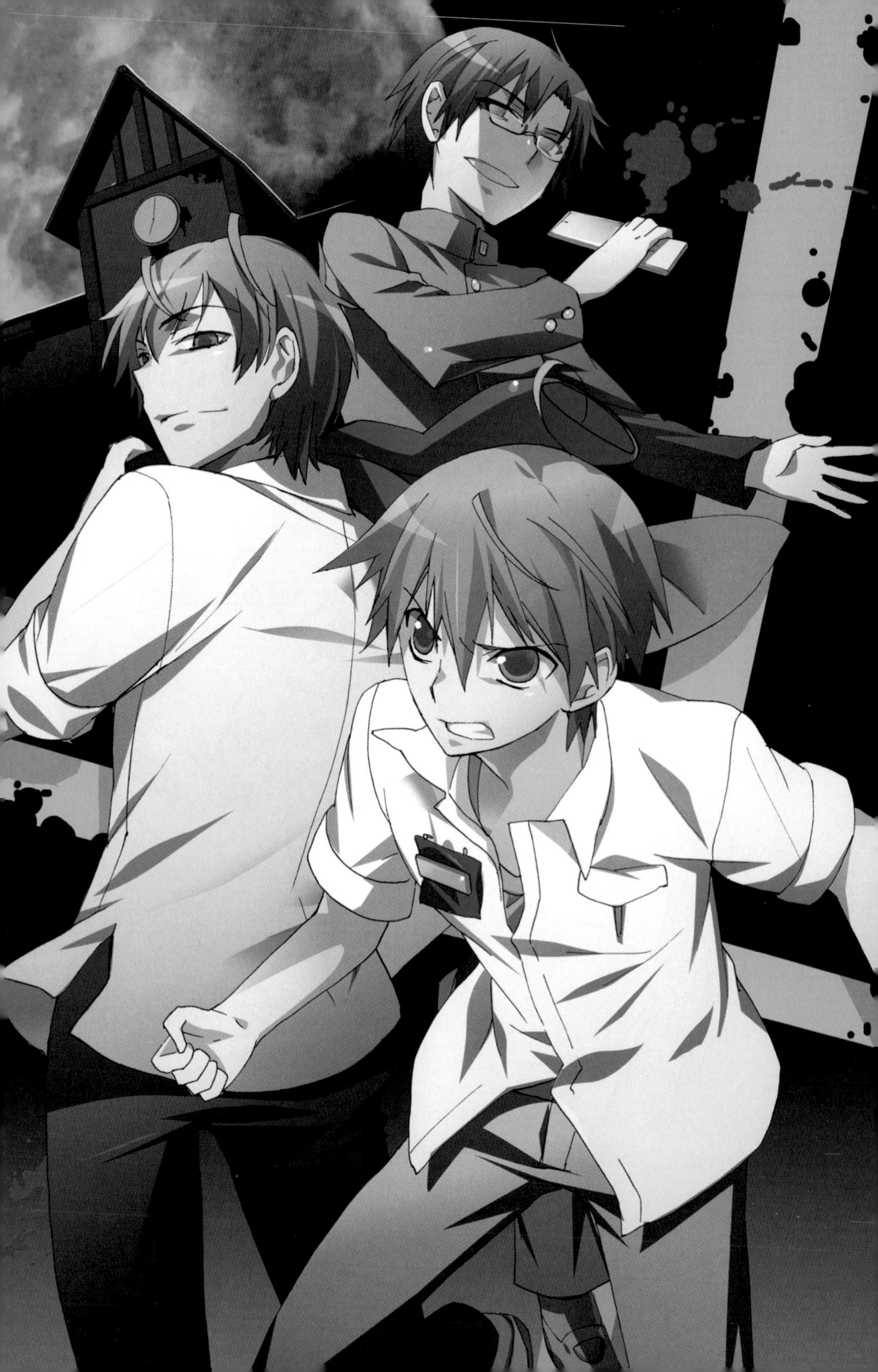

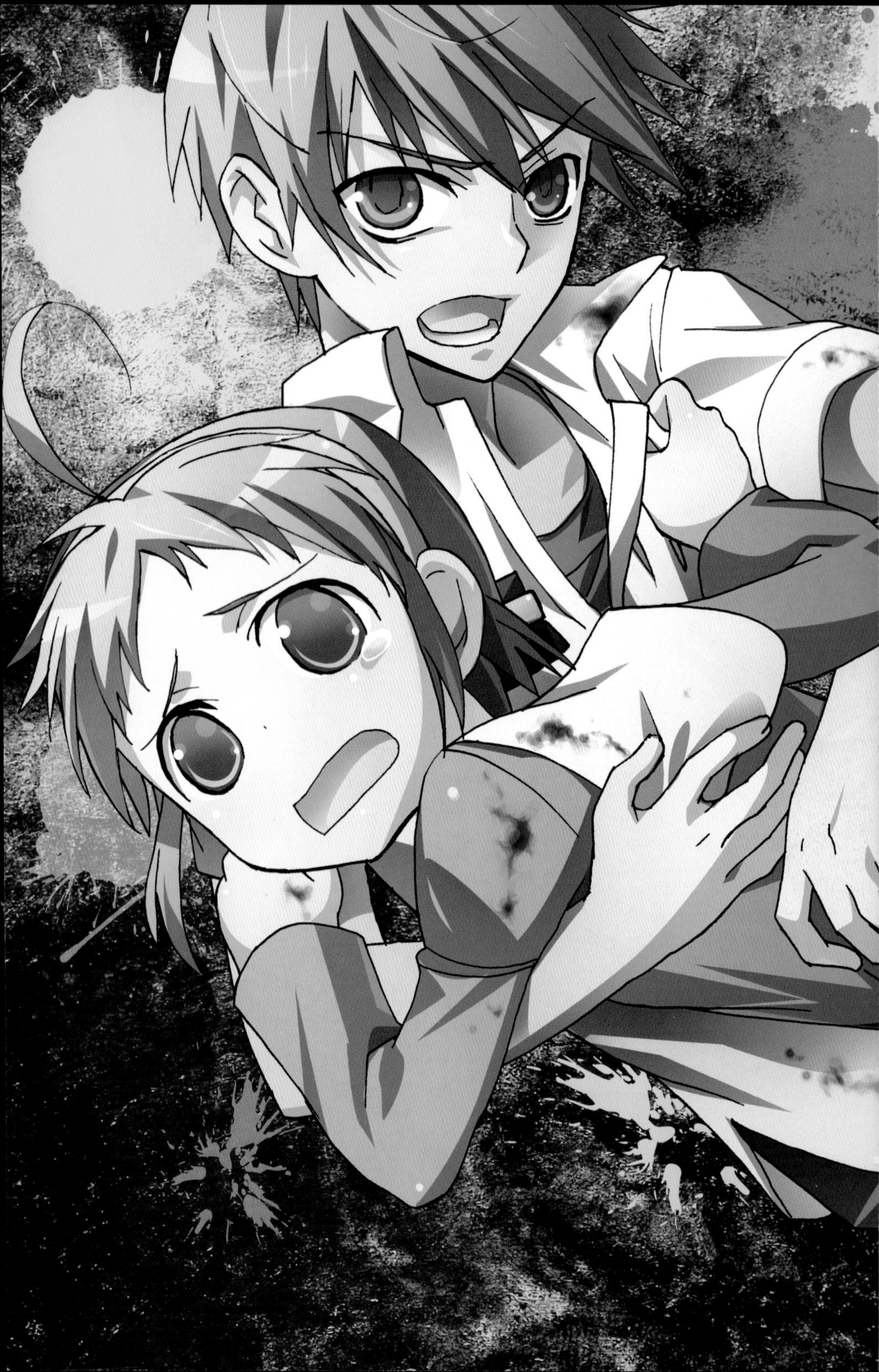

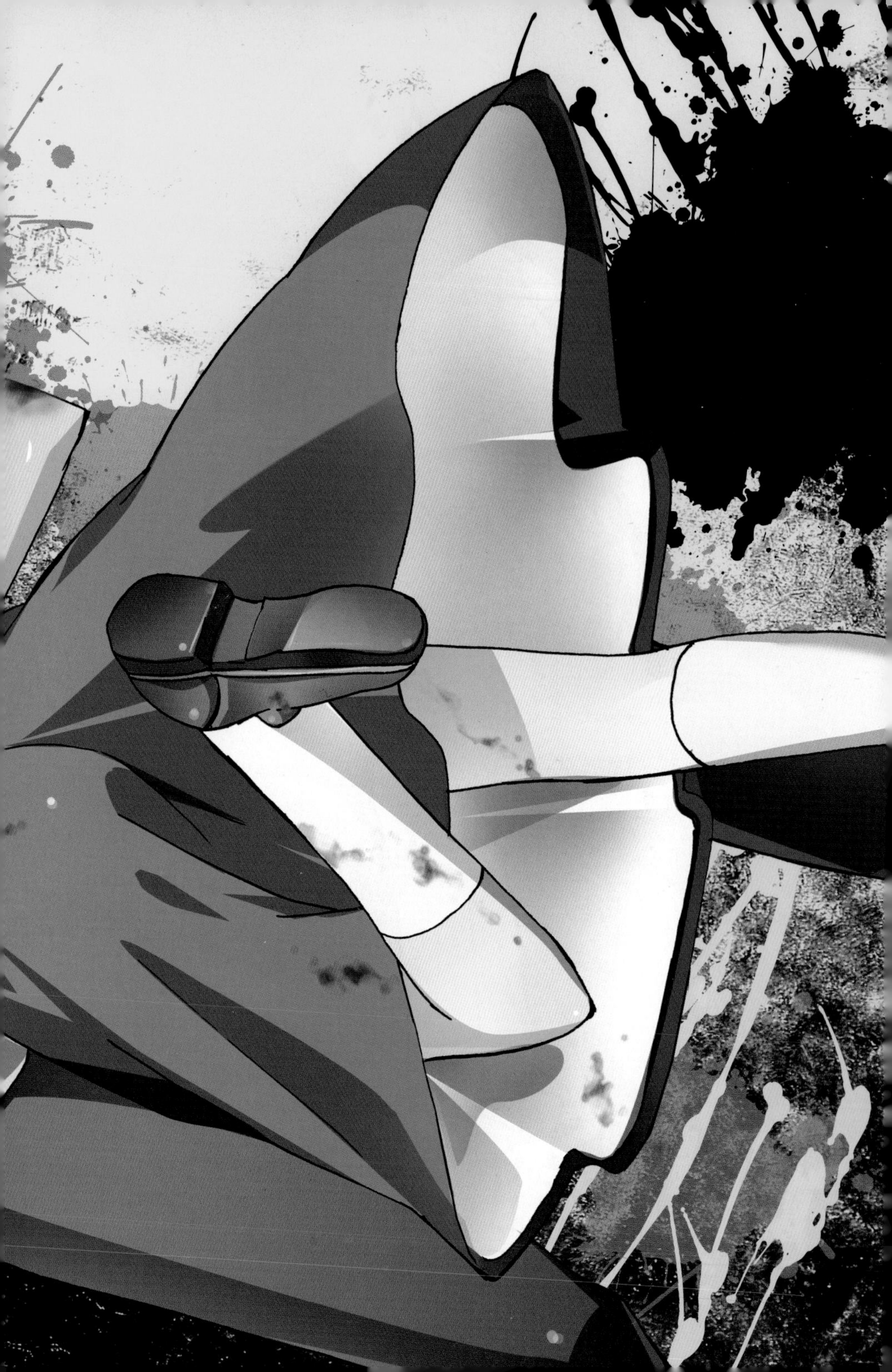

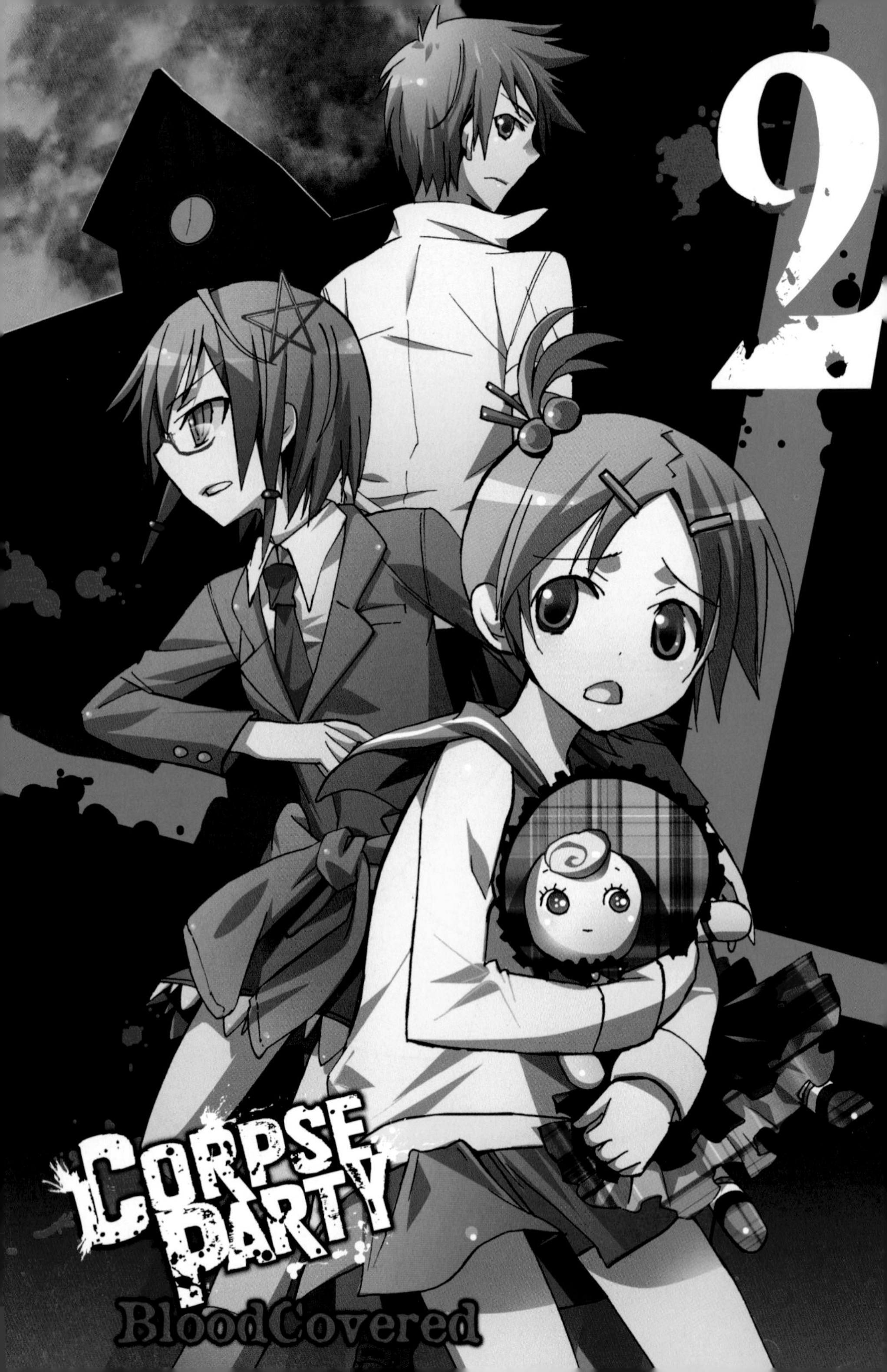
2
CORPSE PARTY
BloodCovered